"An ambitious book . . . *Bowling Alone* is a prodigious achievement. Mr. Putnam's scholarship is wide-ranging, his intelligence luminous, his tone modest, his prose unpretentious and frequently funny."

—*The Economist*

"An important work that is likely to be the center of much debate . . . Books of sociological insight as readable and significant as David Reisman's *Lonely Crowd* and C. Wright Mills's *Power Elite* come along seldom. Putnam's work belongs in their company."

—*Kirkus Reviews*

"Putnam can be fliply hip. But mainly he is learned. . . . The book . . . is responsible, intricate, and balanced . . . full of convincing detail."
—Michael Pakenham, *The Baltimore Sun*

"Deserves to be compared to such classic works as *The Lonely Crowd* and *The Affluent Society*."

—John Atlas, *Newark Star-Ledger*

"Its four hundred pages are crammed with statistics and analyses that seek to document civic decline in the United States. . . . *Bowling Alone* is to be commended for stimulating awareness of civic engagement and providing a wealth of data on trends in contemporary America."

—Francis Fukuyama, *The Washington Post*

"A mountainous, momentous work . . . This is no professorial popgun attempting the crossover from classroom to mass market; it is an antitank gun of an argument, relentlessly researched and heavily armored against academic counterassault. . . . A fabric of stunning comprehensiveness. [Putnam's] put his finger on an important sociological development."

—David Nyhan, *The Boston Globe*

"In this alarming and important study, Putnam charts the grievous deterioration over the past two generations of the organized ways in which people relate to one another and partake in civil life in the U.S. . . . Marshalling a plentiful array of facts, figures, charts, and survey results, Putnam delivers his message with verve and clarity . . . [and offers] a ray of hope in what he perceives to be a dire situation."

—*Publishers Weekly*

"A formidable book . . . There is no place, in my knowledge, where so much about the current disconnectedness of American society has been uncovered, assembled, and presented as in the text, charts, and notes within [*Bowling Alone*]."

—Curtis Gans, *Washington Monthly*

"The strength of Putnam's book is not its theoretical or conceptual novelty but its accumulation and sifting of data. . . . [Putnam] lays out with considerable precision and far more subtlety than he has yet been given credit for, the trends in civic engagement and social capital in all aspects of life."

—James Davison Hunter, *The Weekly Standard*

"A powerful sociological portrait of a democracy in imminent decline—a portrait as perspicacious, deeply felt, and firmly rooted in data as the classic American portraits rendered in . . . *The Lonely Crowd*. . . . *Bowling Alone* is a modern classic: a model of fastidious, prudent, self critical social science that manages to be data-rich without being theory-averse, scholarly yet undeniably relevant."

—Benjamin Barber, *The Nation*

"*Bowling Alone* provides important new data on the trends in civic engagement and social capital, a revised analysis of the causes of the decline, an exploration of its consequences, and ideas about what might be done. The book will not settle the debate, but it is a formidable achievement. It will henceforth be impossible to discuss these issues knowledgeably without reading Putnam's book and thinking about it."

—Paul Starr, *The New Republic*

"*Bowling Alone* is well worth the reading. The topic is important, and the passion infectious. Putnam gets you thinking about the challenges to community in a high-tech economy."

—Christopher Farrell, *BusinessWeek*

"*Bowling Alone* [is] . . . a singularly valuable beta test for anyone thinking about applying the idea of social capital to other problems. . . . This is powerful stuff. Indeed, in the wrong hands—those of a purple haired refugee from Seattle demonstrations, perhaps . . . it could be used to make an inflammatory case against corporate America."

—Walter Kiechel, *Harvard Business Review*

"A provocative discussion. [Putnam] shows us the real problems . . . and offers some broad-based goals that will help us to connect better with one another."

—*Inc. Magazine*

"This book deserves a wide audience. It deals seriously and imaginatively with one of the most urgent problems of our time."
— Sanford D. Horwitt, *The Industry Standard*

"Robert Putnam's *Bowling Alone* is an eloquent and powerful contribution to a long tradition of important reassessments of the American condition. His argument — buttressed by impressive scholarly research — that the United States has lost much of the social glue that once allowed our society to cohere, that we are in danger of becoming a nation of strangers to one another without adequate social bonds, is certain to become a central part of our national conversation."
— Alan Brinkley, author of *Liberalism and Its Discontents*

"A marvelously researched and well written book . . . Putnam does a splendid job of explaining our loss of social capital . . . [and] has written an extremely provocative book — one that provides a penetrating insight into the modern American psyche."
— Howard Upton, *Tulsa World*

"Plainly argued and compulsively readable . . . [*Bowling Alone*] is an agenda-setting book that will be the starting point of discussion and debate for years to come."
— Mark Chaves, *The Christian Century*

"*Bowling Alone* is a tour de force. Robert Putnam has amassed an impressive array of evidence for his original and powerful thesis on the decline of social capital and civic engagement in the past several decades. This thought-provoking book will stimulate huge academic and national public policy debates on the crisis of the American community."
— William Julius Wilson, Harvard University

"Robert Putnam's *Bowling Alone* is a must-read."
— Diane Ravitch, author of *Left Back: A Century of Failed School Reforms*

"Whether you agree with the central thesis of *Bowling Alone*, Putnam's argument deserves to be seriously considered by everyone interested in our social well-being. Each of us should read *Bowling Alone* alone — and then discuss it together."
— William Kristol, Editor and Publisher, *The Weekly Standard*

"Concerns about the cost of progress for traditional community spirit and neighborliness are examined in a very readable manner by Robert Putnam's book *Bowling Alone*."
— Irish Prime Minister Bertie Ahern

BOWLING ALONE: Revised and Updated

THE COLLAPSE AND REVIVAL OF AMERICAN COMMUNITY

Robert D. Putnam

SIMON & SCHUSTER PAPERBACKS

NEW YORK   LONDON   TORONTO   SYDNEY   NEW DELHI

To Ruth Swank Putnam
and to the memory of Frank L. Putnam,
Louis Werner, and Zelda Wolock Werner,
exemplars of the long civic generation

Contents

Preface[1]

In 1995 I published an article in a well-respected but somewhat obscure academic journal, summarizing a lecture I had given in Sweden on the topic of civic engagement in America. Throughout the previous year, I had been following a hunch, poking around in various data sets attempting to piece together a picture of how Americans' participation in membership organizations and civic groups had changed over the preceding decades. My preliminary findings seemed to show a steep decline in participation. Based upon previous work I had done in Italy—which argued that healthy democracies depend upon social connectedness—I began to wonder if some of the challenges America was facing as we approached the end of the twentieth century might have their roots in a shrinking stock of social capital.

At the time, I never expected the article to receive much attention. But before I knew it, I found myself in the middle of a deluge of discussion, debate, and dissent around the questions it provoked. Were more and more Americans indeed bowling—as well as worshipping, picnicking, politicking, and engaging in countless other "social" activities—alone (or not at all)? If so, why? And what could it mean for a nation that supposedly counted community and collective action as founding virtues? Suddenly social scientists, politicians, pundits, PTA presidents, and seemingly everyone in between were talking about social capital, "bridging" and "bonding," and the fact that something palpable had begun to change in America.

The article's unexpected reception put me on a winding path to explore these questions in earnest—mining obscure troves of data, developing original methods of measurement, following a fair number of dead ends, and testing every conceivable counterhypothesis. It was a far longer research journey than I had ever imagined it would be, but the story I unearthed— with the considerable and invaluable help of some of the most skilled researchers with whom I've ever had the pleasure of working—confirmed the nascent hypotheses my article had first explored. In 2000, *Bowling Alone* was published.[2]

Academic reception of the book's thesis was nuanced and initially somewhat critical, as was perfectly appropriate. No scientific claim is ever beyond debate. And no analytical debate is ever really concluded. In fact, the only reason for readers to trust me at all is that I agree in advance to subject myself to peer criticism and incorporate both that criticism and emerging new evidence into my own unfolding understanding. That process of self-correction is how good science works. *Bowling Alone* made bold claims about the direction in which our country was headed as we rounded the corner into a new century. And now, twenty years later, we are left to wonder how those claims have held up. Most, it turns out, have held up reasonably well.[3]

- One of the central arguments of the book is that both *civic engagement* and *organizational involvement* experienced marked declines during the second half of the twentieth century.[4] According to the best available evidence, these declines have continued uninterrupted. Since the turn of the twenty-first century, fewer and fewer Americans are socializing through membership organizations.[5]
- The decline in *church membership* and *church attendance*, two other phenomena *Bowling Alone* detailed, has not only continued but sharply accelerated over the past twenty years.[6] Rates of church attendance seemed to be heading back upward as the new century opened but took a nosedive thereafter. I explored this in depth in a 2010 book with David E. Campbell, *American Grace: How Religion Divides and Unites Us*. That work detailed how Americans today are experiencing faith in increasingly individualistic ways. This dramatic "rise of the 'nones' " (a term for those who do not identify with and are not affiliated with any religion) is particularly pronounced among the youngest cohort of Americans, heralding yet further declines in religiosity in the years ahead.
- The decline of *union membership*, another important trend identified in the book, has also accelerated since the first edition of *Bowling Alone*. And the cultural salience of unions has also continued to wane.[7]

- The collapse of *philanthropic generosity*, which *Bowling Alone* laid bare,[8] by some measures paused during the late 1990s and early 2000s, as aggregate philanthropy (measured by total dollars given) was boosted by megagifts from the megawealthy. But after those boom years, aggregate philanthropy declined once again. Meanwhile, measures of charitable donations that looked at giving by the average American (to churches, local fundraising drives, and organizations such as the United Way) continued to fall, just as *Bowling Alone* had anticipated.[9]

- According to the best available evidence, *social trust* has deteriorated further over the past twenty years as well. This continues to be explained in part by generational replacement, as *Bowling Alone* had argued. As more trusting generations have died out, they have been succeeded by less trusting youth cohorts, leaving America a less trusting society, year after year.[10]

- Contrary to these continued declines, the last two decades have seen little to no consistent change in *volunteerism*.[11] Actually, that is consistent with what *Bowling Alone* reported,[12] although few readers remember that exception to the otherwise downward trends the book described.

- While all of the aforementioned trends that *Bowling Alone* identified are still visible more than twenty years later, the verdicts on two other hypothetical downturns are more controversial. *Political participation* is a mixed picture.[13] Since the year 2000, voting levels have gone both up and down, though basically down. Overall, campaign participation has not decreased; but political alienation has grown significantly.[14] So in some cases the declines in political participation have continued, but in other cases not.

- The nature of trends in *informal social connections* remains hotly contested.[15] A great debate between Miller McPherson, Lynn Smith-Lovin, and Matthew E. Brashears (who reported a decline in close personal ties between 1985 and 2004[16]) and Claude Fischer (who denied such a decline[17]) was fought to a draw, in my opinion. Fischer's work showed that *complete* social isolation had not increased during that period, but McPherson et al. argued that, on average, close personal ties had in fact declined. In examining the hypothesis of a decline in informal social connections, *Bowling Alone* drew on many different data sources, but the dispute between Fischer and McPherson et al. raged entirely on the basis of a single data archive: the General Social Survey (GSS). Later work by Brashears[18] and Pew[19] confirmed that while total social isolation had not increased, the average size of Americans' core discussion networks contracted by about one-third after 1985. Moreover, these personal networks had contracted inward, so to speak, with the biggest declines outside the family and the slightest declines inside the family.[20] Thus, as I see it, despite extensive debate and independent confirmation by other scholars, the most balanced judgment about *Bowling Alone*'s claim about a falloff of informal social connections is neither "true" nor "false," but rather merits the Scottish verdict "not proven."

- But by far the most important development over the past two decades—and one that may yet alter the verdict on *Bowling Alone*—is indeed so significant that it deserves an entire chapter of its own in this Twentieth Anniversary Edition. Though it's now hard to imagine American life without it, the Internet was a nascent invention when the book was written, and social media had yet to be invented. Would (will?) the rise of the Internet offset the downward trends *Bowling Alone* reported? When I wrote the original manuscript, I spent a good deal of time looking at the best available evidence on the topic of how the Internet might evolve and thereby affect trends in social connectedness, but my conclusions were at best speculative. Now, with two decades' worth of experience living our lives online, as well as considerable academic research on the effects of the Internet on nearly every aspect of American life, the picture is somewhat clearer— though still a subject of considerable debate. In the afterword to this edition of *Bowling Alone*, Jonah Hahn and I explore in detail the latest evidence on the effects of the *Internet* and *social media* on social capital.

In the end, the most debatable aspect of *Bowling Alone* was perhaps not the trends it identified. More often, both lay readers and academic experts were concerned with the question of causes. *Why* had social capital declined so precipitously during the latter half of the twentieth century? The past two decades have witnessed prodigious discussion and disputation about my lineup of suspects: Was it really TV or instead inequality? Urban sprawl or immigration? Or some other factor? And how about the somewhat mysterious "generational change" explanation, which was not so much a substantive cause as an accounting mechanism pointing uncertainly to the role of history.

My own views about causation have evolved over twenty years. And I have found that by far the most instructive exercise in my exploration of this question has been to widen the lens on the period of history I was aiming to understand and explain. *Bowling Alone* looked specifically at the second half of the twentieth century and saw mostly declines in measures of social capital. But it ignored the equally important first half of the century, when, as I discovered, almost all of the measures I identified as trending downward were in fact moving in the opposite direction. The story of social capital in America during the past 125 years turns out to look like an inverted U-curve—starting the century at nearly the same low we experience today, growing until roughly the mid-1960s, then declining again.

And, even more remarkably, this essentially steady rise in America's social capital during the first two-thirds of the century and precipitous fall during the last third turns out to be mirrored in both shape and timing by trends in income equality, political comity, and even cultural communitarianism. This fact was a truly breathtaking discovery for me and launched yet another scholarly journey that produced a book of its own. Thus my latest and fullest interpretation of *why* social capital has been declining over the past half century looks at the interplay among all of these trends—through both their upswing and their downward slide. I therefore encourage readers who are curious about the broader story of change over time in America's social capital to look at my latest book, *The Upswing: How America Came Together a Century Ago and How We Can Do It Again*, which I coauthored with Shaylyn Romney Garrett. It is being published contemporaneously with this new edition of *Bowling Alone*.

The lively scholarly discussions *Bowling Alone* inspired, the seemingly endless lines of research it prompted, and the public policy debates it came to inform enriched my professional life more than I could possibly have hoped. But by far the most rewarding aspect of becoming a champion of community in America was to witness the effect it had on the lives of lay readers—both in America and far beyond.

For many years after *Bowling Alone* hit the shelves, I received countless calls, emails, and letters from individuals, community groups, and institutions of all kinds who wanted to share with me how the story of America's lost social capital had resonated with them. Ultimately, the correspondence amounted to a tower of pages nearly two feet tall. And I continue to receive such letters and emails today, some twenty years later.

A great many older Americans wrote to share their personal experience of community decline and disengagement. They related their nostalgia for a bygone America that the data in *Bowling Alone* had captured. "That's exactly how I remember my neighborhood in Oshkosh, Wisconsin, in the 1950s," they'd tell me. On the other hand, a number of my own high school classmates and bowling teammates from Port Clinton, Ohio, wrote to compare notes about whether my rendition of the 1950s was in fact too rosy. Others expressed the view that the solidarity produced by hardship in the Great Depression, or military service in World War II, shaped them into communitarians who now felt unmoored in a more individualistic America.

Baby boomers, who came of age in that individualistic America, often wrote expressing fear and concern about growing social divisions and political apathy. But they also shared a sense that they had somehow been un-witting accomplices to the unraveling of the social fabric. "You've described my life," I would often hear. "My mother belonged to Hadassah and went to meetings every week. My dad was active in Rotary and bowled in a league. I've not done any of those things as an adult, and I've often felt guilty about it. I thought it was just me, but after reading your book I now know that it's the whole country."

For the great mainline civic and religious organizations that dominated midcentury America, *Bowling Alone* articulated publicly a crisis that had long hovered just below the radar. Local newspapers across the country ran stories about local chapters of the Lions and even the Optimists dying out. Organizations like Rotary and the League of Women Voters sought my advice about how to stanch their membership losses.

College students and young people from all over the country contacted me to say that the book had inspired them to reinvest in civic engagement, localism, and relationships. They sought advice about how to enter a public service career. In fact, *Bowling Alone* seems to have had a special impact on American college campuses. Institutionally speaking, the book became, as the *Democrat and Chronicle* of Rochester, New York, wrote, "a wake-up call for universities . . . part of the reason for the increasing [nationwide] emphasis on [community] service."[21] Shortly after the book's publication, the dean of Harvard College sent me a long autobiographical account of social capital in his own life, followed by an intensive discussion of the implication of *Bowling Alone* for Harvard's policies on such topics as extracurricular activities and the promotion of public service among undergraduates.

And in an unusual example of the curricular impact of *Bowling Alone*, a group of Michigan State students were taking an open-book exam for a course in American Politics, for which they had read *Bowling Alone*. One of the questions on the final exam was, "What would Robert Putnam say about _____?" The students decided in mid-exam to call my office to *ask me* what I would say!

I heard from a great many people wanting to connect with me personally, reaching out to build social capital with a chronicler of its decline. Writers sent me piles of manuscripts, asking for advice and feedback. Readers sent me lists of books they thought I'd enjoy. People everywhere invited me to have coffee on my next visit to their hometown. Several wanted me to come play cards with their bridge group or participate in their meditation circle or attend a meeting at their local Elks Lodge. And I was sent numerous photos of bulletin boards announcing church sermons on *Bowling Alone*.

I also received myriad requests for autographed copies of the book—often to give as a gift to an inspiring civics teacher or a member of the Greatest Generation. I received fan mail from an incredibly diverse group—from a home-maker in Windermere, England, to Neil Bush of Kennebunkport, Maine. I was moved by how many readers (like a firefighter from Erie, Pennsylvania) took the time to tell me that the book had changed their life. Occasionally, readers even wrote to ask for personal advice about how to increase their own social capital. Indeed, in the very week that I drafted this preface, two decades after the publication of *Bowling Alone,* a Canadian expatriate emailed me to ask whether she should stay in London or return to Toronto for a better social-capital experience.

From Buffalo, New York, to Amarillo, Texas, scores of local papers re-viewed the book and connected it to homegrown anecdotes about mounting loneliness, isolation, and alienation. On the other hand, when *USA Today* ran a *Bowling Alone*–linked story asking readers to say why they loved their communities, they were inundated with responses, most of which described the generosity, kindness, and trust that characterized the respondents' home-towns.

In fact, *Bowling Alone* stimulated scores of communities in America to reflect on their past strengths and plans for future renewal. For exam-ple, a civic leader in North Carolina wrote, "What a great crusade you have embarked on! I look forward to tracking your progress and the success of Winston-Salem in building social capital across our entire community." The book also inspired (and my research group at Harvard helped organize) a group of more than three dozen towns and cities nationwide to use scientific methods to evaluate their own levels of social capital. Participants included places as diverse as Baton Rouge, Louisiana; Duluth, Minnesota; Lewiston, Maine; San Diego, California; Chicago, Illinois; and Yakima, Washington. This effort ultimately produced the Social Capital Community Benchmark Survey,[22] an unparalleled trove of data for ongoing study of community vi-tality across America. Furthermore, the Social Capital Index, which was an original scholarly contribution of the book[23] and combined several metrics and indicators to create a broad measuring tool for understanding commu-nity vitality, has been confirmed and reused multiple times in the past twenty years.

This pattern of communities taking inspiration from *Bowling Alone* to assess and restore their social capital extended abroad as well—to Ottawa, Canada, and even to Ireland, where the then taoiseach (prime minister) in-troduced me to the classic Irish "third place" by taking me from pub to pub in Dublin and invited me to address his party convention on the topic of social capital. He said publicly that *Bowling Alone* was the most important book he'd ever read. Later an Irish journalist deflated my ego a bit by telling me that the taoiseach hardly ever read anything.

It was gratifying to see social entrepreneurs developing tools and initiatives based on the ideas they encountered in *Bowling Alone*. The Internet site Meetup was conceived by entrepreneur Scott Heiferman, who happened to be reading *Bowling Alone* just after 9/11. "Putnam," he said, "basically sold me on the idea that local community is important."[24] Given his technical expertise, it seemed obvious to him that he could help restore local community. Joseph Kopser, a former student of mine and a U.S. Army veteran, wrote a guide to a more community-friendly strategy for counterinsurgency warfare based on the principles of social capital. Sachin Jain, another former student, built outreach programs for lonely senior citizens as the CEO of a health care company called CareMore. Eric Liu, who also studied with me, founded Citizen University, an initiative to revive civics education, and Civic Saturdays, to offer Americans a secular analog to church. And in 2004 David Crowley, a remarkable social entrepreneur from my own city of Boston, used the language and arguments of *Bowling Alone* to jump-start a highly successful new form of community engagement entitled SCI: Social Capital Inc.

Bowling Alone also sparked an interest in social capital in the most far-flung institutional settings. The American Library Association used the book as a resource in crafting its vision of a library for the Internet age, whose focus is on gathering and building community among readers, not storing dead trees. And PBS drew on *Bowling Alone* for inspiration and guidance in reinventing public broadcasting in a more individualistic world. The Franconia (NH) Heritage Council was inspired to compile a two-century history of local organizations and informal groups.[25] *Wellness Bound*, a magazine focused on healthy lifestyles, devoted an entire issue to "Why Social Capital Matters to America."[26] Numerous law review articles reflected on the implications of *Bowling Alone* for jurisprudence, both in the United States and abroad.[27] And in 2004 the Whitney Museum of American Art curated *Social Capital: Forms of Interaction, Relations in Contemporary Art*, an exhibition at the City University of New York.

Twenty-five years ago, I was an unknown academic with no pretensions of being a public intellectual. But the absolutely overwhelming response to the book thrust me into the limelight and changed the course of my career. And I've long reflected on the question of why *Bowling Alone* struck such a chord.

I tried conscientiously to write simultaneously for two different audiences—the scholarly and the public. The former turns out to have been unexpectedly powerful in explaining the "best-seller" status of the book. In fact, the lion's share of sales have been due to its inclusion as supplementary reading on the syllabi of college courses. Ironically, even though the book has been controversial among sociologists, they have assigned it overwhelmingly in their classes. As a result, a surprising proportion of college graduates have become familiar with the book, which is an important part

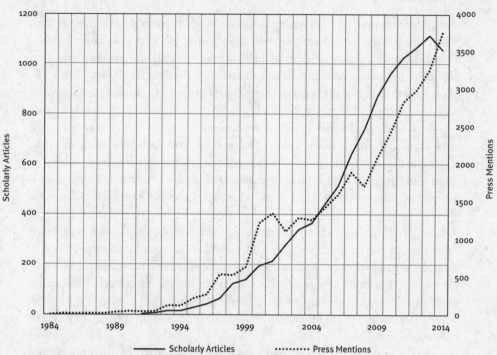

Figure A: Growth in Scholarly and Public Attention to "Social Capital" (1985–2014)

of the reason that the core ideas (and the term "bowling alone") have over time become common currency among ordinary Americans, as figure A illustrates.

Bowling Alone was fortuitously timed to resonate far beyond academia. Before I had anything of substance to say on the matter, many Americans had already noticed that they were less civically engaged than their parents had been. So when a Harvard professor came along with a tome full of charts and graphs that said, in effect, "It's not just you, it's all of us," it hit a nerve. *Bowling Alone* had unwittingly spoken to the Zeitgeist of an anxious nation slowly waking up to its own fraying social fabric.

The book's message also happened to fit the political mood of the day: the "Third Way" of Bill Clinton, Tony Blair, and their contemporaries, as well as our nation's hunger for common ground in the wake of 9/11, which happened a month after the book came out in paperback. Many people were attracted to a communitarian perspective that was orthogonal to conventional party lines, and the book's "purple" policy approach was endorsed by conservatives and liberals alike. I've never hidden the fact that my own views are progressive and democratic, nor my collaboration with President Obama; but many leading conservatives have praised my work. Jeb Bush has attributed his political and ideological resurrection after losing his first campaign for the Florida governor's post in 1994 to having read the original article "Bowling Alone,"[28] and even Rush Limbaugh flirted with the *Bowling Alone* diagnosis of modern American ills, before rejecting its proposed remedies as warmed-over liberalism.[29]

This wide and fertile ground motivated me to become something of a modern-day circuit rider, sharing what I'd found with tens of thousands of people in hundreds of local communities from coast to coast, "an Old Testament prophet with charts," in the words of one observer.[30] I cofounded the Saguaro Seminar, a think tank based at Harvard's Kennedy School of Government, which brought together some of the brightest minds working to rebuild community across the country. One member of the seminar went on to occupy the Oval Office. With Lew Feldstein, a veteran community activist, I wrote a follow-up to *Bowling Alone* entitled *Better Together*, in which we highlighted examples of several successful initiatives aimed at restoring our nation's stock of social capital.[31] *Bowling Alone* was translated into nine languages, and political leaders on five continents sought advice (or at least validation) from me.

Along the way I began to embrace the idea captured by the epitaph on Marx's gravestone—that he sought not merely to interpret the world but to change it. My purpose, of course, was to try to contribute to a "revival of American community," as the subtitle of *Bowling Alone* signaled. It is now perfectly plain that, in that sense, I have so far failed.

In the words of reviewer Alan Ryan, "Putnam is too good a social scientist to be an entirely persuasive preacher."[32] Indeed, my latest book (*The Upswing*, coauthored with Shaylyn Romney Garrett) shows unequivocally just how thoroughly America has continued to regress in the intervening twenty years—a downward plunge resulting not merely in fraying community ties but also in worsening economic inequality, greater political polarization, and more cultural individualism.

The most common criticism of *Bowling Alone* has been that the prescriptive, hortatory last chapter was simply inadequate to the scope of the problem. And the problem today is even bigger than it was when those critiques were written. But perhaps greater, too, is our sense of urgency and our call to creative collective action. We have now witnessed a further two decades of the bitter fruits seeded by a disconnected and divided society. And in a full realization of where we're likely headed, we may yet find the inspiration we need to restore our bonds, mend our bridges, and bend the course of history.

The tremendous response to this book has always felt like a testament to America's embattled but never vanquished community spirit, and the inextricable place of social capital in the success or failure of our democratic experiment. It is my sincere hope that in the season of this twentieth anniversary of *Bowling Alone*, America may at last return to "the better angels of our nature," in Lincoln's words, and revive the Tocquevillian virtues that the book's introductory chapter evokes.

SECTION ONE

Introduction

CHAPTER 1

Thinking about Social Change in America

NO ONE IS LEFT from the Glenn Valley, Pennsylvania, Bridge Club who can tell us precisely when or why the group broke up, even though its forty-odd members were still playing regularly as recently as 1990, just as they had done for more than half a century. The shock in the Little Rock, Arkansas, Sertoma club, however, is still painful: in the mid-1980s, nearly fifty people had attended the weekly luncheon to plan activities to help the hearing- and speech-impaired, but a decade later only seven regulars continued to show up.

The Roanoke, Virginia, chapter of the National Association for the Advancement of Colored People (NAACP) had been an active force for civil rights since 1918, but during the 1990s membership withered from about 2,500 to a few hundred. By November 1998 even a heated contest for president drew only fifty-seven voting members. Black city councillor Carroll Swain observed ruefully, "Some people today are a wee bit complacent until something jumps up and bites them." VFW Post 2378 in Berwyn, Illinois, a blue-collar suburb of Chicago, was long a bustling "home away from home" for local veterans and a kind of working-class country club for the neighborhood, hosting wedding receptions and class reunions. By 1999, however, membership had so dwindled that it was a struggle just to pay taxes on the yellow brick post hall. Although numerous veterans of Vietnam and the post-Vietnam military lived in the area, Tom Kissell, national membership director for the VFW, observed, "Kids today just aren't joiners."[1]

The Charity League of Dallas had met every Friday morning for fifty-seven years to sew, knit, and visit, but on April 30, 1999, they held their last meeting; the average age of the group had risen to eighty, the last new member had joined two years earlier, and president Pat Dilbeck said ruefully, "I feel like this is a sinking ship." Precisely three days later and 1,200 miles to the northeast, the Vassar alumnae of Washington, D.C., closed down their fifty-first—and last—annual book sale. Even though they aimed to sell more than one hundred thousand books to benefit college scholarships in the 1999 event, co-chair Alix Myerson explained, the volunteers who ran the program "are in their sixties, seventies, and eighties. They're dying, and they're not replaceable." Meanwhile, as Tewksbury Memorial High School (TMHS), just north of Boston, opened in the fall of 1999, forty brand-new royal blue uniforms newly purchased for the marching band remained in storage, since only four students signed up to play. Roger Whittlesey, TMHS band director, recalled that twenty years earlier the band numbered more than eighty, but participation had waned ever since.[2] Somehow in the last several decades of the twentieth century all these community groups and tens of thousands like them across America began to fade.

It wasn't so much that old members dropped out—at least not any more rapidly than age and the accidents of life had always meant. But community organizations were no longer continuously revitalized, as they had been in the past, by freshets of new members. Organizational leaders were flummoxed. For years they assumed that their problem must have local roots or at least that it was peculiar to their organization, so they commissioned dozens of studies to recommend reforms.[3] The slowdown was puzzling because for as long as anyone could remember, membership rolls and activity lists had lengthened steadily.

In the 1960s, in fact, community groups across America had seemed to stand on the threshold of a new era of expanded involvement. Except for the civic drought induced by the Great Depression, their activity had shot up year after year, cultivated by assiduous civic gardeners and watered by increasing affluence and education. Each annual report registered rising membership. Churches and synagogues were packed, as more Americans worshiped together than only a few decades earlier, perhaps more than ever in American history.

Moreover, Americans seemed to have time on their hands. A 1958 study under the auspices of the newly inaugurated Center for the Study of Leisure at the University of Chicago fretted that "the most dangerous threat hanging over American society is the threat of leisure," a startling claim in the decade in which the Soviets got the bomb.[4] *Life* magazine echoed the warning about the new challenge of free time: "Americans now face a glut of leisure," ran a headline in February 1964. "The task ahead: how to take life easy."

> As a matter of fact, mankind now possesses for the first time the tools and knowledge to create whatever kind of world he wants. . . . Despite our Protestant ethic, there are many signs that the message is beginning to

get through to some people. . . . Not only are Americans flocking into bowling leagues and garden clubs, they are satisfying their gregarious urges in countless neighborhood committees to improve the local roads and garbage collections and to hound their public servants into doing what the name implies.[5]

The civic-minded World War II generation was, as its own John F. Kennedy proclaimed at his inauguration, picking up the torch of leadership, not only in the nation's highest office, but in cities and towns across the land. Summarizing dozens of studies, political scientist Robert E. Lane wrote in 1959 that "the ratio of political activists to the general population, and even the ratio of male activists to the male population, has generally increased over the past fifty years." As the 1960s ended, sociologists Daniel Bell and Virginia Held reported that "there is more participation than ever before in America . . . and more opportunity for the active interested person to express his personal and political concerns."[6] Even the simplest political act, voting, was becoming ever more common. From 1920, when women got the vote, through 1960, turnout in presidential elections had risen at the rate of 1.6 percent every four years, so on a simple straight-line projection it seemed reasonable, as a leading political scientist later observed, to expect turnout to be nearly 70 percent and rising on the nation's two hundredth birthday in 1976.[7]

By 1965 disrespect for public life, so endemic in our history, seemed to be waning. Gallup pollsters discovered that the number of Americans who would like to see their children "go into politics as a life's work" had nearly doubled over little more than a decade. Although this gauge of esteem for politics stood at only 36 percent, it had never before been recorded so high, nor has it since. More strikingly, Americans felt increased confidence in their neighbors. The proportion that agreed that "most people can be trusted," for example, rose from an already high 66 percent during and after World War II to a peak of 77 percent in 1964.[8]

The fifties and sixties were hardly a "golden age," especially for those Americans who were marginalized because of their race or gender or social class or sexual orientation. Segregation, by race legally and by gender socially, was the norm, and intolerance, though declining, was still disturbingly high. Environmental degradation had only just been exposed by Rachel Carson, and Betty Friedan had not yet deconstructed the feminine mystique. Grinding rural poverty had still to be discovered by the national media. Infant mortality, a standard measure of public health, stood at twenty-six per one thousand births—forty-four per one thousand for black infants—in 1960, nearly four times worse than those indexes would be at the end of the century. America in *Life* was white, straight, Christian, comfortable, and (in the public square, at least) male.[9] Social reformers had their work cut out for them. However, engagement in community affairs and the sense of shared identity and reciprocity had never been greater in modern America, so the prospects for broad-based civic mobilization to address our national failings seemed bright.

The signs of burgeoning civic vitality were also favorable among the younger generation, as the first of the baby boomers approached college. Dozens of studies confirmed that education was by far the best predictor of engagement in civic life, and universities were in the midst of the most far-reaching expansion in American history. Education seemed the key to both greater tolerance and greater social involvement. Simultaneously shamed and inspired by the quickening struggle for civil rights launched by young African Americans in the South, white colleges in the North began to awaken from the silence of the fifties. Describing the induction of this new generation into the civil rights struggles of the 1960s, sociologist Doug McAdam emphasizes their self-assurance:

> We were a "can do" people, who accomplished whatever we set out to do. We had licked the Depression, turned the tide in World War II, and rebuilt Europe after the war. . . . Freedom Summer was an audacious undertaking consistent with the exaggerated sense of importance and potency shared by the privileged members of America's postwar generation.[10]

The baby boom meant that America's population was unusually young, whereas civic involvement generally doesn't bloom until middle age. In the short run, therefore, our youthful demography actually tended to dampen the ebullience of civil society. But that very bulge at the bottom of the nation's demographic pyramid boded well for the future of community organizations, for they could look forward to swelling membership rolls in the 1980s, when the boomers would reach the peak "joining" years of the life cycle. And in the meantime, the bull session buzz about "participatory democracy" and "all power to the people" seemed to augur ever more widespread engagement in community affairs. One of America's most acute social observers prophesied in 1968, "Participatory democracy has all along been the political style (if not the slogan) of the American middle and upper class. It will become a more wide-spread style as more persons enter into those classes."[11] Never in our history had the future of civic life looked brighter.

WHAT HAPPENED NEXT to civic and social life in American communities is the subject of this book. In recent years social scientists have framed concerns about the changing character of American society in terms of the concept of "social capital." By analogy with notions of physical capital and human capital—tools and training that enhance individual productivity—the core idea of social capital theory is that social networks have value. Just as a screwdriver (physical capital) or a college education (human capital) can increase productivity (both individual and collective), so too social contacts affect the productivity of individuals and groups.

Whereas physical capital refers to physical objects and human capital refers to properties of individuals, social capital refers to connections among individuals—social networks and the norms of reciprocity and trustworthiness that arise from them. In that sense social capital is closely related to what some have called "civic virtue." The difference is that "social capital" calls attention to the fact that civic virtue is most powerful when embedded in a dense network of reciprocal social relations. A society of many virtuous but isolated individuals is not necessarily rich in social capital.

The term *social capital* itself turns out to have been independently invented at least six times over the twentieth century, each time to call attention to the ways in which our lives are made more productive by social ties. The first known use of the concept was not by some cloistered theoretician, but by a practical reformer of the Progressive Era—L. J. Hanifan, state supervisor of rural schools in West Virginia. Writing in 1916 to urge the importance of community involvement for successful schools, Hanifan invoked the idea of "social capital" to explain why. For Hanifan, social capital referred to

> those tangible substances [that] count for most in the daily lives of people: namely good will, fellowship, sympathy, and social intercourse among the individuals and families who make up a social unit. . . . The individual is helpless socially, if left to himself. . . . If he comes into contact with his neighbor, and they with other neighbors, there will be an accumulation of social capital, which may immediately satisfy his social needs and which may bear a social potentiality sufficient to the substantial improvement of living conditions in the whole community. The community as a whole will benefit by the coöperation of all its parts, while the individual will find in his associations the advantages of the help, the sympathy, and the fellowship of his neighbors.[12]

Hanifan's account of social capital anticipated virtually all the crucial elements in later interpretations, but his conceptual invention apparently attracted no notice from other social commentators and disappeared without a trace. But like sunken treasure recurrently revealed by shifting sands and tides, the same idea was independently rediscovered in the 1950s by Canadian sociologists to characterize the club memberships of arriviste suburbanites, in the 1960s by urbanist Jane Jacobs to laud neighborliness in the modern metropolis, in the 1970s by economist Glenn Loury to analyze the social legacy of slavery, and in the 1980s by French social theorist Pierre Bourdieu and by German economist Ekkehart Schlicht to underline the social and economic resources embodied in social networks. Sociologist James S. Coleman put the term firmly and finally on the intellectual agenda in the late 1980s, using it (as Hanifan had originally done) to highlight the social context of education.[13]

As this array of independent coinages indicates, social capital has both an individual and a collective aspect—a private face and a public face. First, individuals form connections that benefit our own interests. One pervasive strategem of ambitious job seekers is "networking," for most of us get our jobs because of whom we know, not what we know—that is, our social capital, not our human capital. Economic sociologist Ronald Burt has shown that executives with bounteous Rolodex files enjoy faster career advancement. Nor is the private return to social capital limited to economic rewards. As Claude S. Fischer, a sociologist of friendship, has noted, "Social networks are important in all our lives, often for finding jobs, more often for finding a helping hand, companionship, or a shoulder to cry on."[14]

If individual clout and companionship were all there were to social capital, we'd expect foresighted, self-interested individuals to invest the right amount of time and energy in creating or acquiring it. However, social capital also can have "externalities" that affect the wider community, so that not all the costs and benefits of social connections accrue to the person making the contact.[15] As we shall see later in this book, a well-connected individual in a poorly connected society is not as productive as a well-connected individual in a well-connected society. And even a poorly connected individual may derive some of the spillover benefits from living in a well-connected community. If the crime rate in my neighborhood is lowered by neighbors keeping an eye on one another's homes, I benefit even if I personally spend most of my time on the road and never even nod to another resident on the street.

Social capital can thus be simultaneously a "private good" and a "public good." Some of the benefit from an investment in social capital goes to bystanders, while some of the benefit redounds to the immediate interest of the person making the investment. For example, service clubs, like Rotary or Lions, mobilize local energies to raise scholarships or fight disease at the same time that they provide members with friendships and business connections that pay off personally.

Social connections are also important for the rules of conduct that they sustain. Networks involve (almost by definition) mutual obligations; they are not interesting as mere "contacts." Networks of community engagement foster sturdy norms of reciprocity: I'll do this for you now, in the expectation that you (or perhaps someone else) will return the favor. "Social capital is akin to what Tom Wolfe called 'the favor bank' in his novel *The Bonfire of the Vanities*," notes economist Robert Frank.[16] It was, however, neither a novelist nor an economist, but Yogi Berra who offered the most succinct definition of reciprocity: "If you don't go to somebody's funeral, they won't come to yours."

Sometimes, as in these cases, reciprocity is *specific*: I'll do this for you if you do that for me. Even more valuable, however, is a norm of *generalized* reciprocity: I'll do this for you without expecting anything specific back from you, in the confident expectation that someone else will do something for me down the road. The Golden Rule is one formulation of generalized reciprocity. Equally instructive is the T-shirt slogan used by the Gold Beach, Oregon, Volunteer Fire Department to publicize their annual fund-raising effort: "Come to our breakfast, we'll come to your fire." "We act on a norm of specific reciprocity," the firefighters seem to be saying, but onlookers smile because they recognize the underlying norm of generalized reciprocity—the firefighters will come even if *you* don't. When Blanche DuBois depended on the kindness of strangers, she too was relying on generalized reciprocity.

A society characterized by generalized reciprocity is more efficient than a distrustful society, for the same reason that money is more efficient than barter. If we don't have to balance every exchange instantly, we can get a lot more accomplished. Trustworthiness lubricates social life. Frequent interaction among a diverse set of people tends to produce a norm of generalized reciprocity. Civic engagement and social capital entail mutual obligation and responsibility for action. As L. J. Hanifan and his successors recognized, social networks and norms of reciprocity can facilitate cooperation for mutual benefit. When economic and political dealing is embedded in dense networks of social interaction, incentives for opportunism and malfeasance are reduced. This is why the diamond trade, with its extreme possibilities for fraud, is concentrated within close-knit ethnic enclaves. Dense social ties facilitate gossip and other valuable ways of cultivating reputation—an essential foundation for trust in a complex society.

Physical capital is not a single "thing," and different forms of physical capital are not interchangeable. An eggbeater and an aircraft carrier both appear as physical capital in our national accounts, but the eggbeater is not much use for national defense, and the carrier would not be much help with your morning omelet. Similarly, social capital—that is, social networks and the associated norms of reciprocity—comes in many different shapes and sizes with many different uses. Your extended family represents a form of social capital, as do your Sunday school class, the regulars who play poker on your commuter train, your college roommates, the civic organizations to which you belong, the Internet chat group in which you participate, and the network of professional acquaintances recorded in your address book.

Sometimes "social capital," like its conceptual cousin "community," sounds warm and cuddly. Urban sociologist Xavier de Souza Briggs, however, properly warns us to beware of a treacly sweet, "kumbaya" interpretation of social capital.[17] Networks and the associated norms of reciprocity are generally good for those inside the network, but the external effects of social capital are by no means always positive. It was social capital, for example, that enabled Timothy McVeigh to bomb the Alfred P. Murrah Federal Building in Oklahoma City. McVeigh's network of friends, bound together by a norm of reciprocity, enabled him to do what he could not have done alone. Similarly, urban gangs, NIMBY ("not in my backyard") movements, and power elites often exploit social capital to achieve ends that are antisocial from a wider perspective. Indeed, it is rhetorically useful for such groups to obscure the difference between the pro-social and antisocial consequences of community organizations. When Floridians objected to plans by the Ku Klux Klan to "adopt a highway," Jeff Coleman, grand wizard of the Royal Knights of the KKK, protested, "Really, we're just like the Lions or the Elks. We want to be involved in the community."[18]

Social capital, in short, can be directed toward malevolent, antisocial purposes, just like any other form of capital.[19] (McVeigh also relied on physical capital, like the explosive-laden truck, and human capital, like bomb-making expertise, to achieve his purposes.) Therefore it is important to ask how the positive consequences of social capital—mutual support, cooperation, trust, institutional effectiveness—can be maximized and the negative manifestations—sectarianism, ethnocentrism, corruption—minimized. Toward this end, scholars have begun to distinguish many different forms of social capital.

Some forms involve repeated, intensive, multistranded networks—like a group of steelworkers who meet for drinks every Friday after work and see each other at mass on Sunday—and some are episodic, single stranded, and anonymous, like the faintly familiar face you see several times a month in the supermarket checkout line. Some types of social capital, like a Parent-Teacher Association, are formally organized, with incorporation papers, regular meetings, a written constitution, and connection to a national federation, whereas others, like a pickup basketball game, are more informal. Some forms of social capital, like a volunteer ambulance squad, have explicit public-regarding purposes; some, like a bridge club, exist for the private enjoyment of the members; and some, like the Rotary club mentioned earlier, serve both public and private ends.

Of all the dimensions along which forms of social capital vary, perhaps the most important is the distinction between *bridging* (or inclusive) and *bonding* (or exclusive).[20] Some forms of social capital are, by choice or necessity, inward looking and tend to reinforce exclusive identities and homogeneous groups. Examples of bonding social capital include ethnic fraternal organizations, church-based women's reading groups, and fashionable country clubs. Other networks are outward looking and encompass people across diverse social cleavages. Examples of bridging social capital include the civil rights movement, many youth service groups, and ecumenical religious organizations.

Bonding social capital is good for undergirding specific reciprocity and mobilizing solidarity. Dense networks in ethnic enclaves, for example, provide crucial social and psychological support for less fortunate members of the community, while furnishing start-up financing, markets, and reliable labor for local entrepreneurs. Bridging networks, by contrast, are better for linkage to external assets and for information diffusion. Economic sociologist Mark Granovetter has pointed out that when seeking jobs—or political allies—the "weak" ties that link me to distant acquaintances who move in different circles from mine are actually more valuable than the "strong" ties that link me to relatives and intimate friends whose sociological niche is very like my own. Bonding social capital is, as Xavier de Souza Briggs puts it, good for "getting by," but bridging social capital is crucial for "getting ahead."[21]

Moreover, bridging social capital can generate broader identities and reciprocity, whereas bonding social capital bolsters our narrower selves. In 1829 at the founding of a community lyceum in the bustling whaling port of New Bedford, Massachusetts, Thomas Greene eloquently expressed this crucial insight:

> We come from all the divisions, ranks and classes of society . . . to teach and to be taught in our turn. While we mingle together in these pursuits, we shall learn to know each other more intimately; we shall remove many of the prejudices which ignorance or partial acquaintance with each other had fostered. . . . In the parties and sects into which we are divided, we sometimes learn to love our brother at the expense of him whom we do not in so many respects regard as a brother. . . . We may return to our homes and firesides [from the lyceum] with kindlier feelings toward one another, because we have learned to know one another better.[22]

Bonding social capital constitutes a kind of sociological superglue, whereas bridging social capital provides a sociological WD-40. Bonding social capital, by creating strong in-group loyalty, may also create strong out-group antagonism, as Thomas Greene and his neighbors in New Bedford knew, and for that reason we might expect negative external effects to be more common with this form of social capital. Nevertheless, under many circumstances both bridging and bonding social capital can have powerfully positive social effects.

Many groups simultaneously bond along some social dimensions and bridge across others. The black church, for example, brings together people of the same race and religion across class lines. The Knights of Columbus was created to bridge cleavages among different ethnic communities while bonding along religious and gender lines. Internet chat groups may bridge across geography, gender, age, and religion, while being tightly homogeneous in education and ideology. In short, bonding and bridging are not "either-or" categories into which social networks can be neatly divided, but "more or less" dimensions along which we can compare different forms of social capital.

It would obviously be valuable to have distinct measures of the evolution of these various forms of social capital over time. However, like researchers on global warming, we must make do with the imperfect evidence that we can find, not merely lament its deficiencies. Exhaustive descriptions of social networks in America—even at a single point in time—do not exist. I have found no reliable, comprehensive, nationwide measures of social capital that neatly distinguish "bridgingness" and "bondingness." In our empirical account of recent social trends in this book, therefore, this distinction will be less prominent than I would prefer. On the other hand, we must keep this conceptual differentiation at the back of our minds as we proceed, recognizing that bridging and bonding social capital are not interchangeable.

"SOCIAL CAPITAL" is to some extent merely new language for a very old debate in American intellectual circles. Community has warred incessantly with individualism for preeminence in our political hagiology. Liberation from ossified community bonds is a recurrent and honored theme in our culture, from the Pilgrims' storied escape from religious convention in the seventeenth century to the lyric nineteenth-century paeans to individualism by Emerson ("Self-Reliance"), Thoreau ("Civil Disobedience"), and Whitman ("Song of Myself") to Sherwood Anderson's twentieth-century celebration of the struggle against conformism by ordinary citizens in *Winesburg, Ohio* to the latest Clint Eastwood film. Even Alexis de Tocqueville, patron saint of American communitarians, acknowledged the uniquely democratic claim of individualism, "a calm and considered feeling which disposes each citizen to isolate himself from the mass of his fellows and withdraw into the circle of family and friends; with this little society formed to his taste, he gladly leaves the greater society to look after itself."[23]

Our national myths often exaggerate the role of individual heroes and understate the importance of collective effort. Historian David Hackett Fischer's gripping account of opening night in the American Revolution, for example, reminds us that Paul Revere's alarum was successful only because of networks of civic engagement in the Middlesex villages. Towns without well-organized local militia, no matter how patriotic their inhabitants, were AWOL from Lexington and Concord.[24] Nevertheless, the myth of rugged individualism continues to strike a powerful inner chord in the American psyche.

Debates about the waxing and waning of "community" have been endemic for at least two centuries. "Declensionist narratives"—postmodernist jargon for tales of decline and fall—have a long pedigree in our letters. We seem perennially tempted to contrast our tawdry todays with past golden ages. We apparently share this nostalgic predilection with the rest of humanity. As sociologist Barry Wellman observes,

> It is likely that pundits have worried about the impact of social change on communities ever since human beings ventured beyond their caves. . . .
> In the [past] two centuries many leading social commentators have been gainfully employed suggesting various ways in which large-scale social

changes associated with the Industrial Revolution may have affected the structure and operation of communities. . . . This ambivalence about the consequences of large-scale changes continued well into the twentieth century. Analysts have kept asking if things have, in fact, fallen apart.[25]

At the conclusion of the twentieth century, ordinary Americans shared this sense of civic malaise. We were reasonably content about our economic prospects, hardly a surprise after an expansion of unprecedented length, but we were not equally convinced that we were on the right track morally or culturally. Of baby boomers interviewed in 1987, 53 percent thought their parents' generation was better in terms of "being a concerned citizen, involved in helping others in the community," as compared with only 21 percent who thought their own generation was better. Fully 77 percent said the nation was worse off because of "less involvement in community activities." In 1992 three-quarters of the U.S. workforce said that "the breakdown of community" and "selfishness" were "serious" or "extremely serious" problems in America. In 1996 only 8 percent of all Americans said that "the honesty and integrity of the average American" were improving, as compared with 50 percent of us who thought we were becoming less trustworthy. Those of us who said that people had become less civil over the preceding ten years outnumbered those who thought people had become more civil, 80 percent to 12 percent. In several surveys in 1999 two-thirds of Americans said that America's civic life had weakened in recent years, that social and moral values were higher when they were growing up, and that our society was focused more on the individual than the community. More than 80 percent said there should be more emphasis on community, even if that put more demands on individuals.[26] Americans' concern about weakening community bonds may be misplaced or exaggerated, but a decent respect for the opinion of our fellow citizens suggests that we should explore the issue more thoroughly.

It is emphatically not my view that community bonds in America have weakened steadily throughout our history—or even throughout the last hundred years. On the contrary, American history carefully examined is a story of ups and downs in civic engagement, *not just downs*—a story of collapse *and* of renewal. As I have already hinted in the opening pages of this book, within living memory the bonds of community in America were becoming stronger, not weaker, and as I shall argue in the concluding pages, it is within our power to reverse the decline of the last several decades.

Nevertheless, my argument is, at least in appearance, in the declensionist tradition, so it is important to avoid simple nostalgia. Precisely because the theme of this book might lend itself to gauzy self-deception, our methods must be transparent. Is life in communities as we enter the twenty-first century really so different after all from the reality of American communities in the 1950s and 1960s? One way of curbing nostalgia is to count things. Are club meetings really less crowded today than yesterday, or does it just seem so? Do we really know our neighbors less well than our parents did, or is our childhood recollection of neighborhood barbecues suffused with a golden glow of wishful reminiscence? Are friendly poker games less common now, or is it merely that we ourselves have outgrown poker? League bowling may be passé, but how about softball and soccer? Are strangers less trustworthy now? Are boomers and X'ers really less engaged in community life? After all, it was the preceding generation that was once scorned as "silent." Perhaps the younger generation today is no less engaged than their predecessors, but engaged in new ways. In the chapters that follow we explore these questions with the best available evidence.

THE CHALLENGE of studying the evolving social climate is analogous in some respects to the challenge facing meteorologists who measure global warming: we know what kind of evidence we would ideally want from the past, but time's arrow means that we can't go back to conduct those well-designed studies. Thus if we are to explore how our society is like or unlike our parents', we must make imperfect inferences from all the evidence that we can find.

The most powerful strategy for paleometeorologists seeking to assess global climate change is to triangulate among diverse sources of evidence. If pollen counts in polar ice, and the width of southwestern tree rings, and temperature records of the British Admiralty all point in a similar direction, the inference of global warming is stronger than if the cord of evidence has only a single strand. For much the same reason, prudent journalists follow a "two source" rule: Never report anything unless at least two independent sources confirm it.

In this book I follow that same maxim. Nearly every major generalization here rests on more than one body of independent evidence, and where I have discovered divergent results from credible sources, I note that disparity as well. I have a case to make, but like any officer of the court, I have a professional obligation to present all relevant evidence I have found, exculpatory as well as incriminating. To avoid cluttering the text with masses of redundant evidence, I have typically put confirmatory evidence from multiple studies in the notes, so skeptical "show me" readers should examine those notes as well as the text.[27]

I have sought as diverse a range of evidence as possible on continuities and change in American social life. If the transformation that I discern is as broad and deep as I believe it to be, it ought to show up in many different places, so I have cast a broad net. Of course, social change, like climatic change, is inevitably uneven. Life is not lived in a single dimension. We should not expect to find everything changing in the same direction and at the same speed, but those very anomalies may contain important clues to what is happening.

American society, like the continent on which we live, is massive and polymorphous, and our civic engagement historically has come in many sizes and shapes. A few of us still share plowing chores with neighbors, while many more pitch in to wire classrooms to the Internet. Some of us run for Congress, and others join self-help groups. Some of us hang out at the local bar association and others at the local bar. Some of us attend mass once a day, while others struggle to remember to send holiday greetings once a year. The forms of our social capital—the ways in which we connect with friends and neighbors and strangers—are varied.

So our review of trends in social capital and civic engagement ranges widely across various sectors of this complex society. In the chapters that follow we begin by charting Americans' participation in the most public forum—politics and public affairs. We next turn to the institutions of our communities—clubs and community associations, religious bodies, and work-related organizations, such as unions and professional societies. Then we explore the almost infinite variety of informal ties that link Americans—card parties and bowling leagues, bar cliques and ball games, picnics and parties. Next we examine the changing patterns of trust and altruism in America—philanthropy, volunteering, honesty, reciprocity. Finally we turn to three apparent counterexamples to the decline of connectedness—small groups, social movements, and the Internet.

In each domain we shall encounter currents and crosscurrents and eddies, but in each we shall also discover common, powerful tidal movements that have swept across American society in the twentieth century. The dominant theme is simple: For the first two-thirds of the twentieth century a powerful tide bore Americans into ever deeper engagement in the life of their communities, but a few decades ago—silently, without warning—that tide reversed and we were overtaken by a treacherous rip current. Without at first noticing, we have been pulled apart from one another and from our communities over the last third of the century.

The impact of these tides on all aspects of American society, their causes and consequences and what we might do to reverse them, is the subject of the rest of this book. Section III explores a wide range of possible explanations—from overwork to suburban sprawl, from the welfare state to the women's revolution, from racism to television, from the growth of mobility to the growth of divorce. Some of these factors turn out to have played no significant role at all in the erosion of social capital, but we shall be able to identify three or four critical sources of our problem.

Whereas section III asks "Why?" section IV asks "So What?" Social capital turns out to have forceful, even quantifiable effects on many different aspects of our lives. What is at stake is not merely warm, cuddly feelings or frissons of community pride. We shall review hard evidence that our schools and neighborhoods don't work so well when community bonds slacken, that our economy, our democracy, and even our health and happiness depend on adequate stocks of social capital.

Finally, in section V we turn from the necessary but cheerless task of diagnosis to the more optimistic challenge of contemplating possible therapies. A century ago, it turns out, Americans faced social and political issues that were strikingly similar to those that we must now address. From our predecessors' responses, we have much to learn—not least that civic decay like that around us can be reversed. This volume offers no simple cures for our contemporary ills. In the final section my aim is to provoke (and perhaps contribute to) a period of national deliberation and experimentation about how we can renew American civic engagement and social connectedness in the twenty-first century.

BEFORE OCTOBER 29, 1997, John Lambert and Andy Boschma knew each other only through their local bowling league at the Ypsi-Arbor Lanes in Ypsilanti, Michigan. Lambert, a sixty-four-year-old retired employee of the University of Michigan hospital, had been on a kidney transplant waiting list for three years when Boschma, a thirty-three-year-old accountant, learned casually of Lambert's need and unexpectedly approached him to offer to donate one of his own kidneys.

"Andy saw something in me that others didn't," said Lambert. "When we were in the hospital Andy said to me, 'John, I really like you and have a lot of respect for you. I wouldn't hesitate to do this all over again.' I got choked up." Boschma returned the feeling: "I obviously feel a kinship [with Lambert]. I cared about him before, but now I'm really rooting for him." This moving story speaks for itself, but the photograph that accompanied this report in the *Ann Arbor News* reveals that in addition to their differences in profession and generation, Boschma is white and Lambert is African American. That they bowled together made all the difference.[28] In small ways like this—and in larger ways, too—we Americans need to reconnect with one another. That is the simple argument of this book.

SECTION TWO

Trends
in Civic Engagement
and Social Capital

CHAPTER 2

Political Participation

THE CHARACTER of Americans' involvement with politics and government has been transformed over the past three decades. This is certainly not the only alteration in the way we connect with our communities. It is not even the most dramatic and unequivocal example of change. But it is the most widely discussed, and it is thus a good place to begin.

With the singular exception of voting, American rates of political participation compare favorably with those in other democracies. We have multiple avenues for expressing our views and exercising our rights—contacting local and national officials, working for political parties and other political organizations, discussing politics with our neighbors, attending public meetings, joining in election campaigns, wearing buttons, signing petitions, speaking out on talk radio, and many more. Not all of us do all these things, but more of us are active in these ways than are citizens in many other advanced democracies. We are reminded each election year that fewer voters show up at the polls in America than in most other democracies: our turnout rate ranks us just above the cellar—narrowly besting Switzerland, but below all twenty-two other established democracies.[1] Nevertheless, Americans are fairly active politically outside the ballot booth. However, our interest here is not "How are we doing compared with other countries?" but "How are we doing today compared with our own past?" The answer to that question is less encouraging.

We begin with the most common act of democratic citizenship—voting. In 1960, 62.8 percent of voting-age Americans went to the polls to choose between John F. Kennedy and Richard M. Nixon. In 1996, after decades of slippage, 48.9 percent of voting-age Americans chose among Bill Clinton, Bob Dole, and Ross Perot, very nearly the lowest turnout in the twentieth century. Participation in presidential elections has declined by roughly a quarter over the last thirty-six years. Turnout in off-year and local elections is down by roughly this same amount.[2]

For several reasons, this widely reported fact understates the real decline in Americans' commitment to electoral participation. For most of the twentieth century Americans' access to the voting booth was hampered by burdensome registration requirements. The conventional explanation for our low turnout as compared with other democracies points precisely to the hurdles of registration. Over the last four decades, however, registration requirements in America have been greatly relaxed. The nationwide introduction of "motor voter" registration, on which states have collectively spent $100 million to try to swell the ranks of new voters, is merely the most visible example of this trend. Turnout has declined despite the fact that the most commonly cited barrier to voting has been substantially lowered.[3] Even facing a lower hurdle, fewer Americans are making the jump.

A second qualification is even more important. For much of our history many people in the South, especially blacks, were disenfranchised. To provide an accurate picture of how current voting rates compare with those of the past, figure 1 traces presidential turnout in southern and nonsouthern states over most of the history of the American Republic.

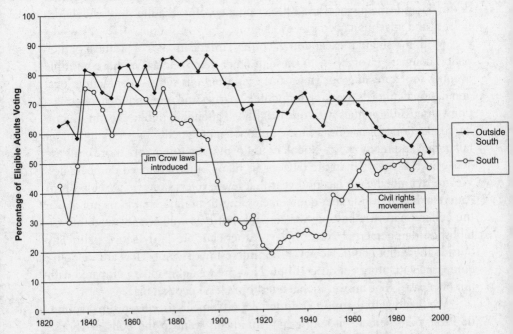

Figure 1: Trends in Presidential Voting (1828–1996), by Region

From the end of the nineteenth century through the middle of the twentieth virtually all African Americans (along with some poor whites) in southern states were prevented from voting by poll taxes, literacy tests, fraud, and violence. This Jim Crow disenfranchisement of southern blacks in the 1890s decimated turnout in the South and artificially depressed the national average for the next seventy years. Since most standard measures of turnout lump those disenfranchised millions with other nonvoters, those measures understate the effective turnout during the first two-thirds of the twentieth century among Americans who were free to vote.[4]

With the civil rights movement of the 1960s and the 1965 Voting Rights Act, millions of newly enfranchised men and women in the South were able for the first time in the twentieth century to exercise the right to vote. This influx of new voters partially masked the decline in turnout among the rest of the American electorate.[5] In effect, American national turnout figures took credit for the inclusion of southern blacks in the electorate, obscuring the fact that fewer and fewer of the rest of us who had had the right to vote all along are now actually exercising it.

Outside the South the slide in electoral participation since 1960 is, by now, the longest decline in American history, and voting in the 1996 and 1998 elections was substantially lower than in any other presidential and off-year elections in nearly two centuries.[6] Even within the South, turnout in 1996 was (except for the period of forced disenfranchisement between 1896 and 1964) very nearly the lowest in 164 years. In short, not in nearly two centuries have so many American citizens freely abstained from voting as in the past few years.

Who are these nonvoters, and why are they missing in action? Many explanations have been offered—growing distrust of government, declining party mobilization, fraying social bonds, political dealignment, and many more. Beneath the ups and downs of individual elections, however, virtually all the long-run decline in turnout is due to the gradual replacement of voters who came of age before or during the New Deal and World War II by the generations who came of age later.

Because generational change will be an important theme in our story, we should pause briefly here to consider how social change and generational change are interrelated. As a matter of simple accounting, any social change—from the rise of rap music to the decline of newspapers—is always produced by some combination of two very different processes. The first is for many individuals to change their tastes and habits in a single direction simultaneously. This sort of social change can occur quickly and be reversed just as quickly. If large numbers of Americans, young and old, fall in love with sport utility vehicles, as they did in the 1990s, the automotive marketplace can be quickly transformed, and it can be transformed in a different direction just as quickly. Sociologists sometimes call this type of change "intracohort," because the change is detectable within each age cohort.

The second sort of social change is slower, more subtle, and harder to reverse. If different generations have different tastes or habits, the social physiology of birth and death will eventually transform society, *even if no individual ever changes*. Much of the change in sexual mores over the last several decades has been of this sort. Relatively few adults changed their views about morality, and most of those who did actually became more conservative. In the aggregate, however, American attitudes toward premarital sex, for example, have been radically liberalized over the last several decades, because a generation with stricter beliefs was gradually replaced by a later generation with more relaxed norms. Sociologists call this type of change "intercohort," because the change is detectable only across different age groups. Precisely because the rhythm of generational change is slower paced, it is more nearly inexorable.[7]

Most social change involves both individual and generational processes. The use of new technology, like the telephone or the Internet, illustrates this sort of mixture. When the innovation is introduced, many people try out the new phone or the new Web browser. As individuals change their behavior, virtually none of the early growth in usage is attributable to generational change. Change is, however, easier for young people, so the immediate impetus for growth is dampened by the ingrained habits of older generations. Many middle-aged Americans today recall how reluctantly their parents picked up the phone for a long-distance call, well after long-distance rates had fallen. Gradually, generational differences became the dominant feature of this social change. Virtually all of the decline in personal letter writing over the past several decades is attributable not to individuals' changing their habits, but to the replacement of one generation accustomed to communicating with distant friends and relatives in writing by a younger generation more accustomed to picking up the phone.[8]

The distinction between intracohort and intercohort change is crucial to understanding what's been happening to turnout in America over the last thirty years. Very little of the net decline in voting is attributable to individual change, and virtually all of it is generational. Throughout their lives and whatever their station in life and their level of political interest, baby boomers and their children have been less likely to vote than their parents and grandparents. As boomers and their children became a larger and larger fraction of the national electorate, the average turnout rate was inexorably driven downward.[9]

This generation gap in civic engagement, as we shall see, is common in American communities these days. It is one reason why the decline in turnout continues so ineluctably, seeming to defy all efforts to reverse it (such as motor voter registration) and why the trend is pervasive, affecting not just presidential politics, but also state and local elections and even voting on bond issues. Whatever the ups and downs of individual candidates and issues, each campaign's efforts to get out the vote must begin at a lower base level, for every year the Grim Reaper removes another swath of the most politically engaged generation in the American electorate.

Voting is by a substantial margin the most common form of political activity, and it embodies the most fundamental democratic principle of equality. Not to vote is to withdraw from the political community. Moreover, like the canary in the mining pit, voting is an instructive proxy measure of broader social change. Compared to demographically matched nonvoters, voters are more likely to be interested in politics, to give to charity, to volunteer, to serve on juries, to attend community school board meetings, to participate in public demonstrations, and to cooperate with their fellow citizens on community affairs. It is sometimes hard to tell whether voting causes community engagement or vice versa, although some recent evidence suggests that the act of voting itself encourages volunteering and other forms of good citizenship. So it is hardly a small matter for American democracy when voting rates decline by 25 percent or more.[10]

On the other hand, in some important respects voting is not a typical mode of political participation. Based on their exhaustive assessment of different forms of participation in American politics, political scientists Sidney Verba, Kay Schlozman, and Henry Brady conclude that "it is incomplete and misleading to understand citizen participation solely through the vote. . . . Compared with those who engage in various other political acts, voters report a different mix of gratification and a different bundle of issue concerns as being behind their activity. . . . [V]oting is sui generis." Declining electoral participation is merely the most visible symptom of a broader disengagement from community life.[11] Like a fever, electoral abstention is even more important as a sign of deeper trouble in the body politic than as a malady itself. It is not just from the voting booth that Americans are increasingly AWOL.

POLITICAL KNOWLEDGE and interest in public affairs are critical preconditions for more active forms of involvement. If you don't know the rules of the game and the players and don't care about the outcome, you're unlikely to try playing yourself. Encouragingly, Americans in the aggregate at century's end are about as likely to know, for example, which party controls the House of Representatives or who their senators are as were their grandparents a half century ago. On the other hand, we are much better educated than our grandparents, and since civics knowledge is boosted by formal education, it is surprising that civics knowledge has not improved accordingly. The average college graduate today knows little more about public affairs than did the average high school graduate in the 1940s.[12]

Roughly every other month from 1974 to 1998 Roper pollsters asked Americans, "Have you recently been taking a good deal of interest in current events and what's happening in the world today, some interest, or not very much interest?" Popular interest in current events naturally tends to rise and fall with what's in the news, so this chart of attention to public affairs looks like the sawtooth traces left by an errant seismograph. Beneath these choppy waves, however, the tide of the public's interest in current events gradually ebbed by roughly 20 percent over this quarter century. Similarly, another long-term series of annual surveys found that political interest steadily slumped by one-fifth between 1975 and 1999.[13] Scandals and war can still rouse our attention, but generally speaking, fewer Americans follow public affairs now than did a quarter century ago.

Even more worrying are intergenerational differences in political knowledge and interest. Like the decline in voting turnout, to which it is linked, the slow slump in interest in politics and current events is due to the replacement of an older generation that was relatively interested in public affairs by a younger generation that is relatively uninterested. Among both young and old, of course, curiosity about public affairs continues to fluctuate in response to daily headlines, but the base level of interest is gradually fading, as an older generation of news and politics junkies passes slowly from the scene. The fact that the decline is generation-specific, rather than nationwide, argues against the view that public affairs have simply become boring in some objective sense.

The post–baby boom generations—roughly speaking, men and women who were born after 1964 and thus came of age in the 1980s and 1990s—are substantially less knowledgeable about public affairs, despite the proliferation of sources of information. Even in the midst of national election campaigns in the 1980s and 1990s, for example, these young people were about a third less likely than their elders to know, for instance, which political party controlled the House of Representatives.[14]

Today's generation gap in political knowledge does not reflect some permanent tendency for the young to be less well informed than their elders but is instead a recent development. From the earliest opinion polls in the 1940s to the mid-1970s, younger people were at least as well informed as their elders were, but that is no longer the case. This news and information gap, affecting not just politics, but even things like airline crashes, terrorism, and financial news, first opened up with the boomers in the 1970s and widened considerably with the advent of the X generation. Daily newspaper readership among people under thirty-five dropped from two-thirds in 1965 to one-third in 1990, at the same time that TV news viewership in this same age group fell from 52 percent to 41 percent. Today's under-thirties pay less attention to the news and know less about current events than their elders do today or than people their age did two or three decades ago.[15]

• • • •

So VOTING IN AMERICA is down by about a quarter, and interest in public affairs by about one-fifth, over the last two or three decades. Not all measures of political interest are declining. Americans seem to follow national election campaigns no less today than three or four decades ago. During the national elections of the 1990s, as many of us said that we "talked about politics" or tried to persuade someone else how to vote as people did in the 1950s and 1960s. But this surface stability conceals a growing generation gap. Members of today's older generation are slightly *more* interested in electoral campaigns than were their predecessors four decades ago, while youths today are *less* interested than youths were in the 1950s and 1960s.[16] This generation gap in civic engagement, if it persists, will further depress political participation in the future.

Voting and following politics are relatively undemanding forms of participation. In fact, they are not, strictly speaking, forms of social capital at all, because they can be done utterly alone. As we have seen, these measures show some thinning of the ranks of political spectators, particularly at the end of the stadium where the younger generation sits. But most of the fans are still in their seats, following the action and chatting about the antics of the star players. How about the grassroots gladiators who volunteer to work for political parties, posting signs, attending campaign rallies, and the like? What is the evidence on trends in partisan participation?

On the positive side of the ledger, one might argue, party organizations themselves are as strong as ever at both state and local levels. Over the last thirty to forty years these organizations have become bigger, richer, and more professional. During presidential campaigns from the late 1950s to the late 1970s, more and more voters reported being contacted by one or both of the major political parties. After a slump from 1980 to 1992, this measure of party vitality soared nearly to an all-time high in 1996, as GOTV ("Get out the vote") activities blossomed.[17]

Party finances, too, skyrocketed in the 1970s and 1980s. Between 1976 and 1986, for example, the Democrats' intake rose at more than twice the rate of inflation, while the Republicans' rose at more than four times the rate of inflation. More money meant more staff, more polling, more advertising, better candidate recruitment and training, and more party outreach. The number of political organizations, partisan and nonpartisan, with regular paid staff has exploded over the last two decades. Nearly every election year since 1980 has set a new record by this standard of organizational proliferation, and the pace of growth has clearly tended to accelerate. The growth chart for this political "industry" (see figure 2) exhibits an ebullience more familiar in Silicon Valley. The business of politics in America has never been healthier, or so it would seem.[18]

Yet viewed by the "consumers" in the political marketplace, this picture of vigorous health seems a bizarre parody. The rate of party identification—the

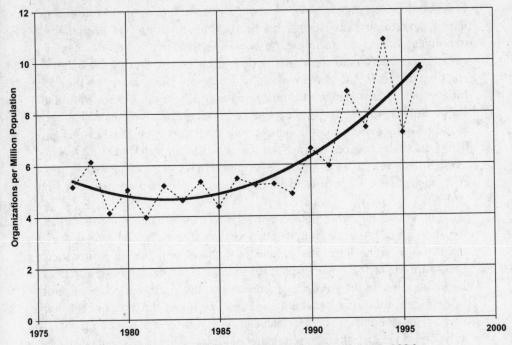

Figure 2: Political Organizations with Regular Paid Staff, 1977–1996

voter's sense of commitment to her own team—fell from more than 75 percent around 1960 to less than 65 percent in the late 1990s. Despite a partial recovery in the late 1980s, at century's end party "brand loyalty" remained well below the levels of the 1950s and early 1960s. What is more, this form of political engagement is significantly lower in more recent cohorts, so that as older, more partisan voters depart from the electorate to be replaced by younger independents, the net attachment to the parties may continue to decline.[19] Again, the Grim Reaper is silently at work, lowering political involvement.

Beyond party identification, at the grassroots level attending a campaign meeting or volunteering to work for a political party has become much rarer over the last thirty years. From the 1950s to the 1960s growing numbers of Americans worked for a political party during election campaigns, ringing doorbells, stuffing envelopes, and the like. Since 1968, however, that form of political engagement has plunged, reaching an all-time low for a presidential election year in 1996. Attendance at political meetings and campaign rallies has followed a similar trajectory over the last half century—up from the 1950s to the 1960s, instability in the 1970s, and general decline since the 1980s.[20] (Figure 3 charts these trends.) In short, while the parties themselves are better financed and more professionally staffed than ever, fewer and fewer Americans participate in partisan political activities.

How can we reconcile these two conflicting pictures—organizational

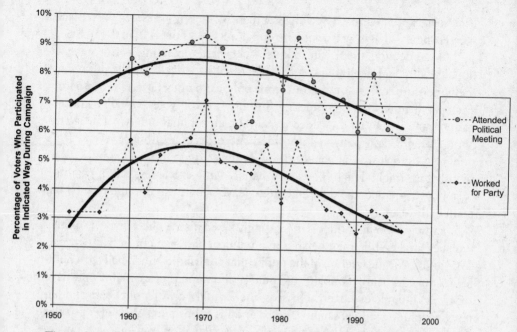

Figure 3: Citizen Participation in Campaign Activities, 1952–1996

health, as seen from the parties, and organizational decay, as seen from the voters' side? One clue to this paradox is the ratio of voters who say they have been *contacted by* a party in the latest campaign to voters who say that they have *worked for* a party in that same campaign. The last three decades of the twentieth century witnessed an accelerating trend toward more and more voter contacts but fewer and fewer party workers. By 1996 this ratio was 2.5 times greater than the equivalent figure in 1968.[21]

At first blush one might admire the growing "productivity" in this flourishing industry. Each "worker" seems to be producing more and more "contacts." In reality, however, this trend is evidence of the professionalization and commercialization of politics in America. The "contacts" that voters report are, in fact, less and less likely to be a visit from a neighborhood party worker and more and more likely to be an anonymous call from a paid phone bank. Less and less party activity involves volunteer collaboration among committed partisans. More and more involves the skilled (and expensive) techniques of effective mass marketing. This trend goes hand in hand with the explosive growth of direct-mail fund-raising and political action committees (PACs) formed to channel financial support to party organizations. During the same period that citizen involvement in party activities was slumping by more than half, spending on presidential nomination and election campaigns exploded from $35 million in 1964 to over $700 million in 1996, a nearly fivefold increase even in constant dollars. The bottom line in the political industry is this:

Financial capital—the wherewithal for mass marketing—has steadily replaced social capital—that is, grassroots citizen networks—as the coin of the realm.[22]

On reflection, then, the contrast between increasing party organizational vitality and declining voter involvement is perfectly intelligible. Since their "consumers" are tuning out from politics, parties have to work harder and spend much more, competing furiously to woo votes, workers, and donations, and to do that they need a (paid) organizational infrastructure. Party-as-organization and party-in-government have become stronger, even as the public has grown less attached to the parties.[23] If we think of politics as an industry, we might delight in its new "labor-saving efficiency," but if we think of politics as democratic deliberation, to leave people out is to miss the whole point of the exercise.

Participation in politics is increasingly based on the checkbook, as money replaces time. While membership in a political club was cut in half between 1967 and 1987, the fraction of the public that contributed financially to a political campaign nearly doubled. "Nationalization and professionalization have redefined the role of citizen activist as, increasingly, a writer of checks and letters," conclude political scientist Verba and his colleagues. "Whatever puzzles there may be concerning the trajectory of participation over the past few decades, there was an unambiguous increase in the amount of money donated to politics over the period from the late 1970s to the late 1980s."[24] There may be nearly as many fans in the political stadium nowadays, but they are not watching an amateur or even a semipro match. Whether the slick professional game they have become accustomed to watching is worth the increasingly high admission price is another matter.

So FAR we have been considering political participation from the important but limited perspective of partisan and electoral activities. For most Americans, however, national election campaigns occupy only a small part of their time and attention. What about trends in political participation outside the context of national elections, especially at the local level? Until recently we lacked any systematic evidence of long-term trends in how involved Americans are in community affairs. However, a recently retrieved archive of unparalleled depth enables us to track in great detail a wide range of civic activities.

Roughly every month from 1973 through 1994 the Roper survey organization presented thousands of Americans with a simple checklist of a dozen different civic activities—from signing a petition or attending a public meeting to working for a political party or running for office.[25] "Which, if any, of these things have you happened to do in the past year?" the pollsters asked. Some of the activities are relatively common: each year across these two decades roughly one in three of us has signed a petition and roughly one in six has attended a public meeting on town or school affairs. On the other hand, some items on the checklist are quite rare. For example, fewer than one American in a hundred has run for public office in the past twelve months. Altogether these more than four hundred thousand interviews provide exceptionally rich raw material for compiling detailed civic statistics for Americans over more than two decades.

How did patterns of civic and political participation change over this period? The answer is simple: *The frequency of virtually every form of community involvement measured in the Roper polls declined significantly, from the most common—petition signing—to the least common—running for office.* Americans are playing virtually every aspect of the civic game less frequently today than we did two decades ago.

Consider first the new evidence on trends in partisan and campaign activities. (Figure 4 charts these trends.) [26] In round numbers, Americans were roughly half as likely to work for a political party or attend a political rally or speech in the 1990s as in the 1970s. Barely two decades ago election campaigns were for millions of Americans an occasion for active participation in national deliberation. Campaigning was something we did, not something we merely witnessed. Now for almost all Americans, an election campaign is something that happens around us, a grating element in the background noise of everyday life, a fleeting image on a TV screen. Strikingly, the dropout rate from these campaign activities (about 50 percent) is even greater than the dropout rate in the voting booth itself (25 percent).

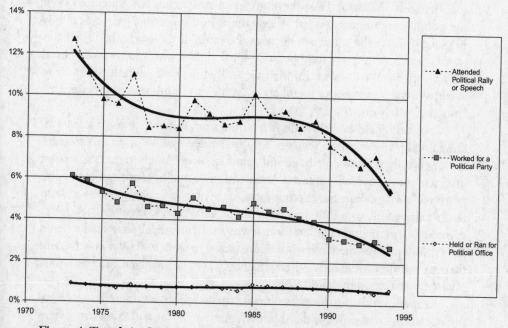

Figure 4: Trends in Civic Engagement I: Partisan Activities

The new evidence also includes a much more demanding measure of political involvement—that is, actually running for or holding office. So few people ever become this involved politically that it takes a social microscope like that provided by the Roper archive to discover that even this intense form of participation has faded. Over the last two decades the number of office seekers in any year at all levels in the American body politic—from school board to town council—shrank by perhaps 15 percent.[27] As a result of this decline, Americans lost more than a quarter million candidates annually to choose among. It is impossible to know what price we paid collectively for the loss of those potential grassroots leaders—not only in terms of talent and creativity, but also in terms of competitive pressure on incumbent officeholders—but it is hard to believe that there was no loss at all.

That Americans in recent years have deserted party politics is perhaps not astonishing news, for antiparty sentiments had become a commonplace of punditry even before Ross Perot rode the antiparty bandwagon to national prominence in 1992. But how about communal forms of activity, like attending local meetings, serving local organizations, and taking part in "good government" activities? Here the new evidence is startling, for involvement in these everyday forms of community life has dwindled as rapidly as has partisan and electoral participation. (The relevant evidence is summarized in figure 5.) The pattern is broadly similar to that for campaign activities—a slump in the late 1970s, a pause in the early 1980s, and then a renewed and intensified decline from the late 1980s into the 1990s.

Between 1973 and 1994 the number of Americans who attended even one public meeting on town or school affairs in the previous year was cut by 40 percent. Over the same two decades the ranks of those who had served as an officer or a committee member for a local club or organization—*any* local club or organization—were thinned by an identical 40 percent. Over these twenty years the number of members of "some group interested in better government" fell by one-third.[28]

Like battlefield casualties dryly reported from someone else's distant war, these unadorned numbers scarcely convey the decimation of American community life they represent. In round numbers every single percentage-point drop represents two million fewer Americans involved in some aspect of community life every year. So, the numbers imply, we now have sixteen million fewer participants in public meetings about local affairs, eight million fewer committee members, eight million fewer local organizational leaders, and three million fewer men and women organized to work for better government than we would have had if Americans had stayed as involved in community affairs as we were in the mid-1970s.

Keep in mind, too, that these surveys invited people to mention *any* local organization—not only "old-fashioned" garden clubs and Shriners lodges with their odd hats, but also trendy upstarts, like environmental action com-

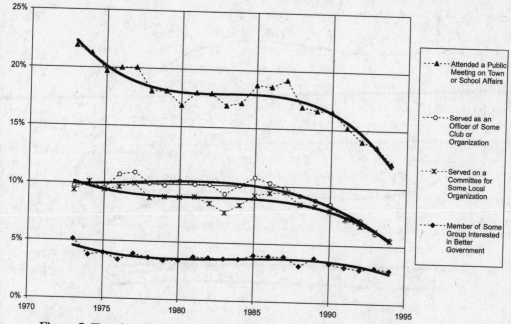

Figure 5: Trends in Civic Engagement II: Communal Participation

mittees and local branches of the antiabortion movement. People were asked whether they had attended *any* public meeting on town or school affairs in the last year—not merely droning sessions of the planning board, but also angry protests against condom distribution in the high school or debates about curbside recycling. Year after year, fewer and fewer of us took part in the everyday deliberations that constitute grassroots democracy. In effect, more than a third of America's civic infrastructure simply evaporated between the mid-1970s and the mid-1990s.

Finally, the Roper surveys also shed light on trends in various forms of public expression—signing petitions, writing Congress, writing an article or a letter to the editor, and making a speech. Once again, each of these types of activity has become less common over these twenty years. (See figure 6 for details.) This is most visible in the case of petition signing, because it is the single most common form of political activity measured in the Roper surveys, but the decline is also clear in the case of letters to Congress. In both cases, however, the chart is essentially flat for the first half of this period and then steadily downward in the second half. Much smaller proportions of the population claim to have given a speech or written a letter to the editor or an article for a newspaper or magazine within the previous year, so clear trends are harder to spot at this degree of magnification, though here too the general tendency is downward.[29]

The changes in American political participation traced in the Roper ar-

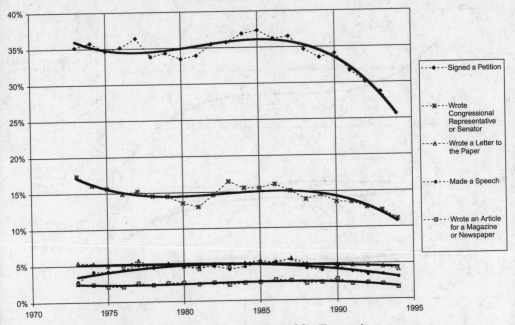

Figure 6: Trends in Civic Engagement III: Public Expression

chive are not identical across all forms of involvement. In some cases, such as attending a public meeting or a political rally, the trend is more or less steadily downward across the two decades, but in other cases, such as signing a petition, the drop is concentrated in the latter half of the period. And in some cases, such as running for office or writing an article for a magazine or newspaper, the decline is quite modest. Across the entire repertoire, however, the decline appears to have accelerated after 1985. Across the twelve separate activities, the average decline was 10 percent between 1973–74 and 1983–84, compared with 24 percent between 1983–84 and 1993–94.

The fraction of the American public utterly uninvolved in any of these civic activities rose by nearly one-third over these two decades. In 1973 most Americans engaged in at least one of these forms of civic involvement every year. By 1994 *most did not engage in any.* Thirty-two million fewer American adults were involved in community affairs in the mid-1990s than would have been involved at the proportional rate of two decades earlier.

We can get a better clue as to the implications of this loss of community life by arraying the dozen activities according to the degree of decline. (See table 1.) Strikingly, the forms of participation that have withered most notice-ably reflect organized activities at the community level. The verbs describing these modes of involvement in the top half of the table reflect action in coop-eration with others: "serve," "work," "attend." Each of these activities can be undertaken only if others in the community are also active. Conversely, the activities (in the bottom half of the table) that have declined most slowly are, for the most part, actions that one can undertake as an individual. Indeed, most of these activities merely require a pen or a keyboard, for the most common verb in this section of the list is "write."

In other words, the more that my activities depend on the actions of others, the greater the drop-off in my participation.[30] Even if everyone else in my town is a civic dropout, I can still write my congressman—or even run for Congress myself. On the other hand, if I'm the only member of a committee, it's not a "committee," and if no one else comes to a meeting on the bond issue, it is not a "meeting," even if I show up. Knowing that, I may well back out, too. In other words, it is precisely those forms of civic engagement most vulnerable to coordination problems and free riding—those activities that brought citizens *together*, those activities that most clearly embody social capital—that have declined most rapidly.[31]

One politically important consequence is that "cooperative" forms of behavior, like serving on committees, have declined more rapidly than "expressive" forms of behavior, like writing letters. It takes (at least) two to cooperate, but only one to express himself. Collaborative forms of political involvement engage broader public interests, whereas expressive forms are more individualistic and correspond to more narrowly defined interests. Any political system needs to counterpoise moments for articulating grievances and moments for resolving differences.

The changing pattern of civic participation in American communities

Table 1: Trends in political and community participation

	Relative change 1973–74 to 1993–94
served as an officer of some club or organization	−42%
worked for a political party	−42%
served on a committee for some local organization	−39%
attended a public meeting on town or school affairs	−35%
attended a political rally or speech	−34%
participated in at least one of these twelve activities	−25%
made a speech	−24%
wrote congressman or senator	−23%
signed a petition	−22%
was a member of some "better government" group	−19%
held or ran for political office	−16%
wrote a letter to the paper	−14%
wrote an article for a magazine or newspaper	−10%

Source: Roper Social and Political Trends surveys, 1973–1994

over the last two decades has shifted the balance in the larger society between the articulation of grievances and the aggregation of coalitions to address those grievances. In this sense, this disjunctive pattern of decline—cooperation falling more rapidly than self-expression—may well have encouraged the single-issue blare and declining civility of contemporary political discourse.[32]

These declines in participation appear all along the spectrum from hyperactivists to civic slugs. The fraction of the public who engaged in *none* of these dozen forms of civic participation rose by more than one-third over this period (from 46 percent in 1973 to 64 percent in 1994), while the band of civic activists who engaged in at least three different types of activity was cut nearly in half (from 20 percent to 11 percent). Moreover, these trends appear consistently in all sections of the population and all areas of the country—men and women, blacks and whites, central cities, suburbs, and rural areas, Northeast, South, Midwest, and West, upper class and lower class, and so on.

In absolute terms, the declines are greatest among the better educated. Among the college educated, attendance at public meetings was nearly halved from 34 percent to 18 percent. On the other hand, because the less educated were less involved to begin with, in relative terms their rates of participation have been even harder hit. Attendance at public meetings fell from 20 percent to 8 percent among those whose education ended in high school and from 7 percent to 3 percent among those who attended only elementary school. The last several decades have witnessed a serious deterioration of community involvement among Americans from all walks of life.

Let's sum up what we've learned about trends in political participation. On the positive side of the ledger, Americans today score about as well on a civics test as our parents and grandparents did, though our self-congratulation should be restrained, since we have on average four more years of formal schooling than they had.[33] Moreover, at election time we are no less likely than they were to talk politics or express interest in the campaign. On the other hand, since the mid-1960s, the weight of the evidence suggests, despite the rapid rise in levels of education Americans have become perhaps 10–15 percent less likely to voice our views publicly by running for office or writing Congress or the local newspaper, 15–20 percent less interested in politics and public affairs, roughly 25 percent less likely to vote, roughly 35 percent less likely to attend public meetings, both partisan and nonpartisan, and roughly 40 percent less engaged in party politics and indeed in political and civic organizations of all sorts. We remain, in short, reasonably well-informed spectators of public affairs, but many fewer of us actually partake in the game.

Might all this be explained as a natural consequence of rising public alienation from politics and declining confidence in political activity of all sorts? Perhaps the trends we have reviewed thus far simply reflect the fact that more Americans than ever before are "turned off" and "tuned out" from politics. Certainly political unhappiness of all sorts has mushroomed during these past three decades. Americans in the mid-1960s were strikingly confident in the benevolence and responsiveness of their political institutions. Only about one in four agreed then with sentiments like "People like me don't have much say in government" and "Public officials don't care what people like me think." Three in four said that you *could* "trust the government in Washington to do what is right all or most of the time." Whether or not they were fooling themselves, Americans in the 1960s felt politically effective.

Such views nowadays seem antiquated or naive. In virtually every case the proportions agreeing and disagreeing with such ideas essentially have been reversed. In the 1990s roughly three in four Americans *didn't* trust the government to do what is right most of the time. A single comparison captures the transformation: In April 1966, with the Vietnam War raging and race riots in Cleveland, Chicago, and Atlanta, 66 percent of Americans *rejected* the view that "the people running the country don't really care what happens to you." In December 1997, in the midst of the longest period of peace and prosperity in more than two generations, 57 percent of Americans *endorsed* that same view.[34] Today's cynical views may or may not be more accurate than the Pollyannaish views of the early sixties, but they undermine the political confidence necessary to motivate and sustain political involvement.

So perhaps because of the dysfunctional ugliness of contemporary politics and the absence of large, compelling collective projects, we have redirected our energies away from conventional politics into less formal, more voluntary, more effective channels. Whether the story of our disengagement from public affairs is as straightforward as that depends on what we find when we turn next to trends in social and civic involvement.

CHAPTER 3

Civic Participation

> Americans of all ages, all stations in life, and all types of disposition are
> forever forming associations. There are not only commercial and indus-
> trial associations in which all take part, but others of a thousand different
> types—religious, moral, serious, futile, very general and very limited, im-
> mensely large and very minute. . . . Nothing, in my view, deserves more
> attention than the intellectual and moral associations in America.[1]

THESE LINES from Alexis de Tocqueville, a perceptive French visitor to early-
nineteenth-century America, are often quoted by social scientists because they
capture an important and enduring fact about our country. Today, as 170 years
ago, Americans are more likely to be involved in voluntary associations than
are citizens of most other nations; only the small nations of northern Europe
outrank us as joiners.[2]

The ingenuity of Americans in creating organizations knows no bounds.
Wandering through the World Almanac list of 2,380 groups with some national
visibility from the Aaron Burr Society to the Zionist Organization of America,
one discovers such intriguing bodies as the Grand United Order of Antelopes,
the Elvis Presley Burning Love Fan Club, the Polish Army Veterans Association of America, the Southern Appalachian Dulcimer Association, and the
National Association for Outlaw and Lawman History. Some of these groups
may be the organizational equivalent of vanity press publications, but surveys
of American communities over the decades have uncovered an impressive
organizational vitality at the grassroots level. Many Americans today are ac-

tively involved in educational or school service groups like PTAs, recreational groups, work-related groups, such as labor unions and professional organizations, religious groups (in addition to churches), youth groups, service and fraternal clubs, neighborhood or homeowners groups, and other charitable organizations. Generally speaking, this same array of organizational affiliations has characterized Americans since at least the 1950s.[3]

Official membership in formal organizations is only one facet of social capital, but it is usually regarded as a useful barometer of community involvement. What can we learn from organizational records and social surveys about Americans' participation in the organized life of their communities? Broadly speaking, American voluntary associations may be divided into three categories: community based, church based, and work based. Let us begin with the most heterogeneous, all those social, civic, and leisure groups that are community based—everything from B'nai B'rith to the Parent-Teacher Association.

The record appears to show an impressive increase in the sheer number of voluntary associations over the last three decades. The number of nonprofit organizations of national scope listed in the *Encyclopedia of Associations* more than doubled from 10,299 to 22,901 between 1968 and 1997. Even taking account of the increase in population during this period, the number of national organizations per capita has increased by nearly two-thirds over the last three decades (see figure 7). Excited by this fact, some observers speak, perhaps too hastily, of a "participation revolution" in American politics and society. This impression of a rapid growth in American organizational life is reinforced—but also qualified—by numerous recent studies of the explosion of interest groups represented in Washington since the 1960s. What these studies reveal is ever more groups speaking (or claiming to speak) on behalf of ever more categories of citizens.[4]

In fact, relatively few of the tens of thousands of nonprofit associations whose proliferation is traced in figure 7 actually have mass membership. Many, such as the Animal Nutrition Research Council, the National Conference on Uniform Traffic Accident Statistics, and the National Slag Association, have no individual members at all. A close student of associations in America, David Horton Smith, found that barely half of the groups in the 1988 *Encyclopedia of Associations* actually had individual members. The median membership of national associations in the 1988 *Encyclopedia* was only one thousand. A comparable study of associations represented in the 1962 *Encyclopedia of Associations* had found a median size of roughly ten thousand members.[5] In other words, over this quarter century the number of voluntary associations roughly tripled, but the average membership seems to be roughly one-tenth as large— more groups, but most of them much smaller. The organizational eruption between the 1960s and the 1990s represented a proliferation of letterheads, not a boom of grassroots participation.

Also revealing is the increasing geographic concentration of national

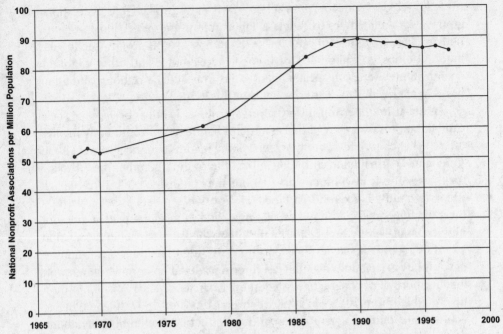

Figure 7: The Growth of National Nonprofit Associations, 1968–1997

headquarters. Membership organizations with local chapters and substantial grassroots activity are headquartered in places like Irving, Texas (Boy Scouts); New Haven, Connecticut (Knights of Columbus); Indianapolis, Indiana (American Legion and Kiwanis); Birmingham, Alabama (Civitan); Tulsa, Oklahoma (Jaycees); Oak Brook, Illinois (Lions Clubs); St. Louis, Missouri (Optimists); Baltimore, Maryland (NAACP); Kansas City, Missouri (the Veterans of Foreign Wars and the Camp Fire Boys and Girls); Atlanta, Georgia (Boys and Girls Clubs); or even New York City (Hadassah and Alcoholics Anonymous). These venerable organizations are headquartered near important concentrations of their members.

The headquarters of the nation's largest organization and one of the most rapidly growing, the American Association of Retired Persons (AARP), however, is not in Florida or California or Arizona (where its constituents are concentrated), but at 6th and E Streets in Washington, a few minutes' walk from Capitol Hill. Similarly, the most visible newcomers to the national associational scene are headquartered within ten blocks of the intersection of 14th and K Streets in Washington: the Children's Defense Fund, Common Cause, the National Organization for Women, the National Wildlife Federation, Greenpeace, Friends of the Earth, the National Gay and Lesbian Task Force, the National Trust for Historic Preservation, the Wilderness Society, the National Right to Life Committee, and Zero Population Growth. The "new associationism" is almost entirely a denizen of the Washington hothouse.[6] The proliferating new organizations are professionally staffed advocacy organizations, not member-centered, locally based associations.[7] The newer groups focus on expressing policy views in the national political debate, not on providing regular connection *among* individual members at the grass roots.

Though these new groups often depend on financial support from ordinary citizens and may speak faithfully on their behalf, they are not really composed of citizen members in the same sense that a church congregation or a reading group or a fraternal organization is. One distinctive feature of a social-capital-creating formal organization is that it includes local chapters in which members can meet one another. Of eighty-three public-interest groups in the early 1970s (including virtually all such organizations at the national level, from the Agribusiness Accountability Project to Zero Population Growth and from the American Civil Liberties Union and Common Cause to the Liberty Lobby and Young Americans for Freedom), two-thirds had no local chapters at all, and another 12 percent had no more than twenty-five chapters nationwide, or an average of one for every two states. Only nine of the eighty-three groups had as many as one hundred local chapters nationwide.[8] By way of comparison, there are seven thousand local Rotary chapters in America, to take a typical "old-fashioned," chapter-based civic organization. In other words, *Rotary alone has nearly twice as many chapters as all eighty-three public-interest groups combined.*

Another survey of 205 national "citizens groups" in 1985 confirmed that less than one-third of them had chapters to which individual members belonged and paid dues. Moreover, the more recently founded the citizens group, the *less* likely it was to be chapter based, so that among all citizens' groups founded after 1965, barely one in four had chapters with individual members.[9] These are mailing list organizations, in which membership means essentially contributing money to a national office to support a cause. Membership in the newer groups means moving a pen, not making a meeting.

These new mass-membership organizations are plainly of growing political importance. Probably the most dramatic example is the AARP, which grew from four hundred thousand card-carrying members in 1960 to thirty-three million in the mid-1990s. But membership in good standing in the AARP requires only a few seconds annually—as long as it takes to sign a check. The AARP is politically significant, but it demands little of its members' energies and contributes little to their social capital. Less than 10 percent of the AARP's members belong to local chapters, and according to AARP staff, the organization's grassroots activities were on life support even during the period of maximum membership growth. In many respects, such organizations have more in common with mail-order commercial organizations than with old-fashioned face-to-face associations. Some of the new organizations actually have their roots in commercial ventures. The AARP, for example, was originally founded as a mail-order insurance firm.[10] Similarly, although the American Automobile Association has the form of an association with members, it is essentially a commercial organization, providing services in exchange for fees.

The national administrators of such organizations are among the most feared lobbyists in Washington, in large part because of their massive mailing lists. Ironically, group involvement with government has exploded at the same time that citizen involvement with both government and groups has diminished. To be sure, political representation is not a new role for voluntary associations. Among the most energetic examples of voluntary association in American history are the abolitionist and temperance movements of the early nineteenth century. Much of the best (as well as some of the worst) in our current national politics is embodied in those advocacy organizations around 14th and K Streets.

From the point of view of social connectedness, however, the new organizations are sufficiently different from classic "secondary associations" that we need to invent a new label—perhaps "tertiary associations."[11] For the vast majority of their members, the only act of membership consists of writing a check for dues or perhaps occasionally reading a newsletter.[12] Few ever attend any meetings of such organizations—many never have meetings at all—and most members are unlikely ever knowingly to encounter any other member. The bond between any two members of the National Wildlife Federation or the National Rifle Association is less like the bond between two members of a gardening club or prayer group and more like the bond between two Yankees fans on opposite coasts (or perhaps two devoted L. L. Bean catalog users): they share some of the same interests, but they are unaware of each other's existence. Their ties are to common symbols, common leaders, and perhaps common ideals, but *not* to each other.

So the vigor of the new Washington-based organizations, though they are large, proliferating, and powerful, is an unreliable guide to the vitality of social connectedness and civic engagement in American communities. Several illustrations may clarify.

According to the *Encyclopedia of Associations*, the number of independent veterans' organizations nearly tripled between 1980 and 1997. This was the single most vigorous sector of organizational growth during this period, at least measured by numbers of organizations. In fact, however, careful national surveys over this same period show that the rate of membership in veterans' organizations among American men and women *fell* by roughly 10 percent. This slump is not surprising, since the number of living veterans fell by 9 percent across these same eighteen years. Explosive growth of organizations claiming to speak on behalf of veterans coincided with declining involvement by veterans. Similarly, the number of trade unions cataloged in the *Encyclopedia of Associations* grew by 4 percent between 1980 and 1997, while the fraction of employees belonging to unions plummeted by more than 35 percent.[13] More organizations do not mean more members.

ENVIRONMENTAL ORGANIZATIONS have been among the growth stocks in the associational world over the last several decades. In tracking the expansion of several of the most dynamic associations, we noted several periods of rapid growth, presumably reflecting major shifts in grassroots engagement with environmental issues. Probing further reveals that mail-order "membership" turns out to be a poor measure of civic engagement. For example, membership in the Environmental Defense Fund (EDF) tripled from one hundred thousand in 1988 to three hundred thousand in 1995. EDF officials, however, attribute this breathtaking expansion to "better marketing efforts," including a switch to "front-end prospecting" (providing a free gift to nonmembers and then asking for a donation) instead of "back-end prospecting" (sending the gifts after donations have been received). Greenpeace became the largest environmental organization in America, accounting for more than one-third of all members in national environmental groups at its peak in 1990, through an extremely aggressive direct-mail program. At that point Greenpeace leaders, concerned about the spectacle of an environmental group printing tons of junk mail, temporarily cut back on direct-mail solicitation. Almost immediately their membership began to hemorrhage, and by 1998 Greenpeace membership had plummeted by 85 percent.[14]

Trends in numbers of voluntary associations nationwide are not a reliable guide to trends in social capital, especially for associations that lack a structure of local chapters in which members can actually participate. What evidence can we glean from organizations that *do* involve their members directly in community-based activity? The membership rolls of such associations across the twentieth century reveal a strikingly parallel pattern across many different civic associations. This pattern is summarized in figure 8, which is a composite of the changing membership rates for thirty-two diverse national, chapter-based organizations throughout the twentieth century, ranging from B'nai B'rith and the Knights of Columbus to the Elks club and the Parent-Teacher Association.[15] In each case we measure membership as a fraction of the pool of members in the population—4-H membership as a fraction of all rural youth, Hadassah membership as a fraction of all Jewish women, and so on. Embodied in the broad outline are a number of crucial facts about associational life in American communities throughout the twentieth century.

For most of the twentieth century growing numbers of Americans were involved in such chapter-based associations.[16] Of course, the U.S. population was growing, too, but our analysis here eliminates that inflation factor by considering the membership rate as a percentage of the relevant population. So the

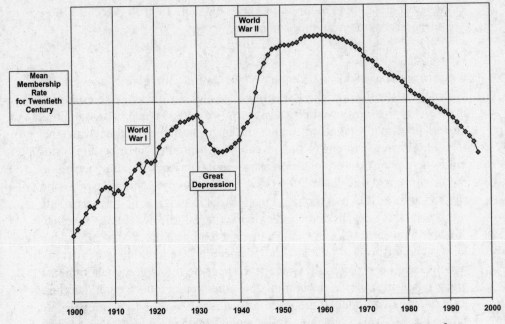

Figure 8: Average Membership Rate in Thirty-two National Chapter-Based Associations, 1900–1997

long upward wave in this figure reflects the fact that more and more women belonged to women's clubs, more rural residents belonged to the Grange, more youths belonged to the Scouts, more Jews belonged to Hadassah and B'nai B'rith, and more men belonged to service clubs. Probably one important factor in this steady growth was the continuing rise in educational levels, but in the aggregate the increase in membership exceeded even that. As the decades passed, America seemed more and more to fit Tocqueville's description.

The sharp dip in this generally rising line of civic involvement in the 1930s is evidence of the traumatic impact of the Great Depression on American communities. The membership records of virtually every adult organization in this sample bear the scars of that period. In some cases the effect was a brief pause in ebullient growth, but in others the reversal was extraordinary. Membership in the League of Women Voters, for example, was cut in half between 1930 and 1935, as was membership in the Elks, the Moose, and the Knights of Columbus. This period of history underlines the effects of acute economic distress on civic engagement, a topic to which we shall return in chapter 11.

Most of these losses had been recouped, however, by the early 1940s. World War II occasioned a massive outpouring of patriotism and collective solidarity. At war's end those energies were redirected into community life. The two decades following 1945 witnessed one of the most vital periods of community involvement in American history. As a fraction of potential membership, the "market share" for these thirty-two organizations skyrocketed. Because of growing population, the increase was even more dramatic. The breadth of this civic explosion encompassed virtually every organization on the list, from "old-fashioned" ones like the Grange and the Elks (roughly a century old in the 1960s) to the newer service clubs like the Lions and the League of Women Voters (roughly four decades old in the 1960s).

By the late 1950s, however, this burst of community involvement began to tail off, even though absolute membership continued to rise for a while. By the late 1960s and early 1970s membership growth began to fall further behind population growth. At first, club secretaries long accustomed to announcing new membership records with monotonous annual regularity did not notice that their organizations were failing to keep pace with population growth. As the decline deepened, however, absolute membership began to slip and then to plummet. By century's close the massive postwar boom in membership rates in these organizations had been eliminated.[17]

On average, across all these organizations, membership rates began to plateau in 1957, peaked in the early 1960s, and began the period of sustained decline by 1969. On average, membership rates more than doubled between 1940–45 and the peak and were slightly less than halved between the peak and 1997. These averages conceal some important differences among the experience of the various organizations. For example, the effects of the Great Depression varied from organization to organization, with massive declines in the Masons and Hadassah, while membership in youth organizations like the 4-H, Boy Scouts, and Girl Scouts seems to have been immune to the economic distress affecting adults. The postwar boom appears in virtually every case, but for the Grange and the General Federation of Women's Clubs the good times had ended by the mid-1950s, whereas other organizations, like Rotary and Optimists, remained on a higher plateau until the 1980s. NAACP membership spiked sharply during World War II, collapsed in the early 1950s, regained its highest levels in the early 1960s, and then stagnated and slumped again from the 1970s onward. These organizational peculiarities remind us that behind each of these membership declines are scores of individual tales of leadership success and failure, organizational tenacity and strategic blunders, and the vicissitudes of social life and politics.

One useful illustration is provided by the Parent-Teacher Association (PTA). In the middle years of the twentieth century the local PTA was among the most common of community organizations. For example, one grassroots survey of associational membership in the early 1960s found that the PTA had more members than any other secular organization. More than one in every six adult Nebraskans reported membership in their local PTA.[18] That the absolute number of PTA members was relatively high during the baby boom is, of course, no surprise at all—more parents, more PTA members. What is more striking, however, is that the *percentage* of parents nationwide who joined the PTA more than doubled between 1945 and 1960, continuing the vertiginous and almost uninterrupted growth of this organization since its founding in 1910. On average, every year throughout the quarter century up to 1960 another 1.6 percent of all American families with kids—more than 400,000 families a year—was added to the PTA membership rolls. Year after year, more and more parents became involved in this way in their children's education.

The reversal of six decades of organizational growth—captured graphically in figure 9—came with shocking suddenness in 1960. When the subsequent decline finally leveled off two decades later, membership in the PTA had returned to the level of 1943, utterly erasing the postwar gains. A brief rebound in the 1980s had all but vanished by the late 1990s. On average, every year throughout the quarter century after 1960 another 1.2 percent of all American families with kids—more than 250,000 families a year—dropped out of the PTA. The best recent study of the PTA concludes that

> membership declined from a high in the early 1960s of almost fifty members per 100 families with children under eighteen to fewer than twenty members per 100 families with children under eighteen in the early 1980s. Although participation rebounded somewhat in the 1980s and the early 1990s, the organization never recaptured its membership heights of the late 1950s and early 1960s. [Recently the organization has experienced renewed decline.] Between 1990 and 1997, the PTA lost half a million members, even though the number of families with children under eighteen grew by over 2 million and public school enrollment grew by over 5 million.[19]

The explosive growth of the PTA was one of the most impressive organizational success stories in American history, its unabated, almost exponential growth over the first six decades of the twentieth century interrupted with only the briefest of pauses during the Great Depression and for a single year during World War II. This success—membership encompassing eventually nearly half the families in America—was due no doubt to the fact that this form of connectedness appealed to millions of parents who wanted to be engaged in some way in their children's education. It is easy in our cynical era to sneer at cookies, cider, and small talk, but membership in the PTA betokened a commitment to participate in a practical, child-focused form of community life.

Yet the PTA's collapse in the last third of the century is no less sensational than its earlier growth. What could account for this dramatic turnaround? Some part of the decline in rates of membership in the PTA is an optical illusion. Parental involvement in local school service organizations (not all of which are affiliated with the national Parent-Teacher Association) did not fall as rapidly as membership in PTA-affiliated groups. First, during the 1970s, following disagreements about school politics, as well as about national dues,

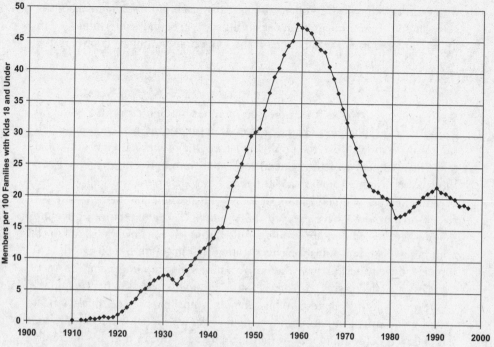

Figure 9: The Rise and Fall of the PTA, 1910–1997

some local parent-teacher organizations disaffiliated from the national PTA either to join competing organizations or to remain wholly independent. As a result, many of the missing local PTAs reappeared as local PTOs (parent-teacher organizations unaffiliated with the national PTA), although many of these now independent local associations themselves subsequently withered. Moreover, bitter battles over school desegregation in the 1960s caused wholesale disaffiliation from the national PTA in several southern states. While a genuine organizational loss, this development may not have marked the withdrawal of southern parents from the organizational life of local schools. Nevertheless, after accounting for all these specific gains and losses, it is reasonably clear that parental participation in parent-teacher groups of all sorts suffered a substantial decline in the decades after 1960.[20] One need not romanticize PTA meetings of the 1950s to recognize that many Americans nowadays are less involved with their kids' education.

No doubt diligent detective work would turn up equally interesting and nuanced stories behind each of the plunging memberships, but the common features across these very diverse organizations—rapid growth to the 1960s, abruptly halted, followed by rapid decline—is a significant piece in the mosaic of evidence on changing civic involvement in American communities. Even after we had explored the details of each organization's rise and decline,

we would be left with the remarkable fact that each of these organizations—
very different from one another in constituency, age, and leadership—seems
to have entered rough water at about the same time in the last quarter of the
twentieth century.

IN TWO IMPORTANT RESPECTS, however, membership figures for individual organizations are an uncertain guide to trends in Americans' involvement in voluntary associations. First, the popularity of specific groups may wax and wane
quite independently of the general level of community engagement. Even
though our historical analysis so far has cast as wide a net as possible in terms
of different types of organizations, it is certainly possible that newer, more dynamic organizations have escaped our scrutiny. If so, the picture of decline
that we have traced may apply only to "old-fashioned" organizations, not to all
community-based organizations. As sociologist Tom Smith has observed, "Ultimately, if we want to know whether group membership *in general* has been
increasing [or decreasing], we have to study group membership *in general*."[21]

Second, formal "card-carrying" membership may not accurately reflect
actual involvement in community activities. An individual who "belongs to"
half a dozen community groups may actually be active in none. What really
matters from the point of view of social capital and civic engagement is not
merely nominal membership, but active and involved membership. To address these two issues, we need to turn from formal organizational records to
social surveys, which can encompass organizational affiliations of all sorts and
can distinguish formal membership from actual involvement.

Several reviews of national surveys conducted between the early 1950s
and the early 1970s found evidence of steady and sustained growth in organizational memberships of all sorts, but other scholars have questioned whether
changes in survey wording might undermine this conclusion.[22] In other words,
subtle shifts in the lens of our social time-lapse camera may have sufficiently
blurred the successive images that we cannot be sure about the trends during
the 1950s and 1960s. However, in 1957 a team of University of Michigan researchers conducted a careful nationwide survey on behalf of the National Institute of Mental Health (NIMH), and in 1976 a group led by one of the earlier
researchers replicated the 1957 study, taking great care to make the studies as
nearly identical as possible.[23] The first wave of surveys was carried out roughly
a decade before what organizational records suggest was the postwar peak of
civic engagement, whereas the second was conducted roughly a decade after
the peak.

In many respects, the Michigan-NIMH study found considerable stabil-
ity in the life experiences of Americans across these two turbulent decades.
Nevertheless, one of their central findings was a "reduced integration of
American adults into the social structure."[24] Over these two decades informal

socializing with friends and relatives declined by about 10 percent, organizational memberships fell by 16 percent, and church attendance (a topic that we shall address more directly in a moment) declined by 20 percent. Examined more closely, these surveys found significant declines in membership in unions; church groups; fraternal and veterans organizations; civic groups, such as PTAs; youth groups; charities; and a catch-all "other" category.[25] Thus the best available survey evidence is consistent with the organizational record that membership in voluntary associations among ordinary Americans declined modestly between the mid-1950s and the mid-1970s.

For the years after the mid-1970s, the survey evidence becomes substantially richer, and our judgments about trends in this quarter century can be fuller and more confident. Three major survey archives contain relevant information: the General Social Survey (GSS), the Roper Social and Political Trends archive, and the DDB Needham Life Style archive.[26]

How has group membership in general changed over the last quarter century? The GSS provides the most comprehensive measure of trends in Americans' formal membership in many different types of groups. The short answer is that formal membership rates have not changed much, at least if we ignore rising educational levels. The percentage of the public who claim formal membership in at least one organization has fallen a bit, but that trend has been glacial so far, from a little less than 75 percent in the mid-1970s to a little less than 70 percent in the early 1990s.[27] Membership in church-related groups, labor unions, fraternal organizations, and veterans groups has declined, but this decline has been mostly offset by increases in professional, ethnic, service, hobby, sports, school fraternity, and other groups. To be sure, the only substantial increase is in the domain of professional organizations, and as we shall see later, that growth has barely kept pace with occupational growth in the professions themselves. If we take into account the rise in educational levels in this period—on the assumption that many more Americans nowadays have the skills and interests that traditionally brought people into civic life—the overall declines are more marked. Among college graduates, for example, organizational membership has declined by roughly 30 percent, while among high school dropouts the decline has been roughly the same. Nevertheless, the net decline in formal organizational membership is modest at best.

This ambiguous conclusion, however, is drastically altered when we examine evidence on more active forms of participation than mere card-carrying membership. Service as an organizational officer or committee member is very common among active members of American organizations. In 1987, 61 percent of all organization members had served on a committee at some time or other, and 46 percent had served as an officer.[28] Among self-described "active" members—roughly half of the adult population—73 percent had served at some time as a committee member, 58 percent had served at some time as an officer, and only 21 percent had never served as either an officer or a committee member. Sooner or later, in short, the overwhelming majority of active members in most voluntary associations in America are cajoled into playing some leadership role in the organization.

How has the number of Americans who fit this bill changed over the last few decades? Between 1973 and 1994 the number of men and women who took *any* leadership role in *any* local organization—from "old-fashioned" fraternal organizations to new age encounter groups—was sliced by more than 50 percent.[29] (Figure 10 summarizes this evidence by showing the changing fraction of the population who have been actively involved in organizational life as either a local officer or a local committee member.) This dismaying trend began to accelerate after 1985: in the ten short years between 1985 and 1994, active involvement in community organizations in this country fell by 45 percent. By this measure, at least, nearly half of America's civic infrastructure was obliterated in barely a decade.

Eighty percent of life, Woody Allen once quipped,[30] is simply showing up. The same might be said of civic engagement, and "showing up" provides a useful standard for evaluating trends in associational life in our communities. In twenty-five annual surveys between 1975 and 1999 the DDB Needham Life Style surveys asked more than eighty-seven thousand Americans, "How many times in the last year did you attend a club meeting?" Figure 11 shows how this form of civic engagement has dwindled over the last quarter of the twentieth

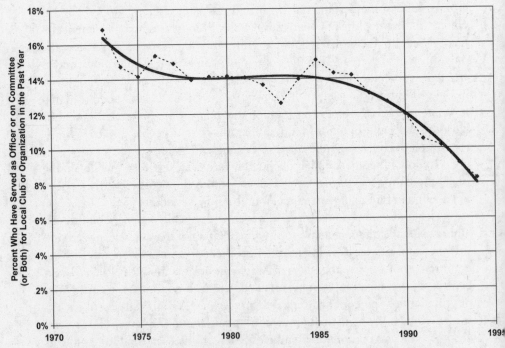

Figure 10: Active Organizational Involvement, 1973–1994

century. In 1975–76 American men and women attended twelve club meetings on average each year—essentially once a month.[31] By 1999 that figure had shrunk by fully 58 percent to five meetings per year. In 1975–76, 64 percent of all Americans still attended at least *one* club meeting in the previous year. By 1999 that figure had fallen to 38 percent. In short, in the mid-1970s nearly two-thirds of all Americans attended club meetings, but by the late 1990s nearly two-thirds of all Americans *never* do. By comparison with other countries, we may still seem a nation of joiners, but by comparison with our own recent past, we are not—at least if "joining" means more than nominal affiliation.

Thus two different survey archives suggest that active involvement in local clubs and organizations of all sorts fell by more than half in the last several decades of the twentieth century. This estimate is remarkably consistent with evidence of an entirely unexpected sort. Each decade between 1965 and 1995, national samples of Americans were asked to complete "time diaries," recording how they spent every minute of a randomly chosen "diary day." From these sets of diaries we can reconstruct how the average American's use of time gradually evolved over the three decades between 1965 and 1995.[32]

Broadly speaking, as John Robinson, director of the time diary project, has shown, our time allocations have not changed dramatically over this period—we have averaged just about exactly eight hours of sleep a night throughout the decades, for example—but there are some important exceptions. Watching

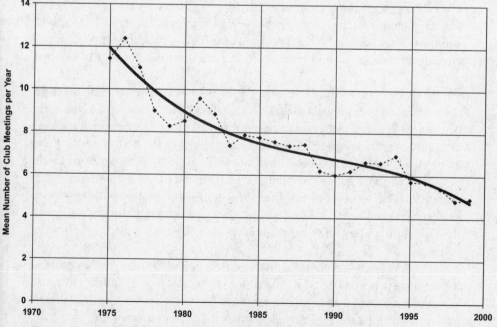

Figure 11: Club Meeting Attendance Dwindles, 1975–1999

TV consumes more time now than it used to, while we spend less time now on housework and child care. The slice of time devoted to organizational activity has always been relatively modest on any given day, since even faithful reading groups or service clubs usually meet only once a week or once a month, not once a day. Nevertheless, the diaries show clearly that the time we devote to community organizations has fallen steadily over this period.[33]

Measured in terms of hours per month, the average American's investment in organizational life (apart from religious groups, which we shall examine separately) fell from 3.7 hours per month in 1965 to 2.9 in 1975 to 2.3 in 1985 and 1995. On an average day in 1965, 7 percent of Americans spent some time in a community organization. By 1995 that figure had fallen to 3 percent of all Americans. Those numbers suggest that nearly half of all Americans in the 1960s invested some time each week in clubs and local associations, as compared to less than one-quarter in the 1990s.[34] Further analysis of the time diary evidence suggests that virtually all of this decline is attributable to generational replacement: members of any given generation are investing as much time in organizational activity as they ever were, but each successive generation is investing less.

If we take into account the rapid growth in educational levels over this period, all these slumps in associational involvement (leadership involvement, meeting attendance, time spent, and so on) are even more dramatic. Among the burgeoning numbers of college graduates, the average number of club meetings per year fell by 55 percent (from thirteen meetings per year to six), while among high school graduates, the drop in annual meeting attendance was 60 percent (from ten meetings per year to four), and among the dwindling number of Americans who had not completed high school, the drop in annual meeting attendance was 73 percent (from nine meetings per year to two per year).

In absolute terms the declines in organizational activity and club meeting attendance were roughly parallel at all educational and social levels. However, because the less well educated were less involved in community organizations to begin with, the relative decline was even greater at the bottom of the hierarchy. A similar pattern appears in the time diary data—declines at all levels in the educational hierarchy, though slightly greater in this case among the more educated. In other words, the gross decline in community involvement has been masked to some degree by the fact that more and more Americans have the skills and social resources that traditionally encouraged participation in community affairs.

In community life, as in the stock market, past performance is no guarantee of future performance, so it is hazardous to assume that trends over the next several decades will mirror those over the last several. Nevertheless, the downtrend shown in figure 11 has been more or less uninterrupted for more than a quarter century, and if the current rate of decline were to continue, clubs would become extinct in America within less than twenty years. Considering that such local associations have been a feature of American community life for several hundred years, it is remarkable to see them so high on the endangered species list.

The organizational slumps reported here come from four entirely different streams of evidence—different sampling techniques, different survey organizations, different questions—but each is based on tens of thousands of interviews in scores of independent surveys, and together they cover associational involvement of all sorts. That they converge so closely in their estimate that active involvement in local organizations fell by more than half in the last several decades of the twentieth century is as striking and persuasive as if southwestern tree rings and Arctic ice cores and British Admiralty records all confirmed the same rate of global warming.

Another "hard" indicator of the priority Americans attribute to organizational involvement is the fraction of our leisure dollar that we spend on dues, a measure that the Commerce Department has tracked for the last seventy years. In 1929, 6 cents of every dollar of consumer spending for leisure and recreation was for club and fraternal dues. With the arrival of television in the 1950s (and the nationwide explosion in sales of TV sets), this figure fell to 4 cents, but by the end of that decade it had risen back to 5 cents, in accord with the 1950s–1960s civic boom that appears repeatedly in our evidence. During the last three decades of the century, however, this figure fell to 3 cents, so that by 1997 this measure of the relative priority that Americans give to our organizational commitments was down 40 percent from its postwar peak in 1958.[35]

To summarize: Organizational records suggest that for the first two-thirds of the twentieth century Americans' involvement in civic associations of all sorts rose steadily, except for the parenthesis of the Great Depression. In the last third of the century, by contrast, only mailing list membership has continued to expand, with the creation of an entirely new species of "tertiary" association whose members never actually meet. At the same time, active involvement in face-to-face organizations has plummeted, whether we consider organizational records, survey reports, time diaries, or consumer expenditures. We could surely find individual exceptions—specific organizations that successfully sailed against the prevailing winds and tides—but the broad picture is one of declining membership in community organizations. During the last third of the twentieth century formal membership in organizations in general has edged downward by perhaps 10–20 percent. More important, active involvement in clubs and other voluntary associations has collapsed at an astonishing rate, more than halving most indexes of participation within barely a few decades.

Many Americans continue to claim that we are "members" of various organizations, but most Americans no longer spend much time in community organizations—we've stopped doing committee work, stopped serving as officers, and stopped going to meetings. And all this despite rapid increases in education that have given more of us than ever before the skills, the resources, and the interests that once fostered civic engagement. In short, Americans have been dropping out in droves, not merely from political life, but from organized community life more generally.

Before reaching any firm conclusion about trends in Americans' involvement in formal social organizations, however, we need to consider changes in the worlds of religion and work. Religion remains today, as in the past, an extremely important sector of American civil society, and work has come to occupy an ever more important place in the lives of many Americans, so trends in those two domains will have an important effect on our collective stock of social capital.

CHAPTER 4

Religious Participation

CHURCHES AND OTHER religious organizations have a unique importance in American civil society. America is one of the most religiously observant countries in the contemporary world. With the exception of "a few agrarian states such as Ireland and Poland," observes one scholar, "the United States has been the most God-believing and religion-adhering, fundamentalist, and religiously traditional country in Christendom," as well as "the most religiously fecund country" where "more new religions have been born . . . than in any other society."[1]

American churches* over the centuries have been incredibly robust social institutions. Tocqueville himself commented at length on Americans' religiosity. Religious historian Phillip Hammond observes that "ever since the nation's founding, a higher and higher proportion of Americans have affiliated with a church or synagogue—right through the 1950s."[2] Although most often we think of the colonists as a deeply religious people, one systematic study of the history of religious observance in America estimates that the rate of formal religious adherence *grew* steadily from 17 percent in 1776 to 62 percent in 1980.[3] Other observers, such as E. Brooks Holifield, argue that the meaning of church "membership" has become less stringent over time and conclude that "from the seventeenth century through the twentieth, participation in congregations has probably remained relatively constant. For most of the

---

* For simplicity's sake I use the term church here to refer to all religious institutions of whatever faith, including mosques, temples, and synagogues.

past three hundred years, from 35 to 40 percent of the population has probably participated in congregations with some degree of regularity."[4] In either case, one reason for this resilience is that religion in America (unlike in most other advanced Western nations) has been pluralistic and constantly evolving, expressed in a kaleidoscopic series of revivals and awakenings rather than a single-state religion that could become ossified.[5]

Faith communities in which people worship together are arguably the single most important repository of social capital in America. "The church is people," says Reverend Craig McMullen, the activist co-pastor of the Dorchester Temple Baptist Church in Boston. "It's not a building; it's not an institution, even. It is relationships between one person and the next."[6] As a rough rule of thumb, our evidence shows, nearly half of all associational memberships in America are church related, half of all personal philanthropy is religious in character, and half of all volunteering occurs in a religious context. So how involved we are in religion today matters a lot for America's social capital.

Religious institutions directly support a wide range of social activities well beyond conventional worship. Among the entries on the weekly calendar for October 14, 1990, of the Riverside Church in New York City, a mainline Protestant congregation, were meetings of the Social Service Training Session, the AIDS Awareness Seminar, the Ecology Task Force, the Chinese Christian Fellowship, Narcotics Anonymous, Riverside Business and Professional Women's Club, Gulf Crisis Study Series, Adult Children of Alcoholics, and Martial Arts Class for Adults and Teens. In January 1991 the weekly calendar of the Crystal Cathedral, an evangelical church in Garden Grove, California, included sessions devoted to Women in the Marketplace, Conquering Compulsive Behaviors, Career Builders' Workshop, Stretch and Walk Time for Women, Cancer Conquerors, Positive Christian Singles, Gamblers Anonymous, Women Who Love Too Much, Overeaters Anonymous, and Friday Night Live (for junior high schoolers). The Garden Grove Crystal Cathedral complex also includes restaurants and a Family Life Center with a swimming pool, weight room, saunas, and steamrooms. In at least one new megachurch, social activism has extended even to classes in charm, modeling, and cake decorating and the inclusion of a bowling alley in a seven-story recreational center.[7]

Churches provide an important incubator for civic skills, civic norms, community interests, and civic recruitment. Religiously active men and women learn to give speeches, run meetings, manage disagreements, and bear administrative responsibility. They also befriend others who are in turn likely to recruit them into other forms of community activity. In part for these reasons, churchgoers are substantially more likely to be involved in secular organizations, to vote and participate politically in other ways, and to have deeper informal social connections.[8]

Regular worshipers and people who say that religion is very important to them are much more likely than other people to visit friends, to entertain at home, to attend club meetings, and to belong to sports groups; professional and academic societies; school service groups; youth groups; service clubs; hobby or garden clubs; literary, art, discussion, and study groups; school fraternities and sororities; farm organizations; political clubs; nationality groups; and other miscellaneous groups.[9] In one survey of twenty-two different types of voluntary associations, from hobby groups to professional associations to veterans groups to self-help groups to sports clubs to service clubs, it was membership in religious groups that was most closely associated with other forms of civic involvement, like voting, jury service, community projects, talking with neighbors, and giving to charity.[10]

Religiosity rivals education as a powerful correlate of most forms of civic engagement.[11] In fact, religiously involved people seem simply to know more people. One intriguing survey that asked people to enumerate all individuals with whom they had had a face-to-face conversation in the course of the day found that religious attendance was the most powerful predictor of the number of one's daily personal encounters.[12] Regular church attendees reported talking with 40 percent more people in the course of the day. These studies cannot show conclusively that churchgoing itself "produces" social connectivity— probably the causal arrow between the two points in both directions—but it is clear that religious people are unusually active social capitalists.

Religious involvement is an especially strong predictor of volunteering and philanthropy. About 75–80 percent of church members give to charity, as compared with 55–60 percent of nonmembers, and 50–60 percent of church members volunteer, while only 30–35 percent of nonmembers do. In part, of course, this is because churches themselves do things that require funds and volunteers, but religious adherents are also more likely to contribute time and money to activities beyond their own congregation. Even excluding contributions to religious causes, active involvement in religious organizations is among the strongest predictors of both philanthropy and volunteering.[13]

In part, the tie between religion and altruism embodies the power of religious values. As Kenneth Wald, a close student of religion, observes, "Religious ideals are potentially powerful sources of commitment and motivation," so that "human beings will make enormous sacrifices if they believe themselves to be driven by a divine force."[14] But the social ties embodied in religious communities are at least as important as religious beliefs per se in accounting for volunteerism and philanthropy.[15] Connectedness, not merely faith, is responsible for the beneficence of church people. Once again, the evidence does not prove beyond all doubt that churchgoing itself produces generosity, but religious involvement is certainly associated with greater attention to the needs of our brothers and sisters.

Churches have been and continue to be important institutional providers of social services. American religious communities spend roughly $15–$20 billion annually on social services. Nationwide in 1998 nearly 60 percent of all congregations (and an even higher proportion of larger congregations) reported contributing to social service, community development, or neighborhood organizing projects. Congregations representing 33 percent of all churchgoers support food programs for the hungry, and congregations representing 18 percent of all churchgoers support housing programs like Habitat for Humanity. Partners for Sacred Places found that the overwhelming majority (93 percent) of older urban congregations provide community services, such as food pantries, self-help groups, and recreational programs, and that 80 percent of the beneficiaries of these programs are not members of the congregations. Black churches have been especially prominent in recent efforts to rebuild inner-city communities, such as the Boston 10-Point Coalition. What is widely regarded as the most successful model for grassroots community organizing in America—the Industrial Areas Foundation—is rooted institutionally in local parishes and congregations.[16]

Churches have provided the organizational and philosophical bases for a wide range of powerful social movements throughout American history, from abolition and temperance in the nineteenth century to civil rights and right-to-life in the twentieth century. According to one of the leading analysts of the civil rights movement of the 1950s and 1960s,

> [T]he Black church functioned as the institutional center of the modern civil rights movement. . . . Churches provided the movement with an organized mass base; a leadership of clergymen largely economically independent of the larger white society and skilled in the art of managing people and resources; an institutionalized financial base through which protest was financed; and meeting places where the masses planned tactics and strategies and collectively committed themselves to the struggle.[17]

Faith-based organizations are particularly central to social capital and civic engagement in the African American community. The church is the oldest and most resilient social institution in black America, not least because it was traditionally the only black-controlled institution of a historically oppressed people. African Americans in all social strata are more religiously observant than other Americans. The black religious tradition distinctively encourages mixing religion and community affairs and invigorates civic activism. Both during and after the civil rights struggle, church involvement among blacks has been strongly associated with civic engagement, in part because the church provides a unique opportunity for blacks to exercise civic skills.[18] C. Eric Lincoln, the sociologist of religion, says:

> Beyond its purely religious function, as critical as that function has been, the Black church in its historical role as lyceum, conservatory, forum, so-

cial service center, political academy, and financial institution, has been and is for Black America the mother of our culture, the champion of our Freedom, and hallmark of our civilization.[19]

In sum, religious involvement is a crucial dimension of civic engagement. Thus trends in civic engagement are closely tied to changing patterns of religious involvement.

MEASURED BY THE YARDSTICK of personal beliefs, Americans' religious commitment has been reasonably stable over the last half century—certainly much more so than one might assume from some public commentary about the secularization of American life. Virtually all Americans say they believe in God, and three out of four say they believe in immortality. There is no evidence that these beliefs have wavered over the last half century. The Gallup poll and other survey organizations have asked Americans repeatedly over the decades how "important religion is in [their] life," and the responses suggest only a modest slippage in this metric of religiosity.[20] However, as one of the leading American religious historians has observed, "Unless religious impulses find a home in more than the individual heart or soul, they will have few long-lasting public consequences."[21] What does the evidence tell us not just about religious beliefs, but about participation in religious institutions?

Trends in religious behavior have been hotly debated among specialists for many years. The classical sociological theory of secularization—that as society becomes modern, it becomes more secular—fits the experience of Western Europe reasonably well, but even in the 1950s and 1960s many observers expressed doubt about whether it fit the facts in this country. In recent years the continuing vitality of religion in America has been "rediscovered" by academic specialists, and by century's end, as America's leading sociologist of religion observed, "Scholars have had it with talk of secularization. They earn their spurs by telling what's good about churches."[22] Because of these quasi-religious struggles about religion's fate, it is important to weigh carefully the conflicting evidence about trends in participation in religious institutions over the last half century or so.

Both sides in the "secularization" debate agree that church membership was very likely at an all-time high in the 1950s, and both discern what stock market gurus would term a modest "market correction" (that is, a falloff in religious observance) in the 1960s and early 1970s. Trends over the last quarter century are more controversial, in part because of uncertainties about the reliability of available evidence. Denominational membership figures are debatable because denominations vary in the strictness of their definition of membership, membership figures are only irregularly updated, self-reports may be inflated, and not all churches keep or report accurate records. Poll data

avoid some of these drawbacks but generally record higher membership figures than the ecclesiastical records, probably because many lapsed members
continue to identify themselves as Presbyterian, or Jewish, or Catholic.[23]

Despite these ambiguities, however, as figure 12 shows, survey evidence
and denominational reports are generally consistent in showing a rise in
church membership from the 1930s to about 1960, followed by a plateau and
then a long, slow slump of roughly 10 percent in church membership between
the 1960s and the 1990s. The percentage of Americans who identify themselves as having "no religion" has risen steadily and sharply from 2 percent in
1967 to 11 percent by the 1990s.[24]

Just as in the case of secular organizations, however, we need to go beyond formal membership to actual participation if we are to assay trends in
religious participation. Five independent survey archives, covering much of
the last half century, generally agree that in any given week over these five
decades, roughly 40–45 percent of Americans claim to have attended religious
services.[25] The earliest surveys show a sharp rise of 15–20 percent in the rate
of church attendance from the 1950s to the 1960s and a decline of that same
magnitude by the early 1970s.[26] The five archives produce slightly divergent estimates of the trends after 1975, but the most reasonable summary is that attendance has slumped—modestly but unmistakably—by roughly 10–12 percent

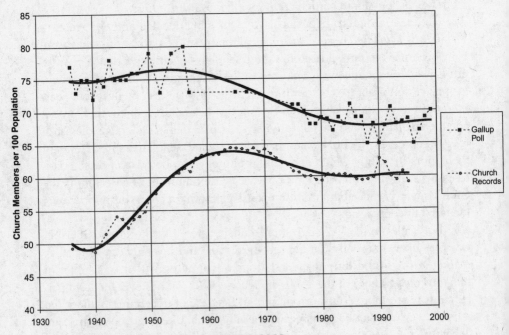

Figure 12: Church Membership, 1936–1999:
Church Records and Survey Data

over the last quarter century.[27] The slump appears to have been more marked in the second half of this period—that is, from the mid-1980s to the mid-1990s.

To put these recent trends into a somewhat longer perspective, figure 13 charts the consolidated evidence from these five archives over the last half of the twentieth century.[28] The surveys converge in suggesting a sharp rise in church attendance in the first several decades after World War II, followed by a decline in church attendance of roughly one-third between the late 1950s and the late 1990s, with more than half of the total decline occurring in the 1960s.

Recently some skeptical sociologists have begun to question whether Americans really are as religiously observant as surveys suggest. Careful comparisons of survey responses with actual counts of parishioners in the pews suggest that many of us "misremember" whether we actually did make it to services last week. Estimates of the overreporting of church attendance range as high as 50 percent.[29] Some scholars believe that the rate of overreporting is actually higher today than a generation ago, and if that is so, then the survey evidence may underestimate the falloff in actual church attendance. In short, participation in organized worship services is probably lower today than it was twenty-five years ago and is surely lower than it was forty years ago.

Americans' involvement in the social life of the church beyond worship itself—in Sunday schools, Bible study groups, "church socials," and the like— appears to have fallen at least as fast as church membership and attendance at

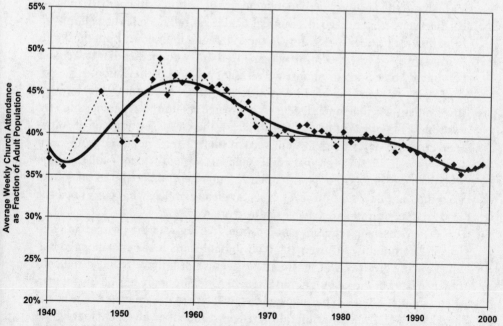

Figure 13: Trends in Church Attendance, 1940–1999

worship services. In the 1950s roughly one in every four Americans reported membership in such church-related groups, apart from church membership itself. By the late 1980s and 1990s comparable studies found that that figure had been cut in half to roughly one in eight.[30] The carefully controlled University of Michigan–NIMH study of change in personal behavior between 1957 and 1976 found a decline of 50 percent in membership in church-related groups. The General Social Survey reports that between 1974 and 1996 membership in church-related groups fell by at least 20 percent.[31] Americans' involvement in the social life of their religious institutions apart from formal worship services has fallen, probably by one-third since the 1960s and by one-half or more since the 1950s.

These results are fully confirmed by evidence from the time diaries completed by samples of Americans in 1965, 1975, 1985, and 1995. Americans in 1995 devoted on average only two-thirds as much time to religion (both worship and religiously related social activities) as we did in 1965 — a steady decline from one hour and thirty-seven minutes a week in 1965 to one hour and seven minutes in 1995.[32] It is not that sermons were getting shorter; rather, the fraction of the population that spent any time on religion at all fell by nearly one-half.

In sum, over the last three to four decades Americans have become about 10 percent less likely to claim church membership, while our actual attendance and involvement in religious activities has fallen by roughly 25 to 50 percent. Virtually all the postwar boom in religious participation — and perhaps more — has been erased. This broad historical pattern in religious participation — up from the first third of the century to the 1960s and then down from the 1960s to the 1990s — is very much the same pattern that we noted earlier for secular community-based organizations, as well as for political participation.

What is more, in all three cases, the more demanding the form of involvement — actual attendance as compared to formal membership, for example — the greater the decline. In effect, the classic institutions of American civic life, both religious and secular, have been "hollowed out." Seen from without, the institutional edifice appears virtually intact — little decline in professions of faith, formal membership down just a bit, and so on. When examined more closely, however, it seems clear that decay has consumed the load-bearing beams of our civic infrastructure.

The decline in religious participation, like many of the changes in political and community involvement, is attributable largely to generational differences.[33] Any given cohort of Americans seems not to have reduced religious observance over the years, but more recent generations are less observant than their parents. The slow but inexorable replacement of one generation by the next has gradually but inevitably lowered our national involvement in religious activities.

Assessments of trends in religious behavior are inevitably controversial because many people have strong personal stakes on one side or the other of the debate, but one special complexity is a well-established "life cycle" pattern in religiosity.[34] Generally speaking, marriage and children encourage greater involvement in church activities. In addition, middle-aged and older people (perhaps more conscious of our own mortality) seem more drawn to religion than are younger people. In order to detect significant long-run change, we must compare rates of religious participation among people of the same age in different eras. If the younger people today are less observant than people their age used to be, then in all likelihood even if today's young people themselves gradually become more religiously involved as they age, they may well never catch up with the pace of their predecessors, and thus the aggregate level of religious engagement in society will tend to fall over time. Between the 1970s and the 1990s, church attendance among people under sixty dropped by roughly 10–20 percent, whereas among people sixty and over church attendance increased slightly.[35] That modest increase in religious involvement among the oldest generation in the population—those born in the 1930s or earlier—was not enough to counterbalance the declining involvement of their children and grandchildren.

This pattern applies in particular to the religious habits of the baby boomers. When they were in their twenties (in the 1960s and 1970s), boomers were more disaffected from religious institutions than their predecessors had been in *their* twenties. As the boomers married, had children, and settled down, they tended to become more involved with organized religion, just as their parents had, but the boomers began this life cycle move toward the church at a much lower level of religious involvement and have never closed the gap. Even now, in their forties and fifties, though (as we would expect) more religious than they once were, boomers remain less religiously involved than middle-aged people were a generation ago. Sociologist Wade Clark Roof estimates that two-thirds of all boomers reared in a religious tradition dropped out, while something less than half have returned.[36] So as the boomers' more religious parents depart from the scene, the average level of religious engagement continues to decline.

Wade Clark Roof and William McKinney summarize American religious behavior in this era:

> Large numbers of young, well-educated, middle-class youth . . . defected from the churches in the late sixties and the seventies. . . . Some joined new religious movements, others sought personal enlightenment through various spiritual therapies and disciplines, but most simply "dropped out" of organized religion altogether. . . . [The consequence was a] tendency toward highly individualized religious psychology with-

out the benefits of strong supportive attachments to believing communities. A major impetus in this direction in the post-1960s was the thrust toward greater personal fulfillment and quest for the ideal self. . . . In this climate of expressive individualism, religion tends to become "privatized," or more anchored in the personal realms.[37]

Privatized religion may be morally compelling and psychically fulfilling, but it embodies less social capital. More people are "surfing" from congregation to congregation more frequently, so that while they may still be "religious," they are less committed to a particular community of believers. The last several decades have witnessed a flourishing of publicity about various cult groups, from transcendental meditation to the Unification Church of the Reverend Moon, but careful studies have shown that none of these movements attracted an enduring American membership of more than a few thousand, an infinitesimal fraction in an adult population of two hundred million.[38] Even for those who remain religiously inclined, "privatized religion knows little of communal support, and exists by and large independent of institutionalized religious forms; it may provide meaning to the believer and personal orientation, but it is not a shared faith, and thus not likely to inspire strong group involvement. . . . 'Believers' perhaps, but 'belongers,' not."[39]

It is not my argument here that privatized religion is morally or theologically frivolous, or that inherited religious traditions are inherently superior. On the contrary, as Stephen Warner, an admirer of the freer market for self-determined religious affiliation, argues, "There is considerable evidence that religious switchers are morally serious."[40] But by most accounts, "the big 'winner' in the switching game is the growing secular constituency."[41]

As Phillip Hammond reports from a survey of churchgoers in North Carolina, Massachusetts, Ohio, and California, "The social revolution of the 1960s and 1970s accelerated the shifting balance between [the collective and individual role of the church], doing so by greatly escalating a phenomenon we will call 'personal autonomy.' Personal autonomy thus has not only led to a decline in parish involvement . . . but it has also led to an alteration in the meaning of that involvement." Active involvement in the life of the parish depends heavily on the degree to which a person is linked to the broader social context—having friends in the parish, in the neighborhood, at work, being part of a closely knit personal network. As we shall see in the next two chapters, those supporting beams for religiously based social involvement have themselves been weakened in recent decades. The bottom line: While for many boomers privatized religion is a worthy expression of autonomous moral judgment, institutionalized religion is less central to their lives than it was to their parents' lives.[42]

• • •

THE RELIGIOUS ORIENTATIONS of the so-called Generation X strongly suggest that this long-run ratcheting down of religious involvement has not yet run its course. For more than three decades college freshmen across America have filled out a standard questionnaire about their senior year in high school — grades, career interests, life goals, social activities, and so on. When the boomers entering college in 1968 completed this questionnaire, 9 percent said that they "never" attended church services. By the late 1990s, when the boomers' children were filling out that same questionnaire, this same index of complete disengagement from organized religion had doubled to 18 percent. Similarly, the fraction of college freshmen who avowed "none" as their religious preference doubled from 7 percent in 1966 to 14 percent in 1997. Another rigorous series of annual surveys has found the fraction of high schoolers who attend church services every week fell from 40 percent in the late 1970s to 32 percent in the early 1990s.[43]

I have generalized about trends in American religious participation in the aggregate over the last three decades, but in at least two important respects that is an oversimplification. First, not everyone in American society has been affected equally by the trends I have described so far. While one group of Americans has tended to withdraw from active involvement in faith-based communities, another group is as fully involved as ever. While the fraction of the population that is entirely disconnected from organized religion has increased, the fraction that is intensely involved has been relatively stable. In other words, religious dropouts have come at the expense of those whose religious involvement was modest but conventional. The result is that the country is becoming ever more clearly divided into two groups—the devoutly observant and the entirely unchurched.[44] (Some might see here a certain parallel to trends in politics—more true believers, more dropouts, and fewer moderates.) This is the sociological substratum that underlies the much discussed "culture wars" of recent years. Although this polarization should not be exaggerated, it may also have a regional dimension, since there is some evidence that religious disengagement has been most marked in the North (especially the Northeast) and most limited in the southern Bible Belt.[45]

Second, the pace and direction of change has varied markedly among different denominations. Protestant and Jewish congregations have lost market share in terms of membership, while Catholics and other religions have gained. Since World War II the percentage of Protestants in the U.S. population has fallen by roughly 3 to 4 percentage points per decade, a decline of roughly one-quarter overall, while the percentage of Jews has fallen by about .5 percentage point per decade, a decline of roughly half overall. By contrast, the Catholic share of the population has risen by 1 to 1.5 percentage points per decade, an increase of roughly one-third overall, while "no religion" rose by about 2 percentage points per decade, roughly quadrupling. The fraction of the U.S. population that claimed to be Protestant fell by 12 to 15 percentage points (or nearly one-fifth) in the last third of the twentieth century, probably the sharpest such decline in U.S. history.[46]

In some measure, these divergent growth rates are influenced by immigration from Latin America for Catholics and from Asia for other religions. By some estimates, for example, Hispanics now constitute one-quarter of American Catholics. Their involvement means that the Catholic Church is once again playing an important role in connecting immigrants to the broader American society, and in that sense continuing to contribute to social capital formation, but this new influx only partially conceals the degree to which native-born Americans are becoming less involved in the church.

The shifts have been even more marked within the broad family of Protestant denominations. Over the last forty years mainline denominations (Methodist, Presbyterian, Episcopal, Lutheran, Congregational, American Baptist, and so on) have heavily lost "market share," while evangelical and fundamentalist groups (Southern Baptist, Pentecostal, Holiness, Assemblies of God, and Church of God in Christ, as well as Jehovah's Witnesses, Mormons, and independent congregations) have continued to grow, although sometimes at a pace slower than before and now barely matching national population growth. While mainline Protestantism still is a significant part of the religious landscape, these congregations are dwindling, aging, and less involved in religious activities. The fraction of all church members who belong to evangelical churches has risen—probably by roughly one-third in the quarter century after 1960—but for Protestants as a whole, the evangelical gains were not enough to offset the mainline losses. One result is that growth has occurred at both ends of the religious spectrum, the most orthodox and the most secular, while the middle has collapsed.[47]

Measures of church attendance tell a slightly different story. While the numbers of self-identified Catholics have continued to grow, the traditionally high Catholic rate of observance as measured by attendance at mass has declined steadily. Among the dwindling number of Protestants, the rate of weekly attendance has held up reasonably well, in part because of the shift among Protestant denominations toward more evangelical congregations; but since there are fewer self-identified Protestants now, the fraction of Americans who attend Protestant worship services regularly has declined significantly over the last three to four decades. In other words, more and more Catholics are becoming merely nominal church members, while a large and steadily growing number of Protestants and Jews are abandoning their religion entirely.[48]

These declines in religious involvement characterize blacks at least as much as whites, even though blacks continue to be more religiously observant than whites. The decline in church attendance between the mid-1970s and the mid-1990s was nearly as great among blacks as among whites, and membership losses from church groups were slightly greater among blacks. Also, among blacks as among whites, mainline Protestant denominations seem to have suffered relative decline, while evangelical congregations have surged.[49]

The revitalization of evangelical religion is perhaps the most notable feature of American religious life in the last half of the twentieth century. As church historians Roger Finke and Rodney Stark have argued, this development is merely the latest reenactment of a familiar drama from American religious history: an insurgent, more disciplined, more sectlike, less "secularized" religious movement overtakes more worldly, establishmentarian denominations. The Methodists did this to the Episcopalians in the mid–nineteenth century, and now the fundamentalists have done it to the Methodists.

From one perspective this development reinvigorates religion and creates vibrant social capital within the new evangelical churches. The achievements of evangelicals over the last several decades in creating energetic religious communities are justly admired by religious leaders across the spectrum. Many of the most important episodes of social capital formation in American history have been rooted in religious revivals, and we may be on the cusp of another such period.[50]

However, as Wade Clark Roof has observed, "Conservative religious energies are channeled in the direction of recovery of faith *within* the religious tradition and of reaffirmation of religious and life-style boundaries within the dominant culture. . . . Growing churches and synagogues are usually exclusive in character, capable of drawing both social and religious boundaries."[51] Historically, mainline Protestant church people provided a disproportionate share of leadership to the wider civic community, whereas both evangelical and Catholic churches put more emphasis on church-centered activities. Reviewing the sweep of American history, Robert Wuthnow, one of the country's most acute and sympathetic observers of religion, concludes that "whereas the mainline churches participated in progressive social betterment programs during the first half of the twentieth century, evangelical churches focused more on individual piety."[52]

Both individually and congregationally, evangelicals are more likely to be involved in activities within their own religious community but are less likely to be involved in the broader community.[53] Evangelicals attend church more regularly than mainline Protestants, are far more generous philanthropically (giving an average of 2.8 percent of family income vs. 1.6 percent), attend Sunday school and Bible study groups more regularly, and have more close friends in the same congregation. According to George Marsden, "The fundamentalist churches offer far stronger community to their members than do their moderate-liberal Protestant counterparts. . . . [They] are some of the most cohesive non-ethnic communities in America."[54]

The social capital of evangelicals, however, is invested at home more than in the wider community. Among evangelicals, church attendance is *not* correlated with membership in community organizations. There are exceptions to the generalization that evangelicals don't reach out: Charles Colson's Prison Fellowship Ministries, for example, is widely praised for working across denominational and racial lines in six hundred prisons nationwide to restore inmates to membership in the community. Most evangelical volunteering, however, supports the religious life of the congregation itself—teaching Sunday school, singing in the choir, ushering at worship services—but does not extend to the broader community as much as volunteering by members of other faiths.[55]

Today's mainline Protestants and Catholics are more likely to be involved in volunteering and service in the wider community. Among mainline Protestants, and to a lesser extent Catholics, church attendance is less closely tied to religious volunteering but more closely tied to secular volunteering. In these faiths, church attendance is correlated with membership and indeed leadership in secular groups. In both evangelical and mainline congregations, the religiously involved learn transferable civic skills, such as management and public speaking, but mainline Protestants are more likely to transfer them to the wider community. As Robert Wuthnow concludes: "Mainline Protestant churches encourage civic engagement in the wider community, whereas evangelical churches apparently do not."[56]

The same contrast appears at the congregational level: self-described conservative congregations are less likely than liberal or moderate congregations to offer social outreach services or programs, with the notable exception of right-to-life activities. (We shall look more closely at the political participation of evangelical Christians in chapter 9.) Similarly, during the civil rights era, black civic engagement was positively correlated with involvement in mainline black churches, but negatively associated with involvement in black fundamentalist denominations. Thus the fact that evangelical Christianity is rising and mainline Christianity is falling means that religion is less effective now as a foundation for civic engagement and "bridging" social capital. Wuthnow gets to the heart of the matter:

> Religion may have a salutary effect on civil society by encouraging its members to worship, to spend time with their families, and to learn the moral lessons embedded in religious traditions. But religion is likely to have a diminished impact on society if that is the only role it plays. What interested Tocqueville about voluntary organizations was . . . their ability to forge connections across large segments of the population, spanning communities and regions, and drawing together people from different ethnic backgrounds and occupations.[57]

It is that broader civic role that, with few exceptions, evangelical religion has not yet come to play in contemporary America.

• • •

LET US SUMMARIZE what we have learned about the religious entry in America's social capital ledger. First, religion is today, as it has traditionally been, a central fount of American community life and health. Faith-based organizations serve civic life both directly, by providing social support to their members and social services to the wider community, and indirectly, by nurturing civic skills, inculcating moral values, encouraging altruism, and fostering civic recruitment among church people.

Second, the broad oscillations in religious participation during the twentieth century mirror trends in secular civic life—flowering during the first six decades of the century and especially in the two decades after World War II, but then fading over the last three or four decades. As in secular life, the more intense the form of involvement, the greater the recent decline, even though a minority of the population continues to find demanding denominations especially appealing. Moreover, as in politics and society generally, this disengagement appears tied to generational succession. For the most part younger generations ("younger" here includes the boomers) are less involved both in religious and in secular social activities than were their predecessors at the same age.

Finally, American religious life over this period has also reenacted the historically familiar drama by which more dynamic and demanding forms of faith have surged to supplant more mundane forms. At least so far, however, the community-building efforts of the new denominations have been directed inward rather than outward, thus limiting their otherwise salutary effects on America's stock of social capital. In short, as the twenty-first century opens, Americans are going to church less often than we did three or four decades ago, and the churches we go to are less engaged with the wider community. Trends in religious life reinforce rather than counterbalance the ominous plunge in social connectedness in the secular community.

CHAPTER 5

Connections
in the Workplace

WORK-RELATED ORGANIZATIONS are conventionally seen through two different lenses. Economically, unions and professional societies are sometimes criticized as a form of monopoly cartel, as a modern-day guild, a means by which workers in a particular industry or profession can combine to suppress competition and boost income. Sociologically, however, these organizations are an important locus of social solidarity, a mechanism for mutual assistance and shared expertise. Fundamentally, of course, these two images are mutually reinforcing, since solidarity is a crucial precondition for economic collaboration. Even those who bemoan the economic consequences of teachers' unions or bar associations might acknowledge the social capital they represent.

Work-related organizations, both unions and business and professional organizations, have traditionally been among the most common forms of civic connectedness in America. In our inventory of social capital, this is an important ledger. Figure 14 summarizes trends in the rate of union membership in the United States over the course of the twentieth century. The details of this historical profile are linked to the specific history of American labor, such as the favorable effects of two world wars and the New Deal on collective bargaining.[1] However, the broad pattern is reminiscent of the pattern we have noted for both community-based and religious organizations: modest growth in the first third of the century; rapid growth coming out of the Depression and World War II; a high plateau from the 1950s into the 1960s; and a sharp, sustained decline during the last third of the century.

For many years, labor unions provided one of the most common orga-

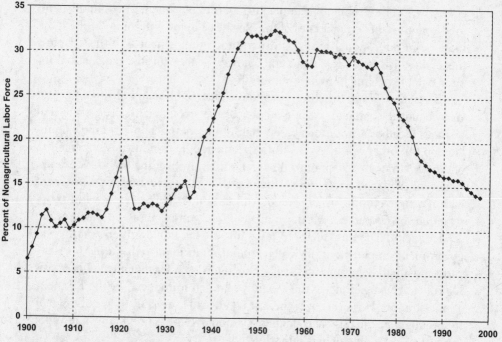

Figure 14: Union Membership in the United States, 1900–1998

nizational affiliations among American working men (and less so, working women), and to some extent that has remained true in recent decades.[2] However, the rate of union membership has been falling for more than four decades, with the steepest decline occurring since 1975. Since the mid-1950s, when union membership peaked, the unionized portion of the workforce in America has nose-dived from 32.5 percent to 14.1 percent. By now, virtually all of the explosive growth in union membership that was associated with the New Deal has been erased. Moreover, the type of involvement in unions has slackened. Unions are now seen mostly as hired bargaining agents, not as a social movement. Although unions, like other voluntary associations, have often been plagued by oligarchy, apathy, and corruption, historically they both created and depended upon social capital—that is, networks of reciprocity. By the end of the twentieth century, however, this once central element in the social life of working Americans had virtually vanished. The solidarity of union halls is now mostly a fading memory of aging men.

But isn't this decline in unionization simply a natural reflection of the changing structure of the postindustrial American economy? Many people consider collective bargaining "primarily suited for the male, blue-collar, production workers in the goods producing industry—the bastion of unions in the '50s—and of little interest to the female, white-collar, knowledge worker in the service industries—the vanguard of the new labor force in the post-industrial economy."[3] The decline of manufacturing, the movement of commerce and jobs from the smokestack states of the Northeast to the antiunion Sunbelt, the increase in educational levels, and part-time employment—all those factors that economists refer to as "structural changes"—are plausible explanations for an inevitable decline in union membership.

In fact, however, the strictly economic change from an industrial to a service economy is only about one-quarter of the story, and all these structural changes together account for barely half of the total decline in union membership.[4] In other words, even within specific jobs and industries, the fraction of the workforce that is unionized has fallen sharply over the last four decades. Between 1953 and 1997 union membership rates declined by 62 percent within manufacturing, by 79 percent within mining, by 78 percent within construction, by 60 percent within transportation, and by 40 percent within the service sector. The only sector to resist this ebbing tide even temporarily was government employment, in which unionization increased sharply for a decade and a half between 1962 and 1979, following a legal change in the basis for collective bargaining in the executive branch introduced by the Kennedy administration. However, over the last two decades even in the public sector union membership has been stagnant. Union decline is not mainly a result of the bleaching of blue collars into white collars.[5]

Labor economists have offered a variety of other interpretations of the decline in unionization—adverse changes in public policy, such as the anti-strike policy introduced by the Reagan administration during the air traffic controllers strike of 1982, virulent employer resistance, flaccid union strategy, and so on. There is some truth in each of these interpretations, but despite much debate, no consensus yet exists among the experts as to their relative weight, and this is not the place to sort them all out. Interestingly, however, one comprehensive study concluded that "virtually all the decline in unionization between 1977 and 1991 seems to be due to decline in demand for union representation"[6]—fewer union members because fewer workers want to join.

Might this decline in "demand" reflect public disgust at improper union influence, featherbedding, corruption, and the like? At one time that explanation might have been plausible, but public resentment of union power has declined steadily for more than two decades, while membership has continued to plunge. Public resentment may have been a consequence of union power, but it is not a cause of continuing union decline. Perhaps the problem with union membership is not so much skepticism about the idea of "union" as skepticism about the idea of "membership." As labor economist Peter Pestillo presciently observed two decades ago, "The young worker thinks primarily of himself. We are experiencing the cult of the individual, and labor is taking a beating preaching the comfort of coalition."[7]

. . .

THE RECENT HISTORY of professional associations seems at first glance entirely different. The percentage of Americans who belong to professional associations and other economic organizations (apart from unions) has doubled over the last four decades. During the 1950s and 1960s most surveys found roughly 8–10 percent membership rates in such organizations, whereas in the 1980s and 1990s virtually all surveys reported equivalent rates of 16–20 percent.[8] The rate of membership in professional and academic societies in the general population rose from 13 percent in 1974 to 18 percent in 1994, an increase of nearly 50 percent in barely two decades.[9]

This impression of rapid growth in professional associations seems confirmed by the membership rolls of the major national professional organizations. Total membership in the American Medical Association rose from 126,042 in 1945 to 201,955 in 1965 and then to a record 296,637 in 1995. The American Institute of Architects is smaller, but its growth has been equally impressive—from 8,500 in 1950 to 23,300 in 1970 and then to a record 47,271 in 1997. Membership in the American Society of Mechanical Engineers nearly tripled from 19,688 in 1945 to 53,810 in 1968 and then doubled again over the next three decades to 107,383 in 1997. For the Institute of Electrical and Electronic Engineers the equivalent jump was from 111,610 in 1963 to 242,800 in 1997. Growth of the American Bar Association (ABA) was even more breathtaking, as total membership quadrupled from 34,134 in 1945 to 118,916 in 1965 and then tripled again to 357,933 in 1991. And so it goes for most major professional organizations. Here at last, it seems, we find welling up unstaunched in the late twentieth century America's Tocquevillean energies.

Before reaching this conclusion, we must, as always, take into account changes in the size of the relevant constituencies, for these same decades have witnessed massive increases in the numbers of people in professional occupations. The more relevant question for our purposes is not "How big is the ABA?" but "How big is the ABA compared to the number of lawyers in America?" And indeed, the changing rate of membership in professional associations *among* members of a given profession turns out to have followed a surprisingly familiar path.

For roughly the first two-thirds of the century the percentage of practicing physicians, lawyers, architects, accountants, and dentists who belonged to the relevant professional association rose sharply and steadily, except for the familiar slump during the Great Depression. (Figure 15 displays the average market share of eight major professional associations over much of the twentieth century.)[10] Typically this increase was about tenfold, from roughly 5–10 percent early in the century to 50–90 percent by the 1960s. Strikingly, in virtually every case one can detect the same postwar acceleration in membership growth between the 1940s and the 1960s that we have already seen in community-based and religious organizations. Generally speaking, membership rates in professional associations roughly doubled between 1945 and 1965, just about the

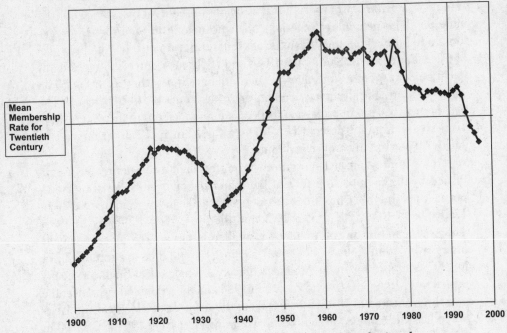

Mean
Membership
Rate for
Twentieth
Century

1900   1910   1920   1930   1940   1950   1960   1970   1980   1990   2000

Figure 15: Average Membership Rate in Eight National Professional Associations, 1900–1997

same rate of growth as we observed earlier in the case of community organizations.

Then in each case the postwar membership boom suddenly slowed, halted, and in almost all cases reversed. First to reach its peak and begin to decline was the American Medical Association (AMA) in 1959, followed by the American Dental Association and the American Institute of Architects (both in 1970), the American Bar Association (ABA) in 1977, and finally the American Institute of Certified Public Accountants in 1993. While the number of registered nurses in America doubled from 1 million in 1977 to 2 million in 1998, membership in the American Nurses Association (ANA) fell from 190,000 to 175,000, so that the ANA's "market share" was cut exactly in half from 18 percent of all RNs in 1977 to 9 percent in 1998. In the case of the American Society of Mechanical Engineers (ASME), the postwar boom had essentially ended by the 1950s, and ASME's market share never regained its pre-Depression peak. The Institute of Electrical and Electronic Engineers (IEEE) was formed in 1963 from the merger of two older organizations, both of which had grown very rapidly in the preceding two decades, but the familiar decline in market share began at the very birth of the IEEE itself.

The downturn in membership rates after 1970 was initially masked by rapid growth in the national pool of professionals. Even if the rate of catch was declining, the fishing was still very good. For example, membership in the

American Institute of Architects more than doubled between 1970 and 1997, although the fraction of architects who were members fell from 41 percent to 28 percent over this period. Membership in the IEEE, drawing on the ebullient electronics industry, more than doubled from 1963 to 1997, even though its "market share" was falling from 51 percent to 37 percent.[11]

Gradually the staff and leadership of each association began to notice their declining membership rates, and eventually in every case relative decline turned into absolute decline, even though the underlying profession continued to burgeon. Thus, just as the leadership of Kiwanis and the League of Women Voters and the Parent-Teacher Association had begun to fret in the 1960s and 1970s about how to reverse their membership slowdown, so too the leadership of the AMA, the ANA, the ABA, and so on now began to discuss what could be causing their slippage.[12]

In each case a broadly similar list of suspects was interrogated — excessive dues, stale programs, competing local or more specialized associations. One common theme was the possibility that as the underlying professions were becoming bigger and more complex, members had shifted their interests and professional identity from, say, medicine to perinatal anesthesiology or from law in general to, say, the intellectual property bar of New York City. I cannot entirely exclude this interpretation, but some initial probes that we conducted were not consistent with it. For example, even specialized groups like the American College of Surgeons and the American Society of Anesthesiology have experienced stagnating or even declining membership rates in recent decades.[13]

So while the absolute number of Americans who belong to professional associations has grown significantly over the last thirty years — and in that sense, this domain is a singular exception to the general pattern we have seen of declining membership — this is the exception that proves the rule, since even in this area of apparent growth, we see the same pattern of growth in sociability during the first two-thirds of the century, followed by sudden stagnation and then decline during the last third. (I leave aside here the familiar issue of whether membership in unions and professional associations today betokens active membership in local chapters, as it once did.)

THUS, SOCIAL CAPITAL in the shape of formal organizations of employees has not increased to offset the declines in political, civic, and religious organizational activity that we noted in earlier chapters. Perhaps, however, a more subtle shift has occurred between residence-based and workplace-based networks, a shift from locational communities to vocational communities. Since more of us are working outside the home today than a generation ago, perhaps we have simply transferred more of our friendships, more of our civic discussions, and more of our community ties from the front porch to the water cooler.[14]

When sociologist Alan Wolfe spoke with several hundred middle-class suburbanites around the country in 1995–96, he encountered a number of people who expressed this thesis. Jeremy Toole of Cobb County, Georgia, estimated that "these days people get about 90 percent of their social connections from the workplace." Diana Hamilton of Sand Springs, Oklahoma, ruminated that "I think people's lives revolve around their work. They make their friends at work, they do their community service through work." And Elizabeth Tyler of Brookline, Massachusetts, added, "I feel very much like I belong to a community of work . . . to a community with my own office, with my own company, within my own industry." [15]

In one sense, such a trend might not be surprising. The Industrial Revolution itself began the process of separating place of work from place of residence, and more and more of our time was spent in factories and offices away from home. By the end of the twentieth century more Americans were in the labor force than ever before—67 percent in 1997, compared with 59 percent in 1950.[16] Professionals and blue-collar workers alike are putting in long hours together, eating lunch and dinner together, traveling together, arriving early, and staying late. What is more, people are divorcing more often, marrying later (if at all), and living alone in unprecedented numbers. Work is where the hearth is, then, for many solitary souls. Even for the minority of Americans who live with spouse and children, argues sociologist Arlie Russell Hochschild, the workplace increasingly serves as a sanctuary from the stresses of marriage, children, and housework.[17] "As more Americans spend more of their time 'at work,'" hypothesizes one thoughtful observer, "work gradually becomes less of a one-dimensional activity and assumes more of the concerns and activities of both private (family) and public (social and political) life." [18]

Changes in the character of work, not just its quantity, might mean that it could account for a greater fraction of our social interaction. After a solitary day's plowing, a farmer might welcome a church social or a Grange meeting, but many of us nowadays work in large, complex organizations, and attending yet another meeting in the evening is the last thing on our minds. Moreover, in the 1980s and 1990s "total quality management," "quality circles," and "team building" became all the rage in management circles. Books with titles like *The Search for Meaning in the Workplace, Creating Community Anywhere,* and *Business as a Calling* urged executives to "establish within the firm a sense of community and respect for the dignity of persons." [19] Many firms put such ideas into practice; by 1992 one survey found that 55 percent of all business establishments had teams (41 percent for a majority of their core workers) and that 41 percent had "quality circles." Architects specializing in office design began to configure the workplace to bolster employees' sense of connectedness, creating spaces with such evocative labels as "watering holes," "conversation pits," and "campfires" where employees come to warm their hands. Sociologist Hochschild concludes that these "new management techniques so pervasive

in corporate life have helped transform the workplace into a more apprecia-
tive, personal sort of social world."[20]

The modern workplace thus encourages regular collaborative contacts
among peers—ideal conditions, one might think, for social capital creation.
Many people form rewarding friendships at work, feel a sense of community
among co-workers, and enjoy norms of mutual help and reciprocity on the job.
According to several surveys in the 1990s by the Families and Work Institute,
nine out of ten employees agree that "I look forward to being with the people
I work with each day" and that "I feel I'm really part of the group of people I
work with." Several studies of friendship and support networks have found that
about half of all workers have at least one close personal tie at work. According to a 1997 survey that asked people to enumerate all their conversations
on a given day, just over half took place in the workplace. When just working adults were considered, that fraction jumped to more than two-thirds.[21]
Clearly many of us have close personal connections at work. From a broader
societal perspective, an added benefit of workplace-based connections is that
the workplace is much more diverse, racially and even politically, than most
other social settings.[22]

Before concluding, however, that the line at the copying machine has replaced the back fence as the locus for social capital in contemporary America,
we need to consider three additional factors. First, I know of *no evidence whatever* that socializing in the workplace, however common, has actually *increased*
over the last several decades. Indeed, of all the domains of social and community connectedness surveyed in this book, systematic long-term evidence on
workplace-based connections has proven the most difficult to find. Many of us
today have friends at work, but it is unclear whether we are more likely to have
friends at work than our parents did. (Some indirect evidence discussed later in
this section actually suggests a trend in the opposite direction.)[23]

Second, social connectedness in the workplace might be described as a
glass half-empty, not merely as a glass half-full. Most studies of personal networks find that co-workers account for less than 10 percent of our friends.
Workplace ties tend to be casual and enjoyable, but not intimate and deeply
supportive. In the most careful study, when people were asked to list their
closest friends, less than half of all full-time workers put even one co-worker
on the list. On average, neighbors were more likely to appear on the list than
co-workers. When people were asked to whom they would turn to discuss
"important matters," less than half of all full-time workers listed even a single co-worker. In short, though most of us who work outside the home have
acquaintances among our workmates, for only a small minority of us does the
workplace account for most of our close personal ties. Americans' most important personal networks are *not* centered mainly in the workplace.[24]

Third, several important trends in the American workplace over the last decade or two have been quite damaging to social ties there. The nature of the implicit employment contract governing many Americans' work lives was transformed during the 1980s and 1990s by downsizing, "right sizing," "reengineering," and other economic restructuring. During the 1980s layoffs and job uncertainty grew primarily because of the business cycle, but during the 1990s restructuring came to be a regular tool of management, even during prosperous times. In fact, one study found that even in the boom year of 1993–94 nearly half of all firms laid off workers. And these were big cuts, averaging 10 percent of each company's workforce. The old employment contract was not in writing—it didn't have to be—but it was the central organizing principle of employee-management relations and was understood by all. World War II veterans joining IBM were instructed to consult with their wives before taking the job, because "once you came aboard you were a member of the corporate family for life."[25]

A half century later increased competition in the global marketplace, improved information technology, greater focus on short-term financial returns, and new management techniques have combined to make virtually all jobs more "contingent." Perhaps the most telling statistic is this: One of the fastest-growing industries in the 1980s was "outplacement" services. These firms' revenues grew from just $35 million in 1980 to a whopping $350 million in 1989. As management scholar Peter Cappelli sums up more than a decade of research on changing employment practices, particularly among white-collar workers, "The old employment system of secure, lifetime jobs with predictable advancement and stable pay is dead."[26]

One consequence of these changes has been increased employee anxiety, but there have been winners as well as losers. More independence from the firm, flatter hierarchies, less paternalism, and more reward for merit and creativity rather than seniority and loyalty have been good for many firms and their employees. Even when corporate morale and employee commitment have been badly damaged, as they typically are, research often finds that corporate productivity has improved. My purpose here is to evaluate not the economic consequences of these changes, but rather their impact on trust and social connectedness in the workplace.[27] On that score, the balance sheet is negative.

In hundreds of interviews with white-collar workers in firms undergoing restructuring—some ultimately successfully, some not—Charles Heckscher found that the most common reaction to the changed social contract was to "put your head down," focusing more and more narrowly on one's own job. Even workers whose jobs were spared often experienced what is called "survivor shock." While some employees relished the independence and greater opportunity afforded to individuals under the new system, most middle managers even in successful firms agreed with the view expressed by one: "We're all alone out here. It's been very stressful." Said another, "The reorganization disrupted the network of relationships among people at all levels." Relationships with peers became more distant. "Rather than turning on each other, most people drifted apart, becoming more isolated and wanting to be left alone."[28]

In addition to the effects of the changed employment contract on social capital in the workplace, the change is not good for involvement in the broader community. As Peter Cappelli points out,

> Much of contemporary American society has been built on stable employment relationships characterized by predictable career advancement and steady growth in wages. Long-term individual investments such as home ownership and college educations for children, community ties and the stability they bring, and quality of life outside of work have all been enhanced by reducing risk and uncertainty on the job.[29]

All that tends to be undermined by the new deal at work.

The workplace remains a significant recruiting ground for volunteers, and an overwhelming majority (92 percent) of corporate executives say they encourage their employees to become involved in community service. On the other hand, according to the most comprehensive national survey of volunteers, the fraction recruited by someone at work slipped from 15 percent in 1991 to 12 percent in 1999.[30] No doubt firms and work-based volunteer recruiters have good intentions, but so far, at least, the workplace remains far less important than churches and other civic organizations as recruitment networks for volunteerism. Whether recent efforts to increase workplace-based volunteering have made a visible impact on the aggregate level of volunteering in the society will become clearer in chapter 7.

Not all employees in America have been affected by these changes in the implicit employment contract. Blue-collar workers have long faced the job insecurity that has recently hit middle management. Nevertheless, over the last three decades job stability at all educational levels in the American workforce has declined. Fewer and fewer of us remain very long in the same job or even in the same company. In fact, although job instability remains higher among blue-collar workers, it has increased much more rapidly among white-collar workers, who account for a growing fraction of the workforce and who have traditionally contributed disproportionately to civic life. This trend toward "job churning" is concentrated among men, who previously had been in more stable jobs, but women continue to have much lower job tenure than men, primarily because they are more likely to move in and out of the labor market. Moreover, what economists call "the returns to tenure" (that is, the wage and salary benefits from seniority) have fallen, as more and more of our income depends on what we've done recently and less and less on how long we've been in our job. One consequence of performance-based pay and performance-based job security is to increase, if only implicitly, the degree of competition among peers. Teamwork stops feeling so amicable when you are subtly competing with your teammates for your livelihood.[31]

In addition, a surprisingly large and growing fraction of the American workforce has "contingent" or "nonstandard" jobs—part-time employees, temps, "independent contractors" (consultants), "on-call" workers (such as substitute teachers), and the like. The best recent studies suggest that nearly 30 percent of all U.S. workers fall into this broad category, about one-half of them part-timers and another one-quarter independent contractors. Temping and part-time work both appear to be growing. Many workers—software programmers, for example, or management consultants, or parents who seek to combine work and family obligations—are in these irregular jobs by choice and find them rewarding both personally and financially. Apart from high-status consultants, however, most people in nonstandard jobs say that they would prefer regular, full-time, noncontingent employment.[32]

More important for our purposes, *all* these structural changes in the workplace—shorter job tenure, more part-time and temporary jobs, and even independent consultancy—inhibit workplace-based social ties. Three-quarters of all independent contractors have no regular work colleagues. Part-time workers have only two-thirds as many friends from work as do full-time workers. Friendships at work decrease with job instability, even when the job changes are voluntary. None of these patterns is surprising in the least, since successful investment in social capital takes time and concerted effort. Birds of passage, whether by choice or by necessity, generally don't nest. The implication is clear—nearly one-third of all U.S. workers have jobs that discourage durable social connections, and that fraction is rising.[33]

In short, some features of contemporary American work life—more time at work, more emphasis on teamwork—would seem to foster informal workplace social capital, while other features—downsizing, the fraying of ties to a particular firm, the rise of contingent work—point in the opposite direction. The impact of another potentially important factor—changing office technology, especially email—is harder to evaluate systematically at this point; the general effect of computer-mediated communication on social capital is discussed in chapter 9.

As I have noted, hard evidence on long-term trends in the frequency of water-cooler discussions of civic affairs or the incidence of close friendships among co-workers is apparently nonexistent. A weaker form of indirect evidence, however, is available through surveys of job satisfaction. Many studies have shown that social connections with co-workers are a strong predictor—some would say the strongest single predictor—of job satisfaction. People with friends at work are happier at work.[34] If social capital at work has risen significantly in recent decades, presumably that should show up in warmer feelings about work, at least if we control for adverse changes in financial and job security.

In 1955 and again in the 1990s Gallup pollsters asked working Americans, "Which do you enjoy more, the hours when you are on your job, or the hours when you are not on your job?" In 1955, 44 percent of all workers said they preferred the hours on the job, but by 1999 barely one-third as many (16 percent) felt that way. According to Roper polls, the proportion of Americans "completely satisfied" with their job fell from 46 percent in the mid-1970s to 36 percent in 1992. Some of this disaffection is traceable to concerns about job security and personal finances, but even controlling for financial security, the General Social Survey reveals a modest long-term slippage (roughly 10 percent overall) in job satisfaction between 1972 and 1998. Recent surveys suggest that as many as one in four employees are chronically angry on the job, and many researchers believe that incivility and aggression in the workplace are on the rise.[35] Not all survey data point in the same direction, but the balance of evidence appears to be that, quite apart from material insecurity, American workers are certainly no happier in the workplace today than a generation ago and probably are less happy. That evidence is hard to square with the hypothesis that the workplace has become the new locus of Americans' social solidarity and sense of community.

Our judgment must be cautious here. Unlike most other domains of sociability discussed in this volume, in this particular area we lack definitive evidence one way or the other. As will become clear in section V, my own view is that any solution to the problem of civic disengagement in contemporary America must include better integration between our work lives and our community and social lives. Nevertheless, a final note of skepticism is necessary about the workplace as the new public square for American communities. In the end, "work" entails time and effort destined to serve primarily material, not social, ends. Work-based networks are often used for instrumental purposes, thus somewhat undercutting their value for community and social purposes. As Alan Wolfe observes:

> Because we form such ties to promote the highly secular activities of getting and spending, friendships and connections developed at work are generally assumed to have a more instrumental character: we use people, and they use us, to solicit more business, advance our careers, sell more products, or demonstrate our popularity. . . . If so, it follows that even if the decline of civil ties in the neighborhood is being compensated by new ties formed at work, the instrumental character of the latter cannot be an adequate substitute for the loss of the former.[36]

Moreover, when at work, our time is our employer's, not our own. We are paid to work, not to build social capital, and our employer has the legal right to draw the line between the two. Court decisions have given employers wide latitude to monitor and control communications in the workplace, and monitoring is in fact increasing rapidly, facilitated by the ease of intercepting electronic communications. A private employer may fire workers for what they say, as well as for their political views or activities. According to a 1999 survey by the American Management Association, two-thirds of employers record employee voice mail, email, or phone calls, review computer files, or videotape workers, and such surveillance is becoming more common. Rights of free speech and privacy that are essential to public deliberation and private solidarity are, to put it mildly, insecure in the workplace. Substantial reforms in public law and private practice would be necessary before the water cooler could become the equivalent of the back fence or the town square.[37]

Most of us nowadays are employed, and most of the time most of us work with other people. In that fundamental sense, the workplace is a natural site for connecting with others. However, the balance of the evidence speaks against the hopeful hypothesis that American social capital has not disappeared but simply moved into the workplace. Americans at the beginning of the twenty-first century are demonstrably less likely than our parents were to join with our co-workers in formal associations. New forces that might foster socializing in the workplace are counterbalanced by equally new forces that inhibit the types of social ties, durable yet flexible and wide-ranging, that are important to civic life and personal well-being. In addition, for the one American adult in three who is not employed, workplace ties are nonexistent. The workplace is not the salvation for our fraying civil society.

CHAPTER 6

Informal

Social Connections

SO FAR we have mostly explored the formal ways in which Americans connect with their communities—through political parties, civic associations, churches, unions, and the like. Far more frequent, however, are the informal connections that we strike up—getting together for drinks after work, having coffee with the regulars at the diner, playing poker every Tuesday night, gossiping with the next-door neighbor, having friends over to watch TV, sharing a barbecue picnic on a hot summer evening, gathering in a reading group at the bookstore, even simply nodding to another regular jogger on the same daily route. Like pennies dropped in a cookie jar, each of these encounters is a tiny investment in social capital.*

In Yiddish, men and women who invest lots of time in formal organizations are often termed *machers*—that is, people who make things happen in the community. By contrast, those who spend many hours in informal conversation and communion are termed *schmoozers*. This distinction mirrors an important reality in American social life.[1] *Machers* follow current events, attend church and club meetings, volunteer, give to charity, work on community projects, give blood, read the newspaper, give speeches, follow politics, and frequent local

---

*Experimental social psychologists have uncovered striking evidence that even the most casual social interaction can have a powerful effect on reciprocity. When a confederate "stranger" speaks briefly in the hallway to an unwitting subject, the subject is quicker to provide help when she subsequently "overhears" the confederate having an apparent seizure than if there had been no previous contact. See Bibb Latané and John M. Darley, The Unresponsive Bystander: Why Doesn't He Help? (Englewood Cliffs, N.J.: Prentice-Hall, 1970), 107–109.

meetings. Statistically speaking, doing any one of these activities substantially increases your likelihood of doing the others. People who work on community projects are likely to be churchgoers, newspaper readers to be volunteers, club-goers to be interested in politics, and blood givers to attend meetings. *Machers* are the all-around good citizens of their communities.

Schmoozers have an active social life, but by contrast to *machers*, their engagement is less organized and purposeful, more spontaneous and flexible. They give dinner parties, hang out with friends, play cards, frequent bars and night spots, hold barbecues, visit relatives, and send greeting cards. Again, doing any one of these things is significantly associated with doing the others, too. All involve, in the felicitous expression of Alexander Pope, "the flow of soul."

The two types of social involvement overlap to some extent—major-league *machers* are often world-class *schmoozers*, and vice versa. Some social settings fall into a gray area between the formal and the informal—a bridge club or a Shriners gathering, for example. Nevertheless, as an empirical matter, the two syndromes are largely distinct—many people are active in one sphere but not the other. And many people do neither; they are not involved in community affairs, and they don't spend much time with friends and acquaintances.

This distinction between *machers* and *schmoozers*—between formal and informal social connectedness—reflects differences in social standing, life cycle, and community attachment.[2] *Machers* tend to be better educated and to have higher incomes, whereas informal social involvement is common at all levels in the social hierarchy. Formal community involvement is relatively modest early in life, peaks in late middle age, and then declines with retirement. Informal social involvement follows the opposite path over the life cycle, peaking among young adults, entering a long decline as family and community obligations press in, then rising again with retirement and widowhood. Single people spend more time and energy in *schmoozing*. For both men and women, marriage increases time spent at home and in formal community organizations, while reducing the time spent with friends. Having children cuts further into informal social connectedness, while adding to formal community involvement. *Machers* are disproportionately homeowners and longtime residents, *schmoozers* are renters and frequent movers. "Settling down" means, among other things, exchanging informal ties for more formal ones, shifting the balance between hanging out with friends and participating in community affairs.

Historically, *machers* (except for those involved in religious life) have tended to be disproportionately male, but the entry of women into the paid labor force has shown that employment, not gender, is the primary key to formal community involvement. Informal social connections are much more frequent among women, regardless of their job and marital status. Married or single, employed or not, women make 10–20 percent more long-distance calls to family and friends than men, are responsible for nearly three times as many greeting cards and gifts, and write two to four times as many personal letters as men. Women spend more time visiting with friends, though full-time work blurs this gender difference, by trimming friendship time for both sexes. Keeping up with friends and relatives continues to be socially defined as women's work.* Even in adolescence (and not only in the United States), women are more likely to express a sense of concern and responsibility for the welfare of others—for example, by doing volunteer work more frequently. Although American boys and girls in the 1990s used computers almost equally, boys were more likely to use them to play games, while girls were more likely to use them for email. Sociologist Claude S. Fischer concludes that "discounting their fewer opportunities for social contact, women are more socially adept and intimate than men, for whatever reasons—psychological constitution, social structure, childhood experiences, or cultural norms." In short, women are more avid social capitalists than men.[3]

Both the *macher* and the *schmoozer* can be found in all corners of our society. Businessmen *schmooze* in country clubs in Palm Springs, and young welfare moms are *machers* in community-based organizations in Appalachia. The highest frequency of card playing in America is among working-class housewives of the Great Plains.[4] When philosophers speak in exalted tones of "civic engagement" and "democratic deliberation," we are inclined to think of community associations and public life as the higher form of social involvement, but in everyday life, friendship and other informal types of sociability provide crucial social support. To be sure, informal connections generally do not build civic skills in the ways that involvement in a club, a political group, a union, or a church can, but informal connections are very important in sustaining social networks. So in our inventory of social capital in America, we need to pay special attention to trends in *schmoozing*.

VISITING WITH FRIENDS and acquaintances has long been one of the most important social practices in America. The early nineteenth century in New England, as historian Karen V. Hansen has shown, was "a very social time."

> The many types of visiting ranged from pure socializing to communal labor: visitors took afternoon tea, made informal Sunday visits, attended maple sugar parties and cider tastings, stayed for extended visits, offered assistance in giving birth, paid their respects to the family of the deceased, participated in quilting parties, and raised houses and barns.

---

*While marriage increases the frequency with which women send greeting cards, it cuts in half the frequency with which men do so, regardless of whether their wives work or not. This sociological "finding" will hardly be news to most couples.

Visits lasted from a brief stopover, or a "call," to a leisurely afternoon, to a month-long stay. Visitors frequently stayed overnight. The difficulty of travel—particularly in winter, by foot, horse, stage, wagon, or train— created barriers to visiting but did not deter visitors who highly valued their contact with neighbors and kin. It was through visiting, in fact, that they created their communities.[5]

Some early sociologists thought that this thicket of informal social connection would not survive a transplant to the anonymous city, that urbanization would doom both friendship and extended kinship. However, experience showed that even in the most densely populated urban settings, social filaments linking residents were steadily regenerated.[6] The density of social connections is lower in cities—the average resident of Los Angeles knows a smaller fraction of her neighbors than does the average resident of a farming village in the Central Valley, and the Angeleña's friends are likely to live farther away—but twentieth-century urbanization was not fatal to friendship. Urban settings sustain not a single, tightly integrated community, but a mosaic of loosely coupled communities. As mobility, divorce, and smaller families have reduced the relative importance of kinship ties, especially among the more educated, friendship may actually have gained importance in the modern metropolis.[7] The passage in popular culture from *I Love Lucy* and *All in the Family* to *Cheers*, *Seinfeld*, and *Friends* exalts informal social ties.

Like our New England forebears, Americans spend lots of time visiting. Five times during the 1980s and 1990s Roper pollsters asked Americans, "During the past week, how many times would you say you have gone out for entertainment—to a movie, to visit friends, to a sports event, to dinner, or whatever?" Nearly two-thirds of us reported going out at least once in the last week, and of those, fully half had gone to the home of friends for dinner, visiting, playing cards, and the like. Among other destinations for a night out, 4 percent had gone to a play or live concert, 11 percent to a sports event, 17 percent to a bar, disco, or other place of public entertainment, 18 percent to a movie, and slightly more than half to a restaurant for dinner.[8] Across America, from big cities to tiny hamlets, spending an evening at home with friends is five to ten times more common than is going to the theater or a ball game.

Several surveys between 1986 and 1990 also showed that *schmoozers* are more common than *machers* in contemporary America.[9] (Figure 16 summarizes these results, highlighting the most relevant social activities.) Slightly more than one-quarter of all Americans had attended at least one meeting of a club or civic organization in the preceding month, and slightly more than one-third had gone to a church social function in that period—a respectable showing for such civic-minded events. During that same month, more than half of all Americans had had friends in for an evening, and nearly two-thirds had gone out to a friend's home for an evening.[10] One way or another, three-quarters of all Americans got together at home with friends at least once during that month, and the national average was three such soirees per month. Similarly, according to time diary data collected between 1965 and 1995, the average American spent roughly half an hour each week on organizational activity (not counting religion), but more than three hours a week visiting with friends.[11]

Comparable estimates of a broader array of social connections (as summarized in figure 17) show that, on average, during the last quarter of the twentieth century Americans attended church services and visited with relatives nearly every other week; ate dinner out, sent a greeting card to someone, and wrote a letter to a friend or relative about once every three weeks; played cards about once a month and entertained at home just about that often; attended a club meeting about every other month and had a drink in a bar almost that often; gave or attended a dinner party, went to the movies, and attended a sporting event roughly every two or three months; worked on some community project and played some team sport roughly twice a year; and wrote a letter to the editor every other year.[12]

The average American in recent decades has been far from isolated civically or socially, but we seem more engaged with one another as friends (or *schmoozers*) than as citizens (or *machers*). We get together with friends about twice as often as we attend organized meetings, we hang out in bars about

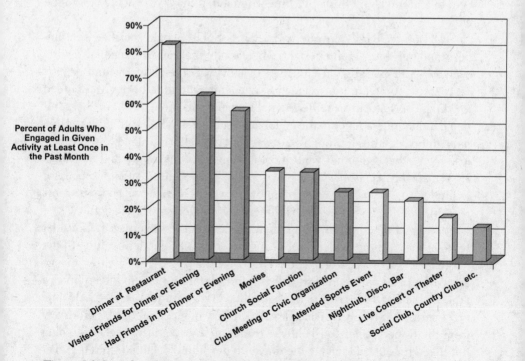

Figure 16: Social and Leisure Activities of American Adults (1986–1990)

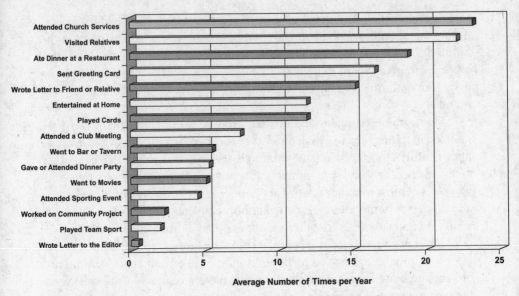

Figure 17: Frequency of Selected Formal and Informal Social Activities, 1975–1998

three times as often as we work on community projects, and we send a greeting card to a friend about thirty-five times more often than we send a letter to the editor.

Of course, hardly anyone is "average." Some people socialize continuously and join every group in sight, whereas others are more detached. Nearly everyone is a "specialist" in some type of activity. Some of us write our parents every week, some are movie fanatics, and some attend a lot of civic-minded meetings. To take an extreme example of specialization, 1/300 of the adult population writes a letter to the editor at least once a month, but this infinitesimal group accounts for roughly 20 percent of all letters to all editors in America.[13] Nevertheless, homey ways of connecting with our friends and neighbors are remarkably widespread. Despite the much hyped allure of Hollywood, for example, Americans play cards more than twice as often as we go to the movies.[14] In sum, the good news is that Americans connect with one another.

The bad news is that we are doing so less and less every year. Consider some of the startling evidence of change over the last quarter century. In the mid- to late 1970s, according to the DDB Needham Life Style archive, the average American entertained friends at home about fourteen to fifteen times a year. By the late 1990s that figure had fallen to eight times per year, a decline of 45 percent in barely two decades. An entirely independent series of surveys from the Roper Social and Political Trends archive confirms that both going out to see friends and having them over to our home declined from the mid-1970s to the mid-1990s. (See figure 18 for details.) Yet a third archive (that of

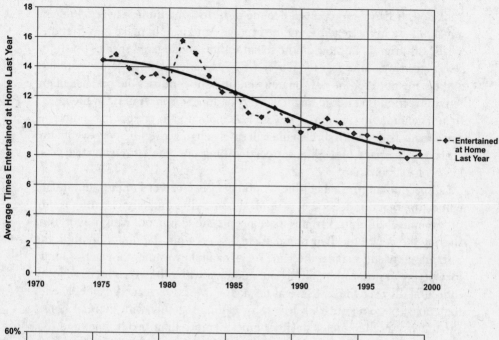

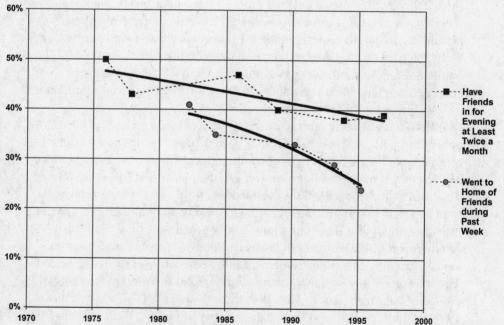

Figure 18: Social Visiting Declines, 1975–1999

Yankelovich Partners) reports a decline of nearly one-third between 1985–86 and 1998–99 in the readiness of the average American to make new friends.[15] Visits with friends are now on the social capital endangered species list. If the sharp, steady declines registered over the *past* quarter century were to continue at the same pace for the *next* quarter century, our centuries-old practice of entertaining friends at home might entirely disappear from American life in less than a generation. Of course, it would be foolhardy to predict that outcome, since many things in American life will surely change over the next twenty-five years, but the pace of decline in social visiting over the last twenty-five years has been extraordinary.

Recognizing the scheduling conflicts of two-career families, one might conjecture that this decline in reciprocal home visits and dinner parties is simply an optical illusion. Perhaps more people are dining out with friends, thus shifting the venue for their prandial encounters from the dining room to the restaurant but still making the same social capital investment. In fact, contrary to widespread impression, dining out (alone or with others) has increased very little if at all over the last several decades.[16] Moreover, faced explicitly with the choice of going out with friends or getting together with them at home, Americans say they prefer staying home by more than two to one, and that stay-at-home margin is rising, not falling.[17] Thus the practice of entertaining friends has not simply moved outside the home, but seems to be vanishing entirely. Informal outings, like picnics, also seem on the path to extinction. The number of picnics per capita was slashed by nearly 60 percent between 1975 and 1999.[18] Americans are spending a lot less time breaking bread with friends than we did twenty or thirty years ago.

Even more startling, this same trend can be observed closer to home. As figure 19 reports, the past two decades have witnessed a dramatic change in one traditionally important form of family connectedness—the evening meal. The fraction of married Americans who say "definitely" that "our whole family usually eats dinner together" has declined by a third over the last twenty years, from about 50 percent to 34 percent.[19] Conversely, the number who disagree with the proposition that "our whole family usually eats dinner together"—in other words, those for whom this is definitely not a customary practice—has increased by half (from 16 percent to 27 percent) over this same period. The ratio of families who customarily dine together to those who customarily dine apart has dropped from more than three to one in 1977–78 to half that in 1998–99. In fact, striking as these data are, they understate the real change in American dining customs, since they refer only to the behavior of married couples, whereas the proportion of adults living (and therefore presumably dining) alone has roughly doubled during this period.[20] Since the evening meal has been a communal experience in virtually all societies for a very long time, the fact that it has visibly diminished in the course of a single generation in our

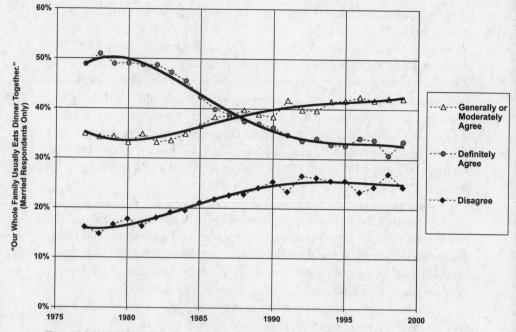

Figure 19: Family Dinners Become Less Common, 1977–1999

country is remarkable evidence of how rapidly our social connectedness has been changing.

Beyond mealtime, virtually all forms of family togetherness became less common over the last quarter of the twentieth century. Between 1976 and 1997, according to Roper polls of families with children aged eight to seventeen, vacationing together fell from 53 percent to 38 percent, watching TV together from 54 percent to 41 percent, attending religious services together from 38 percent to 31 percent, and "just sitting and talking" together from 53 percent to 43 percent. It is hard not to read these figures as evidence of rapidly loosening family bonds.[21]

How about schmoozing at the real-life equivalent of Cheers, the neighborhood bar "where everybody knows your name"? That, too, is becoming a thing of the past. Three independent series of surveys from the mid-1970s to the late 1990s substantiate that conclusion: the frequency with which Americans, both married and single, went out to bars, nightclubs, discos, taverns, and the like declined by about 40–50 percent over the last decade or two.[22] Whether we live alone or not, Americans are staying home in the evening, and Cheers has become a period piece.

Since good food and drink are often accompaniments of good schmoozing, trends in the numbers of various sorts of eating and drinking establishments in America over the last quarter century are both startling and suggestive. (See figure 20.) Between 1970 and 1998 the number of full-service restaurants per one hundred thousand population fell by one-quarter, and the numbers of bars and luncheonettes were cut in half. Meanwhile the per capita number of fast-food outlets, those "personal refueling stations" of modern society, doubled. From the point of view of conversational opportunities, the decline of conventional eating places has to some extent been offset by the proliferation of new wave coffee bars, like the cappuccino bar in Minneapolis that hosts neighborhood discussion groups. As figure 20 shows, however, even accounting for such growth, the net decline in eating and drinking establishments has been substantial.[23]

Unlike the "regulars" at the local bar or café, few of the other people waiting impatiently in line at McDonald's are likely to know your name or even to care that they don't.[24] These cold numbers confirm the gradual disappearance of what social commentator Ray Oldenburg calls "the great good place," those hangouts that "get you through the day."[25] In effect, Americans have increasingly chosen to grab a bite and run rather than sit a while and chat.

Perhaps the most revealing trend in our use of leisure time is the fate of card games. A survey of residents in twenty-four American cities in 1940 found

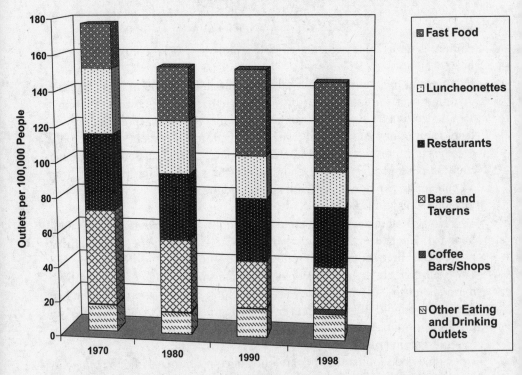

Figure 20: Bars, Restaurants, and Luncheonettes Give Way to Fast Food, 1970–1998

that cards were the nation's favorite form of social recreation. According to that survey, a deck of playing cards was found in 87 percent of American homes, as compared, for example, to radios (83 percent) and telephones (36 percent). On average, over the first half of the twentieth century one pack of cards was sold *each year* for every two Americans aged fourteen and over.[26] Strikingly, trends in playing card sales track almost precisely the trends we spotted earlier in formal civic involvement—steady growth in the first three decades of the century, a slump during the Great Depression, and then explosive growth in the years after World War II. (See figure 21.)

Although poker and gin rummy were popular, the biggest boom was in bridge, a four-handed game that had become extremely popular by the 1950s. By 1958, according to the most modest estimate, thirty-five million Americans—nearly one-third of all adults—were bridge players. Millions of Americans, both men and women, belonged to regular card clubs—in fact, one of the earliest scientific surveys of social involvement found that in 1961 nearly one in every five adults (in Nebraska, at least) was a member of a regular foursome. In dorms and student unions of the 1960s and 1970s hundreds of thousands of college students spent millions of nights in seemingly endless games of bridge. The primary attraction of bridge and other card games was that they were highly social pastimes. "Mixed doubles" clubs were, in that

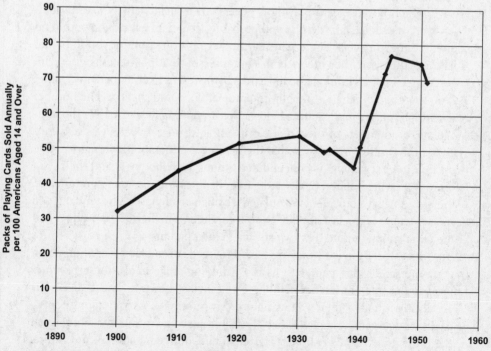

Figure 21: The Rise of Card Games in America, 1900–1951

more gendered world, one of the most important sites for men and women to gather informally. The rules encouraged conversation about topics other than the game itself, since "table talk" about the state of play was generally frowned on. "Serious" bridge players played in silence, but for most players, the weekly or monthly evening of bridge provided a valued opportunity to *schmooze* with friends and neighbors, mostly about personal matters but occasionally about issues of broader concern, including politics.[27]

As recently as the mid-1970s nearly 40 percent of all American adults played cards at least once a month, and the ratio of monthly card players to monthly moviegoers was four to one. Between 1981 and 1999, however, the average frequency of card playing among American adults plunged from sixteen times per year to eight times per year. By 1999 card playing still outdrew movies four to three, but the gap was closing fast. Were this same steady rate of annual decline to continue unabated, card playing would disappear entirely in less than two decades. For a social practice that is more than six centuries old—and one that was booming only a few decades ago—the end is coming with dramatic suddenness.[28] American adults still play five hundred million card games a year, but that figure is falling by twenty-five million games a year.[29] Even if we assume, conservatively, that community issues come up in conversation only once every ten card games, the decline of card playing implies fifty million fewer "microdeliberations" about community affairs each year now than two decades ago.

In fact, because card playing is necessarily a social activity (except for a few solitaire addicts), its demise will probably accelerate toward the end. If no one else in your social circle plays cards, there is no reason for you to bother learning the game. For precisely the same reason that populations of endangered species often implode, so too card playing seems likely to become extinct even more rapidly than a straight-line projection would suggest. The number of card players is rapidly falling below a self-sustaining level. In 1999 the average age of members of the American Contract Bridge League was sixty-four and rising steadily, a sure sign that the decline is generational in nature. The decline in card playing is concentrated among baby boomers and their children. A growing fraction of all card games occurs in retirement communities, the sociological equivalent of isolated ecological niches where endangered species often make a last stand.[30] To college students in the 1990s, "bridge" had the same antique sound that "whist" had to their parents.

Substitutes for card playing have emerged, of course, everything from computer and video games to casino gambling. Like cards, these pastimes provide the spice of chance. Unlike card playing, however, these successors are distinguished by their solitary nature. My informal observation of Internet-based bridge games suggests that electronic players are focused entirely on the game itself, with very little social small talk, unlike traditional card games. Even fanatics of Microsoft Solitaire rarely play in a group, and any visitor to the new megacasinos that dot the land has chilling memories of acres of lonely "players" hunched in silence over one-armed bandits. (Figure 22 summarizes illustrative trends in card playing, casino going, video games, and moviegoing over the last quarter century.) Bridge, poker, gin rummy, and canasta are not being replaced by some equally "*schmoozable*" leisure activity.[31]

Yet another unobtrusive indicator of social connectedness is the practice of sending greeting cards. Sending greeting cards has declined by about 15–20 percent among both married and single people over the last decade or two. (This downtrend predates the advent of the Internet and email by at least a decade, so it represents more than merely a shift from real to virtual greetings.) Individuals send more greeting cards as they age, especially if they are living alone, so card sales have been boosted in an aging America. However, at any given age Americans are now sending fewer greeting cards than people of that age did a generation ago.[32] Yet again we see evidence of generational differences underlying the transformation of social customs in contemporary America.

So much for friends. How about neighbors? According to the General Social Survey, between 1974 and 1998 the frequency with which Americans "spend a social evening with someone who lives in your neighborhood" fell by about one-third—from about thirty times a year to about twenty times a year among married people and from about fifty times a year to about thirty-five times a year among single people.[33] (See figure 23.) Scattered evidence further

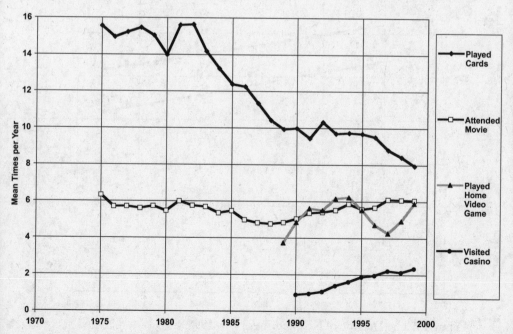

Figure 22: Card Playing and Other Leisure Activities, 1975–1999

suggests that this decline had actually begun twenty years earlier, so that when compared with neighborliness in the mid-1950s, neighborhood ties in the 1990s are perhaps less than half as strong.[34] The average American still socializes with her neighbors every couple of weeks, but as in the case of friendship, these ties are measurably more feeble now than a generation ago.

Recent years have seen much publicity given to "neighborhood associations," and some observers claim that these are more common now than some years ago. One recent survey suggests that as many as one adult in eight is involved with a neighborhood, community, homeowners association, or block club.[35] However, similar associations were frequent in the earlier decades, too; recall that *Life* magazine paean to Americans of the 1960s "satisfying their gregarious urges in countless neighborhood committees." Urban sociologist Barrett A. Lee and his colleagues point out that

recent proliferation of social science literature on neighborhood organizations implies that these groups are newcomers to the urban scene. However, even the slightest amount of digging will suffice to correct that misleading impression. . . . [N]eighborhood organizations first appeared near the end of the last century and were well represented in most large cities prior to the Great Depression.

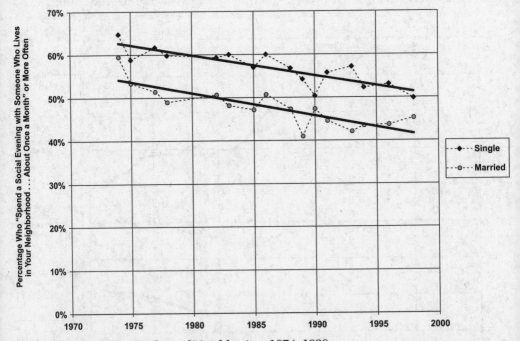

Figure 23: The Decline of Neighboring, 1974–1998

Long-term studies of neighborhood life from Boston to Seattle show that although neighborhoods at the end of the twentieth century were occasionally mobilized for *political* purposes, organized *social* life at the neighborhood level—street carnivals, amateur theatricals, picnics, potlucks, dances, and the like—was much more vibrant in the first half of the twentieth century than in its waning years.[36]

"Neighborhood watch" groups have become more common over the last twenty years, and they often have an immediate impact in reducing crime. A 1998 Department of Justice survey of twelve cities nationwide found that 11 percent of all residents had ever attended a neighborhood watch meeting to help protect themselves from crime (6 percent in the last year), as compared with 14 percent who kept a weapon at home, 15 percent who owned a guard dog, and 41 percent who installed extra locks.[37] In short, we invest more in guns, dogs, and locks than in social capital for crime defense. Perhaps partly for this reason, participation in neighborhood watch programs almost always decays after an initial burst of enthusiasm, unless rooted in neighborhood organization of a more comprehensive sort.[38] Crime watch groups may have become more common, but they provide a frail replacement for the vanished social capital of traditional neighborhoods—sociological AstroTurf, suitable only where the real thing won't grow.

As is true of formal social involvement, the picture that has emerged thus far of waning investments in *schmoozing* is wholly confirmed by studies of American time budgets over the last thirty years. The percentage of Americans who on a "diary day" recorded any time at all spent in informal socializing (including visiting with friends, attending parties, hanging out at bars, informal conversation, and so on) fell steadily from about 65 percent in 1965 to 39 percent in 1995. The average daily time devoted to such activities fell from about eighty to eighty-five minutes in 1965 to fifty-seven minutes in 1995. (See figure 24.) We spent only two-thirds as much time on informal socializing at century's end as we had three decades earlier.[39]

This striking shift in the way we allocate our time—toward ourselves and our immediate family and away from the wider community—is confirmed by a survey of twenty-four thousand time diaries conducted by the NPD Group between 1992 and 1999.[40] Over the course of the 1990s the average American came to spend nearly 15 percent more time on child or pet care (probably because of the "baby echo"—the recent spurt of children of the baby boomers) and roughly 5–7 percent more time each on personal grooming, entertainment, sleep, exercise, and transportation. By contrast, the largest changes of all involve time spent at worship and visiting with friends, both of which fell by more than 20 percent, according to this evidence.

The density of informal social connections varies somewhat, as we noticed earlier, among different social categories—higher among women than

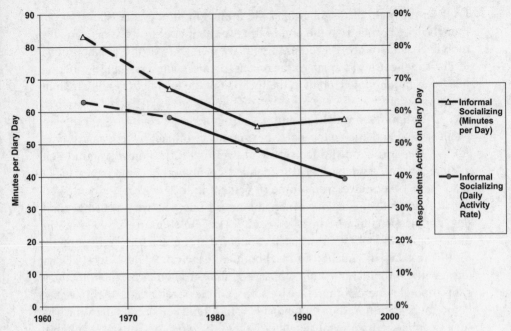

Figure 24: Informal Socializing as Measured in Time Diary Studies, 1965–1995

among men, higher among young people and retired people than among the middle-aged, and so on. Even though the *level* of *schmoozing* differs across these categories, however, the *trends* in *schmoozing* (namely, downward) are very similar in all segments of society—down among both women and men, down in all age categories, down in all social classes, down in all parts of the country, down in big cities and suburbs and small towns, down among both married couples and single people.[41] In short, informal social connectedness has declined in all parts of American society.

We noted earlier the paradox that the strongest predictor of formal community involvement—education—had expanded sharply over the last twenty years and that nevertheless formal community involvement is down sharply. One implication is that without the boost provided by higher educational levels, formal involvement might have declined even more rapidly. We see a similar paradox in the case of informal social involvement: *schmoozing* is higher among single and childless people, and the number of single and childless people has risen significantly over the last two decades.[42] Other things being equal, these trends should have led to *increased* informal social interaction, exactly the opposite of what we have found. As conventional family life has become rarer, we might have expected the real-life equivalent of *Cheers* and *Friends* to take the place of civic organizations and dinner parties, but in fact

we have witnessed the decline of the latter without a compensating increase in
the former. The implication: Something else must be even more powerfully
depressing the rate of *schmoozing* in contemporary America.

So WE ARE SPENDING significantly less time nowadays with friends and neighbors than we used to. What might we be doing instead that has implications for
social capital? One common form of leisure activity is participation in sports.
What can we learn about trends in social capital from an examination of Americans at play? Have we perhaps shifted the locus of our social encounters from
the card table or the neighborhood bar to the softball diamond or the exercise
class?

Some evidence suggests that sports clubs have become slightly more
common over the last two decades; according to the General Social Survey,
membership in such clubs grew from 19 percent in 1974–75 to 21 percent in
1993–94. On the other hand, many studies have found, somewhat surprisingly,
that participation rates in most sports have actually fallen in recent decades.[43]
Since the population is growing, the gross number of participants is also growing in some cases, but as a fraction of the population, participation in all of
the following sports has fallen by 10–20 percent over the last decade or two:
softball, tennis (and other racket games, like table tennis), volleyball, football,
bicycling, skiing (downhill, cross-country, and water), hunting, fishing, camping, canoeing, jogging, and swimming. For example, long-term surveys from
the National Sporting Goods Association, the Sporting Goods Manufacturers
Association, the DDB Needham Life Style studies, and the National Center
for Health Statistics all agree that nationwide participation in softball dropped
by roughly one-third between the mid-1980s and the late 1990s.[44]

A few new sports have become popular—in-line skating and snowboard-
ing among younger, more agile Americans, fitness walking and gym activities among the more health-conscious, golf among senior citizens. However,
most of the new sports are not as "social" as many traditional athletic activities.
Indeed, the most dramatic increases in sports-related purchases over the last
decade have involved "in-home" activities, like treadmills and workout equipment.[45] Moreover, except for walking, none of them attracts nearly as many
participants as the declining traditional sports. Among team sports, soccer and
basketball are up, but not enough to offset simultaneous falloffs in all other
major team sports—softball, baseball, volleyball, and football. All in all, sports
participation is modestly but unambiguously down over the last decade or so,
and this decline has particularly affected team and group sports.[46]

This decline in sports participation is not due to the aging of the U.S. population. On the contrary, the declines are sharpest among the young, whereas
athleticism is actually growing among older Americans. Among twenty-

somethings, average attendance at exercise classes was more than halved from eight times a year in the mid-1980s to three in 1998, whereas over this same period attendance doubled from two to four among Americans sixty and over. Swimming and attendance at health clubs display this same generational discrepancy—down among the younger, steady or up among the older. For physiological reasons, sports participation (except for exercise walking) declines with age, but overlaid on that life cycle pattern is the same generational profile (down among boomers and X'ers, up among their parents and grandparents) that we noted earlier for other forms of social and political participation. There is, in fact, some reason to believe that these twin trends—rising recreational activity among the older generation, falling among the younger generation—have been under way since the early 1960s.[47]

Although it is not our primary concern here, rates of participation in most youth sports seem to have been stagnant or declining over the last several decades.[48] Surprisingly, after an exponential increase in youth soccer in the 1980s, even participation in that fashionable sport slowed in the 1990s.[49] At the same time, most other major sports suffered significant declines in adolescent participation in recent years. One important exception to this general picture is growth in organized school-based sports for women, in part as a consequence of Title IX requiring equal opportunity for women in federally funded athletic programs; but even this major initiative has not offset the more general decline in formal and informal sports participation among American youth.[50] Because of the "baby echo" the absolute number of participants in many youth sports has risen, but what is relevant to our story is that *rates* of participation have been declining.

Fitness was discussed more in the 1990s than it was in the 1970s, and health clubs are all the rage.[51] Could this trend perhaps offset the slumps in other forms of social connection? The empirical evidence suggests not. First, all fitness activities combined (apart from walking) are much less common than the more prosaic activities of card playing or dinner parties. Even with the 1990s' bust in card playing and boom in health clubs, for example, three times as many Americans play cards regularly as visit a health club regularly. Only among single, twenty-something, college graduates are visits to a health club more common than card games, and despite what one might infer from the mass media, only one American adult in every fifteen falls into that demographic category. Even if health clubs offered limitless opportunities for *schmooz*ing (rather than merely staring at a monitor while working out in silence), the growth in health clubs is dwarfed by the collapse of less trendy forms of informal connectedness.

Second, the 1980s and 1990s witnessed no net gain in the number of times that the average American jogs, attends exercise and aerobic classes, or visits a health club. The rise in health clubs in these years was offset by a decline in jogging and exercise classes. (See figure 25.) The less fashionable activity of "walking more than a mile for exercise" is more common than all other forms of workout combined, and in fact, walking for exercise has increased by about one-third over the last decade. However, the increasing popularity of walking (and golf, too) is due entirely to the fitness boom among older Americans, precisely the group that has most resisted the nationwide decline in connectedness. The trends in athletic activity that we have reviewed—down nationwide, down even faster among young adults, down least (or not at all) among senior citizens—have their visible counterpart in the "obesity epidemic" that has swept over America in recent decades—up nationwide, up even faster among young adults, up least of all among older Americans. Fitness is not a domain that has offset the erosion of social capital elsewhere in American society.[52]

Virtually alone among major sports, only bowling has come close to holding its own in recent years.[53] Bowling is the most popular competitive sport in America. Bowlers outnumber joggers, golfers, or softball players more than two to one, soccer players (including kids) by more than three to one, and tennis players or skiers by four to one.[54] Despite bowling's "retro" image, in 1996 even twenty-somethings went bowling about 40 percent more often than they went in-line skating. More recently, even greater numbers of young people have reportedly been attracted by a high-tech combination called "cosmic bowling" or "Rock 'N' Bowl." Moreover, participation in all other major sports is more highly concentrated among either young men, or the upper middle class, or

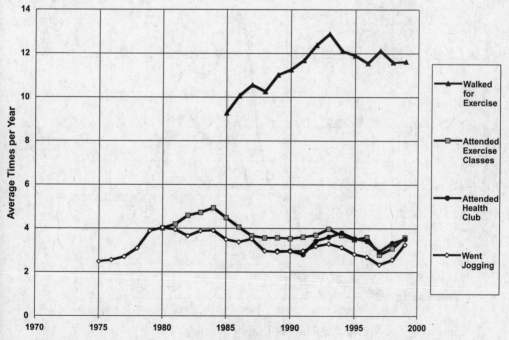

Figure 25: Stagnation in Fitness (Except Walking)

both. Unlike health clubs, bicycling, jogging, exercise, swimming, tennis, golf, softball, and all other major sports, bowling is solidly middle-American—common among both men and women, couples and singles, working-class and middle-class, young and old.[55]

Given population growth, more Americans are bowling than ever before, but *league* bowling has plummeted in the last ten to fifteen years. Between 1980 and 1993 the total number of bowlers in America increased by 10 percent, while league bowling decreased by more than 40 percent.[56] Figure 26 shows the long-run trend in league bowling in America, a profile that precisely matches the trends in other forms of social capital that we have already examined—steady growth from the beginning of the century (except during the Depression and World War II), explosive growth between 1945 and 1965, stagnation until the late 1970s, and then a precipitous plunge over the last two decades of the century. At the peak in the mid-1960s, 8 percent of all American men and nearly 5 percent of all American women were members of bowling teams. Yet as the projections in figure 26 indicate, if the steady decline in league bowling were to continue at the pace of the last fifteen years, league bowling would vanish entirely within the first decade of the new century.

Lest bowling be thought a wholly trivial example, I should note that, according to the American Bowling Congress, ninety-one million Americans

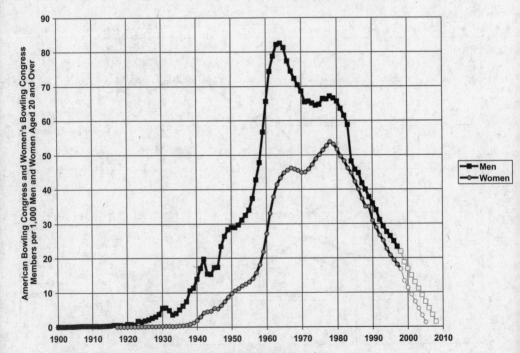

Figure 26: The Rise and Decline of League Bowling

bowled at some point during 1996, *over 25 percent more than voted in the 1998 congressional elections.*[57] Even after the 1980s' plunge in league bowling, between 2 and 3 percent of American adults regularly bowled in leagues, although as we have seen, that figure was dropping fast. The decline in league bowling threatens the livelihood of bowling lane proprietors, because according to the owner of one of the nation's largest bowling lane chains, league bowlers consume three times as much beer and pizza as do solo bowlers, and the money in bowling is in the beer and pizza, not the balls and shoes. The broader social significance, however, lies in the social interaction and even occasionally civic conversations over beer and pizza that solo bowlers forgo. Whether or not bowling beats balloting in the eyes of most Americans, bowling teams illustrate yet another vanishing form of social capital.

Strictly speaking, only poetic license authorizes my description of non-league bowling as "bowling alone." Any observant visitor to her local bowling alley can confirm that informal groups outnumber solo bowlers. Insofar as such informal groups represent what I have called *schmoozing*, the fact that participation in bowling has held more or less steady in recent years actually represents an exception to the general diminishment of informal ties. On the other hand, league bowling, by requiring regular participation with a diverse set of acquaintances, did represent a form of sustained social capital that is not matched by an occasional pickup game.

While Americans are spending less time *doing* sports, we are spending more time and money *watching* sports now than we were only a few decades ago. Sports spectatorship has been rising rapidly, which helps explain the rapid rise in the salaries of professional athletes. In part, the growth in spectatorship reflects our television viewing habits, but it is also reflected in live attendance figures. Adjusted for population growth, attendance at major sporting events has nearly doubled since the 1960s.[58] The year-to-year fortunes of individual sports have varied with the excitement of the season and the vicissitudes of labor-management relations, but virtually all major sports have seen growth in per capita attendance over the last four decades—professional baseball, basketball, football, hockey, and stock-car racing, as well as college football and basketball. Figure 27 summarizes this trend—at last, a trend line that is rising, if only for the passive spectator.

This increase in sports spectatorship is not a dead loss from the point of view of social capital.[59] Sitting with friends in the bleachers for a Friday night high school football game might be just as productive of community as sitting across a poker table. Moreover, at least for the fans of winning teams, the sense of shared enthusiasm for a common passion can generate a certain sense of community. As long-suffering Red Sox fans know, even shared adversity can build community. On the other hand, it is striking that the same changing balance between active participation and passive spectatorship that we earlier

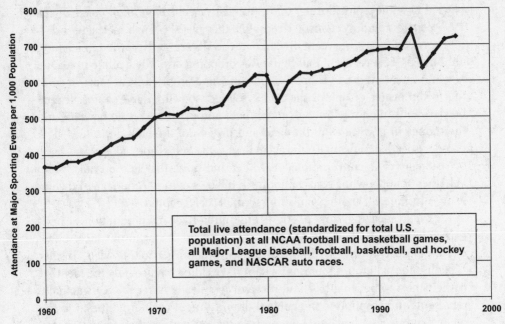

Figure 27: The Growth of Spectator Sports, 1960–1997

noted in the political sphere can be found in the sphere of sports itself. In football, as in politics, watching a team play is not the same thing as playing on a team.

This same phenomenon—observing up, doing down—appears in other spheres of American life. In both popular and high culture, audience growth has generally matched or exceeded population growth. Surveys suggest steady or even increasing per capita attendance at art museums, pop and rock concerts, and movies. Between 1986 and 1998, while churchgoing was falling by 10 percent, museumgoing was up by 10 percent; while home entertaining was down by a quarter, moviegoing was up by a quarter; and while club meeting attendance was down by a third, pop/rock concert attendance was up by a third.[60]

On the other hand, by many measures, "doing" culture (as opposed to merely consuming it) has been declining. Take town bands or jazz jamming or simply gathering around the piano, once classic examples of community and social involvement. According to surveys conducted every year over the last quarter century, the average frequency of playing a musical instrument has been cut from nearly six times per year in 1976 to barely three times per year in 1999. The percentage of Americans who play an instrument at all has fallen by fully one-third (from 30 percent to 20) percent over this period, and exposure to music lessons has been dropping in recent generations.[61] According to surveys commissioned by the National Association of Music Merchants, the fraction of households in which even one person plays an instrument has fallen steadily from 51 percent in 1978 to 38 percent in 1997.[62] We certainly have not lost our taste for *listening* to music, any more than for watching sports, but fewer and fewer of us play together.

When Aristotle observed that man is by nature a political animal, he was almost surely not thinking of *schmoozing*. Nevertheless, our evidence suggests that most Americans connect with their fellows in myriad informal ways. Human nature being what it is, we are unlikely to become hermits. On the other hand, our evidence also suggests that across a very wide range of activities, the last several decades have witnessed a striking diminution of regular contacts with our friends and neighbors. We spend less time in conversation over meals, we exchange visits less often, we engage less often in leisure activities that encourage casual social interaction, we spend more time watching (admittedly, some of it in the presence of others) and less time doing. We know our neighbors less well, and we see old friends less often. In short, it is not merely "do good" civic activities that engage us less, but also informal connecting. Whether this silent withdrawal from social intercourse has affected our propensity to pitch in on common tasks and to show consideration for bystanders is the question to which we turn in the next two chapters.

CHAPTER 7

Altruism, Volunteering, and Philanthropy

ALTRUISM, VOLUNTEERING, AND PHILANTHROPY—our readiness to help others—is by some interpretations a central measure of social capital. Social philosopher John Dewey, however, rightly emphasized the distinction between "doing with" and "doing for." The significance of this distinction is highlighted in a recent development in a close-knit Jewish neighborhood of Providence, Rhode Island.[1]

To celebrate the festival of Purim, Jews of this neighborhood historically exchanged visits, bringing one another gifts of fruit and pastries (Mishloach Manot) in accordance with a religious mitzvah (commandment). In recent years, however, this custom has been interrupted by pressures of time, family vacations, and the like. Nowadays, as Purim approaches, a resident is likely to receive an engraved note from neighbors, like this one:

> We will be in New York for Purim. It will not be possible for us to fulfill the mitzvah of Mishloach Manot this year. Please do not leave any Mishloach Manot outside our door this year. The squirrels, dogs, cats, and rabbits will eat them. Instead of Mishloach Manot, we have donated to the Jewish Theological Seminary in your name.

The philanthropic purpose is admirable. The traditional visits, however, also reinforced bonds within this community. A check in an envelope, no matter how generous, cannot have that same effect. Social capital refers to networks of social connection—doing *with*. Doing good *for* other people, however laudable, is not part of the *definition* of social capital.

As an empirical matter, however, social networks provide the channels through which we recruit one another for good deeds, and social networks foster norms of reciprocity that encourage attention to others' welfare. Thus, as we shall shortly see in more detail, volunteering and philanthropy and even spontaneous "helping" are all strongly predicted by civic engagement. As a matter of fact in contemporary America, those of us who belong to formal and informal social networks are more likely to give our time and money to good causes than those of us who are isolated socially. For this reason, altruism (and honesty, discussed in the next chapter) is an important diagnostic sign of social capital. Thus any assessment of trends in social capital must include an examination of trends in volunteering, philanthropy, and altruism.

Giving time and money to help others is a long and distinguished tradition in American society. Both philanthropy and volunteering are roughly twice as common among Americans as among the citizens of other countries.[2] For the first several centuries of our national experience the social context for volunteering and philanthropy was primarily religious. Caring for others is a central tenet of all our faiths. Toward the end of the nineteenth century a new theme became a more prominent part of the rationale for altruism—helping the less fortunate was a part of our civic duty. As Andrew Carnegie, one of the new millionaires who emerged from the period of rapid growth following the Civil War, proclaimed in his 1889 essay "The Gospel of Wealth," wealth was a sacred trust which its possessor was bound to administer for the good of the community.[3]

During the twentieth century both volunteering and philanthropy became more organized and professionalized. Modern philanthropy began at the turn of the century, not merely with the accumulation of new wealth spawned by the Industrial Revolution, but also with the invention of new techniques for stimulating financial giving by ordinary Americans—the "community chest" (forerunner of the United Way), the community foundation, and the gradual professionalization of fund-raising and volunteer management. The number of community chests exploded from 39 nationwide in 1920 to 1,318 by 1950, covering 57 percent of the U.S. population.[4] While the church remained the single most important locus of volunteering and philanthropy, it was joined by new institutions for organized altruism—the foundation, the corporation, and community organizations of all sorts.

Many of the civic associations whose growth and recent decline we chronicled in an earlier chapter—the Scouts, the Red Cross, "service clubs" (Rotary, Kiwanis, and Lions), the PTA, and so on—were active in mobilizing volunteer energies. Throughout the twentieth century new organizations of collective altruism continued to emerge in response to new needs and renewed idealism—

from the March of Dimes in the 1930s to World Vision in the 1950s to Habitat for Humanity in the 1970s to Teach for America in the 1990s. Between 1989 and 1994 the number of public charities in America grew nearly six times as fast as the U.S. population, and by 1996 a total of 654,186 public charities (not counting churches) were registered in the United States.[5]

Americans are a generous people. Nearly half of us claim to undertake some sort of volunteer work, including both volunteering in organized settings, like churches and hospitals, and informal helping behavior, like baby-sitting a neighbor's plants. According to one widely cited estimate, ninety-three million of us volunteered a total of twenty billion hours in 1995. Moreover, we give an impressive amount of money to good causes. In 1997 American individuals, corporations, and foundations gave $143.5 billion to charity, of which more than three-quarters ($109 billion) was donated by living individuals. In 1992 Americans gave 1.5 million gallons of blood, and the overwhelming majority of blood donors say that their main motivation is simply "wanting to help others." In 1989, 74 percent of Americans reported giving money (not counting contributions to religious and political organizations), 35 percent reported volunteering, and 23 percent reported giving blood. We seem to be living up to Tocqueville's observation more than a century and a half ago:

> Americans enjoy explaining almost every act of their lives on the principle of self-interest properly understood. It gives them great pleasure to point out how an enlightened self-love continually leads them to help one another and disposes them freely to give part of their time and wealth for the good of the state.[6]

Amid the pressures of everyday life, giving time and giving money often seem alternative avenues for generosity. If we lack one, we can give the other. Generally speaking, however, volunteering and philanthropy are complements, not substitutes. Some of us give lots of both, while others give little of either. In 1995 volunteers contributed two or three times as much of their household income to charity as did nonvolunteers. Conversely, 63 percent of all financial donors also volunteered, as compared with only 17 percent of noncontributors. Volunteering is among the strongest predictors of philanthropy, and vice versa. Analogously, active blood donors are more likely to volunteer time and give to philanthropy than nondonors. Altruistic behaviors tend to go together.[7]

Who among us are most generous with our toil and treasure?[8] Not surprisingly, well-to-do, highly educated people—those who have more personal and financial resources—are more likely to volunteer, to donate money, and to give blood. In particular, education is one of the most powerful predictors of virtually all forms of altruistic behavior, even after controlling for other possible predictors. College graduates, for example, are twice as likely as people with a high school education or less to have volunteered in the past year (71 percent compared with 36 percent) or to be blood donors (13–18 percent compared with 6–10 percent). On the other hand, material resources are not the most important predictor of altruism. As a matter of fact, because of their relatively active church involvement, the poor give no less a fraction of their income than the wealthy.[9]

Size of community makes a difference: formal volunteering, working on community projects, informal helping behavior (like coming to the aid of a stranger), charitable giving, and perhaps blood donation are all more common in small towns than in big cities.[10] Age makes a difference: volunteering and blood donation generally follow an inverted U-shaped life cycle pattern, reaching a peak in one's late thirties or early forties. Volunteering is especially common among parents of school-age children, and youth activities are second only to religion as a focus of volunteering. Philanthropy, on the other hand, typically accelerates with age, as disposable wealth accumulates.[11] Employment increases the likelihood of volunteering, probably because it exposes workers to diverse social networks, but among volunteers there is a trade-off between time spent working and time spent volunteering, so the highest rate of volunteering is among part-time workers.[12]

More important than wealth, education, community size, age, family status, and employment, however, by far the most consistent predictor of giving time and money is involvement in community life. Social recluses are rarely major donors or active volunteers, but *schmoozers* and *machers* are typically both.

In 1996, 73 percent of members of secular organizations and 55 percent of members of religious groups said that they volunteered, as compared with only 19 percent of other Americans.[13] As figure 28 shows, Americans who regularly attend both church and clubs volunteer an average of 17 times per year, ten times as often as those who are involved in neither church nor club, who volunteer on average 1.7 times per year. Secular involvement seems to have an even greater effect than religious involvement, for "pure" churchgoers volunteer an average of 5 times per year, while "pure" clubgoers average 12 times per year. Moreover, involvement in secular organizations is closely associated with participation with community projects, while involvement in religious organizations is not.[14] People active in religious organizations volunteer for ushering in church or visiting shut-in parishioners, whereas people active in secular organizations are most likely to work on cleaning up the local playground.

Schmoozing is also closely associated with volunteering.[15] For example, as figure 29 shows, Americans who entertain friends at home are much more likely to work on community projects and to volunteer in other ways. Moreover, people who are actively involved in community and social networks are more likely not only to volunteer in the first place, but also to *stick with* vol-

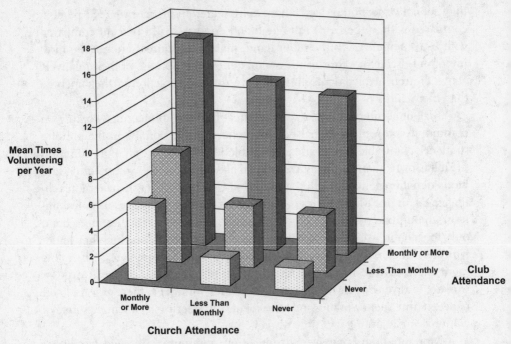

Figure 28: Volunteering Fostered by Clubgoing and Churchgoing

unteering over a period of years, whereas people who are isolated socially are more likely to engage in purely episodic volunteering.[16]

Philanthropy is also tied closely to organizational involvement. In 1996, 87 percent of members of secular organizations and 76 percent of members of religious organizations made some charitable contribution, as compared with only 37 percent of nonmembers. Members of religious organizations donated an average of 1.9 percent of their annual household income ($802) to charity, and members of secular organizations gave an even more impressive 2.3 percent (or $1,167), compared with 0.4 percent ($139) for other Americans.[17] In round numbers, *joiners are nearly ten times more generous with their time and money than nonjoiners.* Social capital is a more powerful predictor of philanthropy than is financial capital.

Altruism of all sorts is encouraged by social and community involvement. Churchgoing and clubgoing, for example, are among the strongest predictors of giving blood, controlling for other background factors, such as age, education, sex, and so on. (See figure 30.) Americans active in community affairs are twice as likely to give blood as their stay-at-home neighbors. Even informal helping, like providing emotional support in the aftermath of a natural disaster or keeping an eye on a neighbor's house, is strongly correlated with the size of one's network of friends and acquaintances.[18] To predict whether I am likely to give time, money, blood, or even a minor favor, you need to know, above all,

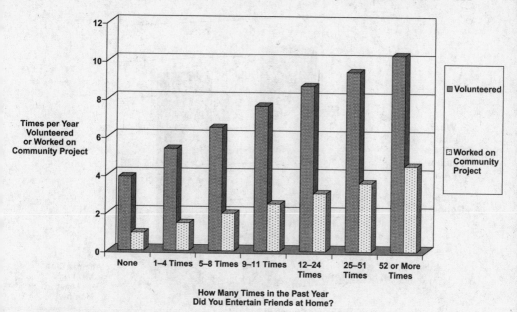

Figure 29: *Schmoozing* and Good Works

how active I am in community life and how strong my ties to family, friends, and neighbors are.

Social connections encourage giving for many reasons. Joiners may be generous souls by nature, but involvement in social networks is a stronger predictor of volunteering and philanthropy than altruistic attitudes per se.[19] As fund-raisers and volunteer organizers know well, simply being asked to give is a powerful stimulus to volunteering and philanthropy. When volunteers are asked how they happened to get involved in their particular activity, the most common answer is, "Someone asked me." Conversely, when potential blood donors are asked why they haven't given blood, the most common response is, "Nobody asked."[20]

Fund-raising typically means friend-raising. So the more involved I am in social and community networks, both formal and informal, the more likely I am to be asked. And I'm more likely to agree if the recruiter is part of my network of friends. Community organizations need time and money, and members call upon one another to pitch in, not only for that organization, but also for others. If I join the PTA, I'm very likely to be asked to volunteer for the fund-raising picnic, and someone I meet there may well invite me to help with the Cancer Society walk-a-thon. Once on the list of usual suspects, I'm likely to stay there.

Volunteering fosters more volunteering, in both formal and informal settings.[21] Organizational involvement seems to inculcate civic skills and a lifelong disposition toward altruism, for adult volunteers and givers are par-

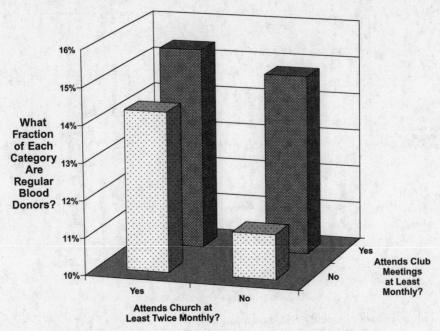

Figure 30: Blood Donation Fostered by Clubgoing and Churchgoing

ticularly distinguished by their civic involvement as youth. Those of us who were involved in youth groups or did youthful volunteering are half again as likely to donate to charity as adults and twice as likely to volunteer as those of us who were not so involved as youngsters. Finally, careful studies have shown that (with other social and personality traits held constant) people who have received help are themselves more likely to help others, so that simple acts of kindness have a ripple effect. In short, giving, volunteering, and joining are mutually reinforcing and habit-forming—as Tocqueville put it, "the habits of the heart."

AGAINST THIS BACKDROP, what have been the trends in giving and volunteering over recent decades? Let's begin with philanthropy. Each year American charities brag about new records in money raised and spent for worthy causes. For as long as records have been kept, total giving in current dollars has risen steadily. Even in dollars adjusted for inflation and population growth, the trend has been generally upward, with only temporary dips around recession years. According to one enthusiastic cheerleader for American generosity, per capita charitable giving in constant 1993 dollars nearly doubled between 1960 ($280) and 1995 ($522).[22]

On the other hand, the growth in charitable giving, even in constant dollars, is hardly surprising, for our income has also risen and, along with it, our spending on practically everything. For example, over those same years (1960–1995) in which real per capita giving doubled, real per capita spending on flowers, seeds, and potted plants almost tripled, and real per capita spending on all recreational goods and services combined—from daffodils to Disneyland and from toys to TV repairs—nearly quadrupled.[23] To measure our philanthropic generosity, we need to know how our giving compares to our income, not merely how many dollars we are handing out. If my income quadruples, while my weekly church offering increases by only a quarter, most reasonable people would say I'm becoming stingier, not more generous. "Tithing," after all, is about relative, not absolute, numbers.[24]

Trends in American philanthropy relative to our resources are dismaying, for in the 1990s Americans donated a smaller share of our personal income than at any time since the 1940s. The long-run trends in personal philanthropy are reminiscent of the evolution of other aspects of American civic engagement, as figure 31 reveals.[25] The first half of the twentieth century was an era of increasing national generosity. As a share of income, personal philanthropy nearly doubled in the three decades between 1929 and 1960. After brief disruptions associated with the Great Depression and World War II, American giving, relative to our means, rose sharply and steadily after the war, increasing by nearly 50 percent between 1944 and 1960. (Since this was a period of rapid economic growth, in real terms the increase was even sharper.) Beginning in 1961, however, philanthropy's share of Americans' income has fallen steadily for nearly four decades, entirely erasing the postwar gains. Total giving by living individuals as a fraction of national income fell from 2.26 percent in 1964 to 1.61 percent in 1998, a relative fall of 29 percent. In 1960 we gave away about $1 for every $2 we spent on recreation; in 1997 we gave away less than $.50 for every $2 we spent on recreation.

The parallel between the timing and direction of trends in philanthropy and the nearly simultaneous ups and downs of American community involvement and social connectedness we reviewed in earlier chapters is uncanny. By contrast, the long-run ups and downs of philanthropy are quite disconnected from the ups and downs of the economy. Hit by the Great Depression, American real per capita income fell by 3 percent between 1929 and 1939, while the share of income that we gave to charity rose by more than a quarter. Over the next two decades real per capita income soared by 74 percent, yet personal giving as a fraction of income continued to rise at just about the same long-run pace as during the Depression years. Through bad times and good, Americans grew steadily more generous. Conversely, after 1960 our generosity has steadily shriveled. Through the booms of the sixties and eighties, as well as the busts of the seventies and early nineties, this inexorable retreat was disrupted only briefly during the middle eighties in response to passing changes in the federal tax code. In short, the waxing and waning of American generosity over the last seventy years coincides closely with the ups and downs in our stock of

Figure 31: The Rise and Fall of Philanthropic Generosity, 1929–1998

social capital and not at all with the ups and downs in our stock of financial capital.

The subsidence of American philanthropic impulses since 1960 has been very pervasive, affecting many different communities of givers and many different recipients. In round numbers, half of all charitable giving in America is religious in nature, so we can get some additional insight (and confirm the general picture) by focusing separately on trends in giving to the major faiths, as well as trends in giving to secular community activities. Figure 32 arrays the best available evidence on long-term trends in giving to major Protestant denominations, to Catholic causes, and to United Way, the most extensive community-based fund-raising operation in America and a good proxy for secular giving.[26] The rhythms of giving in the first half of the century vary across these institutional settings, but the postwar boom in giving is apparent, as is the timing and extent of the post-1960 plunge in generosity relative to means.

After falling sharply from 1960 to 1972, Protestant giving *per member* has stagnated since the early 1970s. On the other hand, as we noted earlier, membership itself in Protestant denominations has continued to fall steadily throughout this period, so Protestant giving as a fraction of national income has continued to fall; in that sense, figure 32 understates the decline in Protestant philanthropy. In other words, if a Protestant deserts her church entirely, as many have in recent years, the financial repercussions of that apostasy are not reflected in figure 32.

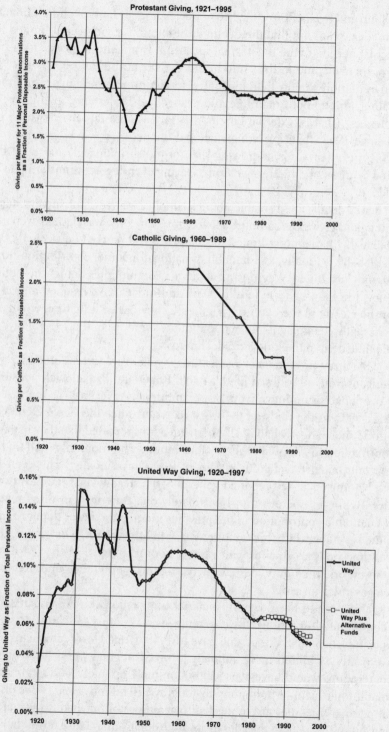

Figure 32: Trends in Protestant, Catholic, and United Way Giving,
1920s–1990s

John and Sylvia Ronsvalle, two of the leading students of church finances in America, point out that the decline in Protestant giving is not limited to a particular portion of the theological spectrum. Evangelicals give a larger fraction of their income to the church, but their contribution per member has fallen even more rapidly than the figures for mainline Protestants.[27] Still more revealing, among both mainline and evangelical Protestants, giving for "benevolences" (that is, external charity) has fallen more rapidly (down 38 percent since 1968) than for "congregational finances" (down 12 percent since 1968).[28] In other words, a growing slice of the shrinking pie has been consumed by internal church operations, leaving even less for ministering to the world.

Fewer details are available about Catholic finances, but surveys suggest that religious giving by Catholics as a fraction of income was slashed even more dramatically than among Protestants, falling by 59 percent between 1960–63 and 1988–89.[29] Finally, as a fraction of national income, contributions to the thousands of United Way organizations in communities across the country are now less than half the level of 1960 and in fact have reached a level not seen since early in the century. (Figure 32 shows as well that the emergence of "alternative campaigns" for activist nonprofit groups in the 1980s and 1990s made little dent in the long-term decline.)

This array of evidence on declining generosity is reinforced by what Americans from all walks of life have told Roper and Yankelovich pollsters in the two longest-running surveys of philanthropy. As recently as the first half of the 1980s, in the midst of the worst recession since the Great Depression, figure 33 shows, nearly half of all American adults reported that they had made a contribution to charity in the previous month, and more than half said that they contributed to religious groups at least "occasionally." However, both these barometers of self-reported generosity fell steadily over the next two decades. By the prosperous mid-1990s barely one American in three reported any charitable contribution in the previous month, and fewer than two in five claimed even occasional religious giving.[30] In other words, what donors themselves told pollsters squares with reports from recipients: In the last decades of the twentieth century, despite increasing prosperity, the generosity of the average American sank.

This decline has powerful material implications for American support of community institutions. If we were giving, at century's end, the same fraction of our income as our parents gave in 1960, United Way campaigns would have nearly $4 billion more annually to invest in good works, U.S. religious congregations would have over $20 billion more annually, and total national philanthropic giving would jump by roughly $50 billion a year.[31] Because our real personal incomes are more than twice those of our parents, we are still contributing more than they did in absolute dollars. In relative terms, however, our spending for others has lagged well behind our spending on ourselves.

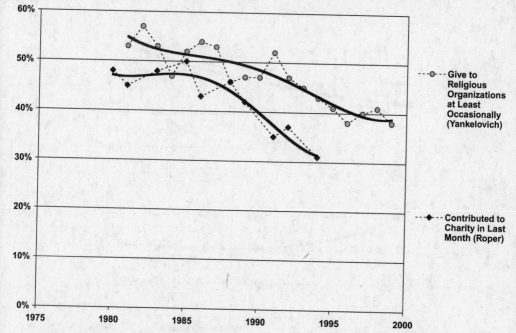

Figure 33: Reported Charitable Giving Declined in the 1980s and 1990s

Idiosyncratic explanations have been offered for each of these instances of declining generosity. Decline in Protestant giving has been linked to inadequate emphasis on "stewardship," particularly among congregational leaders.[32] Decline in Catholic giving has been attributed to disaffection with church doctrine, particularly on birth control and male hegemony.[33] Decline in United Way giving has been blamed on a sex-and-embezzlement scandal in 1992, as well as on competition from the proliferation of "alternative" campaigns. However, given the breadth and simultaneity of the post-1960 declines in giving by Americans, it is more plausible to seek the explanation in some wider social change rather than in the foibles of a particular recipient organization. After years of high and rising generosity for many good causes, over the last four decades Americans have become steadily more tight-fisted, precisely when we have also disengaged from the social life of our communities.

TRENDS IN VOLUNTEERING over the last several decades are more complicated and in some respects more intriguing than the uniform decline that characterizes most dimensions of social capital in America in this period. Americans have worked on fewer and fewer community projects over these decades, corresponding to the trends in declining community involvement that we have already reviewed. In 1975–76 more than two in every five American adults said

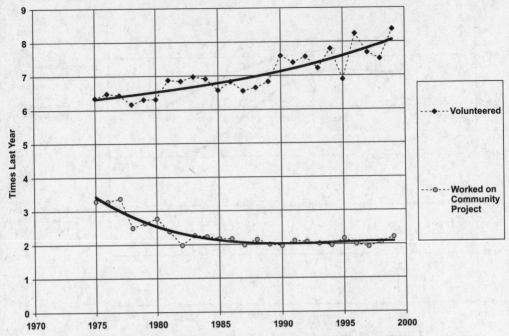

Figure 34: Volunteering Up, Community Projects Down, 1975–1999

that they had worked on some community project in the previous year, but by 1998–99 that figure had dropped to fewer than one in three. (Figure 34 shows that the average number of such projects per year fell by more than 40 percent.)

By contrast, these same people report a steady *increase* in volunteering over this same period. That "volunteering" is reported two to three times more frequently than "working on a community project" suggests that most people see their volunteering as providing personal rather than community service. That volunteering and community projects are moving in opposite directions implies that one-on-one volunteering is increasingly common. Whatever the venue, the average American volunteered a little over six times per year in the 1970s, but by the 1990s that figure had risen to nearly eight times per year. (See figure 34.) This conclusion is broadly consistent with reports from the Gallup poll that the fraction of Americans who say they are "involved in any charity or social service activities, such as helping the poor, the sick, or the elderly" rose steadily from 26 percent in 1977 to 46 percent in 1991.[34]

Coupled with the declining involvement in churches and clubs that we have already noted, this growth of volunteerism poses an explanatory puzzle. Today, as two decades ago, the vast majority of volunteers are recruited through local networks of religious and other civic associations. These recruitment pools have been shrinking rapidly over the same period that volunteering has been on the rise. How could volunteerism be increasing while the primary channels of volunteer recruitment are drying up?

Faced with a shrinking pool of church and club activists, volunteer recruiters could have stepped up their efforts among the remaining activists, or they could have reached outside the usual organizational networks. For the most part, the evidence suggests, they did the latter. Although the rate of volunteering among the shrinking number of people who regularly attend *both* church *and* club meetings rose by more than half between 1975 and 1999, the rate of volunteering among the growing number of people who *never* attend *either* church *or* club meetings more than tripled over this same period.[35] Church- and clubgoers still provide the most regular volunteers, but compared with two decades ago, organizations are less exclusively the route to volunteering. Optimistically we might say that volunteerism has begun to spread beyond the bounds of traditional community organizations. A less optimistic interpretation would add that commitments to volunteerism are more fragile and more sporadic now that they depend on single-stranded obligations, without reinforcement from well-woven cords of organizational involvement.[36]

Who are these new volunteers, sailing so boldly against the tide of civic disengagement? In fact, they turn out to be a familiar group, for virtually the entire increase is concentrated among people aged sixty and over. Volunteering among seniors has nearly doubled over the last quarter century (from an average of 6 times per year to an average of 12 times per year). At the same time, volunteering has grown modestly (from roughly 3.5 to roughly 4.5 times per year) among twenty-somethings and has actually declined among the rest of us (aged thirty to fifty-nine). Figure 35 arrays the net trends in volunteering in the last quarter century by various age brackets.[37] In effect, this graph holds constant any effect of aging per se and compares the frequency of volunteering among people of a certain age in 1998 with the frequency of volunteering among people of that same age in 1975. Thus, for example, people in their early twenties in 1998 volunteered 39 percent more frequently than had people that age in 1975. Similarly, people over seventy-five in 1998 volunteered 140 percent more frequently than people that age had in 1975. Conversely, people in their early thirties in 1998 volunteered 29 percent *less* often than people that same age had done in 1975.

Because different generations of Americans were passing through each of these age-defined windows during these years, we can identify the trends by generation. Americans born in the first third of the twentieth century and (to a lesser extent) their grandchildren in the so-called millennial generation demonstrated *higher* levels of volunteerism in 1998 than people their age had shown in the 1970s, but volunteerism among the late baby boomers (in their thirties and forties in the 1990s) is actually *lower* now than among people of that age in 1975.

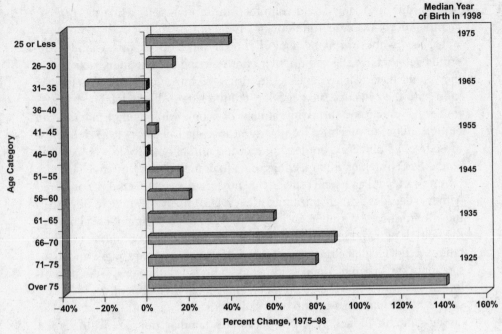

Figure 35: Trends in Volunteering by Age Category, 1975–1998

As we noted earlier, participation in community projects (unlike volunteering in general) has declined over the last quarter century. The generational patterns underlying that decline turn out to be exactly parallel to the patterns underlying the changes in volunteering. As figure 36 shows, participation in community projects has declined in all age categories, but the decline is especially dramatic among people in their thirties and most limited among people over sixty-five. In other words, although participation in community projects is less common today than a quarter century ago, members of the long civic generation continue to contribute to such projects in disproportionate numbers, whereas boomers are much less likely to show up than people their age were a quarter century ago.

Traditionally, retirement has meant withdrawal from civic activity, and historically, volunteering declined after age fifty, but the current generation of seniors has turned that conventional wisdom on its head. They are largely responsible for the boom in volunteering in recent decades, and they have resisted most staunchly the decline in participation in community projects.

On the other hand, physically demanding forms of volunteering have entered hard times in recent years, probably because they could not cushion the fall in younger volunteers by drawing on the boom in older volunteers. For example, although more than 40 percent of the U.S. population is protected by all- or mostly volunteer fire departments, the nationwide ratio of volun-

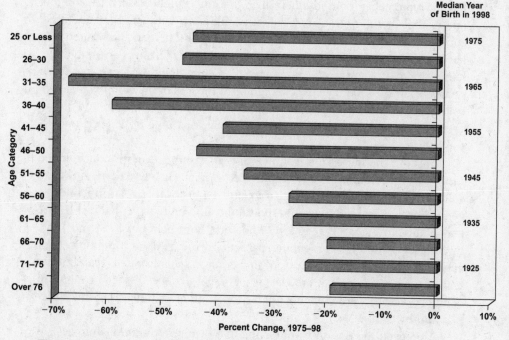

Figure 36: Trends in Participation in Community Projects by Age Category, 1975–1998

teers to professional firefighters fell by a quarter between 1983 and 1997, as fewer younger volunteers signed up to replace their elders and communities were forced to hire professionals. Similarly, nationwide blood donations per one thousand adults declined steadily from eighty units in 1987 to sixty-two units in 1997, even though fear of contracting AIDS through blood donation, a major inhibitor of blood donation in the 1980s, fell substantially over these same years. One cause of declining blood donations appears to be the failure of younger generations to replace the aging long civic generation.[38] In short, volunteering that can be done by senior citizens, such as youth mentoring, is up. Volunteering that requires a younger constitution, such as fighting fires or giving blood, is down.

WHY DID PEOPLE OVER sixty volunteer in greater numbers in the 1990s than in the 1970s? Several factors are relevant, though none seems entirely to explain the trend.[39] Time diary studies have shown a significant growth in free time among people over sixty over the last twenty to thirty years—roughly ten more hours a week between 1975 and 1995—in part because of earlier retirement (voluntary and involuntary).[40] Marked improvements in the health and finances of the elderly over the last several decades have enabled them to enjoy longer, more active postretirement lives than their predecessors. In addition, one central theme of this book is that people born between 1910 and 1940 constitute a "long civic generation"—that is, a cohort of men and women who have been more engaged in civic affairs throughout their lives—voting more, joining more, trusting more, and so on—than either their predecessors or their successors in the sequence of generations. At the end of the century, that generation comprised virtually the entire cohort of people aged sixty and above. True to their own past, even in retirement they continue to be exceptionally good citizens.

In short, the increase in volunteering in recent decades is concentrated in the one generation most resistant to civic disengagement. The growth of volunteerism in the face of church and club debility is mostly attributable to a generation predisposed to civic responsibility and enjoying enhanced leisure and vitality. In the swollen cohort of boomers born between 1950 and 1965, by contrast, volunteerism is ebbing, particularly if it involves community projects. In that sense, the growth of volunteering in recent years is real, but not really an exception to the broader generational decline in social capital. At century's end we were enjoying not a springtime of volunteerism, but an Indian summer.

Moreover, the type of volunteering that involves community projects, as distinct from assistance from one individual to another, has actually declined. In chapter 2 (table 1) we saw that individualized civic acts, such as writing to the editor, have diminished less rapidly than collective civic acts, such as attending a public meeting or working in a local organization. Similarly, we have now discovered, while individualized acts of benevolence, such as reading to a shut-in, have resisted the nationwide decline in civic involvement, community projects that require collective effort, such as refurbishing a neighborhood park, have not.

The rise in volunteering is sometimes interpreted as a natural counterweight to the decline in other forms of civic participation. Disenchanted with government, it is said, members of the younger generation are rolling up their sleeves to get the job done themselves. The profile of the new volunteerism directly contradicts that optimistic thesis. First, the rise in volunteering is concentrated among the boomers' aging, civic parents, whereas the civic dropouts are drawn disproportionately from the boomers.

Second, volunteering is part of the syndrome of good citizenship and political involvement, not an alternative to it. Volunteers are *more* interested in politics and *less* cynical about political leaders than nonvolunteers are. Volunteering is a sign of positive engagement with politics, not a sign of rejection of politics. This is as true for young adults as anyone else, and it is as true at the turn of the century as it was twenty-five years earlier. Conversely, political cynics, even young cynics, are *less* likely than other people to volunteer. Political alienation rose over the last several decades of the twentieth century, and so did volunteering, but volunteering rose *despite* the greater alienation, not *because* of it.[41]

This evidence also deflates any easy optimism about the future of volunteerism, for the recent growth has depended upon a generation fated to pass from the scene over the next decade or two. It is, of course, possible that when boomers reach retirement age after 2010 they too will increase their level of volunteering. Indeed, compared with *their own* preretirement levels, they probably will. Compared with their elders, however, they probably will *not*. So far, the boomer cohort continues to be less disposed to civic engagement than their parents and even to some extent less than their own children, so it is hazardous to assume that the rising tide of volunteerism of the past two decades will persist in the next two.

One may hope—indeed, I do—that a new spirit of volunteerism is beginning to bubble up from the millennial generation. A wide range of evidence (including that summarized in figure 35 and figure 36, as well as evidence summarized in chapter 14) suggests that young Americans in the 1990s displayed a commitment to volunteerism without parallel among their immediate predecessors. This development is the most promising sign of any that I have discovered that America might be on the cusp of a new period of civic renewal, especially if this youthful volunteerism persists into adulthood and begins to expand beyond individual caregiving to broader engagement with social and political issues. However, the millennial generation will have their hands full if they are to make up for the impending departure of their highly civic grandparents and the longtime *incivisme* of their parents' generation.

CHAPTER **8**

Reciprocity,
Honesty, and Trust

Your corn is ripe to-day; mine will be so to-morrow. 'Tis profitable for us both, that I shou'd labour with you to-day, and that you shou'd aid me to-morrow. I have no kindness for you, and know you have as little for me. I will not, therefore, take any pains upon your account; and should I labour with you upon my own account, in expectation of a return, I know I shou'd be disappointed, and that I shou'd in vain depend upon your gratitude. Here then I leave you to labour alone; you treat me in the same manner. The seasons change; and both of us lose our harvests for want of mutual confidence and security.

—DAVID HUME[1]

THE TOUCHSTONE of social capital is the principle of generalized reciprocity— I'll do this for you now, without expecting anything immediately in return and perhaps without even knowing you, confident that down the road you or someone else will return the favor. As philosopher Michael Taylor has pointed out,

Each individual act in a system of reciprocity is usually characterized by a combination of what one might call short-term altruism and long-term self-interest: I help you out now in the (possibly vague, uncertain, and uncalculating) expectation that you will help me out in the future. Reciprocity is made up of a series of acts each of which is short-run altruistic (benefiting others at a cost to the altruist), but which together typically make every participant better off.[2]

The norm of generalized reciprocity is so fundamental to civilized life that all prominent moral codes contain some equivalent of the Golden Rule. Conversely, the ironic perversion of this principle—"Do unto others before they do unto you"—came to epitomize the self-interested "me decade." When Alexis de Tocqueville visited the United States in the early nineteenth century, he was struck by how Americans resisted temptation to take advantage of each other and instead looked out for their neighbors. As Tocqueville pointed out, however, American democracy worked not because Americans obeyed some impossibly idealistic rule of selflessness, but rather because we pursued "self-interest rightly understood."[3]

Members of a community that follows the principle of generalized reciprocity—raking your leaves before they blow onto your neighbors' yard, lending a dime to a stranger for a parking meter, buying a round of drinks the week you earn overtime, keeping an eye on a friend's house, taking turns bringing snacks to Sunday school, caring for the child of the crack-head one flight down—find that their self-interest is served, just as Hume's farmers would both have been better off by sharing their labors.

In some cases, like neighborhood lawn raking, the return of the favor is immediate and the calculation straightforward, but in some cases the return is long-term and conjectural, like the benefit of living in the kind of community where people care for neglected children. At this extreme, generalized reciprocity becomes hard to distinguish from altruism and difficult to cast as self-interest. Nevertheless, this is what Tocqueville, insightfully, meant by "self-interest rightly understood."

When each of us can relax her guard a little, what economists term "transaction costs"—the costs of the everyday business of life, as well as the costs of commercial transactions—are reduced. This is no doubt why, as economists have recently discovered, trusting communities, other things being equal, have a measurable economic advantage.[4] The almost imperceptible background stress of daily "transaction costs"—from worrying about whether you got back the right change from the clerk to double-checking that you locked the car door—may also help explain why students of public health find that life expectancy itself is enhanced in more trustful communities.[5] A society that relies on generalized reciprocity is more efficient than a distrustful society, for the same reason that money is more efficient than barter. Honesty and trust lubricate the inevitable frictions of social life.

"Honesty is the best policy" turns out to be a wise maxim rather than a mawkish platitude, but only if others follow the same principle. Social trust is a valuable community asset if—but only if—it is warranted. You and I will both be better off if we are honest toward one another than if—each fearing betrayal—we decline to cooperate. However, only a seeker of sainthood will be better off being honest in the face of persistent dishonesty. *Generalized reciprocity is a community asset, but generalized gullibility is not.*[6] Trustworthiness, not simply trust, is the key ingredient.[7]

In a society of fallible humans, what kind of assurance can each of us have in the good faith of others? A legal system, complete with courts and law enforcement, provides one strong answer. However, if we needed legal advice and a police presence to formulate and enforce the simplest agreement—like whether to rake our respective lawns or share Sunday snack duties—escalating transaction costs would surely preclude much mutually beneficial cooperation. As Diego Gambetta, a student of trust (and of the Mafia), points out, "Societies which rely heavily on the use of force are likely to be less efficient, more costly, and more unpleasant than those where trust is maintained by other means."[8]

Another solution, social science has recently recognized, inheres in the social fabric in which our daily transactions are embedded.[9] An effective norm of generalized reciprocity is bolstered by dense networks of social exchange. If two would-be collaborators are members of a tightly knit community, they are likely to encounter one another in the future—or to hear about one another through the grapevine. Thus they have reputations at stake that are almost surely worth more than gains from momentary treachery. In that sense, honesty is encouraged by dense social networks.

There is an important difference between honesty based on personal experience and honesty based on a general community norm—between trusting Max at the corner store because you've known him for years and trusting someone to whom you nodded for the first time at the coffee shop last week. Trust embedded in personal relations that are strong, frequent, and nested in wider networks is sometimes called "thick trust."[10] On the other hand, a thinner trust in "the generalized other," like your new acquaintance from the coffee shop, also rests implicitly on some background of shared social networks and expectations of reciprocity.[11] Thin trust is even more useful than thick trust, because it extends the radius of trust beyond the roster of people whom we can know personally.[12] As the social fabric of a community becomes more threadbare, however, its effectiveness in transmitting and sustaining reputations declines, and its power to undergird norms of honesty, generalized reciprocity, and thin trust is enfeebled.

Referring to what I have labeled "thin trust," political scientists Wendy Rahn and John Transue observe that "social, or generalized, trust can be viewed as a 'standing decision' to give most people—even those whom one does not know from direct experience—the benefit of the doubt."[13] Social trust in this sense is strongly associated with many other forms of civic engagement and social capital. Other things being equal, people who trust their fellow citizens volunteer more often, contribute more to charity, participate more often in politics and community organizations, serve more readily on juries, give blood more frequently, comply more fully with their tax obligations, are more tolerant of minority views, and display many other forms of civic virtue. Moreover, people who are more active in community life are less likely (even in private) to condone cheating on taxes, insurance claims, bank loan forms, and employment applications. Conversely, experimental psychologists have shown that people who believe that others are honest are themselves less likely to lie, cheat, or steal and are more likely to respect the rights of others. In that sense, honesty, civic engagement, and social trust are mutually reinforcing.[14]

In short, people who trust others are all-round good citizens, and those more engaged in community life are both more trusting and more trustworthy. Conversely, the civically disengaged believe themselves to be surrounded by miscreants and feel less constrained to be honest themselves. The causal arrows among civic involvement, reciprocity, honesty, and social trust are as tangled as well-tossed spaghetti. Only careful, even experimental, research will be able to sort them apart definitively.[15] For present purposes, however, we need to recognize that they form a coherent syndrome.

For all these reasons, an important diagnostic test for trends in social capital in America in recent decades is how reciprocity and social trust have evolved—not merely thick trust in people whom we know intimately, but thin trust in the anonymous other. The central question in this chapter is this: How are the trends in social capital and civic engagement that we have already discovered reflected in trends in honesty and social trust in America?

OUR SUBJECT HERE is social trust, *not* trust in government or other social institutions. Trust in other people is logically quite different from trust in institutions and political authorities. One could easily trust one's neighbor and distrust city hall, or vice versa. Empirically, social and political trust may or may not be correlated, but theoretically, they must be kept distinct. Trust in government may be a cause or a consequence of social trust, but it is not *the same thing* as social trust.[16]

Fortunately, pollsters have been asking Americans standard questions about social trust and honesty for many decades. Unfortunately, the responses contain an irreducible element of ambiguity. Take, for example, the most common survey question: "Generally speaking, would you say that most people can be trusted, or that you can't be too careful in dealing with people?" This question clearly taps feelings about the trustworthiness of the generalized other—thin trust[17]—but the meaning of the responses remains murky in one respect. If fewer survey respondents nowadays say, "Most people can be trusted," that might mean any one of three things: 1) the respondents are accurately reporting that honesty is rarer these days; or 2) other people's behavior hasn't really changed, but we have become more paranoid; or 3) neither our ethical demands nor other people's behavior have actually changed, but we now have more information about their treachery, perhaps because of more lurid media reports.

It is not easy to sort out what's going on here, any more than when your kindergartner complains that a playmate acted unfairly. However, the social geography of social trust suggests that survey reports about honesty and trust should be interpreted prima facie as accurate accounts of the respondents' social experiences. In virtually all societies "have-nots" are less trusting than "haves," probably because haves are treated by others with more honesty and respect.[18] In America blacks express less social trust than whites, the financially distressed less than the financially comfortable, people in big cities less than small-town dwellers, and people who have been victims of a crime or been through a divorce less than those who haven't had these experiences.[19] It is reasonable to assume that in each case these patterns reflect actual experience rather than different psychic predispositions to distrust. When such people tell pollsters that most people can't be trusted, they are not hallucinating—they are merely reporting their experience.

Take, for instance, the case of city size. As we noted in the previous chapter, virtually all forms of altruism—volunteerism, community projects, philanthropy, directions for strangers, aid for the afflicted, and so on—are demonstrably more common in small towns. Crime rates of all sorts are two or three times higher in cities. (Not surprisingly, victims of crime and violence—wherever they live—express reduced social trust, a perfectly intelligible updating of their views about the trustworthiness of others.) Store clerks in small towns are more likely to return overpayment than their urban counterparts. People in small towns are more likely to assist a "wrong number" phone caller than urban dwellers. Cheating on taxes, employment forms, insurance claims, and bank loan applications are three times more likely to be condoned in cities than in small towns. Car dealers in small towns perform far fewer unnecessary repairs than big-city dealerships.[20]

In short, the somewhat greater mistrust of the generalized other expressed by residents of big cities is not some peculiar paranoia that arises from urban living, but a realistic account of their actual experience and of social norms in their surroundings. To be sure, weaker informal social control in cities also makes them freer places to live—"City air liberates," as the medieval proverb had it. Enfeebled thin trust may be a fair price for that freedom. Nevertheless, when urbanites express social distrust, they are accurately reporting something about their social environment.[21]

To be sure, social distrust is not purely objective. It also to some extent reflects personal cynicism, paranoia, and even projections of one's own dishonest inclinations.[22] People who feel themselves to be untrustworthy are less trusting of others.[23] In fact, social trust can easily generate vicious spirals (or virtuous circles), as my expectations of others' trustworthiness influences my trustworthiness, which in turn influences others' behavior. We should begin, however, with the simpler presumption that both those who report that "most people are honest" and those who say that "you can't be too careful" are sincerely summarizing their own experiences. It is reasonable to suppose, too, that views about something as basic as reciprocity and generalized trust are especially influenced by personal experience and social customs early in life. That, after all, is why we call them the "formative" years.

Most Americans today believe that we live in a less trustworthy society than our parents did.[24] In 1952, as figure 37 shows, Americans were split about fifty-fifty on the issue of whether our society was then as upright morally as it had been in the past. In 1998, however, after nearly four decades of growing cynicism, we believe by a margin of three to one that our society is less honest and moral than it used to be. But perhaps that only proves that nostalgia is in fashion.

Survey archives allow us to screen out that "golden glow," at least to some extent, by comparing our feelings today, not with how we imagine an earlier generation might have felt, but rather with what that generation actually said in response to identical questions. The best evidence suggests that social trust rose from the mid-1940s to the mid-1960s, peaking in 1964 just as many other mea-

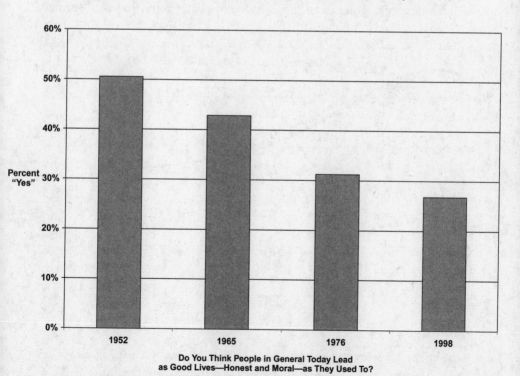

Figure 37: Declining Perceptions of Honesty and Morality, 1952–1998

sures of social capital did. Middle-aged Americans in the 1960s were probably living in a *more* trusting society than the one in which they had grown up.[25]

In the mid-1960s, however, this beneficent trend was reversed, initiating a long-term decline in social trust.[26] (See figure 38.) Every year fewer and fewer of us aver that "most people can be trusted." Every year more and more of us caution that "you can't be too careful in dealing with people." If generalized reciprocity and honesty are important social lubricants, Americans today are experiencing more friction in our daily lives than our parents and grandparents did a generation ago. As figure 38 makes plain, this decline in social trust has been even steeper among younger Americans than among the rest of us, especially since about 1985.[27]

Most, if not all, of the decline in American social trust since the 1960s is attributable to generational succession.[28] Moreover, that generational decline has tended to accelerate in the last decade or two. In the 1970s roughly 80 percent of Americans born in the first third of the century believed that "most people are honest," and in the late 1990s they continued to hold that optimistic view in almost undiminished degree. (See figure 39.) However, their share in the population had fallen from nearly one in every two adults in 1975 to barely one in every eight adults in 1998. At the same time, in the 1970s roughly 75 percent of those born between 1930 and 1945 believed in the essential honesty of others, and their views also changed little over subsequent

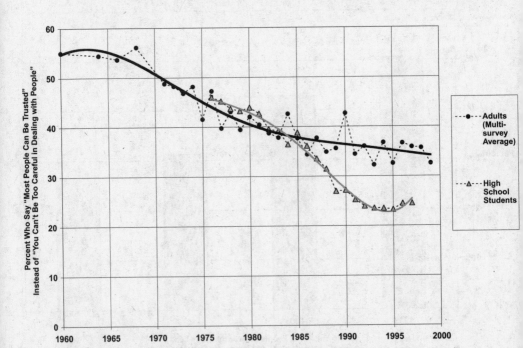

Figure 38: Four Decades of Dwindling Trust: Adults and Teenagers, 1960–1999

decades. Roughly 60 percent of the baby boomers (born 1946–1960) agreed in the 1970s that "most people are honest," and their views were unchanged in the late 1990s. Finally, at the bottom of the generational hierarchy, Americans born after 1960 were not out of adolescence in the mid-1970s, but ever since their cohort began to reach adulthood in the mid-1980s, roughly half of them have denied that "most people are honest." By 1999 this mistrustful younger generation already constituted nearly one-third of the adult population.

Examining the views of the postboomers in finer detail only reinforces the picture of accelerating generational decline. By 1998–99 respondents born in the 1970s—who had been less than five years old when this series of surveys started—constituted a rapidly rising 10 percent of the total population, and only 40 percent of them agreed that "most people are honest." In short, at century's end, a generation with a trust quotient of nearly 80 percent was being rapidly replaced by one with a trust quotient of barely half that. The inevitable result is steadily declining social trust, *even though each individual cohort is almost as trusting as it ever was.*

On the interpretive assumption that expressions of social trust are, in the first instance, reflections of personal experience, weighted perhaps by early impressions, the social distrust among America's youth should be seen not as a character flaw, but rather as a mirror held up to social mores of recent decades.

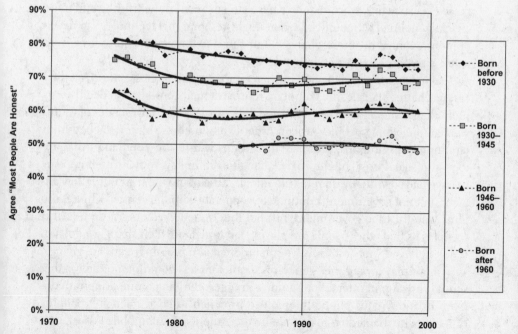

Figure 39: Generational Succession Explains Most of the Decline in Social Trust

Our youth are, in effect, telling us that in their experience most people really *aren't* trustworthy. Perhaps thick trust—confidence in personal friends—is as strong as ever, as some Gen X'ers believe. However, thin trust—the tenuous bond between you and your nodding acquaintance from the coffee shop, that crucial emollient for large, complex societies like ours—is becoming rarer.

The evidence of declining generalized trust and reciprocity also shows up in refusal rates for opinion surveys themselves, which have more than doubled since the 1960s. Cooperation rates may have risen slightly from the 1940s to the 1960s—perhaps not coincidentally the same period in which many of the other indicators of social trust and social capital were rising—but response rates were certainly declining by the 1970s. The most exhaustive recent study of survey response rates confirms the trend and adds that social disconnectedness seems to be part of the reason.[29] Intriguingly, the rise in refusals in recent years has plagued face-to-face and telephone interviews, but *not* mail surveys. This pattern suggests that these refusals may be due more to the vague menace of personal contact with anonymous strangers than to the simple inconvenience of answering questions.

Apprehensiveness may also help explain why the proportion of unlisted phone numbers has grown by two-thirds in the last two decades and why call screening more than tripled from the late 1980s to the late 1990s. Interestingly, the best predictor of the use of call screening is not affluence or even urbanism, but youth. People under forty-five are twice as likely to screen calls as those over sixty-five, who are (as we have already seen) more trusting and more civically inclined.[30] Superficially one might respond that technological development enabled all these changes, but those technologies themselves were surely a response to market demand.

Other signs, too, of the decline of reciprocity (and its close cousin, civility) can be charted statistically. Voluntary returns of mail census forms declined by more than a quarter between 1960 and 1990. In 1990 the lowest rates of return were among young people, African Americans, and those of us detached from community institutions, precisely the groups within the population that are lowest in social trust. Interestingly, alienation from government itself appears to have played virtually no role.[31] In effect, those of us who trust our fellow citizens, but not government, continue to cooperate with the census, while those of us who trust the government, but not the "generalized other," do not. If it seems to us that other people are playing fair and doing their share, we do, too. If not, not. And "not" is the answer that more and more Americans are giving.

If fair play toward the "generalized other" is less common nowadays, that should show up in interactions among strangers. Driving is one important domain of anonymous public intercourse in which to chart changing patterns of reciprocity. According to a study by the American Automobile Association Foundation for Traffic Safety, "violent aggressive driving" increased more than 50 percent between 1990 and 1996. The head of the National Highway Traffic

Safety Administration conjectures that "road rage" (now common enough to have acquired a name) is a factor in twenty-eight thousand deaths per year. Speeding on the open highway has long been tolerated by large majorities of Americans, but during the 1990s tolerance of speeding in town rose sharply. In 1953, 25 percent of Americans told George Gallup that they had driven over eighty-five miles an hour, compared with 49 percent in a similar 1991 Gallup poll. Older Americans are far less likely to think that you can flagrantly violate the law. In the 1991 Gallup poll 54 percent of all drivers under thirty estimated that you could get away with driving ten miles an hour over the speed limit, compared with only 28 percent of drivers fifty and over. By 1997, drivers who reported that other people were driving more aggressively than five years earlier massively outnumbered those who reported an improvement in civility on the road, 74 percent to 3 percent.[32] In short, we all know that other drivers are less courteous nowadays, and "we" are, collectively, they.

Droll confirmation of declining civility on the highway comes from a long-term study of drivers' behavior at stop signs at several intersections in suburban New York, as summarized in figure 40. In 1979, 37 percent of all motorists made a full stop, 34 percent a rolling stop, and 29 percent no stop at all. By 1996, 97 percent made no stop at all at the very same intersections.[33] Another automotive indicator of the decline in thin trust and reciprocity—the virtual disappearance of hitchhiking—seems to have left no statistical trace but is undeniable to motorists who lived through the 1940s and 1950s.

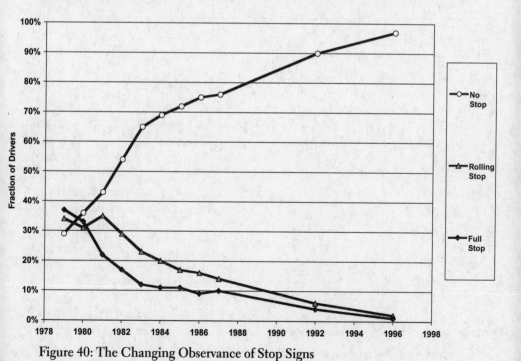

Figure 40: The Changing Observance of Stop Signs

To be sure, for each of these measures one might find a plausible specific explanation—the growth of telephone solicitation, more media attention to angry drivers, rising insurance rates, cheaper gas and more cars, the changing demography of New York suburbs, and so on. In the aggregate, however, these trends suggest that the undeniable decrease in thin trust that appears in the survey record has affected our actual behavior vis-à-vis strangers.

ONE POTENTIAL YARDSTICK for honesty and trustworthiness is the crime rate. As figure 41 shows, crime rates in America began to rise sharply in the middle 1960s, just about the time that other measures of social capital, trust, and trustworthiness began to turn down.[34] In some measure, crime itself may be a symptom of this syndrome of weakened social control. On the other hand, crime rates are highly responsive to other factors, including the youthfulness of the national population, the evolution of illegal drug use (especially crack cocaine), and the rate of incarceration of career criminals.[35] It seems unlikely that more than a fraction of the post-1960 increase in crime is attributable to a generic drop in national honesty. Conversely, it is premature to herald the welcome drop in crime during the 1990s as a harbinger of a nationwide sea change in law-abidingness.

As we noted earlier, one alternative to generalized reciprocity and socially

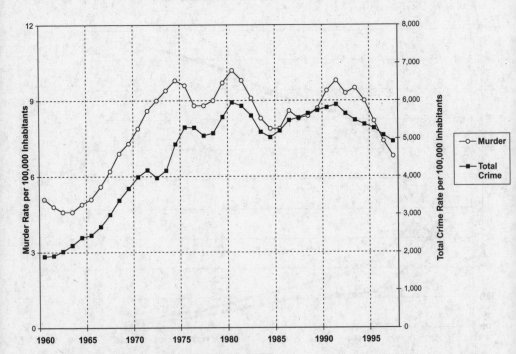

Figure 41: U.S. Crime Rates, 1960–1997

embedded honesty is the rule of law—formal contracts, courts, litigation, adjudication, and enforcement by the state. Thus, if the lubricant of thin trust is evaporating from American society, we might expect to find greater reliance on law as the basis for cooperation. If the handshake is no longer binding and reassuring, perhaps the notarized contract, the deposition, and the subpoena will work almost as well. One way to explore this hypothesis is to examine our changing national investment in the legal system.[36]

The twentieth century was, for America, the century of industrialization and urbanism, of big government and big business. Given folk fears of the licentiousness of the swelling cities, the litigiousness of modern commerce, and the pettifoggery of welfare-state bureaucrats, one might conjecture that the share of legal "transaction costs" in the U.S. economy must have grown steadily throughout the century. In fact, however, as figure 42 plainly shows, as a fraction of the total U.S. workforce, employment of guards, police, and lawyers grew relatively little for most of the twentieth century.

Astonishingly, America had fewer lawyers per capita in 1970 than in 1900.[37] Two world wars; the extraordinary booms of the 1920s and the 1950s; one Great Depression; one New Deal; our metamorphosis from a rustic nation (with 60 percent of its inhabitants living in hamlets of fewer than 2,500 souls) to a metropolitan nation (with nearly half its population in cities an order of magnitude larger); the transformation of our economy from gaslights, horse-

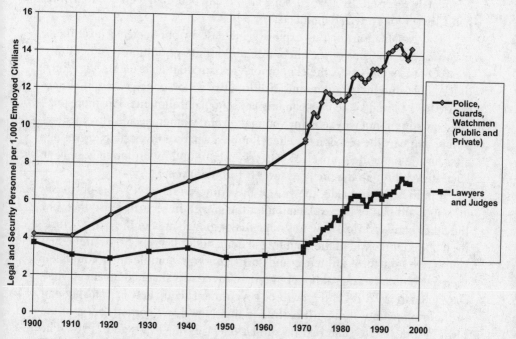

Figure 42: Employment in Policing and the Law Soared After 1970

drawn buggies, and the general store to GE, GM, and Kmart—none of these economic, social, and cultural revolutions raised the lawyering ratio in the American economy by a single iota. After 1970, however, the ratio of lawyers to the rest of us suddenly exploded, more than doubling in the next quarter century and bloating this entry in our national "transaction cost" accounts.

The post-1970 acceleration in employment for providing security was not quite so marked. Nevertheless, during the 1980s both public and private spending on security rose rapidly as a share of GNP—yet another "transaction cost" excrescence. By 1995 America had 40 percent more police and guards and 150 percent more lawyers and judges than would have been projected in 1970, even given the growth of population and the economy.

Moreover, the massive expansion of the legal profession was *not* simply part of the growth of all professions, for no other major profession experienced this same post-1970 explosion. After 1970 the legal profession grew three times faster than the professions as a whole.[38] For the first seven decades of the twentieth century the legal and medical professions grew roughly in tandem, but after 1970 the legal profession grew twice as fast as the medical profession. In 1970 there were 3 percent *fewer* lawyers than doctors in the United States, but by 1995 there were 34 percent *more* lawyers than doctors. For the first seven decades of the twentieth century the ratio of lawyers to engineers fell steadily, as our economy became more "technology intensive." By 1970 America had 1 lawyer for every 4.5 engineers. At that point, however, the century's trend was completely reversed. By 1995, despite all the talk of a high-tech economy, we had 1 lawyer for every 2.1 engineers.[39]

The explanation for this explosive increase in our society's investment in formal mechanisms of social control and dispute resolution is not entirely clear. On the supply side, the clamor for Vietnam draft deferments, the glitter of *L.A. Law*, and the requirements of affirmative action policies are sometimes said to have played a role in expanding law school enrollments. The more puzzling question is not why so many young men and women decided to enter law school, but why the rest of us in effect doubled what we invested in lawyering, after having contented ourselves with a constant (and much lower) supply of legal advice through the previous seventy turbulent years.

On the demand side, the rise of the crime rate after 1970 is obviously an important part of the explanation for the growth in security personnel. On the other hand, criminal law was not a major growth area of the bar, so crime itself played little role in the doubling of demand for lawyers. Some argue that simply the growth of affluence and socioeconomic complexity accounts for the growth of lawyering, although it is hard to see why that had no effect whatsoever before 1970.[40] The growth of government regulation is probably part of the explanation, though it is striking that New Deal corporatism and the birth of the welfare state had no similar effect in the 1930s and 1940s. The rapid increase in divorce in the 1970s is part of the story, a development itself closely tied to changes in American social capital. Despite talk of a "litigation explosion," careful research thus far has cast some doubt on the idea that court dockets in general are more crowded today.[41]

In fact, the largest increase on the demand side for legal work seems to have been in what is gently termed "preventive lawyering." Throughout the American society and economy, beginning around 1970, informal understandings no longer seemed adequate or prudent. The suddenness of the change and its timing seem uncannily similar to trends in other measures of social capital that we have examined. Spouses, neighbors, business partners and would-be partners, parents and children, pastors and parishioners, donors and recipients—all of us abruptly began to demand to "get it in writing." As law professor Marc Galanter summarizes the expanded role of the lawyer,

> Like the provider of artificial hormones that supplement the diminished supply coursing through the body, the lawyer contrives enforceability to supplement the failing supply of reciprocity, moral obligation, and fellow-feeling. . . . Lawyers contrive to provide "artificial trust." . . . Because lawyers are producers and vendors of impersonal "cool" trust, they are the beneficiaries of the decline of its low-cost rival.[42]

Ironically, even trust among lawyers themselves seems to have been impaired by the decline of social capital. Law professors R. J. Gilson and Robert Mnookin report that as the stability of social networks has declined and the number of one-time-only encounters among lawyers has increased, lawyers worry less about their own reputation for honesty, and knowing this, they too trust one another less and cooperate less.[43]

Almost imperceptibly, the treasure that we spend on getting it in writing has steadily expanded since 1970, as has the amount that we spend on getting lawyers to anticipate and manage our disputes. In some respects, this development may be one of the most revealing indicators of the fraying of our social fabric. For better or worse, we rely increasingly—we are forced to rely increasingly—on formal institutions, and above all on the law, to accomplish what we used to accomplish through informal networks reinforced by generalized reciprocity—that is, through social capital.

CHAPTER 9

Against the Tide?
Small Groups, Social Movements,
and the Net

NOT ALL ORGANIZATIONS in America have lost membership over the last quarter century, and not all personal relationships have atrophied. In this chapter we examine three important countertrends that must be weighed in any comprehensive balance of social capital. At one end of the spectrum of size, privacy, and informality is the plethora of encounter groups, reading groups, support groups, self-help groups, and the like that have become important anchors in the emotional and social lives of millions of Americans. At the opposite end of the spectrum is the succession of great social movements that swept across the land in the last third of the twentieth century, beginning with the black civil rights movement, followed by the student movement, the peace movement, the women's movement, the gay and lesbian movement, the abortion and right-to-life movements, the religious conservative movement, the environmental movement, the animal rights movement, and innumerable others. Finally, how is our story affected by the explosive growth in telecommunications in recent years, especially the Internet (or as it is fondly known among the cognoscenti, "computer-mediated communication," or CMC)? Could new "virtual communities" simply be replacing the old-fashioned physical communities in which our parents lived? In short, how do small groups, social movements, and telecommunications qualify our judgment about declining social connectedness and civic engagement?

Sociologist Robert Wuthnow, the leading student of the small-group movement, reports that fully 40 percent of all Americans claim to be "currently involved in [a] small group that meets regularly and provides support or caring for those who participate in it." Roughly half of these groups are Sunday school classes, prayer fellowships, Bible study groups, and other church-related groups of the sort whose decline we discussed in chapter 4. On the other hand, nearly 5 percent of all the people with whom Wuthnow spoke claimed to participate regularly in a self-help group, such as Alcoholics Anonymous or a local chapter of the Association for Retarded Citizens, and nearly as many said they belonged to book discussion groups and hobby clubs. Although Wuthnow's evidence represents only a single snapshot, he eloquently describes the small-group movement as a "quiet revolution" in American society, redefining community in a more fluid way, an antidote to social disconnectedness. Nearly two out of five members of such groups reported that other members had helped them out when someone was sick, three in five said that their group had extended help to someone outside the group, and four out of five agreed that the group made them "feel like you weren't alone."[1] Small groups like this surely represent an important stock of social capital. We earlier reflected on the strengths and limitations of religious forms of social connectedness in contemporary America. What about secular support and discussion groups?

Reading circles emerged as an important feature of middle-class American life in the second half of the nineteenth century, as the spread of education combined with the growth of leisure time. Then, as now, reading groups attracted predominantly women. In the first several decades after the Civil War participants concentrated on intellectual "self-improvement," but the groups also encouraged self-expression, intense friendship, and what a later generation would call "consciousness-raising." Their focus gradually widened from literary pursuits to encompass community service and civic betterment, as part of a quickening movement for social and political reform. By the turn of the century one newly elected president exclaimed to her group, "I have an important piece of news for you. Dante is dead. He has been dead for several centuries, and I think it is time that we dropped the study of *his* Inferno and turned our attention to our own." Another echoed, "We prefer Doing to Dante, Being to Browning. . . . We've soaked in literary effort long enough." From such groups in such moments were born the suffrage movement and numerous other civic-minded initiatives of the Progressive Era.[2]

Informal literary groups can be extremely long lived. One self-rejuvenating group of thirty-five in Fayetteville, Arkansas, for example, has met twice a month since 1926.[3] Intense personal, intellectual, and occasionally even political bonds are forged in these lively discussions. Regular participants become more involved in wider community affairs as well, moving from Dante to Doing.[4] In short, by converting a solitary intellectual activity (reading) into one that is social and even civic, discussion groups provide a fertile forcing bed for both *schmoozers* and *machers*.

Many observers believe that America is now in the midst of another boom in reading groups, much like the end of the previous century, and several grass-roots organizations are striving to make it so.[5] Sadly, evidence to support this hopeful view turns out to be hard to find. Although the numbers are a bit uncertain, it appears that as many Americans were involved in literary, artistic, and discussion groups in the 1960s and 1970s as in the late 1990s. In fact, since participation in such groups is heaviest among single women and college graduates, and since those categories encompass a higher portion of Americans today than three or four decades ago, it is somewhat surprising that the popularity of such groups has not blossomed more than it has. The proportion of single female college graduates who belong to a literary, artistic, study, or discussion group actually fell from one in three in 1974 to one in four in 1994. Our verdict on this form of small group must be mixed: such groups surely contribute to civic engagement and social capital, but there is little evidence that they have grown in numbers that would significantly offset the civic decay of the past several decades.[6]

By contrast, participation in self-help and support groups has unquestionably grown in recent years. The most common of these organizations are "twelve-step" groups, such as Alcoholics Anonymous (founded in 1935) and the more than 130 national analogues that have proliferated for other addictions, such as Gamblers Anonymous and Co-Dependents Anonymous. Alcoholics Anonymous (AA) itself claims roughly one million members in the United States, and its Al-Anon cousin for the family and friends of alcoholics counts another four hundred thousand members.[7] Also relevant are the many support groups for victims of specific diseases or other problems, such as muscular dystrophy, AIDS, and single parenting. Finally there are commercially organized self-help groups, like Jenny Craig, Weight Watchers, and some therapy groups. Firm numbers on all these groups are hard to come by, but one recent national survey found that 2 percent of all adults were currently active in some support or self-help group, and another comprehensive survey found a *lifetime* rate of usage of about 3 percent.[8] (For some perspective, it is worth noting that all participants in self-help groups, newcomers and old-timers combined, are outnumbered two to one by the dropouts from league bowling over the last two decades, to say nothing of other, more "civic" forms of engagement.)

Self-help groups certainly provide emotional support and interpersonal ties that are invaluable to the participants. Wuthnow avers that "the small group movement is thus adding an important element to the way in which modern life is organized. It is extending the principles of formal organization into an arena of interpersonal life that was largely spontaneous and unorganized until very recently."[9] Although some medical professionals still debate the advantages of this lay support versus professional therapy, in practice the two approaches are converging; one comprehensive study of self-help groups in California found that more than 60 percent have professional leaders, blurring the line between self-help and group therapy. An increasing body of evidence suggests that support groups—and especially the interpersonal ties that they offer—provide measurable health and emotional benefits to many participants.[10]

In some respects support groups substitute for other intimate ties that have been weakened in our fragmented society, serving people who are disconnected from more conventional social networks. For example, the rate of participation in such groups is two to four times higher among divorced and single people than among married people. In their sympathetic overview of self-help groups, Alfred H. Katz and Eugene I. Bender ask us to recognize that "to be physically handicapped, poor, a former mental patient, or an object of exploitation or social disapproval is an identity that society forces on many unwilling 'deviants.' . . . We see self-help groups as vehicles through which these outcast persons can claim and grow toward new identities, redefining themselves and society; can overcome solitariness through identification with a reference group; and sometimes can work toward social ends or social change that they see as important."[11]

The growth of these groups reflects the application of social capital remedies to a set of previously neglected problems. Gay support groups, the Association for Retarded Citizens, and overweight people's support groups bring problems hitherto dealt with in isolation into a communal forum. Just as AA helped recast alcoholism as a social problem needing social and spiritual remedies, these newer support groups bring what were thought to be private problems into the public realm. Thus support groups serve an important range of needs for many people who might otherwise lack access to social capital.

In some cases, such groups also come to pursue broader civic goals. Mothers Against Drunk Driving and the Association for Retarded Citizens illustrate the range of public purposes and activities that have emerged from this sector of American life.[12] On the other hand, self-help and support groups do not typically play the same role as traditional civic associations. Alone among twenty-two different sorts of groups to which Americans belong, membership in self-help groups is completely unrelated to any other form of group affiliation. Self-help groups are not nearly so closely associated with regular community involvement such as voting, volunteering, giving to charity, working on community problems, or talking with neighbors, as are more traditional civic associations, such as religious, youth, neighborhood, school service, fraternal, and service groups.[13] As Robert Wuthnow emphasizes,

> [T]he kind of community [these small groups] create is quite different from the communities in which people have lived in the past. These communities are more fluid and more concerned with the emotional

states of the individual. . . . The communities they create are seldom frail. People feel cared for. They help one another. They share their intimate problems. . . . But in another sense small groups may not be fostering community as effectively as many of their proponents would like. Some small groups merely provide occasions for individuals to focus on themselves in the presence of others. The social contract binding members together asserts only the weakest of obligations. Come if you have time. Talk if you feel like it. Respect everyone's opinion. Never criticize. Leave quietly if you become dissatisfied. . . . We can imagine that [these small groups] really substitute for families, neighborhoods, and broader community attachments that may demand lifelong commitments, when, in fact, they do not.[14]

IF THE LINKAGE OF SMALL GROUPS to public life is sometimes tenuous and hard to detect, the comparable connection for social movements is omnipresent. Although all social movements have historical roots, and nearly all epochs witness grassroots organization for social change, the sixties was without doubt the most portentous decade in the twentieth century from the perspective of grassroots social change. Beginning with the successes of the black civil rights movement, wave after wave of popular mobilization swelled and crested in the ensuing years—from the Free Speech Movement in Berkeley in 1964 to the Vietnam protests in Chicago in 1968 and then in Washington, D.C., and hundreds of other towns and cities in the 1970s, from the Stonewall Inn uprising for gay rights in 1969 to the mass demonstrations for environmental quality on Earth Day 1970, from anguished debates about women's liberation in boardrooms and bedrooms across the country throughout the 1970s to the massive and widespread demonstrations for and against abortion during the 1980s.[15]

The social activism of the sixties greatly expanded the repertoire of readily available and legitimate forms of civic engagement. Boycotts that began with blacks and buses in Alabama were then applied by farmworkers to grapes in California, abortion advocates to pizza in Michigan, and upholders of traditional family values to amusement parks in Florida. Protest marches that once outraged authorities in scores of local communities became so routine that police and demonstrators became joint choreographers. Segments of the American population, on both the Left and the Right, who had been quiescent or silently suppressed, suddenly felt empowered and plunged into public life. Standing at the close of the century, it is virtually impossible to overstate the impact of these social movements on the lives of most American communities and most American citizens. In our most private moments, as in our most public ones, our behavior and our values bear the imprint of those movements.[16]

Social movements and social capital are so closely connected that it is sometimes hard to see which is chicken and which egg. Social networks are the quintessential resource of movement organizers. Reading groups became sinews of the suffrage movement. Friendship networks, not environmental sympathies, accounted for which Pennsylvanians became involved in grass-roots protest after the Three Mile Island nuclear accident. Social ties more than ideals or self-interest explain who was recruited to Freedom Summer, a climactic moment in the civil rights movement. Local church connections account for the solidarity that underlies the Christian Coalition.[17] Precisely because social capital is essential for social movements, its erosion could shroud their prospects for the future.

Social movements also *create* social capital, by fostering new identities and extending social networks.[18] Not only did preexisting interpersonal ties bring volunteers to Mississippi to participate in Freedom Summer, but the annealing heat of that tumultuous summer forged lifelong identities and solidarities. "Mississippi exposed them to a way of life and a vision of community that most of the volunteers found enormously appealing," reports Doug McAdam, collective biographer of the volunteers, and they carried that vision with them into the student movement, the peace movement, the women's movement, the environmental movement, and many more. Moreover, "the volunteers left Mississippi not only more disposed toward more activism, but in a better structural position, by virtue of their links to one another, to act on these inclinations." As sociologist Kenneth Andrews has shown, the community infrastructure generated by the Mississippi civil rights movement in the early 1960s had an impact on local African American political power for decades to come.[19]

Whether among gays marching in San Francisco or evangelicals praying together on the Mall or, in an earlier era, autoworkers downing tools in Flint, the act of collective protest itself creates enduring bonds of solidarity. Ironically, many now domesticated sing-along favorites have their origins in highly contentious social movements: "Oh! Susanna!," "Battle Hymn of the Republic," "We Shall Overcome," "Blowin' in the Wind." Collective protest strengthens shared identity, certainly for the participants and sometimes for their heirs, "anchoring individuals in participatory cultures."[20] In short, social movements with grassroots involvement both embody and produce social capital.

Whether national "social movement organizations"—from Greenpeace to the Moral Majority—do so as well is another matter. Even sympathetic commentators on the maturing movements of the sixties, like sociologist Margit Mayer, have observed that their organizational legacy was often Washington-based, full-time, professional, staff-run organizations, with "social entrepreneurs" cultivating comfortable conscience constituencies and "concentrat[ing] on manipulating the mass media so as to influence public opinion and to generate elite responses and policy changes."[21] Indeed, sociologist John McCarthy has argued that professional social movement organizations arise precisely as a response to a "social infrastructural deficit"—that is, cases in which "widespread sentiment exists favoring or opposing a social change, but the lack of available infrastructures inhibits the mobilization of the sentiment."[22]

McCarthy points out that although pro-choice and pro-life positions both garner substantial support in opinion polls, the two movements are structured quite differently. The pro-life movement rests on thousands of church-based grassroots organizations and can efficiently mobilize its supporters for direct action on the basis of those preexisting social networks. To take a single example, in 1993 the National Right to Life Committee claimed 13 million members and 7,000 local chapters. By contrast, the pro-choice movement (particularly with the demise in the 1980s of the organized grassroots women's liberation movement) lacks a preexisting social infrastructure and therefore must rely more heavily on national advocacy organizations, using the technology of direct mail, telemarketing, media campaigns, and the like.[23] Membership in the National Abortion and Reproductive Rights Action League, for example, more than tripled from 132,000 in 1989 to nearly 500,000 in 1996, but within two years membership had plunged to 190,000, of whom state leaders estimated that only about 3–5 percent had done more than write a check.[24] Such volatility in membership is emblematic of affiliation based on symbolic identification rather than on personal networks. As sociologist Debra Minkoff correctly observes, "In the absence of the opportunity or resources to establish face-to-face interactions, such symbolic affiliation may be the only available mobilizing structure that can link isolated individuals."[25] However, we should not mistake symbolic ties for personal ones.

Neither of these approaches—what political consultants sometimes label the "ground war" strategy and the "air war" strategy—is politically or morally superior. Rather, they are adapted to different resource endowments. The pro-life ground war (like the civil rights ground war before it) is adapted for a "social capital rich" environment with dense preexisting social networks of reciprocity, while the pro-choice air war is adapted to a "social capital poor" environment. In the latter case, the existence of a well-developed national social movement organization using "air war" techniques is a sign not of the presence of grassroots engagement, but of its absence.

By COMMON CONSENT, the sixties (and early seventies) were a period of uncommon social and political mobilization. What was the historical significance of this period and what was to be its sequel? Did the movements of those years represent the cresting of a long wave of rising civic involvement—indeed, the very same upwelling whose conventional contours we traced in earlier chapters? And did this cycle of protest then recede, leaving behind it only professionalized and bureaucratized interest groups, still bearing the banners of social movements but deployed now as a defensive light air force, not a massed infantry for change? Is all that remains of that proud period of deepened citizenship now captured by the camp bumper sticker—"Nuke the gay whales for Jesus"? Or instead did the sixties produce a durable and more advanced repertoire of civic engagement, leaving as its legacy many rich new forms of connectedness, a "movement society" in which "elite challenging" behavior becomes perpetual, conventional, routinely deployed by advocates of many different causes?[26] In short, did the sixties mark the birth of an era or merely the climax of one?

This question is surprisingly difficult to answer rigorously. Perhaps because most of the best academic research of the last two decades has been produced by children of the sixties, much of it takes for granted that a new era of expanded participation dawned in 1968. To be sure, case studies of specific movements sometimes describe backlash, weakening, retreat, even quietism. Most social historians, for example, agree that as an organized, grassroots effort, the civil rights movement was receding by 1970, and the women's movement began to decline with the defeat of the Equal Rights Amendment in 1982.[27] By contrast, most studies of the environmental movement tout its continuing ability to rouse millions of Americans to civic activity.

The development of the American environmental movement over the last four decades of the twentieth century provides instructive insights into the fate of the social movements of the 1960s. Although a number of important grassroots conservation organizations, such as the Sierra Club and the National Audubon Society (NAS), were founded at the turn of the twentieth century, the modern era of environmentalism began during the 1960s and was punctuated by the exclamation point of Earth Day 1970, celebrated by a reported twenty million participants across the country. With the ensuing acceptance of environmentalism in Washington and then the onset of the energy crisis, membership growth of the movement itself lagged during the 1970s, but under the threat to environmental gains posed by the Reagan administration, the movement rebounded during the 1980s. By 1990, according to one estimate, the environmental movement counted more than ten thousand organizations nationwide.[28]

Over these four decades, as figure 43 shows, membership in national environmental organizations exploded.[29] Membership in the major organizations rose from about 125,000 in 1960 to 1 million in 1970, then doubled to 2 million in 1980 and more than tripled again to 6.5 million in 1990. Although growth slowed substantially in the 1990s, in quantitative terms this remains a remarkable organizational success story rivaling, for example, the PTA from the 1930s to the 1960s. This remarkable boom led some enthusiastic observers to speak of "participatory environmentalism."

Greenpeace illustrates the development in a nutshell. Founded in 1972, it tripled its membership in barely five years from 800,000 in 1985 to 2,350,000 in 1990, bounding past rival groups that had dwarfed it a decade before and becoming by far the largest U.S. environmental organization, more than twice as big as its nearest competitor, the National Wildlife Federation. This phenomenal growth in environmental organizations occurred precisely in the period in which many other civic organizations were withering, and even the women's movement had wilted. At first blush, figure 43 seems strong evidence that the last several decades have witnessed, *not* a general decline in civic engagement, but merely a reorientation from "old-fashioned" to "contemporary" affiliations, away from Rotary and the League of Women Voters to Greenpeace and the Sierra Club.

Unfortunately, in the main this ebullient growth swelled the mailing lists of what we earlier termed "tertiary" organizations—that is, organizations in which "membership" is essentially an honorific rhetorical device for fundraising. Affiliation with Greenpeace (and its peers elsewhere on the ideological spectrum) does not represent the sort of interpersonal solidarity and intense civic commitment that brought millions of students, African Americans, gays and lesbians, peace activists, and right-to-lifers to thousands of marches and rallies and sit-ins as part of the social movements of the sixties and seventies. The crucial innovation that explains the trend in figure 43 is not a deeper civic consciousness, but direct mail.

In 1965 the National Audubon Society mailed one million invitations to membership, an extraordinary number for an organization that then counted fewer than fifty thousand members. Within six years its postage bill had doubled, as Audubon headquarters sent out two million letters in 1971. By then, with the stimulus of direct mail boosting growth to almost 25 percent a year,

Figure 43: Explosive Growth of National Environmental Organizations, 1960–1998

Audubon membership had ballooned to more than two hundred thousand. The technique spread across the spectrum of environmental associations, and by 1990 Greenpeace was mailing out forty-eight million letters annually.[30]

Virtually all the major American environmental groups (as well as dozens of smaller organizations dedicated to "charismatic" animals, like the Mountain Lion Foundation, Save the Manatee, and Pheasants Forever) are addicted to direct mail as a tool of mobilization and membership retention.[31] Indeed, the few national environmental organizations, such as the Izaak Walton League, that have forsworn direct mail have experienced no growth whatsoever over the last thirty years. In 1960 the Izaak Walton League, for example, had 51,000 members, as compared with 15,000 for the Sierra Club. By 1990, after three decades of direct-mail growth hormones, Sierra Club membership stood at 560,000, as compared with 50,000 for the Izaak Walton League.[32]

Direct mail serves multiple purposes. The leading academic expert on environmental fund-raising, Christopher Bosso, says that "direct mail has been a lucrative, relatively low cost way to educate the public about both an issue and a group; it lowers the cost of individual participation to just writing a check." Whether the technique is "low cost" for the organization depends on how we do the accounting. Typically these organizations allocate 20–30 percent of their budget to fund-raising and associated advertising.[33] Typically, too, the rate of return is 1 percent to 3 percent, depending on how well the mailing list has been chosen. Adding a "front-end" or "back-end" premium can double the rate of return. Once signed up, new "members" have a loyal organizational pen pal, for the average environmental organization requests money from its "members" nine times a year. (Fair is fair: eight of every nine direct mail appeals from non-profit organizations are thrown away unopened.)[34] Typically the dropout rate after the first year is 30 percent, although in some cases (like Common Cause in the 1980s) dropout can exceed 50 percent.[35] On the other hand, members who stay past the first year are more reliable sources of revenue. As one environmental strategist said, "We know what it costs us to bring in a member; we know we lose money to bring people in, [but] it is an investment program."

Recruiting "members" (actually, "donors" or "supporters" would be a more accurate term) has become an exact science. "We know how many new people we have to bring in each year," explained one membership director. "A large percentage are from direct mail. We are trying to get away from mailing so many pieces, but right now it is the most effective way to bring in new members." Added another, "We have a certain amount of attrition . . . and we have a certain amount of desired growth, and based on our response rate we have to mail that number of pieces to maintain our membership level and growth rate." A third wrote me with disarming candor, "Although our membership is not declining, it is becoming increasingly more challenging to bring in new members at an affordable cost per donor. . . . Whoever finds a new niche market is the winner!!!"[36]

As one might expect from this process of recruiting "members," organizational commitment is low. Compared with members recruited through face-to-face social networks (including recipients of gift memberships from friends and relatives), direct-mail recruits drop out more readily, participate in fewer activities, and feel less attachment to the group. Direct-mail recruits also hold more extreme and intolerant political views than members recruited through social networks.[37] It is thus perhaps less surprising that Greenpeace, which had tripled in membership to 2,350,000 between 1985 and 1990, then *lost 85 percent of its members in the next eight years.*

By contrast, *none* of the "old-fashioned" chapter-based organizations that attained record membership after World War II and whose travails we summarized in figure 8 lost as much as 85 percent of its membership in the *three or four decades* from its postwar peak to the end of the century.[38] The reason is obvious and yet crucial in understanding the difference between the older and newer organizational types: Members of the Moose Club or Hadassah are joined to the organization not merely by symbolic ties, but by real ties to real people—that is, by social capital. Members of the local American Legion post are kept there, not mainly by patriotism or by a desire to lobby for more funds for the Veterans Administration, but by long-standing personal ties among the guys. The tensile strength of the newer organizations is much weaker. As Christopher Bosso concludes, supporters of mail-order organizations are less "members" than "consumers" of a cause. "The sharp decline in Greenpeace's numbers in the 1990s may reflect a market axiom that today's hot product is tomorrow's remaindered bin."[39]

Most affiliates of tertiary associations do not even consider themselves "members." More than half of Environmental Defense Fund "members" say that "I don't really think of myself as a member; the money I send is just a contribution." Another survey of "members" of five top environmental organizations found that they averaged less than three years' affiliation, that more than half were affiliated with four or more such groups, and that only 8 percent described themselves as "active," all of which is consistent with a purely "checkbook affiliation."[40] (The remarkable overlap in membership among different groups is due, of course, to direct-mail recruitment, since the groups are prospecting from the same mailing lists.) They are valued supporters and genuine rooters for environmentalism as a good cause, but they are not themselves active in the cause.[41] They don't see themselves as movement foot soldiers in any sense like the young African Americans who sat in lunch counters in Greensboro in 1960, and neither should we.

Minimal commitment among mail-order members is hardly unique to environmental groups. For example, only one out of five Common Cause members said that they would like to be more active in the group, if given an opportunity. Membership in the National Rifle Association tripled between 1977 and 1996—despite (or because of) a national trend in favor of gun control—but the annual renewal rate of NRA members is barely 25 percent.[42] Scarcely half of the "members" of the National Abortion Rights Action League (NARAL) describe themselves as members. Three-quarters of NARAL affiliates have no idea how many of their friends are also members, and two-thirds have never encouraged friends to join. As sociologist John McCarthy, who conducted these polls, concluded, the results "strongly suggest that [NARAL members] did not talk with their friends about membership in the organization."[43] And indeed, why should they, if they think of themselves as fans, not players?

It is sometimes suggested that members of groups like Greenpeace are engaged in "proxy" political participation.[44] In fact, neither the groups' leaders nor the members see the group as a vehicle for participatory democracy. Barely one in every five members of Friends of the Earth and Amnesty International say that "being politically active" is an important reason why they joined.[45] As two close students of tertiary groups conclude,

> Mail-order groups permit a form of political participation which can be labeled cheap participation. For a cost below the threshold of serious analysis by the relatively affluent potential member, they can make a political statement of preference, without engaging in the costs (time and money) of "real" participation. . . . It is the casual nature of the engagement rather than subsequent disillusionment that accounts for turnover.[46]

Even early observers of the sixties raised questions about how truly participatory those movements had become. In their classic analysis in the early 1970s, sociologists John McCarthy and Mayer Zald emphasized that "the functions historically served by a social movement membership base have been . . . increasingly taken over by paid functionaries, by the 'bureaucratization of social discontent,' by mass promotion campaigns, by full-time employees whose professional careers are defined in terms of social movement participation, by philanthropic foundations, and by government itself." By the 1990s, political scientist Ronald Shaiko reported, "The era of flannel-shirted, 'Flower Power' antiestablishmentarianism has virtually vanished. Today . . . public interest organizations are hiring economists, Ivy League lawyers, management consultants, direct mail specialists, and communications directors."[47]

Some critics object to the new tertiary organizations as oligarchic and unresponsive, a product of political betrayal or "selling out." That is not my view. On the contrary, as political scientist Christopher Bosso explains, "The major environmental groups in fact are playing roles that one expects of mature organizations within a political context that forces groups to grow and professionalize or die."[48] Competition for dues makes tertiary organizations sensitive to their constituents, and those that fail to win support die. Moreover, traditional civic organizations had important oligarchic features. Robert Michels's famous "iron law of oligarchy," after all, was coined to describe organizations with active grassroots affiliates.[49] My argument is not that direct-mail organizations are morally evil or politically ineffective. It may be more efficient technically for us to hire other people to act for us politically. However, such organizations provide neither connectedness among members nor direct engagement in civic give-and-take, and they certainly do not represent "participatory democracy." Citizenship by proxy is an oxymoron.

Only two or three of the dozen or so major environmental organizations whose massive membership growth is charted in figure 43 have any local chapters at all. As the membership director of one explained wearily when we asked about membership activities, "*Membership* simply means that you gave us some money at least once in the last two years." Even where a formal structure of state and local chapters exists, it has atrophied. A 1989 membership survey by the Sierra Club itself found that although its members were much more active politically than the average American, only 13 percent had ever attended even a single Sierra Club meeting. The National Audubon Society claims hundreds of chapters nationwide, but of the twenty-eight thousand NAS members in Texas, for example, state officials of the organization estimate that only 3–4 percent are active. In other words, fewer than one Texan in fifteen thousand is active in the one environmental organization with the sturdiest surviving local structure. By comparison, *every week twenty times as many* Texans gather for lunch at "old-fashioned" Rotary clubs.[50]

Close observers of the environmental movement claim that "a fundamental change in environmentalism since 1970 has been a rapid increase in the number and prominence of *grassroots* organizations."[51] At least on the surface, public support for environmentalism seems strong, although it weakened noticeably as the twentieth century ended. By 1990 three-quarters of Americans told the Gallup poll that we considered ourselves "environmentalists," although this figure fell sharply and steadily during the 1990s, so that by the end of the decade the number of self-declared environmentalists had fallen by one-third to only 50 percent.[52] More than 60 percent of us claim that we often make a special effort to recycle, half claim to have given money to an environmental group in the past five years, 30 percent claim to have signed a petition about an environmental issue, 10 percent claim to be a member of a proenvironmental group, and 3 percent claim to have taken part in an environmental protest or demonstration.[53]

There is, however, some reason to believe that these estimates may be exaggerated. Although local groups seem to have become more numerous on issues like toxic waste and land conservation in recent years, I have been able to find no hard evidence that grassroots environmentalism in general has grown. In fact, the only systematic evidence I have found on trends in conservation and environmental organizations at the state and local level and on environmental activism tends to suggest a *decline* over the last several decades. For example, according to annual surveys by Yankelovich Partners, the fraction of Americans who agreed that "I'm concerned about what I myself can do to protect our environment and natural resources" rose unevenly from 50 percent in 1981 to 55 percent in 1990–92 and then fell steadily to 40 percent in 1999, the lowest recording on that barometer in nearly two decades.[54] The gentlest verdict on the claim of growing grassroots environmental activism is "not proved."

If the evidence for grassroots involvement in "progressive" social movements is weak, the comparable evidence for grassroots vitality among religious conservatives is much stronger. In the 1950s and 1960s McCarthyism, the John Birch Society, White Citizens' councils, and the Wallace presidential campaign represented mass-based conservative, anti-Communist, and segregationist movements, but each of those groups mobilized at most several hundred thousand participants and many fewer activists. In the 1970s, riding a wave of religious fundamentalism, the Christian Right emerged as a political force, but organizationally it consisted of a few centralized national direct-mail operations, particularly the Moral Majority headed by Jerry Falwell. However, the 1980s saw the formation of several genuinely grassroots conservative evangelical organizations, ranging from the violently antiabortion Operation Rescue to the more mainstream Christian Coalition, headed by Pat Robertson and Ralph Reed, and the nominally apolitical Promise-Keepers. The Christian Coalition and Promise-Keepers each claimed several million active participants, an order of magnitude larger than any previous mass-based conservative movement in the twentieth century. The fate of these specific organizations, each founded less than a decade ago, is uncertain. What they (and other, smaller religiously based organizations of both the Left and Right) signify, however, is much more important—the appearance of a substantial cadre of highly motivated citizen-activists.[55]

As part of the religious boom in America after World War II, the center of gravity of Protestant evangelicalism gradually moved from the rural and socially peripheral fringes of fundamentalism toward middle-class suburban communities. Membership in denominations associated with the National Association of Evangelicals (the evangelical equivalent of the mainstream National Council of Churches) more than tripled from the 1940s to 1970s, and as we saw earlier, evangelical churches have been hit less hard by the subsequent decline in religious observance.[56] More important, the traditional repugnance of fundamentalism for political involvement was gradually reversed.

Prior to 1974, as sociologist Robert Wuthnow has pointed out, most studies found evangelicals less disposed to political participation than other Americans—less likely to vote, to join political groups, to write to public officials, and to favor religious involvement in politics. After 1974, by contrast, most studies have found them *more* involved politically than other Americans.[57] This historic change is due in part to the expansion of evangelicalism into social strata more accustomed to political participation, but also evangelicalism itself has become more sympathetic to civic engagement. As Christian Smith, author of the most recent study of evangelical involvement in public life, has observed, "Which Christian tradition is actually doing the work of trying to influence American society? It is the evangelicals who are most walking their talk." [58]

This important change in the social bases of American politics aptly illustrates how social capital, civic engagement, and social movements feed on one another. In part, the political mobilization of evangelicals illustrates the effects of new issues (abortion, sexual morality, "family values"), new techniques (television and other instruments of contemporary political organizing), and a new generation of political entrepreneurs. On the other hand, unlike other newly mobilized groups, such as environmentalists, firm and enduring organizational foundations for the politicization of the evangelical community already existed. As several close observers of the new evangelical activism have noted, "Religious people are enmeshed in webs of local churches, channels of religious information, and networks of religious associations that make them readily available for mobilization." [59] So this social movement is both drawing on and replenishing stocks of social capital in at least one portion of American society.

In some respects, evangelical activists look very much like other activists in America—older, whiter, more educated, more affluent—but religion is extraordinarily important in their lives. Of one national sample of religious activists, 60 to 70 percent attended church *more than once a week*, compared with less than 5 percent of other Americans. And in a development that would have astounded and probably appalled their fundamentalist forebears, they are three to five times more active than the average American in virtually all forms of civic and political life.[60]

In the 1996 election evangelicals were more than twice as likely as other Americans to discuss the election in church with a friend and to be contacted by a religious interest group. They were, in fact, more likely to be contacted about the campaign by religious groups than by parties or candidates. The most important predictor of this contact was neither demography nor theology, but simply social engagement in the religious community. And these religious contacts—especially talking politics in church with a friend—had a demonstrable impact on who voted and for whom. The link between involvement in the church community and political mobilization was powerful and direct.[61] Religious conservatives have created the largest, best-organized grassroots social movement of the last quarter century. It is, in short, among evangelical Christians, rather than among the ideological heirs of the sixties, that we find the strongest evidence of an upwelling of civic engagement against the ebb tide described in earlier chapters.

What of the broader hypothesis that modes of "elite-challenging" participation introduced by the social movements of the sixties are now conventional across the political spectrum? One measure seems to support this hypothesis, for popular initiatives and referenda came to play a bigger role in politics in the 1980s and 1990s. In fact, as figure 44 shows, the frequency of statewide ballot initiatives over the twentieth century is the mirror image of virtually all the other trends in civic engagement we have explored—*falling* from the first decade of the century until the late 1960s (except for a *rise* during the Great Depression), then skyrocketing in the last third of the century.[62] According to some political rhetoric, this rise of ballot initiatives is an institutionalized form of "all power to the people."[63]

Contrary to their populist pedigree, however, these devices cannot be taken as a reliable sign of widespread civic engagement. In the first place, five states account for more than half of all ballot initiatives nationwide in the twentieth century—California, Oregon, North Dakota, Colorado, and Arizona—and much of the recent growth is attributable to California alone, so the use of referenda is not necessarily a good metric for citizen involvement everywhere.[64] Second, although civic activists have sometimes placed issues like coastal management and term limits on the ballot, most scholars agree that

> [in] the past two decades, virtually all successful drives have relied, at least predominantly, on professional circulation firms. One study [by the California Commission on Campaign Financing] concluded, ". . . Any

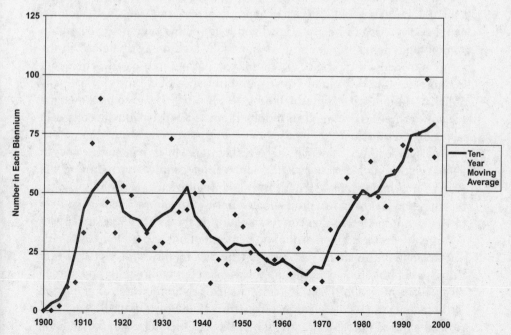

Figure 44: Initiatives on Statewide Ballots in the United States, 1900–1998

individual, corporation, or organization with approximately $1 million to spend can now place any issue on the ballot. .... *Qualifying an initiative for the statewide ballot is thus no longer so much a measure of general citizen interest as it is a test of fundraising ability.*"[65]

Although one might imagine that such ballot contests might spark widespread political discussion by ordinary citizens, studies show that most signers don't read what they sign. During the campaign itself, direct-mail and radio and television sound-bite advertising, much of it deceptive, is more important than grassroots activity. It is thus hardly surprising that campaign spending is a strong predictor of the outcome and that surveys indicate "a very low degree of voter sophistication" on referenda issues.[66] Based on detailed study of ballot initiatives in Massachusetts, Michigan, Oregon, and California in 1976–1982, political scientist Betty Zisk concluded, "Far from replacing group lobbying efforts vis-à-vis the legislature, the initiative and referenda campaigns seem to *provide an alternative channel* for the very group activities the reformers denounced. .... The opportunity for direct participation does not seem to have galvanized large numbers of voters."[67] In short, the rise of ballot initiatives is a better measure of the power of well-financed special interests than of civic engagement.

Demonstrations and other public protests in Washington have become somewhat larger and more frequent since the late 1960s, as media-savvy protest organizers have become more sophisticated about how to garner national television coverage.[68] On the other hand, the great civil rights and Vietnam marches of the sixties were preceded and followed by continuing activism in communities across the country, whereas a "March on Washington" in the 1990s provided no assurance of continuing, community-based action. For example, less than six months after sponsoring the "Stand in the Gap" rally of half a million men on the Mall on October 4, 1997, said to be the largest religious gathering in American history, Promise-Keepers virtually collapsed, laying off its entire staff.[69]

Available survey evidence suggests slight growth in nationwide rates of demonstration and protest over the last quarter century. According to the Roper Social and Political Trends survey archive, the fraction of adults who say that they had *ever* been in a protest march or sit-in rose from 7 percent in 1978 to 10 percent in 1994. Other surveys, too, during the 1970s, 1980s, and 1990s consistently estimated participation in demonstrations and protests at roughly one in ten to fifteen adults, with a slight tendency for the estimates to rise over the years. The abortion issue alone appears to account for roughly one-third of all such activities. On the other hand, the explanation for the rising fraction of the population who have ever protested is the departure of the *pre*-1960s generation of *non*protesters at the top of the age hierarchy, *not* the addition of new protesters at the bottom. As figure 45 shows, protesting is *less* common among twenty-somethings now than it was among people that age in the sixties and seventies, but protesting has become *more* common among middle-aged and older people, as the sixties generation itself aged. Protest marchers have steadily and rapidly grayed over the past several decades.[70]

Strikingly, protests and demonstrations are not an *alternative* to conventional politics, but a complement, in the sense that protesters are unusually active politically in more ordinary ways, too. Even though participation in demonstrations and forms of civil disobedience is not much more common nowadays than in the sixties, it is more widely seen as legitimate by nonparticipants. These days "movement-type" political actions are accepted as "standard operating procedure" across the political spectrum, unlike three or four decades ago. On the other hand, actual involvement is limited to a small and aging fraction of the population. Moreover, as we noted in chapter 2, petitioning and participation at local public meetings have slumped over the last decade or two. As David Meyer and Sidney Tarrow, proponents of the "movement society" hypothesis, ultimately concede, "The amount of highly contentious forms accepted and actually used by citizens seems to be more circumscribed than it was two decades ago."[71]

The decline of grassroots protest should not be exaggerated. The 1990s saw much activity by gay and lesbian activists and pro-lifers, as well as a steady low level of local and campus activism. Grassroots social protest may well be as

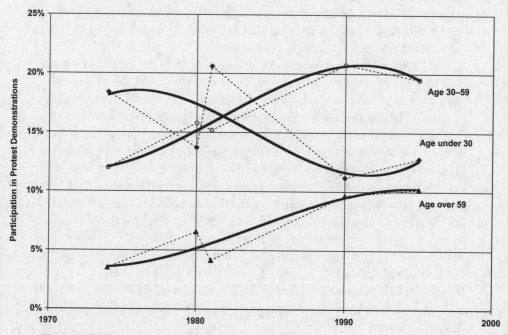

Figure 45: The Graying of Protest Demonstrations

common today as during the 1960s and 1970s, and tolerance for such protest is clearly up. However, I know of no evidence that actual participation in grassroots social movements has grown in the past few decades to offset the massive declines in more conventional forms of social and political participation.

TELECOMMUNICATIONS CONSTITUTES the third countertrend toward greater social connectedness considered in this chapter, and by all odds it is the most important. The humble telephone provides one instructive example. Throughout the twentieth century, telephone use grew exponentially. As the first half of figure 46 shows, the diffusion of phones into American homes followed a familiar trajectory—rising steadily for the first two-thirds of the century, except for the Great Depression reversal. Between 1945 and 1998 local calls per capita climbed from 304 to 2,023 annually, while annual long-distance calls per capita exploded from 13 to 353. Most of this growth represented business and commercial communication, but purely social calls also increased. By 1982 almost half of all American adults talked on the phone (locally or long-distance) with friends or relatives virtually every day. Ties among distant friends and relatives were transformed from the written to the spoken word over the last quarter of the century, as the second half of figure 46 shows, accelerating after the deregulation of the long-distance telephone industry in 1984 before apparently leveling off in the 1990s. The rapid pace of technological innovation—especially the diffusion of cell phones in the 1990s—continued to make the telephone nearly ubiquitous. By 1998 the Pew Research Center for the People & the Press reported that two-thirds of all adults had called a friend or relative the previous day "just to talk."[72]

For nearly half a century after its invention in 1876 the telephone's social implications were badly misjudged by analysts and even by the phone company itself. For those of us who wish to anticipate the impact of the Internet on social relations, the astounding series of poor predictions about the social consequences of the telephone is a deeply cautionary tale. Alexander Graham Bell himself originally expected the telephone to serve the sort of broadcasting function that would later become the province of radio—"music on tap." Well into the twentieth century, telephone executives were so convinced that their primary customer was the businessman that they actually discouraged "socializing" by telephone. As Claude Fischer, the leading sociologist of the telephone, summarizes, "[F]or a generation or more there was a mismatch between the ways people actually used the telephone and how industry men imagined it would or should be used."[73]

Even with the benefit of hindsight it is surprisingly difficult to evaluate the effects of the telephone on social relations. Ithiel de Sola Pool, a pioneer in this field, observed:

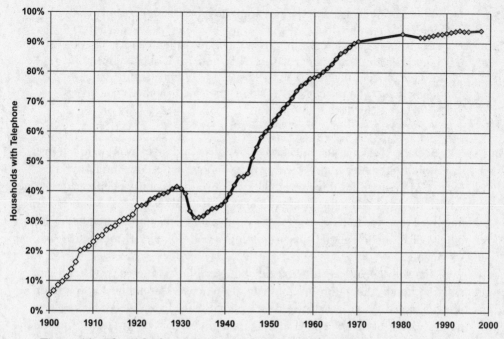

Figure 46a: The Telephone Penetrates American Households

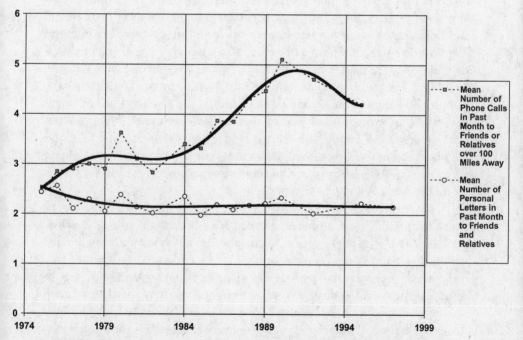

Figure 46b: Trends in Long-Distance Personal Phone Calls and Letters

Wherever we look, the telephone seems to have effects in diametrically opposite directions. It saves physicians from making house-calls, but physicians initially believed it increased them, for patients could summon the doctor to them rather than travel to him. . . . It allows dispersal of centers of authority, but it also allows tight continuous supervision of field offices from the center. . . . No matter what hypothesis one begins with, reverse tendencies also appear.[74]

Socially speaking, the telephone both gives and takes away. When a fire in a switching center unexpectedly cut telephone service on the Lower East Side of Manhattan for three weeks in 1975, two-thirds of the people who lost service reported that being without a telephone made them feel isolated, but one-third reported that they visited other people in person more frequently. In other words, the telephone appears to reduce both loneliness and face-to-face socializing.[75]

Many observers have theorized that the telephone fostered "psychological neighborhoods," liberating our intimate social networks from the constraints of physical space. As early as 1891 one telephone official suggested that the technology would bring an "epoch of neighborship without propinquity." In fact, however, the first comprehensive study of the social impact of the telephone (in 1933) found that this point-to-point medium (unlike the mass media) reinforced existing local ties more than distant ones. In the mid-1970s phone company records were said to show that between 40 and 50 percent of all phone calls originating from a household were made within a two-mile radius, and 70 percent were made within a five-mile radius. Roughly 20 percent of all residential calls were made to a single number, and roughly half were made to one of only five numbers. Concludes Martin Mayer, summarizing these data, "People make most of their telephone calls within the neighborhood in which they live." The type of household that makes heaviest use of the telephone, Mayer reports, is a family with teenagers that has recently moved to a new neighborhood in the same metropolitan area—in other words, the telephone is used to maintain personal relationships now severed by space. "One does not meet new friends on the telephone."[76]

Thus, somewhat paradoxically, the telephone seems to have had the effect of reinforcing, not transforming or replacing, existing personal networks. Compare the top half of figure 46 on the diffusion of the telephone in the first two-thirds of the twentieth century with any of our earlier charts of community engagement over this same period, and the conclusion is obvious: At least in those years, telecommunications and conventional forms of social connectedness were complements, not alternatives. Similarly, Claude Fischer's historical analysis of the social impact of the telephone concludes that although the telephone vastly expanded the possibilities for personal communication, it "did not radically alter American ways of life. Rather, Americans used it to more vigorously pursue their characteristic ways of life."

> The adoption of the telephone probably led people to hold more frequent personal conversations with friends and kin than had previously been customary, even if it also led them to curtail some visits. . . . In total, calling probably led to more social conversations with more people than before. Perhaps these calls substituted for longer visits or chats with family members, or perhaps they simply took up time that would have been spent alone.
>
> The telephone appears to be implicated more in another trend, that of increasing privatism . . . the participation in and valuation of private social worlds as opposed to the larger, public community. . . . There is little evidence that the telephone enabled people to become involved in distinctively new organizational commitments. . . . The home telephone allowed subscribers to maintain more frequent contact with kin and friends by chatting briefly perhaps a few times a week instead of at greater length once a week. There is little sign that telephone calling opened up new social contacts.[77]

In sum, the telephone has without doubt facilitated *schmoozing* with old friends, and in that sense it has offset some of the disconnection described in chapter 6. On the other hand, it has not engendered new friendships, nor has it substantially altered the characteristic activities of *machers*. Historian Daniel Boorstin summarizes the surprisingly mundane impact of the phone on Americans' social capital: "The telephone was only a convenience, permitting Americans to do more casually and with less effort what they had already been doing before."[78]

As the twenty-first century opens we are only a few years into the era of widespread access to the Internet, yet it is hard to avoid speculating that the implications of this new technology of communication may dwarf the effects of the telephone on American society. The speed of diffusion of this new technology has been substantially greater than that of almost any other consumer technology in history—rivaled only by television. To go from 1 percent market penetration to 75 percent required nearly seven decades for the telephone; for Internet access the equivalent passage will require little more than seven years. One survey organization reported that nearly one-third of the adult population (about sixty-four million people) had used the Internet as of the spring of 1999, up by more than ten million users from barely six months earlier.[79]

Like virtually all technical consumer innovations, this one caught on most rapidly and fully among younger generations. One study in 1999 found that although young people were in general much less likely to seek out political information than older cohorts, they were more likely to use the Internet as their preferred means of access. On the other hand, at about the same time the Web site of the American Association of Retired Persons reportedly was already receiving half a million individual visitors every month.[80] The new medium drew, as if mesmerized, people of all generations.

Within a few years of the Internet's launch, simulacra of most classic forms of social connectedness and civic engagement could be found online. Mourners could attend virtual funerals over the Web; a reporter for *Today in Funeral Service* told the Associated Press that the online funeral "kind of depersonalizes it, but it's better than missing it." Virtual vows arrived; America Online in June 1997 held the largest cyberwedding to date, marrying thousands of couples simultaneously while spectators "watched" and "cheered" from their virtual pews. At last count Yahoo mentioned more than five hundred places where one could pray virtually, including one—Yaale Ve'Yavo, an Orthodox Jewish site—that forwards email prayers to Jerusalem to be affixed to the Western Wall. Easter services and Passover seders; grief counseling and cancer support groups; volunteering, cyberromance, and hundreds of thousands of chat groups; voting, lobbying, and even an AIDS Action Council "virtual march on Washington" that logged over twenty-three thousand "poster-carrying marchers"—all these forms of virtual social capital and more could be found in cyberspace.[81]

One central question, of course, is whether "virtual social capital" is itself a contradiction in terms. There is no easy answer. The early, deeply flawed conjectures about the social implications of the telephone warn us that our own equally early conjectures about the Internet are likely to be similarly flawed. Very few things can yet be said with any confidence about the connection between social capital and Internet technology. One truism, however, is this: The timing of the Internet explosion means that it cannot possibly be causally linked to the crumbling of social connectedness described in previous chapters. Voting, giving, trusting, meeting, visiting, and so on had all begun to decline while Bill Gates was still in grade school. By the time that the Internet reached 10 percent of American adults in 1996, the nationwide decline in social connectedness and civic engagement had been under way for at least a quarter of a century. Whatever the future implications of the Internet, social intercourse over the last several decades of the twentieth century was not simply displaced from physical space to cyberspace. The Internet may be part of the solution to our civic problem, or it may exacerbate it, but the cyberrevolution was not the cause.

We also know that early users of Internet technology were no less (and no more) civically engaged than anyone else. By 1999 three independent studies (including my own) had confirmed that once we control for the higher educational levels of Internet users, they are indistinguishable from nonusers when it comes to civic engagement.[82] On the other hand, these oft ballyhooed results prove little about the *effects* of the Net, because of the likelihood that

Internet users are self-selected in relevant ways. The absence of any correlation between Internet usage and civic engagement could mean that the Internet attracts reclusive nerds and energizes them, but it could also mean that the Net disproportionately attracts civic dynamos and sedates them. In any event, it is much too early to assess the long-run social effects of the Internet empirically. Hence I consider here some of the *potential* advantages and disadvantages of computer-mediated communication for American civic life, recognizing in advance that neither the apocalyptic "gloom and doom" prognosticators nor the utopian "brave new virtual community" advocates are probably on target. How are "virtual" communities likely to be different from the "real" thing?

Community, communion, and communication are intimately as well as etymologically related. Communication is a fundamental prerequisite for social and emotional connections. Telecommunications in general and the Internet in particular substantially enhance our ability to communicate; thus it seems reasonable to assume that their net effect will be to enhance community, perhaps even dramatically. Social capital is about networks, and the Net is the network to end all networks. By removing barriers of time and distance, students of computer-mediated communication like sociologist Barry Wellman maintain, "Computer-supported social networks sustain strong, intermediate, and weak ties that provide information and social support in both specialized and broadly based relationships. . . . Computer-mediated communication accelerates the ways in which people operate at the centers of partial, personal communities, switching rapidly and frequently between groups of ties."[83]

Very much like nineteenth-century futurists contemplating the vistas opened by the telephone, enthusiasts for "virtual community" see computer networks as the basis for a kind of utopian communitarianism. Starr Roxanne Hiltz and Murray Turoff, early prophets of computer-mediated communication, predicted that "we will become the Network Nation, exchanging vast amounts of both information and socioemotional communications with colleagues, friends and 'strangers,' who share similar interests . . . we will become a 'global village.'" Internet theorist Michael Strangelove wrote:

> The Internet is not about technology, it is not about information, it is about communication—people talking with each other, people exchanging e-mail. . . . The Internet is mass participation in fully bidirectional, uncensored mass communication. Communication is the basis, the foundation, the radical ground and root upon which all community stands, grows, and thrives. The Internet is a community of chronic communicators.[84]

Howard Rheingold, self-described "homesteader on the electronic frontier," reported, "The idea of a community accessible only via my computer screen sounded cold to me at first, but I learned quickly that people can feel passionately about e-mail and computer conferences. I've become one of them. I care about these people I met through my computer." John Perry Barlow, cofounder of the Electronic Frontier Foundation, found no parallel in recorded history for the advent of computer-mediated communication: "We are in the middle of the most transforming technological event since the capture of fire." [85]

The Internet is a powerful tool for the transmission of information among physically distant people. The tougher question is whether that flow of information itself fosters social capital and genuine community. Information is, of course, important, but as John Seeley Brown and Paul Duguid of Xerox's famed Palo Alto Research Center emphasize, information itself needs a social context to be meaningful: "The tight focus on information, with the implicit assumption that if we look after information everything else will fall into place, is ultimately a sort of social and moral blindness." At its best, computer-mediated communication allows wider, more efficient networks that strengthen our ties to the social world and increase our "intellectual capital," for information can be shared at virtually no cost. People with different pieces of the puzzle can collaborate more easily. Computer-mediated communication can support large, dense, yet fluid groups that cut across existing organizational and geographic boundaries, increasing the involvement of otherwise peripheral participants, such as the recent retirees studied in one corporate experiment in electronic communication.[86]

Social networks based on computer-mediated communication can be organized by shared interests rather than by shared space. By century's end thousands of far-flung, functionally defined networks had sprung up, linking like-minded people as disparate as BMW fanciers, bird-watchers, and white supremacists. Echoing precisely (but perhaps unconsciously) early speculations about the effects of the telephone, MIT computer scientist Michael L. Dertouzos speculated about millions of "virtual neighborhoods" based on shared avocations rather than shared space.[87] Certainly cyberspace already hosts thousands of hobby and other special interest groups, and if participation in such groups becomes widespread and durable, then perhaps the prediction may be right this time.

Virtual communities may also be more egalitarian than the real communities in which we live. At least for the foreseeable future, computer-mediated communication drastically truncates information about one's discussion partners. Rheingold argues that the invisibility of text-based communication prevents people from forming prejudices prior to their encounters. As the canine cybernaut in the famous New Yorker cartoon put it, "On the Internet no one knows you're a dog." Thus, assuming widespread cyberaccess, "virtual communities" may be more heterogeneous with regard to such physical factors as race, gender, and age, although as we shall see later, they may be more homogeneous with respect to interests and values.[88]

Anonymity and the absence of social cues inhibit social control—that is, after all, why we have the secret ballot—and thus cyberspace seems in some respects more democratic. (Ironically, this advantage of computer-mediated communication depends on the fact that at least with current technology, it actually transmits *less* information among participants than face-to-face communication does.) Research has shown that online discussions tend to be more frank and egalitarian than face-to-face meetings. Thus computer-mediated communication may lead to flatter hierarchies. In workplace networks, experiments have shown, computer-mediated communication is less hierarchical, more participatory, more candid, and less biased by status differences. Women, for example, are less likely to be interrupted in cyberspace discussions.[89]

Some of the allegedly greater democracy in cyberspace is based more on hope and hype than on careful research. The political culture of the Internet, at least in its early stages, is astringently libertarian, and in some respects cyberspace represents a Hobbesian state of nature, not a Lockean one. As Peter Kollock and Marc Smith, two of the more thoughtful observers of community on the Internet, observe, "It is widely believed and hoped that the ease of communicating and interacting online will lead to a flourishing of democratic institutions, heralding a new and vital arena of public discourse. But to date, most online groups have the structure of either an anarchy [if unmoderated] or a dictatorship [if moderated]."[90]

The high speed, low cost, and broad scope of mobilization that is possible on the Internet can be an advantage for political organizers, by reducing transaction costs, particularly for widely scattered groups of like-minded citizens. For example, the 1997 Nobel Prize–winning International Campaign to Ban Landmines was organized by Jody Williams primarily over the Internet from her home in rural Vermont. As early as 1995, Mark Bonchek reported, "27,000 people read the alt.politics.homosexuality newsgroup regularly with an average of 75 messages per day. As its name suggests, alt.politics.homosexuality is a forum for people to discuss issues and distribute information related to politics and homosexuality." Bonchek found a surprising range of positions on these issues in the postings to this forum, both sympathetic and hostile toward homosexuality.[91]

On the other hand, computer-mediated communication so lowers the threshold for voicing opinions that, like talk radio, it may lead not to deliberation, but to din. Consider, for example, the following advertisement that appeared on the inside back cover of *Mother Jones* in April 1999:

> If you care
> you can do something . . . easy!
> *www.ifnotnow.com*
> Be a full-time citizen activist . . .
> . . . for 5 minutes a week!

> Over a dozen of the best social advocacy groups
> provide the information
> —you read alerts, send letters, get responses,
> and monitor results—all at the click of a button.
> It's a one-stop shop for staying involved.
> We want to make it easy for you to make a difference!
> Make your voice heard!
> *www.ifnotnow.com*
> Sign up for a free trial now!

If generalized, this shortcut to civic expression would simply exacerbate the imbalance between talking and listening that is a prominent feature of contemporary civic disengagement, as we noted in chapter 2 and table 1. John Seeley Brown and Paul Duguid point out that "the ability to send a message to president@whitehouse.gov . . . can give the illusion of much more access, participation, and social proximity than is actually available."[92] Millions more of us can express our views with the click of a mouse, but is anyone listening?

Nevertheless, the potential benefits of computer-mediated communication for civic engagement and social connectedness are impressive. The Internet offers a low-cost and in many respects egalitarian way of connecting with millions of one's fellow citizens, particularly those with whom one shares interests but not space or time. In fact, liberating our social ties from the constraints of time—through what the experts term "asynchronous communication"—may turn out to be a more important effect of the Internet than liberation from the constraints of space.

AGAINST THIS PROMISE, on the other hand, must be weighed four serious challenges to the hope that computer-mediated communication will breed new and improved communities. I shall discuss them in order of increasing complexity.

The "digital divide" refers to the social inequality of access to cyberspace. Certainly in the early years of the Internet heavy users were predominantly younger, highly educated, upper-income white males. An exhaustive 1997 study by the Census Bureau found that the least connected groups in American society were the rural poor, rural and inner-city racial minorities, and young, female-headed households. Moreover, these gaps by education, income, race, and family structure appeared to be widening, not narrowing. Media specialist Pippa Norris found that both in the United States and in Europe the Internet has *not* mobilized previously inactive groups (with the partial exception of young people) but has instead reinforced existing biases in political participation. Sociologist Manuel Castells argues forcefully that because access to computer-mediated communication is culturally, educationally, and economically restrictive, and will be so for a long time, the most important cultural impact of computer-mediated communication could be potentially the reinforcement of the culturally dominant social networks.[93]

This specter of a kind of cyberapartheid, in which bridging social capital is diminished as elite networks become less accessible to the have-nots, is indeed frightening. For that very reason, however, it is widely recognized as a key challenge that must be addressed. Given political will, this problem is tractable. If the Internet is seen as a kind of twenty-first-century public utility, then inexpensive, subsidized access (including both hardware and user-friendly software) can be made available in libraries, community centers, Laundromats, and even private residences, much as low-cost telephone service was subsidized in the twentieth century. This first challenge of the Internet to community connectedness is serious but not insurmountable.

The second challenge is technically more difficult to resolve. Computer-mediated communication transmits much less nonverbal information than face-to-face communication. MIT's Dertouzos asks the right question: "Which qualities of human relationships will pass well through tomorrow's information infrastructures and which ones will not?"[94]

Humans are remarkably effective at sensing nonverbal messages from one another, particularly about emotions, cooperation, and trustworthiness. (It seems possible that the ability to spot nonverbal signs of mendacity offered a significant survival advantage during the long course of human evolution.) Psychologist Albert Mehrabian writes in *Silent Messages: Implicit Communication of Emotions and Attitudes* that in the "realm of feelings" our "facial and vocal expressions, postures, movements, and gestures" are crucial. When our words "contradict the messages contained within them, others mistrust what we say—they rely almost completely on what we do."[95]

Computer-mediated communication, now and for the foreseeable future, masks the enormous amount of nonverbal communication that takes place during even the most casual face-to-face encounter. (Emoticons in email, like :), implicitly acknowledge this fact, but provide only the faintest trace of the information in actual facial expression.) Eye contact, gestures (both intentional and unintentional), nods, a faint furrowing of the brow, body language, seating arrangements, even hesitation measured in milliseconds—none of this mass of information that we ordinarily process almost without thinking in face-to-face encounters is captured in text.

Moreover, as organization theorists Nitin Nohria and Robert G. Eccles point out, face-to-face encounters provide a depth and speed of feedback that is impossible in computer-mediated communication.

Relative to electronically mediated exchange, the structure of face-to-face interaction offers an unusual capacity for interruption, repair, feedback, and learning. In contrast to interactions that are largely sequential, face-to-face interaction makes it possible for two people to be sending and delivering messages simultaneously. The cycle of interruption, feedback, and repair possible in face-to-face interaction is so quick that it is virtually instantaneous. As [sociologist Erving] Goffman notes, "a speaker can see how others are responding to her message even before it is done and alter it midstream to elicit a different response." When interaction takes place in a group setting, the number of "conversations" that can be going on simultaneously when the interactants are face-to-face is even harder to replicate in other media.

The poverty of social cues in computer-mediated communication inhibits interpersonal collaboration and trust, especially when the interaction is anonymous and not nested in a wider social context. Experiments that compare face-to-face and computer-mediated communication confirm that the richer the medium of communication, the more sociable, personal, trusting, and friendly the encounter.[96]

Computer-mediated communication is, to be sure, more egalitarian, frank, and task oriented than face-to-face communication. Participants in computer-based groups often come up with a wider range of alternatives. However, because of the paucity of social cues and social communication, participants in computer-based groups find it harder to reach consensus and feel less solidarity with one another. They develop a sense of "depersonalization" and are less satisfied with the group's accomplishments. Computer-based groups are quicker to reach an intellectual understanding of their shared problems—probably because they are less distracted by "extraneous" social communication—but they are much worse at generating the trust and reciprocity necessary to implement that understanding.

Cheating and reneging are more common in computer-mediated communication, where misrepresentation and misunderstanding are easier. Participants in computer-based settings are less inhibited by social niceties and quicker to resort to extreme language and invective—"flaming" is the commonly used term among cybernauts, a compelling image of communication as hand-to-hand combat with flamethrowers. Computer-mediated communication is good for sharing information, gathering opinions, and debating alternatives, but building trust and goodwill is not easy in cyberspace. John Seeley Brown and Paul Duguid point out that "interactions over the Net, financial or social, will be as secure not as its digital encryption, which is a relatively cheap fix, but as the infrastructure—social as well as technical—encompassing that interaction."[97]

For these reasons, Nohria and Eccles suggest, widespread use of computer-mediated communication will actually require *more frequent* face-to-face encounters: "an extensive, deep, robust social infrastructure of relationships must exist so that those using the electronic media will truly understand what others are communicating to them." Experience in the Blacksburg, Virginia, electronic community network suggests that "when you overlay an electronic community directly on top of a physical community, that creates a very powerful social pressure to be civil. If you're going to yell at somebody on the Net, or flame them out, you may run into them at the grocery store, and they may turn out to be your neighbor."[98] In other words, social capital may turn out to be a *prerequisite for*, rather than a *consequence of*, effective computer-mediated communication.

All these problems are less serious in dealing with clear, practical issues, but more serious in situations of uncertainty and ambiguity. If computer-mediated communication is nested within an ongoing face-to-face relationship, the complications are much reduced. Arranging to meet your spouse at the restaurant might be easily handled via computer-mediated communication, but wrangling with a new neighbor about her loud parties would not. The archetypal interaction with a new pal on the Internet lacks precisely the social embeddedness that seems essential to overcome the lack of social cues within the medium itself. Face-to-face networks tend to be dense and bounded, whereas computer-mediated communication networks tend to be sparse and unbounded. Anonymity and fluidity in the virtual world encourage "easy in, easy out," "drive-by" relationships. That very casualness is the appeal of computer-mediated communication for some denizens of cyberspace, but it discourages the creation of social capital. If entry and exit are too easy, commitment, trustworthiness, and reciprocity will not develop.[99]

Video and audio enhancements of computer-mediated communication may in time reduce these difficulties, but that is unlikely to happen soon. The "bandwidth" requirements (communications capacity) necessary for even poor-quality video are so high that it is unlikely to be commonly and cheaply available for at least a decade or more. Moreover, some experimental evidence suggests that the negative effects of computer-mediated communication—depersonalization, psychological distance, weak social cues, and so on—are reduced but not eliminated even by high-quality video.[100] The pace and breadth of technological change make predictions about the effects of computer-mediated communication on social exchange risky, but this second obstacle to community building in cyberspace looks even more forbidding than the digital divide.

The third obstacle goes by the evocative label of "cyberbalkanization."[101] The Internet enables us to confine our communication to people who share precisely our interests—not just other BMW owners, but owners of BMW 2002s and perhaps even owners of turbocharged 1973 2002s, regardless of where they live and what other interests they and we have. That powerful specialization is one of the medium's great attractions, but also one of its subtler threats to bridging social capital. A comment about Thunderbirds in a BMW chat group risks being flamed as "off topic." Imagine, by contrast, the guffaws if a member of a bowling team or a Sunday school class tried to rule out a casual conversation gambit as off-topic.

Real-world interactions often force us to deal with diversity, whereas the virtual world may be more homogeneous, not in demographic terms, but in terms of interest and outlook. Place-based communities may be supplanted by interest-based communities. As communications specialist Stephen Doheny-Farina, a thoughtful and sympathetic commentator on the prospects for cyber-community, observes:

> In physical communities we are forced to live with people who may differ from us in many ways. But virtual communities offer us the opportunity to construct utopian collectivities—communities of interest, education, tastes, beliefs, and skills. In cyberspace we can remake the world out of an unsettled landscape.[102]

Interaction in cyberspace is typically single stranded. Members of my e-group on nineteenth-century American history are connected to me only in terms of *that* topic, unlike my neighbor, who may also meet me at the supermarket, in church, or on the ball field. We cannot be sure, of course, how Internet communities will evolve, but if virtual communities do turn out to be more single stranded than real-world communities, that will probably increase cyberbalkanization.

Local heterogeneity may give way to more focused virtual homogeneity as communities coalesce across space. Internet technology allows and encourages infrared astronomers, oenophiles, Trekkies, and white supremacists to narrow their circle to like-minded intimates. New "filtering" technologies that automate the screening of "irrelevant" messages make the problem worse. Serendipitous connections become less likely as increased communication narrows our tastes and interests—knowing and caring more and more about less and less. This tendency may increase productivity in a narrow sense, while decreasing social cohesion.

On the other hand, we should not romanticize the heterogeneity of the real-world communities in which we now live. "Birds of a feather flock together" is a folk adage that reminds us that tendencies toward community homogeneity long predate the Internet. Whether the *possibility* of even more narrowly focused communities in cyberspace will turn into reality will depend in large part on how the "virtual" facet of our lives fits into our broader social reality, as well as on our fundamental values. Moreover, as computer scientist Paul Resnick has pointed out, perhaps what will evolve are neither all-encompassing "cybercommunities," nor watertight "cyberghettos," but multiple "cyberclubs" with partially overlapping memberships. In this sort of world, weak ties that bridge among distinct groups might create an interwoven community of communities.[103]

The final potential obstacle is more conjectural and yet more ominous: Will the Internet in practice turn out to be a niftier telephone or a niftier television? In other words, will the Internet become predominantly a means of active, social communication or a means of passive, private entertainment? Will computer-mediated communication "crowd out" face-to-face ties? It is, in this domain especially, much too early to know. Very preliminary evidence suggests, hopefully, that time on the Internet may displace time in front of the tube: one survey in 1999 found that among Internet users, 42 percent said they watched less TV as a result, compared with only 19 percent who said they read fewer magazines and 16 percent who said they read fewer newspapers. On the other hand, an early experimental study found that extensive Internet usage seemed to cause greater social isolation and even depression.[104] Amid these scattered straws in the wind, a final caution: The commercial incentives that currently govern Internet development seem destined to emphasize individualized entertainment and commerce rather than community engagement. If more community-friendly technology is to be developed, the incentive may need to come from outside the marketplace.

Having explored both optimistic and pessimistic scenarios, what can we conclude about the probable effects of telecommunications on social connectedness and civic engagement? The history of the telephone reminds us that both utopianism and jeremiads are very likely misplaced. Moreover, it is a fundamental mistake to suppose that the question before us is computer-mediated communication *versus* face-to-face interaction. Both the history of the telephone and the early evidence on Internet usage strongly suggest that computer-mediated communication will turn out to *complement*, not *replace*, face-to-face communities.

In a particularly striking parallel to the use of the telephone, a careful study by sociologist Barry Wellman and his colleagues of the use of computer-mediated communication by research scholars found that

> although the Internet helps scholars to maintain ties over great distances, physical proximity still matters. Those scholars who see each other often or work nearer to each other email each other more often. Frequent contact on the Internet is a complement to frequent face-to-face contact, not a substitute for it.[105]

This finding is wholly consistent with the informed prediction by MIT researcher Dertouzos, an enthusiastic champion of computer-mediated communication: "[T]hough some unimportant business relationships and casual social relationships will be established and maintained on a purely virtual basis, physical proximity will be needed to cement and reinforce the more important professional and social encounters." "Dan Huttenlocher, professor of computer science at Cornell, argues that digital technologies are adept at maintaining communities already formed. They are less good at making them."[106] If the primary effect of computer-mediated communication is to reinforce rather than replace face-to-face relationships, however, then the Net is unlikely in itself to reverse the deterioration of our social capital.

Finally, we must not assume that the future of the Internet will be determined by some mindless, external "technological imperative." The most important question is not what the Internet will do to us, but what we will do with it. How can we use the enormous potential of computer-mediated communication to make our investments in social capital more productive? How can we harness this promising technology for thickening community ties? How can we develop the technology to enhance social presence, social feedback, and social cues? How can we use the prospect of fast, cheap communication to enhance the now fraying fabric of our real communities, instead of being seduced by the mirage of some otherworldly "virtual community"? In short, how can we make the Internet a part of the solution? As the new century opens, some of the most exciting work in the field of computer-mediated communication is addressing precisely these issues. In the final chapter of this book, I shall say a bit about some of those prospects. For the moment, I conclude that the Internet will not *automatically* offset the decline in more conventional forms of social capital, but that it has that potential. In fact, it is hard to imagine solving our contemporary civic dilemmas without computer-mediated communication.

The evidence on small groups, social movements, and telecommunications is more ambiguous than the evidence in earlier chapters. All things considered, the clearest exceptions to the trend toward civic disengagement are 1) the rise in youth volunteering discussed in chapter 7; 2) the growth of telecommunication, particularly the Internet; 3) the vigorous growth of grassroots activity among evangelical conservatives; and 4) the increase in self-help support groups. These diverse countercurrents are a valuable reminder that society evolves in multiple ways simultaneously. These exceptions to the generally depressing story I have recounted alert us to a heartening potential for civic renewal. Even so, these developments hardly outweigh the many other ways in which most Americans are less connected to our communities than we were two or three decades ago. Before exploring possible avenues for reform, we need to understand the origins of that ebb tide. What can explain the reversal in recent decades of the civic-minded trends that characterized the first two-thirds of the twentieth century? We turn to that conundrum in the next section of this book.

SECTION THREE

Why?

CHAPTER 10

Introduction

SOMETHING IMPORTANT HAPPENED to social bonds and civic engagement in America over the last third of the twentieth century. Before exploring why, let's summarize what we have learned.

During the first two-thirds of the century Americans took a more and more active role in the social and political life of their communities—in churches and union halls, in bowling alleys and clubrooms, around committee tables and card tables and dinner tables. Year by year we gave more generously to charity, we pitched in more often on community projects, and (insofar as we can still find reliable evidence) we behaved in an increasingly trustworthy way toward one another. Then, mysteriously and more or less simultaneously, we began to do all those things less often.

We are still more civically engaged than citizens in many other countries, but compared with our own recent past, we are less connected. We remain interested and critical spectators of the public scene. We kibitz, but we don't play. We maintain a facade of formal affiliation, but we rarely show up. We have invented new ways of expressing our demands that demand less of us. We are less likely to turn out for collective deliberation—whether in the voting booth or the meeting hall—and when we do, we find that discouragingly few of our friends and neighbors have shown up. We are less generous with our money and (with the important exception of senior citizens) with our time, and we are less likely to give strangers the benefit of the doubt. They, of course, return the favor.

Not all social networks have atrophied. Thin, single-stranded, surf-by interactions are gradually replacing dense, multistranded, well-exercised bonds. More of our social connectedness is one shot, special purpose, and self oriented. As sociologist Morris Janowitz foresaw several decades ago, we have developed "communities of limited liability," or what sociologists Claude Fischer, Robert Jackson, and their colleagues describe more hopefully as "personal communities."[1] Large groups with local chapters, long histories, multiple objectives, and diverse constituencies are being replaced by more evanescent, single-purpose organizations, smaller groups that "reflect the fluidity of our lives by allowing us to bond easily but to break our attachments with equivalent ease."[2] Grassroots groups that once brought us face-to-face with our neighbors, the agreeable and disagreeable alike, are overshadowed by the vertiginous rise of staff-led interest groups purpose built to represent our narrower selves. Place-based social capital is being supplanted by function-based social capital. We are withdrawing from those networks of reciprocity that once constituted our communities.

Most puzzling, unlike the declines of community that earlier Jeremiahs thought they discerned, this erosion of social capital did not begin when the Pilgrims first stepped ashore. On the contrary, within living memory the tide was strongly moving in the opposite direction—toward more active social and political participation, more fulsome generosity and trustfulness, greater connectedness. Whatever one's detailed assessment of the reversal of tide in the last two or three decades, its very suddenness, thoroughness, and unexpectedness constitute an intriguing mystery. Why, beginning in the 1960s and 1970s and accelerating in the 1980s and 1990s, did the fabric of American community life begin to unravel? Before we can consider reweaving the fabric, we need to address this mystery.

It is, if I am right, a puzzle of some importance to the future of American democracy. It is a classic brainteaser, with a corpus delicti, a crime scene strewn with clues, and many potential suspects. As in all good detective stories, however, some plausible miscreants turn out to have impeccable alibis, and some important clues hint at portentous developments that occurred long before the curtain rose. Moreover, as in Agatha Christie's *Murder on the Orient Express*, this crime turns out to have had more than one perpetrator, so that we shall need to sort out ringleaders from accomplices. Finally, I need to make clear at the outset that I have not entirely solved the mystery, so I invite your help in sifting clues.

WHEN SEEKING TO SOLVE a serial crime (or, for that matter, to understand a public health epidemic) investigators typically look for common features among the victims—were they all blondes, or seafood aficionados, or left-handed? Similarly, social scientists, faced with a trend like declining social participation, look for concentrations of effects. If the drop in participation is greatest among suburbanites, that might suggest one explanation, whereas if it is greatest among (say) working women, another interpretation becomes more plausible. I too shall follow that broad strategy, looking to see whether the declines in civic engagement are correlated across time and space with certain social characteristics. We must recognize at the outset, however, two weaknesses in this strategy.

First, effects triggered by social change often spread well beyond the point of initial contact. If, for example, the dinner party has been undermined by the movement of women into the paid labor force—and we shall find some evidence for that view—such a development might well inhibit dinner parties not only among women who work outside the home, but also among stay-at-homes, tired of doing all the inviting. In that event, work and dinner parties might be only loosely correlated across individuals, even though (by hypothesis) the former had undermined the latter. Similarly, if commuting or TV triggered the collapse of fraternal clubs, the effects would eventually be visible among noncommuters and non–TV watchers, since once the club started downhill, even those otherwise ready to show up wouldn't. We saw in earlier chapters evidence of just such "synergistic" effects, such as the more rapid decline in *collective* activities (like public meetings) than in *individual* activities (like letters to the editor). Unfortunately for our detective strategy, synergistic effects (rather like an epidemic that has spread beyond its initial carrier) thwart unequivocal verdicts.[3]

Second, in our routine screening of the usual suspects, *none* stands out in the initial lineup. Civic disengagement appears to be an equal opportunity affliction. The sharp, steady declines in club meetings, visits with friends, committee service, church attendance, philanthropic generosity, card games, and electoral turnout have hit virtually all sectors of American society over the last several decades and in roughly equal measure. The trends are down among women and down among men, down on the two coasts and down in the heartland, down among renters and down among homeowners, down in black ghettos and down in white suburbs, down in small towns and down in metropolitan areas, down among Protestants and down among Catholics, down among the affluent and down among the impoverished, down among singles and down among married couples, down among unskilled laborers and down among small-business people and down among top managers, down among Republicans and down among Democrats and down among independents, down among parents and down among the childless, down among full-time workers and down among homemakers.[4]

To be sure, the *levels* of civic engagement differ across these categories, as we have already noted—more informal socializing among women, more civic involvement among the well-to-do, less social trust among African Americans, less voting among independents, more altruism in small towns, more church attendance among parents, and so on. But the *trends* in civic engagement are very similar. For example, on average between 1974 and 1994, 18 percent of whites reported having attended a public meeting on local affairs in the previous year, as compared with only 13 percent of blacks, but each race's rate of attendance was cut in half over those two decades. More people take part in local politics in rural Vermont in 1999 than in metropolitan Boston, but *fewer* people take part in local politics in rural Vermont in 1999 than did in 1959. In short, with respect to *change* in civic engagement, we do not find any readily identifiable "hot spots" on the demographic map of this anticivic epidemic that might provide easy clues as to its origins.

A plausible place to begin our inquiry, for example, might be with education. Education is one of the most important predictors—usually, in fact, *the* most important predictor—of many forms of social participation—from voting to associational membership, to chairing a local committee to hosting a dinner party to giving blood. To be sure, education has little effect on *schmoozing*—that is, informal social connectedness, like visiting friends or family dining—or on church attendance, although education *is* positively correlated with membership in church-related groups. On the other hand, education is an especially powerful predictor of participation in public, formally organized activities. Having four additional years of education (say, going to college) is associated with 30 percent more interest in politics, 40 percent more club attendance, and 45 percent more volunteering. College graduates are more than twice as likely to serve as an officer or committee member of a local organization, to attend a public meeting, to write Congress, or to attend a political rally. The same basic pattern applies to both men and women and to all races and generations. Education, in short, is an extremely powerful predictor of civic engagement.[5]

Why does education have such a massive effect on social connectedness?[6] Education is in part a proxy for privilege—for social class and economic advantage—but when income, social status, and education are used together to predict various forms of civic engagement, education stands out as the primary influence. Educational attainment may conceivably be a marker of unusual ambition or energy or some other innate trait that also encourages civic involvement. Finally, educated people are more engaged with the community at least in part because of the skills, resources, and inclinations that were imparted to them at home and in school. In any event, whether across individuals or across states and localities or (during the first two-thirds of the twentieth century) across time, more education means more participation.

Although it is widely recognized that Americans today are better educated than our parents and grandparents, it is less often appreciated how massively and rapidly this trend transformed the educational composition of the adult population. As recently as 1960, only 41 percent of American adults had graduated from high school; in 1998, 82 percent had. In 1960, only 8 percent of American adults had a college degree; in 1998, 24 percent had. Between 1972 and 1998 the proportion of all adults with fewer than twelve years of education was cut in half, falling from 40 percent to 18 percent, while the proportion with more than twelve years nearly doubled, rising from 28 percent to 50 percent, as the generation of Americans educated around the dawn of the twentieth century (most of whom did not finish high school) passed from the scene and were replaced by the baby boomers and their successors (most of whom attended college).[7]

Thus education boosts civic engagement sharply, and educational levels have risen massively. Unfortunately, these two plain facts only deepen our central mystery. If anything, the growth in education should have increased civic engagement. Thus this first investigative foray leaves us more mystified than before. Whatever forces lie behind the slump in civic engagement and social capital, those forces have affected all levels in American society. Social capital has eroded among the one in every twelve Americans who have enjoyed the advantages of graduate study, it has eroded among the one in every eight Americans who did not even make it into high school, and it has eroded among all strata in between. The mysterious disengagement of the last third of a century has afflicted all echelons of our society.

Many possible answers have been suggested for this puzzle:

- Busyness and time pressure
- Economic hard times
- The movement of women into the paid labor force and the stresses of two-career families
- Residential mobility
- Suburbanization and sprawl
- Television, the electronic revolution, and other technological changes
- Changes in the structure and scale of the American economy, such as the rise of chain stores, branch firms, and the service sector, or globalization
- Disruption of marriage and family ties
- Growth of the welfare state
- The civil rights revolution
- The sixties (most of which actually happened in the seventies), including
  - Vietnam, Watergate, and disillusion with public life
  - The cultural revolt against authority (sex, drugs, and so on)

Most respectable mystery writers would hesitate to tally up this many plausible suspects, no matter how energetic their detective. I am not in a position to address all these theories—certainly not in any definitive form—but we must begin to winnow the list. It is tempting to assume that one big effect (like civic disengagement) has one big cause (like two-career families or materialism or

TV), but that is usually a fallacy. A social trend as pervasive as the one we are investigating probably has multiple causes, so our task is to assess the relative importance of such factors.

A solution, even a partial one, to our mystery must pass several tests.

- *Is the proposed explanatory factor correlated with social capital and civic engagement?* If not, it is difficult to see why that factor should even be placed in the lineup. For example, many women have entered the paid labor force during the period in question, but if working women turned out to be no less engaged in community life than housewives, it would be harder to attribute the downturn in community organizations to the rise of two-career families.[8]

- *Is the correlation spurious?* If parents, for example, were more likely to be joiners than childless people, that might be an important clue. However, if the correlation between parental status and civic engagement turned out to be entirely due to the effects of age, for example, we would have to remove the declining birth rate from our list of suspects.

- *Is the proposed explanatory factor changing in the relevant way?* Suppose, for instance, that people who often move have shallower community roots. That could be an important part of the answer to our mystery, but *only if* residential mobility itself had risen during this period. (Failure to clear this hurdle is what led us to dismiss any indictment against education.)

- *Is it possible that the proposed explanatory factor is the* result *of civic disengagement, not the* cause? For example, even if newspaper readership were closely correlated with civic engagement across individuals and across time, we would need to weigh the possibility that reduced newspaper circulation is the result (not the cause) of disengagement.

Against that set of benchmarks, the next five chapters examine potential influences on the creation and destruction of social capital.

CHAPTER **11**

Pressures of Time and Money

THE MOST OBVIOUS SUSPECT behind our tendency to drop out of community affairs is pervasive busyness. This is everybody's favorite explanation for social disengagement. "I don't have enough time" is the reason that Americans cite most often for our failure to participate. "Too busy" is by far the most common explanation we offer for not volunteering. We certainly *feel* busier now than Americans did a generation ago: the proportion of us who say we "always feel rushed" jumped by more than half between the mid-1960s and the mid-1990s. Throughout the 1980s and 1990s more and more of us reported that we "work very hard most of the time" and that we frequently "stayed late at work." The groups that feel most harried are full-time workers (especially those with advanced education), women, people aged twenty-five to fifty-four, and parents of younger children, especially single parents.[1] These patterns are hardly surprising, yet these same groups have historically been especially active in community life. Perhaps the villain of the piece is simply overwork.

Related potential causes of disengagement are endemic economic pressures, job insecurity, and declining real wages, especially among the lower two-thirds of the income distribution. The economic climate in America from the middle 1970s to the middle 1990s was one of increasing anxiety. So perhaps the combined pressures of time and money are (just as we tell pollsters) the main explanation for our civic disengagement. However, finding sufficient evidence to convict (or acquit) these suspects—that we have less time for friends, neighbors, and civic affairs simply because we're running harder than ever to keep up economically—turns out to be unexpectedly difficult. Because of crosscurrents in the relevant evidence, I ask the reader to withhold final judgment on this interpretation until the end of this chapter.

First, it is not at all clear whether, in the aggregate, Americans are working harder than our parents did at the height of the civic boom in the 1960s. Economists Ellen McGrattan and Richard Rogerson report that in the aggregate, "the number of weekly hours of market work per person in the United States has been roughly constant since World War II," a half century during which (as we have seen) civic engagement first ballooned and then shriveled.[2] Beneath this aggregate stability there have been important shifts in the distribution of paid work, from men to women and from older to younger people. Men as a whole spent fewer hours in paid work in the 1990s than in the 1950s. In particular, men over fifty-five have far more leisure time today, mainly because of early retirement, some of it involuntary. Clearly women work more hours outside the home now than thirty years ago, a development we shall address in more detail later. Whether *men and women who are in the labor force* are working longer now than a generation ago is a matter of debate among economists, but probably the best guess is that there has not been much change. Time diary studies suggest that nonwork time burdens have been reduced, including housework and (since we have fewer children today) child care. In fact, John Robinson and Geoffrey Godbey report a 6.2-hour-per-week *gain* in free time between 1965 and 1995 for the average American—4.5 hours for women and 7.9 hours for men—due mostly to less housework and earlier retirement.[3]

The Robinson-Godbey claim that Americans have *more* leisure time now than several decades ago is contested by other observers, but there is surely no evidence that we have *less*. Harris polls have found that the median time that Americans say we have "available to relax, watch TV, take part in sports or hobbies, go swimming or skiing, go to the movies, theater, concerts, or other forms of entertainment, get together with friends, and so forth" has remained rock-steady at nineteen to twenty hours per week over the last quarter century. (Time diary studies suggest that we actually have up to twice that much free time.) Despite somewhat conflicting evidence, it seems reasonable to conclude that *the last three decades have seen no general decline in free time in America that might explain civic disengagement.*[4] In fact, there may well have been a significant net increase in leisure time over these years. Before releasing the suspect, however, we need to identify specifically how the gains and losses in free time have been distributed.

First, much of the new "free time" has come in forms that are not easily convertible to civic engagement. Some of it has come in a thousand scattered moments amid a harried schedule and some of it in large, involuntary chunks to older men forced to take early retirement. Second, all sides in the debates about work hours agree that less educated Americans have gained free time, whereas their college-educated counterparts, for the most part, have lost it. The hours-per-week edge of college-educated Americans over high school dropouts lengthened from six hours in 1969 to thirteen hours in 1998. As Robinson and Godbey note, the "working class" has less work and the "leisure class" less leisure. Third, dual-career families are more common and are spending more time at work than they used to: married couples average fourteen more hours at work each week in 1998 than 1969. In other words, for that segment of society—well-educated middle-class parents—whose energies historically provided a disproportionate share of the community infrastructure, the time bind is real. Perhaps we've witnessed a redistribution of free time from people (mostly younger, more educated women) who would have invested it in community engagement toward people (mostly older, less educated men) more likely to consume it privately.[5]

Finally, even if all of us have enough free hours to invest in community activities, my free hours are not necessarily *the same hours* as yours, so coordinating schedules has become more burdensome. That interpretation is consistent with the fact noted earlier that *collective* forms of civic engagement have declined more rapidly than *individual* forms.[6]

Two additional streams of evidence, however, are not entirely consistent with this "hassle" theory of civic disengagement. First, heavy time demands are *not* associated with lessened involvement in civic life, even among people with identical levels of education and income. Quite the reverse: Employed people are *more* active civically and socially than those outside the paid labor force, and among workers, longer hours are often linked to *more* civic engagement, not less. People who report the heaviest time pressure are *more* likely, not less likely, to participate in community projects, to attend church and club meetings, to follow politics, to spend time visiting friends, to entertain at home, and the like.[7] Contrary to standard economic theory, one study has found that people with longer paid work hours are actually more likely to volunteer, and people with two jobs are likelier to volunteer than people with only one. In an exhaustive study of the determinants of participation, political scientist Sidney Verba and his colleagues found that the amount of free time a person has seems to have little or no effect on whether he or she becomes civically active or not. Just about the only social activity that busy, harried people engage in *less* than other people is dinner with their families.[8]

The positive correlation between civic activity and work hours certainly does not mean that working longer *causes* greater civic involvement. We all know that the way to get something done is to give it to a busy person. One reason that some of us are harried is precisely that we are civically engaged. Neither fact implies that if we became even busier (by working much longer hours, for example), we would also become more involved in community life, since at some point the twenty-four-hour constraint would become binding. On the other hand, evidence shows that hard work does not *prevent* civic engagement. Time diary studies show that, unsurprisingly, people who spend more time at work do feel more rushed, and these harried souls do spend less time eating, sleeping, reading books, engaging in hobbies, and just doing nothing. Compared with the rest of the population, they also spend a lot less time watching television—almost 30 percent less. However, they do *not* spend less time on organizational activity.[9] In short, those who are always on the run forgo *ER* before the Red Cross and *Friends* before friends. Busy people tend to forgo the one activity—TV watching—that is (as we shall see in chapter 13) most lethal to community involvement.

A second reason for doubting that the hecticness of contemporary life explains much of the decline in civic involvement is that the civic decline is virtually as steep among those who feel *least* harried as among those who feel *most* harried. The falloff in civic and social involvement is perfectly mirrored among full-time workers, among part-time workers, and among those outside the paid labor force. Even among the one-third of the American population who report that they have "a lot of spare time," church attendance has dropped by 15–20 percent, clubgoing by 30 percent, and entertaining friends by 35 percent over the last two decades.[10] If people are dropping out of community life, long hours and hectic schedules cannot be the sole reason. Although these may be contributing factors, especially for the sorts of people who have historically borne a disproportionate share of the organizational burden in America, they are certainly not the sole cause.

IF TIME PRESSURE is not the main culprit we seek, how about financial pressures? Several important clues point in this direction. First, financial anxieties clearly rose over the last quarter of the twentieth century. In the early 1970s inflation triggered by the Vietnam War plus two massive global oil shocks brought down the curtain on the ebullient economic prosperity of the 1950s and 1960s. In biblical fashion, two fat and happy decades were followed by two lean and nervous decades. Throughout the 1970s and 1980s financial anxieties mounted among Americans of all walks of life, and even the recovery of the 1990s did not erase the pervasive uneasiness left by those two decades. In early 1975, at the bottom of the most serious recession in forty years, 74 percent of Americans still said that "our family income is high enough to satisfy nearly all our important desires," but by 1999, despite eight uninterrupted years of growth, that very same barometer of economic satisfaction had fallen to 61 percent.[11] In the midst of the boom of the 1990s, Americans remained more troubled and skittish economically than we had been thirty years earlier, perhaps because our material aspirations had expanded in the meantime.[12]

It is also true that financial worries and economic troubles have a profoundly depressing effect on social involvement, both formal and informal. As we saw in chapter 3, the Great Depression triggered the only significant interruption in the rising tide of civic participation and social connectedness during the first two-thirds of the twentieth century. Contrary to expectations that unemployment would radicalize its victims, social psychologists found that the jobless became passive and withdrawn, socially as well as politically.[13] As my economic situation becomes more dire, my focus narrows to personal and family survival. People with lower incomes and those who feel financially strapped are much less engaged in all forms of social and community life than those who are better off. For example, even comparing people with identical levels of income and education, men and women in the financially most worried third of the population attend only two-thirds as many club meetings as people in the least worried third of the population.[14]

Financial anxiety is associated not merely with less frequent moviegoing—perhaps the natural consequence of a thinner wallet—but also with less time spent with friends, less card playing, less home entertaining, less frequent attendance at church, less volunteering, and less interest in politics. Even social activities with little or no financial cost are inhibited by financial distress. In fact, the only leisure activity positively correlated with financial anxiety is watching TV. Furthermore, when we combine financial worries, income, and education to predict various forms of civic engagement and social connectedness, income itself becomes insignificant. In other words, it is not low income per se, but the financial worry that it engenders, that inhibits social engagement. Even among the well-to-do, a sense of financial vulnerability dampens community involvement.

This bill of particulars is powerful.[15] Economic hard times lower our incomes, raise our debt levels, and make our jobs more precarious (and perhaps more demanding). Stress rises, and civic engagement falls. The case seems open and shut. However, the defense has some strong counterevidence. First, the decline in civic engagement in its various forms appears to have begun before the economic troubles of the 1970s, and the decline continued unabated during the booms of the mid-1980s and late 1990s. The economy went up and down and up and down, but social capital only went down.

Second, the declines in engagement and connectedness are virtually as great among the affluent segments of the American public as among the poor and middle-income wage earners, with very little sign that disengagement is concentrated among those who have borne the brunt of the economic distress of the last two decades. For example, among the third of the U.S. population *least* troubled by financial worries, attendance at club meetings fell from thirteen times per year to six times per year, while among the *most* troubled financially, the decline was from nine times per year to four times per year. Even among the fortunate one in every eighteen Americans who avows that his family "definitely" has "more to spend on extras than most of our neighbors do," the pace of entertaining at home fell from seventeen times per year in 1975 to ten times per year in 1999, while their annual club attendance was falling from thirteen to five.[16] Economic good fortune has not guaranteed continued civic engagement.

Some observers of trends in social capital argue that its decline in the last twenty years has been concentrated among the more "marginalized" sectors of the population.[17] Others, by contrast, blame civic disengagement on an AWOL, self-centered, upper-middle-class elite who have abandoned their traditional civic responsibilities.[18] The balance of evidence, in my opinion, speaks against both those views, for the central fact is that by virtually all measures of civic disengagement and all measures of socioeconomic status, the trends are very similar at all levels. Examined with a microscope, the dropouts may be faintly greater among the financially distressed, but the differences are slight and inconsistent.[19] Certainly the comfortable are not dropping out *more* rapidly than the afflicted, but neither are they dropping out much *less*.

Holding both real income and financial satisfaction constant (a trick done more easily in the statistical world than in the real world) does little to attenuate the fall in civic engagement and social connectedness. At most, the spread of financial anxiety might account for 5–10 percent of the total decline in church attendance, club membership, home entertaining, and the like.[20] Neither objective nor subjective economic well-being has inoculated Americans against the virus of civic disengagement. Pressures of time and money are supporting actors in our mystery story, but neither is easily cast in the lead.

THE MOVEMENT OF WOMEN out of the home into the paid labor force is the most portentous social change of the last half century. The fraction of women who work outside the home doubled from fewer than one in three in the 1950s to nearly two in three in the 1990s. On average, women are spending roughly one more hour per day in paid labor in the 1990s than in the 1960s, and since there are only twenty-four hours in a day, something had to give. Most, if not all, of that additional time at work was recouped by cutting back on household chores and child care, but it seems plausible that the cutbacks also affected community involvement.[21] Most of our mothers were homemakers, and most of them invested heavily in social-capital formation—a jargony way of referring to countless unpaid hours in church suppers, PTA meetings, neighborhood kaffeeklatsches, and visits to friends and relatives. However welcome and overdue the feminist revolution may be, it is hard to believe that it has had no impact on social connectedness. Could this be the primary reason for the decline of social capital over the last generation?

Getting a job outside the home has two opposing effects on community involvement—it *increases opportunity* for making new connections and getting involved, while at the same time it *decreases time* available for exploring those opportunities.

Generally speaking, people active in the workforce are more involved in community life. The role of housewife is often socially isolating. Homemakers belong to different types of groups from those working women belong to (more PTAs, for example, and fewer professional associations), but in the aggregate working women belong to slightly more voluntary associations. Earlier in the twentieth century, men belonged to more civic and professional organizations and took a more active role in public life, but that sex difference has faded as women have moved into the paid workforce.[22]

The "public involvement" gap has narrowed downward over the last several decades, as activities like working for a political party or serving as a local organizational leader have faded more rapidly among men than among women, some of whom had only recently entered work-related circles of influence. While the number of men running for public office fell by about one-quarter between 1974 and 1994, the number of female candidates actually rose over these years, sharply narrowing the gender gap, at least at the local level.[23] Similarly, even though membership in the bar association has lagged behind the growth of lawyers, more women lawyers has meant relatively more women active in the bar association. In this sense, the movement of women toward professional equality has tended to increase their civic involvement.

In one specific and expanding category—single moms—the evidence is quite strong that work outside the home has a positive effect on virtually all forms of civic engagement, from club membership to political interest.[24] With kids to care for and without a spouse to help, these women are often isolated socially except for their connections at work. In short, work outside the home means exposure to a wider array of social and community networks. Insofar as this factor is dominant, the movement of women into the paid labor force certainly did not contribute to the national decline of social capital and civic engagement and may actually have muted that decline.

On the other hand, women have traditionally invested more time than men in social connectedness. Although men belong to more organizations, women spend more time in them. Women also spend more time than men in informal conversation and other forms of *schmoozing*, and they participate more in religious activities.[25] Precisely because women's traditional investments in social capital were so time-intensive, their rate of investment has been reduced by their movement into the paid labor force.

Comparing two women of the same age, education, financial security, and marital and parental status, full-time employment appears to cut home entertaining by roughly 10 percent, club and church attendance by roughly 15 percent, informal visiting with friends by 25 percent, and volunteering by more than 50 percent. Moreover, husbands of women who work full-time are, like their wives, less likely to attend church, volunteer, and entertain at home. Conversely, other things being equal, women who work full-time (and their husbands) spend more time on personal relaxation, such as videos, movies,

TV, and shopping—in short, zoning out. When both members of a couple have worked in high-stress jobs all day, relaxation, not frenetic civic engagement, is understandably a preferred leisure activity. These sorts of evidence make it plausible to suppose that the movement of women into the paid labor force has been a significant contributor to the national decline in community involvement.[26]

In short, work outside the home, especially full-time work, is a double-edged sword with respect to civic engagement—more opportunity, but less time. In part because of these crosscurrents, some detailed evidence is hard to reconcile with the theory that women's liberation caused our civic crisis. For example, time diary data between 1965 and 1985 show that while the decline in actual organizational activity in recent years is concentrated among women, employed women are actually spending more time on organizations than before, while nonemployed women are spending less. Moreover, the time diary data suggest that the decline in *schmoozing* since 1965 has also been concentrated among nonemployed women. The decline in PTA membership and in club attendance actually has been greatest among "traditional moms"—that is, married women with kids at home and no paid employment.[27] These figures suggest that women who work full-time may have been more resistant to the slump than those who do not.

These patterns might be, at least in part, an optical illusion, because women who have chosen to enter the workforce doubtlessly differ in many respects from women who have chosen to stay home. Perhaps some forms of community involvement appear to be rising among working women and declining among housewives precisely because the sort of women who, in an earlier era, were most involved with their communities have been disproportionately likely to enter the workforce, thus simultaneously lowering the average level of civic engagement among the remaining homemakers and raising the average among women in the workplace. Obviously we have not been running a great national controlled experiment on the effects of work on women's civic engagement, in which women were randomly assigned to work or to stay home, so questions of self-selection and causality are difficult to resolve.

We can get further insight into the implications of employment for women's civic and social life if we consider simultaneously two dimensions of women's work life:

1. Amount of time spent in work outside the home.
2. Preference for employment outside the home.

The DDB Needham Life Style data permit us to measure these two dimensions simultaneously. First, all women in the survey are asked whether they are full-time employees, part-time employees, or full-time homemakers. Those who are employed either full- or part-time are then asked whether they work primarily for personal satisfaction or primarily for financial necessity.

Those who are full-time homemakers are asked whether they stay at home primarily for personal satisfaction or primarily to take care of children. Of course, in the real world such decisions are doubtless made for a mixture of all these motivations and others besides.[28] Nevertheless, as a crude first cut, this standard question distinguishes between women who are working (or not working) mainly because they *want* to and those who are working (or not working) mainly because they *have* to.

Figure 47 shows how women are distributed across these two dimensions. Column A represents women who are employed full-time primarily out of financial necessity; over the last two decades they have constituted on average 31 percent of all women. This average is somewhat misleading, however, since their numbers almost doubled from about 21 percent of all women in 1978 to 36 percent in 1999; the arrow on the column represents this trend. Column B represents women who are employed full-time primarily for personal satisfaction; they constitute 11 percent of the total sample, a figure that has not changed much over these two decades. In other words, of all women who work full-time, the fraction who say that they are doing so primarily out of financial necessity has risen from two-thirds to more than three-quarters. (Figure 48 summarizes this trend.) At least in these surveys, *virtually all the increase in full-time employment of American women over the last twenty years is attributable to financial pressures, not personal fulfillment.*[29]

Column C represents women who work part-time outside the home and

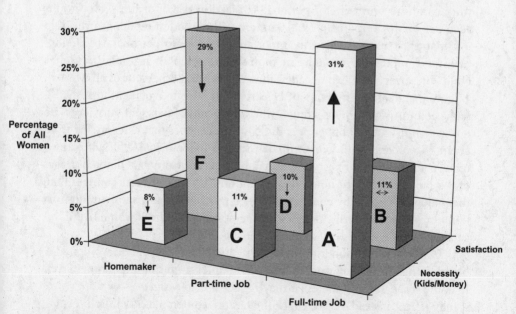

Figure 47: Working by Choice and by Necessity Among American Women, 1978–1999

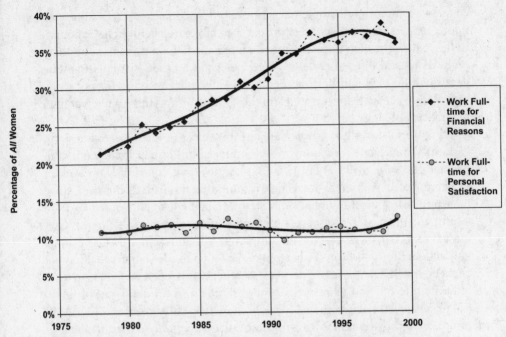

Figure 48: More Women Work Because They Must, 1978–1999

do so primarily for financial reasons, while column D represents those who work part-time primarily for personal satisfaction. Each of these two groups accounts for 10–11 percent of all women, with a modest tendency over time for financial reasons to gain in importance relative to personal satisfaction. Column E represents stay-at-home moms who say that their primary reason is child care; over these two decades, they represented 8 percent of all women, a figure that declined from about 11 percent in 1978 to 7 percent in 1999. Finally, column F represents women who for reasons of personal satisfaction do not work outside the home. Over the past two decades that category fell from about 37 percent of all women in 1978 to 23 percent in 1999. Not surprisingly, columns E and F disproportionately represent women at different stages of the life cycle. Stay-at-home moms (column E) are ten years younger than the national average. By contrast, the category of personally satisfied full-time homemakers (column F) includes a large number of retired women, and this category is ten years older than the national average.

One difficult conundrum in studying the effects of work on women's behavior is this: If working women turn out to differ from full-time homemakers in some respect, that difference may reflect the *consequences* of working, or it may reflect instead *self-selection*. If working women attend church less frequently than full-time homemakers, for example, is that because of the pressures of time and competing obligations, or is it because religiously devout women are less likely to work outside the home? Here the distinction made in figure 47 between women who are working (or not working) because they *want* to (columns F, D, and B) and those who are working (or not working) because they *have* to (columns E, C, and A) provides some useful analytic leverage.

If we compare column A with column B, we are comparing women all of whom are working full-time, but some (column A) by necessity and some (column B) by choice. That is, we are comparing women whose work circumstances are similar, but whose preferences differ. Similarly, if we compare column A with column F, we are comparing women who would all apparently prefer not to work outside the home, but some (column A) are employed by necessity, whereas others (column F) are contentedly remaining at home. That is, we are comparing women whose preferences are similar, but whose work circumstances differ. To be sure, life is more complicated than can be encompassed in any simple chart. Most women (like most men) have mixed and very complex feelings about both work and home, and the distinction between "personal satisfaction" and "necessity" is much too crude to capture the underlying motivations. I do not offer figure 47 as a comprehensive account of the complicated choices (some of them not actually "choices" in a full sense) that women must make in the real world. However, it does provide a useful template for considering now the implication of women's work for civic engagement.

Consider, first, the relationship between work and clubgoing. Women working full-time attend fewer club meetings than other women. Figure 49 illustrates in more detail how clubgoing varies with both the nature of a woman's employment and her motivations. For each category, the height of the column represents those women's relative frequency of attendance at club meetings. (Some standard of comparison is necessary, so arbitrarily we compare each category to the average frequency of clubgoing among all men, represented by the floor in figure 49. In order to concentrate our attention on the effects of work per se, our statistical analysis holds constant other factors that affect community involvement, including education, year of birth, year of survey, marital and parental status, financial worries, and community rootedness).[30] Thus women who work full-time out of financial necessity attend, on average, .7 more club meetings per year than the typical man. Women who are full-time homemakers by choice (back row of figure 49, far left), by contrast, attend 2.7 more club meetings per year than the average man, or 2 more meetings per year than their counterparts who are working full-time by necessity. (Since we have already controlled for both education and financial worries, we can be confident this difference does not simply reflect a social class discrepancy between the two groups.)

Several important conclusions can be drawn from figure 49. First, *all* the columns rise above the standard of comparison (the floor of the graph) that

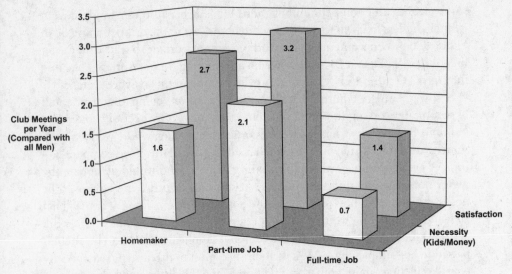

Figure 49: Working Full-Time Reduces Community Involvement

represents the level of involvement of the average man. Whether working full-time, part-time, or not at all outside the home, and whether by choice or necessity, women invest more time in associational life than the average man.

Second, full-time work significantly depresses club attendance, regardless of whether work is a choice or a necessity. (Graphically this is represented by the sharp falloff in the two right-hand columns.) Moreover, women whose work status represents a personal choice (whether at home full-time, in the workplace full-time, or some combination of the two) are more involved in organizational life than women in the same situation out of necessity. (Graphically this is represented by the greater height of the columns in the back row.) The least involvement is found among women who are working full-time not because they want to, but because they have to. Women who work full-time by necessity—the fastest-growing group of women and by now the largest—incur the steepest civic penalty. More and more women are—by necessity, not by choice—in precisely the category that most inhibits social connectedness.

Finally, figure 49 also shows that the greatest involvement is found among part-time workers, especially those for whom work is a choice, not a necessity. We can guess that these women are striving to balance conflicting obligations to family, community, and self *and* have a certain amount of maneuvering room in which to do so. At least from the point of view of civic engagement, part-time work seems like a "golden mean."[31]

These fundamental findings about club attendance turn out to apply to other modes of community involvement, both formal and informal, including church attendance, entertaining at home, visiting with friends, and volunteering. Other things being equal, women employed full-time attend church four fewer times a year, entertain at home one or two fewer times a year, spend about one-third less time visiting with friends, and volunteer about four fewer times per year than other women.[32] The fact that full-time work reduces community involvement among both women working by choice and those working by necessity suggests that the correlation is not primarily a result of self-selection. In fact, since as figure 48 showed, virtually all the increase in female employment over the last two decades of the twentieth century was by necessity, not by choice, self-selection must have played a minor role at best during this period.

Women working by choice are more involved with clubs, church, friends, home entertaining, and volunteering than are women who are working out of necessity. This fact, illustrated by the difference between the front and back columns on the far right of figure 49, is a rough measure of the degree of self-selection underlying the correlation between civic involvement and work. This evidence suggests that socially active women were somewhat more likely to choose to enter the workforce than their less civic-minded sisters, but that compared to the effect of work itself, the effect of self-selection is modest.

Women who must work full-time are the least likely to visit with friends, to entertain at home, or to volunteer, just as they are least involved in club life. Women who work part-time, especially those who do so by choice, volunteer more, entertain more, and visit more with friends than do full-time employees or full-time homemakers.[33] With only a very few exceptions, women in *all* categories are more involved than men in all these forms of community activity.

In short, full-time work inhibits a woman's social involvement, both formal and informal.[34] However, the degree to which a woman works by *choice* is also closely associated with community engagement. In fact, the greatest community involvement is found among women who are working part-time by choice. (Recall that we are here holding constant other features of the woman's circumstances, including her education, marital and parental status, and financial situation, so the civic advantage of part-time work is *not* due merely to the kind of women who are able to choose part-time work.) This striking fact suggests that *one practical way to increase community engagement in America would be to make it easier for women (and men too) to work part-time if they wished.*[35]

Several important qualifications must be added to our conclusions about women's work and civic engagement.

First, to avoid misunderstanding, I explicitly disclaim the view that working women are "to blame" for our civic disengagement. Obviously full-time employment reduces the time available for other activities. Although the mothers of the current generation of American adults were usually not part of the paid labor force, they engaged in many socially productive activities. As their daughters have assumed a greater share of work outside the home, one might have expected their sons to assume a greater share of other social and community responsibilities, but (as our evidence shows) that has not happened. The movement of women toward professional equality has released much creative energy and increased individual autonomy and has been a net plus for American society. The broader social ledger of costs and benefits, however, must include not merely the benefits of women's new roles, but also the costs of social and community activities collectively foregone.

Second, full-time employment has not inhibited all forms of organizational involvement. As we noted earlier, women's participation in the more public sorts of civic activities has been enhanced by full-time employment. The same is true for formal membership in many professional and service organizations.[36] In other words, to some extent, as women's place of work has moved outside the home into the public sphere, so too has the locus of their community engagement. For some working women the increase in *opportunity* for involvement in community life has outweighed the decrease in *time*, and they have swum against the society-wide current of community disengagement.

Third, and most important, neither the movement of women into the paid labor force nor the increase in financial distress discussed earlier can be the main reason for the basic decline in American civic engagement over the last two decades. In fact, based on the evidence now available, my best guess is that both factors together account for less than *one-tenth* of the total decline.[37] In short, *the emergence of two-career families over the last quarter of the twentieth century played a visible but quite modest role in the erosion of social capital and civic engagement.*

One way to see the limited potential of these explanations is to focus on the two social categories least affected by them—namely, unmarried men and married women without full-time employment who are financially comfortable. Bachelors and affluent housewives constitute only small fractions of the American population, but their testimony is important to our case, for they have been relatively shielded from the forces for civic disengagement we have been examining in this chapter, especially the movement of women into the workplace.

The *level* of social engagement is higher among affluent housewives than among other women—they spend more time visiting friends, entertaining at home, attending club meetings, and so on. So the long-term movement of women out of the category of "affluent housewife" into other social categories has tended to depress civic engagement. However, the *declines* in home entertaining, clubgoing, community projects, visiting with friends, and so forth are virtually as great among these women who have been least affected by the rise of two-career families or by the roughly simultaneous rise in financial distress as among other women. In fact, the dropout rate from public meetings, party work, local leadership, and other kinds of involvement has been almost as great among affluent housewives as among the rest of the population. Similarly, the decline in club meetings, visiting friends, working on community projects, serving as a local leader, signing petitions, and the like has been at least as great among bachelors as among the rest of Americans. None of this is consistent with the hypothesis that our national civic disengagement over the past several decades can be attributed primarily to the movement of women into the paid labor force.[38]

To sum up: The available evidence suggests that busyness, economic distress, and the pressures associated with two-career families are a modest part of the explanation for declining social connectedness. These pressures have targeted the kinds of people (especially highly educated women) who in the past bore a disproportionate share of the responsibility for community involvement, and in that sense this development has no doubt had synergistic effects that spread beyond those people themselves. With fewer educated, dynamic women with enough free time to organize civic activity, plan dinner parties, and the like, the rest of us, too, have gradually disengaged. At the same time, the evidence also suggests that neither time pressures nor financial distress nor the movement of women into the paid labor force is *the* primary cause of civic disengagement over the last two decades.[39] The central exculpatory fact is that civic engagement and social connectedness have diminished almost equally for both women and men, working or not, married or single, financially stressed or financially comfortable.

CHAPTER 12

Mobility and Sprawl

COMPARED WITH THE CITIZENS of most other countries, Americans have always lived a nomadic existence. Nearly one in five of us move each year and, having done so, are likely to pick up and move again. More than two in five of us expect to move in the next five years.[1] As a result, compared with other peoples, Americans have become accustomed to pitching camp quickly and making friends easily. From our frontier and immigrant past we have learned to plunge into new community institutions when we move.

Nevertheless, for people as for plants, frequent repotting disrupts root systems. It takes time for a mobile individual to put down new roots. As a result, residential stability is strongly associated with civic engagement. Recent arrivals in any community are less likely to vote, less likely to have supportive networks of friends and neighbors, less likely to belong to civic organizations. People who expect to move in the next five years are 20–25 percent less likely to attend church, attend club meetings, volunteer, or work on community projects than those who expect to stay put. Homeowners are much more rooted than renters, even holding other social and economic circumstances constant. Among homeowners, only one in four expects to move in the next five years, compared with two-thirds of renters. Because of their greater rootedness, homeowners are substantially more likely to be involved in community affairs than are renters.[2]

Just as frequent movers have weaker community ties, so too communities with higher rates of residential turnover are less well integrated. Mobile communities seem less friendly to their inhabitants than do more stable communities. Crime rates are higher, and school performance is lower, in high-mobility communities. In such communities, even longtime residents have fewer ties with their neighbors.[3] So mobility undermines civic engagement and community-based social capital.

Could rising mobility thus be the central villain of our mystery? The answer is unequivocal: No. Residential mobility can be entirely exonerated from any responsibility for our fading civic engagement, because mobility has not increased at all over the last fifty years. In fact, census records show that both long-distance and short-distance mobility have slightly *declined* over the last five decades.

During the 1950s, 20 percent of Americans changed residence each year, 7 percent moving to a different county or state. During the 1990s the comparable figures are 16 percent and 6 percent. Americans today are, if anything, slightly *more* rooted residentially than a generation ago. In 1968 (when civic engagement was near its peak) the average American adult had lived in the same locality for twenty-two years; three decades later that figure remained essentially unchanged. Although historical data on residential mobility are incomplete, residential mobility may never have been lower in our national history than it is at the close of the twentieth century. Homeownership also rose over the last few decades to set an all-time record high of 67 percent in 1999. Americans' expectations about the likelihood of moving over the next five years have been steady for at least the last quarter century.[4] If our verdicts on pressures of time and money had to be nuanced, the verdict on mobility is unequivocal: This theory is simply wrong.

But if moving itself has not eroded our social capital, have we perhaps moved to places that are less congenial to social connectedness? Now, as in the past, connectedness does differ by community type. Compared with other Americans, residents of the nation's largest metropolitan areas (*both* central cities *and* their suburbs) report 10–15 percent fewer group memberships, attend 10–15 percent fewer club meetings, attend church about 10–20 percent less frequently, and are 30–40 percent less likely to serve as officers or committee members of local organizations or to attend public meetings on local affairs. (Figure 50 and figure 51 illustrate these differences.) As we noted in chapter 7, residents of small towns and rural areas are more altruistic, honest, and trusting than other Americans. In fact, even among suburbs, smaller is better from a social capital point of view.[5] Getting involved in community affairs is more inviting—or abstention less attractive—when the scale of everyday life is smaller and more intimate.

Is this pattern perhaps spurious? Could it be that the *type* of people who congregate in the biggest metropolitan areas are somehow predisposed against civic engagement? To rule this out, we reexamined the evidence, simultaneously holding constant a wide range of individual characteristics—age, gender, education, race, marital status, job status, parental status, financial circum-

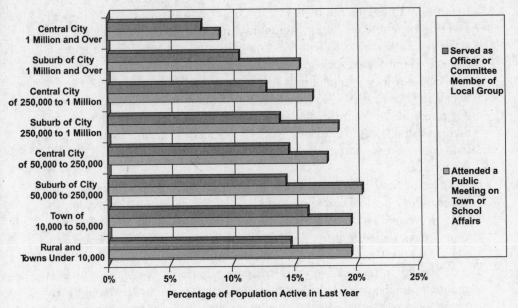

Figure 50: Community Involvement Is Lower in Major Metropolitan Areas

stances, homeownership, region of the country. Comparing two people identical in all these respects, the resident of a major metropolitan area, either in the central city or in a suburb, is significantly less likely to attend public meetings, to be active in community organizations, to attend church, to sign a petition, to volunteer, to attend club meetings, to work on community projects, or even to visit friends.[6] Metropolitans are less engaged because of where they are, not who they are.

We can also discount the possibility that small towns simply attract more gregarious people. Holding constant where people now live, civic engagement is *not* correlated with whether one would *prefer* living in a big city, a suburb, or a small town. Most people live in the size of place that they prefer, but where preferences and reality diverge, it is reality, not preferences, that determines civic engagement.[7] Living in a major metropolitan agglomeration somehow weakens civic engagement and social capital.

More and more Americans live in precisely such settings. Figure 52 traces changes in where Americans have lived over the last half of the twentieth century, distinguishing among three broad categories: 1) those who live outside metropolitan agglomerations as defined by the Census Bureau—that is, in small towns and rural areas—have fallen from 44 percent of the population in 1950 to 20 percent in 1996; 2) those who live in the central city of a metropolitan area have slumped slightly from 33 percent in 1950 to 31 percent in 1996; 3) those who live in some metropolitan area, but outside the central city—

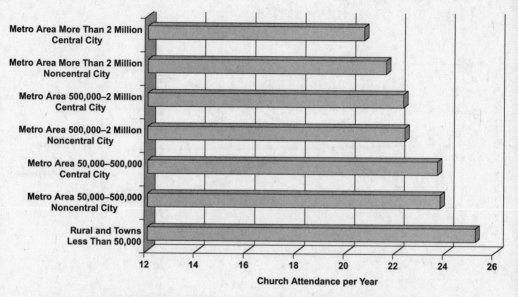

Figure 51: Church Attendance Is Lower in Major Metropolitan Areas

that is, in the suburbs—have more than doubled from 23 percent in 1950 to 49 percent in 1996. In the 1950s barely half of all Americans lived in a metropolitan area, whereas in the 1990s roughly four in five of us did. Throughout this era we have been moving to places that appear to be less hospitable to civic engagement. Moreover, the best available research found no evidence of suburbanization abating in the 1990s.[8] Thus the decline in social connectedness over the last third of the twentieth century might be attributable to the continuing eclipse of small-town America.

Americans have been moving from the countryside to the city for more than a century amid constant jeremiads from antiurban prophets of social doom. "[New York] is a splendid desert—a domed and steepled solitude, where a stranger is lonely in the midst of a million of his race," wrote Mark Twain in 1867. "A man walks his tedious miles through the same interminable street every day, elbowing his way through a buzzing multitude of men, yet never seeing a familiar face, and never seeing a strange one the second time. . . . The natural result is . . . the serene indifference of the New Yorker to everybody and everything without the pale of his private and individual circle." A few years later social philosopher Henry George broadened the indictment of American urbanization beyond Gotham: "Squalor and misery, and the vices and crimes that spring from them, everywhere increase as the village grows to the city."[9]

At least until recently, however, urbanization appears to have had no deleterious effect on our civic involvement. In fact, Americans were moving

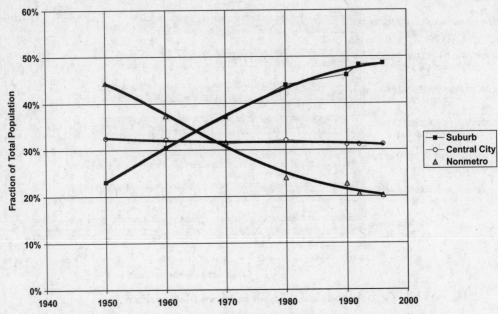

Figure 52: The Suburbanization of America, 1950–1996

into the city in great numbers throughout the first two-thirds of the twentieth century, all the while that civic engagement was high and rising. Moreover, the recent declines in all forms of civic engagement are virtually identical everywhere—in cities, big and small, in suburbs, in small towns, and in the countryside.[10] No part of America, from the smallest hamlet on up the scale, has been immune from this epidemic. So more must surely be involved than simply urbanization.

Could disengagement perhaps be linked not to urbanization, but to suburbanization? Suburbs have been a feature of American life since the mid–nineteenth century, driven in large measure by revolutions in transportation. First the streetcar and later the automobile enabled millions of us to live on the leafy urban periphery, while enjoying the economic, commercial, and cultural advantages of the city. After World War II widespread car ownership combined with a government-subsidized road- and home-building boom to produce accelerated movement to the suburbs, not different in kind from the earlier trends, but different in degree.

Suburbanization meant greater separation of workplace and residence and greater segregation by race and class. Such segregation was hardly new to American cities, but increasingly in the postwar period it took on a new character. In the classic American city neighborhoods tended to be homogeneous, but municipalities were heterogeneous, often in a crazy-quilt pattern with Ukrainian blocks adjacent to Irish areas, Jewish neighborhoods next to black ones, and servants living near the upper-class homes they served. In a suburbanized America municipalities were increasingly homogeneous in ethnic and class terms.

Initially, the postwar wave of suburbanization produced a frontierlike enthusiasm for civic engagement. The booster mythology fostered by suburban developers was positively communitarian. Ran one ad for Park Forest, the Chicago suburb closely studied by urbanist William Whyte for *The Organization Man:*

YOU BELONG IN PARK FOREST!

The moment you come to our town you know:
    You're welcome
    You're a part of the big group
You can live in a friendly small town
    Instead of a lonely big city
You can have friends who want you—
    And you can enjoy being with them.
Come out. Find out about the spirit of Park Forest.[11]

This was not mere hype, for Whyte reported that Park Forest was a "hotbed of participation. With sixty-six adult organizations and a population turnover that makes each one of them insatiable for new members, Park Forest probably swallows up more civic energy per hundred people than any other community in the country." A few years later sociologist Herbert Gans, who had actually moved into Levittown, New Jersey, to study its social life, reported that Levittowners were "hyperactive joiners." The image of suburban life that emerged from studies of the 1960s was one of unusually active involvement in neighborhood activities.[12] Americans, it seemed, were rediscovering the civic virtues of small-town life.

As suburbanization continued, however, the suburbs themselves fragmented into a sociological mosaic—collectively heterogeneous but individually homogeneous, as people fleeing the city sorted themselves into more and more finely distinguished "lifestyle enclaves," segregated by race, class, education, life stage, and so on. So-called white flight was only the most visible form of this movement toward metropolitan differentiation. At century's end some suburbs were upper-middle-class, but many others were middle-middle, lower-middle, or even working-class. Some suburbs were white, but others were black, Hispanic, or Asian. Some were child focused, but others were composed predominantly of swinging singles or affluent empty nesters or retirees. Many suburbs had come to resemble theme parks, with uniform architecture and coordinated amenities and boutiques. In the 1980s "common interest developments" and "gated communities" began to proliferate, in which private homeowner associations and visible physical barriers manned by guards supplemented the invisible sociological barriers that distinguished each community from its neighbors. In 1983, 15 percent of the development projects in Orange County, California, were gated communities, and within five years this fraction had doubled.[13]

One might expect the numbing homogeneity of these new suburban enclaves to encourage a certain social connectedness, if only of the "bonding," not the "bridging," sort. Suburban developers in the 1990s, like their predecessors in the 1950s, continued to sell community. "Remember the street you grew up on?" ran one Internet ad. "Where neighbors knew neighbors. Live there again—at Greenfield at The Wheatlands. Greenfield is a traditional hometown for families who aspire to the good life."[14]

Most evidence, however, actually points in the opposite direction. Not only are canvasing politicians and Girl Scouts selling cookies excluded from exclusive communities, but the affluent residents themselves also appear to have a surprisingly low rate of civic engagement and neighborliness even within their boundaries. In a careful survey of community involvement in suburbs across America, political scientist Eric Oliver found that the greater the social homogeneity of a community, the lower the level of political involvement: "By creating communities of homogeneous political interests, suburbanization reduces the local conflicts that engage and draw the citizenry into the public realm."[15]

When ethnographer M. P. Baumgartner lived in a suburban New Jersey community in the 1980s, rather than the compulsive togetherness ascribed to the classic suburbs of the 1950s, she found a culture of atomized isolation, self-restraint, and "moral minimalism." Far from seeking small-town connectedness, suburbanites kept to themselves, asking little of their neighbors and expecting little in return. "The suburb is the last word in privatization, perhaps even its lethal consummation," argue new urbanist architects Andres Duany and Elizabeth Plater-Zyberk, "and it spells the end of authentic civic life."[16]

More than sixty years ago urbanist Lewis Mumford observed that "suburbia is a collective effort to lead a private life." Now, however, the privatization of suburban life has become formalized and impersonal. Gated communities are innately introverted, as traditional urban neighborhoods were innately extroverted. As two close students of gated communities, Robert Lang and Karen Danielsen, report, "In the past, suburbanites used gentle nudges to prod neighbors to act responsibly—when their grass grew a bit too high, for instance. Now a representative from the community association comes by to precisely measure grass and, for a fee, will mow lawns that have grown unruly. The whole process formalizes a social exchange that has historically been informal."[17]

The preeminent historian of the American suburb, Kenneth T. Jackson, concludes:

> [A] major casualty of America's drive-in culture is the weakened "sense of community" which prevails in most metropolitan areas. I refer to a tendency for social life to become "privatized," and to a reduced feeling of concern and responsibility among families for their neighbors and among suburbanites in general for residents of the inner city. . . . The real shift, however, is the way in which our lives are now centered inside the house, rather than on the neighborhood or the community. With increased use of automobiles, the life of the sidewalk and the front yard has largely disappeared, and the social intercourse that used to be the main characteristic of urban life has vanished. . . . There are few places as desolate and lonely as a suburban street on a hot afternoon.[18]

In the earlier postwar period the larger structure of the typical metropolitan area remained monocentric—people lived in the suburbs but continued to travel into the central city for work and commerce. Gradually, however, both jobs and shops migrated into the suburbs, too, producing agglomerations of shopping malls, corporate headquarters, and office and industrial parks—what urbanist Joel Garreau calls "edge cities." The older, radially structured urban areas of the Northeast were succeeded by the sprawling, polycentric megalopolises of the Sunbelt. At the beginning of the twenty-first century more and more of us commute from one suburb to another. More and more of our shopping is done in a megamall in yet a third suburb. Segregatory zoning policies have excluded such gathering places as local shops and restaurants from residential areas, at the same time that federal tax policy encouraged the shopping center boom.

Rather than at the grocery store or five-and-dime on Main Street, where faces were familiar, today's suburbanites shop in large, impersonal malls. Although malls constitute America's most distinctive contemporary public space, they are carefully designed for one primary, private purpose—to direct consumers to buy. Despite the aspirations of some developers, mall culture is not about overcoming isolation and connecting with others, but about privately surfing from store to store—in the presence of others, but not in their company. The suburban shopping experience does not consist of interaction with people embedded in a common social network. Fewer and fewer of us actually spend much time in the central city or in any other single site. As one Californian observed, "I live in Garden Grove, work in Irvine, shop in Santa Ana, go to the dentist in Anaheim, my husband works in Long Beach, and I used to be the president of the League of Women Voters in Fullerton." Our lives are increasingly traced in large suburban triangles, as we move daily from home to work to shop to home.[19]

It is difficult to overstate the symbiosis between the automobile and the suburb. We went from a society of one car per household in 1969 to nearly two cars per household in 1995, even though the size of the average household was shrinking over this period. Between 1973 and 1996 the fraction of Americans describing a second automobile as "a necessity," not "a luxury," nearly doubled from 20 percent to 37 percent. By 1990 America had more cars than drivers. Much of this change has occurred quite recently. As late as 1985 only 55 percent of all new single-family homes included space for two or more cars, but by 1998 that index of automotive dominance was 79 percent and rising.[20]

Suburbanization of the last thirty years has increased not only our financial investment in the automobile, but also our investment of time. Between 1969 and 1995, according to government surveys of vehicle usage, the length of the average trip to work increased by 26 percent, while the average shopping trip increased by 29 percent. While the number of commuting trips per household rose 24 percent over this quarter century, the number of shopping trips per household almost doubled, and the number of other trips for personal or family business more than doubled. And each trip was much more likely to be made alone, for the average vehicle occupancy fell from 1.9 in 1977 to 1.6 in 1995; for trips to and from work, the average occupancy fell from 1.3 to 1.15. (Since vehicle occupancy cannot fall below 1.0, these figures represent a decline of a third in passenger occupancy for all trips and a decline of 50 percent in passenger commuting.)

One inevitable consequence of how we have come to organize our lives spatially is that we spend measurably more of every day shuttling alone in metal boxes among the vertices of our private triangles. American adults average seventy-two minutes every day behind the wheel, according to the Department of Transportation's Personal Transportation Survey. This is, according to time diary studies, more than we spend cooking or eating and more than twice as much as the average parent spends with the kids. Private cars account for 86 percent of all trips in America, and two-thirds of all car trips are made alone, a fraction that has been rising steadily.

Commuting accounts for little more than one-quarter of all personal trips, but for the structure of the lives of working Americans it is the single most important trip of the day. (The number of people who work at home has risen, but the proportion remains tiny—less than 4 percent of the workforce in 1997 worked even *one* day a week at home. In any event, home-based workers drive as much as conventional workers, more trips to the mall offsetting fewer trips to work.) Over the last two or three decades driving alone has become overwhelmingly the dominant mode of travel to work for most Americans. The fraction of us who travel to work in a private vehicle rose from 61 percent in 1960 to 91 percent in 1995, while all other forms of commuting—public transit, walking, and so on—declined. Mass transit plays a small and declining role in the transportation of most metropolitan areas nationwide; in 1995, 3.5 percent of all commuting trips were on mass transit. Carpooling too has fallen steadily for more than two decades. The fraction of all commuters who carpool has been cut in half since the mid-1970s and is projected to reach only 7–8 percent by 2000. The bottom line: By the end of the 1990s, 80–90 percent of all Americans drove to work alone, up from 64 percent as recently as 1980.

We are also commuting farther. From 1960 to 1990 the number of workers who commute across county lines more than tripled. Between 1983 and 1995 the average commuting trip grew 37 percent longer in miles. Ironically, travel time increased by only 14 percent, because the speed of the average commute, by all modes of transportation combined, increased by nearly one-quarter. Three factors have made for faster travel, at least in the recent past—the switch from carpools and mass transit to single-occupancy vehicles, which are quicker for the individual worker though socially inefficient; the increase in suburb-to-suburb commuting; and greater flexibility in work hours. On the other hand, traffic congestion has metastasized everywhere. In a study of sixty-eight urban areas from Los Angeles to Corpus Christi to Cleveland to Providence, annual congestion-related delay per driver rose steadily from sixteen hours in 1982 to forty-five hours per driver in 1997.[21]

In short, we are spending more and more time alone in the car. And on the whole, many of us see this as a time for quiet relaxation, especially those of us who came of age in the midst of this driving boom. According to one survey in 1997, 45 percent of all drivers—61 percent of those aged eighteen to twenty-four, though only 36 percent of those aged fifty-five and over—agreed that "driving is my time to think and enjoy being alone."[22]

The car and the commute, however, are demonstrably bad for community life. In round numbers the evidence suggests that *each additional ten minutes in daily commuting time cuts involvement in community affairs by 10 percent*—fewer public meetings attended, fewer committees chaired, fewer petitions signed, fewer church services attended, less volunteering, and so on. In fact, although commuting time is not quite as powerful an influence on civic involvement as education, it is more important than almost any other demographic factor. And time diary studies suggest that there is a similarly strong negative effect of commuting time on informal social interaction.[23]

Strikingly, increased commuting time among the residents of a community lowers average levels of civic involvement even among noncommuters. In fact, the "civic penalty" associated with high-commute communities is almost as great for retired residents and others who are outside the workforce as for full-time workers, and virtually as great for weekend church attendance as for involvement in secular organizations. In other words, this appears to be a classic "synergistic effect," in which the consequences of individual actions spill beyond the individuals in question. In the language of economists, commuting has negative externalities.

This otherwise puzzling fact is actually an important clue that it is not simply time spent in the car itself, but also spatial fragmentation between home and workplace, that is bad for community life. Lexington, Massachusetts, for example, has been transformed over the last fifty years from a Middlesex country town to a bedroom suburb for MIT, Harvard, and the high-tech suburbs along route 128. Though still a pleasant place in which to live, it is less self-sufficient civically than it was when most residents worked in town. Now that most residents commute out each day, many civic organizations have fallen on harder times, a fact that affects even those residents who still do work in town. Moreover, work-based ties now compete with place-based ties rather than reinforcing them. If your co-workers come from all over the metropolitan area, you must choose—spend an evening with neighbors *or* spend an evening with colleagues. (Of course, tired from a harried commute, you may well decide to just stay at home by yourself.) In short, sprawl is a collective bad, both for commuters and for stay-at-homes.

To be sure, suburbs, automobiles, and the associated sprawl are not without benefits. Americans *chose* to move to the suburbs and to spend more time driving, presumably because we found the greater space, larger homes, lower-cost shopping and housing—and perhaps, too, the greater class and racial segregation—worth the collective price we have paid in terms of community. On the other hand, DDB Needham Life Style survey data on locational preferences suggest that during the last quarter of the twentieth century—the years of rapid suburbanization—suburban living gradually became less attractive compared to residence in either the central city or smaller towns.[24] Whatever our private preferences, however, metropolitan sprawl appears to have been a significant contributor to civic disengagement over the last three or four decades for at least three distinct reasons.

First, sprawl takes time. More time spent alone in the car means less time for friends and neighbors, for meetings, for community projects, and so on. Though this is the most obvious link between sprawl and disengagement, it is probably not the most important.

Second, sprawl is associated with increasing social segregation, and social homogeneity appears to reduce incentives for civic involvement, as well as opportunities for social networks that cut across class and racial lines. Sprawl has been especially toxic for bridging social capital.

Third, most subtly but probably most powerfully, sprawl disrupts community "boundedness." Commuting time is important in large part as a proxy for the growing separation between work and home and shops. More than three decades ago, when (we now know in retrospect) civic engagement was at full flood, political scientists Sidney Verba and Norman Nie showed that residents of "well-defined and bounded" communities were much more likely to be involved in local affairs. In fact, Verba and Nie found commuting itself to be a powerful negative influence on participation. Presciently, they wrote that "communities that appear to foster participation—the small and relatively independent communities—are becoming rarer and rarer."[25] Three decades later this physical fragmentation of our daily lives has had a visible dampening effect on community involvement.

The residents of large metropolitan areas incur a "sprawl civic penalty" of roughly 20 percent on most measures of community involvement. More and more of us have come to incur this penalty over the last thirty years. Coupled with the suburbanization of the American population represented in figure 52, the direct civic penalty associated with sprawl probably accounts for something less than one-tenth of the total disengagement outlined in section II of this book.[26] It, like the pressures of time and money, helps explain our national civic disengagement. Yet it cannot account for more than a small fraction of the decline, for civic disengagement is perfectly visible in smaller towns and rural areas as yet untouched by sprawl. Our roundup of suspects is not yet complete.

CHAPTER 13

Technology and Mass Media

WHEN THE HISTORY of the twentieth century is written with greater perspective than we now enjoy, the impact of technology on communications and leisure will almost surely be a major theme. At the beginning of the century the communications and entertainment industries hardly existed outside small publishing houses and music halls. The first quarter of the century had nearly passed before the term *mass media* was invented. At the end of the century, by contrast, the gradual merger of the massive telecommunications and entertainment industries had become the very foundation for a new economic era.

Among the effects of this century-long transformation, two are especially relevant here. First, news and entertainment have become increasingly individualized. No longer must we coordinate our tastes and timing with others in order to enjoy the rarest culture or the most esoteric information. In 1900 music lovers needed to sit with scores of other people at fixed times listening to fixed programs, and if they lived in small towns as most Americans did, the music was likely to be supplied by enthusiastic local amateurs.* In 2000, with my hi-fi Walkman CD, wherever I live I can listen to precisely what I want when I want and where I want. As late as 1975 Americans nationwide chose among a handful of television programs. Barely a quarter century later, cable, satellite, video, and the Internet provide an exploding array of individual choice.

---

* Virtually all small towns in New Hampshire, where I am writing this book, supported town bands in that era; few do now.

Second, electronic technology allows us to consume this hand-tailored entertainment in private, even utterly alone. As late as the middle of the twentieth century, low-cost entertainment was available primarily in public settings, like the baseball park, the dance hall, the movie theater, and the amusement park, although by the 1930s radio was rapidly becoming an important alternative, the first of a series of electronic inventions that would transform American leisure. In the last half of the century television and its offspring moved leisure into the privacy of our homes. As the poet T. S. Eliot observed early in the television age, "It is a medium of entertainment which permits millions of people to listen to the same joke at the same time, and yet remain lonesome."[1] The artifice of canned laughter reflected both the enduring fact that mirth is enhanced by companionship and the novel fact that companionship could now be simulated electronically. At an accelerating pace throughout the century, the electronic transmission of news and entertainment changed virtually all features of American life.

The pace of this transformation was astonishing, even by the standards of modern technology. Table 2 shows the speed at which a range of modern appliances diffused into American households during the twentieth century.[2] Those that provided electronic entertainment—radio, the video recorder, and, above all, television—spread into homes at all levels in American society five to ten times more quickly than other devices that are now nearly as ubiquitous. Even more than the automobile, these innovations are transforming how we spend our days. In this chapter we investigate whether they are implicated in the erosion of America's social capital as well.

ALTHOUGH MODERN MEDIA offer both information and entertainment—indeed, they increasingly blur the line between the two—it is important from the point of view of civic engagement to treat the two somewhat separately.

The first means of mass communication and entertainment, of course,

Table 2: Pace of Introduction of Selected Consumer Goods

Technological Invention	Household Penetration Begins (1 Percent)	Years to Reach 75 Percent of American Households
Telephone	1890	67
Automobile	1908	52
Vacuum cleaner	1913	48
Air conditioner	1952	~48
Refrigerator	1925	23
Radio	1923	14
VCR	1980	12
Television	1948	7

was not electronic, but the printed word and, above all, the newspaper. Alexis de Tocqueville saw clearly the importance of mass communication for civic engagement:

> When no firm and lasting ties any longer unite men, it is impossible to obtain the cooperation of any great number of them unless you can persuade every man whose help is required that he serves his private interests by voluntarily uniting his efforts to those of all the others. That cannot be done habitually and conveniently without the help of a newspaper. Only a newspaper can put the same thought at the same time before a thousand readers. . . . So hardly any democratic association can carry on without a newspaper.[3]

Nearly two centuries later newspaper readership remains a mark of substantial civic engagement. Newspaper readers are older, more educated, and more rooted in their communities than is the average American. Even holding age, education, and rootedness constant, however, those who *read* the news are more engaged and knowledgeable about the world than those who only *watch* the news. Compared to demographically identical nonreaders, regular newspaper readers belong to more organizations, participate more actively in clubs and civic associations, attend local meetings more frequently, vote more regularly, volunteer and work on community projects more often, and even visit with friends more frequently and trust their neighbors more.[4] Newspaper readers are *machers and schmoozers.*

Without controlled experiments, we can't be certain which causes which. Virtually all nonexperimental studies of the media find it hard to distinguish between "selection effects" (people with a certain trait seek out a particular medium) and "media effects" (people develop that trait by being exposed to that medium). We shall have to grapple with that analytic problem repeatedly in this chapter. Nevertheless, the evidence makes quite clear that newspaper reading and good citizenship go together.

We should probably not be altogether surprised, therefore, that newspaper readership has been plunging in recent decades, along with most other measures of social capital and civic engagement. In 1948, when the median American adult had nine years of formal schooling, daily newspaper circulation was 1.3 papers per household. That is, a half century ago the *average* American family read *more* than one newspaper a day. Fifty years later schooling had risen by 50 percent, but newspaper readership had fallen by 57 percent, despite the fact that newspaper reading is highly correlated with education.[5]

Newspaper reading is a lasting habit established early in adult life. If we start young, we generally continue. Virtually none of the precipitous decline in newspaper circulation over the last half century can be traced to declining readership by individuals. Virtually all of the decline is due to the by now familiar pattern of generational succession. As figure 53 shows, three out of every four Americans born in the first third of the twentieth century continue to read a daily newspaper as the century closes, just as that generation did decades ago. Fewer than half of their boomer children are carrying on the tradition, however, a fraction that has dwindled to one in four among their X'er grandchildren. Since more recent cohorts show no sign of becoming newspaper readers as they age, circulation continues to plunge as the generation of readers is replaced by the generation of nonreaders.[6] Reversing that slump will not be easy, since each year the ground is slipping away beneath our feet.

One might imagine that the explanation for this trend is simple: TV. We're now watching news, not reading it. The facts, however, are more complicated. Americans have not simply shifted their news consumption from the printed page to the glowing screen. In fact, Americans who watch the news on television are *more* likely to read the daily newspaper than are other Americans, not *less* likely.[7] In the lingo of economics, TV news and the daily newspaper are complements, not substitutes. Some of us are newshounds, and some are not.

It is not just newspaper readership, but interest in the news per se that is declining generationally. As figure 54 shows, when people are asked whether they "need to get the news (world, national, sports, and so on) every day," the answer turns out to depend on when they were born. A more or less steady two-

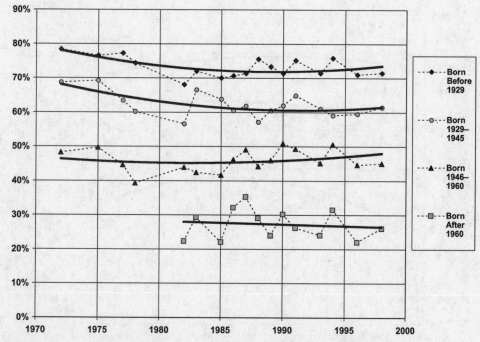

Figure 53: Generational Succession Explains the Demise of Newspapers

thirds of people born before 1930 say "definitely" or "generally" yes. Among the generation of their children and grandchildren (born after 1960), news interest is barely half as great. Moreover, figure 54 shows absolutely no evidence of a life cycle growth in news interest among the younger generations that might eventually bring them to the level of their parents and grandparents.

Since watching the news and reading the news are both elements in the same syndrome, it is hardly surprising that TV news viewing is positively associated with civic involvement. Those of us who rely solely on TV news are not quite as civic in our behavior as our fellow citizens who rely on newspapers, but we news watchers are nevertheless more civic than most other Americans. Regular viewers of network newscasts (as well as followers of National Public Radio and even of the local TV news) spend more time on community projects, attend more club meetings, and follow politics much more closely than other Americans (even when matched in terms of age, education, sex, income, and so on). Americans who follow news on television (compared with those who don't) are more knowledgeable about public affairs, vote more regularly, and are generally more active in community affairs, though they are not quite as distinctively civic as newspaper readers.[8]

Unfortunately, like news readership, news viewership is on the decline, as we would predict from figure 54. In recent years the falloff in the audience for network news has been even faster than the decline in newspaper circula-

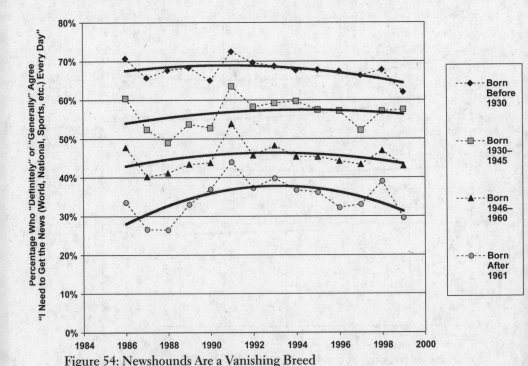

Figure 54: Newshounds Are a Vanishing Breed

tion: for example, the regular audience for nightly network news plunged from 60 percent of adults in 1993 to 38 percent in 1998. Moreover, as with newspaper circulation, much of the decline in television news viewing is driven by generational differences. The audience for network news is aging rapidly, as one might easily guess from the health aid advertising that supports Brokaw, Jennings, and Rather. According to a 1997 study by NBC News, while the average age of the audience for all prime-time programs was forty-two, the average age of the audience for nightly newscasts was fifty-seven. Moreover, newscast viewers nowadays are poised to switch away at a moment's notice: half of all Americans report that they watch the news with a remote control in hand.[9]

Some see hope in the rise of news on the Internet or the all-news cable channels. It is still too early to predict the long-run effects of these new channels. That said, the early returns are not encouraging. First, just as TV newshounds are disproportionately newspaper readers, most people who follow news on the Internet or on all-news cable channels also are "generalists" in their news consumption. CNN viewers, for example, are twice as likely as other Americans to watch the evening network newscasts. Even enthusiasts for Internet news concede that "the Internet is emerging as a supplement to—not a substitute for—other traditional news sources." In fact, as usage of the Internet expanded in the second half of the 1900s, usage of it to follow public affairs became relatively *less* important.[10] In short, the newer media are mainly drawing on the steadily shrinking traditional audience for news, not expanding it.

Moreover, unlike those who rely on newspapers, radio, and television for news, those few technologically proficient Americans who rely *primarily* on the Internet for news are actually *less* likely than their fellow citizens to be civically involved.[11] Of course, this does not prove that the Net is socially demobilizing. These "early adopters" of Internet news may well have been socially withdrawn to begin with. Nevertheless, Internet and cable news outlets seem unlikely to offset the civic losses from the shrinking audiences for network broadcast and print news.

MOST OF THE TIME, energy, and creativity of the electronic media, however, is devoted not to news, but to entertainment. Watching the news is not harmful to your civic health. What about television entertainment? Here we must begin with the most fundamental fact about the impact of television on Americans: Nothing else in the twentieth century so rapidly and profoundly affected our leisure.

In 1950 barely 10 percent of American homes had television sets, but by 1959, 90 percent did, probably the fastest diffusion of a technological innovation ever recorded. (The spread of Internet access will rival TV's record but probably not surpass it.) The reverberations from this lightning bolt continued unabated for decades, as per capita viewing hours grew by 17–20 percent during the 1960s, by an additional 7–8 percent during the 1970s, and by another 7–8 percent from the early 1980s to the late 1990s. (For one measure of this steady growth, see the Nielsen ratings for household viewing hours in figure 55.) In the early years TV watching was concentrated among the less educated sectors of the population, but during the 1970s the viewing time of the more educated sectors of the population began to converge upward. Television viewing increases with age, particularly upon retirement, but each generation since the introduction of television has begun its life cycle at a higher starting point. Partly because of these generational differences, the fraction of American adults who watch "whatever's on"—that is, those of us who turn on the TV with no particular program in mind—jumped from 29 percent in 1979 to 43 percent by the end of the 1980s. By 1995 viewing per TV household was more than 50 percent higher than it had been in the 1950s.[12]

Most studies estimate that the average American now watches roughly four hours per day, very nearly the highest viewership anywhere in the world. Time researchers John Robinson and Geoffrey Godbey, using the more conservative time diary technique for determining how people allocate their time, offer an estimate closer to three hours per day but conclude that as a primary activity, television absorbed almost 40 percent of the average American's free time in 1995, an increase of roughly one-third since 1965. Between 1965 and 1995 we gained an average of six hours a week in added leisure time, and we

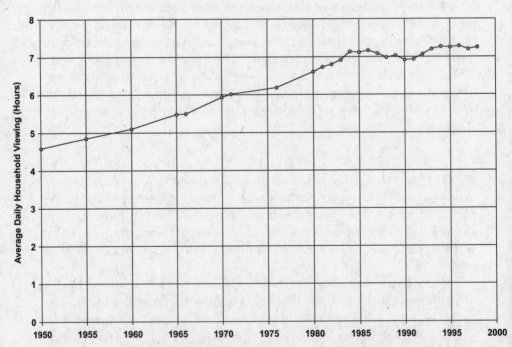

Figure 55: A Half Century's Growth in Television Watching, 1950–1998

spent almost all six of those additional hours watching TV. In short, as Robinson and Godbey conclude, "Television is the 800-pound gorilla of leisure time."[13]

Moreover, multiple sets per household have proliferated: by the late 1990s three-quarters of all U.S. homes had more than one set, allowing ever more private viewing. The fraction of sixth-graders with a TV set in their bedroom grew from 6 percent in 1970 to 77 percent in 1999. (Two kids in three aged 8–18 say that TV is usually on during meals in their home.) At the same time, during the 1980s the rapid diffusion of videocassette players and video games into American households added yet other forms of "screen time." Finally, during the 1990s personal computers and Internet access dramatically broadened the types of information and entertainment brought into the American home.[14] (Some of these trends are captured in figure 56.)

The single most important consequence of the television revolution has been to bring us home. As early as 1982, a survey by Scripps-Howard reported that eight out of the ten most popular leisure activities were typically based at home. Amid all the declining graphs for social and community involvement traced in the DDB Needham Life Style surveys from 1975 to 1999, one line stands out: The number of Americans who reported a preference for "spending a quiet evening at home" rose steadily. Not surprisingly, those who said so were heavily dependent on televised entertainment.[15] While early enthusiasts for this

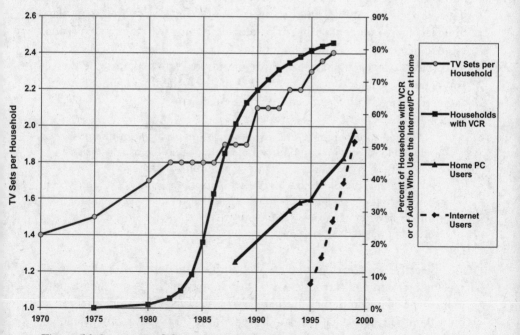

Figure 56: Screens Proliferate in American Homes:
VCRs, PCs, Extra TV Sets, and the Net, 1970–1999

new medium spoke eagerly of television as an "electronic hearth" that would foster family togetherness, the experience of the last half century is cautionary.

Social critic James Howard Kuntsler's polemic is not far off target:

> The American house has been TV-centered for three generations. It is the focus of family life, and the life of the house correspondingly turns inward, away from whatever occurs beyond its four walls. (TV rooms are called "family rooms" in builders' lingo. A friend who is an architect explained to me: "People don't want to admit that what the family does together is watch TV.") At the same time, the television is the family's chief connection with the outside world. The physical envelope of the house itself no longer connects their lives to the outside in any active way; rather, it seals them off from it. The outside world has become an abstraction filtered through television, just as the weather is an abstraction filtered through air conditioning.[16]

Time diaries show that husbands and wives spend three or four times as much time watching television together as they spend talking to each other, and six to seven times as much as they spend in community activities outside the home. Moreover, as the number of TV sets per household multiplies, even watching together becomes rarer. More and more of our television viewing is done entirely alone. At least half of all Americans usually watch by themselves, one study suggests, while according to another, one-third of all television viewing is done alone. Among children aged 8–18 the figures are even more startling: less than 5 percent of their TV-watching is done with their parents, and more than one-third is done entirely alone.[17]

Television viewing has steadily become a more habitual, less intentional part of our lives. Four times between 1979 and 1993 the Roper polling organization posed a revealing pair of questions to Americans:

> When you turn the television set on, do you usually turn it on first and then look for something you want to watch, or do you usually turn it on only if you know there's a certain program you want to see?
>
> Some people like to have a TV set on, sort of in the background, even when they're not actually watching it. Do you find you frequently will just have the set on even though you're not really watching it, or [do you either watch it or turn it off]?

Selective viewers (that is, those who turn on the television only to see a specific program and turn it off when they're not watching) are significantly more involved in community life than habitual viewers (those who turn the TV on without regard to what's on and leave it on in the background), even controlling for education and other demographic factors. For example, selective viewers are 23 percent more active in grassroots organizations and 33 percent more likely to attend public meetings than other demographically matched Americans. Habitual viewing is especially detrimental to civic engagement. Indeed, the effect of habitual viewing on civic disengagement is as great as the effect of simply watching more TV.[18]

Year by year we have become more likely to flick on the tube without knowing what we want to see and more likely to leave it on in the background even when we're no longer watching, as figure 57 shows. As recently as the late 1970s selective viewers outnumbered habitual viewers by more than three to two, but by the mid-1990s the proportions were reversed. In 1962, only a few years after television had become nearly ubiquitous, the leading character in *The Manchurian Candidate* could say, "There are two kinds of people in the world—those who walk into a room and turn the TV on, and those who walk into a room and turn the TV off."[19] Four decades later the first kind of people have become more common and the second kind ever rarer.

Habituation to omnipresent television is much more pervasive among younger generations. (Keep in mind in this discussion that "younger" can include people in their forties at the turn of this century.) Even highly educated members of younger generations are much less likely to be selective viewers than less educated people from earlier generations. Of Americans born before 1933 (none of whom grew up with TV), 43 percent were selective viewers in 1993, roughly twice the rate of selective viewing (23 percent) that year among people born after 1963 (all of whom grew up with TV). Those of us who have

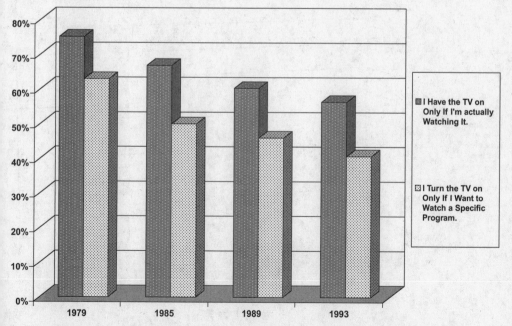

Figure 57: TV Becomes an American Habit, as Selective Viewing Declines

grown up in the television age are more much likely than our elders to consider TV a natural constant companion. This is precisely what we should expect if TV watching is a habit acquired most easily in childhood. In short, even when total TV hours are the same across different age groups—as they often are—different generations use television differently. Since the trend toward habitual TV watching mostly reflects the effects of generational succession, it is unlikely to be reversed any time soon.[20]

Habitual viewing is not the only way in which generations differ in their television-viewing customs. Another is channel surfing. Figure 58, drawn from a 1996 Yankelovich Monitor survey, shows that when they are actually watching TV, younger generations (including boomers, compared with their elders) are more likely to surf from program to program, "grazing" or "multitasking" rather than simply following a single narrative. Other scholars have found that compared with teenagers in the 1950s, young people in the 1990s have fewer, weaker, and more fluid friendships.[21] Although I know no systematic evidence that supports this hunch, I suspect that the link between channel surfing and social surfing is more than metaphorical.

The ubiquity of television in our lives can best by conveyed by examining what proportion of Americans report TV viewing in various slices of time throughout the day. The DDB Needham Life Style surveys from 1993 to 1998 asked respondents to indicate whether or not they had been watching TV

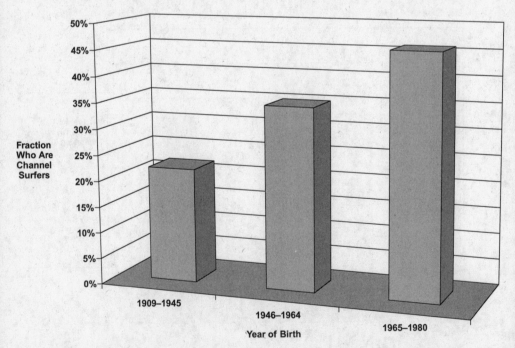

Figure 58: Channel Surfing Is More Common Among Younger Generations

during ten different periods throughout the previous day—from waking up in the morning to going to bed at night. During each period when they reported watching, they were asked whether this was mainly for information, mainly for entertainment, or "just for background." Figure 59 charts the national averages.

During *every* period of the day at least one-quarter of all adults report some TV viewing. After work this fraction rises to more than half, peaking at 86 percent during the aptly named "prime time" hours.[22] In many homes television is merely on in the background, a kind of visual Muzak, but figure 59 shows that such casual usage accounts for a relatively small fraction of reported viewership. These averages include both working and nonworking Americans, though obviously the figures for workers are lower during the workday. Roughly half of all Americans—married and single, parents and childless—report watching television while eating dinner, and nearly one-third do so during breakfast and lunch.[23] By the end of the twentieth century television had become omnipresent in Americans' lives.

Another way of seeing the dominance of television viewing in Americans' lives is to compare it with other ways in which we spend our evenings. Figure 60 shows that 81 percent of all Americans report that most evenings they watch TV, as compared with only 56 percent who talk with family members, 36 percent who have a snack, 27 percent who do household chores, and 7 per-

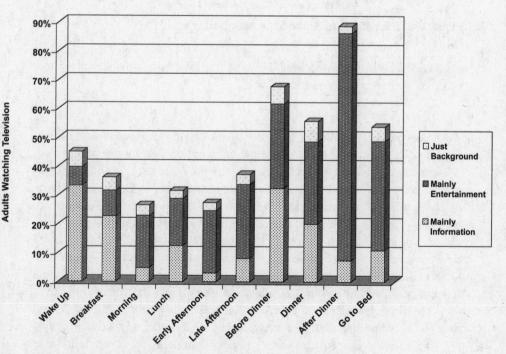

Figure 59: America Watches TV All Day Every Day

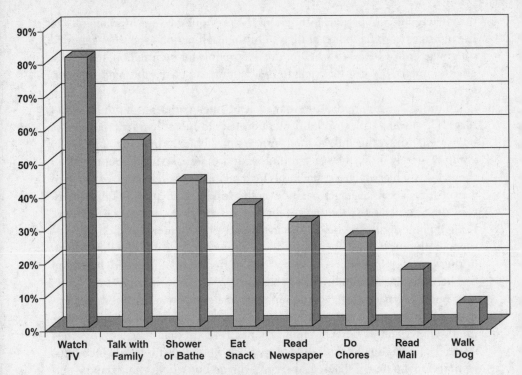

Which of These Things Do You Do Most Weeknights
After Your Evening Meal and Before Bedtime?

Figure 60: In the Evening Americans, Above All, Watch TV

cent who walk the dog. Watching TV at night has become one of the few universals of contemporary American life.[24]

THIS MASSIVE CHANGE in the way Americans spend our days and nights occurred precisely during the years of generational civic disengagement. How is television viewing related to civic engagement? In a correlational sense, the answer is simple: More television watching means less of virtually every form of civic participation and social involvement. Television viewing is also correlated with other factors that depress civic involvement, including poverty, old age, low education, and so on. Thus in order to isolate the specific connection between television and social participation, we need to hold those other factors constant, statistically speaking. Other things being equal, such analysis suggests, each additional hour of television viewing per day means roughly a 10 percent reduction in most forms of civic activism—fewer public meetings, fewer local committee members, fewer letters to Congress, and so on.[25]

If the time diary estimates are correct that Americans spent nearly an hour more per day in front of the tube in 1995 than in 1965, then that factor alone might account for perhaps one-quarter of the entire drop in civic engagement over this period.[26] I must, however, add two qualifications to this estimate, one that might bias it upward and one that might bias it downward. On the one hand, I have as yet offered no evidence that the causal arrow runs from TV watching to civic disengagement rather than the reverse. On the other hand, this estimate presumes that the only effect of TV on civic engagement comes from the number of hours watched, rather than something about the character of the watching, the watcher, and the watched.

Before we turn to these important subtleties, figure 61 presents some of the evidence linking TV watching and civic disengagement. In order to screen out the effects of life cycle and education, we confine our attention here to working-age, college-educated Americans. (The pattern is even more marked within other, more TV-dependent segments of the population, such as retired people or the less well educated.) In this group those who watch an hour or less of television per day are half again as active civically as those who watch three hours or more a day. For example, 39 percent of the light viewers attended some public meeting on town or school affairs last year, as compared with only 25 percent of the demographically matched heavy viewers. Of the light viewers, 28 percent wrote Congress last year, compared with 21 percent of the heavy viewers. Of light viewers, 29 percent played a leadership role in some local organization, as contrasted with only 18 percent of heavy viewers. Light viewers were nearly three times more likely to have made a speech last year than were equally well-educated heavy viewers (14 percent to 5 percent).

The significance of these differences between heavy and light viewers is magnified by the fact that even among this select group of well-educated, working-age Americans, heavy viewers outnumber light viewers by nearly two to one. A major commitment to television viewing—such as most of us have come to have—is incompatible with a major commitment to community life.

In chapter 2 we noticed that collective forms of engagement, such as attending meetings, serving on committees, or working for a political party, had diminished much more rapidly over the last several decades than individual forms of engagement, such as writing to Congress or signing a petition. Both types of engagement can have political consequences, but only the former helps to foster and reinforce social connections. Television, it turns out, is bad for both individualized and collective civic engagement, but it is particularly toxic for activities that we do together. Whereas (controlling as always for demographic factors) watching lots of TV cuts individual activities, like letter writing, by roughly 10–15 percent, the same amount of additional TV viewing cuts collective activities, like attending public meetings or taking a leadership role in local organizations, by as much as 40 percent. In short, just as television privatizes our leisure time, it also privatizes our civic activity, dampening our interactions with one another even more than it dampens individual political activities.[27]

As we have seen, newshounds who watch television for information are

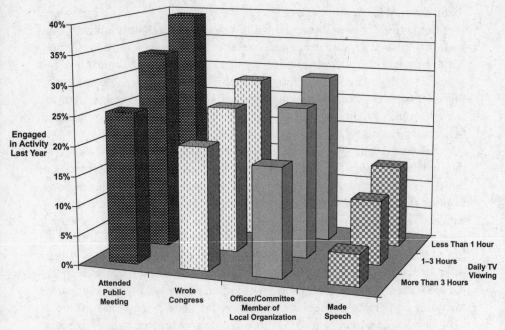

Figure 61: More TV Means Less Civic Engagement (Among College-Educated, Working-Age Adults)

more civic-minded than most other Americans. But most of us watch television for entertainment, not news. Of all Americans, 7 percent say that they watch primarily for information, as compared with 41 percent who say they watch primarily for entertainment. (The rest of us say that we watch for both information and entertainment; the inextricable link between information and entertainment—"infotainment"—is a notable feature of television that distinguishes it from other media, like books or radio.)[28] We have already seen that the news and public affairs programming seems to have, if anything, a positive effect on civic engagement. How about TV entertainment?

One way to detect the effects of television entertainment on social participation is to focus on those people—half of all Americans—who say that "television is my primary form of entertainment." Not surprisingly, these people watch much more TV than other Americans, and they are much more likely to concede that "I'm what you would call a couch potato."[29] In terms of civic engagement these people who are most heavily dependent on televised entertainment turn out to differ most remarkably from the other half of the American population.

Considered in combination with a score of other factors that predict social participation (including education, generation, gender, region, size of hometown, work obligations, marriage, children, income, financial worries, religiosity, race, geographic mobility, commuting time, homeownership, and more), dependence on television for entertainment is not merely *a* significant predictor of civic disengagement. It is *the single most consistent* predictor that I have discovered.

People who say that TV is their "primary form of entertainment" volunteer and work on community projects less often, attend fewer dinner parties and fewer club meetings, spend less time visiting friends, entertain at home less, picnic less, are less interested in politics, give blood less often, write friends less regularly, make fewer long-distance calls, send fewer greeting cards and less email, and express more road rage than demographically matched people who differ only in saying that TV is *not* their primary form of entertainment. TV dependence is associated not merely with less involvement in community life, but with less social communication in all its forms—written, oral, or electronic. This simple question turns out to distinguish those Americans who are most socially isolated from those most involved in their communities, as figures 62 to 66 illustrate. Nothing—not low education, not full-time work, not long commutes in urban agglomerations, not poverty or financial distress—is more broadly associated with civic disengagement and social disconnection than is dependence on television for entertainment.[30]

On average, Americans who definitely *disagree* that "television is my primary form of entertainment"—let's call them TV minimalists—volunteer nine times a year. By contrast, TV maximalists—those who definitely *agree* that TV

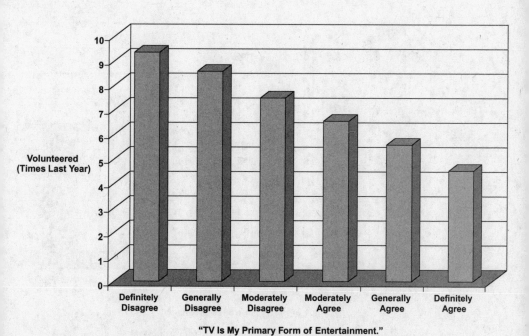

Figure 62: TV Watching and Volunteering Don't Go Together

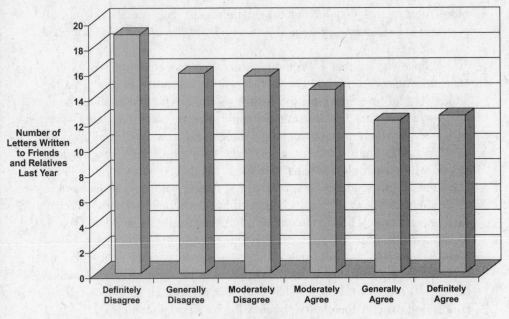

Figure 63: TV Watchers Don't Keep in Touch

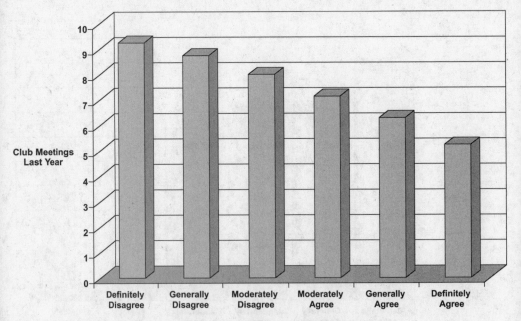

Figure 64: TV Watching and Club Meetings Don't Go Together

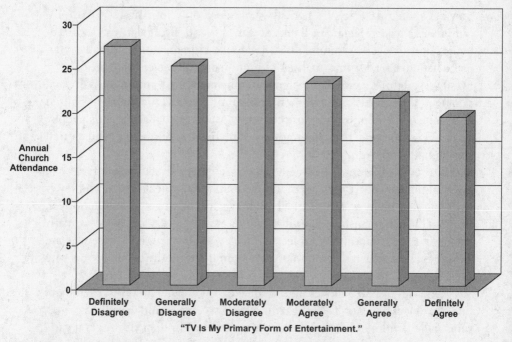

Figure 65: TV Watching and Churchgoing Don't Go Together

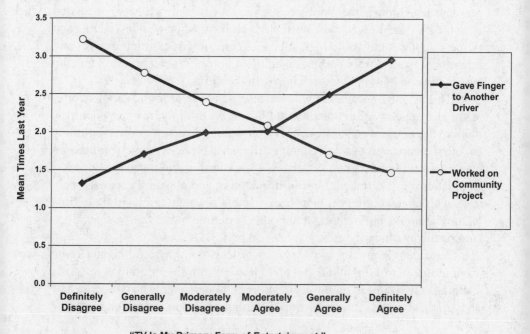

Figure 66: TV Watching and Comity Don't Go Together

provides their prime leisure activity—volunteer only four times a year. TV minimalists average eighteen letters a year to friends and relatives, TV maximalists only twelve. TV minimalists attend nine club meetings annually, compared with five for TV maximalists. TV minimalists attend church, on average, twenty-seven times a year, compared with nineteen for TV maximalists. In fact, reliance on televised entertainment is a strong negative predictor of church attendance, even controlling for religiosity. Among equally religious people, those who report that TV is their primary form of entertainment attend church substantially less often.[31]

The civic differences between the two groups are crystallized in figure 66: TV minimalists report more than three community projects a year and fewer than half that many instances in which they gave the finger to another driver. Among TV maximalists, this civility ratio is exactly reversed—twice as many rude gestures as community projects. *Machers, schmoozers,* and those who are simply civil are drawn disproportionately from the minority of Americans who are TV minimalists.

One can discover niches of resistance to TV dependency, but even there one can detect traces of its disengaging aura. Take, for example, well-educated, financially comfortable women from the Northeast in their thirties and early forties—the single demographic category in the nation most likely to disavow televised entertainment. Even in this select group, more than one in four confess that television is their primary leisure activity. Sure enough, compared with their TV-free sisters, the TV-afflicted volunteer 62 percent less often, go to 37 percent fewer club meetings, attend 27 percent fewer church services and 21 percent fewer dinner parties, entertain at home 20 percent less often, and report 24 percent more dissatisfaction with their lives.[32]

This negative correlation between television watching and social involvement also appears in time diaries and in surveys from many other countries. Both in this country and abroad, heavy television viewers are (even controlling for other demographic factors) significantly less likely to belong to voluntary associations and to trust other people. As TV ownership and usage spread across populations, it was linked, both in this country and abroad, to reduced contacts with relatives, friends, neighbors. More TV watching meant more time not just at home, but indoors, at the expense of time in the yard, on the street, and visiting in others' homes.[33]

A dead-on summary of the impact of television on social capital came from a member of the traditional and close-knit Amish community in southeastern Pennsylvania in response to a visiting ethnographer, who had asked how the Amish know which technological inventions to admit and which to shun.

We can almost always tell if a change will bring good or bad tidings. Certain things we definitely do not want, like the television and the radio.

They would destroy our visiting practices. We would stay at home with the television or radio rather than meet with other people. The visiting practices are important because of the closeness of the people. How can we care for the neighbor if we do not visit them or know what is going on in their lives?[34]

So FAR we have discovered that television watching and especially dependence upon television for entertainment are closely correlated with civic disengagement. Correlation, however, does not prove causation. An alternative interpretation is this: People who are social isolates to begin with gravitate toward the tube as the line of leisurely least resistance. Without true experimental evidence—in which randomly selected individuals are exposed (or not exposed) to television over long periods of time—we cannot be sure that television itself is the *cause* of disengagement. (Since the putative effects of TV presumably build up over years, a few minutes' viewing in a university lab is unlikely to replicate the deeper effects that we're talking about here.)

Truly conclusive evidence on this crucial point is not at hand, and given ethical restrictions on human experimentation, it is not likely to be available any time soon. (It is hard to know whether the louder public outcry against such an experiment would come on behalf of subjects forced to watch TV or those forced *not* to watch.) On the other hand, several sorts of evidence make the attribution of guilt in this case more plausible. First, the epidemic of civic disengagement began little more than a decade after the widespread availability of television. Moreover, as we shall see in more detail in chapter 14, the greater the youthful exposure of any cohort of individuals to television, the greater their degree of disengagement today. We have already noted that younger generations, exposed to television throughout their lives, are more habitual in their television usage and that habitual usage in turn is associated with lesser civic engagement.

Strikingly direct evidence about the causal direction comes from a range of intriguing studies of communities conducted just before and just after television was introduced. The most remarkable of these studies emerged from three isolated communities in northern Canada in the 1970s.[35] Owing only to poor reception, residents of one (given the pseudonym Notel by the researchers) were without television as the study began. The "treatment" whose effects were observed was the introduction of a single channel to Notel residents—the Canadian Broadcasting Corporation (CBC). Life in Notel was compared with that of two other communities, Unitel and Multitel. Though it was very similar to Notel in other respects, during the two years of the study TV reception in Unitel went from CBC only to CBC plus the three American commercial networks. Multitel was similar in all relevant respects to the other two towns, although removed somewhat geographically. Residents of Multitel could receive all four channels throughout the span of the research.

Canadian researcher Tannis MacBeth Williams and her colleagues explained why this triad of towns constituted a true experiment:

> Except for anachronistically lacking television reception in 1973, [Notel] was typical. It was accessible by road, had daily bus service in two directions, and its ethnic mix was not unusual. The town just happened to be located in a valley in such a way that the transmitter meant to serve the area did not provide television reception for most residents.[36]

Significant also is the fact that this study was conducted before the widespread availability of VCRs and satellite dishes. In other words, there will likely never be another example like this of an essentially TV-free community in an industrialized nation. The results clearly showed that the introduction of television deflated Notel residents' participation in community activities. As the researchers report succinctly,

> Before Notel had television, residents in the longitudinal sample attended a greater variety of club and other meetings than did residents of both Unitel and Multitel, who did not differ. There was a significant decline in Notel following the introduction of television, but no change in either Unitel or Multitel.[37]

The researchers also asked whether television affected only those who were peripherally involved in community activities or also the active leaders. Their conclusion:

> Television apparently affects participation in community activities for individuals who are central to those activities, not just those who are more peripherally involved. Residents are more likely to be centrally involved in their community's activities in the absence than in the presence of television.[38]

This study strongly suggests that television is not merely a concomitant of lower community involvement, but actually a cause of it. A major effect of television's arrival was the reduction in participation in social, recreational, and community activities among people of all ages. Television privatizes leisure time.

Comparable though less conclusive evidence comes from studies of the introduction of television in England, South Africa, Scotland, Australia, and the United States.[39] The effects of television on childhood socialization have been hotly debated for more than three decades. The most reasonable conclusion from a welter of sometimes conflicting results appears to be that heavy television watching probably increases aggressiveness (although perhaps not actual violence), that it probably reduces school achievement, and that it is statistically associated with "psychosocial malfunctioning," although how much of this effect is self-selection and how much causal remains controversial. Heavy television watching by young people is associated with civic ignorance, cynicism, and lessened political involvement in later years, along with reduced academic achievement and lower earnings later in life. In an exhaustive review of this interdisciplinary literature on television's effects on American social life, George Comstock and Haejung Paik conclude that the introduction of television has dampened the degree to which people engage in social activities outside of the home. None of these studies provides entirely unassailable support for the thesis that television viewing causes civic disengagement, but taken together the evidence certainly points in that direction.[40]

If television does reduce civic engagement, how does it do so? Broadly speaking, there are three possibilities:

- Television competes for scarce time.
- Television has psychological effects that inhibit social participation.
- Specific programmatic content on television undermines civic motivations.

Let's review the evidence for each of these hypotheses.

Even though there are only twenty-four hours in everyone's day, most forms of social and media participation are positively correlated. People who listen to lots of classical music are more likely, not less likely, than others to attend Cubs games. People who engage in do-it-yourself projects around the house are more likely than others to play a lot of volleyball and to do more public speaking. Even within demographically matched groups, people who attend more movies also attend more club meetings, more dinner parties, more church services, and more public gatherings, give more blood, and visit with friends more often. More than thirty years ago social psychologist Rolf Meyersohn noted this pattern in our leisure activities and dubbed it simply "the more, the more."[41]

Television is, as Meyersohn observed, the principal exception to this generalization—the only leisure activity that seems to inhibit participation in other leisure activities. TV watching comes at the expense of nearly every social activity outside the home, especially social gatherings and informal conversations. The major casualties of increased TV viewing, according to time diaries, are religious participation, social visiting, shopping, parties, sports, and organizational participation. The only activities positively linked to heavy television watching are sleeping, resting, eating, housework, radio listening, and hobbies. Television viewers are anchored at home, and they recognize that fact themselves: heavy viewers generally agree that "I am a homebody," whereas most light viewers don't. Political scientists John Brehm and Wendy Rahn found that TV watching has such a powerful impact on civic engagement that *one hour less* daily viewing is the civic-vitamin equivalent of *five or six more years* of education. There is reason to believe that the displacement effects of television watching may be even more significant with respect to unstructured activities, such as hanging out with friends, than with respect to more formal activities, such as organizational meetings.[42] In short, more time for TV means less time for social life.

Several times throughout the 1970s, just as (we now know) our national civic disengagement was gathering steam, the Roper organization asked Americans how their allocation of time and energy had changed in the recent years. Two broad conclusions emerged. First, as figure 67 shows, we massively shifted toward home-based activities (especially watching TV) and away from socializing outside the home. For example, 47 percent of all Americans reported that they were watching more TV than in the past, compared with only 16 percent who said they were watching less TV, for a net increase of 31 percent. Conversely, only 11 percent said they were spending more time than in the past visiting friends and relatives who did not live "quite nearby," as compared with 38 percent who said they were spending less time in that sort of socializing, for a net decrease of 27 percent. Almost without exception, activities outside the home were fading, while activities at home (especially watching TV) were increasing.[43]

Second, those who said they were spending more time watching TV than in the past were significantly less likely to attend public meetings, to serve in local organizations, to sign petitions, and the like than demographically matched people who said they were spending less time on TV. By contrast, the minority of people who reported spending more time with friends than in the past were also more likely to take part in civic life, even when compared with demographically identical groups.[44] The link between increased television watching and decreased civic engagement at that crucial juncture is unusually clear.

IF TV STEALS TIME, it also seems to encourage lethargy and passivity. Time researchers Robert Kubey and Mihaly Csikszentmihalyi used an ingenious method to track our use of time and its effects on our psychic well-being.[45] They persuaded subjects to carry beepers with them around the clock for a week, and when the beepers were randomly triggered, the subjects wrote down what they were doing and how they felt. Television viewing, Kubey and Csikszentmihalyi found, is a relaxing, low-concentration activity. Viewers feel passive and less alert after watching. On heavy-viewing evenings, people are also likely to engage in other low-energy, even slothful activities, whereas on light-viewing evenings, the same people spent more time outside the home in activ-

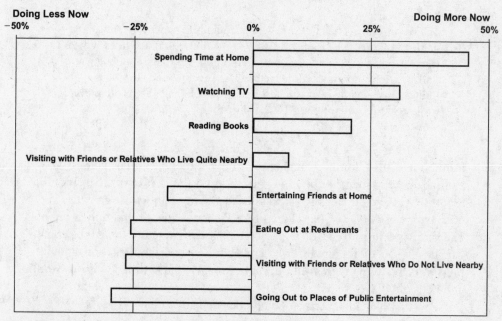

Figure 67: Americans Began Cocooning in the 1970s

ities like sports and club meetings. Heavy viewing is associated with lots of free time, loneliness, and emotional difficulties. TV is apparently especially attractive for people who feel unhappy, particularly when there is nothing else to do.

TV itself is probably not the primary cause of these negative feelings, but it does not help much, either, except as a momentary escape. As Kubey and Csikszentmihalyi summarize their findings,

> Heavy viewers spend more time with TV, but find it is less rewarding. . . . Although . . . feeling badly in unstructured and solitary time leads to the use of television, . . . heavy viewing and the rapid montage of much contemporary television may also help reinforce an intolerance in the heavy viewer for daily moments that are not similarly chocked full of sight and sound. . . . It seems likely that heavy viewing helps perpetuate itself. Some television viewers grow dependent on the ordered stimuli of television or similar entertainments and become increasingly incapable of filling leisure time without external aids.[46]

Kubey and Csikszentmihalyi report that these psychological concomitants of television watching are common in many cultures. British social psychologist Michael Argyle found that TV induces an emotional state best described as "relaxed, drowsy, and passive." British researchers Sue Bowden and Avner Offer report:

> Television is the cheapest and least demanding way of averting boredom. Studies of television find that of all household activities, television requires the lowest level of concentration, alertness, challenge, and skill. . . . Activation rates while viewing are very low, and viewing is experienced as a relaxing release of tension. Metabolic rates appear to plunge while children are watching TV, helping them to gain weight.[47]

As Kubey and Csikszentmihalyi conclude, television is surely habit-forming and may be mildly addictive. In experimental studies viewers generally demand a major bribe to give it up, even though viewers consistently report that television viewing is less satisfying than other leisure activities and even than work. In 1977 the *Detroit Free Press* was able to find only 5 out of 120 families willing to give up television for a month in return for $500. People who do give up TV reportedly experience boredom, anxiety, irritation, and depression. One woman observed, "It was terrible. We did nothing—my husband and I talked."[48]

As with other addictions, conclude Bowden and Offer,

> viewers are prone to habituation, desensitization, and satiation. . . . A researcher reported in 1989 that "virtually everyone in the television industry ardently believes that the audience attention span is growing shorter, and that to hold the audience, television editing must be even faster paced and present more and more exciting visual material." . . . As consumers become accustomed to the new forms of stimulation, they require an ever stronger dose.[49]

Although not immediately relevant to our central concern with civic engagement and social capital, self-avowed dependence on television for entertainment turns out to be correlated with a surprisingly wide range of physical and psychological ills. The DDB Needham Life Style surveys happen to include self-reports on headaches, indigestion, and sleeplessness. (Since the research was originally designed, among other things, to assist pharmaceutical marketers, it is not surprising that these measures were included.) We combined these three reports into a single index of "malaise"—people who score high on this measure are frequent victims of headaches, stomachaches, and insomnia. Figure 68 shows that malaise is closely associated with dependence on televised entertainment.[50]

As always, we checked to see whether this unexpectedly strong correlation might be spurious—perhaps people in poor physical or financial shape have more headaches and also watch more TV. However, among several dozen po-

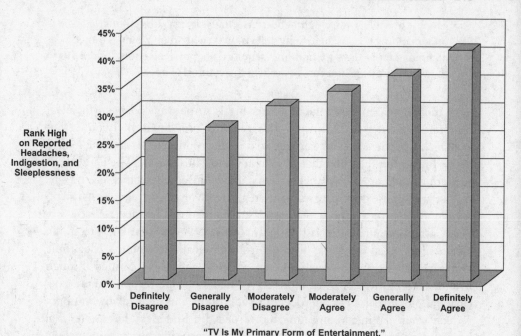

Figure 68: TV Watchers Don't Feel So Great

tential predictors of malaise (including self-described physical health, financial anxiety, frequency of exercise, use of cigarettes, religiosity, various forms of social connectedness, and all standard demographic characteristics), the top four, far above all other factors, turned out to be physical health, financial insecurity, low education (a proxy for social class), and TV dependence. Not surprisingly, physical health was the strongest predictor of malaise, but the other three were essentially equal in predictive power. In other words, TV dependence is as disruptive to one's constitution as financial anxiety and class deprivation. Without experimental research, we cannot prove which way the causal arrow points, but it is not obvious why people with a headache would disproportionately seek solace in TV. (We shall see later some evidence that generational differences are implicated here as well.) But whichever causes what, it is not a little distressing that by the end of the twentieth century more than half of all Americans said that TV was their primary form of entertainment.

Like other addictive or compulsive behaviors, television seems to be a surprisingly unsatisfying experience. Both time diaries and the "beeper" studies find that for the average viewer television is about as enjoyable as housework and cooking, ranking well below all other leisure activities and indeed below work itself.[51] TV's dominance in our lives reflects not its sublime pleasures, but its minimal costs. Time researchers John Robinson and Geoffrey Godbey conclude:

Much of television's attraction is that it is ubiquitous and undemanding. . . . As an activity, television viewing requires no advance planning, costs next to nothing, requires no physical effort, seldom shocks or surprises, and can be done in the comfort of one's own home.[52]

Another reason that television viewing is so negatively linked to social connectedness may be that it provides a kind of pseudopersonal connection to others. Anyone who has encountered a television personality face-to-face knows the powerful feeling that you already know this person. The daily cheer of morning anchors or the weekly drama of well-loved characters reassures us that we know these people, care about them, are involved in their lives—and no doubt they reciprocate those feelings (or so we subconsciously feel).

Communications theorist Joshua Meyrowitz notes that the electronic media allow social ties to be divorced from physical encounters. "Electronic media create ties and associations that compete with those formed through live interaction in specific locations. Live encounters are certainly more 'special' and provide stronger and deeper relationships, but their relative number is decreasing." Political communications specialist Roderick Hart argues that television as a medium creates a false sense of companionship, making people *feel* intimate, informed, clever, busy, and important. The result is a kind of "remote-control politics," in which we as viewers *feel* engaged with our community without the effort of actually *being* engaged.[53] Like junk food, TV, especially TV entertainment, satisfies cravings without real nourishment.

By making us aware of every social and personal problem imaginable, television also makes us less likely to do anything about it. "When the problems of all others become relatively equal in their seeming urgency," Meyrowitz notes, "it is not surprising that many people turn to take care of 'number one.'" In a similar vein, political scientist Shanto Iyengar has shown experimentally that prevailing television coverage of problems such as poverty leads viewers to attribute those problems to individual rather than societal failings and thus to shirk our own responsibility for helping to solve them. Political scientist Allan McBride showed in a careful content analysis of the most popular TV programs that "television programs erode social and political capital by concentrating on characters and stories that portray a way of life that weakens group attachments and social/political commitment." Television purveys a disarmingly direct and personal view of world events in a setting dominated by entertainment values. Television privileges personalities over issues and communities of interest over communities of place. In sum, television viewing may be so strongly linked to civic disengagement because of the psychological impact of the medium itself.[54]

• • •

PERHAPS, TOO, THE MESSAGE—in other words, the specific programmatic content—is also responsible for TV's apparent anticivic effects. The DDB Needham Life Style surveys allow us to explore this possibility because, in addition to questions about social connectedness and civic involvement, the surveys elicit information about which specific programs the respondents "watch because you really like it." While causality is impossible to extract from such evidence, we can construct a rough-and-ready ranking of which programs attract and/or create the most civic and least civic audiences.

At the top of the pro-civic hierarchy (controlling, as always, for standard demographic characteristics, such as age and social class) are news programs and educational television. In the late 1990s the audiences for programs like the network news and public affairs presentations, *NewsHour* and other PBS shows, were generally more engaged in community life than other Americans, in part because these audiences tended to avoid other TV fare. At the other end of the scale fell action dramas (exemplified in an earlier era by *The Dukes of Hazzard* and *Miami Vice*), soap operas (such as *Dallas* and *Melrose Place*), and so-called reality TV (such as *America's Most Wanted* and *A Current Affair*).[55]

One way of gauging the impact of different types of programming on civic engagement (as distinct from simply the amount of time spent before the tube) is to compare the effects of increasing doses of news programs and of daytime TV, controlling not only for education, income, sex, age, race, employment and marital status, and the like, but also for the total time spent watching TV. As figure 69 shows, the more time spent watching news, the more active one is in the community, whereas the more time spent watching soap operas, game shows, and talk shows, the less active one is in the community.[56] In other words, even among people who spend the same number of hours watching TV, what they watch is closely correlated with how active they are in community life.

The clear distinction between the *NewsHour* audience and the *Jerry Springer Show* audience underscores the fact that not all television is antisocial. Experimental research has shown that pro-social programming can have pro-social effects, such as encouraging altruism.[57] Moreover, television (especially, but not only, public affairs programming) can sometimes reinforce a wider sense of community by communicating a common experience to the entire nation, such as happened in the Kennedy assassination, the *Challenger* explosion, and the Oklahoma City bombing. These were shared national experiences only because television brought the same painful images into our homes. Television at its civic best can be a gathering place, a powerful force for bridging social differences, nurturing solidarity, and communicating essential civic information.

To this list of shared experiences, however, we must add the deaths of

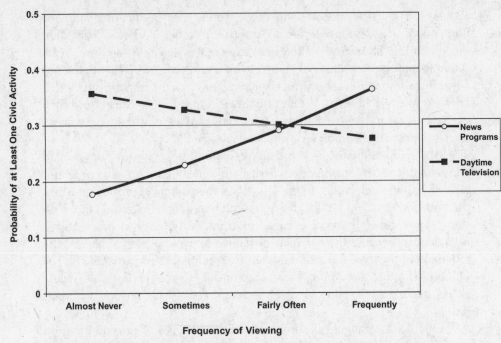

Figure 69: Types of Television Programs and Civic Engagement, Controlling for Time Spent Watching TV

Diana and JFK Jr. and the O.J. trial, all of which purveyed more melodrama than civic enlightenment. The bonds nurtured by these common experiences are psychologically compelling, as virtually all of us can testify. But they are generally not sociologically compelling, in the sense of leading to action. Each episode is captivating, but few lead to enduring changes in the way we behave or connect. Child psychologists speak of a fairly primitive stage of social development called "parallel play"—two kids in a sandbox, each playing with a toy but not really interacting with each other. In healthy development children outgrow parallel play. But the public spectacles of television leave us at that arrested stage of development, rarely moving beyond parallel attentiveness to the same external stimulus.

Television "in the wild," so to speak, is represented mostly by programs that are empirically linked to civic disengagement. Those program types that are most closely associated with civic isolation constitute a massive and growing share of television programming. "Target marketing" and the advent of five-hundred-channel cable TV portend a further fragmentation of audiences along lines of social, economic, and personal interest.[58] According to Nielsen Media Research, the number of channels received by the average household soared from nineteen in 1985 to forty-nine in 1997 and continues to rise. The ability of television to create a single national "water-cooler" culture has shrunk, as fewer and fewer of us watch common programs. In the early 1950s two-thirds of all Americans tuned in and watched the top-rated program (*I Love Lucy*); in the early 1970s the top-rated program (*All in the Family*) drew about half of the national TV audience; by the mid-1990s the audience share of *ER* and *Seinfeld* was barely one-third.[59] This trend toward market segmentation provides choice and presumably thus enhances consumer satisfaction, but it also undercuts TV's once vaunted role in bringing us together.

Another probable effect of television (not just programming, but also the associated advertising) is its encouragement of materialist values. For example, according to media researcher George Gerbner and his colleagues, heavy-viewing adolescents "were more likely to want high status jobs that would give them a chance to earn a lot of money but also wanted to have their jobs be relatively easy with long vacations and time to do other things." As we shall see in more detail in the next chapter, materialism among college freshmen has risen notably during the era of maximum television exposure, and while in college, students who watch more television become even more materialistic, compared with their fellow students who watch less TV or none at all.[60]

In sum, the rise of electronic communications and entertainment is one of the most powerful social trends of the twentieth century. In important respects this revolution has lightened our souls and enlightened our minds, but it has also rendered our leisure more private and passive. More and more of our time and money are spent on goods and services consumed individually, rather than those consumed collectively. Americans' leisure time can increasingly be measured—as do strategic marketers—in terms of "eyeballs," since watching things (especially electronic screens) occupies more and more of our time, while doing things (especially with other people) occupies less and less. This emphasis on visual entertainment seems to be especially common among the generations who have been reared in the last several decades.[61] Watching TV, videos, and computer windows onto cyberspace is ever more common. Sharing communal activities is ever less so.

The apotheosis of these trends can be found, most improbably, at the Holiday Bowling Lanes in New London, Connecticut. Mounted above each lane is a giant television screen displaying the evening's TV fare. Even on a full night of league play, team members are no longer in lively conversation with one another about the day's events, public and private. Instead each stares silently at the screen while awaiting his or her turn. Even while bowling together, they are watching alone.

The effects of these new technologies on Americans' worldview are most marked among the younger generations. Social critic Sven Birkerts emphasizes the historical rupture that the introduction of television signaled:

There is a ledge, a threshold, a point after which everything is different.
I would draw the line, imprecisely, somewhere in the 1950s. That was

when television worked its way into the fabric of American life, when we grew accustomed to the idea of parallel realities—the one that we lived in, the other that we stepped into whenever we wanted a break from our living. People born after the mid-1950s are the carriers of the new; they make up the force that will push us out of our already-fading rural/small-town/urban understanding of social organization. The momentum of change has already made those designations all but meaningless.[62]

Americans at the end of the twentieth century were watching more TV, watching it more habitually, more pervasively, and more often alone, and watching more programs that were associated specifically with civic disengagement (entertainment, as distinct from news). The onset of these trends coincided exactly with the national decline in social connectedness, and the trends were most marked among the younger generations that are (as we shall see in more detail in the next chapter) distinctively disengaged. Moreover, it is precisely those Americans most marked by this dependence on televised entertainment who were most likely to have dropped out of civic and social life—who spent less time with friends, were less involved in community organizations, and were less likely to participate in public affairs.

The evidence is powerful and circumstantial, though because it does not derive from randomized experiments, it cannot be fully conclusive about the causal effects of television and other forms of electronic entertainment. Heavy users of these new forms of entertainment are certainly isolated, passive, and detached from their communities, but we cannot be entirely certain that they would be more sociable in the absence of television. At the very least, television and its electronic cousins are willing accomplices in the civic mystery we have been unraveling, and more likely than not, they are ringleaders.

CHAPTER 14

From Generation
to Generation

OUR EFFORTS THUS FAR to identify the culprits for civic disengagement have been fruitful but inconclusive. Television, sprawl, and pressures of time and money each contributes measurably to the problem. However, even the small, shrinking minority of Americans most insulated from such pressures—affluent single-wage-earner couples who live outside major metropolitan areas and seldom watch TV—have steadily disengaged from community and social life over the last two decades. Seemingly living in comfortably "square" 1950s Pleasantville, even these folks went to half as many club meetings in the 1990s as people like them did in the 1970s and are five times more likely to be entirely disengaged from community life. Even in the tiny, civic-minded hamlets of pastoral Vermont, attendance at town meetings fell by nearly half between the early 1970s and the late 1990s.[1] As we noted earlier, virtually no corner of American society has been immune to this anticivic contagion. It has affected men and women; central cities, suburbs, and small towns; the wealthy, the poor, and the middle class; blacks, whites, and other ethnic groups; people who work and those who don't; married couples and swinging singles; North, South, both coasts, and the heartland.

Age is the one striking exception to this uniformity. Age is second only to education as a predictor of virtually all forms of civic engagement, and trends in civic engagement are *not* uniform across all age categories. Middle-aged and older people are more active in more organizations than younger people, attend church more often, vote more regularly, both read and watch the news more frequently, are less misanthropic and more philanthropic, are more interested in politics, work on more community projects, and volunteer more.[2]

Something about age is clearly a key to our puzzle. However, this clue is fundamentally ambiguous, for it might strengthen either of two quite different interpretations. Do people of different ages behave differently because they are momentarily at different points in a common life cycle or because they enduringly belong to different generations? Age is an exceedingly valuable clue, but it is not so nearly infallible as fingerprints or DNA, so we need to explore the evidence with care.

AT THE END of the twentieth century, American males in their sixties and seventies had much worse eyesight than their grandsons in their twenties and thirties, and the older men were also much more likely to have served in the military than were their grandsons. However, these two age-related patterns have quite different origins. The eyesight effect is due entirely to the life cycle: as we age, virtually everyone's vision deteriorates. On the other hand, the different rates of military service are due to generational differences. About 80 percent of men born in the 1920s served in the military, as compared with about 10 percent of men born in the 1960s, a difference attributable entirely to differences in world affairs when each group reached eighteen. Eyesight reflects the life cycle, whereas military service reflects generations. When the grandsons reach their grandfathers' age, their vision too will blur, but they will never share their grandfathers' military service.

With evidence from a single point in time, we cannot distinguish between life cycle and generational effects, but if we follow a given cohort over the years, we can more readily distinguish the two. And the two effects have dramatically different social consequences. Life cycle effects mean that individuals change, but society as a whole does not. Generational effects mean that society changes, even though individuals do not. There is little reason to believe that average eyesight in America will deteriorate in the early decades of the twenty-first century, but it is virtually certain that veterans will become rarer.

So before we can tell whether the ubiquitous age-related differences in civic engagement are truly generational, and thus producing social change, we need to determine whether these differences are attributable to the normal life cycle. With comparable evidence across several decades, we can follow each cohort as its members move through various stages of life. If successive cohorts generally retrace the same ups and downs as they age, we can be reasonably sure that we are observing a life cycle pattern. If not, it is more likely that age-related differences are generational in origin.[3]

Life cycle patterns in social behavior are typically caused by one of three factors—the demands of family (that is, marriage and parenting), the slackening of energy (declining from adolescence to old age), and the shape of careers (that is, entering and leaving the labor force). Different forms of civic involvement peak at different stages of the life cycle. Sports clubs attract the energies of youth. Time with friends peaks in one's early twenties, declines with marriage and kids, and rebounds in one's sixties with retirement and widowhood. Child-related activities, like parent-teacher meetings, picnicking, and athletic events, are tied to the prime parenting years (twenties and thirties). Membership in civic organizations and professional societies crests among men and women in their forties and fifties. Donation of blood rises to a peak in one's thirties and falls off sharply after fifty, whereas donation of money rises later in life. Church involvement spurts during one's twenties (with the advent of marriage and children), plateaus, and then resumes rising gently among seniors. Volunteering used to have a single peak in one's thirties, reflecting PTA bake sales and Little League coaching, but in recent decades (as we saw in chapter 7) a second, postretirement spurt in volunteering has appeared. Civic engagement in general typically traces a pattern like that in figure 70, rising from early adulthood toward a plateau in middle age, from which it gradually declines. This humpback pattern represents the natural arc of life's engagements.[4]

If this normal cycle of life's events entirely explained age-related differences in civic engagement, older Americans should be much less involved

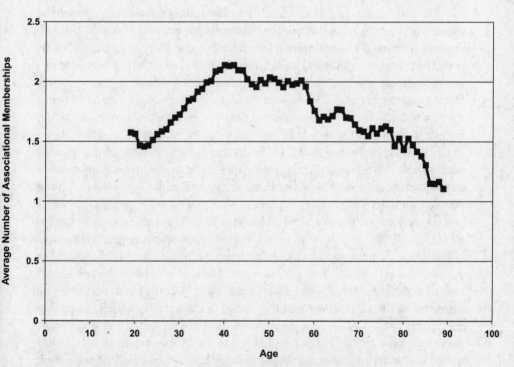

Figure 70: Membership in Associations Rises and Falls with Age

civically than middle-aged people. Classic sociological studies in the 1950s and 1960s found exactly that. By the 1990s, however, middle-aged men and women were, unexpectedly, not much more engaged than their elders.

Moreover, as baby boomers passed through the normal civic life cycle, like a pig through a python, America should have experienced waves of increasing civic involvement, as the boomers ascended the normal life cycle of rising community involvement. We should have seen a boom in PTA membership in the 1970s and 1980s, along with rapidly rising church membership, and a profusion of civic involvement in the 1990s. (By this same logic, we should look forward to a boom in volunteering and philanthropy as the boomers begin to retire in the 2010s.) So far, however, none of those past waves of civic engagement has materialized—quite the contrary, as we have seen throughout this book: the boomers and their successors have not trod the same ascending civic path traced by previous generations. This civic "dog that didn't bark" is an important clue to America's civic decline in the past several decades, for the expected life cycle upswings must have been swamped by unexpected generational downswings. Political interest and participation, church attendance, community projects, charitable giving, organizational involvement—as we have seen, all these forms of civic involvement and more besides have declined largely, if not exclusively, because of the inexorable replacement of a highly civic generation by others that are much less so.[5]

We can see this fact most clearly by examining the civic engagement of successive generations as they pass by fixed milestones in the life cycle. Table 3 presents patterns of change among four different age groups over the last quarter of the twentieth century.[6] This table, though packed with numbers, is worth poring over, for it portrays a striking picture of social change in America over the last quarter century. The table, in effect, holds life cycle differences constant in order to focus on generational differences. The first row in the table, for example, shows the extent of newspaper readership in four different age brackets at the beginning of the 1970s. In that era slightly less than half of all young adults (49 percent) read a newspaper daily, as compared with roughly three-quarters of each of the other three age groups in the population. Among people over sixty, for example, 76 percent were newspaper readers. The second row shows the level of newspaper readership in each of these same age groups in the mid-1990s. In that more recent period readership among young adults had fallen to 21 percent, less than half the figure for young adults two decades earlier, for a relative decline of 57 percent. At the other end of the age hierarchy, newspaper readership had also slipped a bit, but only by 10 percent. The third row in the table shows that the rate of decline in newspaper readership was much faster among younger cohorts than among older cohorts. People over sixty in the 1990s (that is, people born in the 1930s or earlier) were almost as likely to read newspapers as people that age had been in the 1970s. In short, the falloff in newspaper readership in America from the 1970s to the 1990s was heavily concentrated in the younger generations—the younger the cohort, the more rapid the decline over these two decades.

Now scanning down the table, one can see that this same pattern applies to practically every form of civic engagement. In virtually every case, disengagement was concentrated among the younger cohorts and is slightest among men and women born and raised before World War II. Among people over sixty, reading newspapers, signing petitions, and writing letters to the editor and to Congress were almost as common in the 1990s as in the 1970s, but among the youngest category these activities were half as common as they had been. Among the oldest cohort church attendance was essentially unchanged between 1973–74 and 1997–98, whereas among people under thirty it fell by nearly one-third. Even in cases such as union membership and work for a political party, in which every age group shows a falloff in participation, the *rate* of decline was significantly faster among younger cohorts. As the last three rows in the table show, participation in *any* of the twelve civic activities measured in the Roper Social and Political Trends surveys fell by 11 percent among those over sixty, by 22 percent among those aged forty-five to fifty-nine, by 32 percent among those aged thirty to forty-four, and by 44 percent among those under thirty. Reading across the row for the 1970s, we see the familiar life cycle humpback, with the oldest cohort significantly less engaged than the younger ones. By the 1990s, however, the life cycle hump was much flatter, as the younger cohorts were now only slightly more engaged than their elders. The more recent the cohort, the more dramatic its disengagement from community life. This is a strong clue that the overall decline in civic engagement in America over the last several decades had its roots in generational differences.[7]

The key question to ask about generational differences is not *how old are people now*, but *when were they young*.[8] Figure 71 addresses this question, displaying various measures of civic engagement according to the respondents' year of birth.[9] In effect, figure 71 lines up Americans from left to right according to their date of birth, beginning with those born in the first third of the twentieth century and continuing across to the generation of their grandchildren, born in the last third of the century. To each successive birth cohort, we pose a series of tests of social capital and civic engagement: Did you vote in the last presidential election? How often do you read a newspaper? What voluntary associations do you belong to, if any? How often do you attend church? How many times last year did you attend a club meeting? Are you interested in politics? Did you work on any community projects last year? Do you think most people can be trusted or that you can't be too careful?

As we begin moving along this line from the oldest generation toward younger generations—from those born around the turn of the last century to those born during the Roaring Twenties—we at first find high and relatively stable levels of civic engagement and social capital. Then rather abruptly, how-

Table 3: All Forms of Civic Disengagement Are Concentrated in Younger Cohorts

		Age Brackets			
		18–29	30–44	45–59	60+
Read newspaper daily	1972–75	49%	72%	78%	76%
	1996–98	21%	34%	53%	69%
	Relative change	−57%	−52%	−31%	−10%
Attend church weekly	1973–74	36%	43%	47%	48%
	1997–98	25%	32%	37%	47%
	Relative change	−30%	−25%	−22%	−3%
Signed petition	1973–74	42%	42%	34%	22%
	1993–94	23%	30%	31%	22%
	Relative change	−46%	−27%	−8%	0%
Union member	1973–74	15%	18%	19%	10%
	1993–94	5%	10%	13%	6%
	Relative change	−64%	−41%	−32%	−42%
Attended public meeting	1973–74	19%	34%	23%	10%
	1993–94	8%	17%	15%	8%
	Relative change	−57%	−50%	−34%	−21%
Wrote congressman	1973–74	13%	19%	19%	14%
	1993–94	7%	12%	14%	12%
	Relative change	−47%	−34%	−27%	−15%
Officer or committee member of local organization	1973–74	13%	21%	17%	10%
	1993–94	6%	10%	10%	8%
	Relative change	−53%	−53%	−41%	−24%
Wrote letter to newspaper	1973–74	6%	6%	5%	4%
	1993–94	3%	5%	5%	4%
	Relative change	−49%	−18%	−9%	−4%
Worked for political party	1973–74	5%	7%	7%	5%
	1993–94	2%	3%	4%	3%
	Relative change	−64%	−59%	−49%	−36%
Ran for or held public office	1973–74	0.6%	1.5%	0.9%	0.6%
	1993–94	0.3%	0.8%	0.8%	0.5%
	Relative change	−43%	−49%	−8%	−22%
Took part in any of twelve different forms of civic life*	1973–74	56%	61%	54%	37%
	1993–94	31%	42%	42%	33%
	Relative change	−44%	−31%	−22%	−11%

* Wrote Congress, wrote letter to editor, wrote magazine article, gave speech, attended rally, attended public meeting, worked for political party, served as officer or as committee member of local organization, signed petition, ran for office, and/or belonged to good-government organization.

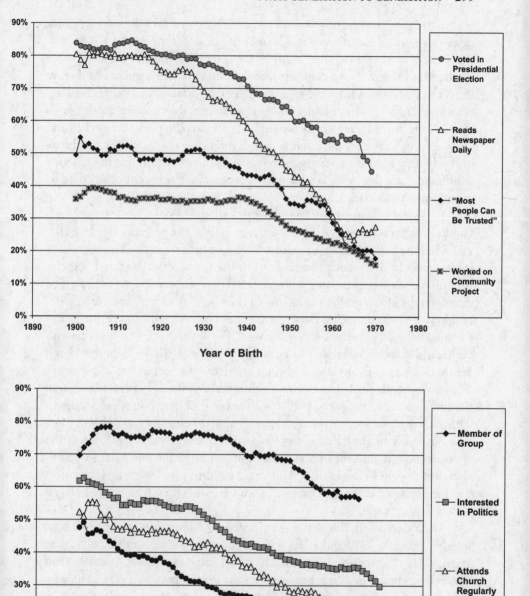

Figure 71: Generational Trends in Civic Engagement (Education Held Constant)

ever, starting with men and women born sometime in the 1930s, we encounter signs of reduced community involvement. These preboomers are still relatively civic, in absolute terms, but they are somewhat less so than their older brothers and sisters. As we continue along the line to the boomers and then to the X'ers, this downward trend in joining, trusting, voting, newspaper reading, church attending, volunteering, and being interested in politics continues almost uninterruptedly for nearly forty years. (Attendance rates at churches and clubs decline across all the cohorts, rather than showing the distinctive break in the 1930s.) Figure 71, in sum, shows that each generation that has reached adulthood since the 1950s has been less engaged in community affairs than its immediate predecessor.

By any standard, these intergenerational differences are extraordinary. Controlling for educational disparities, members of the generation born in the 1920s belong to almost twice as many civic associations as do members of the generation of their grandchildren born in the late 1960s (roughly 1.9 memberships per capita, compared with roughly 1.1 memberships per capita). The grandparents are more than twice as likely to trust other people as the grandchildren are (50 percent vs. 20 percent). They vote at nearly double the rate of the most recent cohorts (80–85 percent vs. 45–50 percent). The grandparents are nearly twice as interested in politics (55 percent vs. 30–35 percent) and nearly twice as likely to attend church regularly (45 percent vs. 25 percent). They are twice as likely to work on a community project (35 percent did so in the previous year, compared with 15–20 percent of the younger generation). The grandparents are the last of the rabid newshounds: they are almost three times as likely to read a daily newspaper (75 percent vs. 25 percent) as the youngest cohort, and they provide the lion's share of the audience for television news.[10] And well-established life cycle patterns give little reason to expect that the youngest generation ever will come to match their grandparents' levels of civic engagement.

Deciphered with this key, figure 71 depicts a long civic generation, born roughly between 1910 and 1940, a broad group of people substantially more engaged in community affairs and more trusting than those younger than they.[11] The core of this civic generation is the cohort born in 1925–1930, who attended grade school during the Great Depression, spent World War II in high school (or on the battlefield), first voted in 1948 or 1952, set up housekeeping in the 1950s, and saw their first television when they were in the late twenties. Since national polling began, this cohort has been exceptionally civic—voting more, joining more, reading more, trusting more, giving more.

What is more, this group has played this leading civic role despite the fact that it received substantially less formal education than its children and grandchildren. Only one-quarter of Americans born between 1900 and 1940 went beyond high school, as compared with more than half of Americans born after that date. As far as formal education is concerned, the members of the long civic generation were "self-made" citizens. As the distinguished sociologist Charles Tilly (born in 1928) has said on behalf of his generation, "We are the last suckers."[12]

These patterns hint that being raised after World War II was a quite different experience from being raised before that watershed. It is as though the postwar generations were exposed to some anticivic X-ray that permanently and increasingly rendered them less likely to connect with the community. Whatever that force might have been, *it*—rather than anything that happened during the 1970s and 1980s—accounts for most of the civic disengagement that lies at the core of our mystery. But why did it take so long for the effects of that mysterious X-ray to become manifest? If the roots of civic disengagement can be traced to the 1940s and 1950s, why did the effects not become conspicuous in PTA meetings and Masonic lodges, in the Red Cross and the bar association, and in polling places and church pews and bowling alleys across the land until the 1960s, 1970s, and 1980s?

The visible effects of generational disengagement were delayed several decades by two important factors. First, the postwar boom in college enrollments gave America a timely civic booster shot that forestalled a cataclysmic decline in political and social involvement that might otherwise have occurred.[13] More important, the effects of generational developments lag several decades after their onset, because it takes that long for a given generation to become numerically dominant in the adult population. The long civic generation (born between 1910 and 1940) did not reach its zenith until 1960, when it comprised two-thirds of those who chose between John Kennedy and Richard Nixon. Not coincidentally, many indexes of social capital that we examined in section II peaked at high noon of the long civic generation's day in the sun.

Only after the mid-1960s did significant numbers of the "postcivic" generation reach adulthood, diluting and then supplanting the civic engagement of older cohorts. By the time that Bill Clinton was elected president in 1992, the long civic generation's share in the electorate had been cut precisely in half compared to 1960. Conversely, in the last quarter of the twentieth century, boomers and X'ers (that is, Americans born after 1945) tripled from one out of every four adults to three out of four. This generational math (coupled with the civic differences among the successive generations) is the single most important explanation for the collapse of civic engagement over the last several decades.

In short, the decades that have seen a national deterioration in social capital are the very decades during which the numerical dominance of an exceptionally civic generation was replaced by the dominion of "postcivic" cohorts. Although the long civic generation has enjoyed unprecedented life expectancy, allowing its members to contribute more than their share to American social capital in recent decades, they are now passing from the scene. Even the youngest members of that generation reached retirement as the century ended. Thus a generational analysis leads almost inevitably to the conclusion that the national slump in civic engagement is likely to continue.

More than a quarter century ago, just as the first signs of disengagement were beginning to appear in American politics, political scientist Ithiel de Sola Pool observed that the central issue would be—it was then too soon to judge, as he rightly noted—whether the development represented a temporary change in the weather or a more enduring change in the climate.[14] It now appears that he had spotted the initial signs of a climatic shift. Moreover, just as the erosion of the ozone layer was not proven scientifically until many years after the proliferation of the chlorofluorocarbons that caused it, so too the erosion of America's social capital became visible only several decades after the underlying process had begun. Like Minerva's owl that flies at dusk, we come to appreciate how important the long civic generation has been to American community life just as its members are retiring. And reversing the effects of their departure will be as difficult as trying to heat a tubful of bathwater that has become cold: a lot of really hot water will have to be added to raise the average temperature. Unless America experiences a dramatic upward boost in civic engagement in the next few years, Americans in the twenty-first century will join, trust, vote, and give even less than we did at the end of the twentieth.

One important consequence is the graying of civic America. Older people have almost always voted somewhat more than younger people, but this generation gap in electoral turnout widened significantly from the 1960s to the 1990s. In fact, civic life in this country has been graying for nearly forty years, partly because seniors remain vigorous longer nowadays, but mainly because younger and middle-aged groups have been dropping out (or not joining in the first place), compared with people that same age a few decades earlier. In the early 1970s people sixty and over provided 12 percent of the officers and committee members of local organizations, 20 percent of all community volunteers, and 24 percent of the attendance at club meetings. By the mid-1990s these figures had risen to 20 percent, 35 percent, and 38 percent, respectively. Even though the seniors' share in the adult population barely budged during these two decades, their contribution to community life almost doubled.[15]

This overrepresentation of the older generation in civic life reflects the free choice of different cohorts about how to spend their time. Indeed, the older generation is upholding more than its share of the civic burden. At the same time, its voice on controversial issues is amplified by its activism. When the interests of the older generation differ from those of younger people—on local taxes to support schools, for example—it is reasonable to suspect that the views of the older generation have greater weight than they had a few decades ago. In the mid-1970s people forty-five and over accounted for one-third of the participants in local meetings about town and school affairs and the same fraction of all letters to the editor, but twenty years later their share in both public meetings and editorial pages had risen to one-half.[16] One does not have to assume that this older civic generation is unusually selfish—the opposite is probably true—to be concerned about the self-disenfranchisement of younger groups.

IF THE LONG CIVIC GENERATION is the first notable actor in our civic morality play, the second is the baby boom generation, born between 1946 and 1964. As the new century opens, the oldest members of this massive cohort are in their mid-fifties, the youngest in their mid-thirties. Boomers constitute more than one-third of the adult population, as they have for the last two decades and as they will for nearly another two decades. They are the best-educated generation in American history. Boomers experienced unprecedented affluence and community vitality in their youth, but as adults they have endured hard times, though less so than their parents did during the Great Depression.[17]

The boomers were the first generation to be exposed to television throughout their lives, and they are much more likely than their elders to turn on the TV without knowing what they are going to watch and to leave it on when they are not watching. Political scientist Paul Light reports that

> by the time the average baby boomer reached age 16, he or she had watched from 12,000 to 15,000 hours of TV, or the equivalent of 24 hours a day for 15 to 20 solid months. . . . There can be little doubt that television reduced the baby boom's contact with its peers and parents, and that the generation made its first contacts with the real world through the medium.[18]

In political terms, this generation was indelibly marked by the events of the sixties—the civil rights movement (which happened while most of them were still in elementary school), the Kennedy and King assassinations, the trauma of Vietnam, and Watergate. Perhaps with reason—they surely think so—they are distrusting of institutions, alienated from politics, and (despite their campus flings of the sixties and seventies) distinctively less involved in civic life—even less so their own children, some of whom have begun (as we saw in chapter 7 and will see again later in this chapter) a boomlet in volunteering. Despite their unusual education, boomers are less knowledgeable about politics than their parents were at a comparable age. As Michael Delli Carpini, the political biographer of the sixties generation, observes, "They are less likely to be interested in politics, less likely to follow politics with any regularity, less likely to express a political opinion, and less likely to have accurate information relevant to politics." [19] They vote less, campaign less, attend political meetings less, contribute less, and in general avoid their civic duties more than other generations. [20] Delli Carpini concludes,

> It is the rejection of mainstream politics rather than the development of an alternative political direction that most clearly distinguishes the sixties generation from preceding cohorts. . . . In short, it is a generation which, relative to earlier generations, rejects the norms and institutions that are central to the political system of which they are a part. What distinguishes this generation most is what it does not like or does not do, and not what it likes or does. [21]

Politics is, however, not the only aspect of community life from which the boomers disengaged. Boomers were slow to marry and quick to divorce. Both marriage and parenthood became choices, not obligations. Although 96 percent of boomers were raised in a religious tradition, 58 percent abandoned that tradition, and only about one in three of the apostates have returned. In their work life they are less comfortable in bureaucracies, less loyal to a particular firm, more insistent on autonomy. Perhaps because of the very uniformity of the postwar society into which they were born—two-parent, two-child families, chrome-laden cars and prefab homes, packed classrooms and I Love Lucy— they put great emphasis on individualism and tolerance for diversity and rejected traditional social roles. One cost of the crowded schools the boomers attended was a reduced opportunity for social learning, for research shows that participation in extracurricular activities is substantially diminished in larger schools. In part because of competitive pressures inherent in their large cohort, boomers have had to endure diminished expectations and economic frustrations. [22]

Throughout their lives they have expressed more libertarian attitudes than their elders and less respect for authority, religion, and patriotism. Comparisons of the high school graduating classes of 1967 and 1973 make clear that even in high school late boomers were less trusting, less participatory, more cynical about authorities, more self-centered, and more materialistic, even by comparison to early boomers. Boomers in general are highly individualistic, more comfortable on their own than on a team, more comfortable with values than with rules. They are less moralistic about drug use, for example, than their parents—more inclined to blame drug problems on society than on the individual and less likely to accept drug testing in the workplace. To their credit, the boomers have been from the beginning an unusually tolerant generation—more open-minded toward racial, sexual, and political minorities, less inclined to impose their own morality on others. [23] We shall examine this admirable facet of their political outlook in more detail in chapter 22.

On any given issue, the tolerant, cynical, "laid-back" boomers may have a point, but as a syndrome their attitudes have had a high social cost. Survey analyst Cheryl Russell perceptively characterizes boomers as "free agents."[24] The evidence on social capital and civic engagement that we have reviewed in earlier chapters makes clear that this free agency has reduced the vitality of American communities—less volunteering, less philanthropy, less trust, less shared responsibility for community life.

Generational nomenclature after the boomers becomes more controversial. At some risk of unintentional insult to its members, I here follow the custom of referring to those born between 1965 and 1980 as the "X Generation." Although X'ers have often been blamed by their elders (especially the boomers) for the troubles of contemporary American society—especially the emphasis on materialism and individualism—the evidence that I have already presented makes clear that this indictment is misplaced. The erosion of American social capital began before any X'er was born, so the X'ers cannot reasonably be blamed for these adverse trends. That said, the X Generation reflects in many respects a continuation of the generational course begun just after World War II.

Closely examined, table 3 clearly shows that almost all forms of civic engagement—from union membership to church attendance to petition signing to public meeting attendance—continued to plummet among young people who were in their twenties in the nineties—that is, Gen X'ers. In many respects this generation accelerated the tendencies to individualism found among boomers, for X'ers are the second consecutive generation of free agents. X'ers have an extremely personal and individualistic view of politics. They came of age in an era that celebrated personal goods and private initiative over shared public concerns. Unlike boomers, who were once engaged, X'ers have never made the connection to politics, so they emphasize the personal and private over the public and collective. Moreover, they are visually oriented, perpetual surfers, multitaskers, interactive media specialists. In both personal and national terms, this generation is shaped by uncertainty (especially given the slow growth, inflation-prone 1970s and 1980s), insecurity (for these are the children of the divorce explosion), and an absence of collective success stories—no victorious D-Day and triumph over Hitler, no exhilarating, liberating marches on Washington and triumph over racism and war, indeed hardly any "great collective events" at all. For understandable reasons, this cohort is very inwardly focused.

Gen X'ers are also more materialist than their predecessors were at this age, although perhaps no more materialist than the boomers themselves have become in middle age. One useful window onto the changing values of American youth over the last three decades is provided by the annual UCLA survey of college freshmen. (See figure 72 for an overview of key trends.) In the late 1960s and early 1970s, as the boomers entered college, 45–50 percent of them rated keeping up-to-date with politics and helping clean up the environment as very important personal objectives, compared with roughly 40 percent of them who rated "being very well off financially" that high. By 1998, as the last of the X'ers entered college, three decades of growing materialism had reduced ratings for politics and the environment to 26 percent and 19 percent, respectively, while financial well-being had shot up to a rating of 75 percent. An independent annual nationwide survey of high school seniors by the University of Michigan confirms this trend toward growing materialism, as the fraction of students who rated "having lots of money" as quite important burgeoned from 46 percent in 1976 to 70 percent in 1990, before drifting back to 60–65 percent in the mid-1990s.[25]

These values are consistent with the self-reported behavior of X'ers. According to the UCLA surveys, political discussions among high school students were only half as common in the late 1990s as in the late 1960s. Participation in student elections plummeted even faster than participation by their parents in national elections, falling from roughly 75 percent in the late 1960s to 20 percent in the late 1990s. When high school seniors were given a long list of potential recipients of charitable donations, from the United Way to citizens' lobbies to the cancer society, the proportion who said that they would "definitely" make such contribution to at least one such organization (or already had) fell by about a quarter between the mid-1970s and the mid-1990s.[26] Most portentous of all, X'ers are much less likely to trust other people than people their age were twenty years ago: the fraction of high school seniors who agreed

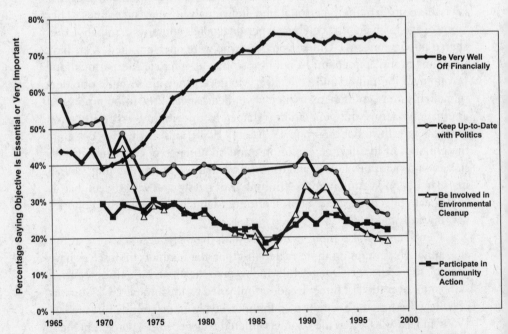

Figure 72: Greed Trumps Community Among College Freshmen, 1966–1998

that "most people can be trusted" was sliced exactly in half between the late boomers of 1976 (of whom 46 percent were trusting) and the late X'ers of 1995 (of whom only 23 percent were trusting).[27]

These distinctions persisted when the X'ers moved into adulthood. Only 54 percent of X'er adults feel guilty when they don't vote, as compared with over 70 percent for older generations, and X'ers are in fact much less likely to vote, particularly in local elections. Compared with older generations—even when those older generations were the same age as the X'ers are now—they are less interested in politics, less informed about current events (except for scandal, personality, and sports), less likely to attend a public meeting, less likely to contact public officials, less likely to attend church, less likely to work with others on some community project, and less likely to contribute financially to a church or charity or political cause. X'ers are *not* especially cynical about politics or critical of political leaders—those are traits they share with their elders—but X'ers *are* less inclined to get involved themselves.[28] Whether these changes are "the fault" of the students themselves or of their parents, teachers, and the broader society is quite another matter—I am inclined to blame the latter, not the former—but the facts appear clear. Collective action—and especially politics—is even more foreign to the X'ers than to the boomers.

Evidence of the distinctive challenges that have faced recent cohorts comes from a quite unexpected source: public health epidemiologists using a variety of different methodologies have confirmed a long-term trend toward increasing depression and suicide that is generationally based. Depression has struck earlier and much more pervasively in each successive generation, beginning with the cohorts born after 1940. For example, one study reported that "of those Americans born before 1955, only 1 percent had suffered a major depression by age 75; of those born after 1955, 6 percent had become depressed by *age 24.*"[29] Psychologist Martin Seligman concludes that "the rate of depression over the last two generations has increased roughly tenfold."[30]

Unfortunately, this same generational trend also appeared as a veritable epidemic of suicide among American youth in the last half of the twentieth century. Between 1950 and 1995 the suicide rate among adolescents aged fifteen to nineteen more than quadrupled, while the rate among young adults aged twenty to twenty-four, beginning at a higher level, nearly tripled. Most, though not all, of this increase was concentrated among young men, although young women attempt suicide more frequently. Was this rise in youthful suicide simply part of a general rise in suicide among Americans in our harried age? Quite the contrary, as figure 73 shows, this explosive growth in youthful suicide coincided with an equally remarkable decline in suicide among older groups.[31]

In the first half of the twentieth century older people had been much more likely to commit suicide than younger people, presumably because of the accumulation of frustrations and physical frailties over the course of the life

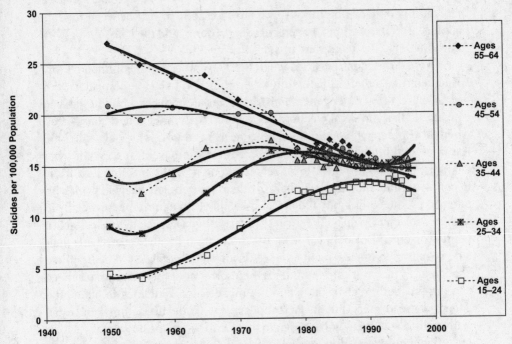

Figure 73: Age-Related Differences in Suicide Rates, 1950–1995

cycle. During the second half of the twentieth century, however, suicide became less and less common among older people and more and more common among younger people. In fact, this is precisely the pattern we might have predicted as the well-integrated long civic generation aged (reducing the traditionally high rates among old people) at the same time that the less well-integrated boomers and X'ers entered the population (raising the traditionally low rates among young people). As the twentieth century ended, Americans born and raised in the 1920s and 1930s were about *half as likely* to commit suicide as people that age had been at midcentury, whereas Americans born and raised in the 1970s and 1980s were *three or four times more* likely to commit suicide as people that age had been at midcentury. Whether or not generational differences in social capital fully account for figure 73, the figure surely shows that the life experiences of people who came of age *after* 1950 were very different from those of people who came of age *before* 1950.

In fact, a broadly similar trend toward youthful suicide at a time when suicide rates for the rest of the population were falling has been found in many Western countries. Since clinical depression is a prime risk factor for suicide, the rise in observed suicide rates for young people is sadly consistent with the generationally based increase in depression. As the leading researchers in the field summarize hundreds of studies in dozens of advanced countries:

It is striking that the rise in psychosocial disorders over the last 50 years is a phenomenon that applies to adolescents and young adults and not to older people. The explanation, therefore, has to lie in social, psychological or biological changes that impinge on younger age groups.[32]

Suicide is a powerful but (fortunately) rare symptom of psychic distress. Less dire, more pervasive symptoms are tapped by the annual DDB Needham Life Style surveys on headaches, indigestion, and sleeplessness—what we term "malaise." As figure 74 shows, in the mid-1970s the frequency of these symptoms did not differ significantly by age. On average, people in their sixties and seventies were neither more nor less likely than their children or grandchildren to be plagued by upset stomachs, migraines, and sleepless nights. Over the ensuing two decades, however, despite short-term fluctuation, among older people these symptoms of malaise tended to fade, while middle-aged and (especially) younger people became more and more afflicted. Between 1975–76 and 1998–99 the fraction of adults under thirty who ranked high on symptoms of malaise jumped from 31 percent to 45 percent, while the comparable index of suffering for adults sixty and over slipped from 33 percent to 30 percent. Slightly more than half of this growing gap can be attributed to the added financial worries that young people have encountered over the last quarter century, but that still leaves a substantial increase in youthful malaise unexplained, for even among the financially comfortable the generation gap in malaise widened steadily.[33]

Over these same years (net of life cycle effects) general contentment with life declined among people under fifty-five, while increasing modestly among people over that age. Surveys in the 1940s and 1950s had found that younger people were *happier* than older people. By 1975 age and happiness were essentially uncorrelated. By 1999, however, younger people were *unhappier* than older people.[34] The bottom line: a widening generation gap in malaise and unhappiness. The trends represented in figure 73 and figure 74 are, sadly, perfectly consistent: The younger you are, the worse things have gotten over the last decades of the twentieth century in terms of headaches, indigestion, sleeplessness, as well as general satisfaction with life and even likelihood of taking your own life.

At midcentury young Americans (those we would come to label as the long civic generation) were happier and better adjusted than other people—less likely to take their own lives, for example. At century's end that same generation (now in retirement) remains distinctively well-adjusted psychologically and physiologically. On the other hand, at century's end the children and grandchildren of the long civics (those we label boomers and X'ers) are much more distressed and more likely to take their own lives than their grandparents had been at their age.

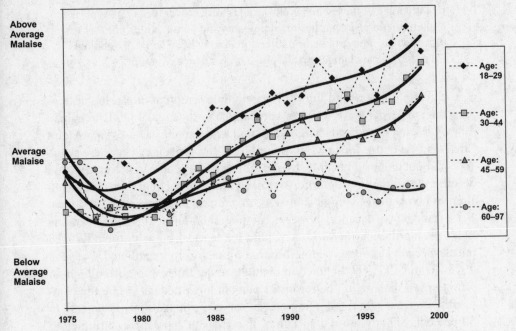

Figure 74: Growing Generation Gap in Malaise (Headaches, Insomnia, Indigestion)

As yet, this remarkable, well-established, and disturbing trend toward sui-cide, depression, and malaise among America's younger generations has no widely accepted interpretation. One plausible explanation, however, is social isolation. Educational sociologists Barbara Schneider and David Stevenson re-cently reported that "the average American teenager typically spends approx-imately three and a half hours alone each day. . . . Adolescents spend more time alone than with family or friends." Compared with teenagers studied in the 1950s, young people in the 1990s reported fewer, weaker, and more fluid friendships. Similarly, Martin Seligman points out that the depression epidemic has spared the close-knit old order Amish community, even though careful studies show that the rate of other mental diseases is no different in that community from that in the wider American society. He traces the growth of depression among younger Americans to "rampant individualism," coupled with "events that have weakened our commitment to the larger, traditional in-stitutions of our society."

Individualism need not lead to depression as long as we can fall back on large institutions—religion, country, family. When you fail to reach some of your personal goals, as we all must, you can turn to these larger institutions for hope. . . . But in a self standing alone without the buffer of larger beliefs, helplessness and failure can all too easily become hopelessness and despair.[35]

Our evidence shows that this trend encompasses not merely the ultimate trauma of suicide, but also chronic symptoms of milder distress.

Social isolation is a well-established risk factor for serious depression. In part, depression causes isolation (partly because depressed people choose isolation and partly because depressed people are not pleasant to be around). However, there is also reason to believe that isolation causes depression.[36] Though all the evidence is not in, it is hard to believe that the generational decline in social connectedness and the concomitant generational increase in suicide, depression, and malaise are unrelated.

Against this bleak picture of social isolation and civic disengagement among recent generations must be set one important countervailing fact: Without any doubt the last ten years have seen a substantial *increase* in volunteering and community service by young people. The annual survey of entering college freshman for 1998 reported that a record proportion of students volunteered during their last year of high school—74 percent, compared with a low of 62 percent in 1989. Volunteerism on a regular basis also is up, with 42 percent of freshmen donating their time for at least one hour a week, compared with 27 percent in 1987. This upturn in volunteering by high school students in the 1990s is also confirmed in the annual Michigan Monitoring the Future surveys, as well as the DDB Needham Life Style surveys.

Why this welcome and encouraging increase in volunteering has occurred is not yet clear. In part it may simply reflect stronger public encouragement (including, in some cases, graduation requirements) for community service. If this youthful volunteering is driven only by official pressure, without the undergirding of a broader civic infrastructure of community organizations, both religious and secular, then one cannot be optimistic that the increase will prove durable. On the other hand, a more optimistic interpretation would be that the forty-year trend toward generational disengagement is at last bottoming out.

GENERATIONAL SUCCESSION is, in sum, a crucial element in our story. However, it has *not* contributed equally powerfully to all forms of civic and social disengagement. The declines in church attendance, voting, political interest, campaign activities, associational membership, and social trust are attributable almost entirely to generational succession. In these cases, social change is driven largely by differences from one generation to another, not by changing habits of individuals. By contrast, the declines in various forms of *schmooz*ing, such as card playing and entertaining at home, are attributable mostly to society-wide changes, as people of all ages and generations tended to shift away from these activities. The declines in club meetings, in dining with family and friends, and in neighboring, bowling, picnicking, visiting with friends, and sending greeting cards are attributable to a complex combination of both society-wide change and generational replacement.

In other words, one set of forces has affected Americans of all ages over the last several decades. These *society-wide* forces have been especially detrimental to private socializing, such as playing cards and entertaining at home. The consequent declines have been moderately strong and visible in the short run, since the behavior of individuals of virtually all generations has been affected. The allure of electronic entertainment is a likely explanation for these trends, as it has transformed the way all of us spend our time.

A second set of forces has produced substantial differences across different generations, while not changing individuals. These *generational* forces have especially affected public engagement, such as religious observance, trust, voting, following the news, and volunteering. Because these forces have operated through generational succession, their effects have been more gradual and less immediately visible. Nevertheless, Americans born in the first half of the twentieth century have been persistently more likely to vote, to go to church, to volunteer, to keep up with public affairs, and to trust other people than Americans born in the second half of the century.

Some activities have been buffeted by *both* the society-wide effects on private socializing *and* the generational effects on public norms. Club meetings, family dining, and local organizational leadership are excellent examples of this type of change. Because such activities have been affected by both short-run and long-run changes, they have evidenced some of the most dramatic changes of all, such as the 60 percent fall in club meetings, the 53 percent fall in service as officer or committee member of a local group, and the 60 percent increase in families that customarily dine apart.

Since the link between generational change and declining civic engagement varies from domain to domain, it is somewhat misleading to form a single summary of the role of generational change in accounting for the declines surveyed in section II of this book. Nevertheless, as a rough summary it seems fair to say that about half of the overall decline in social capital and civic engagement can be traced to generational change.[37] However, to say that civic disengagement in contemporary America is in large measure generational merely reformulates our central puzzle. The roots of our lonely bowling probably date to the 1940s and 1950s, rather than to the 1960s, 1970s, and 1980s, but what force could have affected Americans who came of age after World War II so differently from their parents and even from their older brothers and sisters?

• • •

A NUMBER OF SUPERFICIALLY PLAUSIBLE CANDIDATES fail to fit the timing required by this new formulation of our mystery. Family instability, for example, seems to have an ironclad alibi for what we have now identified as the critical period, for the generational decline in civic engagement began with the children of the maritally stable 1940s and 1950s. The divorce rate in America actually fell after 1945, and the sharpest jump in the divorce rate did not occur until the 1970s, long after the cohorts who show the sharpest declines in civic engagement and social trust had left home. Similarly, working mothers are exonerated by this respecification of our problem, for the plunge in civicness among children of the 1940s, 1950s, and 1960s happened while Mom was still at home. Neither economic adversity nor affluence nor government policies can easily be tied to the generational decline in civic engagement, since the slump seems to have affected in equal measure those who came of age in the placid fifties, the booming sixties, the busted seventies, and the go-go eighties.

Several other factors fit the evidence better. First, the generational reformulation of our central mystery raises the possibility that the wartime Zeitgeist of national unity and patriotism that culminated in 1945 reinforced civic-mindedness. It is a commonplace of sociology that external conflict increases internal cohesion. As sociological pioneer William Graham Sumner wrote in 1906:

> A differentiation arises between ourselves, the we-group, or in-group, and everybody else, or the others-groups, out-groups. . . . The relation of comradeship and peace in the we-group and that of hostility and war towards others-groups are correlative to each other. The exigencies of war with outsiders are what make peace inside. . . . Loyalty to the group, sacrifice for it, hatred and contempt for outsiders, brotherhood within, warlikeness without—all grow together, common products of the same situation.

We noted in chapter 3 that membership in civic associations has spurted after both major wars in the twentieth century, and political scientist Theda Skocpol has extended this argument to the whole of American history. In chapter 5 we observed that union membership has historically grown rapidly during and immediately after major wars. Historians Susan Ellis and Katherine Noyes emphasize that to understand the origins of American volunteering, one must consider the history of American involvement in wars. "Volunteers are frequently active in the movements that lead to war, in the support of efforts to win war, in the protest against war, and in rebuilding society after war." [38]

During the Civil War, women in the North formed Ladies' Aid Societies to make bandages, clothing, and tents for soldiers, and eventually a group of Ladies' Aid Societies banded together to form the U.S. Sanitary Commission, which became the largest relief organization during and after the war. Drawing on her experience as a battlefield nurse with the Sanitary Commission, Clara Barton formed the American Red Cross in 1881. The war also gave a powerful boost to fraternal associations appealing to the spirit of camaraderie and mutual sacrifice fostered by shared wartime adversity. Five of what would become the largest associations of the late nineteenth century and early twentieth century—the Knights of Pythias, the Grange, the Benevolent and Protective Order of Elks, the Ancient Order of United Workmen, and the Grand Army of the Republic—were founded between 1864 and 1868. A similar, if less pronounced, spurt in voluntary activity in civil society was associated with World War I.[39]

The most relevant example, however, is the extraordinary burst of civic activity that (as we saw repeatedly in section II) occurred during and after the Second World War. Virtually every major association whose membership history we examined—from the PTA, the League of Women Voters, and the American Society of Mechanical Engineers to the Lions Club, the American Dental Association, and the Boy Scouts—sharply expanded its "market share" between the mid-1940s and the mid-1960s. As we observed, there were similar postwar spurts in other community activities from league bowling and card playing to churchgoing and United Way giving.

World War II, like earlier major wars in U.S. history, brought shared adversity and a shared enemy.[40] The war ushered in a period of intense patriotism nationally and civic activism locally. It directly touched nearly everyone in the country. Sixteen million men and women served in the armed forces, including six million volunteers. They and their immediate families made up at least one-quarter of the population. Of men born in the 1920s (the cohort that would prove to be the core of the "long civic generation"), nearly 80 percent served in the military.[41] In millions of front windows hung blue stars, emblematic of a son or husband in the armed forces, and a dismaying number of gold stars, signifying a lost loved one. And the agonizing task of deciding which young men would be sent off to war lay in the hands not of a distant federal bureaucracy, but of thousands of lay draft boards across the country.

Patriotic themes, including civilian service—civil defense, rationing, scrap drives, War Bond sales—pervaded popular culture, from radio shows to the comics section of newspapers, from Hollywood to Broadway to Tin Pan Alley. Historian Richard Lingeman reported, "American flags were displayed everywhere—in front of homes, public buildings, fraternal lodges. Elks, Lions, Kiwanis, Rotary, even trailer camps, gas stations, and motor courts had them." The war reinforced solidarity even among strangers: "You just felt that the stranger sitting next to you in a restaurant, or someplace, felt the same way you did about the basic issues."[42]

The government sought whenever possible to use voluntary cooperation and resorted to controls in piecemeal fashion—not least out of careful political calculation. Wrote one Democratic Party operative, opposing gas rationing before the 1942 congressional elections, "An appeal by the President for voluntary cooperation will get patriotic support . . . and will be politically safer."[43]

Treasury secretary Henry Morgenthau pressed for a massive advertising campaign to sell War Bonds in the hope that bond campaigns would "make the country war-minded." Batman flogged war bonds from the cover of his comic book, Betty Grable auctioned off a pair of nylons for $40,000, and Marlene Dietrich toured sixteen Ohio towns in a Jeep. It worked: twenty-five million workers signed up for payroll savings plans, and in 1944 E-bond sales absorbed 7.1 percent of after-tax personal income.[44]

Superstar crooner Bing Crosby was enlisted to rally support for scrap drives:

> Junk ain't junk no more, 'cause junk can win the war.
> What's junk to you has a job to do, 'cause junk ain't junk no more.
> Pots and pans, old garbage cans, the kettle that doesn't pour.
> Collect today for the USA, 'cause junk can win the war.[45]

Hard as it is to believe in our more jaundiced age, such appeals hit the target. Facing a severe shortage of rubber, in June 1942 the president asked the public to turn in "old tires, old rubber raincoats, old garden hose, rubber shoes, bathing caps, gloves — whatever you have that is made of rubber." Boy Scouts were posted at filling stations to remind drivers to donate their car floor mats. Literally millions of Americans responded to the president's appeal, and in less than four weeks roughly four hundred thousand tons of scrap rubber — six pounds for every man, woman, and child in the country (or at the front) — were collected.[46]

Volunteers came in throngs, especially early in the war. In the first six months of 1942 the civilian defense corps expanded from 1.2 million to 7 million, and by mid-1943 more than 12 million Americans were registered. With armbands, whistles, and flashlights, the volunteers set out to supervise blackouts, plan gas decontamination, practice first aid. In Chicago in April 1942 sixteen thousand block captains took the oath of allegiance in a mass ceremony in the Coliseum. Local communities raised funds through "socials" to build observer posts for aircraft spotters. "A recruitment meeting in Hannibal, Missouri, consisting of a parade followed by a town meeting, packed 4,000 people in the armory, and another 15,000 were outside because there was no room for them," recalls Lingeman. Meanwhile, Red Cross volunteers nationwide skyrocketed from 1.1 million in 1940 to 7.5 million in 1945 and set to work rolling bandages, ferrying blood donors to collection sites, training for emergency work.[47]

Young people enlisted in the war effort in myriad ways — the Junior Service Corps, the High School Victory Corps, the Scouts, the Junior Red Cross, and, not least, the 4-H, which took a lead in the Victory Garden program. At its peak this most popular of civilian war efforts generated nearly twenty million Victory Gardens in backyards and vacant lots, yielding 40 percent of all vegetables grown in the country. As an indication of the scope of young people's participation in the war effort, Lingeman lists the activities of Gary, Indiana, eighth-graders over a two-year period:

> taught young girls infant care; collected phonograph records; distributed WAR WORKERS SLEEPING signs; sold war stamps at an exhibition of a captured Japanese submarine; discussed curfew law with City Council; distributed anti-black market pledge cards; took auxiliary fireman and police training courses; collected 500,000 pounds of wastepaper; sold an average of $40,000 worth of war stamps a month; delivered Community Chest material to every home in the city; sponsored a Clean Plate campaign [to discourage food wastage]; participated in War Bond and tin can drives; and collected library books for servicemen.[48]

Wartime civilian volunteerism both drew on prewar associational networks and contributed in turn to the postwar civic frenzy. Social historian Julie Siebel has recounted one unexpectedly instructive example.[49] In prewar America, Junior Leagues had brought together privileged young ladies in communities across the country to socialize and to volunteer for various local "good works." As early as 1929 the Junior Leagues introduced the concept of a "volunteer bureau" to act as a kind of clearinghouse for local volunteerism. Even before Pearl Harbor the American Junior League Association (AJLA) was working with Eleanor Roosevelt (herself a former Junior Leaguer) to convert their existing volunteer bureaus into official Civilian Defense Volunteer Offices (CDVOs).

With the outbreak of war the AJLA became de facto the government's Office of Civilian War Services. By the end of 1943, 4,300 CDVOs had been established nationwide, and their volunteers were fixing school lunches, coordinating day care centers, running scrap drives, and organizing social welfare activities. After the war many of these volunteer bureaus successfully made the transition to peacetime service. In 1947, 390 such bureaus were still in operation, more than five times the number that had existed before the war. Multiply this example manyfold and one can begin to see the organizational mechanisms that undergirded the massive postwar civic renaissance that we observed repeatedly in section II.

My point is not to romanticize the ubiquity or the effectiveness of such efforts, or even the esprit de corps they generated. As the war progressed, it gradually became clear that energies (particularly of the adult volunteers) could be better invested elsewhere in the war effort, and many of these programs had sputtered to a stop by 1944. In the meantime, however, they had demonstrated the mobilizing power of shared adversity. Sociologist Lloyd Warner, studying the impact of the war on one town, reported finding a sense of "unconscious well-being" because "everyone is doing something to help in the common desperate enterprise in a co-operative rather than a private spirit." Adds historian Richard Polenberg, "To a large extent, participation in a common cause tended to enhance feelings of comradeship and well-being."[50] More important to our concerns here, it is almost surely no accident that those Indiana eighth-graders (and their older brothers and sisters) became in later years dependable members of the long civic generation.

The war fostered social solidarity in yet another way—by accentuating civic and economic equality. Symbolically it was important that celebrities like Joe DiMaggio, Clark Gable, William McChesney Martin (head of the New York Stock Exchange), and all four sons of FDR entered the armed services. To be sure, relatively few celebrities saw combat service, but an instructive comparison is with the Vietnam War, in which notorious social inequality in military service contributed directly to widespread cynicism. Materially, the combination of plentiful work in war industries, unionization, high taxes, rationing, and perhaps other factors meant that World War II (coupled to some extent with the prior Great Depression) was probably the most leveling event in American economic history. The fraction of all personal wealth held by the top 1 percent of adults fell from 31 percent in 1939 to 23 percent in 1945, and the share of income received by the top 5 percent fell from 28 percent to 19 percent.[51]

War is a powerful force for social change, and certainly not all the social changes fostered by World War II were good for American social capital. The powerful explosion of solidarity and self-sacrifice triggered by the attack on Pearl Harbor did not continue throughout the war. For example, shortages and rationing led to hoarding and black marketeering. Polenberg notes, "The longer the war lasted, the more the balance shifted from public and collective to private and personal concerns. . . . One in five Americans told interviewers that buying scarce goods at black market prices was sometimes justified."[52] Moreover, vast population shifts disrupted families and communities and exacerbated regional, racial, and class tensions. When massive new war plants sprouted in places like Ypsilanti (Michigan), Pascagoula (Mississippi), and Seneca (Illinois), conflict erupted between old-time residents and newcomers: "Folks in houses think trailer people are vermin" was a typical sentiment.[53] Racial tensions were in some instances heightened by the war—most obviously in the case of the Japanese Americans interned in California, but also in increased anti-Semitism and in violent episodes like the 1943 race riot in Detroit, in which twenty-five blacks and nine whites were killed. On the other hand, in historical perspective the social changes spawned by the war contributed directly to the black civil rights advances of the 1950s and 1960s.

As the twentieth century ends, Americans have learned that no story is all heroes. (Indeed, we sometimes feel that heroes don't really exist.) But most Americans in 1945 felt that the war had been a just one and that their terrible collective sacrifice—all those sons and daughters who would not come home—had been in some measure vindicated by victory. This was not a feeling that would be repeated in the 1950s in Korea or in the 1960s in Vietnam. Long-term research on veterans of these wars suggests that while Vietnam vets have been relatively isolated socially, even decades after the war, vets of the Second World War were more socially integrated.[54]

When twenty-nine-year-old John F. Kennedy, running for Congress in 1946, said, "Most of the courage shown in the war came from men's understanding of their interdependence on each other. Men were saving other men's lives at risk of their own simply because they realized that perhaps the next day their lives would be saved in turn. . . . We must work together. . . . We must have the same unity that we had during the war," most of his listeners must have nodded.[55] He and they had already formed the long civic generation. Fifteen years later, when he admonished the nation, "Ask not what your country can do for you; ask what you can do for your country," to the former Gary eighth-graders, now just turned thirty and settling down, it must have rung true in a way that, sadly, it no longer does to most Americans.

So one plausible explanation for the strong generational effects in civic engagement that pervade our evidence is the replacement of a cohort of men and women whose values and civic habits were formed during a period of heightened civic obligation with others whose formative years were different. In a complementary fashion, the generational patterns outlined in this chapter also reinforce my argument in the previous chapter. The long civic generation was the last cohort of Americans to grow up without television. The more fully that any given generation was exposed to television in its formative years, the lower its civic engagement during adulthood. As we saw in chapter 13, men and women raised in the sixties, seventies, and eighties not only watch television *more* than those born in the thirties, forties, and fifties: they also watch television *differently*—more habitually, even mindlessly—and those different ways in which television is used are linked in turn to different degrees of civic engagement. Although more research is needed to put the issue beyond all reasonable doubt, it seems likely the effect of TV discussed in chapter 13 and the effect of generation discussed in this chapter are in some respects opposite sides of the same coin.

As political scientist Wendy Rahn has shown, those generational differences continue to show up in the values expressed by successive cohorts more than half a century later.[56] (See figure 75.) The changes are probably part of a larger societal shift toward individual and material values and away from communal values. We saw in figure 72 unmistakable evidence of this transformation in the values expressed by college freshmen over the years, and there is comparable evidence of a similar shift across American society. When asked by Roper pollsters in 1975 to identify the elements of "the good life," 38 percent of all adults chose "a lot of money," and an identical 38 percent mentioned "a job that contributes to the welfare of society." The same question was then posed every three years, and by 1996 those who aspired to contribute to society had slipped to 32 percent, while those who aspired to a lot of money had leaped to 63 percent. Other increasingly important elements of the good life included a vacation home (rising from 19 percent in 1975 to 43 percent in 1996), a second color TV (10 percent to 34 percent), a swimming pool (14 percent to 36 percent), a second car (30 percent to 45 percent), travel abroad (30 percent to 44 percent), a job that pays more than average (45 percent to 63 percent), and "really nice" clothes (36 percent to 48 percent). By contrast, a happy marriage (84 percent to 80 percent), children (74 percent to 72 percent), and "an interesting job" (69 percent to 61 percent) all declined. Figure 76 summarizes the changes in the American definition of "the good life" during the last quarter of the twentieth century. Much of this growth in materialism, further analysis shows, is attributable to generational replacement, as a cohort less concerned about material goods passes from the scene and is replaced by a cohort who gives more priority to a second color TV and really nice clothes.[57]

"Community" means different things to different people. We speak of the community of nations, the community of Jamaica Plain, the gay community, the IBM community, the Catholic community, the Yale community, the Af-

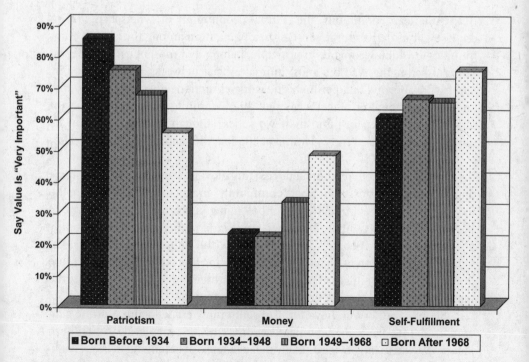

Figure 75: From Generation to Generation, Patriotism Wanes, Materialism Waxes

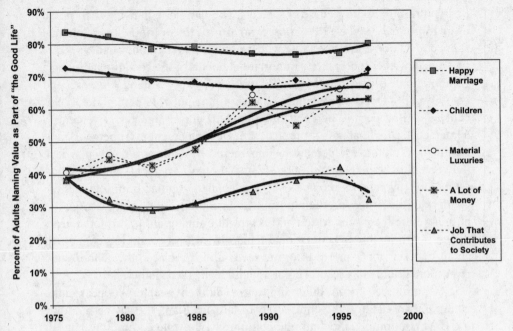

Figure 76: Materialism Grows in the Final Decades of the Twentieth Century

rican American community, the "virtual" community of cyberspace, and so on. Each of us derives some sense of belonging from among the various communities to which we might, in principle, belong. For most of us, our deepest sense of belonging is to our most intimate social networks, especially family and friends. Beyond that perimeter lie work, church, neighborhood, civic life, and the assortment of other "weak ties" that constitute our personal stock of social capital. (Keep in mind that "weak ties," though less intimate, can be quite important collectively.) How, if at all, does the sense of community differ across generations?

As the twentieth century ended, Yankelovich Partners surveyed large numbers of Americans about what "community" meant to them: "What are the ways in which you get a real sense of belonging or a sense of community?"[58] For all generations, as figure 77 shows, family and friends are most commonly cited, followed (for people who work outside the home) by co-workers. (In light of our discussion in chapter 5, it is interesting that co-workers are no more important for the younger generation than for their elders.) At this radius, the sense of belonging does not vary across the generations.

Slightly further out, however, the community embeddedness of the generations differs markedly. Compared with Gen X'ers, men and women born before 1946 are nearly twice as likely to feel a sense of belonging to their neighborhood, to their church, to their local community, and to the various groups

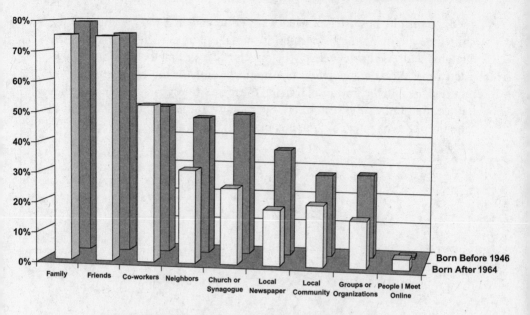

"In What Ways Do You Get a Real Sense of Belonging?"
Figure 77: The Meaning of Community for Successive Generations

and organizations to which they belong. (Baby boomers fall midway between the two in every case.) Among the younger generations, these residential, religious, and organizational ties are more frayed. Not surprisingly, electronic ties are more important to Gen X'ers than to the older generation, but even among the younger cohort, *kith and kin are twenty times more important than cyberfriends* as a source of community. As the new century opened, the younger generation felt less connection to civic communities—residential, religious, organizational—without any apparent offsetting focus of belongingness, beyond the ties to family, friends, and co-workers that they shared with the older generation. For the younger cohort, strong ties still count, but they are no longer complemented and reinforced by ties to the wider community.

To sum up: Much of the decline of civic engagement in America during the last third of the twentieth century is attributable to the replacement of an unusually civic generation by several generations (their children and grandchildren) that are less embedded in community life. In speculating about explanations for this sharp generational discontinuity, I am led to the conclusion that the dynamics of civic engagement in the last several decades have been shaped in part by social habits and values influenced in turn by the great mid-century global cataclysm. It is not, however, my argument that world war is a necessary or a praiseworthy means toward the goal of civic reengagement. We must acknowledge the enduring consequences—some of them, I have argued, powerfully positive—of what we used to call "the war," without at the same time glorifying martial virtues or mortal sacrifice. (This is precisely the dilemma addressed so effectively by director Steven Spielberg in *Saving Private Ryan*.) When a generation of Americans early in the twentieth century reflected on both the horrors of war and the civic virtues that it inculcated, they framed their task as the search for "the moral equivalent of war." [59] Insofar as the story of this chapter contains any practical implication for civic renewal, it is that.

CHAPTER 15

What Killed
Civic Engagement?
Summing Up

WE ARE ABOUT READY to sum up our conclusions about the complex of factors that lies behind the erosion of America's social connectedness and community involvement over the last several decades. First, however, we must review the evidence for and against several additional suspects.

First, the American family structure has changed in several important and potentially relevant ways over the last several decades. The downturn in civic engagement coincided with the breakdown of the traditional family unit—Mom, Dad, and the kids. Since the family itself is, by some accounts, a key form of social capital, perhaps its eclipse is part of the explanation for the reduction in joining and trusting in the wider community. What does the evidence show?

Evidence of the loosening of family bonds is unequivocal. In addition to the century-long increase in divorce rates (which accelerated from the mid-1960s to the mid-1970s and then leveled off), and the more recent increase in single-parent families, the incidence of one-person households has more than doubled since 1950, in part because of the rising number of widows living alone. According to the General Social Survey, the proportion of all American adults who are currently married fell from 74 percent in 1974 to 56 percent in 1998, while the proportion of adults who have children at home fell from 55 percent to 38 percent. The Census Bureau reports that the fraction of adults who are both married and have kids at home—the archetypal Ozzie and Harriet family—was sliced by more than one-third from 40 percent in 1970 to 26 percent in 1997.[1]

It is a commonplace of cocktail conversation that we meet people through our spouses and our children. To what extent has the transformation of American family structure and home life over the last thirty years (fewer marriages, more divorces, fewer children, more people living alone) contributed to the decline of civic engagement? The surprising answer is "Probably not much."

Marriage and children do change the kinds of social networks to which one belongs. Both marriage and children increase time spent in community organizations and at home and decrease time spent in informal socializing with friends. Only two types of organizational affiliations, however, are sufficiently strongly related to marital and parental status to make a real difference in the aggregate: church- and youth-related activities.

Americans who are married and those with children are much more likely to be involved in religious activities, including church membership, church attendance, and church-related social activities. As I will explain momentarily, it is not clear which is cause and which effect, but the link is strong. Not surprisingly, parents are also more involved in school and youth groups (PTA, Scouts, and so on), and they are more likely to "attend public meetings on town *or school* affairs" (emphasis added). Finally, since church- and youth-related activities are the two most common sites for volunteering in America, parents are more likely to volunteer than people of the same age and social status who are single and childless.

On the other hand, neither marital nor parental status boosts membership in other sorts of groups. Holding other demographic features constant, marriage and children are *negatively* correlated with membership in sports, political, and cultural groups, and they are simply unrelated to membership in business and professional groups, service clubs, ethnic organizations, neighborhood associations, and hobby groups. Married people attend *fewer* club meetings than demographically matched single people.

Married people are slightly (but only slightly) more likely to give and attend dinner parties, to entertain at home, and to take an active role in local organizations. On the other hand, married people are *less* likely to spend time informally with friends and neighbors. Married people tend to be homebodies. As the marriage rate declined, therefore, the main effect on social life should have been to move social activities from the home into more public settings, but there should have been no generic effects on civic engagement as such. Interest in politics is actually slightly higher among single and childless adults than among married people and parents, other things being equal. Having kids is more important in inducing local involvement (leadership, meetings, volunteering), as we have seen. Parenthood is marginally more important than marriage per se as an entrée to community life, but the effect does not appear to extend beyond school- and youth-related activities themselves.

Divorce per se is negatively related to involvement in religious organizations but appears to be unrelated (positively or negatively) to other forms of civic involvement, formal or informal. Compared to demographically matched never married people, divorced people don't entertain friends less often (though they do give slightly fewer dinner parties), don't volunteer less, don't attend club meetings less often, don't work on fewer community projects, and actually sign slightly more petitions, attend slightly more public meetings, and write to Congress slightly more often. Divorce itself does not seem to be seriously implicated in the general trend toward civic disengagement.

The traditional family unit is down (a lot) and religious engagement is down (a little), and there is probably some link between the two. However, the nature of that link is quite unclear. It might be that the dissolution of the traditional family has led to lower religious involvement, or it might be that lower religious involvement has led to greater acceptance of divorce and other nontraditional family forms. In other words, the decline of the traditional family may have contributed to the decline of traditional religion, but the reverse is equally possible. In any event, the evidence is *not* consistent with the thesis that the *overall* decline in civic engagement and social connectedness is attributable to the decline in the traditional family. On the contrary, to some extent the decline in family obligations ought to have freed up time for more social and community involvement.

If we could rerun the last thirty or forty years, holding the traditional family structure constant—which we can do statistically by giving extra weight to the married people and parents who appear in our surveys—we might produce more religious participation and we surely would produce more involvement in school and youth groups. For those two reasons, that bit of hypothetical social engineering would modestly increase the average level of volunteering. (Ironically, volunteering is one of the few forms of civic engagement for which there is no decline to explain.) *However,* tinkering with family structure in this way would have virtually no effect on membership or activity in secular organizations (from Kiwanis to the NAACP to the AMA), nor would it halt the decline in political activities such as voting or party work. It would tend to *decrease* the time we spend with friends and neighbors even more than we have in fact witnessed. In short, apart from youth- and church-related engagement, *none* of the major declines in social capital and civic engagement that we need to explain can be accounted for by the decline in the traditional family structure.[2] In my view, there are important reasons for concern about the erosion of traditional family values, but I can find no evidence that civic disengagement is among them.

RACE IS SUCH A FUNDAMENTAL FEATURE of American social history that nearly every other feature of our society is connected to it in some way. Thus it seems intuitively plausible that race might somehow have played a role in the erosion of social capital over the last generation. In fact, the decline in social connectedness and social trust began just after the greatest successes of the civil rights revolution of the 1960s. That coincidence suggests the possibility of a kind of civic "white flight," as legal desegregation of civic life led whites to withdraw from community associations. This racial interpretation of the destruction of social capital is controversial and can hardly be settled within the compass of these brief remarks. Nevertheless the basic facts are these.

First, racial differences in associational membership are not large. At least until the 1980s, controlling for educational and income differences, blacks belonged to more associations on average than whites, essentially because they were more likely than comparably situated whites to belong to both religious and ethnic organizations and no less likely to belong to any other type of group.[3] On the other hand, as we saw in chapter 8, racial differences in social trust are very large indeed, even taking into account differences in education, income, and so on. Clearly these racial differences in social trust reflect not collective paranoia, but real experiences over many generations.

Second, the erosion of social capital has affected all races. This fact is inconsistent with the thesis that "white flight" is a significant cause of civic disengagement, since African Americans have been dropping out of religious and civic organizations and other forms of social connectedness at least as rapidly as white Americans. In fact, the sharpest drop in civic activity between the 1970s and the 1990s was among college-educated African Americans. Even more important, among *whites* the pace of civic disengagement has been uncorrelated with racial intolerance or support for segregation. Avowedly racist or segregationist whites have been no quicker to drop out of community organizations during this period than more tolerant whites. The decline in group membership is essentially identical among whites who favor segregation, whites who oppose segregation, and blacks.[4]

Third, if civic disengagement represented white flight from integrated community life after the civil rights revolution, it is hard to reconcile with the generational differences described in chapter 14. Why should disengagement be hardly visible at all among Americans who came of age in the first half of the century, when American society was objectively more segregated and subjectively more racist than in the 1960s and 1970s? If racial prejudice were responsible for America's civic disengagement, disengagement ought to be especially pronounced among the most bigoted individuals and generations. But it is not.

This evidence is not conclusive, but it does shift the burden of proof onto those who believe that racism is a primary explanation for growing civic disengagement over the last quarter century, however virulent racism continues to be in American society. Equally important, this evidence also suggests that reversing the civil rights gains of the last thirty years would do nothing to reverse the social capital losses.

• • •

CIRCUMSTANTIAL EVIDENCE, particularly the timing of the downturn in social connectedness, has suggested to some observers that an important cause—perhaps even *the* cause—of civic disengagement is big government and the growth of the welfare state.[5] By "crowding out" private initiative, it is argued, state intervention has subverted civil society. This is a much larger topic than I can address in detail here, but a word or two is appropriate.

On the one hand, some government policies have almost certainly had the effect of destroying social capital. For example, the so-called slum clearance policies of the 1950s and 1960s replaced physical capital but destroyed social capital, by disrupting existing community ties. It is also conceivable that certain social expenditures and tax policies may have created disincentives for civic-minded philanthropy. On the other hand, it is much harder to see which government policies might be responsible for the decline in bowling leagues, family dinners, and literary clubs.

One empirical approach to this issue is to examine differences in civic engagement and public policy across different political jurisdictions to see whether swollen government leads to shriveled social capital. Among the U.S. states, however, differences in social capital appear essentially uncorrelated with various measures of welfare spending or government size.[6] Citizens in free-spending states are no more engaged than citizens in frugal ones. Cross-national comparison can also shed light on this question. Among the advanced Western democracies, social trust and group membership are, if anything, *positively* correlated with the size of government; social capital appears to be highest of all in the big-spending welfare states of Scandinavia.[7] This simple analysis, of course, cannot tell us whether social connectedness encourages welfare spending, whether the welfare state fosters civic engagement, or whether both are the result of some other unmeasured factor(s). Sorting out the underlying causal connections would require much more thorough analysis. However, even this simple finding is not easily reconciled with the notion that big government undermines social capital.

Examining trends in the size of American government over the last half century reinforces doubts about the thesis that the welfare state is responsible for our declining social capital. Figure 78 shows that only two things have really changed with respect to the size of government relative to the size of the U.S. economy over the last half century: 1) defense spending generally declined, more or less steadily, from 1951 to 1998; and 2) state and local spending rose steadily from 1947 to 1975. On the other hand, two things have *not* really changed: 1) the size of federal domestic spending (it averaged 2.2 percent of GNP in the late 1940s and in the late 1990s and 2.7 percent at the peak in the mid-1960s); and 2) the relative size of federal vs. state and local spending in the last twenty-five years.

Meanwhile social capital in virtually all its forms increased a lot between 1947 and 1965 and decreased a lot between 1965 and 1998. Thus figure 78

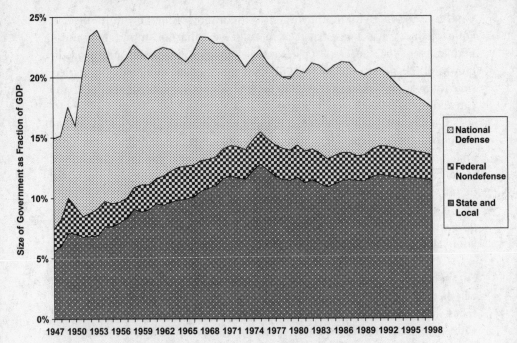

Figure 78: Government Spending, 1947–1998:
State and Local Government Up, National Defense Down

seems to me inconsistent with any theory that blames the decline of social capital or civic engagement on either big government or the relative size of the
federal government, compared with state and local government.

IF BIG GOVERNMENT is not the primary cause of declining civic engagement
in contemporary America, how about big business, capitalism, and the market? Thoughtful social critics have long feared that capitalism would undermine the preconditions for its own success by eroding interpersonal ties and
social trust.[8] Many of the grand masters of nineteenth-century social theory,
from Georg Simmel to Karl Marx, argued that market capitalism had created
a "cold society," lacking the interpersonal warmth necessary for friendship and
devaluing human ties to the status of mere commodities. The problem with
this generic theory of social disconnectedness is that it explains too much:
America has epitomized market capitalism for several centuries, during which
our stocks of social capital and civic engagement have been through great
swings. A constant can't explain a variable.

One version of economic determinism, however, may have more
validity—the gradual but accelerating nationalization and globalization of our
economic structures. The replacement of local banks, shops, and other locally

based firms by far-flung multinational empires often means a decline in civic commitment on the part of business leaders. As Wal-Mart replaces the corner hardware store, Bank of America takes over the First National Bank, and local owners are succeeded by impersonal markets, the incentives for business elites to contribute to community life atrophy. Urbanist Charles Heying has shown, for example, how such "corporate delocalization" in the last third of the twentieth century tended to strip Atlanta of its civic leadership. The social cohesion and civic commitment of Atlanta's elite rose from the 1930s to a peak in the 1960s and then declined to the 1990s, very much the same trajectory as our other measures of social capital. Heying offers suggestive evidence of similar trends in places as diverse as Chicago, Philadelphia, Dayton, and Shreveport. One of Boston's top developers complained to me privately about the demise of "the Vault," a celebrated cabal of local business leaders. "Where are the power elite when you need them?" he said. "They're all off at corporate headquarters in some other state."[9]

I have no doubt that global economic transformations are having an important impact on community life across America. The link is most direct, however, as regards larger philanthropic and civic activities. It is less clear why corporate delocalization should affect, for example, our readiness to attend a church social, or to have friends over for poker, or even to vote for president. Nevertheless, the connection between civic disengagement and corporate disengagement is worth exploring.[10]

LET US SUM UP what we have learned about the factors that have contributed to the decline in civic engagement and social capital traced in section II.

First, pressures of time and money, including the special pressures on two-career families, contributed measurably to the diminution of our social and community involvement during these years. My best guess is that no more than 10 percent of the total decline is attributable to that set of factors.

Second, suburbanization, commuting, and sprawl also played a supporting role. Again, a reasonable estimate is that these factors together might account for perhaps an additional 10 percent of the problem.

Third, the effect of electronic entertainment—above all, television—in privatizing our leisure time has been substantial. My rough estimate is that this factor might account for perhaps 25 percent of the decline.

Fourth and most important, generational change—the slow, steady, and ineluctable replacement of the long civic generation by their less involved children and grandchildren—has been a very powerful factor. The effects of generational succession vary significantly across different measures of civic engagement—greater for more public forms, less for private *schmoozing*—but as a rough rule of thumb we concluded in chapter 14 that this factor might account for perhaps half of the overall decline.

Slightly complicating our accounting for change is the overlap between generational change and the long-term effects of television. Not all of the effects of television are generational—even members of the long civic generation who are heavy TV watchers reduce their civic involvement—and not all of the effects of generational succession can be traced to television. (We speculated that the fading effects of World War II are also quite important, and other factors too may be lurking behind the "generational effect.") Nevertheless, perhaps 10–15 percent of the total change might be attributed to the joint impact of generation and TV—what we might term in shorthand "the TV generation."[11]

All of these estimates should be taken with a few grains of salt, partly because the specific effects vary among different forms of community involvement. Generation is more important in explaining the decline of churchgoing, for example, and less important in explaining the decline in visiting with friends. Nevertheless, figure 79 represents a rough-and-ready image of the relative importance of the factors we have explored. The missing chunk from the pie chart accurately reflects the limits of our current understanding. Work, sprawl, TV, and generational change are all important parts of the story, but important elements in our mystery remain unresolved.

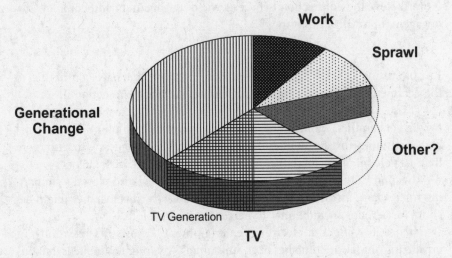

Figure 79: Guesstimated Explanation for Civic Disengagement, 1965–2000

So What?

With the assistance of Kristin A. Goss

CHAPTER 16

Introduction

By VIRTUALLY EVERY CONCEIVABLE MEASURE, social capital has eroded steadily and sometimes dramatically over the past two generations. The quantitative evidence is overwhelming, yet most Americans did not need to see charts and graphs to know that something bad has been happening in their communities and in their country. Americans have had a growing sense at some visceral level of disintegrating social bonds. It is perhaps no coincidence that on the eve of the millennium the market for civic nostalgia was hotter than the market for blue-chip stocks. For example, newscaster Tom Brokaw's book profiling the heroic World War II generation got mixed reviews from critics yet was a runaway best-seller. In Los Angeles there was an on-again, off-again movement to rename the LAX airport after the actor Jimmy Stewart, a military hero in real life who brought civic heroes Jefferson Smith and George Bailey to the silver screen. American nostalgia in the late twentieth century is no run-of-the-mill, rosy-eyed remembrance of things past. It is an attempt to recapture a time when public-spiritedness really did carry more value and when communities really did "work." As we buy books and rename airports, we seem to be saying that at a profound level civic virtue and social capital do matter.

Are we right? Does social capital have salutary effects on individuals, communities, or even entire nations? Yes, an impressive and growing body of research suggests that civic connections help make us healthy, wealthy, and wise. Living without social capital is not easy, whether one is a villager in southern Italy or a poor person in the American inner city or a well-heeled entrepreneur in a high-tech industrial district.

If we are to believe that social capital benefits individuals and communities, we must first understand how social capital works its magic. High levels of trust and citizen participation operate through a variety of mechanisms to produce socially desirable outcomes. Obviously the mechanism(s) at work will vary by the circumstance and outcome in question. But in general social capital has many features that help people translate aspirations into realities.

First, social capital allows citizens to resolve collective problems more easily. Social scientists have long been concerned about "dilemmas" of collective action. Such dilemmas are ubiquitous, and their dynamics are straightforward. People often might all be better off if they cooperate, with each doing her share. But each individual benefits more by shirking her responsibility, hoping that others will do the work for her. Moreover, even if she is wrong and the others shirk, too, she is still better off than if she had been the only sucker. Obviously if every individual thinks that the others will do the work, nobody will end up taking part, and all will be left worse off than if all had contributed.

Supporting government through a tax system is a dilemma of collective action. So is limiting lawn sprinklers and long showers during arid summers. These and other coordination challenges go by various names—"collective-action problems," "the prisoner's dilemma," "the free-rider problem," and "the tragedy of the commons," to name a few. But they all share one feature: They are best solved by an institutional mechanism with the power to ensure compliance with the collectively desirable behavior. Social norms and the networks that enforce them provide such a mechanism.

Second, social capital greases the wheels that allow communities to advance smoothly. Where people are trusting and trustworthy, and where they are subject to repeated interactions with fellow citizens, everyday business and social transactions are less costly. There is no need to spend time and money making sure that others will uphold their end of the arrangement or penalizing them if they don't. Economists such as Oliver Williamson and political scientists such as Elinor Ostrom have demonstrated how social capital translates into financial capital and resource wealth for businesses and self-governing units. Indeed, the Nobel Prize–winning economist Kenneth Arrow has concluded, "Virtually every commercial transaction has within itself an element of trust, certainly any transaction conducted over a period of time. It can be plausibly argued that much of the economic backwardness in the world can be explained by a lack of mutual confidence."[1]

A third way in which social capital improves our lot is by widening our awareness of the many ways in which our fates are linked. People who have active and trusting connections to others—whether family members, friends, or fellow bowlers—develop or maintain character traits that are good for the rest of society. Joiners become more tolerant, less cynical, and more empathetic to the misfortunes of others. When people lack connections to others, they are unable to test the veracity of their own views, whether in the give-and-take of

casual conversation or in more formal deliberation. Without such an opportunity, people are more likely to be swayed by their worst impulses. It is no
coincidence that random acts of violence, such as the 1999 spate of schoolyard
shootings, tend to be committed by people identified, after the fact, as "loners."

The networks that constitute social capital also serve as conduits for the
flow of helpful information that facilitates achieving our goals. For example,
as we shall see in chapter 19, many Americans—perhaps even most of us—get
our jobs through personal connections. If we lack that social capital, economic
sociologists have shown, our economic prospects are seriously reduced, even if
we have lots of talent and training ("human capital"). Similarly, communities
that lack civic interconnections find it harder to share information and thus
mobilize to achieve opportunities or resist threats.

Social capital also operates through psychological and biological processes to improve individuals' lives. Mounting evidence suggests that people
whose lives are rich in social capital cope better with traumas and fight illness
more effectively. Social capital appears to be a complement, if not a substitute,
for Prozac, sleeping pills, antacids, vitamin C, and other drugs we buy at the
corner pharmacy. "Call me [or indeed almost anyone] in the morning" might
actually be better medical advice than "Take two aspirin" as a cure for what
ails us.

To clarify how these mechanisms operate in practice, consider the following stylized example, which, while technically fabricated, depicts reality
for many parents. Bob and Rosemary Smith, parents of six-year-old Jonathan,
live in an urban community that is full of both delights and troubles. Bob and
Rosemary support public education in principle, and they would like their
first-grader to be exposed to children from diverse backgrounds, an opportunity that the public schools provide. But the Smiths' local elementary school
is a shambles: teachers are demoralized, paint is chipping off the walls, and
there is no money for extracurricular activities or computer equipment. Worried about Jonathan's ability to learn and thrive in this environment, Bob and
Rosemary have a choice. They can pull their child out of the public schools
and pay dearly to put him in a private school, or they can stick around and try
to improve the public school. What to do?

Let's suppose that the Smiths want to stick around and start a Parent-
Teacher Association at Jonathan's school. The chances that they will be able
to do so will depend upon two things: the existence of other concerned parents
who are also likely to join; and the likelihood that such an association will be
effective in improving conditions at the school. Here social capital comes in.
The more the Smiths know and trust their neighbors, the greater their ability
to recruit and retain reliable members of the new PTA. In cohesive neighborhoods filled with lots of overlapping connections, individuals more easily learn
who can be counted on, and they can make better use of moral suasion to ensure continued attention to the problems at hand.

Let's assume the Smiths succeed in starting the PTA, and several months later it has an active membership of seventeen parents. What does this new institution, this addition to the stock of social capital, do for the individuals involved and for the community at large? For one, belonging to the PTA almost certainly inculcates civic skills in parents. People who might never have designed a project, given a presentation, lobbied a public official, or even spoken up at a meeting are pressed to do so. What's more, the PTA serves to establish and enforce norms of commitment and performance on the part of school officials, teachers, and perhaps even students. It also allows for the deepening of interpersonal bonds and "we-ness" between families and educators. On a more personal note, the PTA meetings are bound to establish, or strengthen, norms of reciprocity and mutual concern among parents. These connections will almost certainly pay off in myriad unexpected ways in the future. If Bob loses his job, he will now have fifteen other adults upon whom he can call for employment leads or even for simple moral support. If Rosemary decides to start a lobbying group to press for better child health facilities in the city, she will have fifteen other potential lobbyists to aid in her cause. At the very least, Bob and Rosemary will have another couple or two with whom they can catch a movie on Friday nights. All these gains—civic skills, social support, professional contacts, volunteer labor, moviegoing partners—arose because the Smiths wanted to put computers in their kid's school.

Community connectedness is not just about warm fuzzy tales of civic triumph. In measurable and well-documented ways, social capital makes an enormous difference in our lives. This section considers five illustrative fields: child welfare and education; healthy and productive neighborhoods; economic prosperity; health and happiness; and democratic citizenship and government performance. I present evidence that social capital makes us smarter, healthier, safer, richer, and better able to govern a just and stable democracy.

MOST OF THE EVIDENCE that I present is drawn from the work of other scholars in many disciplines. In addition, I seek analytic leverage by comparing differences in social capital and civic engagement across the fifty states. Since those comparisons will appear in several different guises, it is useful to describe the geographic pattern of social capital in contemporary America.

To rate average social capital of the various states, we have combined a number of independent measures, which are summarized in table 4. From a variety of sources we have compiled state-level measures of participation in a range of civic and political activities during the preceding year, including group membership, attendance at public meetings on town or school affairs, service as an officer or committee member for some local organization, attendance at club meetings, volunteer work and community projects,[2] home enter-

Table 4: Measuring Social Capital in the American States

Components of Comprehensive Social Capital Index	Correlation with Index
Measures of community organizational life	
Served on committee of local organization in last year (percent)	0.88
Served as officer of some club or organization in last year (percent)	0.83
Civic and social organizations per 1,000 population	0.78
Mean number of club meetings attended in last year	0.78
Mean number of group memberships	0.74
Measures of engagement in public affairs	
Turnout in presidential elections, 1988 and 1992	0.84
Attended public meeting on town or school affairs in last year (percent)	0.77
Measures of community volunteerism	
Number of nonprofit (501[c]3) organizations per 1,000 population	0.82
Mean number of times worked on community project in last year	0.65
Mean number of times did volunteer work in last year	0.66
Measures of informal sociability	
Agree that "I spend a lot of time visiting friends"	0.73
Mean number of times entertained at home in last year	0.67
Measures of social trust	
Agree that "Most people can be trusted"	0.92
Agree that "Most people are honest"	0.84

taining and socializing with friends,[3] social trust,[4] electoral turnout,[5] and the incidence of nonprofit organizations and civic associations.[6]

These fourteen indicators of formal and informal community networks and social trust are in turn sufficiently intercorrelated that they appear to tap a single underlying dimension. In other words, these fourteen indicators measure related but distinct facets of community-based social capital, and we have combined them into a single Social Capital Index.[7] Table 4 summarizes these fourteen indicators and their correlation with the summary index.

Differences among the states on the underlying measures are substantial, with ratios of roughly three to one between high- and low-ranking states. Social trust, for example, ranges from 17 percent in Mississippi to 67 percent in North Dakota. The average number of associational memberships per capita varies from 1.3 in Louisiana and North Carolina to 3.3 in North Dakota. Turnout in recent presidential elections has varied between 42 percent in South Carolina and 69 percent in Minnesota. The number of nonprofit organizations per 1,000 inhabitants ranges from 1.2 in Mississippi to 3.6 in Vermont. The average number of club meetings attended per year varies from 4 in Nevada to 11 in North and South Dakota. The rate of volunteering varies from 5 times per year in Nevada, Mississippi, and Louisiana to twice that in Utah. The fraction of the population who report attending a public meeting on town or school affairs in the previous year ranges from 10 percent in Georgia and New York to 32 percent in New Hampshire, 29 percent in Utah, and 26 percent in Wisconsin.

The correlations in table 4 imply that these interstate differences go together. Places with dense associational networks tend to have frequent public meetings on local issues, places that have high electoral turnout tend to have high social trust, places with lots of local clubs tend to support many nonprofit organizations, and so on. Figure 80 maps the differences in social capital and civic engagement across the American states, much like a weather map.

Geographically speaking, the national social-capital "barometric map" is fairly straightforward. The primary "high-pressure" zone is centered over the headwaters of the Mississippi and Missouri Rivers and extends east and west along the Canadian border. The primary "low-pressure" area is centered over the Mississippi Delta and extends outward in rising concentric circles through the former Confederacy.[8] California and the mid-Atlantic states lie near the national average.[9] We can explore, at least in a preliminary way, the effects of different levels of social capital by comparing the quality of life in these different states. Minnesota and Mississippi differ from one another in many ways, not merely in their level of social capital, so we must be cautious about inferring causation from mere correlation, but the contrasts summarized in figure 80 provide a useful initial test bed for exploring what difference social capital might make.

Even a cursory glance at this map of America's social-capital resources leads one to ask, "Where in the world did these differences come from?" Answering that question in detail is a task for another day, but this pattern has deep historical roots. Alexis de Tocqueville, patron saint of contemporary social capitalists, observed precisely the same pattern in his travels in the America of the 1830s, attributing it, at least in part, to patterns of settlement:

> As one goes farther south [from New England], one finds a less active municipal life; the township has fewer officials, rights, and duties; the population does not exercise such a direct influence on affairs; the town meetings are less frequent and deal with fewer matters. For this reason the power of the elected official is comparatively greater and that of the voter less; municipal spirit is less wide awake and less strong. . . . Most of

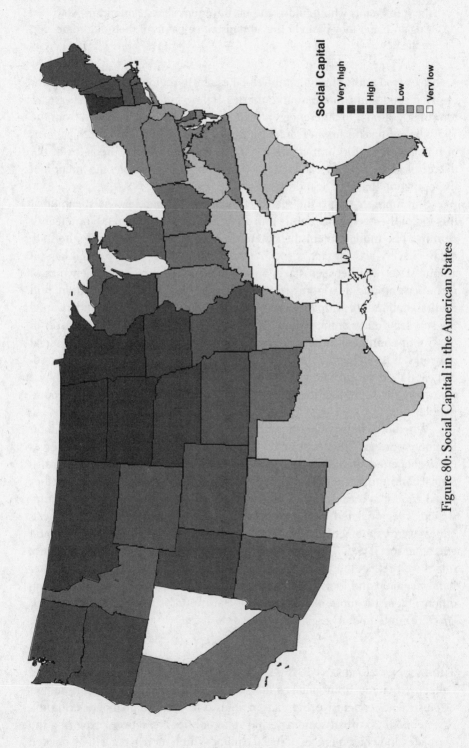

Figure 80: Social Capital in the American States

the immigrants who founded the northwestern states came from New England, and they brought the administrative habits of their old home to the new.[10]

Well-trod paths of migration helped establish regional and local patterns of social capital in contemporary America. These interstate differences are astonishingly similar to differences in "state political culture" as drawn from the 1950s by political historian Daniel Elazar, who traced them in turn to patterns of nineteenth-century immigration. One surprisingly strong predictor of the degree of social capital in any state in the 1990s is, for example, the fraction of its population that is of Scandinavian stock.[11]

Still more striking is the spatial correlation between low social capital at the end of the twentieth century and slavery in the first half of the nineteenth century. The more virulent the system of slavery then, the less civic the state today. Slavery was, in fact, a social system *designed* to destroy social capital among slaves and between slaves and freemen. Well-established networks of reciprocity among the oppressed would have raised the risk of rebellion, and egalitarian bonds of sympathy between slave and free would have undermined the very legitimacy of the system. After emancipation the dominant classes in the South continued to have a strong interest in inhibiting horizontal social networks. It is not happenstance that the lowest levels of community-based social capital are found where a century of plantation slavery was followed by a century of Jim Crow politics. Inequality and social solidarity are deeply incompatible.

Whether patterns of immigration and slavery provide the sole explanation for contemporary differences in levels of social capital is an issue that deserves more concerted attention than I can devote to it here. However, the clear historical continuities are relevant to one aspect of our current inquiry—whether social capital is a cause or merely an effect of contemporary social circumstance. If regional and local patterns of civic engagement and social connectedness were evanescent and mutable, then correlations between social capital and other social facts (like educational performance or public health or crime) might well reflect the *effect* of those factors *on* social capital. If, on the other hand, regional and local profiles of social capital represent long-standing traditions, then it is more plausible that social capital is a *cause*, not merely an *effect*, of contemporary social circumstance.

THE EVIDENCE I PRESENT in this section on the wide range of individual and collective benefits from social capital, while impressive in its scope, is neither exhaustive nor conclusive. Scholars in fields as far-flung as medicine, criminology, economics, urban sociology, and state politics are actively exploring the correlates and consequences of social capital. Much more work will be needed to prove the power of social capital and, in particular, to show in detail how and when its effects are clearest and most beneficial. I do not offer the generalizations in this section as the final word. But the evidence we review shows that in measurable ways it *matters* that social capital and civic engagement have declined in America over the last several decades. The same evidence strongly suggests that in many disparate domains important to Americans today, more social capital and civic engagement would improve things.

CHAPTER 17

Education and Children's Welfare

CHILD DEVELOPMENT is powerfully shaped by social capital. A considerable body of research dating back at least fifty years has demonstrated that trust, networks, and norms of reciprocity within a child's family, school, peer group, and larger community have wide-ranging effects on the child's opportunities and choices and, hence, on his behavior and development.[1] Although the presence of social capital has been linked to various positive outcomes, particularly in education, most research has focused on the bad things that happen to kids who live and learn in areas where there is a deficit of social capital. The implication is clear: Social capital keeps bad things from happening to good kids.

One indication of the strong connection between social capital and child development is the remarkable convergence between the state-by-state Social Capital Index that we have constructed and a popular measure of child well-being (the Kids Count indexes published annually by the Annie E. Casey Foundation).[2] (Table 5 summarizes the measures that make up the Kids Count index of child welfare.)

STATES THAT SCORE HIGH on the Social Capital Index—that is, states whose residents trust other people, join organizations, volunteer, vote, and socialize with friends—are the same states where children flourish: where babies are born healthy and where teenagers tend not to become parents, drop out of school, get involved in violent crime, or die prematurely due to suicide or homicide. (See figure 81.) Statistically, the correlation between high social capital and

Table 5: Kids Count Index of Child Welfare

Percent low-birth-weight babies

Infant mortality rate (deaths per 1,000 live births)

Child death rate (deaths per 100,000 children ages 1–14)

Deaths per 100,000 teens ages 15–19 by accident, homicide, and suicide

Teen birth rate (births per 1,000 females ages 15–17)

Percent of teens who are high school dropouts (ages 16–19)

Juvenile violent crime arrest rate (arrests per 100,000 youths ages 10–17)

Percent of teens not attending school and not working (ages 16–19)

Percent of children in poverty

Percent of families with children headed by a single parent

---

positive child development is as close to perfect as social scientists ever find in data analyses of this sort.[3] States such as North Dakota, Vermont, Minnesota, Nebraska, and Iowa have healthy civic adults and healthy well-adjusted kids; other states, primarily those in the South, face immense challenges in both the adult and youth populations.

Of course, the mere fact that social capital is correlated with good outcomes for kids does not mean that social capital *causes* these outcomes or, conversely, that a social-capital deficit is leading kids to take wrong turns in life. Besides social capital, states also differ in many other ways that might influence child well-being—parental education levels, poverty rates, family structure, racial composition, and so forth. To make matters more complicated, social capital itself is associated with these factors. Thus states with disproportionately large numbers of poorly educated adults and low-income single-parent families tend not to have as many vibrant civic communities as do states where residents have the economic luxury and practical skills to participate. Because of this complicated set of relationships among child outcomes, social capital, and demographics, we must be vigilant not to draw spurious conclusions from the data. What we really want to know is whether the observed differences across states in child well-being are linked directly to social capital itself or to some other factor or factors that influence both child well-being and social capital.

Fortunately modern statistical tools help us to sort through the confusion by allowing us to hold constant other factors while examining the specific links between social capital and child well-being. In essence, our analysis finds that socioeconomic and demographic characteristics do matter—but so does social capital.[4] Indeed, across the various Kids Count indicators, social capital is second only to poverty in the breadth and depth of its effects on children's lives. While poverty is an especially potent force in increasing youth fertility, mortality, and idleness, community engagement has precisely the opposite effect. Social capital is especially important in keeping children from being born unhealthily small and in keeping teenagers from dropping out of school, hang-

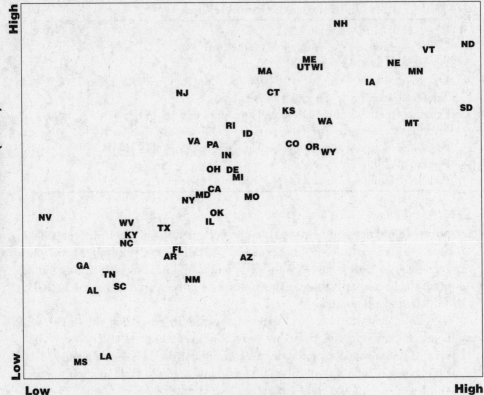

Social Capital Index

Figure 81: Kids Are Better Off in High-Social-Capital States

ing out on the streets, and having babies out of wedlock. A state's racial composition and rate of single-parent families also affect child well-being, though far less consistently or strongly than do poverty and low social capital. In general, the education level of the adult population does not have a significant independent influence on child outcomes, after poverty, social capital, and demographics are taken into account. A state's social infrastructure is far more important than anyone would have predicted in ensuring the healthy development of youth.

Similar conclusions have been reached by scholars studying family life at the level of the neighborhood and even the individual family. Community psychologists have long noted that child abuse rates are higher where neighborhood cohesion is lower.[5] For example, in a widely cited study of two neighborhoods, one with a high child maltreatment rate and the other with a low rate, social capital turned out to be the main factor that distinguished the two communities. These neighborhoods had similar income levels and similar rates of working women and single-parent households. However, in the high-risk neighborhoods, residents were far more reluctant to ask for help from a neighbor. Parents in the high-abuse area were also far less likely to report exchanging child care with a neighbor or allowing their kids to play with others in the neighborhood. Kids in low-risk neighborhoods were more than three times as likely as kids in high-risk areas to find a parent home after school. The authors of the study concluded that in areas with high abuse rates, a "family's own problems seem to be compounded rather than ameliorated by the neighborhood context. Under such circumstances strong support systems are most needed, but least likely to operate."[6] Informal social networks help shield children from their parents' worst moments.

Individual children at risk have proved particularly vulnerable to social-capital deficits. More hopefully, precisely such children are most susceptible to the positive benefits of social connectedness, if it can be provided. Pediatrician Desmond K. Runyan and his colleagues, for example, followed a large group of preschool children identified as at high risk of abuse and neglect. After several years fully 87 percent of these at-risk children were suffering from behavioral and emotional problems. However, the best predictor of which children successfully avoided such problems was the degree to which they and their mothers were enmeshed in a supportive social network, lived in a socially supportive neighborhood, and attended church regularly. As the authors conclude, even in these preschool years "the parents' social capital . . . confers benefits on their off-spring, just as children benefit from their parents' financial and human capital. Social capital may be most crucial for families who have fewer financial and educational resources." Another study found that inner-city African American adolescents living in neighborhoods with relatively high levels of social capital were less depressed than those living in less close-knit neighborhoods; this positive effect of neighborhood support was especially marked for kids who lacked strong family ties. Similar results have been found in both urban and rural settings.[7]

Social capital matters for children's successful development in life. We can draw the same conclusion about the link between social capital and school performance. The quality of American education has been of growing concern in recent decades; in fact, many knowledgeable observers believe that public schooling has reached a crisis.[8]

Yet not all states are faring poorly. Mirroring our findings on healthy children, those states with high social capital have measurably better educational outcomes than do less civic states. The Social Capital Index is highly correlated with student scores on standardized tests taken in elementary school, junior high, and high school, as well as with the rate at which students stay in school.[9] (See figure 82.) The beneficial effects of social capital persist even after accounting for a host of other factors that might affect state educational success—racial composition, affluence, economic inequality, adult educational levels, poverty rates, educational spending, teachers' salaries, class size,

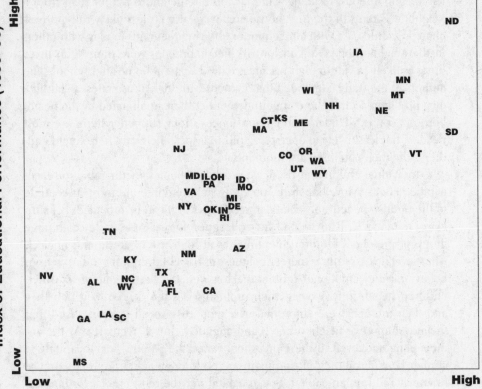

Social Capital Index

Figure 82: Schools Work Better in High-Social-Capital States

family structure, and religious affiliation, as well as the size of the private-school sector (which might "cream" better students from public schools). Not surprisingly, several of these factors had an independent effect on state test scores and dropout rates, but astonishingly, social capital was the single most important explanatory factor. In fact, our analysis suggests that for some outcomes—particularly SAT scores—the impact of race, poverty, and adult education levels is only indirect. These factors seem to influence the level of social capital in a state, and social capital—not poverty or demographic characteristics per se—drives test scores.[10]

Unexpectedly, the level of *informal* social capital in the state is a stronger predictor of student achievement than is the level of *formal* institutionalized social capital. In other words, level of social trust in a state and the frequency with which people connected informally with one another (in card games, visiting with friends, and the like) were even more closely correlated with educational performance than was the amount of time state residents devoted to club meetings, church attendance, and community projects. That is not to say that formal activities were unimportant. Rather, what this admittedly crude evidence is saying is that there is something about communities where people connect with one another—over and above how rich or poor they are materially, how well educated the adults themselves are, what race or religion they are—that positively affects the education of children. Conversely, even communities with many material and cultural advantages do a poor job of educating their kids if the adults in those communities don't connect with one another. Sadly, the evidence of section II is that more and more American communities are like that.

One can see the importance of social capital by comparing specific examples. Take two medium-size states on the East Coast: North Carolina (ranked number forty-one in the nation in terms of SAT scores, achievement tests, and dropout rates) and Connecticut (ranked number nine). Controlling for all the other ways in which the two states differ (wealth and poverty, race, adult educational levels, urbanism, and so on), for North Carolina to see educational outcomes similar to Connecticut's, according to our statistical analysis, residents of the Tar Heel State could do any of the following: increase their turnout in presidential elections by 50 percent; double their frequency of club meeting attendance; triple the number of nonprofit organizations per thousand inhabitants; or attend church two more times per month. These may seem like daunting challenges, requiring a great deal of community organizing, and in any event I do not mean to imply that the link between, say, adult club attendance and school performance is simple, direct, and mechanical. On the other hand, the data also suggest how hard it would be for North Carolina to match Connecticut's performance simply through traditional educational reforms—by decreasing class size, for example. Because the effect of class size on state-level performance is modest by comparison to the effects of social capital, it would be virtually impossible to achieve the same progress simply by reducing class size.[11] In reality, of course, a multipronged approach to improving education is needed, for there are no magic bullets; my point is merely that the potential leverage offered by social capital is surprisingly great compared to more conventional approaches.[12]

Why does the density of social connectedness in a state seem to have such a marked effect on how well its students perform in school? The honest answer is that we are not yet entirely sure, but we have some important clues. First, where civic engagement in community affairs in general is high, teachers report higher levels of parental support and lower levels of student misbehavior, such as bringing weapons to school, engaging in physical violence, playing hooky, and being generally apathetic about education. The correlation between community infrastructure, on the one hand, and student and parental engagement in schools, on the other hand, is very substantial even after taking into account other economic, social, and educational factors, like poverty, racial composition, family structure, educational spending, class size, and so forth. In light of the rash of deadly school violence in 1999 it is worth noting that among all these factors the strongest predictors of student violence across the states are two-parent families and community-based social capital, dwarfing the importance of such social conditions as poverty, urbanism, or levels of parental education. In short, parents in states with high levels of social capital are more engaged with their kids' education, and students in states with high levels of social capital are more likely than students in less civic states to hit the books rather than to hit one another.[13]

A second reason why students perform better in states with high social capital may be that they spend less time watching TV. As figure 83 shows, the negative correlation between the average time that kids spend watching TV and the average level of adult civic engagement and social connectedness is quite powerful. (As always, we have checked to confirm that this relationship is not simply a spurious reflection of some other factor, such as poverty or race.) It seems likely that where community traditions of social involvement remain high, children are naturally drawn into more productive uses of leisure than where social connectedness and civic engagement among adults is limited.

This state-by-state analysis reconfirms decades of research showing that community involvement is crucial to schools' success. These studies have found that student learning is influenced not only by what happens in school and at home, but also by social networks, norms, and trust in the school and in the wider community.[14] Indeed, Parent-Teacher Associations were created to institutionalize social capital among parents, and between parents and teachers, so that schools could better meet their educational goals.

The decline in PTA membership over the past several decades reflects many parents' disengagement from their children's schooling. That decline is a shame, because research suggests that when parents and the wider community work with schools, students benefit in concrete and measurable ways. One of the earliest and most influential studies linking social capital to education was done by James Coleman, the late University of Chicago sociologist who laid the intellectual foundations for the study of social capital and its effects. Coleman was puzzled by the low dropout rates at Catholic and other religiously based high schools. Students in public high schools, for example, were three times as likely as Catholic high school students to drop out; students at non-Catholic private schools were more than twice as likely to drop out. In addition, Catholic schools were shown to be more effective in teaching mathematics and verbal skills to students. Coleman hypothesized that Catholic school success is due not to the particular characteristics of the individual students, but rather to the social structure enveloping the school: the students' parents have multistranded relations with one another, both as fellow members of the local church and as parents of school chums. And these parent communities provide social resources to at-risk students and insulate the schools from pressures to water down their core curricula. In short, Coleman warned,

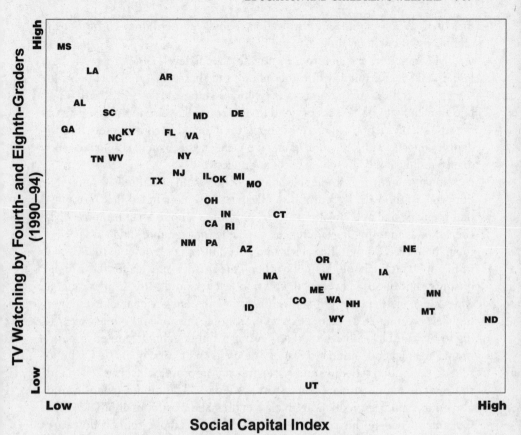

Social Capital Index

Figure 83: Kids Watch Less TV in High-Social-Capital States

we cannot understate "the importance of the embeddedness of young persons in the enclaves of adults most proximate to them, first and most prominently the family and second, a surrounding community of adults (exemplified in all these results by the religious community)."[15] Unfortunately, the "functional communities" from which Catholic school students benefit have been eroding, because both the church and the family have lost strength and cohesion. This trend can be expected to harm kids of all socioeconomic groups, but especially the disadvantaged.

Educational researchers Anne Henderson and Nancy Berla have summarized a large number of studies tending to show that when parents are involved with their children's education, children do better in school and the schools they attend are better. They conclude that "[t]he evidence is now beyond dispute. When schools work together with families to support learning, children tend to succeed not just in school, but throughout life. . . . When parents are involved in their children's education at home, their children do better in school. When parents are involved at school, their children go further in school, and the schools they go to are better."[16]

Moving from the community to the school level, other research has found that social capital within the school walls has a plethora of benefits to students, teachers, and administrators. Studies going back at least thirty years have shown that smaller schools tend to outperform large schools in large part because smaller schools afford more opportunities and encouragement for students to engage with one another in face-to-face extracurricular activities and to take responsibility for school clubs and so forth.[17]

In large, multiyear studies of Chicago schools and of Catholic schools nationwide, Anthony S. Bryk and his colleagues have concluded that "communal" social capital and "relational trust" give some schools an enormous edge, even after accounting for differences in teacher backgrounds and student demographics. As communities of learning, Catholic schools differ in many ways from public high schools. Catholic schools are smaller, provide for more high-quality relationships between students and teachers in diverse settings, offer a wider range of interactive extracurricular programs, and are characterized by a high level of internal agreement about the school's mission and values. According to Bryk and his colleagues, if an "average" public school adopted a "communal organization" similar to that of a demographically comparable Catholic school, the public school would see significant improvements in teacher and staff morale and in student interest in academics. The public school would also enjoy significant reductions in class cutting and classroom disorder.[18] Like Coleman, Bryk and his colleagues conclude that Catholic schools do better than public schools not because the teachers or students are more qualified, but because "Catholic schools benefit from a network of social relations, characterized by trust, that constitute a form of 'social capital.'"[19]

Some cities are using these insights to build social capital and citizen participation within their public schools. In one of the earliest, most successful, and longest-running school reform initiatives, the Yale child psychiatrist James Comer has developed a model of effective linkage among schools, parents, and the community. Two of the guiding principles of a Comer school include "[c]oordination and cooperation among all adults concerned with the child's best educational interests" and "active involvement of parents every step of the way."[20] Comer and his colleagues found that parental participation can improve school performance and family support for kids' achievement—but only if parents are given real decision-making responsibility and are placed in positions suited to their knowledge and skills.[21] Where these elements aren't present, parents tend to become disillusioned and distrustful, undermining the community-based social capital so vital to public schools.

In the late 1980s Chicago launched a path-breaking education reform initiative whose cornerstone is parent participation in decision making. Although the reform plan did not work as well as hoped, evaluators still found that social capital within schools can make a difference. When there is a high level of trust among teachers, parents, and principals, these key players are more committed to the central tenets of school improvement. Teachers in high-trust settings feel loyal to the school, seek innovative approaches to learning, reach out to parents, and have a deep sense of responsibility for students' development. Even after taking into account all the other factors that influence the odds of successful reform, trust remains a key ingredient.[22]

As these studies suggest, parental and community engagement are at the center of current efforts to improve schooling. Indeed, two of the more controversial reform approaches—the creation of charter schools and the provision of publicly financed vouchers for kids to attend private schools—may be viewed as attempts by parents to give their kids the benefits of the "communal orientation" that produces exceptional student behavior and performance. Critics of "choice" programs fear they will only exacerbate existing educational inequities. Supporters argue that putting schooling into the invisible hand of the free market will improve quality for everyone because schools will be forced to compete on outcomes. While it is too soon to tell which side is right, we do have evidence that if "choice" programs work, their success may turn less on the magic of the marketplace than on the magic of social capital. School reform initiatives that encourage kids to attend smaller, more communal schools may have the unintended result of increasing both student and parental involvement in clubs, classroom activities, governing bodies, and education lobbying groups.[23] In this way, such education reform could be an engine of civic reengagement, although if only the most engaged parents removed their children to the new schools, thus also removing the "positive externalities" that their engagement produces for other kids, the net effect could be to exacerbate inequality.

Social capital at the neighborhood or community level clearly has an impact on child learning. But social capital *within* families also powerfully affects youth development.[24] Families that enjoy close social bonds and parents who instill the value of reciprocity in their kids are more likely to "gain a greater degree of compliance and adherence to their values."[25] Even holding constant many other things that affect educational achievement, including parents' education and income, race, family size, region, and gender, children whose parents are closely involved with their kids and their kids' schools are much less likely to drop out of high school than children who lack these forms of social capital. Kids of parents who attend programs at their kids' school, help with homework, and monitor their kids' behavior outside school are likely to have higher grade-point averages, to be more engaged in the classroom, and to shun drugs and delinquent activity.[26] One long-term study of low-income teen mothers in Baltimore found that in those families where high levels of emotional support existed between a mom and her child, and where the mom had a strong support network, the child was dramatically more likely to graduate from high school, go on to college, and have a steady job. In other words, "at risk" children can succeed in life if their mothers have enough social capital.[27]

The beneficial effects of social capital are not limited to deprived communities or to primary and secondary education. Indeed, precisely what many high-achieving suburban school districts have in abundance is social capital, which is educationally more important even than financial capital. Conversely, where social connectedness is lacking, schools work less well, no matter how affluent the community. Moreover, social capital continues to have powerful effects on education during the college years. Extracurricular activities and involvement in peer social networks are powerful predictors of college dropout rates and college success, even holding constant precollegiate factors, including aspirations.[28] In other words, at Harvard as well as in Harlem, social connectedness boosts educational attainment. One of the areas in which America's diminished stock of social capital is likely to have the most damaging consequences is the quality of education (both in school and outside) that our children receive.

CHAPTER 18

Safe and Productive Neighborhoods

As WE SAW in the previous chapter, the healthy development of kids depends in large part on the social context in which they come of age. Neighborhoods with high levels of social capital tend to be good places to raise children. In high-social-capital areas, public spaces are cleaner, people are friendlier, and the streets are safer. How do trust, social networks, and citizen engagement translate into nice, safe neighborhoods?

Scholars, especially criminologists, have puzzled over these questions for years. Most of the early work was concerned with why some neighborhoods seemed to have so much more vandalism, graffiti, street crime, and gang scuffles than did others. These neighborhood characteristics persisted over many decades, despite population turnover. Beginning in the 1920s, some of the nation's leading criminologists began to develop "ecological" theories of crime and juvenile deliquency. The theories varied in their particulars but generally focused on "social disorganization" as the engine of bad behavior. Such disorganization marked many urban communities where population turnover was high, neighbors anonymous, ethnic groups uneasily mixed, local organizations rare, and disadvantaged youths trapped in "subcultures" cut off from the adult world.

Noted criminologist Robert J. Sampson, summarizing many empirical studies, concludes that even controlling for poverty and other factors that might encourage criminal behavior, "communities characterized by (a) anonymity and sparse acquaintanceship networks among residents, (b) unsupervised teenage peer groups and attenuated control of public space, and (c) a weak organizational base and low social participation in local activities face an increased risk of crime and violence." For example, comparing neighborhoods matched on other social and economic factors, national surveys show that living in a neighborhood of high mobility doubles your risk of becoming a victim of crime, compared to living in a more stable neighborhood. However, Sampson adds, the "social disorganization" school did not adequately explain how and why these neighborhood characteristics seemed to produce increased levels of crime.[1]

Jane Jacobs, the great scholar of urban life, offered an answer in her now classic 1961 book, *The Death and Life of Great American Cities.* Jacobs noted that "social capital"—a term of which she is one of the inventors—is what most differentiated safe and organized cities from unsafe and disorganized ones. In a scathing indictment of twentieth-century urban planning and renewal efforts, she argued that where cities are configured to maximize informal contact among neighbors, the streets are safer, children are better taken care of, and people are happier with their surroundings. To Jacobs, regular contact with the local grocer, the families on the front stoop, and the priest walking the blocks of his parish, as well as the presence of street fairs and conveniently traversed parks, developed a sense of continuity and responsibility in local residents. "The sum of such casual, public contact at a local level—most of it fortuitous, most of it associated with errands, all of it metered by the person concerned and not thrust upon him by anyone—is a feeling for the public identity of people, a web of public respect and trust, and a resource in time of personal and neighborhood need."[2]

In the decades since these influential studies, many other scholars across a range of disciplines have elaborated the basic insights. The conclusions of this work are straightforward and just as Jacobs and the early criminologists would have predicted: Higher levels of social capital, all else being equal, translate into lower levels of crime.

A state-level analysis of homicide statistics is illustrative. (Murder rates are generally accepted as the most reliable index of the incidence of crime, the least susceptible to distortion from one jurisdiction to another.) States with more social capital have proportionately fewer murders. (See figure 84.) This inverse relationship is astonishingly strong—as close to perfect as one might find between any two social phenomena.[3] Of course, there are many reasons why states high in social capital might happen to have low homicide rates. States rich in social capital, for example, tend to be wealthier, better educated, less urban, and more egalitarian in their distribution of income. But further analysis, which takes account of these and other factors, finds that the relationship between social capital and safe streets is real. In fact, social capital is about as important as poverty, urbanism, and racial composition as a determinant of homicide prevalence. Surprisingly, social capital is *more important* than a state's education level, rate of single-parent households, and income inequality

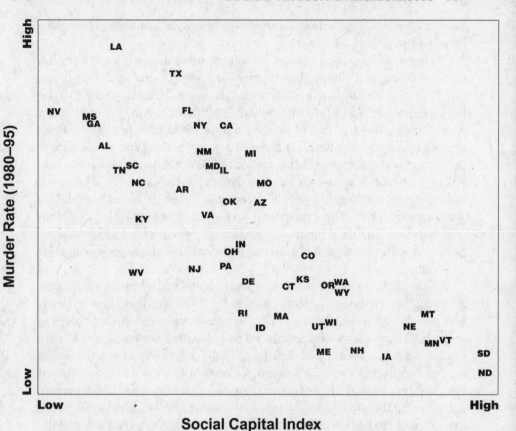

Social Capital Index

Figure 84: Violent Crime Is Rarer in High-Social-Capital States

in predicting the number of murders per capita during the 1980–95 period. Intriguingly, this correlation remains strong when we control for statewide levels of fear about crime; that unexpected fact implies that the causal arrow runs, at least in part, from social capital to crime.[4]

Our story here intersects with an age-old historical puzzle—why is the South different? Historians have known for more than a century that lethal violence is much more common in the states of the former Confederacy than in the rest of the country. In fact, murder rates have been much higher in the South since well before the Civil War, and this difference continued more or less undiluted throughout the twentieth century. During the 1980s and 1990s, for example, the murder rate in the South was roughly twice that in the North. Moreover, the same regional distinction is found both among whites and among blacks. Many interpretations have been offered—psychological, cultural, societal, economic, even racial. However, the regional difference persists even when we hold constant race, age, economic inequality, urbanization, education, poverty, and other established predictors of murder rates.

Something about "southernness" seems to be associated with high potential for lethal violence.

Some observers have blamed "a southern world view that defines the social, political, and physical environment as hostile . . . the symbiosis of profuse hospitality and intense hostility toward strangers." Others suggest that the key to the puzzle is a distinctive southern "culture of honor," manifest in the nineteenth-century tradition of dueling and traceable perhaps to eighteenth-century immigration patterns.[5] Figure 84 suggests instead that social capital (or, rather, its absence) may be the missing link. Once differences in social capital are taken into account, the hoary regional difference vanishes. The South is no more violent than you would expect it to be, given its well-established social-capital deficit. This explanation accounts not only for the gross difference between North and South, but also for differences *within* the North and South.[6] In other words, lethal violence is endemic wherever social capital is deficient.

To probe further the link between social capital and violence, we can take advantage of a charming question posed in the DDB Needham Life Style surveys over the last several decades. "Do you agree or disagree with the following sentence?" respondents were asked: "I'd do better than average in a fist fight." On average, 38 percent of all Americans pick the pugnacious alternative. (Men are twice as likely to agree as women, 53 percent to 26 percent, but women have slowly narrowed the truculence gap, rising steadily from 20–25 percent agreement in the late 1970s to 30 percent in the late 1990s.) More to the point, there turn out to be significant differences from state to state. At the top of the scale, nearly half of the residents of Louisiana, West Virginia, and New Mexico agree with that sentence, as compared with less than a third of residents in South Dakota, Maine, Iowa, Minnesota, New Hampshire, and Nebraska. As figure 85 shows, pugnacity is strongly correlated with low social capital, perhaps because in the absence of the emollient effects of community connectedness and social trust a self-help system of enforcing social order has emerged. In any event, citizens in states characterized by low levels of social capital are readier for a fight (perhaps because they need to be), and they are predisposed to mayhem.[7]

These state differences dovetail nicely with a body of research that has examined crime and delinquency rates at the local or even census-tract level. Besides looking at criminal misbehavior, these studies have used sophisticated statistical techniques to explore "neighborhood effects" on other problems that beset American cities—everything from child abuse, to dropout rates, to teen pregnancy, to drug use.[8] The unifying premise of these studies is that a person's behavior depends not only on his own characteristics, but also on the characteristics of those around him—his neighbors, school peers, and so forth.

These studies have been at the center of a rigorous debate, mostly over whether they have actually proven anything besides the tendency of like-

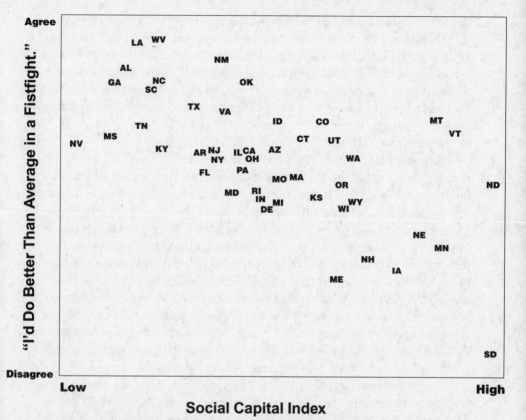

Social Capital Index

Figure 85: States High in Social Capital Are Less Pugnacious

minded people to congregate in the same places. This criticism is as follows: Sure, teenage dropouts tend to be found in the same neighborhoods, but it's not because these kids are influencing each other to leave school. Rather, the clustering appears because families with similar values or parenting practices feel more comfortable living near one another. Critics rightly note that the most sophisticated statistical analysis has trouble identifying the invisible forces that might cause "birds of a feather" to flock together. What is more, even if neighborhood effects do exist, they might be trivial compared to "family effects" such as parental nurturing and guidance.[9]

I take these critiques seriously. Nonetheless, the sheer number and diversity of studies that have found neighborhood effects on crime have persuaded me that these effects are real. Although the magnitude of the neighborhood influence varies, scholars have been able to demonstrate that, over and above their individual predisposition to engage in risky behaviors, kids who live amid other risk-taking kids are more likely to fall into bad patterns. In Boston, for example, kids whose neighborhood peers use drugs, commit crimes, and befriend gang members are themselves substantially more likely to do so as well, regardless of their initial proclivities. In Chicago young black men who live in neighborhoods with lots of white-collar professionals are more than three times as likely to graduate from high school than are comparable young men who live in neighborhoods with less educated residents.[10] These and dozens more studies suggest that people are profoundly motivated not merely by their own choices and circumstances, but also by the choices and circumstances of their neighbors. My fate depends on not only whether *I* study, stay off drugs, go to church, but also on whether my neighbors do these things.

Although the methods of analysis have not always allowed researchers to pinpoint how neighborhood effects work, there have been recent scholarly efforts to understand those processes better.[11] Researchers have come to believe that social capital—or lack of it—is a big piece of the puzzle. On one hand, the presence of social capital—individuals connected to one another through trusting networks and common values—allows for the enforcement of positive standards for youths and offers them access to mentors, role models, educational sponsors, and job contacts outside the neighborhood.[12] Social networks may also provide emotional and financial support for individuals and supply political leverage and volunteers for community institutions.[13] By contrast, the absence of positive norms, community associations, and informal adult friendship and kin networks leaves kids to their own devices. It is in such settings that youths are most likely to act on shortsighted or self-destructive impulses.

It is in such settings too that youths are most prone to create their own social capital in the form of gangs or neighborhood "crews." As sociologist Robert Sampson states: "Lack of social capital is one of the primary features of socially disorganized communities."[14] The best evidence available on changing levels of neighborhood connectedness suggests that most Americans are less embedded in their neighborhood than they were a generation ago.[15] This is due in part to the fact that women—long the stalwart neighborhood builders—are now much more likely to be away at work during the day than their mothers were. And professional men, who once lent their skills to neighborhood associations, are spending longer hours on the job than their fathers did. As we noted in section II, people are less likely today to socialize with neighbors and to work on community projects.

Indeed, the decline in neighborhood social capital—community monitoring, socializing, mentoring, and organizing—is one important feature of the inner-city crisis, in addition to purely economic factors. Many students of urban life have commented on the flight of jobs and middle-class families from American cities. Their departure represents a drain of both human and financial capital and, by extension, social capital. The nation's leading urban sociologist, William Julius Wilson, described the downward spiral in his 1987 classic *The Truly Disadvantaged*: "The basic thesis is not that ghetto culture went unchecked following the removal of higher-income families in the inner city, but that the removal of these families made it more difficult to sustain the basic institutions in the inner city (including churches, stores, schools, recreational facilities, etc.) in the face of prolonged joblessness. And as the basic institutions declined, the social organization of inner-city neighborhoods (defined here to include a sense of community, positive neighborhood identification, and explicit norms and sanctions against aberrant behavior) likewise declined."[16]

Based on years of studying inner-city Philadelphia, the urban ethnographer Elijah Anderson also has documented a steady erosion in the "moral cohesion" of low-income neighborhoods. He, too, links the decline of social capital to the exodus of financial and human capital. The departure of middle-class blacks, he concludes, "has diminished an extremely important source of moral and social leadership within the black community." Meanwhile the senior statesmen and stateswomen of the neighborhood—the "old heads," as Anderson calls them—have stuck around, but their numbers are dwindling, and they have lost their moral authority. The male "old head" was "a man of stable means who was strongly committed to family life, to church, and, most important, to passing on his philosophy, developed through his own rewarding experience with work, to young boys he found worthy." He has "been losing prestige and credibility as a role model" as legitimate jobs have disappeared and illicit economic activity has proved highly lucrative. At the same time, the community "mothers," who once occupied porch stoops and served as the neighborhood's eyes and ears, have become "overwhelmed by a virtual proliferation of 'street kids'—children almost totally without parental supervision, left to their own devices." These women no longer enjoy the informal permission they once had to intervene on behalf of neighbors. "As family caretakers and role models disappear or decline in influence, and as unemployment and poverty become more persistent," Anderson concludes, "the community, particularly its children, becomes vulnerable to a variety of social ills, including crime, drugs, family disorganization, generalized demoralization, and unemployment."[17]

People who live and work in inner cities recognize the people and processes that Anderson describes. Moreover, it is not only in minority and impoverished neighborhoods that social-capital deficits lead to crime and other social pathologies. Anderson's ground-level insights about how social capital underpins healthy neighborhoods have been quantified in scores of sophisticated analyses of neighborhood and individual data.

One of the best is a widely noted study of Chicago neighborhoods by Robert J. Sampson, Stephen Raudenbush, and Felton Earls. Based on extensive survey and crime data, the study found that two characteristics—mutual trust and altruism among neighbors, and their willingness to intervene when they see children misbehaving—went a long way to explain why some neighborhoods are less crime prone than are others. Indeed, a neighborhood's "collective efficacy" was a better predictor than was its poverty or residential instability of whether a person is likely to be victimized in the neighborhood. In this Chicago study other measures of social capital—such as individual participation in local organizations, number of neighborhood-based programs, and extent of kin and friendship ties in the neighborhood—didn't seem to make much of a difference. Rather, the authors conclude, "Reductions in violence appear to be more directly attributable to informal social control and cohesion among residents."[18]

An earlier study by Sampson and W. Byron Groves found that organizational participation and social ties did make a difference in reducing crime levels. Their analysis of British crime data found that in areas where people are connected through tight bonds of friendship and looser yet more diverse acquaintanceship ties, and where people are active in local committees and clubs, there are fewer muggings, assaults, burglaries, auto thefts, and so forth.[19] What is most interesting about this research is its finding that traditional neighborhood "risk factors"—such as high poverty and residential mobility—may not be as big a part of the crime problem as most people assume. Sampson and Groves's analysis suggests that while poorer, less stable areas do have substantially higher rates of street robbery, this is not simply because of poverty and instability per se. Rather, these places have higher crime rates in large part because adults don't participate in community organizations, don't supervise teenagers, and aren't linked through networks of friends. Similarly, a study of a dozen New York neighborhoods found that participation in community organizations helped to lessen the effects of socioeconomic disadvantage on juvenile delinquency.[20] Put another way, young people rob and steal not only because they are poor, but also because adult networks and institutions have broken down.

Just as neighborhoods can affect families, so can families affect neighborhoods. In economists' terms, family social capital has "positive externalities," spilling out of the home and into the streets. In Northern California scholars have found that the presence of lots of stable families in a neighborhood is associated with lower levels of youthful lawbreaking, not because the adults serve as role models or supervisors, but because the adults rear well-adjusted and well-behaved kids. Thus "good families" have a ripple effect by increasing the pool of "good peers" that other families' kids can befriend.[21] If we think of youthful troublemaking as a communicable disease—a sort of behavioral chicken pox that spreads through high schools and friendship groups—then stable families provide the vaccines that reduce the number of contagious kids capable of infecting others.

Yet the integration of families into neighborhoods may not always be beneficial. If the neighborhood norms and networks are at odds with what ethnographer Anderson calls "decent" values,[22] then families who become enmeshed in the community may run afoul of their own better natures. One study of Northern California high school students found that the extent to which parents knew their child's friends, and knew the parents of those friends, was a strong indicator of the child's classroom engagement and refusal to use alcohol and drugs. But such positive effects of "parents knowing parents" were found only in areas where school engagement and substance abuse were not a problem. In areas where students were more troubled, the social integration of parents actually exacerbated the problems of living in a community with poorly adjusted peers.[23] In other words, social integration into a community of bad actors may not produce good results.

Inner-city gangs might also be seen as a misguided attempt at neighborhood-based social capital building in areas where constructive institutions are sadly lacking. Although experts agree that gangs are hard to identify and even harder to count, most evidence suggests that their numbers are growing.[24] Some of these gangs are hierarchical enterprises whose sole business is business, especially marketing drugs and guns. But other gangs are closer to mutual aid societies based on horizontal bonds of interpersonal trust, reciprocity, and friendship that is defended to the death.[25] In many cases gang members are tolerated and well integrated into the mainstream community.[26]

In her excellent study of Latino gangs in Chicago, Ruth Horowitz describes the extensive social capital that existed within them:

> The Lions have been together as a group for almost ten years and during that time there has been a continual exchange, both individual and collective, of goods, services, and personal information. Small exchanges have occurred continuously but the larger obligations often take years to fulfill. The constant lending of money or buying of rounds of beer provides a daily continuity of social relationships and the flow of exchanges. Whoever has cash pays for the beer; no questions are asked, no accounts are recorded. The same is true of small loans and meals. The more serious mutual obligations, such as owing someone for help in an ongoing struggle for precedence or for going to jail without revealing the names of the other participants, are often continued over an extended period.[27]

A former Los Angeles gang member, Sanyika Shakur, explained such long-term obligations in the language of the streets: "If you are in this 'hood, and you leave and . . . are successful, you're obligated. You have double indemnity: you have the cultural obligation, and . . . you have the 'hood obligation. . . . So, the cultural obligation: If you don't come back and . . . contribute, you'll get your 'guild pass' revoked. Then you have the responsibility for the 'hood thing, which can get you murdered if you don't come back."[28]

The reciprocal obligations described in these accounts of gang life represent, I must underline, forms of social capital. In many respects these networks and norms of reciprocity serve the interests of the members in much the same way that social capital embodied in bowling teams helps their members. The purposes to which gang solidarity are directed are, however, typically more harmful to bystanders. This example reminds us that not all the *external* effects of social capital are beneficial.

Other students of gang activity have suggested that gangs represent an important social institution in neighborhoods where young men have little chance of connecting with wider society[29] and where other "mainstream" institutions, such as neighborhood associations and fraternal societies, are debilitated or absent.[30] Gang members have been used by ward politicians as soldiers in political organizing,[31] by organized crime syndicates as entry-level employees in illicit enterprises,[32] and by community groups as sources of volunteer labor, money, and protection.[33] The latter point is particularly telling. One study of women activists in Washington, D.C., public-housing developments found that drug gangs were important benefactors, providing crucial money for children's after-school programs that the women were organizing. One activist invited the drug dealers to tour her fledgling children's center, and they reciprocated by putting out the word that the woman's organizing was to go forward without any trouble from the street toughs.[34] In short, even as they sell drugs and carry out violent wars on the streets, gangs represent a form of social capital, providing networks of reciprocity, charity, organizing, and social control—albeit on their own, often destructive, terms. Where constructive social capital and institutions are allowed to wither, gangs emerge to fill the void.

All this is not to suggest that America's inner cities lack constructive forms of social capital. American ghettos are far more diverse than is commonly appreciated. Most residents work; most families are not on welfare; most teenagers are in school.[35] And ethnographers of minority communities, especially in American cities, have found rich spiritual and emotional networks that sustain people stung by economic dislocations and the indifference of "mainstream" white institutions. More than two decades ago Carol Stack's classic study, *All Our Kin*, introduced white America to the elaborate and nurturing support networks developed by the black families of "the Flats," an inner-city neighborhood in the Midwest. Most of the people Stack met and lived among for three years were second-generation northerners. Most were single women raising children, and most were on public assistance. Stack discovered numerous "alliances of individuals trading and exchanging goods, resources, and the care of children." She was impressed by "the intensity of their acts of domestic cooperation, and the exchange of goods and services among these persons, both kin and non-kin."[36]

Although students of urban life frequently note the high level of distrust that exists among the urban poor, Stack countered that residents of the Flats must have high levels of trust to maintain their exchange networks, since a gift is rarely repaid right away. And far from being *disorganized*, Stack argued, inner cities are (or at least were then) marked by well-organized, though often invisible, networks of altruism and obligation.[37] These networks took the form of extended, socially constructed, and well-recognized "kin groups," made up of one's relatives, one's romantic partners and their family members, one's friends, and the family members and friends of one's friends. Stack noted how the urban poor, knowing that they cannot make it on their own, are constantly seeking to expand their network. Network members might provide child care, cash assistance, temporary shelter, and other forms of assistance. Meanwhile members of the network monitored one another for evidence of shirking, imposing strong sanctions against those who take more than they give. In sum, the Flats offered a richly textured depiction of a wealth of social capital among the struggling poor.[38]

Unfortunately, more recent studies suggest that inner-city social networks are not nearly as dense or effective as those Stack found in the late 1960s,[39] for like the sprawling suburbs and small villages in the heartland, inner cities too have less social capital nowadays than they once did. Where these reciprocity systems persist, however, they remain an important asset to poor people, an asset that is too often overlooked in popular accounts of the urban underclass.

In short, social capital is a good thing, far more often than not, for disadvantaged neighbors. In areas where social capital is lacking, the effects of poverty, adult unemployment, and family breakdown are magnified, making life that much worse for children and adults alike. As we have seen, there is preliminary yet intriguing evidence that social trust, organizational participation, and neighborhood cohesion can help to break the link between economic disadvantage and teenage troublemaking. The problem, of course, is that social capital is often lacking in disadvantaged areas, and it is difficult to build. A review of "neighborhood crime watch" programs found that they are most likely to succeed in areas where they are least needed—middle-class, stable neighborhoods that already benefit from social trust and networks of association.[40] Instead of a "virtuous circle," in which existing social capital facilitates the creation of more social capital, inner cities are too often marked by a vicious circle, in which low levels of trust and cohesion lead to higher levels of crime, which lead to even lower levels of trust and cohesion. Social-capital-intensive strategies may help to "unwind" this negative spiral, but they are challenging strategies to pursue.

During the 1980s, under the rubric of "community policing," police departments across the country began to implement a kind of "applied social capitalism," seeking to fight crime by building working partnerships between law enforcement officials and community residents. Some evidence suggests that community policing does reduce social disorder and crime, at least in part through the creation and activation of local social capital. Evaluating the Chicago experiment in community policing, the so-called Chicago Alternative Policing Strategy (CAPS), Wesley Skogan and Susan Harnett report that "by creating relatively uniform opportunities for participation, CAPS took the first step toward mobilizing wider participation among all segments of the community." Similarly, Jenny Berrien and Christopher Winship report promising results from Boston's 10-Point Coalition, a working partnership between the police and the public, brokered by local ministers. Only these local ministers, they argue, had the connections and trust within the community—the social capital—to make the strategy work. One reason for the drop in crime in America's big cities in the 1990s may well be that their residents and their leaders have learned to capitalize more effectively on local stocks of social capital, dwindling or not.[41]

In this chapter we have reviewed some of the most salient evidence that social capital contributes to safe and productive neighborhoods, while its absence hampers efforts at improvement. (Of course, social capital is not the only factor that affects crime rates, so a decline in social capital will lead to a rise in crime only if other relevant factors remain unchanged.) Much of my evidence has been drawn from studies of inner cities and their residents, because for more than a generation scholarly energies have been invested in studying the problems of those settings. In seeking evidence of the impact of social connectedness on community well-being, I have found in this body of literature a wealth of empirical evidence and sensitive interpretation. However, it is worth underlining that had the "culture of suburbia" and the social pathologies of middle-class white communities attracted equal attention, we would be able to draw a more balanced assessment of the impact of social-capital deficits in Grosse Point as well as in the central city of Detroit. There is no reason to suppose that the effects (good and bad) of social capital on neighborhood life are limited to poor or minority communities.

A second reason for emphasizing the role of social capital in poor communities is this: Precisely because poor people (by definition) have little economic capital and face formidable obstacles in acquiring human capital (that is, education), *social* capital is disproportionately important to their welfare. Thus, while our evidence in sections II and III makes clear that the erosion of social capital and community engagement has affected Grosse Point in essentially the same degree as inner-city Detroit, the *impact* of that development has so far been greater in the inner city, which lacks the cushioning of other forms of capital. The shooting sprees that affected schools in suburban and rural communities as the twentieth century ended are a reminder that as the breakdown of community continues in more privileged settings, affluence and education are insufficient to prevent collective tragedy.

CHAPTER 19

Economic Prosperity

JUST AS AREAS HIGH IN SOCIAL CAPITAL are good at maintaining livable spaces, they are also good at getting ahead. A growing body of research suggests that where trust and social networks flourish, individuals, firms, neighborhoods, and even nations prosper.[1] What's more, as we have seen in the previous chapter, social capital can help to mitigate the insidious effects of socioeconomic disadvantage.

At the individual level, social connections affect one's life chances. People who grow up in well-to-do families with economically valuable social ties are more likely to succeed in the economic marketplace, not merely because they tend to be richer and better educated, but also because they can and will ply their connections. Conversely, individuals who grow up in socially isolated rural and inner-city areas are held back, not merely because they tend to be financially and educationally deprived, but also because they are relatively poor in social ties that can provide a "hand up."[2]

Economists have developed an impressive body of research suggesting that social ties can influence who gets a job, a bonus, a promotion, and other employment benefits.[3] Social networks provide people with advice, job leads, strategic information, and letters of recommendation. In his pioneering work on job searchers during the 1970s, Mark Granovetter documented the counterintuitive fact that casual acquaintances can be more important assets than close friends and family for individuals in search of employment.[4] My closest friends and kin—my "strong ties"—are likely to know the same people and hear of the same opportunities I do. More distant acquaintances—my "weak ties"—are more likely to link me to unexpected opportunities, and thus those weak ties are actually more valuable to me.

Granovetter's "strength of weak ties" finding has been replicated and expanded upon by other researchers interested in social mobility. Recently studies have found that such "weak ties" have an especially strong impact on the fortunes of people at the margins of mainstream economic and social institutions.[5] As is usually the case, there is a lively debate over precisely how much job networks—or isolation therefrom—really influence the employment prospects of inner-city residents. Skeptics have argued that employer racism,[6] the educational requirements of new urban jobs,[7] and city dwellers' lack of access to suburban growth centers[8] are equally or more important obstacles. Yet a mounting body of evidence suggests that social capital does matter, and its presence may help to surmount these employment barriers.[9]

For example, researchers have shown that when social networks and institutions are present, unemployed people take advantage of them to good ends. One sees this most in ethnic immigrant communities, where employers rely on their employees to recruit and train new workers. This social-capital approach is said to speed training, improve employee morale, and enhance loyalty to the company. The practice of using ethnic networks as employment networks goes a long way to explain why certain ethnic groups perennially dominate certain services and industries, the Chinese "rag trade" in New York being a good example. One study of niche economies found that for most ethnic groups such solidaristic hiring practices actually boosted immigrants' wages to the level of similarly skilled whites. Immigrant networks also provide financing to entrepreneurs, whether in the form of gifts from family members or loans from rotating credit associations.[10] (A rotating credit association is a group, often ethnically based, in which members make regular contributions to a common fund, which is then made available, in whole or in part, to each contributor in rotation. Such self-help microlending arrangements are widespread throughout the world wherever formal credit institutions are unwilling or unable to provide credit to small borrowers.) A study of Korean business owners found that about 70 percent used debt financing to start their enterprises and that of those who borrowed, 41 percent got their money from family and 24 percent from friends (compared with 37 percent from a financial institution).

The economic advantages of social ties extend beyond ethnic enclaves. Surveys of unemployed people have found, for example, that they look first to friends and relatives for leads on job openings. Fully 85 percent of young men in one survey used personal networks to find employment, compared with just 54–58 percent who said they used state agencies and newspapers. In Los Angeles two-thirds of white and black women who had looked for a job in the past five years landed their latest or current position with the help of someone they knew in the firm. Interestingly, for most of these women, the person who was of the most direct help lived outside their own neighborhoods.[11] All told, data from diverse surveys suggest that roughly one-half of people get their jobs through a friend or relative.[12] Other studies have examined the importance of institutionalized social-capital networks for job attainment. For example, the frequency of church attendance is one of the strongest predictors of whether inner-city black youths will become gainfully employed. The youths' religious beliefs have almost no impact on employment, suggesting that it is the social networking aspect of churchgoing, not the religious aspect, that is behind these youths' economic success.[13]

Nor is the economic value of social networks limited to the have-nots. Sociologist Ronald S. Burt has demonstrated that the social and organizational ties embodied in a business executive's Rolodex are at least as important in determining her career success as her educational qualifications and experience. Dozens of studies from Albany to Singapore and from Dresden to Detroit have found that at all levels in the social hierarchy and in all parts of the economy, social capital is a powerful resource for achieving occupational advancement, social status, and economic rewards—perhaps even more important than human capital (education and experience). Studying banking in Chicago, Brian Uzzi found that "firms that embed their commercial transactions with their lender in social attachments receive lower interest rates on loans." Even in buying and selling, especially for major purchases or risky transactions, we prefer to deal with people we know. Sociologists Paul Dimaggio and Hugh Louch found that "people who transact with friends and relatives report greater satisfaction with the results than do people who transact with strangers."[14]

These studies provide solid evidence that social capital matters because our networks, if they are extensive enough, connect us to potential economic partners, provide high-quality information, and vouch for us.[15] Moreover, for many white-collar jobs, our connections—our access to other people and institutions—is what our employer actually is hiring us for. In short, social networks have undeniable monetary value.

One problem, as the leading scholars of urban life have noted, is that these social networks are absent in precisely the places where they are needed most. In Chicago, for example, blacks who live in extreme poverty—Wilson's "truly disadvantaged"—were substantially less likely than blacks in low-poverty areas to have a current partner or best friend. If the extreme poverty resident did have a partner or best friend, that partner/friend was substantially less likely to have completed high school or to have steady work than the partners and friends of blacks in less destitute neighborhoods. The data suggest "that not only do residents of extreme-poverty areas have fewer social ties but also that they tend to have ties of less social worth, as measured by the social position of their partners, parents, siblings, and best friends, for instance. In short, they possess lower volumes of social capital."[16] Scholars in other cities have reached similar conclusions. A study of the impoverished and socially isolated Red Hook section of Brooklyn, for example, has documented the deterioration of neighborhood associations and church activities. Their decline has inhibited the growth of social networks just as employers were making most of their hires through "word of mouth."[17] And a study of Los Angeles County found that neighborhood poverty kept workers' wages down not because they lacked transportation to well-paying jobs, but because these workers lacked access to networks of people who could tell them about good job opportunities in the first place.[18] Social contacts can be extremely lucrative in theory—an Atlanta study found that each employed person in one's social network increases one's annual income by $1,400.[19] But networks tend to be more lucrative for whites than for members of minority groups. Blacks who gain job information from their neighbors tend to earn less than blacks who obtain their jobs through contacts outside the neighborhood.[20] This suggests that among the disadvantaged, "bridging" social capital may be the most lucrative form. All told, people in economically disadvantaged areas appear to suffer doubly. They lack the material resources to get ahead, and they lack the social resources that might enable them to amass these material resources.

In some ways social capital may be economically counterproductive. Some scholars who study ethnic "niche" economies—retail, manufacturing, or service sectors dominated by one immigrant group—have questioned whether their tight bonds of trust and solidarity might restrict growth and mobility. Although ethnic enclaves provide start-up capital and customers to their own entrepreneurs, the pressures of solidarity can drag down individuals and businesses that succeed "too much" or that try to expand beyond the immediate ethnically based market.[21] Some sociologists have also noted that less successful members of the community sometimes take advantage of the bonds of obligation and responsibility felt by more successful members. Thus, fast-rising entrepreneurs often face excessive demands for jobs, money, and other favors from struggling family members and neighbors. To realize their full potential, entrepreneurs may have to reach beyond their own ethnic groups or neighborhoods and forge ties to the broader world—customers, financial institutions, and civic associations.[22] Where social capital is not productive, it must be sought elsewhere.

Tight networks also may be exploited by commercial concerns seeking easy profits. For example, Amway and other businesses rely on quasi-independent agents to recruit others into merchandising. In these cases agents are asked to call upon friends and neighbors to buy and sell products, a situation that some view as anathema to the tacit norms of reciprocity and altruism that govern good social relations. These exceptions aside, however, most researchers agree that social capital does help individuals to prosper. The only real debate is over how big a role social capital plays relative to human or financial capital.

Given that social capital can benefit individuals, it is perhaps no surprise that it also can help neighborhoods, and even entire nations, to create wealth. This happens in many different ways. At the neighborhood level social capital is a marketable asset for homeowners. A Pittsburgh study found that, other things being equal, neighborhoods with high social capital were far less likely to decline than were low-social-capital areas.[23] In areas where residents vote, sustain vibrant neighborhood associations, feel attached to their neighborhood, and see it as a good place to live, other people want to move in, and housing values therefore remain comparatively high. The positive impact of social engagement held even after accounting for other factors that might affect housing prices, such as proximity to downtown, racial composition, and residents' socioeconomic status. The lesson is clear: Homeowners who are also good neighbors take their social capital to the bank.

At the local or regional level, there is mounting evidence that social capital among economic actors can produce aggregate economic growth. This is not to say that having more bowling leagues and PTAs will necessarily cause the town economy to prosper. But it is to say that, under certain conditions, cooperation among economic actors might be a better engine of growth than free-market competition. Consider two telling examples.

In 1940 Tupelo, Mississippi, was one of the poorest counties in the poorest state in the nation.[24] It had no exceptional natural resources, no great university or industrial concern to anchor its development, no major highways or population centers nearby. What was worse, in 1936 it had been ravaged by the fourth deadliest tornado in U.S. history, and the following year its only significant factory closed after a deeply divisive strike. A university-trained sociologist and native son, George McLean, returned home around this time to run the local newspaper. Through exceptional leadership he united Tupelo's business and civic leaders around the idea that the town and surrounding Lee County would never develop economically until they had developed as a community. Concerned about the dim prospects of the county's cotton economy, McLean initially persuaded local business leaders and farmers to pool their money to buy a siring bull. That move proved the start of a lucrative dairy industry that improved local incomes and therefore made businesses more prosperous. To create a less hierarchical social order, the town's elite Chamber of Commerce was disbanded and a Community Development Foundation open to everyone was started in its place. The foundation set to work improving local schools, starting community organizations, building a medical center, and establishing a vocational education center. At the same time, businesses were welcomed into town only if they paid high wages to all employees and shared this as a goal. Rural Development Councils were set up in outlying areas to encourage self-help collective action—from technical training to local cleanup campaigns—in a setting in which cooperative action for shared goals had been countercultural.

Over the next fifty years, under McLean's and his successors' leadership, Tupelo has become a national model of community and economic development, garnering numerous awards and attracting a constant stream of visitors eager to copy the town's success in their own communities. Since 1983 Lee County has added one thousand industrial jobs a year, garnered hundreds of millions of dollars of new investment, produced arguably the best school system in Mississippi, constructed a world-class hospital, and kept unemployment and poverty rates well below the state (and sometimes even the national) average. The community's success was based on its unwavering commitment to the idea that citizens would not benefit individually unless they pursued their goals collectively. Today it is unthinkable that one could enjoy social prominence in Tupelo without also getting involved in community leadership. Tupelo residents invested in social capital—networks of cooperation and mutual trust—and reaped tangible economic returns.

Another, slightly different "social-capital approach" is at the root of the economic miracle in California's Silicon Valley. Led by a small group of computer entrepreneurs, and aided by a resource-rich university community, Silicon Valley emerged as the world capital of high-tech development and manufacturing. The success is due largely to the horizontal networks of informal and formal cooperation that developed among fledgling companies in the area. Although nominally competitors, these companies' leaders shared information, problem-solving techniques, and, perhaps just as important, beers after work. They developed trade associations, industry conferences, and even a "Homebrew Computer Club," a hobbyists' group from whose ranks came the leaders of more than twenty computer companies. In an industry where job turnover is high, the key players had repeated interactions with one another in a variety of settings: "a colleague might become a customer or a competitor; today's boss could be tomorrow's subordinate." Far from producing anxiety and distrust, this "continual shuffling and reshuffling tended to reinforce the value of personal relationships and networks."[25] These informal networks expanded to include firms on the periphery of the high-tech nexus: lawyers specializing in intellectual property and business incorporation, venture capitalists, suppliers, and so forth. In the early 1990s, when Silicon Valley's economic condition began to slip, local businesses under the aegis of the San Jose Chamber of Commerce traded on their existing stock of social capital and created Joint Venture: Silicon Valley. That nonprofit networking organization helped to enhance public-private cooperation on everything from taxes to building permits to literacy.[26]

Silicon Valley's major U.S. competitor, the route 128 corridor outside Boston, did not develop such interfirm social capital. Rather it maintained traditional norms of corporate hierarchy, secrecy, self-sufficiency, and territoriality. Employees rarely went out after work with one another or with people from other firms. Route 128's "I'll succeed on my own" philosophy is largely responsible for its poor performance relative to Silicon Valley's, according to the leading study of the two high-tech centers. "The contrasting experience of Silicon Valley and Route 128 suggests that industrial systems built on regional networks are more flexible and technologically dynamic than those in which experimentation and learning are confined to individual firms."[27] The great British economist Alfred Marshall long ago recognized the advantages of such "industrial districts," which allow for information flows, mutual learning, and economies of scale.[28] Even before Silicon Valley, the model had succeeded in north-central Italy (crafts and consumer goods), western Michigan (furniture), and Rochester, New York (optics).

These are cooperative models for an increasingly competitive global economy. Social commentator Francis Fukuyama has argued that economies whose citizens have high levels of social trust—high social capital—will dominate the twenty-first century. When we can't trust our employees or other market players, we end up squandering our wealth on surveillance equipment, compliance structures, insurance, legal services, and enforcement of government regulations.[29] Conversely, studies of the biotech industry by organization theorists like Walter Powell and Jane Fountain have shown that social networks that embody a norm of reciprocity—that is, social capital—are "key enablers" of innovation, mutual learning, and productivity growth, as important as physical and human capital, particularly in rapidly evolving fields.[30]

Understanding the detailed linkages between social capital and economic performance is a lively field of inquiry at the moment, so it would be premature to claim too much for the efficacy of social capital or to describe exactly when and how networks of social connectedness boost the aggregate productivity of an economy. Research on social capital and economic development in what we once called the "Third World" is appearing at a rapid rate, based on work in such far-flung sites as South Africa, Indonesia, Russia, India, and Burkina Faso. Similarly rich work is under way on how Americans might improve the plight of our poorest communities by enabling those communities to invest in social capital and empowering them to capitalize on the social assets they already have.[31] For the moment, the links between social networks and economic success at the individual level are understood. You can be reasonably confident that you will benefit if you acquire a richer social network, but it is not yet entirely clear whether that reflects merely your ability to grab a larger share of a fixed pie, or whether if we all have richer social networks, we all gain. The early returns, however, encourage the view that social capital of the right sort boosts economic efficiency, so that if our networks of reciprocity deepen, we all benefit, and if they atrophy, we all pay dearly.

CHAPTER 20

Health and Happiness

OF ALL THE DOMAINS in which I have traced the consequences of social capital, in none is the importance of social connectedness so well established as in the case of health and well-being. Scientific studies of the effects of social cohesion on physical and mental health can be traced to the seminal work of the nineteenth-century sociologist Émile Durkheim, *Suicide*. Self-destruction is not merely a personal tragedy, he found, but a sociologically predictable consequence of the degree to which one is integrated into society—rarer among married people, rarer in more tightly knit religious communities, rarer in times of national unity, and more frequent when rapid social change disrupts the social fabric. Social connectedness matters to our lives in the most profound way.

In recent decades public health researchers have extended this initial insight to virtually all aspects of health, physical as well as psychological. Dozens of painstaking studies from Alameda (California) to Tecumseh (Michigan) have established beyond reasonable doubt that social connectedness is one of the most powerful determinants of our well-being. The more integrated we are with our community, the less likely we are to experience colds, heart attacks, strokes, cancer, depression, and premature death of all sorts. Such protective effects have been confirmed for close family ties, for friendship networks, for participation in social events, and even for simple affiliation with religious and other civic associations. In other words, both *machers* and *schmoozers* enjoy these remarkable health benefits.

After reviewing dozens of scientific studies, sociologist James House and his colleagues have concluded that the *positive* contributions to health made by social integration and social support rival in strength the *detrimental* contributions of well-established biomedical risk factors like cigarette smoking, obesity, elevated blood pressure, and physical inactivity. Statistically speaking, the evidence for the health consequences of social connectedness is as strong today as was the evidence for the health consequences of smoking at the time of the first surgeon general's report on smoking. If the trends in social disconnection are as pervasive as I argued in section II, then "bowling alone" represents one of the nation's most serious public health challenges.[1]

Although researchers aren't entirely sure why social cohesion matters for health, they have a number of plausible theories. First, social networks furnish tangible assistance, such as money, convalescent care, and transportation, which reduces psychic and physical stress and provides a safety net. If you go to church regularly, and then you slip in the bathtub and miss a Sunday, someone is more likely to notice. Social networks also may reinforce healthy norms— socially isolated people are more likely to smoke, drink, overeat, and engage in other health-damaging behaviors. And socially cohesive communities are best able to organize politically to ensure first-rate medical services.[2]

Finally, and most intriguingly, social capital might actually serve as a physiological triggering mechanism, stimulating people's immune systems to fight disease and buffer stress. Research now under way suggests that social isolation has measurable biochemical effects on the body. Animals who have been isolated develop more extensive atherosclerosis (hardening of the arteries) than less isolated animals, and among both animals and humans loneliness appears to decrease the immune response and increase blood pressure. Lisa Berkman, one of the leading researchers in the field, has speculated that social isolation is "a chronically stressful condition to which the organism respond[s] by aging faster."[3]

Some studies have documented the strong correlation between connectedness and health at the community level. Others have zeroed in on individuals, both in natural settings and in experimental conditions. These studies are for the most part careful to account for confounding factors—the panoply of other physiological, economic, institutional, behavioral, and demographic forces that might also affect an individual's health. In many cases these studies are longitudinal: they check on people over many years to get a better understanding of what lifestyle changes might have caused people's health to improve or decline. Thus researchers have been able to show that social isolation *precedes* illness to rule out the possibility that the isolation was caused by illness. Over the last twenty years more than a dozen large studies of this sort in the United States, Scandinavia, and Japan have shown that *people who are socially disconnected are between two and five times more likely to die from all causes, compared with matched individuals who have close ties with family, friends, and the community.*[4]

A recent study by researchers at the Harvard School of Public Health provides an excellent overview of the link between social capital and physical health across the United States.[5] Using survey data from nearly 170,000 individuals in all fifty states, these researchers found, as expected, that people who are African American, lack health insurance, are overweight, smoke, have a low income, or lack a college education are at greater risk for illness than are more socioeconomically advantaged individuals. But these researchers also found an astonishingly strong relationship between poor health and low social capital. States whose residents were most likely to report fair or poor health were the same states in which residents were most likely to distrust others.[6] Moving from a state with a wealth of social capital to a state with very little social capital (low trust, low voluntary group membership) increased one's chances of poor to middling health by roughly 40–70 percent. When the researchers accounted for individual residents' risk factors, the relationship between social capital and individual health remained. Indeed, the researchers concluded that if one wanted to improve one's health, moving to a high-social-capital state would do almost as much good as quitting smoking. These authors' conclusion is complemented by our own analysis. We found a strong positive relationship between a comprehensive index of public health and the Social Capital Index, along with a strong negative correlation between the Social Capital Index and all-cause mortality rates.[7] (See table 6 for the measure of public health and

Table 6: Which State Has the Best Health and Health Care?

Morgan-Quitno Healthiest State Rankings (1993–1998):

1. Births of low birth weight as a percent of all births (−)
2. Births to teenage mothers as a percent of live births (−)
3. Percent of mothers receiving late or no prenatal care (−)
4. Death rate (−)
5. Infant mortality rate (−)
6. Estimated age adjusted death rate by cancer (−)
7. Death rate by suicide (−)
8. Percent of population not covered by health insurance (−)
9. Change in percent of population uninsured (−)
10. Health care expenditures as percent of gross state product (−)
11. Per capita personal health expenditures (−)
12. Estimated rate of new cancer cases (−)
13. AIDS rate (−)
14. Sexually transmitted disease rate (−)
15. Percent of population lacking access to primary care (−)
16. Percent of adults who are binge drinkers (−)
17. Percent of adults who smoke (−)
18. Percent of adults overweight (−)
19. Days in past month when physical health was "not good" (−)
20. Community hospitals per 1,000 square miles (+)
21. Beds in community hospitals per 100,000 population (+)
22. Percent of children aged 19–35 months fully immunized (+)
23. Safety belt usage rate (+)

health care and figure 86 for the correlations of public health and mortality with social capital.)

The state-level findings are suggestive, but far more definitive evidence of the benefits of community cohesion is provided by a wealth of studies that examine individual health as a function of individual social-capital resources. Nowhere is the connection better illustrated than in Roseto, Pennsylvania.[8] This small Italian American community has been the subject of nearly forty years of in-depth study, beginning in the 1950s when medical researchers noticed a happy but puzzling phenomenon. Compared with residents of neighboring towns, Rosetans just didn't die of heart attacks. Their (age-adjusted) heart attack rate was less than half that of their neighbors; over a seven-year period not a single Roseto resident under forty-seven had died of a heart attack. The researchers looked for the usual explanations: diet, exercise, weight, smoking, genetic predisposition, and so forth. But none of these explanations held the answer—indeed, Rosetans were actually more likely to have some of these risk factors than were people in neighboring towns. The researchers then began to explore Roseto's social dynamics. The town had been founded in the nineteenth century by people from the same southern Italian village. Through local leadership these immigrants had created a mutual aid society, churches, sports clubs, a labor union, a newspaper, Scout troops, and a park and athletic field. The residents had also developed a tight-knit community where conspicuous displays of wealth were scorned and family values and good behaviors reinforced. Rosetans learned to draw on one another for financial, emotional, and other forms of support. By day they congregated on front porches to watch the comings and goings, and by night they gravitated to local social clubs. In the 1960s the researchers began to suspect that social capital (though they didn't use the term) was the key to Rosetans' healthy hearts. And the researchers worried that as socially mobile young people began to reject the tight-knit Italian folkways, the heart attack rate would begin to rise. Sure enough, by the 1980s Roseto's new generation of adults had a heart attack rate above that of their neighbors in a nearby and demographically similar town.

The Roseto story is a particularly vivid and compelling one, but numerous other studies have supported the medical researchers' intuition that social cohesion matters, not just in preventing premature death, but also in preventing disease and speeding recovery. For example, a long-term study in California found that people with the fewest social ties have the highest risk of dying from heart disease, circulatory problems, and cancer (in women), even after accounting for individual health status, socioeconomic factors, and use of preventive health care.[9] Other studies have linked lower death rates with membership in voluntary groups and engagement in cultural activities;[10] church attendance;[11] phone calls and visits with friends and relatives;[12] and general sociability such as holding parties at home, attending union meetings, visiting friends, participating in organized sports, or being members of highly cohesive

Public health is better in high-social-capital states

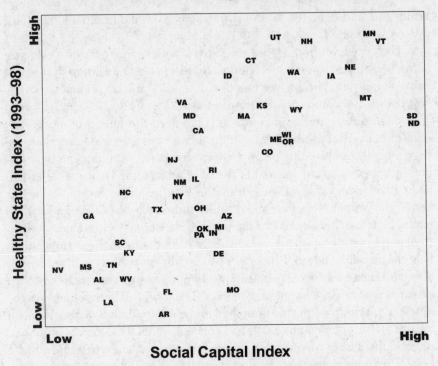

Healthy State Index (1993–98)

High

Low

Social Capital Index

Low   High

Mortality is lower in high-social-capital states

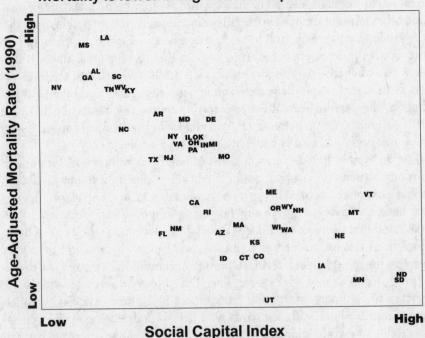

Age-Adjusted Mortality Rate (1990)

High

Low

Social Capital Index

Low   High

Figure 86: Health Is Better in High-Social-Capital States

military units.[13] The connection with social capital persisted even when the studies examined other factors that might influence mortality, such as social class, race, gender, smoking and drinking, obesity, lack of exercise, and (significantly) health problems. In other words, it is not simply that healthy, health-conscious, privileged people (who might happen also to be more socially engaged) tend to live longer. The broad range of illnesses shown to be affected by social support and the fact that the link is even tighter with death than with sickness tend to suggest that the effect operates at a quite fundamental level of general bodily resistance. What these studies tell us is that social engagement actually has an independent influence on how long we live.

Social networks help you stay healthy. The finding by a team of researchers at Carnegie Mellon University that people with more diverse social ties get fewer colds is by no means unique.[14] For example, stroke victims who had strong support networks functioned better after the stroke, and recovered more physical capacities, than did stroke victims with thin social networks.[15] Older people who are involved with clubs, volunteer work, and local politics consider themselves to be in better general health than do uninvolved people, even after accounting for socioeconomic status, demographics, level of medical care use, and years of retirement.[16]

The bottom line from this multitude of studies: As a rough rule of thumb, if you belong to no groups but decide to join one, you cut your risk of dying over the next year *in half.* If you smoke and belong to no groups, it's a toss-up statistically whether you should stop smoking or start joining. These findings are in some ways heartening: it's easier to join a group than to lose weight, exercise regularly, or quit smoking.

But the findings are sobering, too. As we saw in section II, there has been a general decline in social participation over the past twenty-five years. Figure 87 shows that this same period witnessed a significant decline in self-reported health, despite tremendous gains in medical diagnosis and treatment. Of course, by many objective measures, including life expectancy, Americans are healthier than ever before, but these self-reports indicate that we are feeling worse.[17] These self-reports are in turn closely linked to social connectedness, in the sense that it is precisely less connected Americans who are feeling worse. These facts alone do not *prove* that we are suffering physically from our growing disconnectedness, but taken in conjunction with the more systematic evidence of the health effects of social capital, this evidence is another link in the argument that the erosion of social capital has measurable ill effects.

We observed in chapter 14 the remarkable coincidence that during the same years that social connectedness has been declining, depression and even suicide have been increasing. We also noted that this coincidence has deep generational roots, in the sense that the generations most disconnected socially also suffer most from what some public health experts call "Agent Blue." In any given year 10 percent of Americans now suffer from major depression, and

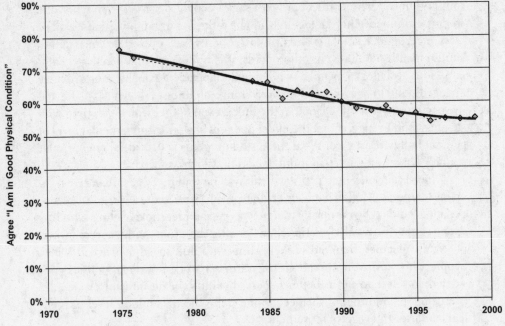

Figure 87: Americans Don't Feel as Healthy as We Used To

depression imposes the fourth largest total burden of any disease on Americans overall. Much research has shown that social connections inhibit depression. Low levels of social support directly predict depression, even controlling for other risk factors, and high levels of social support lessen the severity of symptoms and speed recovery. Social support buffers us from the stresses of daily life. Face-to-face ties seem to be more therapeutic than ties that are geographically distant. In short, even within the single domain of depression, we pay a very high price for our slackening social connectedness.[18]

Countless studies document the link between society and psyche: people who have close friends and confidants, friendly neighbors, and supportive co-workers are less likely to experience sadness, loneliness, low self-esteem, and problems with eating and sleeping. Married people are consistently happier than people who are unattached, all else being equal. These findings will hardly surprise most Americans, for in study after study people themselves report that good relationships with family members, friends, or romantic partners—far more than money or fame—are prerequisites for their happiness.[19] The single most common finding from a half century's research on the correlates of life satisfaction, not only in the United States but around the world, is that happiness is best predicted by the breadth and depth of one's social connections.[20]

We can see how social capital ranks as a producer of warm, fuzzy feelings by examining a number of questions from the DDB Needham Life Style survey archives:

"I wish I could leave my present life and do something entirely different."
"I am very satisfied with the way things are going in my life these days."
"If I had my life to live over, I would sure do things differently."
"I am much happier now than I ever was before."

Responses to these items are strongly intercorrelated, so I combined them into a single index of happiness with life. Happiness in this sense is correlated with material well-being. Generally speaking, as one rises up the income hierarchy, life contentment increases. So money can buy happiness after all. But not as much as marriage. Controlling for education, age, gender, marital status, income, and civic engagement, the marginal "effect" of marriage on life contentment is equivalent to moving roughly seventy percentiles up the income hierarchy—say, from the fifteenth percentile to the eighty-fifth percentile.[21] In round numbers, getting married is the "happiness equivalent" of quadrupling your annual income.[22]

What about education and contentment? Education has important indirect links to happiness through increased earning power, but controlling for income (as well as age, gender, and the rest), what is the marginal correlation of education itself with life satisfaction? In round numbers the answer is that four additional years of education—attending college, for example—is the "happiness equivalent" of roughly doubling your annual income.

Having assessed in rough-and-ready terms the correlations of financial capital (income), human capital (education), and one form of social capital (marriage) with life contentment, we can now ask equivalent questions about the correlations between happiness and various forms of social interaction. Let us ask about regular club members (those who attend monthly), regular volunteers (those who do so monthly), people who entertain regularly at home (say, monthly), and regular (say, biweekly) churchgoers. The differences are astonishingly large. Regular club attendance, volunteering, entertaining, or church attendance is the happiness equivalent of getting a college degree or more than doubling your income. Civic connections rival marriage and affluence as predictors of life happiness.[23]

If monthly club meetings are good, are daily club meetings thirty times better? The answer is no. Figure 88 shows what economists might call the "declining marginal productivity" of social interaction with respect to happiness. The biggest happiness returns to volunteering, clubgoing, and entertaining at home appear to come between "never" and "once a month." There is very little gain in happiness after about one club meeting (or party or volunteer effort) every three weeks. After fortnightly encounters, the marginal correlation of ad-

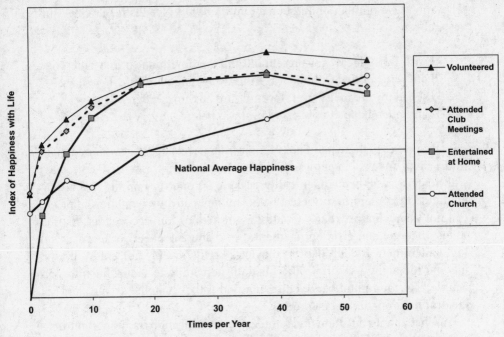

Figure 88: Social Connectedness (at Least in Moderation) Fosters Happiness

ditional social interaction with happiness is actually negative—another finding that is consistent with common experience! Churchgoing, on the other hand, is somewhat different, in that at least up through weekly attendance, the more the merrier.

This analysis is, of course, phrased intentionally in round numbers, for the underlying calculations are rough and ready. Moreover the direction of causation remains ambiguous. Perhaps happy people are more likely than unhappy people to get married, win raises at work, continue in school, attend church, join clubs, host parties, and so on. My present purpose is merely to illustrate that social connections have profound links with psychological well-being. The Beatles got it right: we all "get by with a little help from our friends."

In the decades since the Fab Four topped the charts, life satisfaction among adult Americans has declined steadily. Roughly half the decline in contentment is associated with financial worries, and half is associated with declines in social capital: lower marriage rates and decreasing connectedness to friends and community. Not all segments of the population are equally gloomy. Survey data show that the slump has been greatest among young and middle-aged adults (twenty to fifty-five). People over fifty-five—our familiar friends from the long civic generation—are actually *happier* than were people their age a generation ago.[24]

Some of the generational discrepancy is due to money worries: despite rising prosperity, young and middle-aged people feel less secure financially. But some of the disparity is also due to social connectedness. Young and middle-aged adults today are simply less likely to have friends over, attend church, or go to club meetings than were earlier generations. Psychologist Martin Seligman argues that more of us are feeling down because modern society encourages a belief in personal control and autonomy more than a commitment to duty and common enterprise. This transformation heightens our expectations about what we can achieve through choice and grit and leaves us unprepared to deal with life's inevitable failures. Where once we could fall back on social capital—families, churches, friends—these no longer are strong enough to cushion our fall.[25] In our personal lives as well as in our collective life, the evidence of this chapter suggests, we are paying a significant price for a quarter century's disengagement from one another.

CHAPTER 21

Democracy

THE PLAYWRIGHT OSCAR WILDE is said to have mused, "The trouble with socialism is that it would take too many evenings."[1] Fair enough, but how many evenings does liberal democracy take? That democratic self-government requires an actively engaged citizenry has been a truism for centuries. (Not until the middle of the twentieth century did some political theorists begin to assert that good citizenship requires simply choosing among competing teams of politicians at the ballot box, as one might choose among competing brands of toothpaste.)[2] In this chapter I consider both the conventional claim that the health of American democracy requires citizens to perform our *public* duties and the more expansive and controversial claim that the health of our *public* institutions depends, at least in part, on widespread participation in *private* voluntary groups—those networks of civic engagement that embody social capital.

The ideal of participatory democracy has deep roots in American political philosophy. With our experiment in democracy still in its infancy, Thomas Jefferson proposed amending the Constitution to facilitate grassroots democracy. In an 1816 letter he suggested that "counties be divided into wards of such size that every citizen can attend, when called on, and act in person." The ward governments would have been charged with everything from running schools to caring for the poor to operating police and military forces to maintaining public roads. Jefferson believed that "making every citizen an acting member of the government, and in the offices nearest and most interesting to him, will attach him by his strongest feelings to the independence of his country, and its republican constitution."[3]

Visiting American shores a decade later, Alexis de Tocqueville struck a similar note, suggesting that even in the absence of Jeffersonian ward governments, Americans' local civic activity served as the handmaiden of their national democratic community: "It is difficult to draw a man out of his own circle to interest him in the destiny of the state," Tocqueville observed, "because he does not clearly understand what influence the destiny of the state can have upon his own lot. But if it is proposed to make a road cross the end of his estate, he will see at a glance that there is a connection between the small public affair and his greatest private affairs; and he will discover, without its being shown to him, the close tie that unites private to general interest."[4]

British political philosopher John Stuart Mill lauded the effects of participatory democracy on character. Without shared participation in public life, Mill wrote, a citizen "never thinks of any collective interest, of any objects to be pursued jointly with others but only in competition with them, and in some measure at their expense. . . . A neighbour, not being an ally or an associate, since he is never engaged in any common undertaking for joint benefit, is therefore only a rival." The engaged citizen, by contrast, "is called upon . . . to weigh interests not his own; to be guided, in case of conflicting claims, by another rule than his private partialities. . . . He is made to feel himself one of the public, and whatever is for their benefit to be for his benefit."[5]

The eminent Progressive philosopher John Dewey grappled with a conundrum that remains timely today—how to reconcile modern, large-scale, technologically advanced society with the exigencies of democracy. "Fraternity, liberty and equality isolated from communal life are hopeless abstractions. . . . Democracy must begin at home, and its home is the neighborly community." "Only in local, face-to-face associations," adds Dewey's biographer Robert Westbrook, "could members of a public participate in dialogues with their fellows, and such dialogues were crucial to the formation and organization of the public."[6]

Many of America's Founding Fathers, however, didn't think much of voluntary associations. They were famously opposed to political parties and local political committees, as well as to any other group whose members might combine to threaten political stability. James Madison called groups organized around particular interests or passions "mischiefs of faction," whose presence must be tolerated in the name of liberty, but whose effects must be controlled.[7] Madison's fear, which reverberates among today's critics of Washington lobbyists and special interest groups, was that elected representatives, swayed by these "factions," would sacrifice the good of the whole for the pet projects of the few. In his comprehensive history of civic life in America, Michael Schudson concludes that the Founders "were far from sharing a pluralist vision, still attached as they were to the notions of consensus, property, virtue, and deference that came naturally to them."[8] As we shall shortly see, the Founders' concerns about "the mischiefs of faction" reappear in the contemporary debate about social capital and democracy.

Echoing Tocqueville's observations, many contemporary students of democracy have come to celebrate "mediating" or "intermediary" associations, be they self-consciously or only indirectly political, as fundamental to maintaining a vibrant democracy.[9] Voluntary associations and the social networks of civil society that we have been calling "social capital" contribute to democracy in two different ways: they have "external" effects on the larger polity, and they have "internal" effects on participants themselves.

Externally, voluntary associations, from churches and professional societies to Elks clubs and reading groups, allow individuals to express their interests and demands on government and to protect themselves from abuses of power by their political leaders. Political information flows through social networks, and in these networks public life is discussed. As so often, Tocqueville saw this point clearly: "When some view is represented by an association, it must take clearer and more precise shape. It counts its supporters and involves them in its cause; these supporters get to know one another, and numbers increase zeal. An association unites the energies of divergent minds and vigorously directs them toward a clearly indicated goal."[10]

When people associate in neighborhood groups, PTAs, political parties, or even national advocacy groups, their individual and otherwise quiet voices multiply and are amplified. "Without access to an association that is willing and able to speak up for our views and values," writes political philosopher Amy Gutmann, "we have a very limited ability to be heard by many other people or to influence the political process, unless we happen to be rich or famous."[11] Citizen connectedness does not require formal institutions to be effective. A study of the democracy movement in East Germany before the collapse of the Berlin Wall, for example, found that recruitment took place through friendship networks and that these informal bonds were more important than ideological commitment, fear of repression, or formal organizing efforts in determining who joined the cause.[12]

Internally, associations and less formal networks of civic engagement instill in their members habits of cooperation and public-spiritedness, as well as the practical skills necessary to partake in public life. Tocqueville observed that "feelings and ideas are renewed, the heart enlarged, and the understanding developed only by the reciprocal action of men one upon another."[13] Prophylactically, community bonds keep individuals from falling prey to extremist groups that target isolated and untethered individuals. Studies of political psychology over the last forty years have suggested that "people divorced from community, occupation, and association are first and foremost among the supporters of extremism."[14]

More positively, voluntary associations are places where social and civic skills are learned—"schools for democracy." Members learn how to run meetings, speak in public, write letters, organize projects, and debate public issues with civility.[15] William Muraskin's description of the effects of Prince Hall Masonry on the civic skills of African Americans applies much more broadly:

> Masonry as an institution has been concerned with . . . inspiring and training its membership in leadership roles. Through the fraternity, members have learned to perform many bourgeois social roles with which they have limited or no prior experience. By teaching these roles, and by promoting an arena for their enactment, Masonry has worked to bring leadership potential within its membership to practical fruition.[16]

The most systematic study of civic skills in contemporary America suggests that for working-class Americans voluntary associations and churches offer the best opportunities for civic skill building, and even for professionals such groups are second only to the workplace as sites for civic learning. Two-thirds or more of the members of religious, literary, youth, and fraternal/service organizations exercised such civic skills as giving a presentation or running a meeting.[17] Churches, in particular, are one of the few vital institutions left in which low-income, minority, and disadvantaged citizens of all races can learn politically relevant skills and be recruited into political action.[18] The implication is vitally important to anyone who values egalitarian democracy: without such institutions, the class bias in American politics would be much greater.[19]

Just as associations inculcate democratic habits, they also serve as forums for thoughtful deliberation over vital public issues. Political theorists have lately renewed their attention to the promise and pitfalls of "deliberative democracy."[20] Some argue that voluntary associations best enhance deliberation when they are microcosms of the nation, economically, ethnically, and religiously.[21] Others argue that even homogeneous organizations can enhance deliberative democracy by making our public interactions more inclusive. When minority groups, for example, push for nondiscrimination regulations and mandatory inclusion of ethnic interests in school curricula and on government boards, they are in effect widening the circle of participants.[22]

Voluntary associations may serve not only as forums for deliberation, but also as occasions for learning civic virtues, such as active participation in public life.[23] A follow-up study of high school seniors found that regardless of the students' social class, academic background, and self-esteem, those who took part in voluntary associations in school were far more likely than nonparticipants to vote, take part in political campaigns, and discuss public issues two years after graduating.[24] Another civic virtue is trustworthiness. Much research suggests that when people have repeated interactions, they are far less likely to shirk or cheat.[25] A third civic virtue acquired through social connectedness is reciprocity. As we saw repeatedly in chapter 7, the more people are involved in networks of civic engagement (from club meetings to church picnics to informal get-togethers with friends), the more likely they are to display concern for the generalized other—to volunteer, give blood, contribute to charity, and so on. To political theorists, reciprocity has another meaning as well—the willingness of opposing sides in a democratic debate to agree on the ground rules for seeking mutual accommodation after sufficient discussion, even (or especially) when they don't agree on what is to be done.[26] Regular connections with my fellow citizens don't *ensure* that I will be able to put myself in their shoes, but social isolation virtually guarantees that I will not.

On the other hand, numerous sensible critics have raised doubts about whether voluntary associations are necessarily good for democracy.[27] Most obviously, some groups are overtly antidemocratic—the KKK is everyone's favorite example. No sensible theorist has ever claimed that *every* group works to foster democratic values. But even if we restrict our attention to groups that act within the norms of democracy, one common concern is that associations—or interest groups—distort governmental decision making. From Theodore Lowi's *End of Liberalism* in the 1960s to Jonathan Rauch's *Demosclerosis* in the 1990s, critics of American pluralism have argued that the constant and conflicting pleas of ever more specialized lobbies have paralyzed even well-intentioned public officials and stifled efforts to cut or improve ineffective government programs.[28] This complaint is reminiscent of Madison's worry that mischievous "factions" would profit at the expense of the commonweal. Contrary to the pluralists' ideal, wherein bargaining among diverse groups leads to the greatest good for the greatest number, we end up instead with the greatest goodies for the best-organized few.

A second concern is that associational ties benefit those who are best equipped by nature or circumstance to organize and make their voices heard. People with education, money, status, and close ties with fellow members of their community of interest will be far more likely to benefit politically under pluralism than will the uneducated, the poor, and the unconnected.[29] In our words, social capital is self-reinforcing and benefits most those who already have a stock on which to trade. As long as associationalism is class biased, as virtually every study suggests it is,[30] then pluralist democracy will be less than egalitarian. In the famous words of the political scientist E. E. Schattschneider: "The flaw in the pluralist heaven is that the heavenly chorus sings with a strong upper-class accent."[31]

Finally, critics of pluralism have suggested that it can trigger political polarization and cynicism. Political scientists concerned about the decline in mass political parties as forces for organizing politics argue that citizen group politics is almost by nature extremist politics, since people with strongly held views tend to be the leaders and activists. Evidence from the Roper Social and Political Trends archives indeed suggests that ideological extremism and civic participation are correlated, although as we shall shortly see, that fact turns out to have unexpected implications for our current predicament.

If participation and extremism are linked, there are a number of important repercussions. First, voluntary organizations that are ideologically homogeneous may reinforce members' views and isolate them from potentially enlightening alternative viewpoints.[32] In some cases such parochialism may nurture paranoia and obstruction. In a polarized voluntary group universe, reasonable deliberation and bargaining toward a mutually acceptable compromise is well nigh impossible, as each side refuses "on principle" to give ground. Moreover, political polarization may increase cynicism about government's ability to solve problems and decrease confidence that civic engagement makes any difference.[33]

These are all serious concerns. Voluntary associations are not everywhere and always good. They can reinforce antiliberal tendencies; and they can be abused by antidemocratic forces. Further, not everyone who participates will walk away a better person: some people who join self-help groups, for example, will learn compassion and cooperation, while others will become more narcissistic. In the words of political theorist Nancy Rosenblum: "The moral uses of associational life by members are indeterminate."[34]

Voluntary groups are not a panacea for what ails our democracy. And the absence of social capital—norms, trust, networks of association—does not eliminate politics. But without social capital we are more likely to have politics of a certain type. American democracy evolved historically in an environment unusually rich in social capital, and many of our institutions and practices— such as the unusual degree of decentralization in our governmental processes, compared with that of other industrialized countries—represent adaptations to such a setting. Like a plant overtaken by climatic change, our political practices would have to change if social capital were permanently diminished. How might the American polity function in a setting of much lower social capital and civic engagement?

A politics without face-to-face socializing and organizing might take the form of a Perot-style electronic town hall, a kind of plebiscitary democracy. Many opinions would be heard, but only as a muddle of disembodied voices, neither engaging with one another nor offering much guidance to decision makers. TV-based politics is to political action as watching ER is to saving someone in distress. Just as one cannot restart a heart with one's remote control, one cannot jump-start republican citizenship without direct, face-to-face participation. Citizenship is not a spectator sport.

Politics without social capital is politics at a distance. Conversations among callers to a studio in Dallas or New York are not responsible, since these "participants" need never meaningfully engage with opposing views and hence learn from that engagement. Real conversations—the kind that take place in community meetings about crack houses or school budgets—are more "realistic" from the perspective of democratic problem solving. Without such face-to-face interaction, without immediate feedback, without being forced to examine our opinions under the light of other citizens' scrutiny, we find it easier to hawk quick fixes and to demonize anyone who disagrees. Anonymity is fundamentally anathema to deliberation.

If participation in political deliberation declines—if fewer and fewer voices engage in democratic debate—our politics will become more shrill and less balanced. When most people skip the meeting, those who are left tend to be more extreme, because they care most about the outcome. Political scientist Morris Fiorina describes, for example, how a generally popular proposal to expand a nature reserve in Concord, Massachusetts, where he lived, became bogged down in protracted and costly controversy perpetuated by a tiny group of environmentalist "true believers." [35]

The Roper Social and Political Trends surveys show that Fiorina's experience is typical: Americans at the political poles are more engaged in civic life, whereas moderates have tended to drop out. Controlling for all the standard demographic characteristics—income, education, size of city, region, age, sex, race, and job, marital, and parental status—Americans who describe themselves as "very" liberal or "very" conservative are more likely to attend public meetings, write Congress, be active in local civic organizations, and even attend church than their fellow citizens of more moderate views. Moreover, this correlation between ideological "extremism" and participation strengthened over the last quarter of the twentieth century, as people who characterize themselves as being "middle of the road" ideologically have disproportionately disappeared from public meetings, local organizations, political parties, rallies, and the like. [36]

In the 1990s self-described middle-of-the-roaders were about *one-half* as likely to participate in public meetings, local civic organizations, and political parties as in the mid-1970s. Participation by self-described "moderate" liberals or conservatives declined by about *one-third*. The declines were smallest—averaging less than *one-fifth*—among people who described themselves as "very" liberal or "very" conservative. Writing to a newspaper, writing to Congress, or even giving a speech declined by a scant 2 percent among people who described themselves as "very" liberal or conservative, by about 15 percent among people who described themselves as "moderately" liberal or conservative, and by about 30 percent among self-described "middle-of-the-roaders." [37]

Ironically, more and more Americans describe their political views as middle of the road or moderate, but the more polarized extremes on the ideological spectrum account for a bigger and bigger share of those who attend meetings, write letters, serve on committees, and so on. The more extreme views have gradually become more dominant in grassroots American civic life as more moderate voices have fallen silent. In this sense civic disengagement is exacerbating the classic problem of "faction" that worried the Founders.

Just as important as actual engagement is psychic engagement. Social capital is also key here. Surveys show that most of our political discussions take place informally, around the dinner table or the office water cooler. We learn about politics through casual conversation. You tell me what you've heard and what you think, and what your friends have heard and what they think, and I accommodate that new information into my mental database as I ponder and revise my position on an issue. In a world of civic networks, both formal and informal, our views are formed through interchange with friends and neighbors. Social capital allows political information to spread.[38]

However, as political scientists Cathy J. Cohen and Michael C. Dawson have pointed out, these informal networks are not available to everyone. African Americans who live in clusters of poverty in American inner cities suffer not only from economic deprivation, but also from a dearth of political information and opportunity. Their study of Detroit neighborhoods with concentrated poverty found that even residents not themselves destitute are far less likely to attend church, belong to a voluntary organization, attend public meetings, and talk about politics than similar people in more advantaged neighborhoods.[39] People in high-poverty neighborhoods feel cut off from their political representatives and see political and community engagement as futile. In part a realistic assessment of the nation's long-standing inattention to the truly disadvantaged, this alienated apathy also reflects the fact that inner-city neighborhoods often lack institutions to mobilize citizens into political action. In other words, people don't participate because they're not mobilized, and not mobilized, they can never savor the fruits of participation.

But perhaps face-to-face mobilization isn't necessary for effective democracy. It is sufficient, the argument goes, for large national membership groups, such as the American Association of Retired Persons, the Audubon Society, and the NAACP, to represent the interests of their diffuse membership. Just as you and I hire a mechanic to fix our cars and money managers to husband our wealth, so, too, one might argue, it is simply a sensible division of labor for us to hire the AARP to defend our interests as prospective retirees, the Audubon Society our environmentalist views, the NAACP our sympathies on racial issues, and so on. "This is not Tocquevillian democracy," concedes Michael Schudson, "but these organizations may be a highly efficient use of civic energy. The citizen who joins them may get the same civic payoff for less personal hassle. This is especially so if we conceive of politics as a set of public policies. The citizen may be able to influence government more satisfactorily with the annual membership in the Sierra Club or the National Rifle Association than by attending the local club luncheons."[40] To some intellectuals, citizenship by proxy has a certain allure.[41]

But if we have a broader conception of politics and democracy than merely the advocacy of narrow interests, then the explosion of staff-led, professionalized, Washington-based advocacy organizations may not be as satisfactory, for it was in those local luncheons that civic skills were honed and genuine give-and-take deliberation occurred. As Theda Skocpol argues:

> In classic civic America, millions of ordinary men and women could in-teract with one another, participate in groups side by side with the more privileged, and exercise influence in both community and national af-fairs. . . . In recent times the old civic America has been bypassed and shoved to the side by a gaggle of professionally dominated advocacy groups and nonprofit institutions rarely attached to memberships worthy of the name. Ideas of shared citizenship and possibilities for democratic leverage have been compromised in the process.[42]

Peter Skerry has argued that broad national membership organizations tend to be dominated not by member input—which is, after all, usually just a check sent in for their dues—but by headquarters staff. These people are inevitably pulled toward the wishes of their major patrons: wealthy individuals, foundations, even the government agencies that indirectly fund many of them. Because the voluntary organizations' members are geographically dispersed, these organizations also tend to rely on media strategies to push their agendas. Media strategies to generate more contributions often emphasize threats from the group's "enemies" and in the process give us a politics fraught with postur-ing and confrontation, rather than reasoned debate.[43]

There is another reason why large "tertiary" organizations are no substi-tute for more personal forms of political engagement: Most political decision making does not take place in Washington. To be effective, therefore, politi-cal activity cannot be confined to mailing one's dues to an inside-the-Beltway interest group. For example, economist James T. Hamilton discovered that neighborhoods where people owned their homes and voted were (holding con-stant many other factors) less likely to get hazardous waste plants than neigh-borhoods where people rented and rarely voted. He concluded that in deciding where to locate, hazardous waste companies look to locate in places in which they can expect the least locally organized opposition.[44] In this way, civic dis-engagement at the local level undermines neighborhood empowerment. Of course, the reverse is true as well, for disengagement and disempowerment are two sides of the same coin.

SOCIAL CAPITAL AFFECTS NOT ONLY what goes into politics, but also what comes out of it. The best illustration of the powerful impact of civic engage-ment on government performance comes not from the United States, but from an investigation that several colleagues and I conducted on the seemingly ar-cane subject of Italian regional government.[45]

Beginning in 1970, Italians established a nationwide set of potentially powerful regional governments. These twenty new institutions were virtually identical in form, but the social, economic, political, and cultural contexts in which they were implanted differed dramatically, ranging from the preindustrial to the postindustrial, from the devoutly Catholic to the ardently Communist, from the inertly feudal to the frenetically modern. Just as a botanist might investigate plant development by measuring the growth of genetically identical seeds sown in different plots, we sought to understand government performance by studying how these new institutions evolved in their diverse settings. As we expected, some of the new governments proved to be dismal failures—inefficient, lethargic, and corrupt. Others were remarkably successful, however, creating innovative day care programs and job training centers, promoting investment and economic development, pioneering environmental standards and family clinics—managing the public's business efficiently and satisfying their constituents.

What could account for these stark differences in quality of government? Some seemingly obvious answers turned out to be irrelevant. Government organization was too similar from region to region for that to explain the contrasts in performance. Party politics or ideology made little difference. Affluence and prosperity had no direct effect. Social stability or political harmony or population movements were not the key. None of these factors was correlated with good government as we had anticipated. Instead the best predictor is one that Alexis de Tocqueville might have expected. Strong traditions of civic engagement—voter turnout, newspaper readership, membership in choral societies and literary circles, Lions Clubs, and soccer clubs—were the hallmarks of a successful region.

Some regions of Italy, such as Emilia-Romagna and Tuscany, have many active community organizations. Citizens in these regions are engaged by public issues, not by patronage. They trust one another to act fairly and obey the law. Leaders in these communities are relatively honest and committed to equality. Social and political networks are organized horizontally, not hierarchically. These "civic communities" value solidarity, civic participation, and integrity. And here democracy works.

At the other pole are "uncivic" regions, like Calabria and Sicily, aptly characterized by the French term *incivisme*. The very concept of citizenship is stunted there. Engagement in social and cultural associations is meager. From the point of view of the inhabitants, public affairs is somebody else's business—that of *i notabili*, "the bosses," "the politicians"—but not theirs. Laws, almost everyone agrees, are made to be broken, but fearing others' lawlessness, everyone demands sterner discipline. Trapped in these interlocking vicious circles, nearly everyone feels powerless, exploited, and unhappy. It is hardly surprising that representative government here is less effective than in more civic communities.

The historical roots of the civic community are astonishingly deep. Enduring traditions of civic involvement and social solidarity can be traced back nearly a millennium to the eleventh century, when communal republics were established in places like Florence, Bologna, and Genoa, exactly the communities that today enjoy civic engagement and successful government. At the core of this civic heritage are rich networks of organized reciprocity and civic solidarity—guilds, religious fraternities, and tower societies for self-defense in the medieval communes; cooperatives, mutual aid societies, neighborhood associations, and choral societies in the twentieth century.

Civic engagement matters on both the demand side and the supply side of government. On the demand side, citizens in civic communities expect better government, and (in part through their own efforts) they get it. As we saw earlier in the hazardous waste study, if decision makers expect citizens to hold them politically accountable, they are more inclined to temper their worst impulses rather than face public protests. On the supply side, the performance of representative government is facilitated by the social infrastructure of civic communities and by the democratic values of both officials and citizens. In the language of economics, social capital lowers transaction costs and eases dilemmas of collection action. Where people know one another, interact with one another each week at choir practice or sports matches, and trust one another to behave honorably, they have a model and a moral foundation upon which to base further cooperative enterprises. Light-touch government works more efficiently in the presence of social capital. Police close more cases when citizens monitor neighborhood comings and goings. Child welfare departments do a better job of "family preservation" when neighbors and relatives provide social support to troubled parents. Public schools teach better when parents volunteer in classrooms and ensure that kids do their homework. When community involvement is lacking, the burdens on government employees—bureaucrats, social workers, teachers, and so forth—are that much greater and success that much more elusive.

Civic traditions seem to matter in the United States as well. As I explained briefly in chapter 16, in the 1950s political scientist Daniel Elazar did a pathbreaking study of American "political cultures."[46] He concluded that there were three cultures: a "traditionalistic" culture in the South; an "individualistic" culture in the mid-Atlantic and western states; and a "moralistic" culture concentrated in the Northeast, upper Midwest, and Pacific Northwest. Strikingly, Elazar's political-culture map looks much like the distribution of social capital portrayed in figure 80. The traditionalistic states, where politics tends to be dominated by elites resistant to innovation, are also the states that tend to be lowest in social capital. The individualistic states, where politics is run by strong parties and professional politicians and focused on economic growth, tend to have moderate levels of social capital. The moralistic states— in which "good government," issue-based campaigning, and social innovation are prized—tend to have comparatively high levels of social capital. The correlation between the political-culture index derived from Elazar's study[47] and our Social Capital Index is strikingly large.[48]

Do civic traditions also predict the character of governments in the United States? Suggestive studies have found that the social capital–rich "moralistic" states tend to be unusually innovative in public policy and to have merit systems governing the hiring of government employees. Politics in these states is more issue oriented, focused on social and educational services, and apparently less corrupt. Preliminary studies suggest that states high in social capital sustain governments that are more effective and innovative.[49]

At the municipal level, too, research has found that high levels of grassroots involvement tend to blunt patronage politics[50] and secure a fairer distribution of federal community development grants.[51] And cities that have institutionalized neighborhood organizations, such as Portland (Oregon) and St. Paul (Minnesota), are more effective at passing proposals that local people want. These cities also enjoy higher levels of support for and trust in municipal government.[52]

The connection between high social capital and effective government performance begs an obvious question: Is there a similar link between declining social capital and declining trust in government? Is there a connection between our democratic discontent and civic disengagement? It is commonly assumed that cynicism toward government has caused our disengagement from politics, but the converse is just as likely: that we are disaffected because as we and our neighbors have dropped out, the real performance of government has suffered. As Pogo said, "We have met the enemy and he is us."

Social capital affects government in many ways. We all agree that the country is better off when everyone pays the taxes they owe. Nobody wants to subsidize tax cheats. The legitimacy of the tax system turns in part on the belief that we all do our share. Yet we know that the IRS cannot possibly audit everyone, so rational citizens have every reason to believe that if they pay their share, they will indeed be subsidizing those who are not so honor bound. It is a recipe for disillusionment with the IRS and the tax system in general.

Yet not everyone is equally disillusioned. It turns out that in states where citizens view other people as basically honest, tax compliance is higher than in low-social-capital states. (See figure 89.) If we consider state differences in social capital, per capita income, income inequality, racial composition, urbanism, and education levels, *social capital is the only factor that successfully predicts tax compliance.*[53] Similarly, surveys have found that individual taxpayers who believe that others are dishonest or are distrustful of government are more likely themselves to cheat.[54] My willingness to pay my share depends crucially on my perception that others are doing the same. In effect, in a community rich in social capital, government is "we," not "they." In this way social capital reinforces government legitimacy: I pay my taxes because I believe that most other people do, and I see the tax system as basically working as it should.

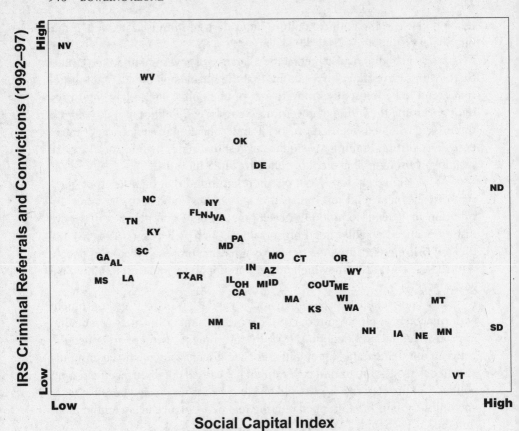

Social Capital Index

Figure 89: Tax Evasion Is Low Where Social Capital Is High

Conversely, in a community that lacks bonds of reciprocity among its inhabitants, I won't feel bound to pay taxes voluntarily, because I believe that most people cheat, and I will see the tax system as yet another broken government program, instituted by "them," not "us."

In this context it is not surprising that one of the best predictors of cooperation with the decennial census is one's level of civic participation. Even more striking is the finding that communities that rank high on measures of social capital, such as turnout and social trust, provide significantly higher contributions to public broadcasting, even when we control for all the other factors that are said to affect audience preferences and expenditures—education, affluence, race, tax deductibility, and public spending.[55] Public broadcasting is a classic example of a public good—I obtain the benefit whether or not I pay, and my contribution in itself is unlikely to keep the station on the air. Why should any rational, self-interested listener, even one addicted to Jim Lehrer, send off a check to the local station? The answer appears to be that, at least in communities that are rich in social capital, civic norms sustain an expanded sense of "self-interest" and a firmer confidence in reciprocity. Thus if our stocks of social capital diminish, more and more of us will be tempted to "free-ride," not merely by ignoring the appeals to "viewers like you," but by neglecting the myriad civic duties that allow our democracy to work.

Similarly, research has found that military units are more effective when bonds of solidarity and trust are high, and that communities with strong social networks and grassroots associations are better at confronting unexpected crises than communities that lack such civic resources.[56] In all these instances our collective interest requires actions that violate our immediate self-interest and that assume our neighbors will act collectively, too. Modern society is replete with opportunities for free-riding and opportunism. Democracy does not require that citizens be selfless saints, but in many modest ways it does assume that most of us much of the time will resist the temptation to cheat. Social capital, the evidence increasingly suggests, strengthens our better, more expansive selves. The performance of our democratic institutions depends in measurable ways upon social capital.

CHAPTER 22

The Dark Side of Social Capital

THE DOLTISH, NARROW-MINDED, materialistic, snobbish, glad-handing, big-oted, middle-class joiner is a stock figure in American letters. The 1998 movie *Pleasantville* lampooned the 1950s as provincial, misogynist, racist, proto-fascist, and (worst of all) boring, compared with the enlightened, liberated, Technicolor 1990s. The satirical theme was hardly original. As early as 1865 Henry David Thoreau wrote contemptuously in the *Atlantic Monthly* that "the American has dwindled into an Odd Fellow, one who may be known by the development of his organ of gregariousness and his manifest lack of intellect."[1]

Sinclair Lewis, the first American Nobel laureate for literature, added "babbittry" to our language with his 1922 novel about George F. Babbitt, re-altor, 100 percent booster of Zenith, Ohio, and of the Republican Party, who wore on his watch chain

> a large, yellowish elk's-tooth—proclamation of his membership in the Brotherly and Protective Order of Elks, and on the lapel of his well-cut, well-made, undistinguished grey suit stuck his Boosters' Club button. With the conciseness of great art the button displayed two words: "Boosters-Pep!" It made Babbitt feel loyal and important. It associated him with Good Fellows, with men who were nice and human and im-portant in business circles. It was his V.C., his Legion of Honor ribbon, his Phi Beta Kappa key.
>
> His clubs and associations were food comfortable to his spirit. Of a decent man in Zenith it was required that he should belong to one, pref-erably two or three, of the innumerous "lodges" and prosperity-boosting

lunch-clubs; to the Rotarians, the Kiwanis, or the Boosters; to the Odd-fellows, Moose, Masons, Red Men, Woodmen, Owls, Eagles, Macca-bees, Knights of Pythias, Knights of Columbus, and other secret orders characterized by a high degree of heartiness, sound morals, and rever-ence for the Constitution. There were four reasons for joining these or-ders: It was the thing to do. It was good for business, since lodge-brothers frequently became customers. It gave to Americans unable to become Geheimräte or Commendatori such unctuous honorifics as High Wor-thy Recording Scribe and Grand Hoogow to add to the commonplace distinctions of Colonel, Judge, and Professor. And it permitted the swad-dled American husband to stay away from home for one evening a week. The lodge was his piazza, his pavement café. He could shoot pool and talk man-talk and be obscene and valiant. Babbitt was what he called a "joiner" for all these reasons.[2]

Figures like George Babbitt give social capital a bad name. They force us to examine carefully what vices might be hidden on the dark side of civic virtue.

ON THE BANNERS of the French Revolution was inscribed a triad of ideals—liberty, equality, and fraternity. Fraternity, as the French democrats intended it, was another name for what I term "social capital." The question not resolved on those banners, or in subsequent philosophical debates, is whether those three good things always go together. Much of Western political debate for two hundred years has revolved about the trade-offs between liberty and equality. Too much liberty, or at least too much liberty in certain forms, may undermine equality. Too much equality, or at least too much equality in certain forms, may undermine liberty. Less familiar but no less portentous are the trade-offs involving the third value of the triad: Is too much fraternity bad for liberty and equality? All good things don't necessarily go together, so perhaps a single-minded pursuit of social capital might unacceptably infringe on freedom and justice. This chapter addresses some of those difficult normative issues.

Is social capital at war with liberty and tolerance? This was and remains the classic liberal objection to community ties: community restricts freedom and encourages intolerance. The discerning nineteenth-century Englishman Walter Bagehot described how oppressive the soft shackles of community could be.

You may talk of the tyranny of Nero and Tiberius; but the real tyranny is the tyranny of your next-door neighbour. What law is so cruel as the law of doing what he does? What yoke is so galling as the necessity of being like him? What espionage of despotism comes to your door so effectually as the eye of the man who lives at your door? Public opinion is a permeating influence, and it exacts obedience to itself; it requires us to think other men's thoughts, to speak other men's words, to follow other men's habits.[3]

In small-town America in the 1950s people were deeply engaged in community life, but to many this surfeit of social capital seemed to impose conformity and social division. Then in the sixties tolerance and diversity blossomed, matching almost precisely the decline in social capital.[4] Thoughtful commentators like Michael Schudson and Alan Wolfe have suggested that in the ensuing years Americans have become more tolerant while becoming less connected with one another.[5] "Might not the gain in liberty be worth the cost in community?" they have asked.

Without a doubt America in the 1990s was a more tolerant place than America in the 1950s or even the 1970s. Drawing on the General Social Survey archive, table 7 summarizes three broad measures of support for racial integration, gender equality, and civil liberties, that is, freedom of speech and writing in support of controversial views. Figure 90 provides an overview of how Americans' views in each of these three domains changed over the last quarter of the twentieth century. In fact, attitudes on all twenty-one questions summarized in table 7 moved in a more tolerant direction over the last quarter of the twentieth century: more tolerance for racial intermarriage, more tolerance for working women, more tolerance for homosexuality, and so on.

The increase in tolerance in recent decades has been stark and broad. In 1956, 50 percent of white Americans said that whites and blacks should go to separate schools; in 1995, only 4 percent said so. In 1963, 45 percent of white Americans said they would move out if blacks moved in next door; in 1997, 1 percent said the same thing. In 1973, only 20 percent of Americans reported that someone of another race had been to their house for dinner recently, but by 1996 that had more than doubled to 42 percent. As recently as 1987, 46 percent of all Americans opposed interracial dating, but by 1999 that figure had been cut in half to 23 percent. In 1963, 61 percent of Americans supported laws banning interracial marriage, but by 1998 only 11 percent did. Interracial social bridges were being strengthened, even though—or perhaps because— most forms of social capital were becoming attenuated.

In 1973 nearly half of all Americans (45 percent) favored banning from the local public library books that advocated homosexuality, but twenty-five years later that figure had fallen to 26 percent. Between 1987 and 1999 the fraction of Americans who favored firing homosexual teachers fell from more than half to less than one in three. In 1975 half of all Americans still agreed that "most men are better suited emotionally for politics than most women" and that "a woman's place is in the home." By 1999 less than one-quarter endorsed these views. Behind each of these statistical trends stands a category of Americans increasingly liberated from stigma and oppression.[6]

Table 7: Indexes of Tolerance for Racial Integration, Gender Equality, and Civil Liberties

A. Tolerance for racial integration (whites only)
  1. White people have a right to keep [Negroes/blacks/African Americans] out of their neighborhoods if they want to, and [Negroes/blacks/African Americans] should respect that right. (agree/disagree)
  2. Do you think there should be laws against marriages between [Negroes/blacks/African Americans] and whites? (yes/no)
  3. During the last few years, has anyone in your family brought a friend who was a [Negro/black/African American] home for dinner? (yes/no)
  4. Suppose there is a community-wide vote on the general housing issue. There are two possible laws to vote on. One law says that a homeowner can decide for himself whom to sell his house to, even if he prefers not to sell to [Negroes/blacks/African Americans]; the second law says that a homeowner cannot refuse to sell to someone because of his or her race or color. Which law would you vote for?
  5. If your party nominated a [Negro/black/African American] for president, would you vote for him if he were qualified for the job? (yes/no)
  6. If you and your friends belonged to a social club that would not let [Negroes/blacks/African Americans] join, would you try to change the rules so that [Negroes/blacks/African Americans] could join? (yes/no)
B. Tolerance for feminism
  1. Women should take care of running their homes and leave running the country up to men. (agree/disagree)
  2. Do you approve or disapprove of a married woman earning money in business or industry if she has a husband capable of supporting her? (approve/disapprove)
  3. If your party nominated a woman for president, would you vote for her if she were qualified for the job? (yes/no)
  4. Most men are better suited emotionally for politics than are most women. (agree/disagree)
  5. It is much better for everyone involved if the man is the achiever outside the home and the woman takes care of the home and family. (agree/disagree)
C. Tolerance for civil liberties
  1. There are always some people whose ideas are considered bad or dangerous by other people. For instance, *someone who is against all churches and religion.* If such a person wanted to make a speech in your community against churches and religion, should he be allowed to speak or not?
  2. If some people in your community suggested that a book he wrote against churches and religion should be taken out of your public library, would you favor removing this book or not?
  This same pair of questions was also posed about
  - a person who believes that blacks are genetically inferior.
  - a man who admits that he is a Communist.
  - a person who advocates doing away with elections and letting the military run the country.
  - a man who admits that he is a homosexual.

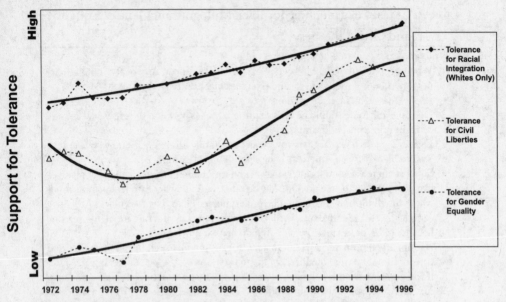

Figure 90: Tolerance Grows for Racial Integration, Civil Liberties, and Gender Equality

So between the mid-1960s and the late 1990s Americans became substantially more tolerant, precisely the same period when (as we saw in section II) they were becoming disconnected from civic life and from one another. Can it be a coincidence that as social capital has crumbled, tolerance has increased? Didn't the decline of old-fashioned clubs simply reflect people dropping out (or never joining) because they were more tolerant of women, blacks, and so on than their parents had been, while the clubs weren't? Didn't we become more tolerant precisely *because* we were freed from the suffocating, parochial influences of those hermetic social compartments? Is there not, in short, a kind of iron law linking social capital and intolerance, so that the decline of social capital is simply an inevitable concomitant of the rise of tolerant individualism? Don't we face in the end a painful and even arbitrary choice of values— community or individualism, but not both? Liberty or fraternity, but not both. If we aspire to the close-knit community of Salem, isn't it just part of the deal, as Arthur Miller argued in 1953 in *The Crucible*, that we shun "witches"—that is, anyone who does not fit in? No "witches," no Salem.[7]

If this conceptual framework is accurate, then those who care about both liberty and community face a painful trade-off, but every cloud has a silver lining. Michael Schudson argues, "The decline in organizational solidarity is truly a loss, but *is also the flip side of a rise in individual freedom*, which is truly a gain."[8] We no longer connect, but at least I don't bother you and you don't bother me.

Table 8: Social Capital and Tolerance: Four Types of Society

	Low Social Capital	High Social Capital
High tolerance	(1) *Individualistic:* You do your thing, and I'll do mine	(3) *Civic community* (Salem without "witches")
Low tolerance	(2) *Anarchic:* War of all against all	(4) *Sectarian community* (in-group vs. out-group; Salem with "witches")

But does solidarity inevitably come at the cost of freedom, just as heads inevitably comes at the cost of tails? Is disengagement really just "the flip side" of liberation? Before accepting this beguiling interpretation, consider table 8. Conceptually, at least, tolerance and social capital are not opposite ends of a single continuum from extreme individualism to extreme sectarianism. In fact, there are four logically possible types of society. The simple "liberty vs. community" interpretation highlights cells (1) and (4)—the individualistic society with much liberty but little community, and the sectarian society with much community but little liberty. But we should not too quickly dismiss the other two types, especially the attractive cell (3) that combines social capital with tolerance. Might community and liberty, at least under some circumstances, be compatible?

The first evidence in favor of this more hopeful interpretation is that individuals who are more engaged with their communities are generally *more* tolerant than their stay-at-home neighbors, not less. Many studies have found that the correlation between social participation and tolerance is, if anything, *positive*, not negative, even holding education constant. The positive link between connectedness and tolerance is especially strong with respect to gender and race: the more people are involved with community organizations, the *more* open they are to gender equality and racial integration.

Social joiners and civic activists are as a rule *more* tolerant of dissent and unconventional behavior than social isolates are, a pattern first discovered by social scientists during the repressive McCarthy period of the 1950s and confirmed repeatedly since then. One comprehensive study of citizen-participation initiatives in five American cities found that, irrespective of socioeconomic status, people who were very active in these initiatives were considerably more tolerant toward the rights of unpopular and controversial speakers than were nonparticipants. Except for the very common finding that religious involvement, especially involvement in fundamentalist churches, is linked to intolerance, I have not found a single empirical study that confirms the supposed link between community involvement and intolerance.[9] George Babbitt may have been arrogant and opinionated, but (the empirical evidence suggests) his bigotry might well have been even worse if he had *not* been exposed to the bustle of Zenith's community life.

The linkage between social capital and civic tolerance is even more posi-

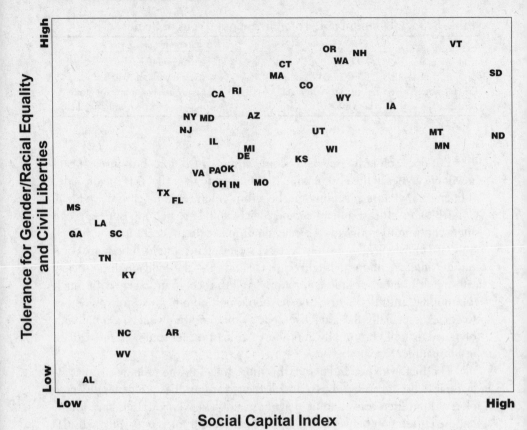

Social Capital Index

Figure 91: Social Capital and Tolerance Go Together

tive at the community level. Figure 91 shows that citizens of high-social-capital states are far more tolerant of civil liberties and far more committed to racial and gender equality than citizens of low-social-capital states. Far from being incompatible, liberty and fraternity are mutually supportive, and this remains true when we control for other factors like education, income, urbanism, and so on. The most tolerant communities in America are precisely the places with the greatest civic involvement. Conversely, communities whose residents bowl alone are the least tolerant places in America.[10]

Moreover, on closer inspection, the trends toward greater tolerance and civic disengagement over the last thirty years are not simply two sides of the same coin. Most of the changes in both tolerance and civic engagement over the last several decades are traceable to generational succession. That is, the main reason that people have become less engaged and more tolerant is that newer, more tolerant, less engaged generations have gradually replaced older, less tolerant, more engaged cohorts. But the generational dividing line between tolerant and intolerant Americans is not the same as the generational dividing line between engaged and disengaged Americans.

The increasing tolerance of the last several decades is almost entirely due to replacement of less tolerant people born in the first half of the twentieth century by more tolerant boomers and X'ers. People born after about 1945 are now and always have been more tolerant than those born before. However, this generational engine producing greater tolerance appears to have halted with the advent of the boomers. As sociologist James C. Davis noted some years ago, *people born in the 1970s or 1980s are no more tolerant than their parents born in the 1940s and 1950s.* The generational turning point is quite different for social capital, as I noted in chapter 14. There is little difference in the civic habits of people born in the 1920s and those born in the 1940s, but those born in the 1940s and even the 1950s are more civic than those born in the 1970s and 1980s.[11]

Something in the *first* half of the twentieth century made successive cohorts of Americans more tolerant, but that generational engine failed to produce further increases in tolerance among those born in the second half of the century. The late X'ers are no more tolerant than the early boomers. So the biggest generational gains in tolerance are already behind us. By contrast, something happened in America in the *second* half of the twentieth century to make people less civically engaged. The late X'ers are a lot less engaged than the early boomers. As a result, the biggest generational losses in engagement still lie ahead.

Virtually no cohort in America is more engaged *or* more tolerant than those born around 1940–45. They are the liberal communitarians par excellence. Their parents were as engaged, but less tolerant. Their children are as tolerant, but less engaged. For some reason, that cohort inherited most of their parents' sense of community, but they discarded their parents' intolerance. For the most part, they successfully passed their tolerance to their children, but they failed to transmit the communitarian habits they had themselves inherited. It was from this liberal communitarian cultural matrix that the civil rights movement emerged. But that cultural matrix has already begun to fade, leaving a nation as we enter the new century that is increasingly disengaged, but no longer increasingly tolerant. Closely examined, the generational roots of the growing tolerance and declining civic engagement of the last several decades are quite distinct. There is no reason to assume that community engagement must necessarily have illiberal consequences. Indeed, looking across the variegated states and communities in this diverse land, precisely the opposite appears true: social capital and tolerance have a symbiotic relationship.

Henry David Thoreau and Sinclair Lewis and Walter Bagehot were not entirely mistaken. No doubt community connections are sometimes oppressive. American clubs and churches are even more racially segregated than our neighborhoods and schools.[12] Bonding social capital (as distinct from bridging social capital) is particularly likely to have illiberal effects. As political philosopher Amy Gutmann has observed:

> Although many associational activities in America are clearly and directly supportive of liberal democracy, others are not so clearly or directly supportive, and still others are downright hostile to, and potentially destructive of, liberal democracy. . . . Other things being equal, the more economically, ethnically, and religiously heterogeneous the membership of an association is, the greater its capacity to cultivate the kind of public discourse and deliberation that is conducive to democratic citizenship.[13]

Community-mongers have fostered intolerance in the past, and their twenty-first-century heirs need to be held to a higher standard. That said, the greatest threat to American liberty comes from the disengaged, not the engaged. The most intolerant individuals and communities in America today are the *least* connected, not the *most* connected. There is no evidence whatever that civic disengagement is a useful tool against bigotry, or even that tolerance is a convenient side effect of disengagement.

Is social capital at war with equality? Thoughtful radicals have long feared so. Social capital, particularly social capital that bonds us with others like us, often reinforces social stratification. The abundant social capital of the 1950s was often exclusionary along racial and gender and class lines. Generally speaking, the haves engage in much more civic activity than the have-nots. Thus, strengthening the social and political power of voluntary associations may well widen class differences.

Liberals and egalitarians have often attacked some forms of social capital (from medieval guilds to neighborhood schools) in the name of individual opportunity. We have not always reckoned with the indirect social costs of our policies, but we were right to be worried about the power of private associations. Social inequalities may be embedded in social capital. Norms and networks that serve some groups may obstruct others, particularly if the norms are discriminatory or the networks socially segregated. A recognition of the importance of social capital in sustaining community life does not exempt us from the need to worry about how that "community" is defined—who is inside and thus benefits from social capital and who is outside and does not.

Does this logic mean that we must in some fundamental sense choose between community and equality? The empirical evidence on recent trends is unambiguous: No. *Community and equality are mutually reinforcing, not mutually incompatible.* Social capital and economic equality moved in tandem through most of the twentieth century. In terms of the distribution of wealth and income, America in the 1950s and 1960s was more egalitarian than it had been in more than a century. As we saw in section II, those same decades were also the high point of social connectedness and civic engagement. Record highs in equality and in social capital coincided. In both cases circumstantial evidence points to the World War II epoch as key.[14]

Conversely, the last third of the twentieth century was a time of growing inequality *and* eroding social capital. By the end of the twentieth century the gap between rich and poor in the United States had been increasing for nearly three decades, the longest sustained increase in inequality in at least a century, coupled with the first sustained decline in social capital in at least that long.[15] The timing of the two trends is striking: Sometime around 1965–70 America reversed course and started becoming both less just economically and less well connected socially and politically. This pair of trends illustrates that fraternity and equality are complementary, not warring values.

This same conclusion is reinforced by comparing equality and social capital across the American states. Figure 92 and figure 93 show that the American states with the highest levels of social capital are precisely the states most characterized by economic and civic equality.[16] Figure 92 shows that income is distributed more equally in high-social-capital states and that the gap between rich and poor is especially large in low-social-capital states. Figure 93 shows that in high-social-capital states people from different social classes are equally likely to attend public meetings, to lead local organizations, and the like, whereas in low-social-capital states civic life is monopolized by the haves, leaving the have-nots out. In short, both across space and across time, equality and fraternity are strongly *positively* correlated.

This simple analysis cannot detect what is causing what here. There are several plausible alternatives. First, social capital may help produce equality. Historically social capital has been the main weapon of the have-nots, who lacked other forms of capital. "Solidarity forever" is a proud, strategically sensible rallying cry for those, such as ethnic minorities or the working class, who lack access to conventional political clout. So it is plausible that well-knit communities can sustain more egalitarian social and political arrangements. Conversely, great disparities of wealth and power are inimical to widespread participation and broadly shared community integration, so it is also plausible that the causal arrow points from equality toward civic engagement and social capital. A third view is that social connectedness and equality are fostered by the same external forces, such as the leveling and annealing effects of massive (and victorious) war.

I cannot here adjudicate this complicated historical question, but the evidence powerfully contradicts the view that community engagement must necessarily amplify inequality. On the contrary, there is every reason to think that the twin master trends of our time—less equality, less engagement—reinforce

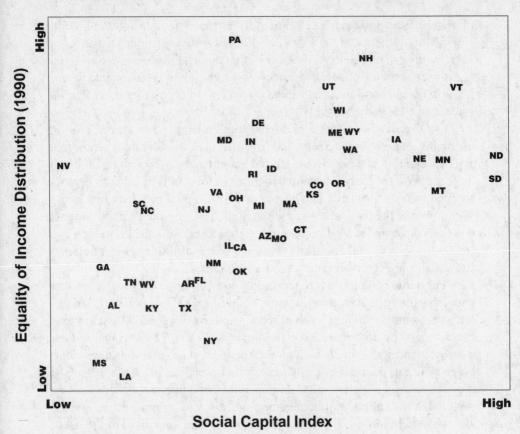

Social Capital Index

Figure 92: Social Capital and Economic Equality Go Together

one another. Thus, efforts to strengthen social capital should go hand in hand with efforts to increase equality.

Many practical tensions may arise between fraternity, on the one hand, and liberty and equality, on the other, for one could easily conceive of initiatives that would foster one of these values at the expense of the others. However, the empirical evidence clearly contradicts the simple view that the *only* way to have more fraternity is to sacrifice liberty and equality. To console ourselves that the collapse of American community has at least brought us a more liberal, egalitarian America is false optimism. To refrain from efforts to rebuild community for fear that such efforts will lead inevitably to intolerance and injustice is false pessimism.

However, we have not yet faced what is in some respects the deepest and most paradoxical indictment that might be made against advocates of fraternity—that is, the view that fraternity is in some sense at war with itself. Social cap-

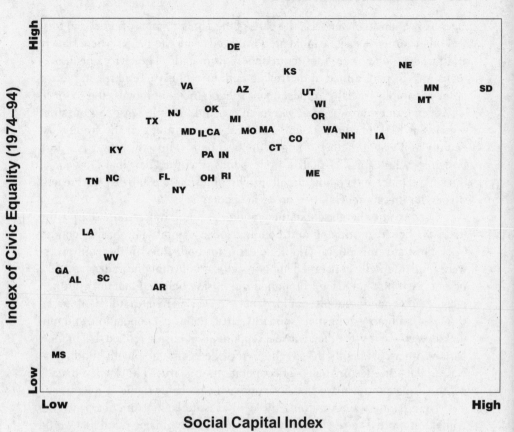

Social Capital Index

Figure 93: Social Capital and Civic Equality Go Together

ital is often most easily created *in opposition* to something or someone else. Fraternity is most natural within socially homogeneous groups. Traditional southern white identity was forged in part in resistance to racial integration, Jews are unified by anti-Semitism, and some African Americans fear that integration might undermine racial solidarity. Social divisiveness is the central normative issue raised by communitarianism. Does the exaltation of social capital and community solidarity lead inevitably to the murderous hatreds of Bosnia and Kosovo?

We need not travel across the Atlantic to find vivid examples of this dilemma, for it is quintessentially, as Gunnar Myrdal entitled his classic analysis of race in our history, "an American dilemma." Race is the most important embodiment of the ethical crosscurrents that swirl around the rocks of social capital in contemporary America. It is perhaps foolhardy to offer a brief interpretation of those issues here, but it would be irresponsible to avoid them.

Slavery and its Jim Crow aftermath had the effect of thwarting connections that might otherwise have been made among the dispossessed of both races. As we saw in chapter 16, the parts of the United States where social trust and other forms of social capital are lowest today are the places where slavery and racialist policy were most entrenched historically. The civil rights movement was, in part, aimed at destroying certain exclusive, nonbridging forms of social capital—racially homegeneous schools, neighborhoods, and so forth. The deeper question was what was to follow, and in some sense this question remains as high on the national agenda at the beginning of the twenty-first century as it was at the beginning of the twentieth. The easy answer is "More bridging social capital"—that is, more bonds of connection that cross racial lines. Workplace integration, for all its difficulties, has been by far the greatest success for this approach, as we noted in chapter 5.

On the other hand, school integration has posed much more sharply the trade-offs between bridging and bonding social capital. The busing controversy illustrates this dilemma quite clearly, for both sides in the controversy were fundamentally concerned about social capital (though, understandably, no one used that language). Proponents of busing believed that only through racially integrated schools could America ever generate sufficient social capital—familiarity, tolerance, solidarity, trust, habits of cooperation, and mutual respect—across the racial divide. Opponents of busing replied that in most parts of America, neighborhood schools provided a unique site for building social capital—friendship, habits of cooperation, solidarity. The deepest tragedy of the busing controversy is that both sides were probably right.

Here is one way of framing the central issue facing America as we become ever more diverse ethnically. If we had a golden magic wand that would miraculously create more bridging social capital, we would surely want to use it. But suppose we had only an aluminum magic wand that could create more social capital, but only of a bonding sort. This second-best magic wand would bring more blacks and more whites to church, but not to the same church, more Hispanics and Anglos to the soccer field, but not the same soccer field. Should we use it? As political scientist Eileen McDonagh has put the point vividly: "Is it better to have neighborhoods legally restricted on the basis of race, but with everyone having everyone else over for dinner, or is it better to have neighborhoods unrestricted on the basis of race, but with very little social interaction going on between neighbors?"[17] That was the dilemma embodied in the busing controversy. If we ignore it, our efforts to reinvigorate community in America may simply lead to a more divided society.

Much of the evidence I have presented suggests that social capital at various levels is mutually reinforcing—that those who reach out to friends and family are often the most active in community outreach as well. But this is by no means always the case. The *fraternity vs. fraternity* dilemma highlights one aspect of this question of scope. Some kinds of bonding social capital may discourage the formation of bridging social capital and vice versa. That's what happened in the case of busing.

Earlier in this book I observed that bridging and bonding social capital are good for different things. Strong ties with intimate friends may ensure chicken soup when you're sick, but weak ties with distant acquaintances are more likely to produce leads for a new job. From a collective point of view the scope of the social capital we need depends on the scale of the problems we face. This maxim should help guide us as we deal with the "aluminum wand" dilemma I describe here. What if we need to choose between policies that build a little bridging social capital and those that build a lot of bonding social capital? For ensuring that small children get the stimulation and structure they need, bonding social capital may be optimal. Here a little "familism" would go a long way, no matter how civically "amoral" it might be. For improving public schools we need social capital at the community level, whether these be residential communities (as in the neighborhood school model) or communities of like-minded families (as in the charter school model). For other issues—such as deciding what sort of safety net, if any, should replace the welfare system—surely it is social capital of the most broad and bridging kind that will most improve the quality of public debate. In short, for our biggest collective problems we need precisely the sort of bridging social capital that is toughest to create.[18] That challenge will be central as we turn in the following section to the most important question of this book: So what do we do now?

SECTION FIVE

What Is to Be Done?

CHAPTER 23

Lessons of History:
The Gilded Age and
the Progressive Era

OVER THE LAST THREE DECADES a variety of social, economic, and technological changes have rendered obsolete a significant stock of America's social capital. Television, two-career families, suburban sprawl, generational changes in values—these and other changes in American society have meant that fewer and fewer of us find that the League of Women Voters, or the United Way, or the Shriners, or the monthly bridge club, or even a Sunday picnic with friends fits the way we have come to live. Our growing social-capital deficit threatens educational performance, safe neighborhoods, equitable tax collection, democratic responsiveness, everyday honesty, and even our health and happiness.

Is erosion of social capital an ineluctable consequence of modernity, or can we do something about it? Sometimes, in the face of fundamental questions like this one, history instructs. In this case, some unexpectedly relevant—and in many respects optimistic—lessons can be found in a period uncannily like our own: the decades at the end of the nineteenth century and beginning of the twentieth century that American historians have dubbed the Gilded Age and the Progressive Era.* In a number of deep respects the challenges facing American society at the end of the nineteenth century foreshadowed those that we face in our own time.

Almost exactly a century ago America had also just experienced a period

---

* Neither term is used with great precision, but roughly speaking, "Gilded Age" refers to the period 1870–1900 and "Progressive Era" to 1900–1915. Like any historical demarcation, this division is not strict, since developments associated with the Progressive movement had clear antecedents during the earlier period, and developments associated with the Gilded Age persisted into the later period.

of dramatic technological, economic, and social change that rendered obsolete a significant stock of social capital. In the three or four decades after the Civil War, the Industrial Revolution, urbanization, and massive waves of immigration transformed American communities. Millions of Americans left family and friends behind on the farm when they moved to Chicago or Milwaukee or Pittsburgh, and millions more left community institutions behind in a Polish shtetl or an Italian village when they moved to the Lower East Side or the North End. America in the last quarter of the nineteenth century suffered from classic symptoms of a social-capital deficit—crime waves, degradation in the cities, inadequate education, a widening gap between rich and poor, what one contemporary called a "Saturnalia" of political corruption.

But even as these problems were erupting, Americans were beginning to fix them. Within a few decades around the turn of the century, a quickening sense of crisis, coupled with inspired grassroots and national leadership, produced an extraordinary burst of social inventiveness and political reform. In fact, most of the major community institutions in American life today were invented or refurbished in that most fecund period of civic innovation in American history. The Progressive Era was not the only example of practical civic enthusiasm in American history, and it was surely not flawless, but (partly for that reason) it contains many instructive parallels to our own era. This chapter tells the story of that exceptional epoch, offering inspiration, enlightenment, and a few cautionary tales that may illumine our own.[1]

DURING THE LAST THIRD of the nineteenth century technological, economic, and social changes transformed American life. Between roughly 1870 and 1900 America evolved rapidly from a rural, localized, traditional society to a modern, industrialized, urban nation. At the end of the Civil War, America remained, as it had been at the time of Tocqueville's visit in the 1830s, predominantly a land of small farms, small towns, and small businesses. By the turn of the century America was rapidly becoming a nation of cities, teeming with immigrants born in villages in Europe or America but now toiling in factories operated by massive industrial combines.

Technological change was one key to this transformation. In the eight decades up to 1870, the U.S. Patent Office had recognized 118,000 inventions. In the next four decades patents were generated at nearly twenty times this rate. Some of the new inventions (like the reaper) revolutionized agricultural productivity. Some (like the sewing machine and canned food) transformed the home. But most momentous of all were the inventions that underlay the American industrial, transportation, and urban revolutions—the steam boiler, steel, electricity, the telegraph and telephone, the elevator, the air brake, and many more. Steel production, for instance, mushroomed from 77,000 tons in 1870 to 11.2 million tons in 1900. The number of factories in America nearly quadrupled from 140,000 in 1865 to 512,000 in 1900, and their size grew even faster. In 1865 the typical New England mill employed only 200 to 300 people. In 1915 the first Ford Motor plant employed no fewer than 15,000.[2]

Just as the sinews of the nation were now made of steel, electricity was transforming its synapses. At the turn of the century, wrote journalist Mark Sullivan,

> electricity was streaking up and down the country, literally like lightning—wires to provide it with a pathway were everywhere being extended, like long nerves of new growth, from central power houses, from the city to the suburb, longer and longer capacity for transmission carrying it to distant villages, from the villages to the farm—everywhere ending in a switch, by the turning of which man could tap for himself a practically limitless reservoir of physical power.[3]

Railroad and telegraph transformed America from small, isolated "island communities" scattered across 3 million square miles to an integrated national economic unit. Between 1870 and 1900 the nationwide rail network grew from 53,000 to 193,000 miles. "A transcontinental railroad network brought farm and factory, country and town, closer together," concludes historian Sean Dennis Cashman. "Telegraph and telephone, electricity and press increased public knowledge, business efficiency, and political debate."[4]

Along with these technological revolutions came a revolution in the scale of enterprise, for this was also the seed time of the modern corporation. Corporate organization decimated many occupations, such as small merchant and independent artisan, while creating new ones, such as company administrator and unskilled industrial worker. Between 1897 and 1904 the first great merger wave in American history swept over Wall Street, leaving in its wake massive new corporations—Standard Oil, General Electric, Du Pont, U.S. Steel, American Tobacco, Nabisco, and many others. In fact, in relationship to the size of the total economy, the merger wave at the end of the nineteenth century was not rivaled until the megamergers of the 1990s.[5]

Economic historian Glenn Porter summarizes the dramatic changes in the structure and scale of the American economy.

> For the first time, whole industries came to be identified with the names of the powerful individuals who dominated them—Cornelius Vanderbilt, E. H. Harriman, and James J. Hill in railroads, Cyrus McCormick in reapers, John D. Rockefeller in oil, J. P. Morgan in finance, James B. Duke in tobacco, Gustavus Swift and Philip Armour in meatpacking, Andrew Carnegie in steel.... Similarly, the improvements in transportation and communications and the growth of cities opened opportunities for mass merchandising in the new fields of department stores, mail-order houses, and chain stores. Montgomery Ward and Sears, Roe-

buck & Company led the way among the mail-order firms, while distributors such as A&P and Woolworth's set new patterns in chain store retailing.[6]

Measured materially, the standard of living in the United States improved substantially during the half century after the close of the Civil War. Per capita wealth increased by some 60 percent, and real per capita GNP rose 133 percent, even as the population swelled with an influx of poor immigrants. From 1871 to 1913 the expansion of the American economy averaged 4.3 percent annually.[7]

These gains were not spread evenly, either across social classes or across time. The gap between rich and poor, and even the gap between skilled and unskilled laborers, widened, in the words of historian Mark Wahlgren Summers, "in work experience, in their satisfaction with American society, in pay scales and control of their own lives." In 1896 Charles B. Spaur estimated that 1 percent of the population owned more than half of all national wealth, while the 44 percent of families at the bottom owned only 1.2 percent. Contemporary economic historians Jeffrey Williamson and Peter Lindert report that economic inequality had increased rapidly during the years of early industrialization prior to the Civil War and continued to rise irregularly to very high levels, probably peaking just before World War I. Not until the final decades of the twentieth century would economic inequality widen as it did during the nineteenth century. Despite the growing maldistribution of well-being, however, the real income and standard of living of American workers did rise significantly in the late nineteenth and early twentieth centuries.[8]

Several severe recessions (or "panics," as they were termed) interrupted the economic progression. Unemployment surpassed 16 percent in the depressions of 1873–77 and 1893–97. No period of economic distress in American history had been as deep and traumatic as the years from 1893 to 1897. On the other hand, that depression was followed by almost two decades of nearly uninterrupted growth.[9] The prosperity of these two decades would produce a society confident and efficient enough to contemplate large-scale innovation to address the problems of the day—crime, violence, disease, urban squalor, political corruption, even the growing inequalities of wealth and power. It also gave birth to a broad and internally diverse Progressive coalition united in the optimistic assumption that society was capable of improvement via intentional reform.

The decades between the Civil War and World War I were also an epoch of rapid population growth and urbanization. Between 1870 and 1900 national population nearly doubled from 40 million to 76 million, while the population of cities tripled from 10 million to 30 million. Large cities grew faster still, and new ones were added to the roles almost yearly. The number of cities with over 50,000 in population tripled from 25 to 78 in this period. In merely twenty years between 1870 and 1890, Boston's population rose by 79 percent to nearly 450,000, San Francisco's doubled to nearly 300,000, Milwaukee's tripled to more than 200,000, and Denver's multiplied twentyfold to 107,000. Chicago, barely a village in 1860, had a population of 2.2 million by 1910. Year after year an endless stream of hopeful emigrants from American farms and European villages poured into the anonymous teeming cities of tenements and skyscrapers.[10] These migrants were living now not merely in a new community, but in a setting so unfamiliar and disjointed that many doubted it deserved the term *community* at all.

Most of the new urban dwellers were also living in a new country. In the thirty years between 1870 and 1900, nearly 12 million persons immigrated to the United States, more than had come to our shores in the previous two and a half centuries. In the following fourteen years nearly another 13 million would arrive. In 1870 one-third of all industrial workers in America were foreign born. By 1900 more than half were. In 1890 immigrant adults actually outnumbered native adults in eighteen of the twenty cities with a population over 100,000.[11]

The immigrants came from a wide variety of European countries as well as Canada and East Asia. Germans, Irish, French Canadians, British, and Scandinavians were most numerous up to 1890, but during the following two decades, as historian Steven Diner points out,

> immigrants, mostly Catholics and Jews from the unfamiliar countries of Southern and Eastern Europe, poured into America in record numbers to work in its expanding industrial economy. Often living in dense urban neighborhoods where foreign tongues predominated, they created their own churches, synagogues, and communal institutions.[12]

By 1890 the cacophony of strange tongues and strange customs of the newcomers had triggered a national debate about "Americanization" and ethnic identity, similar in many respects to the debate about "multiculturalism" and "English only" today. Historian Sean Dennis Cashman reminds us, for example, that "when in 1889 and 1890 the states of Illinois and Wisconsin decided that English was to be the medium of instruction in schools, there was a great outcry from Germans and Scandinavians."[13]

Whether his journey had begun in rural Iowa or rural Slovakia, the new Chicagoan was living a life and facing risks quite different from those that he had been raised to expect. He had come in search of economic opportunity, and often found it, but he also encountered profound insecurity. Urban workers were frequently unemployed. Older systems of "outdoor relief"—local, temporary public assistance programs—were swamped by new demands, as was the newer system of "indoor relief"—the poorhouse. Traditional social safety nets of family, friends, and community institutions no longer fit the way new urban workers had come to live.[14]

On the other hand, the ever-mounting waves of immigrants would have been stilled but for the realistic prospect of better-paying work. New affluence, however unequally distributed, gradually combined with ingenuity to produce a new culture of leisure and materialism. The invention of the phonograph and movies between 1896 and 1902 portended a radical transformation in the nature of mass leisure in the new century. As early as 1908 New York City alone had more than six hundred five-cent storefront movie theaters, or "nickelodeons." In 1914 half a million records were produced annually, and by 1921 this figure would balloon to over one hundred million.[15] As early as 1897 Mr. Dooley (Finley Peter Dunne's fictional Irish American barman) derided the new emphasis on material consumption:

> I have seen America spread out from th' Atlantic to th' Pacific with a branch office iv th' Standard Ile Comp'ny in ivry hamlet. I've seen th' shackles dropped fr'm th' slave, so's he cud by lynched in Ohio. . . . An' th' invintions . . . th' cottongin an' th' gin sour an' th' bicycle an' th' flyin'-machine an' th' nickel-in-th'-slot machine an' th' Croker machine an' th' sody fountain an'—crownin' wurruk iv our civilization—th' cash raygister.[16]

A decade later Harvard philosopher William James would express the same disdain in the elevated language of Yankee reformers, as he bemoaned "the moral flabbiness born of the exclusive worship of the bitch-goddess SUCCESS. That—with the squalid cash interpretation put on the word 'success'—is our national disease." [17]

On the other hand, other cultural changes during the Gilded Age were more progressive. As the Industrial Revolution advanced, middle-class male and female spheres became less rigidly delimited. Women assumed new public roles, demanded the vote, got advanced education, and increasingly worked and played alongside men. Perhaps the critical ingredients in this change were advances in the education of women and (for middle-class women, able to enjoy the fruits of new timesaving domestic appliances) new leisure. During the Gilded Age women began to break out of their traditional "proper sphere," many joining local reform efforts under the banner of "municipal housekeeping" and a few entering the professions, including law and medicine, thus laying the groundwork for the "new woman" of the Progressive Era.[18]

To those who lived through this epoch, what was most striking was simply the overwhelmingly accelerated pace of change itself. We often speak easily about the rapid pace of change in our own time. However, nothing in the experience of the average American at the end of the twentieth century matches the wrenching transformation experienced at the beginning of the century by an immigrant raised as a peasant in a Polish village little changed from the sixteenth century who within a few years was helping to construct the avant-garde skyscrapers of Louis Sullivan in the city of "big shoulders" beside Lake Michigan. Even for native-born Americans, the pace of change in the last decades of the nineteenth century was extraordinary. As Bostonian Henry Adams later wrote of his own boyhood, "The American boy of 1854 stood nearer the year 1 than to the year 1900."[19]

Much of the change was for the better, but much of it was not. Begin—as muckrakers like Lincoln Steffens and Jacob Riis did—with urban degradation. The bursting cities of the Gilded Age were industrial wastelands; centers of vice, poverty, and rampant disease; full of dank, crowded slums; corruptly administered. Infant mortality increased by two-thirds between 1810 and 1870. As early as the late 1860s, New York crusader Charles Loring Brace had warned of children he termed "street Arabs" forming gangs and creating a "dangerous class." Child labor burgeoned: "In 1900 nearly one-fifth of the children under fifteen earned wages in nonagricultural work, and uncounted millions of others worked on farms." Crime surged in turn-of-the-century American cities, just as it did in a number of other Western countries in the throes of industrialization and urbanization. "Some parts of Chicago had three times as many people as the most crowded parts of Tokyo and Calcutta," writes historian Cashman. "Whole neighborhoods were congested, filthy, and foul. Offal and manure littered the street along with trash and garbage. It was hardly surprising that, in the large cities, consumption, pneumonia, bronchitis, and diarrhea were endemic. . . . [For example,] Pittsburgh had the highest mortality rate for typhoid in the world, 1.3 per 1,000."[20]

The most vivid portrayal of American cities in the late nineteenth century remains Danish-born journalist Jacob Riis's 1890 work, *How the Other Half Lives.*

> In the tenements all the influences make for evil; because they are the hot-beds of the epidemics that carry death to rich and poor alike; are the nurseries of pauperism and crime that fill our jails and police courts; that throw off a scum of forty thousand human wrecks to the island asylums and workhouses year by year; that turned out in the last eight years a round half million beggars to prey upon our charities; that maintain a standing army of ten thousand tramps with all that that implies; because, above all, they touch the family life with deadly moral contagion.[21]

Jane Addams, founder of Hull House, decried the lack of public services:

> The streets are inexpressibly dirty, the number of schools inadequate, sanitary legislation unenforced, the street lighting bad, the paving miserable and altogether lacking in the alleys and smaller streets, and the stables foul beyond description. Hundreds of houses are unconnected with the street sewer.[22]

Less sympathetic observers cheered evangelist Josiah Strong's antiurban philippic: "The first city was built by the first murderer, and crime and vice and wretchedness have festered in it ever since." [23]

Developments in the teeming metropolis were especially unsettling to new middle-class professionals. "In their eyes," writes historian Don Kirschner, "the cities were esthetically repulsive, commercially spastic, culturally balkanized, morally depraved, medically lethal, socially oppressive, and politically explosive." To be sure, recent historians have suggested that Progressive Era critics exaggerated the depravity of Gilded Age cities. Jon Tieford, for example, argues that experts in city governments of the nineteenth century had many practical achievements to their credit—clean water, efficient transportation, extensive libraries. Even machine politics had beneficial effects, especially in providing political access for urban immigrants, although as urban historian Robert Barrows notes, "the fact that charitable activity was sometimes a by-product does not excuse the bribery, graft, and general malfeasance associated with late-nineteenth-century urban politics." As the most renowned civic critic, Lincoln Steffens, pointed out, the ultimate responsibility lay not with the politicians, but with the voters themselves. "The misgovernment of the American people is misgovernment *by* the American people." [24]

City machines offered patronage to the urban, immigrant poor, contracts and licenses to legitimate business, and protection to illegitimate business. Meanwhile, rake-offs and corruption were rampant—under Boss Tweed, for example, New York City paid $179,729.60, a colossal sum at the time, for three tables and forty chairs. Historian Steven Diner summarizes the political effects in terms not entirely dissimilar to middle-American political alienation a century later:

> Middle-class Americans . . . watched as the trusts manipulated members of Congress and used the courts and federal power to suppress dissent from farmers and workers. Government, which according to American ideals should represent the will of the people, appeared a captive of special interests. [25]

Gazing enviously upward, the average American saw the almost unimaginable new wealth of the robber barons—Rockefeller, Morgan, Carnegie, and their ilk. Farmers—and into the twentieth century most Americans still lived on the land—had little protection against railroad exploitation, expensive credit, and price deflation. The new industrial trusts stifled competition and transformed economic power into political power. Unorganized, workers were dependent on wages set by massive corporations. They responded with repeated efforts to build unions, but until the turn of the century these efforts were rebuffed with violence and squelched by recurrent depressions that undermined labor's market power. Nevertheless, waves of strikes gave evidence of their discontent.[26]

Peering fearfully downward, many white, native-born Americans were deeply concerned about immigrants and African Americans. As in contemporary America, ethnic cleavages tended to reinforce class lines. As historian Nell Irvin Painter observes, "Whereas the middle and upper classes were largely Protestant, native-born, of British descent, the working classes, particularly the industrial working classes, consisted of many peoples who were foreign, Catholic, or, in the South, black." The last years of the nineteenth century witnessed the rise of a defensive nativism, a heterogeneous alliance of convenience among unions (fearful of low-wage competition from immigrants), Protestant conservatives (hostile toward the rising influx of Jews and "Papists" from southern and Eastern Europe), and even some social reformers (worried that unchecked immigration exacerbated the problems of the cities). By 1894 the nativist American Protective Association, founded in Clinton, Iowa, in 1887, claimed an astonishing 2.5 million members (or roughly 7 percent of all American adults), although it declined rapidly thereafter. Distress about foreign "depravity" helped to fuel the "just say no" temperance movement, which appealed to native-born Protestants fighting against "vices" they saw most clearly in immigrant cultural traditions.[27]

As always in our history, the most virulent ethnocentrism was reserved for race. With the end of Reconstruction in 1877, control by local whites over emancipated blacks became more violent. For southern blacks, historian Richard McCormick reports, "the early 1900s brought nearly complete exclusion from politics, legal segregation of virtually all public and private facilities, and a sickening explosion of race riots and lynchings." On May 18, 1896, in the notorious *Plessy* v. *Ferguson* case, the Supreme Court endorsed "separate, but equal" Jim Crow laws. The stain of segregation spread steadily after the turn of the century—from railcars to streetcars, ferryboats to chain gangs, zoos to theaters, hospitals to jails. White racist vigilantism spread from the South to the Midwest and West. By the 1880s lynchings had become common and peaked between 1889 and 1898. During that decade there was an average of one lynching every other day somewhere in America. Meanwhile, between 1890 and 1908 virtually all southern states disenfranchised African Americans, using new race-based suffrage restrictions—the poll tax, the literacy test, the grandfather clause, and other devices. Throughout the South electoral participation by African Americans fell by an average of 62 percent—by as much as 100 percent in North Carolina, 99 percent in Louisiana, 98 percent in Alabama, and 83 percent in Florida.[28]

The more vicious forms of segregation were concentrated in the South, but in the North many civic institutions explicitly excluded working-class people, as well as African Americans, Jews, and Catholics, from membership. Progressives in the South were intent on excluding blacks from politics, and those in the West were hostile to Asians. At the same time, across the nation racist doctrines gained intellectual credibility. Professor Nathaniel Shaler of Harvard argued that emancipated blacks were reverting to the savages they had once been. "The administrations of T.R. [Teddy Roosevelt] and Woodrow Wilson coincided with what has been, since the abolition of slavery, the nadir of race relations in America," observes political historian Wilson Carey McWilliams. In short, the Progressive Era was intimately associated with exclusion.[29]

Americans at the end of the nineteenth century were divided by class, ethnicity, and race, much as we are today, although today's dividing lines differ in detail from those of a century ago (as Asians and Hispanics, for example, have replaced Jews and Italians as targets of discrimination). Equally evocative of our own social dilemmas were debates about the effects of the transportation and communications revolutions on traditional community bonds. The railroad and rural free delivery, mail-order firms and (somewhat later) chain stores, and the automobile disrupted local commerce and threatened place-based social connections. Sears, Roebuck, Montgomery Ward, the A&P, and Woolworth's were the counterparts to today's Wal-Mart and Amazon.com. Thundered William Allen White, the influential Progressive Kansas journalist,

> The mail order house unrestricted will kill our smaller towns, creating great cities with their ... inevitable caste feeling that comes from the presence of strangers who are rich and poor living side by side. Friendship, neighborliness, fraternity, or whatever you may call that spirit of comradry that comes when men know one another well, is the cement that holds together this union of states.[30]

Editorialized one newspaper in neighboring Iowa, "When your loved one was buried, was it Marshall Field and Co. who dropped a tear of sympathy and uttered the cheering words, or was it your hometown merchant?"[31]

The new communications technology triggered a lively debate among turn-of-the-century social philosophers that prefigured with remarkable fidelity the quickening controversy in contemporary America about the effects of the Internet. On the one hand, optimists enthused that the new technologies of communication would allow human sympathy wider scope. Altruism would expand in a society newly unified by rail, power line, and telegraph.[32] In William Allen White's Utopian vision, the new technological advances in the communications field harbored the possibility of making the

> nation a neighborhood. ... The electric wire, the iron pipe, the street railroad, the daily newspaper, the telephone ... have made us all one body. ... There are no outlanders. It is possible for all men to understand one another. ... Indeed it is but the dawn of a spiritual awakening.[33]

Philosopher Herbert Croly argued that the new communications media would allow an active citizenry to "meet" despite distance and thus would reduce or eliminate the need for representation. Replace electricity and the telephone with the Internet in these arguments, and the thesis sounds exceptionally timely at the beginning of the twenty-first century.

On the other hand, more cautious social observers like John Dewey and Mary Parker Follett were concerned with how to intertwine the new technology with face-to-face ties. Although they recognized and honored the larger new society, they also cherished the smaller, older social networks of neighborhoods.

> The Great Society created by steam and electricity may be a society [wrote Dewey], but it is no community. The invasion of the community by the new and relatively impersonal and mechanical modes of combined human behavior is the outstanding fact of modern life. . . . The machine age in developing the Great Society has invaded and partially disintegrated the small communities of former times without generating a Great Community.[34]
>
> Real solidarity [added Follett] will never be accomplished except by beginning somewhere the joining of one small group with another. . . . Only by actual union, not by appeals to the imagination, can the . . . varied neighborhood groups be made the constituents of a sound, normal, unpartisan city life. Then being a member of a neighborhood group will mean at the same time being a member and a responsible member of the state.[35]

Working in Roxbury, a then new streetcar suburb of Boston, Follett observed that "a free, full community life lived within the sustaining and nourishing power of the community bond . . . is almost unknown now." Seeking to re-create face-to-face neighborhood bonds, historian Jean Quandt reports, Follett

> sought to make [community] centers into institutions for overcoming civic apathy, furthering mutual understanding among groups, and creating a local framework for the integration of churches, trade associations, lodges, and youth groups. . . . [T]he face-to-face communication which started at the level of the community center would remain the surest way of creating solidarity.[36]

Progressives also worried about professionalization and about ordinary men and women forsaking participation for spectatorship and leisure. Sociologist Robert Park wrote: "In politics, religion, art and sport we are represented now by proxies where formerly we participated in person. All the forms of communal and cultural activity in which we . . . formerly shared have been taken over by professionals and the great mass of men are no longer actors, but spectators." A few years later John Dewey, a younger member of the Progressive intellectuals, blamed cheap entertainment for the decline of civic involvement: "The increase in the number, variety, and cheapness of amusements represents a powerful diversion from political concern. The members of an inchoate public have too many ways of enjoyment, as well as of work, to give much thought to organization into an effective public. . . . What is significant is that access to means of amusement has been rendered easy and cheap beyond anything known in the past."[37]

Social reformers in the Progressive Era (as in our own era) were caught on the horns of a dilemma. In social service, in public health, in urban design, in education, in neighborhood organization, in cultural philanthropy, even in lobbying, professional staff could often do a more effective, more efficient job in the task at hand than "well-meaning" volunteers. However, disempowering ordinary members of voluntary associations could easily diminish grassroots civic engagement and foster oligarchy. Progressives struggled with themselves over the choice between professionalism and grassroots democracy, though in the end professionalism would win out.[38]

Beyond these portentous debates about technology and professionalism, many Americans at the close of the nineteenth century felt morality eroding and community fracturing. The dominant public ideology of the Gilded Age had been social Darwinism. Its advocates had argued that social progress required the survival of the fittest—with little or no interference by government with the "natural laws of the marketplace." In a society so organized, the ablest would succeed, the feckless would fail, and the unhindered process of elimination would ensure social progress. In important respects this philosophy foreshadowed the libertarian worship of the unconstrained market that has once again become popular in contemporary America. However, at the end of the nineteenth century, critics of social Darwinism gradually gained the upper hand both intellectually and (increasingly) politically.[35] "At the turn of the century," reports historian Painter, "Americans came increasingly to feel that society needed to be democratized to ensure everyone a decent chance for life, liberty, and the pursuit of happiness."[39]

This philosophical U-turn was triggered in part by the revelations of muckraking journalists—Jacob Riis, whose How the Other Half Lives (1890) portrayed the tragic conditions in slum tenements; Lincoln Steffens, whose Shame of the Cities (1904) censured urban squalor and government corruption; Ida Tarbell, whose exposés in McClure's magazine (1904) attacked the depredations of the Standard Oil trust; Upton Sinclair, whose The Jungle (1905) decried abuses of immigrant laborers; and others.[40] Quite apart from such specific abuses, however, Progressive intellectuals articulated a broader yearning for the community values of small-town life, nostalgia provoked by the materialism, individualism, and "bigness" of the new America.

The pace and degree of the social change through which Americans had just lived a century ago were profoundly disorienting. The transformation of their society affected virtually everyone and tore asunder traditional relationships. They expressed their feelings about the social disjunctures in their lives in remarkably contemporary terms. "We are unsettled to the very roots of our being," wrote Walter Lippmann in 1914.

> There isn't a human relation, whether of parent and child, husband and wife, worker and employer, that doesn't move in a strange situation. We are not used to a complicated civilization, we don't know how to behave when personal contact and eternal authority have disappeared. There are no precedents to guide us, no wisdom that wasn't made for a simpler age. *We have changed our environment more quickly than we know how to change ourselves.*[41]

A year later Booth Tarkington, the Pulitzer Prize–winning Hoosier novelist, reflected on the social changes that had accompanied late-nineteenth-century urbanization in his native Indianapolis.

> Not quite so long ago as a generation, there was no panting giant here, no heaving, grimy city; there was but a pleasant big town of neighborly people who had understanding of one another, being on the whole, much of the same type. It was a leisurely and kindly place—"homelike," it was called. . . . The good burghers were given to jogging comfortably about in phaetons or in surreys for a family drive on Sunday. No one was very rich; few were very poor; the air was clean, and there was time to live.[42]

Urban historian Robert Barrows notes the nostalgic oversimplification in these lines but adds that "Tarkington's lament for a simpler time also reflected a reality that readers of his generation would have accepted without hesitation." Sociologist Charles Horton Cooley, a firsthand witness to the changes, observed in 1912 that "in our own life the intimacy of the neighborhood has been broken up by the growth of an intricate mesh of wider contacts which leaves us strangers to people who live in the same house . . . diminishing our economic and spiritual community with our neighbors."[43] Urbanization, industrialization, and immigration had undermined neighborliness.

Progressive thinkers came mostly from small towns, and they recognized the oppressive features of small-town life—"the small-town herd," as one of them put it. But they also recalled the virtues of a community rooted in interpersonal ties. "Reading of a wedding or the birth of a child," William Allen White noted, "we have that neighborly feeling that breeds the real democracy." Such neighborliness constituted an informal network of mutual aid, social capital in a particularly pure form. In small towns, historian Quandt observes,

[w]ith everyone minding everyone else's business, illness or distress was quickly known and called forth a quick response. Jane Addams remembered the uses of village gossip: it kept men informed about who needed help and enabled them to do "the good lying next at hand." . . . Along with a feeling of intimacy and a sense of classlessness, the small-town ethos which shaped the values of these intellectuals emphasized widespread participation in the public affairs of the community. . . . The result was a political democracy based on an egalitarian rather than a paternalistic sense of community.[44]

The communitarian Progressives decried the erosion of such close-knit ties in urbanizing, industrializing America. The impersonal and attenuated ties of the market replaced the sturdier bonds of family, friendship, and small-town solidarity. Their theories echoed distinctions articulated by contemporaneous social theorists from Europe—Sir Henry Maine's status versus contract, Ferdinand Tönnies's Gemeinschaft versus Gesellschaft, Emile Durkheim's mechanical versus organic solidarity, and Georg Simmel's comparison of town and metropolis, all expounded between 1860 and 1902. Britain, as the first industrializing country, first encountered the modern clash of self-seeking and solidarity. As early as 1845 Benjamin Disraeli, later to become a Victorian reformer, wrote:

In great cities men are brought together by the desire of gain. They are not in a state of co-operation, but of isolation, as to the making of fortunes; and for all the rest they are careless of neighbours. Christianity teaches us to love our neighbour as ourself; modern society acknowledges no neighbour.

In the newer social order, his American successors concurred, "relations tended to be superficial, the restraints imposed by public opinion weak, and common cause with one's neighbor lacking."[45]

Yet these thinkers remained hopeful that social bonds of different form but similar value could be reconstructed even in the arm's-length society that they saw arising around them. Their diagnosis of social change led to prescription, not despair. As historian Quandt describes the optimistic outlook of these reformers, "The easy sense of belonging, the similarity of experience, and the ethic of participation might be more easily maintained in the small locality than anywhere else, but this did not preclude their cultivation in different soil."[46] Finding or shaping new tools for cultivating community in the alien soil of industrial society was, thus, a central task for the Progressives.

Social reformers of the Progressive Era began to see society's ills, poverty and the rest, as reflecting societal and economic causes, not individual moral failings. Rugged individualism seemed increasingly unrealistic in the new, more complex and interdependent circumstances and was gradually supplanted by a more organic conception of society. Progressives did not deny the importance of self-interest but added that men and women were also moved by nonmaterial values—affection, reputation, even altruism.

During the Gilded Age "charity" and "Americanization" had seemed to the comfortable middle classes an adequate response to social ills. "In these decades," writes social historian Paul Boyer, "the middle class was in fact abandoning the immigrant cities and their complex problems—fleeing to the suburbs, retreating into tight neighborhood enclaves, dismissing municipal politics with ridicule, and allowing the industrial capitalism that was shaping the city to proceed unchecked and uncontrolled." But, adds historian Jeffrey A. Charles, "by the turn of the century . . . sociability alone appeared to be an inadequate response to the feeling of crisis that gripped the middle class. . . . [S]ocial redemption required a new type of cooperative activism . . . serving the community."[47]

Campaigning for president in 1912, Woodrow Wilson spoke of the transformation that had overtaken America in the preceding four decades in terms he knew voters would understand.

> We have come upon a very different age from any that preceded us. . . . Yesterday, and ever since history began, men were related to one another as individuals. . . . All over the Union, people are coming to feel they have no control over the course of their affairs. To-day, the everyday relationships of men are largely with great impersonal concerns, with organizations, not with other individual men. Now this is nothing short of a new social age, a new era of human relationships, a new stage-setting for the drama of life.[48]

IT WAS, IN SHORT, A TIME very like our own, brimming with promise of technological advance and unparalleled prosperity, but nostalgic for a more integrated sense of connectedness. Then, as now, new modes of communication seemed to promise new forms of community, but thoughtful men and women wondered whether those new forms would be fool's gold. Then, as now, optimism nurtured by recent economic advances battled pessimism grounded in the hard realities of seemingly intractable social ills.

Then, as now, new concentrations of wealth and corporate power raised questions about the real meaning of democracy. Then, as now, massive urban concentrations of impoverished ethnic minorities posed basic questions of social justice and social stability. Then, as now, the comfortable middle class was torn between the seductive attractions of escape and the deeper demands of redemptive social solidarity.

Then, as now, new forms of commerce, a restructured workplace, and a new spatial organization of human settlement threatened older forms of solidarity. Then, as now, waves of immigration changed the complexion of America and seemed to imperil the *unum* in our *pluribus*. Then, as now, materialism, political cynicism, and a penchant for spectatorship rather than action seemed to thwart idealistic reformism.

Above all, then, as now, older strands of social connection were being abraded—even destroyed—by technological and economic and social change. Serious observers understood that the path from the past could not be retraced, but few saw clearly the path to a better future.

By the turn of the century, complacency bred of technological prowess was succeeded by dissatisfaction, civic inventiveness, and organized reform efforts fueled by a blend of discontent and hopefulness. Over the succeeding decade this flourishing, multifaceted movement—sprouting from seeds sown in the Gilded Age and dependent on new tendrils of social connectedness—would produce the most powerful era of reform in American history.

While reactionary romantics mused about a return to a smaller, simpler, pastoral age, Progressives were too practical to be attracted by that appeal. They admired the virtues of the past but understood that we could not go back. The Industrial Age, despite its defects, had made possible a material prosperity that was an essential precondition for civic progress. The issue was not "modernity, yes or no?" but rather how to reform our institutions and adapt our habits in this new world to secure the enduring values of our tradition.

Their outlook was activist and optimistic, not fatalist and despondent. The distinctive characteristic of the Progressives was their conviction that social evils would not remedy themselves and that it was foolhardy to wait passively for time's cure. As Herbert Croly put it, they did not believe that the future would take care of itself.[49] Neither should we.

Historian Richard McCormick, writing about the final years of the nineteenth century, might have been charting a course for Americans entering the twenty-first century:

> Amid hard times, many Americans questioned the adequacy of their institutions and wondered whether democracy and economic equality were possible in an industrial society. Answering these questions with hope and hard work, some men and women began to experiment with new methods for solving the problems at hand. Hundreds poured their energies into settlement houses where they lived and worked among the urban poor. From their pulpits a new generation of ministers sought to make Christianity relevant to this world, not only the next, by aligning their churches actively on the side of the disadvantaged. Across the country the movement for municipal reform entered a new phase as businessmen and professionals tried to reach beyond their own ranks and enlist broad support for varied programs of urban improvement. Women's clubs increasingly turned their attention from discussing liter-

ature to addressing social problems. Although these middle- and upper-class endeavors would not reach a peak of strength for another decade, the seeds of Progressivism were planted during the depression of the 1890s.[50]

One striking feature of the revitalization of civic life in America in the last decades of the nineteenth century was a veritable "boom" in association building. The American penchant for clubs dated to the earliest years of the Republic.[51] Some Progressive Era associations (like the Independent Order of Odd Fellows) dated from the first third of the nineteenth century, and many others dated from the Civil War and its aftermath. As we noted in chapter 14, the Knights of Pythias, the Grange, the Benevolent and Protective Order of Elks, the Ancient Order of United Workmen, and the Grand Army of the Republic (GAR) all had been founded between 1864 and 1868. The nineteenth-century equivalent of the American Legion, the GAR, had well over three hundred thousand members by 1885.[52]

Historians agree, however, that on these earlier foundations was built a massive new structure of civic associations in the late nineteenth and early twentieth centuries.[53] Social clubs were not new to American life, but community histories regularly note their proliferation in this period. A so-called club movement swept across the land in the late nineteenth century, emphasizing self-help and amateurism. In 1876 Henry Martyn Robert published *Robert's Rules of Order* to bring order to the mushrooming anarchy of club and committee meetings. Handbooks appeared on how to establish a boys' club or a women's club. College fraternities and sororities expanded rapidly in the 1880s and 1890s.

In the last decades of the nineteenth century Americans created and joined an unprecedented number of voluntary associations. Beginning in the 1870s and extending into the 1910s, new types of association multiplied, chapters of preexisting associations proliferated, and associations increasingly federated into state and national organizations. In Peoria and St. Louis, Boston and Boise and Bath and Bowling Green, Americans organized clubs and churches and lodges and veterans groups. Everywhere, from the great entrepôt metropolises to small towns in the heartland, the number of voluntary associations grew even faster than the rapidly growing population. Thus the per capita density of associations—fraternal, religious, ethnic, labor, professional, civic, and so on—rose sharply through the second half of the nineteenth century. Then, shortly after the turn of the century, the density of associations began to stagnate. (Figure 94 shows the growth in the number of local organizations per capita in a sample of twenty-six diverse communities across the country.)[54]

Standing at the verge of another century, we can see that the foundation stone of twentieth-century civil society was set in place by the generation of

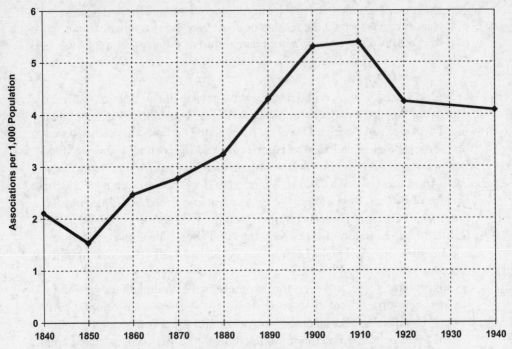

Figure 94: Associational Density in Twenty-six American Communities, 1840–1940

1870–1900. This period of institutional ferment ended in the early twentieth century, but then (as we have seen earlier in this book) a long period of in-filling followed, as the organizations founded in the Gilded Age and Progres-sive Era added to their membership ranks. That figure 94 traces not merely an arc of association building, but an arc of civic creativity and entrepreneurship is suggested by the fact that it mirrors perfectly an explosive growth in U.S. local newspapers from 1880 to 1910, followed by a period of some stagnation between 1920 and 1940.[55]

During the years from 1870 to 1920 civic inventiveness reached a cre-scendo unmatched in American history, not merely in terms of numbers of clubs, but in the range and durability of the newly founded organizations. Political scientist Theda Skocpol and her colleagues have shown that half of *all* the largest mass membership organizations in two centuries of American history—associations that *ever* enrolled at least 1 percent of the adult male or female population—were founded in the decades between 1870 and 1920.[56] As figure 95 shows, the number of such large membership associations grew dramatically in the late nineteenth century, reaching a plateau in the 1920s from which it hardly budged during the rest of the twentieth century.

Indeed, it is hardly an exaggeration to say that most major, broad-gauged civic institutions of American life today were founded in several decades of

Number of groups founded

Number over one percent

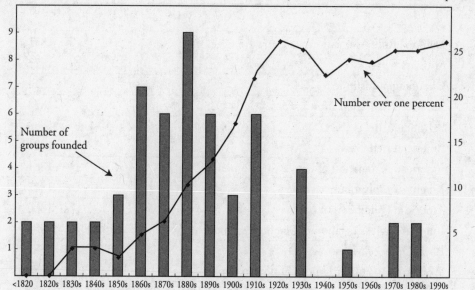

Source: Civic Engagement Project, Harvard University; data as of July 1999.

Figure 95: Founding and Cumulative Incidence of Large Membership Associations

exceptional social creativity around the turn of the twentieth century. Table 9 displays evidence for this generalization. From the Red Cross to the NAACP, from the Knights of Columbus to Hadassah, from Boy Scouts to the Rotary club, from the PTA to the Sierra Club, from the Gideon Society to the Audubon Society, from the American Bar Association to the Farm Bureau Federation, from Big Brothers to the League of Women Voters, from the Teamsters Union to the Campfire Girls, it is hard to name a major mainline civic institution in American life today that was *not* invented in these few decades.

Furthermore, organizations founded in that fecund period at the turn of the twentieth century have been unusually long-lived. For example, of all 506 contemporary national "societies and associations" listed in the *Encarta 2000 World Almanac*—large and small; with chapters and without; religious, professional, social, political, and so on—almost twice as many were founded in the thirty years between 1890 and 1920 as in the thirty years between 1960 and 1990. Figure 96, which shows the distribution of founding dates for all 506 associations, reveals that to a remarkable extent American civil society at the close of the twentieth century still rested on organizational foundations laid at the beginning of the century.[57] An age distribution of this sort—where the elderly outnumber the youthful—implies that the birth rate has declined, or that the infant mortality rate has risen, or both. In other words, compared with or-

Table 9: Social Capital Innovations, 1870–1920

Organization	Founding date
National Rifle Association	1871
Shriners	1872
Chautauqua Institute	1874
American Bar Association	1878
Salvation Army (U.S.)	1880
American Red Cross	1881
American Association of University Women	1881
Knights of Columbus	1882
American Federation of Labor	1886
International Association of Machinists [and later Aerospace Workers]	1888
Loyal Order of Moose	1888
Women's Missionary Union (Southern Baptist)	1888
Hull House (other settlement houses founded within a few years)	1889
General Federation of Women's Clubs	1890
United Mine Workers	1890
International Brotherhood of Electrical Workers	1891
International Longshoremen's Association	1892
Sierra Club	1892
National Council of Jewish Women	1893
National Civic League	1894
American Bowling Congress	1895
Sons of Norway	1895
American Nurses Association	1896
Volunteers of America	1896
Irish-American Historical Society	1897
Parent-Teacher Association (originally National Congress of Mothers)	1897
Fraternal Order of Eagles	1898
Gideon Society	1899
Veterans of Foreign Wars	1899
National Consumers League	1899
International Ladies Garment Workers Union	1900
4-H	1901
Aid Association of Lutherans	1902

Goodwill Industries	1902
National Farmers Union	1902
Big Brothers	1903
International Brotherhood of Teamsters	1903
Sons of Poland	1903
National Audubon Society	1905
Rotary	1905
Sons of Italy	1905
Boys Clubs of America	1906
YWCA	1906
Big Sisters	1908
NAACP	1909
American Camping Association	1910
Boy Scouts	1910
Campfire Girls	1910
Urban League	1910
Girl Scouts	1912
Hadassah	1912
Community Chest (later United Way)	1913
Community foundations (Cleveland, Boston, Los Angeles, etc.)	1914–15
American Association of University Professors	1915
Junior Chamber of Commerce (Jaycees)	1915
Kiwanis	1915
Ku Klux Klan (second)	1915
Women's International Bowling Congress	1916
Civitan	1917
Lions Club	1917
American Legion	1919
Optimists	1919
Business and Professional Women (BPW)	1919
American Civil Liberties Union	1920
American Farm Bureau Federation	1920
League of Women Voters	1920

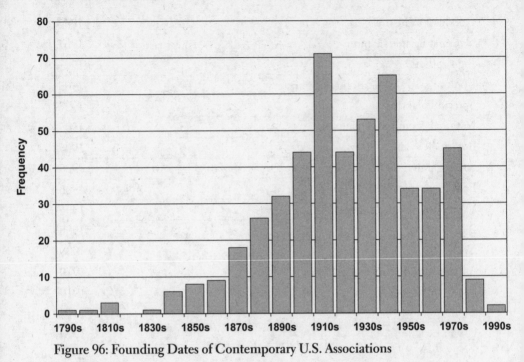

Figure 96: Founding Dates of Contemporary U.S. Associations

ganizational entrepreneurs in our own time, organization builders at the turn of the century were more prolific or more successful or both.

Moreover, the newer groups listed in recent almanacs, however worthy, are either mailing list groups, like People for the American Way, or narrowly defined and evanescent, like the Association for Investment Management and Research, the International Society of Sand Castle Builders, New Age Walkers, or the Group Against Smokers' Pollution (GASP). The groups founded between 1890 and 1920—which, after all, have endured for roughly a century by now—are more likely to be broad-based professional, civic, or service organizations, like the Boy Scouts, the National Association of Grocers, the Red Cross, or the Lions Club. (Is it really plausible to think that New Age Walkers or even GASP will still be around in 2099?)

To spot lessons in the burst of social-capital investment at the turn of the twentieth century, note first the wide variety of guises in which it appeared. America a century ago was a more gendered place than our own, and most of the organizations founded in that period were segregated by sex. It is thus not surprising that the most prominent example of organizational proliferation in that era were fraternal groups. Although Freemasonry had much earlier origins, the Gilded Age ushered in a period of massive expansion of fraternal groups. "Every fifth, or possibly every eighth, man you meet is identified with some fraternal organization," W. S. Harwood wrote in 1897. By 1910, historian

David Beito calculates, "a conservative estimate would be that one third of all adult males over age nineteen were members."

In part, fraternalism represented a reaction against the individualism and anomie of this era of rapid social change, asylum from a disordered and uncertain world. Fraternal groups provided both material benefits (for example, life and health insurance) and social solidarity and ritual. Mutual aid, resting on the principle of reciprocity—today's recipient, tomorrow's donor—was a core feature of the groups. Historian Beito observes, "They successfully created vast social and mutual aid networks among the poor." The nation's largest fraternal organizations—the Masons, Odd Fellows, Knights of Pythias, Ancient Order of United Workmen, Modern Woodmen of America—each reported hundreds of thousands of members in local chapters across the land. Notes Beito, this "geographically extended structure . . . facilitated a kind of coinsurance to mitigate local crises such as natural disasters or epidemics." Finally, Beito adds,

> By joining a lodge, an initiate adopted, at least implicitly, a set of values. Societies dedicated themselves to the advancement of mutualism, self-reliance, business training, thrift, leadership skills, self-government, self-control, and good moral character. These values reflected a fraternal consensus that cut across such seemingly intractable divisions as race, gender, and income.

Men of all social ranks joined these societies. Fraternal organizations encompassed both middle-class and working-class members. They were typically segregated by race and gender. On the other hand, as Beito has shown, there were many comparable organizations for African Americans and women that served the same functions of mutual aid and moral uplift. The segregation may be repugnant to our values, but as an ascendant form of social capital, fraternal organization was definitely not limited to middle-class white males. As illustrated by the Knights of Columbus, B'nai B'rith, and Prince Hall Freemasonry (an organization for black Masons), various ethnic groups tended to spawn their own fraternal organizations. By the early twentieth century fraternal organizations were challenged by new service clubs (Rotary, Kiwanis, Lions, the Jaycees, and the like) and by professional associations. These newer groups offered business contacts, a more modern face, and more outward civic zeal, though this came at the expense of the "brotherhood" of fraternalism.[58]

Among women, a more or less spontaneous grassroots crusade of 1873–74 across the Midwest reinvigorated the temperance movement and resulted in the formation of the Woman's Christian Temperance Union (WCTU), which quickly expanded as a vehicle for broader moral and social reform. Frances Willard, its activist leader, adopted a national policy of "Do Everything," and WCTU women did—advocating prison reform, forming youth groups, establishing kindergartens, even endorsing labor reform. In the 1890s the WCTU began to decline, and with Willard's death in 1898, it narrowed its focus to temperance and prohibition. Meanwhile, however, new women's groups began to appear, emerging in part from the many independent reading and study groups described in chapter 9. In 1890 this translocal network of women's organizations was linked together to form the General Federation of Women's Clubs. During this period women's associations turned toward explicit involvement in public affairs, campaigning on issues like child labor, women's employment, kindergartens, and myriad other social reforms including women's suffrage.[59]

Immigrant and ethnic associations illustrate other aspects of social capital building at the end of the last century. Generally speaking, emigration devalues one's social capital, for most of one's social connections must be left behind. Thus immigrants rationally strive to conserve social capital. So-called chain migration, whereby immigrants from a given locale in the "old country" settle near one another in their new homeland, was and remains one common coping strategy. In addition, the benevolent society for mutual aid was the bedrock of many immigrant communities, providing financial security, camaraderie, and even political representation. A member of a Chinese tong expressed the essential value of social capital for immigrants in a remark in the early twentieth century: "We are strangers in a strange country. We must have an organization (tong) to control our country fellows and develop our friendship."[60]

According to historian Rowland Berthoff, "The immigrants, who had been accustomed to a more tightly knit communal life than almost any American could now recall, were quick to adopt the fraternal form of the American voluntary association in order to bind together their local ethnic communities against the unpredictable looseness of life in America." Germans, who constituted the largest ethnic minority throughout this era, were especially associational. When Italians, Jews, Poles, and others from southern and Eastern Europe arrived around the turn of the century, they too quickly organized mutual aid societies, free loan societies, burial societies, social, sports, and recreational clubs, foreign-language newspapers, churches, and synagogues. By 1910 two-thirds of all Poles in America were said to belong to at least one of the approximately seven thousand Polish associations, and there were similar figures for Jews, Slovaks, Croats, and so on. In addition, national fraternal organizations, like B'nai B'rith, Hadassah, and the Knights of Columbus, attracted large numbers after the turn of the century.[61]

The building of associations among freed blacks followed much the same pattern, including mutual aid, burial, and social associations and black fraternal and women's groups. Released from bondage, exercising newly acquired civic freedoms, and facing profound social dislocation, blacks founded and joined associations in great numbers in both North and South between 1870 and 1900. In his classic study of *The Philadelphia Negro* at the turn of the century, W. E. B. Du Bois emphasized the importance of black secret societies, such as the Odd Fellows and Freemasons, in furnishing "pastime from the monotony of work, a field for ambition and intrigue, a chance for parade, and insurance against misfortune"—virtually the same boons that attracted millions of whites into such organizations in these years. As we discussed in earlier chapters, the church played a role of unique importance in social-capital formation within the African American community. At the same time, associations arose that linked blacks and whites together in support of social reform—above all, the NAACP and the Urban League.[62]

Although the culture of industrial America was becoming in some respects more secular, religion played a substantial role in the civic revitalization of the period quite apart from the devotional activities of local parishes and congregations. The Salvation Army, an evangelical Protestant movement ministering to the unchurched urban poor with missionary zeal and unorthodox mass marketing—marches, brass bands, and "Hallelujah lassies"—spread from Britain to America in 1880. This was the epoch of the "Social Gospel" and "muscular Christianity." The Social Gospel movement embodied a turn-of-the-century effort by liberal Protestant theologians and ministers to bring pressing social problems such as urban poverty to the attention of their middle-class parishioners. The Social Gospel represented a reaction against individualism, laissez-faire, and inequality, and an attempt to make religion relevant to new social and intellectual circumstances.

It was in this period that many churches took on the character of what religious historian E. Brooks Holifield terms "the social congregation."

> In the late nineteenth century, thousands of congregations transformed themselves into centers that not only were open for worship but also were available for Sunday school, concerts, church socials, women's meetings, youth groups, girls' guilds, boys' brigades, sewing circles, benevolent societies, day schools, temperance societies, athletic clubs, scout troops, and nameless other activities. . . . Henry Ward Beecher advised the seminarians at Yale to "multiply picnics" in their parishes, and many congregations of every variety proceeded beyond picnics to gymnasiums, parish houses, camps, baseball teams, and military drill groups. . . . They also gave increasing amounts of money for purposes other than their own maintenance: both in the cities and in the country churches, Protestant congregations by 1923 gave 25 to 35 percent of their offerings to missions and benevolent causes, up from 14 to 18 percent at the turn of the century.[63]

Religious inspiration, self-improvement, and civic engagement were closely intertwined in this period. The Chautauqua movement, founded in upstate New York in 1874 as a summer institute for Methodist Sunday school teachers, spawned a nationwide series of extension schools, study groups, and

tent lecture circuits, on which speakers ranging from Eugene Debs to Warren Harding regularly traveled. By 1919 one commentator estimated that "one
out of every eleven persons in the country, man, woman, or child, attended a
lyceum or Chautauqua program every year." Radio (and later television) would
provide more alluring entertainment, though less opportunity for grassroots,
cross-class civic deliberation.

Catholics tended to be even more sympathetic to the plight of the poor
than did Protestants, not least because more Catholics belonged to the labor-
ing classes. As always, the church played a special role in the black community.
Evelyn Higginbotham, a leading historian of the black church, observes that
"it housed a diversity of programs including schools, circulating libraries, concerts, restaurants, insurance companies, vocational training, athletic clubs—
all catering to a population much broader than the membership of individual
churches. The church . . . held political rallies, clubwomen's conferences,
and school graduations." In short, a socially reformist Christianity was a central inspiration for much of the social activism of the period. On the verge of
nominating Theodore Roosevelt as a full-throated reform candidate for president in 1912, delegates to the Progressive convention broke spontaneously into
an emotional chorus of "Onward, Christian Soldiers!" [64]

This was also the era in which the organized labor movement became
a serious force in American life. The Knights of Labor, based on the premise
that workers of all types should be enrolled in "one big union," had boomed
from 28,100 members in 1880 to 729,000 six years later, but then fell back to
100,000 in 1890 and collapsed in 1894 in the face of internal conflicts between
the skilled and unskilled, as well as between blacks and whites. Its leading role
was soon taken over by the American Federation of Labor, along with a series
of unions organized along craft and industrial lines—mine workers (founded
in 1890), electrical workers (1891), longshoremen (1892), garment workers
(1900), teamsters (1903), and so on. In barely seven years (1897–1904) nationwide union membership almost quadrupled from 3.5 percent of the nonagricultural workforce to 12.3 percent. This time union efforts proved more
durable, and union membership would not fall below the new plateau for the
rest of the century. [65]

Historians Thomas Cochran and William Miller make clear that unions
were a part of their members' social lives, not merely a means to gain material
improvements:

> Collective action by labor had roots far more complex than simple ques-
> tions of wages and hours. . . . Labor unions were but a part of the mass
> movement into clubs, lodges and fraternal orders. Working for the union
> and empowering the delegates to do battle with the boss was a reassertion
> of the individual's power over his environment. Mutual benefit policies

gave a feeling of security in the face of industrial accidents and seasonal unemployment, while union socials, dances, picnics and lectures offered stimulating leisure-time activity.[66]

Because Progressive Era reformers were especially aware of the importance of youth development, that was a special focus of their organizational energies. In an extraordinary burst of creativity, in less than a decade (1901–10) most of the nationwide youth organizations that were to dominate the twentieth century were founded—the Boy Scouts and Girl Scouts, Campfire Girls, the 4-H, Boys Clubs and Girls Clubs, Big Brothers and Big Sisters, and the American Camping Association, the organizational crystallization of the movement for summer camps that had rapidly developed in the previous two decades.

In these years, too, the kindergarten and the high school became recognizable elements in American public schooling and the playground a commonplace of American towns and cities. Beginning with the creation of sand gardens in Boston in 1885, organized playgrounds spread rapidly to New York, Chicago, Philadelphia, Los Angeles, and beyond, and by 1906 the Playground Association of America had been founded. Through the creation of such public recreation centers, reformers hoped to involve the entire family in wholesome leisure, rather than leaving kids unsupervised in dangerous streets. In the face of newly recognized child abuse, the New York Society for the Prevention of Cruelty to Children, founded in 1874 after the model of the New York Society for the Prevention of Cruelty to Animals, was followed by similar organizations elsewhere, and by 1908 there were fifty-five local societies for the prevention of cruelty to children. In short, Americans of that era did not simply bemoan "the way kids are today," or long nostalgically for the lost social control of the village. Rather, the Progressives devoted their intellectual, organizational, and financial energies to blazing constructive new paths for youth. In a stroke of marketing genius, the new organizations combined enduring social values—"A Scout is trustworthy, loyal, helpful, friendly, courteous . . ."—with the pure fun of camping, sports, and play.[67]

One of the most notable social inventions of the Progressive Era were settlement houses, an idea imported from mid-Victorian England. Settlement houses hosted idealistic young middle-class men and women who lived for several years in urban slums seeking to bring education and "moral uplift" to the immigrant poor. Hull House, founded by Jane Addams in Chicago in 1889, was quickly followed by a proliferation of similar experiments in other cities—six by 1891, seventy-four by 1897, and approximately four hundred by 1910. Initially the primary purpose of the settlers was to teach English and the civic knowledge necessary for citizenship, but their activities broadened rapidly, as historian Mark Wahlgren Summers describes:

Settlement house workers set up debate societies and lecture series, taught slum mothers the importance of bathing and sanitation, trained them in manual skills to compete in the job market, and ran kindergartens and daycare centers for the children of working parents. Soon an art gallery joined Hull House's main dormitory, then a coffeehouse, a gymnasium, and a nursery.[68]

Settlement houses made valuable contributions to the lives of the urban poor. Settlements like Pittsburgh's Kingsley House ran summer "fresh air" programs for thousands of children and their parents. A Hull House club gave Benny Goodman his first clarinet. Ironically, however, the most significant long-term effect of the settlement house movement was not on the recipients of service, but on the service givers. Jane Addams had hoped that firsthand contact with the harsher realities of life would give meaning to the lives of young college graduates. The range of leaders who came out of the experience of the settlement houses was extraordinary—not merely scores of social reformers like Florence Kelley and Eleanor Roosevelt, but also future public-spirited business magnates like Gerard Swope (president of General Electric, 1922–1944) and Walter Sherman Gifford (president of AT&T, 1925–1948). Historian Richard McCormick summarizes the settlements' longer-term impact:

> For men and women alike, the settlements served as training grounds. From them, residents moved into every conceivable Progressive social reform: the improvement of tenement houses, the public playground movement, the crusade to abolish child labor, the demand for better hours and wages for working women, and many more. . . . Often their values and activities must have seemed alien to the immigrant working people whom they sought to assist. But no other Americans in the early 1900s tried so hard or so successfully to devise solutions for urban, industrial problems as did the women and men of the settlement movement.[69]

As a social movement, Progressivism was broad and variegated. As political philosopher Peter Levine has observed, "Any movement that attracted Upton Sinclair and J. Edgar Hoover, W. E. B. Du Bois and Robert Taft, Herbert Hoover and the young Franklin D. Roosevelt can hardly be called a movement at all."[70] Any simple interpretation thus risks being misleading and incomplete. From our point of view, however, the Progressive Era represented a civic communitarian reaction to the ideological individualism of the Gilded Age. Although it culminated in a specifically political movement, it began with social goals that were both broader and more immediate. In the successful efforts to establish playgrounds, civic museums, kindergartens, public parks, and the like, an important part of the rationale was to strengthen habits of co-operation, while not stifling individualism. Frederick Law Olmsted, designer of New York's Central Park (opened in 1876) and first commissioner of Yosemite National Park (1890), crusaded for parks and recreation areas as a means to overcome isolation and suspicion. Similarly, one enthusiastic supporter of the playground movement exclaimed that playgrounds

> are actually coming in considerable numbers and in all parts of the country, and everywhere they produce the same social results. That is, they bring about fine community spirit, awaken civic consciousness and co-operation, and make for a whole-souled companionship instead of individualism and isolation. If we could see the playground idea prevail . . . the gain to the nation through the ever increasing number of cheerful, contented, industrious, patriotic citizens will be far greater than if mines of fabulous wealth were uncovered or all the commerce of the world were brought under our flag.[71]

In short, though they did not generally use this terminology, an important goal of Progressives was to strengthen social capital.[72] Recall that the term *social capital* was itself invented by a Progressive Era educator, L. J. Hanifan, expounding the value of community centers.

The impulse to educate and assimilate may have reached its greatest flowering in the kindergarten movement. Borrowed from an institution invented by German progressive educators, the first American kindergarten was launched by Elizabeth Palmer Peabody, a "lady bountiful" in Boston. By the late 1870s this kindergarten movement was spreading rapidly across the country, and by 1908 more than four hundred kindergartens were run by women's clubs, temperance groups, churches, and other organizations. In their early years kindergartens were inspired by an innovative educational philosophy that encouraged childhood creativity. Their volunteer organizers sought both to provide a wholesome educational environment for immigrant children and to influence the child-rearing techniques of their parents. Around the kindergartens grew up an array of new forms of adult connectedness—mothers' clubs, sewing clubs, and so on. Some of the most innovative features of the movement, including its legion of volunteers and its emphasis on childhood creativity, rather than just school readiness, fell away as kindergartens were increasingly incorporated into the public school system and kindergarten teachers strove for professional recognition; but an important residue remained. The National Congress of Mothers, formed in part from the kindergarten movement in 1897, went on to organize local school groups of parents and teachers. In 1924 the Congress of Mothers was formally renamed the National Congress of Parents and Teachers (later the PTA).[73]

As McCormick reveals, civic engagement was at the heart of the Progressives' approach:

> Progressivism owed much of its success to a distinctive method of reform, variations of which were adopted by the leaders of nearly every cause. They typically began by organizing a voluntary association, investigating a problem, gathering relevant facts, and analyzing them according to the precepts of one of the newer social sciences. From such an analysis a proposed solution would emerge, be popularized through campaigns of education and moral suasion, and—as often as not, if it seemed to work—be taken over by some level of government as a public function.[74]

Social entrepreneurs, both at the grass roots and nationally, built new organizations, often initially for nonpolitical purposes. An early example was the temperance movement, which aimed in part to create "a cohesive structure of reciprocal responsibility" in the face of industrialization and urbanization. Often too the new organizations were built on preexisting social networks, especially religious ones. In turn local and national reform movements were built on the foundations of the informal or nonpolitical groups.

A far from unique example: the transformation of women's reading groups into first a civic movement and then a political force. During the depression of the 1890s, women's reading groups expanded their agenda to include social service and advocacy. The General Federation of Women's Clubs (GFWC), founded in 1890, campaigned for government food inspection, stricter housing codes, safer drinking water, workplace protection for women, and services for the poor, sick, disabled, and children. The National Congress of Mothers, established to educate mothers about child rearing, then sought public support for infant health clinics, juvenile courts, probation homes for children awaiting trial, kindergartens, and playgrounds. Barred by segregation from joining the GFWC, African Americans formed the National Association of Colored Women's Clubs of America in 1896, campaigned against alcoholic consumption, and supported nurseries, kindergartens, and homes for unwed mothers. "Woman's place is in the Home," wrote suffragist Rheta Childe Dorr in 1910, "but Home is not contained within the four walls of an individual home. Home is the community."[75] The suffrage movement, reaching across class lines (though generally not race lines), was merely the most visible culmination of feminist organizing at the turn of the century.

The successive waves of labor mobilization provide another illustration of the interweaving of movements for social solidarity and movements for political reform. The efforts to organize labor in the closing decades of the nineteenth century were hardly tea parties, for this was the most vivid period of class conflict in American history. "The eighties dripped with blood," recalled Ida Tarbell in her memoirs. Despite recurrent efforts to broaden labor's agenda to encompass social reform and class struggle, the most durable nineteenth-century unions had aimed primarily at improved conditions of employment. The burst of unionization at the turn of the century, however, culminated in the election of fifteen unionists to Congress in 1910, and with the threat of "socialism" hanging in the air, the political establishment moved to encompass labor reform among their objectives. Here too alliances across class lines were important. The National Consumers League, founded in 1899 by Florence Kelley, a Hull House settler, aimed to enable middle-class women shoppers to boycott firms that failed to provide decent working conditions for women employees.[76]

As a social movement, Progressivism evades any simple classification as "top down" or "bottom up." Many of the new fraternal, civic, and reform organizations represented the recruiting efforts of national headquarters and national leaders, while others sprang up in response to local initiatives. Some, like the 4-H and the Grange, were actually the creation of the federal government. More important still was the lateral diffusion of initiatives from one community to another. As political scientist Theda Skocpol notes, "This method of organizational expansion was very reminiscent of the techniques used by Methodist and Baptist circuit-riding clergy to disseminate new congregations, like wildfire, across the pre–Civil War United States."[77]

Lateral learning was common in the diffusion of the Progressives' ideas for increasing civic engagement. Initiatives born in one part of the country were picked up and developed in other communities from whence they spread further. We can see this process in action by tracing the evolution of a single civic innovation. In the 1890s, modeled in part on the lectures of scholars like John Dewey at Hull House, the Universities of Wisconsin and Chicago developed university extension schools to deepen ties between the university and adult citizens. In the first decade of the new century Tom Johnson, the renowned Progressive mayor of Cleveland, conceived the idea of periodic tent meetings to draw citizens and political leaders into informal give-and-take on public issues. By 1907, building on these initiatives, civic organizations in Rochester, New York, had established "social centers" in the public schools for regular, publicly funded popular debate about local issues.

Within three years hundreds of such meetings were being held annually in Rochester, as recorded in the *Democrat and Chronicle* of March 20, 1910: "This week's programs in the social centers and civic clubs is a varied one, with evenings devoted to discussions of business conditions, health, art, social organization, high prices, the liquor question and neighborhood problems." Participation in these civic deliberations cut widely across class and educational lines: an observer in 1911 reported laconically "the topic being the commission form of government, a Polish washwoman and the president of the WCTU were opposed by a day cleaner and a college professor." By 1916 the "social center" (or "community center") movement had spread across the country, reaching West Virginia, where, as we have seen, it evoked from L. J. Hanifan the first recorded reference to "social capital."[78]

As this story illustrates, although the major metropolitan and intellectual centers of New York, Boston, and their ilk were part of the process of civic renovation, much of the creative action took place in communities all across the heartland, as local activists intent on rebuilding community ties in the new century learned from one another what worked. In fact, the wave of association building of the late nineteenth century actually had begun in the small towns of the heartland, not in the cosmopolitan metropolis. The high school movement spread most rapidly in small towns in the Midwest and West. Historians Arthur Link and Richard McCormick may exaggerate slightly, but they capture the distinctiveness of the movement when they conclude, "Progressivism was the only reform movement ever experienced by the whole American nation."[79]

As a political movement, the Progressives were responsible for the most thoroughgoing renovation of public policies and institutions in American history, rivaled only by the New Deal. The secret ballot (1888, Kentucky); popular initiative and referendum (1898, South Dakota); presidential primary elections (1900, Minnesota); the city manager system (1903, Galveston, Texas); the direct election of senators (1913); women's suffrage (1893, Colorado; 1920 in the U.S. Constitution)—in a few short decades all these fundamental features of our political process were introduced into state and local politics and then gradually diffused nationwide. Quite apart from these basic political reforms, this was also the most intense period of local administrative reform in our history.[80]

Nationally, the Progressives laid the institutional cornerstones for fiscal and monetary policy with the Federal Reserve (1913), the income tax (1913), and the Bureau of the Budget (1921). The first consumer protection legislation in American history (the Food and Drug Administration and federal meat inspection in 1906, the Federal Trade Commission in 1914); the first environmental legislation (the national forest system in 1905 and the national park system in 1913); the creation of the Departments of Commerce and Labor (1913) and the General Accounting Office (1921); strengthened antitrust regulations (1903); child labor laws (1916); the eight-hour day (beginning with the railways in 1916); workmen's compensation (1916); first federal regulation of the communications industry (1910); the U.S. Bureau of Investigation (1908; renamed the Federal Bureau of Investigation in 1935); federal campaign finance regulation (1907); the biggest trade liberalization in more than half a century (1913); the foundations for federal water policy in the western states (1902); and Mother's Day (1914)—hardly an area of public policy was left untouched by the Progressive avalanche of policy initiatives.[81] Typically, innovation began with experimental reforms in states and local communities, then gathered strength as it thundered toward Washington.

Not all these reforms proved as successful as their advocates had expected, and a few in retrospect look positively pernicious. Nevertheless, taken as a whole, this package of reforms constituted an impressive achievement within a constitutional system that is built to thwart radical change. This achievement rested on a broad-based, grassroots, nationwide political movement that swept through both major political parties in the first decade of the century. In turn, that political mobilization drew on the energies and organizations created during the social capital building of the previous several decades.

Generally speaking, the wave began in the last third of the nineteenth century with organizations (like fraternal and cultural groups) focused primarily on the private concerns of their members, including leisure and self-help. In the last decade of the nineteenth century and the first decade of the twentieth century these associations (and newer ones spawned in that period) gradually turned their attention to community issues and eventually to political reform. The earlier, inward-oriented phase of creating social networks paved the way for the later, outward-oriented phase of political action.[82] Like any stylized historical generalization, this interpretation could be exaggerated, since there were public facets of the Shriners and private facets of the League of Women Voters, but the central fact is that *investment in social capital was not an alternative to, but a prerequisite for, political mobilization and reform.* That too is a crucial lesson for our own times.

WE NEED NOT WHITEWASH the Progressive Era, for debates about the legacy of this movement have preoccupied historians for nearly a century now. Its critics, in the ascendancy among professional historians for much of the last half century, note the propensity of Progressives to favor a technocratic elitism. In proposing "professional," "expert" solutions to social problems, many Progressives adopted an antipolitical stance that had the effect, if not the intention, of demobilizing public participation. After 1896 electoral turnout began a descent from which it has yet to recover. Partisan politics, and especially the party machine, was the great enemy for Progressives, who generally preferred "boards" and "commissions" dominated de facto by middle-class professionals. Progressives were conscious of the corruption and dependency inherent in the machine, but they were blind to the role of the machine in allowing access to the public sphere for the otherwise powerless, especially the immigrant. Historian Philip Ethington has observed that "among the many ironies of the so-called Progressive Era (circa 1890s–1920s), the saddest perhaps is the deep and enduring damage done to democracy by her closest friends," for instead of the deliberative democracy advocated by some Progressives, we ended up instead with the direct, plebiscitary democracy pushed successfully by others.[83]

An even greater debate has raged among historians about whether the Progressive Era was about social reform or social control or social revolution.

Some scholars have argued that middle-class reformers organized voluntary associations to exert social control over rambunctious, uncouth working-class immigrants. Other researchers, while acknowledging that Progressive leadership came from the middle class, emphasize the benevolent aspect of the new institutions, aimed to strengthen immigrant and working-class communities and reduce social inequality. Still others have noted that middle-class reformers were often prodded to action by the demands of their working-class "clients," so that to reduce this dynamic to top-down social control is to ignore the intentions and agency of those whose lives were being changed. "Fear of working-class violence explains much of what has been called progressive reform," concludes historian Painter.[84]

Even those who celebrated the new associationism and its political consequences often recognized the potential for excessive social control and subordination of the individual.[85] The communitarian impulses of the Progressive Era could easily go much too far: during World War I, William Dudley Foulke, president of the National Municipal League, suggested that the draft should be used for public service purposes after the war:

> The public welfare may require of some that they shall marry and rear children for the sake of the community. They must be ready to do it whether they so desire or not. It may require of some, that they shall give up the use of intoxicating liquor or discontinue some other habit that involves extravagance or demoralization . . . whether there is a prohibitory law or not. It may require periods of training either for military service or in organizing the industries of state or city for purposes of defense or social betterment, and those on whom the call is made must be willing to sacrifice their private interests and respond to the appeal.[86]

This "big brother-ism," American style, illustrates the risk of an overdone communitarianism.

Even more troubling is the fact that racial segregation and social exclusion were, as we have seen, so central to the public agenda of the Progressive Era. Jim Crow was legalized in 1896, the NAACP was founded in 1909 to attack legal race discrimination, and in 1915 the second Ku Klux Klan was founded (in part) to enforce it, by illegal means if necessary.[87] Not all the "civic innovations" of the Progressive Era were beneficent and progressive. Those of us who seek inspiration for contemporary America in that earlier epoch of reform must attend to the risk that emphasizing community exacerbates division and exclusion. Since social capital is inevitably easier to foster within homogeneous communities, emphasis on its creation may inadvertently shift the balance in society away from bridging social capital and toward bonding social capital. That is one of the most instructive lessons from that earlier era.

But there are other, more positive lessons as well. The institutions of civil society formed between roughly 1880 and 1910 have lasted for nearly a century. In those few decades the voluntary structures of American society assumed modern form. Essentially, the trends toward civic disengagement reviewed in section II of this book register the decay of that very structure over the last third of the twentieth century. Still, in human affairs it is no small feat to create a set of institutions that can endure and serve society through a century of kaleidoscopic social and economic transformation.

For all the difficulties, errors, and misdeeds of the Progressive Era, its leaders and their immediate forebears in the late nineteenth century correctly diagnosed the problem of a social-capital or civic engagement deficit. It must have been tempting in 1890 to say, "Life was much nicer back in the village. Everybody back to the farm." They resisted that temptation to reverse the tide, choosing instead the harder but surer path of social innovation. Similarly, among those concerned about the social-capital deficit today, it would be tempting to say, "Life was much nicer back in the fifties. Would all women please report to the kitchen, and turn off the TV on the way?" Social dislocation can easily breed a reactionary form of nostalgia.

On the contrary, my message is that we desperately need an era of civic inventiveness to create a renewed set of institutions and channels for a reinvigorated civic life that will fit the way we have come to live. Our challenge now is to reinvent the twenty-first-century equivalent of the Boy Scouts or the settlement house or the playground or Hadassah or the United Mine Workers or the NAACP. What we create may well look nothing like the institutions Progressives invented a century ago, just as their inventions were not carbon copies of the earlier small-town folkways whose passing they mourned. We need to be as ready to experiment as the Progressives were. Willingness to err—and then correct our aim—is the price of success in social reform.

Looking back from the doorstep of the twenty-first century, it is hard to imagine a time without Boy Scouts, but a century ago it must have seemed fanciful that the twentieth-century equivalent of Tom Sawyer's antebellum gang on the Mississippi sandbar would involve beanies, merit badges, and the Scout's oath. Nevertheless, institutions like the Boy Scouts provided a new and successful forum for youthful community building. So too some solutions to today's civic deficit may seem initially preposterous, but we should be wary of straining our civic inventiveness through conventional filters. The specific reforms of the Progressive Era are no longer appropriate for our time, but the practical, enthusiastic idealism of that era—and its achievements—should inspire us.

CHAPTER 24

Toward an Agenda for Social Capitalists

"To EVERYTHING THERE IS A SEASON, and a time for every purpose under the heaven," sang the Hebrew poet in Ecclesiastes. When Pete Seeger put that ancient maxim to folk music in the 1960s, it was, perhaps, a season for Americans to unravel fetters of intrusive togetherness. As we enter a new century, however, it is now past time to begin to reweave the fabric of our communities.

At the outset of our inquiry I noted that most Americans today feel vaguely and uncomfortably disconnected. It seemed to many as the twentieth century closed, just as it did to the young Walter Lippmann at the century's opening, that "we have changed our environment more quickly than we know how to change ourselves." We tell pollsters that we wish we lived in a more civil, more trustworthy, more collectively caring community. The evidence from our inquiry shows that this longing is not simply nostalgia or "false consciousness." Americans are *right* that the bonds of our communities have withered, and we are *right* to fear that this transformation has very real costs. The challenge for us, however, as it was for our predecessors moving from the Gilded Age into the Progressive Era, is not to grieve over social change, but to guide it.

Creating (or re-creating) social capital is no simple task. It would be eased by a palpable national crisis, like war or depression or natural disaster, but for better *and* for worse, America at the dawn of the new century faces no such galvanizing crisis. The ebbing of community over the last several decades has

I want to thank Tom Sander for help in preparing this chapter.

been silent and deceptive. We notice its effects in the strained interstices of our private lives and in the degradation of our public life, but the most serious consequences are reminiscent of the old parlor puzzle: "What's missing from this picture?" Weakened social capital is manifest in the things that have vanished almost unnoticed—neighborhood parties and get-togethers with friends, the unreflective kindness of strangers, the shared pursuit of the public good rather than a solitary quest for private goods. Naming this problem is an essential first step toward confronting it, just as labeling "the environment" allowed Americans to hear the silent spring and naming what Betty Friedan called "the problem that has no name" enabled women to articulate what was wrong with their lives.

Naming our problem, however—and even gauging its dimensions, diagnosing its origins, and assessing its implications, as I have sought to do in this book—is but a preliminary to the tougher challenge. In a world irrevocably changed, a world in which most women are employed, markets global, individuals and firms mobile, entertainment electronic, technology accelerating, and major war (thankfully) absent, how can we nevertheless replenish our stocks of social capital? Like most social issues, this one has two faces—one institutional and one individual. To use the convenient market metaphor, we need to address both the *supply* of opportunities for civic engagement and the *demand* for those opportunities.

Just as did our predecessors in the Progressive Era, we need to create new structures and policies (public and private) to facilitate renewed civic engagement. As I shall explain in more detail in a moment, leaders and activists in every sphere of American life must seek innovative ways to respond to the eroding effectiveness of the civic institutions and practices that we inherited. At the same time we need to fortify our resolve as individuals to reconnect, for we must overcome a familiar paradox of collective action. Even if I privately would prefer a more vibrant community, I cannot accomplish that goal on my own—it's not a meeting, after all, if only I show up, and it's not a club if I'm the only member. It is tempting to retreat to private pleasures that I *can* achieve on my own. But in so doing, I make it even harder for you to solve your version of the same problem. Actions by individuals are not sufficient to restore community, but they *are* necessary.

So our challenge is to restore American community for the twenty-first century through both collective and individual initiative. I recognize the impossibility of proclaiming any panacea for our nation's problems of civic disengagement. On the other hand, because of my experience in spearheading in recent years a concerted nationwide conversation modeled on the intensive interchange among scholars and practitioners in the Progressive Era, I am optimistic that, working together, Americans today can once again be as civically creative as our Progressive forebears. These deliberations, the "Saguaro Seminar: Civic Engagement in America," brought together thinkers and doers from many diverse American communities to shape questions and seek answers.[1] The ensuing discussions have informed my suggestions in this chapter in many ways. The group's objectives have been, first, to make Americans more aware of the collective significance of the myriad minute decisions that we make daily to invest—or disinvest—in social capital and, second, to spark the civic imaginations of our fellow citizens to discover and invent new ways of connecting socially that fit our changed lives.

Figuring out how to renew our stock of social capital is a task for a nation and a decade, not a single scholar, or even a single group. Communitarian scholar-activists, such as Amitai Etzioni and William Galston, have long labored in this vineyard. My intention in this chapter is modest—to identify key facets of the challenge ahead, by sketching briefly six spheres that deserve special attention from aspiring social capitalists: youth and schools; the workplace; urban and metropolitan design; religion; arts and culture; and politics and government. For each, by offering some suggestions of my own, I seek to provoke the reader's own imagination in the hope that together we can produce something even more creative and powerful.

PHILOSOPHERS FROM ARISTOTLE and Rousseau to William James and John Dewey have begun discussions of civics with the education of youth. They have pondered the essential virtues and skills and knowledge and habits of democratic citizens and how to instill them. That starting point is especially appropriate for reformers today, for the single most important cause of our current plight is a pervasive and continuing generational decline in almost all forms of civic engagement. Today's youth did not initiate the erosion of Americans' social capital—their parents did—and it is the obligation of Americans of all ages to help rekindle civic engagement among the generation that will come of age in the early years of the twenty-first century.

So I set before America's parents, educators, and, above all, America's young adults the following challenge: *Let us find ways to ensure that by 2010 the level of civic engagement among Americans then coming of age in all parts of our society will match that of their grandparents when they were that same age, and that at the same time bridging social capital will be substantially greater than it was in their grandparents' era.* One specific test of our success will be whether we can restore electoral turnout to that of the 1960s, but our goal must be to increase participation and deliberation in other, more substantive and fine-grained ways, too—from team sports to choirs and from organized altruism to grassroots social movements.

The means to achieve these goals in the early twenty-first century, and the new forms of connectedness that will mark our success, will almost surely be different from those of the mid-twentieth century. For this reason, success will require the sensibility and skills of Gen X and their successors, even more than of baby boomers and their elders. Nevertheless, some "old-fashioned" ideas are relevant. Take civics education, for example. We know that knowledge about public affairs and practice in everyday civic skills are prerequisites for effective participation. We know, too, that the "civics report card" issued by the U.S. Department of Education for American elementary and high school students at the end of the twentieth century was disappointing.[2] So improved civics education in school should be part of our strategy—not just "how a bill becomes a law," but "How can I participate effectively in the public life of my community?" Imagine, for example, the civic lessons that could be imparted by a teacher in South Central Los Angeles, working with students to *effect* public change that her students think is important, like getting lights for a neighborhood basketball court.

We know other strategies that will work, too. A mounting body of evidence confirms that community service programs really do strengthen the civic muscles of participants, especially if the service is meaningful, regular, and woven into the fabric of the school curriculum. Episodic service has little effect, and it is hard to imagine that baby-sitting and janitorial work—the two most frequent types of "community service" nationwide, according to one 1997 study—have much favorable effect. On the other hand, well-designed service learning programs (the emerging evidence suggests) improve civic knowledge, enhance citizen efficacy, increase social responsibility and self-esteem, teach skills of cooperation and leadership, and may even (one study suggests) reduce racism.[3] Interestingly, voluntary programs seem to work as well as mandatory ones. Volunteering in one's youth is, as we noted in chapter 7, among the strongest predictors of adult volunteering. Intergenerational mentoring, too, can serve civic ends, as in Boston's Citizen Schools program, which enables adult volunteers to work with youth on tangible after-school projects, like storywriting or Web site building.

Participation in extracurricular activities (both school linked and independent) is another proven means to increase civic and social involvement in later life. In fact, participation in high school music groups, athletic teams, service clubs, and the like is among the strongest precursors of adult participation, even when we compare demographically matched groups.[4] From a civic point of view, extracurricular activities are anything but "frills," yet funding for them was decimated during the 1980s and 1990s. Reversing that perverse development would be a good start toward our goal of youthful reengagement by 2010. Finally, we know that smaller schools encourage more active involvement in extracurricular activity than big schools—more students in smaller schools have an opportunity to play trombone or left tackle or King Lear. Smaller schools, like smaller towns, generate higher expectations for mutual reciprocity and collective action. So deconcentrating megaschools or creating smaller "schools within schools" will almost surely produce civic dividends.

Our efforts to increase social participation among youth must not be limited to schooling. Though it is not yet easy to see what the Internet-age equivalent of 4-H or settlement houses might be, we ought to bestow an annual Jane Addams Award on the Gen X'er or Gen Y'er who comes up with the best idea. What we need is not civic broccoli—good for you but unappealing—but an updated version of Scouting's ingenious combination of values and fun. I challenge those who came of age in the civically dispiriting last decade of the twentieth century to invent powerful and enticing ways of increasing civic engagement among their younger brothers and sisters who will come of age in the first decade of the twenty-first century.

THE CHANGING CHARACTER of work and the closely related movement of women into the paid workforce were among the most far-reaching upheavals in American society during the twentieth century. This transformation of the workplace was comparable in magnitude to the metamorphosis of America a century earlier from a nation of farms to one of factories and offices. Yet as the twenty-first century opens, American institutions, both public and private, and norms and practices within the workplace have only begun to adapt to this change. As we saw in chapter 11, this workplace revolution is implicated in the nearly simultaneous decline of social connectedness and civic involvement. So I challenge America's employers, labor leaders, public officials, and employees themselves: *Let us find ways to ensure that by 2010 America's workplace will be substantially more family-friendly and community-congenial, so that American workers will be enabled to replenish our stocks of social capital both within and outside the workplace.*

Fortunately there is some evidence that community- and family-oriented workplace practices benefit the employer as well as the employee. At least in periods of full employment, moreover, such practices become a key ingredient in recruiting and retaining a high-quality, loyal workforce. Happily, the proportion of American workers who reported some flexibility in their work schedules increased from 16 percent in 1990 to 30 percent in 1997.[5] However, many of the benefits of employment practices that encourage social capital formation—stronger families, more effective schools, safer neighborhoods, more vibrant public life—"leak" outside the firm itself, whereas all the costs stay put. This fact gives firms an incentive to underinvest in civic engagement by their employees. Conversely, workplace practices that inhibit community involvement and family connectedness produce a classic case of what economists term "negative externalities," imposing an unrequited cost on society.

In the case of environmental pollution, it is now widely accepted that tax and other financial incentives are an appropriate public response to negative externalities, reinforcing moral suasion as a means of encouraging environmentally friendly behavior. Similarly, we need to rethink how to reward firms that act responsibly toward their employees' family and community commitments and how to encourage other employers to follow their example. Many firms offer released time to employees who volunteer for community service, a valuable practice that should be extended. But volunteering is only one form of civic engagement. Public policies like the Family and Medical Leave Act of 1993 and legal requirements that employers facilitate jury service illustrate that the public interest in civic and social connectedness can justify public regulation of employment contracts. However, caring for sick loved ones is not the only family responsibility, and jury service is not the citizen's only duty, and our labor law should recognize that.

Our findings in chapter 11 point unambiguously to the civic as well as the personal dividends associated with part-time employment. For many people, we discovered, part-time work is the best of both worlds—enhancing one's exposure to broader social networks while leaving enough time to pursue those opportunities outside the workplace. We found that part-time workers are typically more involved in community activities than *either* full-time employees *or* people who are not employed at all. Not everyone wants a part-time job, of course, but many do, and America's public, nonprofit, and private institutions have only begun to address the challenge of restructuring work to meet that demand. The new politics of time must be high on the public agenda in the new century.

Civic engagement and social connectedness can be found inside the workplace, not only outside it. Thus our workplace agenda should also include new means of social-capital formation on the job. This is especially true with regard to bridging social capital, since the increasing diversity in the workplace is a valuable and not yet fully exploited asset for social capitalists. As we saw in chapter 5, some encouraging initiatives along these lines—teamwork, architectural restructuring, and the like—are already under way. On the other hand, other changes that we discussed there—especially the proliferation of "contingent" work—heighten the challenge of creating work-based social capital. Employers, labor unions, labor relations experts, and employees themselves need to be more creative in meeting the social connectivity needs of temps, part-timers, and independent contractors.[6] Finally, we need to challenge the notion that civic life has no part in the workplace. Why not employer-provided space and time for civic discussion groups and service clubs? Why not better protection for privacy of employees' communications?

As THE TWENTIETH CENTURY ENDED, Americans gradually began to recognize that the sprawling pattern of metropolitan settlement that we had built for ourselves in the preceding five decades imposes heavy personal and economic costs—pollution, congestion, and lost time. In chapter 12 we discovered that metropolitan sprawl has also damaged the social fabric of our communities. So I challenge America's urban and regional planners, developers, community organizers, and home buyers: *Let us act to ensure that by 2010 Americans will*

*spend less time traveling and more time connecting with our neighbors than we
do today, that we will live in more integrated and pedestrian-friendly areas, and
that the design of our communities and the availability of public space will encourage more casual socializing with friends and neighbors.*[7] One deceptively
simple objective might be this: that more of us know more of our neighbors by
first name than we do today.

Urban designers, marching under the banner of "the new urbanism,"
have produced many creative suggestions along precisely these lines over the
past decade or two.[8] Admittedly, far more time and energy have been invested
so far in articulating and even implementing these ideas than in measuring
their impact on community involvement. It is surely plausible that design innovations like mixed-use zoning, pedestrian-friendly street grids, and more
space for public use should enhance social capital, though it is less obvious
that the cosmetic details of Victorian or colonial design and the echoes of
nineteenth-century public architecture typically found in new urbanist communities like Disney's Celebration, Florida, will necessarily have that effect.
(The brand-new town in Easton, Ohio, includes a town center built to resemble a converted train station, although there was never any train station there.)
In any event it is time to begin assessing rigorously the actual consequences of
these promising initiatives.[9]

The new urbanism is an ongoing experiment to see whether our thirst
for great community life outweighs our hunger for private backyards, discount
megamalls, and easy parking. In the end Americans will get largely the kind
of physical space we demand; if we don't really want more community, we
won't get it. On the other hand, in the past, segregated suburban sprawl was
also powerfully shaped (often unintentionally) by public policies like highway construction, mortgage interest deduction, redlining, and concentrated
public housing. As the costs of sprawl (economic and environmental as well
as social) become clearer, public policies to discourage it will become more
attractive, as they already have in places from Atlanta to Portland. Finally, innovative community thinkers and organizers like Harry Boyte, Ernesto Cortes,
and John McKnight have devoted much effort to finding and exploiting unexpected assets in disadvantaged communities. Community Development Corporations, created in the 1970s to foster physical reconstruction of blighted
neighborhoods, are now turning their attention to investing in social capital,
too, and groups like the Local Initiatives Support Corporation (LISC) have
had some success in that area.[10] I challenge all of us to add to that good work
the objective of creating networks that bridge the racial, social, and geographic
cleavages that fracture our metropolitan areas.

FAITH-BASED COMMUNITIES REMAIN such a crucial reservoir of social capital in
America that it is hard to see how we could redress the erosion of the last sev-

eral decades without a major religious contribution. Particularly in the public realm, Americans cherish the First Amendment strictures that have enabled us to combine unparalleled religiosity and denominational pluralism with a minimum of religious warfare. On the other hand, it is undeniable that religion has played a major role in every period of civic revival in American history. So I challenge America's clergy, lay leaders, theologians, and ordinary worshipers: *Let us spur a new, pluralistic, socially responsible "great awakening," so that by 2010 Americans will be more deeply engaged than we are today in one or another spiritual community of meaning, while at the same time becoming more tolerant of the faiths and practices of other Americans.*

In our national history, religion has contributed to social-capital creation, above all, in three dramatic and fervent "awakenings." During the Great Awakening from 1730 to 1760, revivals "explode[d] like a string of firecrackers" into "massive and continuous revival meetings . . . kept in motion by traveling preachers." The Second Great Awakening from 1800 to 1830 was an equally frothy period of engagement, in which "circuit riders" carried the new gospel from one churchless frontier settlement to another. Circuit riders formed groups of ten to twelve converts to reinforce each other's spiritual seeking until regular churches could be established. Historians debate the motivation and even the religiosity of these evangelists, but the movement inspired many to turn toward the poor, reject slavery, and found missionary and temperance societies. One notable invention was the Sunday school movement, integrating revivalism with a desire to teach literacy to those excluded from common schools, including women (black and white), factory children, and frontiersmen.[11]

In the previous chapter we observed a third major period of religious engagement with social issues at the end of the nineteenth century, embodied in activities like the Social Gospel movement and the Salvation Army—the so-called church of the poor that focused on the "submerged tenth" of American life, buffeted by the strains of urbanization and industrialization. The Salvation Army, "saving the world one soul at a time," was an interesting hybrid of doctrinal fundamentalism, liturgical heterodoxy (with marching bands and "hallelujah lassies"), and progressive beliefs about helping the poor, raising the religious status of women, and ministering to white and black alike.[12]

Are there the ingredients in America at the beginning of the twenty-first century for another Great Awakening? Megachurches, to take a single example, use contemporary marketing and entertainment techniques to craft an accessible religious experience for their typically suburban, middle-class market. (Though initially focused on the white population, megachurches are increasingly attracting people of color.) While their church services, by dint of size if nothing else, often seem impersonal and theologically bland, megachurch leaders are savvy social capitalists, organizing small group activities that build personal networks and mix religion and socializing (even bowling teams!).

Meanwhile, in a different portion of the religious spectrum, as we saw in chapters 4 and 9, evangelical and fundamentalist churches (along with their counterparts among Jews and other religious traditions) constitute one of the most notable exceptions to the general decline in social capital that I have traced in this book.

From a civic point of view, a new Great Awakening (if it happened) would not be an unmixed blessing. As we noted in chapters 4 and 22, proselytizing religions are better at creating bonding social capital than bridging social capital, and tolerance of unbelievers is not a virtue notably associated with fundamentalism. In our culture, if not our jurisprudence, a new Great Awakening would raise issues about the constitutional separation of church and state, as illustrated by the controversy surrounding the "charitable choice" provision of welfare reform that provides public funds for religiously linked social services. On the other hand, one can also detect signs of a broadly ecumenical and socially engaged religiosity in movements like the evangelical Call to Renewal. In addition, some of the innovations of the Gilded Age and Progressive Era, like the settlement house and the Chautauqua movement, though not narrowly religious, could inspire twenty-first-century equivalents.[13]

No sector of American society will have more influence on the future state of our social capital than the electronic mass media and especially the Internet. If we are to reverse the adverse trends of the last three decades in any fundamental way, the electronic entertainment and telecommunications industry must become a big part of the solution instead of a big part of the problem. So I challenge America's media moguls, journalists, and Internet gurus, along with viewers like you (and me): *Let us find ways to ensure that by 2010 Americans will spend less leisure time sitting passively alone in front of glowing screens and more time in active connection with our fellow citizens. Let us foster new forms of electronic entertainment and communication that reinforce community engagement rather than forestalling it.* The recent flurry of interest in "civic journalism" could be one strand to this strategy, if it is interpreted not as a substitute for genuine grassroots participation, but as a goad and soapbox for such participation.[14] I noted in chapter 13 that, as a technical matter, the extraordinary power of television can encourage as well as discourage civic involvement. Let us challenge those talented people who preside over America's entertainment industry to create new forms of entertainment that draw the viewer off the couch and into his community.

We saw in chapter 9 that the Internet can be used to reinforce real, face-to-face communities, not merely to displace them with a counterfeit "virtual community." Let us challenge software designers and communications technologists to heed the call of University of Michigan computer scientist Paul

Resnick to make the Internet social capital–friendly and to create a Community Information Corps to encourage youthful computer professionals to use their skills to help rebuild community in America.

In chapter 9 I discussed several important obstacles to the use of computer-mediated communication to build social capital. Some of those obstacles, like the digital divide, can (and must) be addressed by public policy. Others, like anonymity and single strandedness, might be amenable to technological "fixes." On the other hand, computer-mediated communication also opens opportunities for hitherto unthinkable forms of democratic deliberation and community building—like citywide citizen debates about local issues or joint explorations of local history or even announcements of a local ultimate Frisbee tournament. Several early studies of well-wired communities suggest—tentatively, but hopefully—that residents who have easy access to local computer-based communication use that new tool to strengthen, not supplant, face-to-face ties with their neighbors and that some of them become more actively involved in community life, precisely as we social capitalists would wish.[15] Electronic support groups for elderly shut-ins might be useful complements to (not substitutes for) regular personal visits. The key, in my view, is to find ways in which Internet technology can reinforce rather than supplant place-based, face-to-face, enduring social networks.

To BUILD BRIDGING SOCIAL CAPITAL requires that we transcend our social and political and professional identities to connect with people unlike ourselves. This is why team sports provide good venues for social-capital creation. Equally important and less exploited in this connection are the arts and cultural activities. Singing together (like bowling together) does not require shared ideology or shared social or ethnic provenance. For this reason, among others, I challenge America's artists, the leaders and funders of our cultural institutions, as well as ordinary Americans: *Let us find ways to ensure that by 2010 significantly more Americans will participate in (not merely consume or "appreciate") cultural activities from group dancing to songfests to community theater to rap festivals. Let us discover new ways to use the arts as a vehicle for convening diverse groups of fellow citizens.*

Art manifestly matters for its own sake, far beyond the favorable effect it can have on rebuilding American communities. Aesthetic objectives, not merely social ones, are obviously important. That said, art is especially useful in transcending conventional social barriers. Moreover, social capital is often a valuable by-product of cultural activities whose main purpose is purely artistic.

Liz Lerman's Dance Exchange has built unlikely community togetherness using community-based modern dance, bringing together, for example, unemployed shipyard workers and white-collar professionals when the closing of the Portsmouth (N.H.) shipyard strained local community bonds. The Roadside Theater Company has mustered diverse local folks in declining towns in Appalachia to celebrate their traditions and restore community confidence through dramatization of local stories and music. The Museum of the National Center for African American Artists in Boston has convened diverse groups of black Americans (Haitians, Jamaicans, Afro-Brazilians, and native African Americans) to build and then parade twenty-foot fish sculptures to the New England Aquarium. Toni Blackman's Freestyle Union in Washington, D.C., uses *ciphering*, a novel combination of hip-hop, rap poetry, and improvisational poetry slams, to attract people from all walks of life, from a Filipino break-dancer to a right-to-life Christian. The Baltimore Museum of Art urges local residents to exploit its public spaces on "Freestyle Thursdays" by inviting local choral groups and others to perform. Chicago's Gallery 37 provides apprenticeships for diverse young budding artists—rich and poor, suburban and inner city, black, white, Latino—to follow their own muses, building social connections among artist-mentors, artist-apprentices, and observers. In the Mattole Valley of northern California, David Simpson has used community theater to build bridges between loggers and environmentalists. Many of these activities produce great art, but all of them produce great bridging social capital—in some respects an even more impressive achievement.[16]

POLITICS AND GOVERNMENT is the domain where our voyage of inquiry about the state of social capital in America began, and it is where I conclude my challenges to readers who are as concerned as I am about restoring community bonds in America. Nowhere is the need to restore connectedness, trust, and civic engagement clearer than in the now often empty public forums of our democracy. So I challenge America's government officials, political consultants, politicians, and (above all) my fellow citizens: *Let us find ways to ensure that by 2010 many more Americans will participate in the public life of our communities—running for office, attending public meetings, serving on committees, campaigning in elections, and even voting.* It is perhaps foolhardy to hope that we could reverse the entire decline of the last three to four decades in ten years, but American democracy would surely feel the beneficent effects of even a partial reversal.

Campaign reform (above all, campaign finance reform) should be aimed at increasing the importance of social capital—and decreasing the importance of financial capital—in our elections, federal, state, and local. Since time is distributed more equally across the population than money, privileging time-based participation over check-based participation would begin to reverse the growing inequality in American politics. Government authority should be decentralized as far as possible to bring decisions to smaller, local jurisdictions, while recognizing and offsetting the potential negative effect of that decentralization on equality and redistribution. Indeed, liberals alert to the benefits of social capital should be readier to transfer governmental authority downward in exactly the same measure that compassionate conservatives should be readier to transfer resources from have to have-not communities. Decentralization of government resources and authority to neighborhood councils has worked in cities like Minneapolis, Portland, and Seattle, creating new social capital in the form of potluck dinners, community gardens, and flea markets, though deft design is needed to be sure that the balance between bridging and bonding does not tip too far toward urban fragmentation.

Policy designers of whatever partisan persuasion should become more social capital–savvy, seeking to do minimum damage to existing stocks of social capital even as they look for opportunities to add new stocks. How about a "social-capital impact statement" for new programs, less bureaucratic and legalistic than environmental impact statements have become, but equally effective at calling attention to unanticipated consequences? For example, the greatest damage to social capital in the inner city of Indianapolis, Indiana, in the last half century was the unintended disruption of neighborhood networks when those neighborhoods were pierced by Interstate 65 in the early 1960s. The Front-Porch Alliance created by former mayor Stephen Goldsmith more than a quarter century later was a worthy effort to help restore some Indianapolis neighborhood institutions, but Goldsmith himself would be the first to say that it would have been better to avoid the damage in the first place.[17]

In all the domains of social-capital creation that I have discussed here all too briefly, social capitalists need to avoid false debates. One such debate is "top-down versus bottom-up." The roles of national and local institutions in restoring American community need to be complementary; neither alone can solve the problem. Another false debate is whether government is the problem or the solution. The accurate answer, judging from the historical record (as I argued in chapter 15), is that it can be both. Many of the most creative investments in social capital in American history—from county agents and the 4-H to community colleges and the March of Dimes—were the direct result of government policy. Government may be responsible for some small portion of the declines in social capital I have traced in this volume, and it cannot be the sole solution, but it is hard to imagine that we can meet the challenges I have set for America in 2010 without using government.

The final false debate to be avoided is whether what is needed to restore trust and community bonds in America is individual change or institutional change. Again, the honest answer is "Both." America's major civic institutions, both public and private, are somewhat antiquated a century after most of them were created, and they need to be reformed in ways that invite more active participation. Whether the specific suggestions I have made for institutional reform are persuasive or not is less important than the possibility that we may have a national debate about how to make our institutions more social capital–friendly. In the end, however, institutional reform will not work—indeed, it will not happen—unless you and I, along with our fellow citizens, resolve to become reconnected with our friends and neighbors. Henry Ward Beecher's advice a century ago to "multiply picnics" is not entirely ridiculous today. We should do this, ironically, not because it will be good for America—though it will be—but because it will be good for us.

Afterword

Has the Internet Reversed the Decline of Social Capital?

Robert D. Putnam and Jonah C. Hahn

Just as we began writing this afterword in February 2020, the coronavirus epidemic and the ensuing months of quarantine unexpectedly threw our draft into disarray. Our principal question was whether virtual ties can replace face-to-face ties—and suddenly the world was in the midst of a massive experiment on precisely that question. Ninety percent and more of Americans reported that, at least initially, they practiced social distancing, stayed home as much as possible, stopped going to bars and restaurants, and so on.[1] As a result—and almost overnight—virtual ties and online connections became a lifeline for millions of isolated Americans. That experience may well cause a long-lasting change in the relationship between virtual and face-to-face ties, but at this writing (July 2020) it is far too soon to know for sure. Marked changes in social capital in the immediate aftermath of 9/11 had vanished within six months.

Nevertheless, we can already glimpse ways in which what we are now reporting might be altered by the epidemic, so we shall conclude with some speculations about possible long-term effects of the nationwide quarantine on virtual and in-person social capital in America. Can technology really create community, or does it create only an unsatisfying illusion of closeness? Are there ways of integrating online and offline connections that might give us the best of both worlds? The experience of the epidemic itself will help us reframe these questions. But let us first consider the pre-epidemic lessons of the two decades between 2000 and 2020.

Has Facebook Replaced Bowling Leagues?

How would the conclusions of *Bowling Alone* be changed if we were to take into account the ensuing two decades of the Internet's growth and development? We begin with a quick summary of what the first edition of *Bowling Alone* said about the Internet. That is followed by an overview of the myriad ways in which the Internet—and especially social media—have exploded over the last twenty years, creating new forms of social engagement that may (or may not) have replaced the missing in-person networks that *Bowling Alone* had emphasized. We introduce the concept of *alloy* to refer to the crucial fact that most actual networks are neither purely virtual nor purely in-person, but combine both types of networks into novel mixtures with unexpected properties. The concept of alloy plays an important role throughout this afterword.

Against this backdrop, we look at the best available evidence about the effects of social media on civic engagement, democracy, and personal and social well-being. Next, we zoom out briefly to understand the broader impact of the Internet on social institutions, especially the structure of commerce and the structure of the workplace. Lastly, we close with a few notes on the role of the Internet during the COVID-19 pandemic so far, and what we imagine the possibilities are going forward. A central theme throughout is *agency*: that the evolution of the Internet and its role in society is fundamentally driven not by impersonal technology but by choices that both users and Internet entrepreneurs make.

The core idea of *Bowling Alone* is social capital; the core component of social capital, as we use the term, is social networks; and the core insight of social capital theory is that social networks have value, both for people in the networks and for bystanders (in the form of what economists call "externalities").[2] The Internet is certainly a network, so it is entirely natural to ask whether it could facilitate social capital.

The basic argument of *Bowling Alone* in 2000 was that American social capital had been in comprehensive and steady decline for roughly three decades. In one chapter devoted to possible exceptions to that argument, twelve pages (169–180 above) were dedicated to the rise of the Internet, then in its infancy. The invention of Facebook and other social media platforms still lay six years in the future, but *Bowling Alone* observed that Internet usage was rapidly rising. We noted that both cyberoptimists and cyberpessimists were common, and we summarized their arguments.

The Internet, we said, had great future potential for flattening hierarchy, encouraging grassroots organizing, and fostering equality, liberty, and democracy. On the other hand, the incipient digital divide might reinforce existing social, educational, and cultural inequalities. What we labeled "cyberbalkanization" (borrowing the term from Marshall van Alstyne and Erik Brynjolfsson)[3] might encourage social fragmentation, favoring bonding social capital at the expense of bridging social capital.[4]

We recognized that the Internet was a powerful tool for the transmission of information, but we asked whether this tool would become what we called a "niftier television" or a "niftier telephone." That is, in the long run would the Internet serve mainly as a tool for passive entertainment, or mainly as a tool for social communication? That question remains open and important today.

We closed our 2000 futurology with two warnings that are even more relevant today than they were two decades ago. First, we objected to framing the issue in dichotomous terms: virtual networks versus "real" networks. On the contrary, we suggested, Internet-based communication worked best when overlaid on in-person connections. In later years we began to use the term *alloys* to describe social networks that integrate face-to-face and virtual connections. This alloy framing will play an even more central role in what follows here.

Second, we rejected technological determinism. "The most important question," we argued, "is not what the Internet will do to us, but what we will do with it."[5] Those words foreshadow our conclusion here—the consequences of the Internet will be determined by the ways in which we use it.

Bowling Alone came out in a climate of extreme cyberoptimism—the Internet would bring global togetherness, peace, and democracy.[6] In the words of noted Internet pioneer John Perry Barlow, "We are creating a world that all may enter without privilege or prejudice accorded by race, economic power, military force, or station of birth."[7] (More circumspect than that, *Bowling Alone* was at the time often read as more skeptical of the Internet than our actual words warranted.) Over the ensuing twenty years, however, the balance of informed opinion shifted sharply toward pessimism. "We were promised community, civics, and convenience," wrote Joseph Bernstein in 2019. "Instead we found ourselves dislocated, distrustful, and disengaged."[8] Here we shall explore, among other things, evidence for and against Bernstein's pessimistic conclusion.

At the publication of the first edition of *Bowling Alone* nearly half (47 percent) of all American adults had *never* used the Internet, and even seven years after publication, a mere 5 percent used anything one could recognize as social media. By 2018, we were in an entirely new online world, as nearly 90 percent of all adults used the Internet and nearly 70 percent used social media.[9] The expansion affected all generations, of course, but was much faster among the youngest cohorts. As of 2018, among teenagers aged thirteen to seventeen, 45 percent used the Internet "almost constantly," 44 percent "several times a day," and only 11 percent once a day or less. "Almost constant" use had doubled in the span of only four years.[10]

Qualitatively, the two biggest changes in this period occurred around 2006, with the near-simultaneous introduction of social media, sometimes labeled as the transition from Web 1.0 to Web 2.0, and the smartphone, enabling the mobile Internet. This transition brought even greater generational differences. By 2019 the fraction of all U.S. adults who used social media ranged from 40 percent among those over sixty-five to 90 percent among those aged eighteen to twenty-nine. By contrast, differences in use of social media by race, gender, education, and income (sometimes referred to as digital divides) were more modest.[11] Surprisingly, teens — by far the heaviest users of social media — were ambivalent about the impact of social media on their lives, with 31 percent saying it was mostly positive, but 24 percent saying mostly negative, and nearly half (45 percent) saying mixed or neither.[12]

Over this period the number of social media platforms exploded, and turnover among the most popular sites has been very high, especially among the youngest generation.[13] Many sites that at one time were enormously popular, such as Myspace or Vine, now either no longer exist or retain only a small, loyal userbase. By 2018–2019, the most-used sites across all generations were YouTube and Facebook, while Snapchat, Instagram, and TikTok were used much more by teenagers, mostly for sharing photos and videos of friends and celebrities.[14] (See figure B.) These latter platforms are generally used for checking in with friends, but, unlike forums and blogging sites such as Reddit or Tumblr, they are not (with the partial exception of Instagram) frequently spaces for extended discussion of issues, either personal or public, with a group of friends or acquaintances. YouTube is mostly an entertainment medium whose algorithms draw casual viewers ever deeper into "rabbit holes,"[15] though it also has an important role in education and self-help. In the aggregate, people worldwide are said to watch more than a billion hours of YouTube videos daily.[16] Facebook, the granddaddy of all social media sites, remains very popular among adults, though its usage has begun to decline among younger Americans.

The fact that Internet usage skyrocketed does not in itself prove, however, that electronic ties effectively replaced the face-to-face social capital that continues to decline.[17] In previous centuries, use of both the telephone and television had skyrocketed, but they did not necessarily supplant earlier forms of social capital. Claude Fischer, reflecting on the history of the telephone at the very start of the Internet revolution, argued that the effects of technological innovation on social relations are generally modest and can even be contradictory. The telephone, for example, seems to have had the effect of reinforcing, not transforming or replacing, existing personal networks.[18]

So for our purposes the key question about the development of the Internet in the last twenty years is not whether usage has grown but whether that growth, both quantitatively and qualitatively, has offset the decline in face-to-face social capital recorded in *Bowling Alone*. Has social media become the friendship-in-a-box or the PTA-in-a-box or the democracy-in-a-box that early Internet enthusiasts expected? Has Facebook simply replaced bowling leagues?

The Internet today is used in ways that could not have been foreseen twenty years ago, enabling types of social connections that could not have existed at the time of the first edition of *Bowling Alone*. The myriad uses of various online platforms are illustrated in the many social connections that

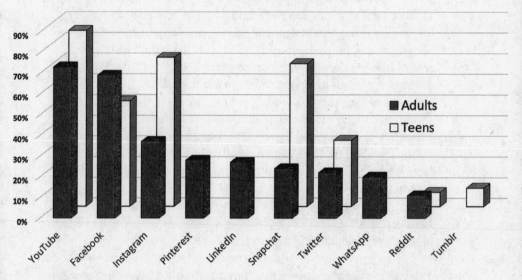

Internet Platform Usage, 2018–2019
Adults and Teens

Figure B: Social Media Platform Usage, 2018–2019: Adults and Teens
Source: See endnote 14.

members of the three-generation Putnam family have today that could not have been made without the endless succession of new apps and online technologies: email (which, strictly speaking, came into widespread use a decade or so earlier), Facebook, Twitter, Instagram (and its offspring finstas), World of Warcraft (and other multiplayer online games), blogs, Snapchat, WhatsApp, Skype, Zoom, podcasts, and so on.

- In 2003, Bob's wife, Rosemary, created a temporary email listserv for a book group composed of spouses of visiting faculty in Cambridge, England. Nearly two decades later, more than a dozen of those "Cambridge ladies," now scattered around the globe, communicate daily with one another on that same listserv. Every day Rosemary also plays Words with Friends with a dozen friends all over America and checks in with many other friends via Facebook.
- Bob's son, Jonathan, now a historical novelist, uses Facebook and Instagram (and more recently Zoom and Twitter) to connect with old college friends and with readers of his books, and to hold meetings with his writing group. Bob's grandson Alonso uses WhatsApp to keep in touch with friends he made while studying in Argentina, India, and Cuba.

- Bob's grandson Noah actively blogs about the Internet, with many subscribers recruited via Twitter, some of whom he's met in person. He also uses iMessage and Snapchat to interact with close friends. Another grandson used a group messaging app (GroupMe) to organize meetings with friends in college, and when he moved to a new city, the same app led him to a pickup soccer game among total strangers.
- Two other grandsons, Gray and Gideon, keep in touch with faraway school friends via competitive video games, using the simultaneous chat feature for off-topic personal conversation. While in college, Bob's granddaughter Miriam began to gather such strong and widespread social support on platforms like Facebook, Twitter, Snapchat, and Instagram that she has become an online professional political organizer. The Putnam grandchildren also listen to podcasts, taking part in the associated communities of fellow listeners, and several have used dating sites.
- Finally, during the 2020 pandemic, the far-flung Putnams celebrated Passover "together" on Zoom, holding a Seder for twenty-five members of the extended family living in ten cities on three continents.

We cite these examples not because the Putnam family is atypical but precisely because it is (for the most part) typical. Several things are worth noting:

- In each case, Internet platforms have been used to create novel connections that could not have existed in a pre-Internet world. They represent real and important additions to social capital that enhance the lives of the Putnam family members.
- Few of the connections are exclusively virtual. Whether the connections began online or offline, almost all involve electronic networks that are used by people to stay in touch with others whom they also have met (or plan to meet) in real life. In other words, virtually all these networks are, in practice, what we earlier termed alloys, composed simultaneously of online and offline connections.
- Most (but not all) are "microcommunities" whose purpose is to connect people with similar interests. They are not used for cruising the world to find new acquaintances or to engage in civic life. Rather, they are what digital strategist Sara Wilson calls "digital campfires."[19]

In short, while they definitely enhance in-person social networks, they are in most cases symbiotic with real-world networks. Most of these virtual communities are not intended to—and really couldn't—*replace* face-to-face networks.

Online platforms have massively proliferated over the last two decades. They are consequential in many aspects of our lives. But much of the Internet is simply not designed to foster social connections. As such, we give very little discussion time to those forms here.

- Information. Platforms that focus primarily on transmitting information include Google, Wikipedia, the New York Times, the Drudge Report, and HOLLIS (the Harvard On-Line Library Information System). Such sites are very important, not least in allowing us to write this chapter while staying informed about the rest of the world in the middle of a pandemic; but, however important, information platforms are not the subject of this afterword.
- Entertainment. Platforms that focus on providing entertainment probably account for a substantial share of Internet traffic. They include streaming services (Netflix, Hulu, Prime Video, and Spotify, for example) and, of course, pornography, which is sometimes said to account for perhaps a quarter of all Internet traffic.[20] The merger of various forms of electronic entertainment is probably the most dramatic Internet-related change in the last twenty years. Roughly speaking, in terms of the allocation of hours in our day, the Internet has essentially replaced simple television over these two decades. However, entertainment platforms are also not the subject of the afterword.
- Business. The massive impact of the Internet on business and commerce is also primarily outside the scope of our discussion. So we are not writing about Amazon or Uber or eBay or Slack, though we will explore briefly some important *indirect* effects of such sites on in-person social capital.

While the platforms just discussed can have an indirect impact on social capital formation, here we focus primarily on social interaction: the platforms and apps termed "social media." These include social networking sites (SNS) such as Facebook, Reddit, Twitter, LinkedIn, and Nextdoor. And they include sites that are primarily about media-sharing (YouTube, Instagram, and TikTok), communication (email, WhatsApp, Snapchat, and Zoom), games and gaming (Xbox Live, Second Life, and Words with Friends), dating (Tinder), and blogs (Tumblr). We focus on social media, since those platforms are the most likely to be able to replace or enhance face-to-face social capital.[21] Looking at social media is the best bet for assessing the plausibility, dynamics, and impact of social-capital formation online.

Partly because they have multiple uses, different sites foster different types of social capital. As technology columnist Kevin Roose has aptly observed, "Not all platforms are created equal. With so much alarming information flying around, private group messages and videoconferences are likely to produce calmer, more nourishing interactions than public platforms like Twitter and

Facebook, both of which are designed to amplify content that is outrageous, divisive or otherwise highly engaging."[22] We aim here to offer a broad synthetic overview of social media, so inevitably some of the subtler differences between platforms will be blurred.

Moving Beyond the "Real" vs. "Virtual" Dichotomy: Alloys

Perhaps the most important confusion about the Internet and social capital is the oft-assumed but false dichotomy between "real" (or offline) social networks and virtual social networks. Studies confirm that people tend to interact with the same individuals both offline and online.[23] Few Americans have an offline life and an entirely separate online life, and indeed, when there is a sharp divide, it's usually a sign of a major problem.[24] Our interactions with friends, family members, colleagues, and even strangers almost always combine electronic networks and face-to-face networks in digital alloys.

In metallurgy, an alloy combines two or more metallic elements in an entirely new metal. Prior to smelting, metalworkers cannot predict the exact characteristics of the alloy, because an alloy possesses properties that are quite different from those of its foundational metals. Even the same two elemental metals can be mixed in different ways to produce different alloys, each with unexpected strengths and weaknesses. Zinc and copper can be mixed to produce different forms of brass, each with unique properties, none of which is identical to either zinc or copper. Similarly, an alloyed social network has effects different from either a purely virtual network or a purely face-to-face network, and not all social alloys are identical.

Take Facebook-based networks, for example. Facebook was originally campus-based, and your Friends on Facebook were almost certainly also your friends in real life. But several years later Facebook went global, and the previous linkage between Friends and friends was broken.[25] Facebook had become a quite different alloy, more heavily based on electronic ties and less based on in-person ties, and Mark Zuckerberg bragged about building a global community.

Nevertheless, unpublished research from Facebook itself found that in 2018 slightly more than half of all Facebook links were between people who lived within fifty miles of each other. Since these networks are geographically bounded, it is very likely that they are an alloy that blends "real" and virtual networks. Indeed, researcher Charles Croom and his colleagues found that Facebook users actually have in-person ties to fully two-thirds of their Friends on the platform.[26] Some research suggests that online social relations are broader but shallower, while offline relations are fewer but more intimate.[27]

In 2017 Mark Zuckerberg acknowledged that social media had not replaced Rotary clubs and churches and PTAs and bowling leagues, alluding (without irony) to evidence from *Bowling Alone*: "Membership in all kinds of groups has declined as much as one-quarter," he said. "That's a lot of people who now need to find a sense of purpose and support somewhere else."[28] He thus set out to create a new type of more genuine "community" based on Facebook Groups that would focus on social connections in in-person communities.[29] The jury is still out on whether that initiative will succeed, but if it did, it would amount to yet another new and different alloy combining real and virtual ties, or indeed perhaps an entire family of new alloys.[30]

Other social media platforms represent other sorts of alloys. For example, Meetup was explicitly designed to create alloys—starting from the Internet and drawing strangers into face-to-face groups which meet regularly about shared interests: chihuahuas, moviegoing, socialism, astrology, and so on. CommonPlace and its later lookalike Nextdoor aimed to create locally-based alloys, but unlike Meetup, these sites began with a real-world neighborhood and added a virtual dimension to it—Marquette CommonPlace (Michigan) or Nextdoor Fairway Oaks–Abilene (Texas).[31] And some social media like Twitter and Instagram are basically not alloys at all: although users sometimes do constitute "communities," most of those communities rarely meet in person. The bottom line: as we compare virtual and real-life social connections, we must keep in mind that rarely are these two distinct categories.

The Effects of Social Media on Social Capital: The Evidence So Far

What does empirical evidence say about how interpersonal relations, civic engagement, social network dynamics, and (more distantly) democracy and inequality have been affected by social media?[32] Does the Internet increase or decrease social capital? We begin our answer to this question with a few words of caution.

First, the vast majority of studies look at the correlation between virtual and in-person connections, but correlation does not prove causation. For example, if intense Facebook users are exceptional real-world civic activists, which is causing which? Do civic activists join Facebook as one aspect of their activism, or did Facebook itself cause them to be activists? If political use of the Internet is correlated with offline political interest, is that correlation causal or spurious? If Internet connections *cause* new face-to-face connections, then the rise of the Internet might indeed offset the decline in in-person ties described in *Bowling Alone*. On the other hand, if the correlation is *not* causal, then it merely means that people who are sociable offline are now also sociable online, but they are not making up for the people who are no longer attending real meetings. Surprisingly few studies have been able to address that conundrum. Many studies simply assume that increasing online connections can replace declining offline connections—Facebook replacing bowling leagues—but few studies have tested the causality, and fewer still have confirmed that causation runs from the virtual world to the real world.

Social media obviously can have important social-capital benefits, as is clear from the Putnam family experiences described above. Even behavioral economist Hunt Allcott and his colleagues, who have done the most rigorous research skeptically examining claims about the effects of social media, emphasize that "Facebook produces large benefits for its users. . . . Any discussion of social media downsides should not obscure the fact that it fulfills deep and widespread needs."[33]

Many studies have found a positive correlation between online and offline socializing.[34] For example, the 2009 Pew Internet Personal Networks and Community survey, led by Keith Hampton, found that "ownership of a mobile phone and participation in a variety of Internet activities were associated with larger and more diverse core discussion networks" and other forms of offline civic engagement. It also found that heavy Internet users have a more extended social network than light users. This study concluded that "people's social worlds are enhanced by new communication technologies." However, that implicit causal claim was imprudent. Because the evidence was based on a single survey at a single point in time, it could not prove any causal link. On the contrary, it seems more likely that online and offline ties were correlated simply because both were more common among more sociable people—the social-capital equivalent of the rich getting richer.[35]

More recent studies that focus most clearly on causation generally find mixed, modest, and even negative effects. A 2015 review of thirty-six separate studies found that among panel studies that offer some leverage in detecting causality, the effect of social networking sites on civic and political participation is minimal.[36] In fact, in an unusually rigorous before-and-after comparison, Andrea Geraci and her colleagues found that increases in Internet access strongly predicted subsequent *declines* in civic engagement, such as associational involvement, which implies in turn that the Internet might even accelerate the civic losses that *Bowling Alone* had described. [37]

Other evidence also suggests that the use of social media tends to displace alternative forms of socializing. Studying long-term trends in the use of time, Scott Wallsten found that time spent in online socializing tended to crowd out offline socializing; "a cost of online activity is less time spent with other people."[38] Conversely, when Hunt Allcott and his colleagues deactivated Facebook accounts for a randomized set of people, they discovered that it opened up an average of sixty minutes per day, which led them to spend more time engaging in face-to-face activities.[39]

Moreover, being in the physical presence of other people no longer guarantees social interaction. Sociologist Sherry Turkle has noted anecdotally how people are often physically together in a collective space—at the breakfast table, in a business meeting, even sitting at a bar—engaged not with others who are present but with a cell phone, surfing the Web. They are alone together. We seem to be communicating more but listening less. Our devices allow the illusion of connection without the demands of friendship and conversation.[40]

Romance provides one of the clearest cases of the Internet supplanting traditional social rituals, especially among younger cohorts. The Pew Research Center found in 2019 that 30 percent of U.S. adults had used a dating app or website, a usage rate that ranged from 9 percent among those over the age of sixty-five to 48 percent among those aged eighteen to twenty-nine.[41] A Stanford study found that by 2017, more couples were meeting online than through family or friends or any other intermediary. The fraction who first met online doubled between 2000 and 2017, while the fraction who first met through family, friends, and co-workers fell by roughly 40 percent, a dramatic indication of how rapidly online connections have displaced offline connections in this domain.[42]

Use is not the same as satisfied use, however. In 2012 Eli Finkel and his colleagues summarized the benefits of online dating compared to conventional offline dating (a larger pool of potential partners and the ability to assess compatibility before meeting face-to-face) and the drawbacks (the availability of a large pool "may lead online daters to objectify potential partners and might even undermine their willingness to commit to one of them").[43] Online dating, in other words, may make romance seem more like a comparative shopping expedition.[44] While a majority of online daters find the experience positive and appreciate certain advantages that come with searching for love online, in the end most people (54 percent) say that online dating is neither better nor worse than offline dating, but only a few (5 percent) say online is better, while a substantial minority (38 percent) say online is worse.[45]

The empirical findings so far on the effects of social media on social capital are not yet conclusive. Nevertheless, the current balance of empirical evidence tends to undercut the argument that socializing of the sort exemplified by league bowling has simply been replaced by online *schmoozing*.

What about the role of social media in political and civic engagement? From the presidential campaigns of Howard Dean in 2004 and Barack Obama in 2008 to the Arab Spring revolutions of 2010 to the massive protests against racism in 2020, social media has played an undisputed central role in civic and political engagement. Most users of social networking sites engage in some form of political expression: by "liking" political material, amplifying get-out-the-vote efforts, posting thoughts about political or social issues, urging friends to get involved in political or social issues, posting content/links related to political news, and so forth. In many ways social media is synonymous with modern political and civic expression. Pew found in 2018 that more than half of U.S. adults (53 percent) engaged in political or civic activities online, with this behavior twice as common among people under fifty as among those over fifty. Thus it is beyond doubt that social media has become part of America's stock of civic and political engagement.[46]

Two important caveats. The first is a slightly different version of the familiar issue of correlation versus causation. Social media did not directly "cause" the protests in Tahrir Square, or the later Black Lives Matter (BLM) protests of 2020, but it certainly facilitated and enabled those protests: the protesters used social media as a highly efficient organizing tool. Studies typically find that offline civic engagement and political activity correlate with online activity and engagement. And yet huge protests were obviously organized in pre-Internet times—think of the 1963 March on Washington or the subsequent Vietnam War protests. Causation may run from the real world to the virtual world. Offline social networks present avenues to engage with politics online—for example, signing an online petition at the behest of an offline friend, another example of an alloy.[47] Careful studies usually find that the causal effect of social media on civic and political participation is quite moderate.[48]

Second, in building durable social movements, it is not clear that virtual ties can reproduce the power of face-to-face ties. Studies of pre-Internet social revolutions, from the 1964 Freedom Summer project during the civil rights movement to the 1989 East German revolution against Communist rule, typically find that the strongest predictor of who sticks with a movement through thick and thin is not ideological commitment but personal ties with other activists.[49] Digital tools, as political scientist David Karpf said of their use in the United States, "can certainly help you mobilize a crowd, but (at least so far) it is less useful for organizing that crowd into a movement or converting that movement energy into long-term victories."[50] The fate of the massive 2020 Black Lives Matter protest marches may provide another test of this hypothesis. Virtual networks, we conclude for now, can help build powerful and enduring social movements, *but only if* they are interlaced with face-to-face networks in potent new alloys.[51]

In 2000 *Bowling Alone* distinguished between two types of civic engagement: expression (for example, writing letters to the editor or signing a petition) versus cooperation and exchange (for instance, working on a committee or attending a civic meeting). Expressive activities, which involve one-way communication, had slipped by 10 to 20 percent over the preceding decades, but cooperative exchange activities, which typically involve listening as well as talking, had plunged 35 to 40 percent.[52]

It is expressive activities that have burgeoned on the Internet, and it turns out that cybertalk can be cheap. One study found that of the 1.2 million members of the Save Darfur "Cause" on Facebook around 2010, "the vast majority . . . recruited no one else into the Cause and contributed no money to it—suggesting that in the case of the Save Darfur campaign, Facebook conjured an illusion of activism rather than facilitating the real thing."[53] Passive online observation became so common that it gave rise to the term "lurking," and online-only, low-effort, low-stakes political involvement became so common that it also got its own name, "slacktivism." Political fundraising in the United States has massively moved online, but much of that fundraising is grounded in real-world networks of friends and acquaintances. We are still early in the era of online fundraising, so we don't yet know in a rigorous way whether those networks are independent of offline networks or are instead a particularly interesting example of an alloy.

In short, there is little evidence that solely online activities have yet replaced the in-person civic life that *Bowling Alone* showed was disappearing. The Internet has vastly increased the ease with which political organizers can get millions of individuals to say "stop," but that is not the same thing as mobilizing those individuals for sustained collective action. As we have repeatedly emphasized, online and offline networks are often alloyed to create powerful new forms of social capital, and as we discuss below, such alloyed civic networks might be one of the most important innovations of the last twenty years. If virtual networks can be combined with in-person networks in what we have been calling alloys, collective action can be sustained to undergird genuine democratic change. As digital organizer Ben McGuire has observed, "Hypothetically, digital organizing creates an attractive scenario for political campaigns: converting a huge and diffuse base of social media followers into volunteers."[54] This is yet another way in which thinking in terms of alloys instead of online and offline networks could have major practical implications.

The Effects of Social Media on Democracy

So far, we've considered the effects of the Internet on civic engagement and political participation. From the point of view of democracy, one equally important consideration is whether the Internet equalizes levels of participation across different social groups or instead reinforces existing racial and class differences. The empirical evidence shows the latter: online political participation—from contacting a government official to engaging in political discussions to blogging—is at least as biased by race and social class as offline participation.[55] The Internet has not created a more equal democracy, and the Twittersphere is far from a representative sample of Americans.

In the early years of the Internet, simple Internet access was unequally distributed, as less educated, rural, and lower-income Americans, especially communities of color, were slower to gain access to the Web.[56] More recently, digital access divides have narrowed, but they have not yet disappeared, and the urban-rural divide is in some respects still widening.[57] However, even equal access to the Internet does not mean that everyone gains equal benefit from that access. Sociologist Eszter Hargittai and her collaborators, experts on how the Internet is actually used, point out that "growth in basic user statistics does not necessarily mean that everybody is taking advantage of the medium in similar ways." Affluent Americans use the Internet in ways that enhance their ability to influence public affairs, whereas poorer, less educated Americans typically use it in ways (especially for entertainment) that do not.[58]

After talking with scores of teenagers nationwide about how they use the Internet, the ethnographer danah boyd concluded that offline inequalities carry over online. "In a world where information is easily available," she writes, "strong personal networks and access to helpful people often matter more than access to the information itself. . . . Those whose networks are vetting information and providing context are more privileged in this information landscape than those whose friends and family have little experience doing such information work. . . . Just because teens can get access to a technology that can connect them to anyone anywhere does not mean that they have equal access to knowledge and opportunity."[59] At least at this point in its evolution, the Internet seems more likely to widen the opportunity gap than close it.

Yet another fundamental question about the effects of the Internet on American democracy takes us to the issues of cyberbalkanization and polarization. The Founders believed that democracy required civil disagreement, not a Hobbesian war of all against all, and civil disagreement in turn required at least some shared values and experiences. But as legal philosopher Cass Sunstein has pointed out, self-selection in Facebook algorithms and Twitter feeds leads to what the technology specialist Nicholas Negroponte has called the "Daily Me," that is, a communication universe that reflects only one's own interests and concerns. The Daily Me phenomenon in turn fosters polarization, because in the virtual world there may be even less exposure to opponents than in the real world. Discussion within homogeneous groups leads the participants to become more extreme; if a liberal group discusses affirmative action, they become even more favorable to it, whereas if a conservative group discusses the same issue, they become even more opposed.[60]

Quite apart from the Internet, perhaps one of the most momentous issues facing American democracy in the opening decades of the twenty-first century is political and social polarization.[61] Over the past half century, Americans have increasingly sorted themselves into two opposing party blocs, while social identities have increasingly overlapped with political loyalties. Rising residential segregation translates into homogeneous enclaves where neighbors often vote for the same candidates, earn similar incomes, and share ethnic backgrounds.[62] Political polarization is more extreme than at any point since the Civil War. Parents worry more about the political affiliation of their child's potential partner than about the partner's race or religion.[63] All that has raised interpersonal partisan hostility.[64]

However, polarization was rising for a quarter century *before* social media was invented, so the Internet certainly did not *cause* polarization. The question here is whether online contacts simply reflect our polarized life in the real world, or whether social media fosters further polarization among users,[65] or, as Yphtach Lelkes and colleagues put it, "the new media environment exacerbates already rising tensions."[66] Disentangling offline polarization from similar online trends is tricky, and there are probably feedback loops and mutual reinforcement.

Let's begin with the fraught topic of "cyberbalkanization," as we labeled it in *Bowling Alone* in 2000. "Homophily" is a bit of social science jargon that simply means "birds of a feather flock together," a very common pattern in social relations.[67] White suburbanites are mostly friends with other white suburbanites; rich folks mostly hang out with one another; Red Sox fans bond with other Red Sox fans (and certainly not with fans of the damned Yankees). Hanging out with people like you tends to reinforce your own sense of who you are—that is, your cultural or social or political identity.

Social and political homophily and ideological segregation are at least as extreme online as offline. One of the early illustrations of homophily was the contrast between Facebook and its rival Myspace; upper-class white teens migrated to Facebook, while lower-class teens of color stuck to Myspace.[68] "Cultural prejudice permeates social media. . . . Many of the social divisions that exist in the offline world have been replicated, and in some cases amplified, online."[69] Barely one-fifth of all Facebook "friendships" cross ideological or political lines, and Facebook users are considerably more likely than nonusers to read and share news articles that are aligned with their ideological positions.[70] The heaviest social media users, who tend to be the most rabid partisans, possess the most polarized social networks.[71] In effect, social media create ideologically and politically segregated echo chambers in which people feel comfortable and thus foster a more constrained sense of "we."[72]

Social psychologist Jonathan Haidt says, "The Internet and especially Twitter are the worst places for this, because you don't have relationships and people are trying to show how smart they are. They're trying to show how devoted they are to their team. So the kind of political engagement, the kind of public square that we get from social media, is generally terrible."[73] In short, social media seem to foster political disagreement, amplify polarizing content, and suppress constructive discourse.[74] Hunt Allcott and his colleagues found that enticing users to leave Facebook for an experimental period modestly reduced their exposure to polarized news content and their polarization on policy views.[75] Even more striking is evidence we shall shortly see that Facebook algorithms actually *cause* further ideological polarization.[76]

Users befriend like-minded individuals at increasingly higher rates, while "unfriending" those who espouse dissenting opinions.[77] Misinformation campaigns like those used during the 2016 election campaign can trigger these unfriending practices. Indeed, Gregory Asmolov concluded that "the purpose of these campaigns is not to shape people's perceptions about reality, but rather to dissolve horizontal ties among people by increasing the impact of conflict-related social categorization."[78] Exploring the ways in which bad actors have exploited the weaknesses of social media—encouraging nativism and undermining democracy—would take much more space than we have here. So, too, would examining the related but distinct topics of privacy, surveillance, and the big Internet conglomerates. But these are obviously major issues for the future of American democracy.

Critics often identify a common perpetrator responsible for this social fracturing: prioritizing algorithms. Such algorithms are silent nudgers. They pull the strings in the selection and curation of content, and thus they are not neutral tools. Since algorithms prioritize high engagement and enticing content, they filter out moderate voices and reaffirm beliefs or values already loved (or hated) by the group, which effectively reinforces users' preferences.[79] They potentially transform popularity into legitimacy, as the sheer number of "likes," upvotes, retweets, and shares signals greater credibility.[80] Social media platforms fed by algorithms amplify human biases about everything from race to politics and "bolster assessments of the political in-group at the expense of denigration of the out-group."[81]

Algorithms appear to boost the reach of misinformation and disinformation among our self-segregated, politically polarized online communities.[82] Moreover, certain features of these algorithms accelerate ideological and social clustering, especially evident in how misinformation spreads, like-minded enclaves form, and polarization widens. Indeed, an internal Facebook research project that showed the polarizing effect of algorithms was so explosive that it was shut down. "Our algorithms exploit the human brain's attraction to divisiveness," reported the team of researchers who were involved with the project. "If left unchecked," Facebook would feed users "more and more divisive content in an effort to gain user attention and increase time on the platform."[83] We will come back to algorithms later when we examine the economic incentives that affect how they are written.

Thus ever more like-minded social networks emerge as a consequence of these algorithm-bred personalized feeds. Networks high in bonding social capital but weak in bridging social capital become susceptible to conspiracy theories and antidemocratic behavior. Ultimately, such content filtering reshapes our sense of civic duty by deemphasizing things we share in common and defining freedom as the satisfaction of private preferences.[84]

The Effects of Social Media on Social Support, Happiness, and Trust

In the preceding section we explored the effects of social media on our social and political behavior. Equally important is the effect of social media on our personal well-being, including our social support, happiness, and trust.

Bowling Alone showed that friendship and other forms of social connectedness increase one's mental and even physical well-being, and more recent research has thoroughly confirmed that fact.[85] But do online connections have the same positive effects? SNS usage is generally positively correlated with offline social connectedness, but, as we have said, that is not surprising, since sociable people are likely to be sociable both online and offline. The more difficult question is whether the well-established benefits of face-to-face connections are mirrored online.

Economists John Helliwell and Haifang Huang directly compared the effects, on happiness, of offline friends and online Friends. They concluded:

> The number of real-life friends is positively correlated with subjective well-being (SWB) even after controlling for income, demographic variables and personality differences. Doubling the number of friends in real life has an equivalent effect on well-being as a 50 percent increase in income. [By contrast,] the size of online networks is largely uncorrelated with subjective well-being.[86]

In short, offline friends matter a lot for our happiness, while online Friends appear to have no such effect. Recent studies that use more sophisticated methods to disentangle correlation from causation find that SNS usage may even lead to *poorer* psychological well-being, not improved well-being.[87] For example, Holly B. Shakya and Nicholas A. Christakis found that measures of physical and mental health and life satisfaction were positively predicted by in-person friendship but negatively predicted by Facebook usage.[88]

In another study that was able to tease apart causality, economists Fabio Sabatini and Francesco Sarracino found that online social networking plays a positive role in subjective well-being *if* the networking is used to facilitate physical interactions (thus creating alloys). At the same time, they found that networking activities that do not facilitate face-to-face interactions tend to erode trust, and that this erosion can then negatively affect subjective well-being (independent of the online social interaction itself). They conclude that "the overall effect of networking on individual welfare is significantly negative."[89] Their findings remind us of the importance of alloys: while purely virtual connections may be injurious, when virtual and real networks are intertwined, good things can happen.

The question about the impact of social media on psychological well-being is fraught, especially with respect to younger generations. Among both children and adults, more screen time is correlated with less happiness and more depression, whereas more in-person social interaction is associated with more happiness.[90] As we noted earlier, growth in social media usage has been much faster among teens than among older adults. Starting around 2011–2012, rapid growth in teen use of smartphones and social media coincided with what some observers describe as a significant decline in in-person social interaction, such as getting together with friends or attending religious services or taking part in sports. Simultaneously, regular surveys of high schoolers found self-described loneliness, unhappiness, and objective symptoms of depression all rising. There is considerable scientific dispute, however, about the "effect size" of Internet usage on psychological well-being among youth.[91]

Causation in this case remains uncertain, but longitudinal studies have found that more digital usage today is associated with lower well-being later, and a number of experimental studies have found that limiting social media use improves psychological well-being.[92] Other studies find more nuanced patterns. For example, Moira Burke and Robert Kraut found that tailored Facebook messages from people you care about improve your psychological well-being. This is not surprising: after all, getting a handwritten note or a call from a friend is a pick-me-up. But, Burke and Kraut say, more impersonal interactions with online friends, such as reading their status updates or receiving a "like," have less effect.[93]

A so-called loneliness epidemic has been widely discussed in recent years. The jury is still out on the hypothesis that loneliness is becoming more common in America, but there is evidence that social isolation linked to Internet usage causes serious problems.[94] Causation may also work in reverse, yielding a vicious circle as social media use leads to loneliness and depression, which leads to more use of social media. Rebecca Nowland and her colleagues argue that while the Internet can displace in-person connections, the effect of social media depends in part on how we use it.

> Lonely people express a preference for using the Internet for social interaction and are more likely to use the Internet in a way that displaces time spent in offline social activities. . . . When the Internet is used as a way station on the route to enhancing existing relationships and forging new social connections, it is a useful tool for reducing loneliness. But when social technologies are used to escape the social world and withdraw from the "social pain" of interaction, feelings of loneliness are increased.[95]

To be sure, in some instances the Internet can reduce isolation, as in the case of a queer teen in a conservative rural community. It is, in the end, perhaps not surprising that social media don't generally deepen human connections — that's not what they were designed to do. As Nicole Carty observed, "Facebook,

Twitter, Instagram and others aren't built to foster deep human connections; they're built to maximize our time on their platforms."[96]

An essential element in connection is trust, especially interpersonal or social trust. Unlike trust in government or institutions, social trust refers to an individual's belief in the trustworthiness, fairness, or honesty of the people in society. Social trust is integral to social capital, enabling the norms of reciprocity essential for democracy. High levels of trust correlate with low levels of corruption and income inequality as well as more robust democracy and political engagement.[97]

But for decades U.S. social trust has declined. In the two decades since 2000, data from the General Social Survey, American National Election Studies, and Monitoring the Future indicate that two conclusions drawn in *Bowling Alone* still hold: social trust continues to wane among adults and teenagers, and generational replacement is a likely explanation for such declines.[98]

How social media affects social trust should not be conflated with the public's trust *in* social media. While the latter is important, here we consider only the first issue. Some studies find that activity on SNS is positively correlated with social trust, but again, few of those studies distinguish between correlation and causation. This is important because it is quite plausible that high-trust people are more likely to be drawn to social networking sites. Studies that test specifically for causation suggest that SNS usage does not increase social trust and may actually decrease it.[99]

Part of the debate about the wider effects of the Internet rests on the role of anonymity. Anonymity is often, though not always, characteristic of social networking sites. As the saying goes, "On the Internet, nobody knows you're a dog." Some social networking sites require users to provide real names in order to register an account. Yet overall trust is eroded, or at least questioned, when users cannot verify for themselves other users' identities. Even in settings like Facebook, which are not necessarily anonymous, people misrepresent themselves online—more benignly as the "curated self," and most insidiously as a form of predation.

Generally speaking, anonymity undermines trust and trustworthiness by eliminating or at least muting the role of reputation. The ability to hide one's true identity invites uninhibited behaviors, since users see themselves as being immune from the consequences of their comments.[100] Anonymity facilitates spamming, impersonation, hate speech, deception, and flaming.[101] In other words, anonymity severs the link between online and offline lives. This is the very opposite of an alloy; in that sense, alloys may be seen as a way of reducing or eliminating the problems associated with anonymity.

Parallel to (but independent of) anonymity and its effects is the ease with which people can leave virtual networks. Easy come, easy go is one of the attractions of the Internet, but it also means that accountability—and thus honesty—is undermined. Dense, bounded networks produce more social control (and hence are better for collective action), while sparse, unbounded networks focus more on private gain (which could be good or bad).

Differences in anonymity across SNSs underlie differences in users' social capital. The lack of connection to in-person networks corresponds to less social capital.[102] Without an offline verification to testify to a user's identity, individuals are more likely to present themselves in misleading ways—for example, to fake an online dating profile.[103] Conversely, impolite comments are left less often on SNSs whose users are more easily identifiable, and aggressive behavior is also less common on such sites.[104]

Andrew Chadwick, a political scientist who has studied the adverse effects of deception on the Internet, warns that "racism, sexism, and all manner of other prejudices flourish online" since "individuals can hide behind the cloak of anonymity or pseudoanonymity."[105] Daegon Cho and K. Hazel Kwon add that "the ease with which Internet anonymity may induce flaming and trolling has become a non-negligible issue especially along with growing concerns about a civility crisis in contemporary politics."[106] Incivility in turn seems to increase polarization.[107]

Users of online discussion boards and chat rooms often attack others with aggressive or insulting comments.[108] A comprehensive analysis of Reddit found a marked increase in incivility there since 2016.[109] Further out at the ideological extremes, Internet-based communication has increasingly led to trolling, slander, abuse, violence, cyberbullying, and cyberstalking, especially by shadowy white supremacist and "incel" groups.[110] Such evidence reinforces the notion that, under anonymous conditions, group identity becomes more significant and users' attitudes become more polarized.[111]

To be sure, anonymity has its advantages. For example, as we have said, it may allow for more social support for minorities who are otherwise socially isolated or afraid to "come out," such as nonbinary persons, and it may provide needed protection for whistleblowers. But more generally, the anonymity associated with purely Internet-based networks tends to undermine trust and increase polarization.

The Effect of the Internet on Social Institutions Such as Commerce and Work

Thus far we have considered how the Internet shapes us by altering our individual social networks. In this section we expand our attention beyond social media to consider the impact of the Internet on a broader set of institutions, especially commerce and work, that shape our social interactions. Instead of considering how the Internet (especially social media) might displace the time we would otherwise spend having neighbors over for dinner, we can also think about how these technologies reshape where and how we meet, work, and shop. Aggregate effects are more speculative, and have not been as carefully studied as the direct effects of social media, but this "Amazon effect" (eliminating offline places, like small stores, that once served as sites for creating social capital) might be more important as a whole than the "Facebook effect."

Even before the coronavirus epidemic, e-commerce, including Amazon and Uber Eats, had been weakening "third places" beyond home and work— bookstores, restaurants, and so forth: that is, places where people traditionally encountered friends and acquaintances and thus created and maintained face-to-face social capital.[112] For example, a traditional shopping mall is comprised of 50 percent apparel, 29 percent accessories, 5 percent restaurants, 2 percent home furnishings, and 1 percent health and personal care. This mix left malls vulnerable to e-commerce, given that online sales for apparel and accessories vastly outperform store sales.[113] By 2019, mall vacancies were at an eight-year high.[114] The Census Bureau found that time spent shopping for consumer goods declined from twelve hours a month in 2003 to ten hours in 2018, an effect even larger among younger Americans aged fifteen to thirty-four.[115] The 2020 quarantine-induced economic crisis accelerated this trend by driving some mall anchors, like JCPenney, into bankruptcy. So the Internet has powerfully affected social capital by eliminating places where we used to meet face-to-face, often incidentally.

On the other hand, the revival of independent bookstores illustrates people's willingness to lean against the "technological" effect of the Internet to meet their own self-defined needs—in this case for community. While Amazon effectively shuttered Borders and drastically weakened Barnes & Noble, small, independent bookstores parried the corporate blow, and their numbers rose rapidly after 2009. Ryan Raffaelli discovered three core features underlying independent bookselling's success: community, curation, and convening. Bookstore owners sold "community" to their customers, emphasizing a collective identity and an ability to sustain local economies. Instead of merely selling nationally best-selling works, indie bookstores refined their selection to reflect the tastes of their clients while also organizing author talks, reading groups, events for families, and children's story times.[116] These spaces have become "anchors of authenticity" because they weave together community threads as arts and culture hubs in addition to selling books.[117] By forgoing the lower prices available online, customers at local bookstores are choosing to pay more for books in return for maintaining social ties. Whether this example will be emulated in other sectors affected by e-commerce remains to be seen, but it's another illustration of our basic point that the effects of the Internet depend upon the choices we make.

Like third places, the workplace has long been another important institutional site of social connections, both formal (unions) and informal (friends at work). This became even more true as the fraction of women working outside the home rose in the last half century.[118] One of the earliest critical responses to *Bowling Alone* was the question "Can the workplace replace bowling?" Another critic responded affirmatively in a book entitled *Working Together*.[119]

The uneven movement of Americans' lives into the workplace, and of work into their lives, continued during the two decades after *Bowling Alone* was first published, at least for younger, better-educated Americans. The fraction of workers telecommuting rose only from 1 percent in the mid-1990s to 7 percent in 2019, but the workplace had gradually become an important channel through which the Internet permeated Americans' lives.[120]

It does *not* follow, however, that proliferating virtual ties in and around the workplace have made up for the disappearance of bowling leagues, any more than Amazon has replaced the lost community of the local bookstore. As in the case of the Amazon effect, surprisingly little systematic research has been done on the effect of the Internet on workplace-based social capital—on whether Slack is as good as the water cooler as a place to build community. A Pew study in 2016 found that only 17 percent of workers ever used social media to "build or strengthen personal relationships with coworkers," 24 percent to "make or support professional connections," and 27 percent to "connect with friends and family at work," whereas 37 percent use social media to "take a mental break from work," probably a euphemism for solitary recreational surfing.[121]

Those data seem to suggest that the workplace has not replaced the bowling alley as a space for finding and sustaining social capital. Coincidentally, the coronavirus shutdown, during which one-third to one-half of workers were telecommuting, provided an unparalleled opportunity to study this issue. Below we will address directly the lessons of the epidemic.

Stepping Back: The Role of Agency and Internet Entrepreneurs

As we implied in the first edition of *Bowling Alone*, the effects of the Internet are determined by how we choose to use it, not wholly by the technology itself. The same is true of social media. As Claude Fischer said at the dawn of the Internet age, "We ought to think more about these technologies as tools people use to pursue their social ends than as forces that control people's actions."[122] Indeed, our choices (as well as the choices of Internet entrepreneurs) are probably the main determinant of what we often term the "effects" of the Internet.

Recall the argument of Rebecca Nowland and her colleagues that while online activities may displace offline connections and thus increase loneliness, online connections can also be used intentionally to nurture social connections that can then reduce loneliness. Moreover, as we have seen, some of the most interesting issues involve not pure virtual connections but alloys, and even less is known about the effects of different alloys. One corollary is that the more we explore different alloys, the greater will be our ability to find and foster alloys that produce social capital. Users' choices affect the broader impact of social media.

Conversely, the impersonal march of technology alone does not determine what apps and platforms exist and what they allow us to do. Internet entrepreneurs are not passively following technological dictates but rather are making design choices based on what they think will sell. They are not necessarily malevolent, but Internet entrepreneurs want us as customers, and their interests are not identical to ours. Kevin Roose has observed that "for many of us, the world has been reduced to what we experience on screens. And the things on those screens are not neutral or inert. They've been put there on purpose and arranged . . . to accomplish some goal. Maybe that goal is to make us click, buy or share. Maybe it's to persuade us, or harden some part of our identity. Most of the time, what these machines want from us appears harmless. Once in a while, it actually is." [123]

Reflecting on the limitations of an approach that emphasizes technological imperatives raises additional questions about the future of the Internet and social capital. It may well be that many of the pernicious effects of social media on social capital or democracy or individual well-being derive from the dominant Internet business model, *not the technology*.[124] Financial incentives drive social media away from social capital and toward consumerism.

This business model, nearly ubiquitous across social media platforms, offers a "free" service to users in that it requires no financial cost to create a profile. But of course the user's account is not free at all. Users avoid a subscription plan or registration fee at the cost of their privacy and data. Social media sites have a high rate of turnover, and few have a sustainable business model if they shun "data grabs." Remember the adage "If you're not paying for the product, you are the product."

Social media companies desire user engagement in large part because they want to acquire more user data to improve advertising metrics to fuel profit. The entire social media model depends upon offering a "free" service funded by selling to vendors the personal information generated by each click, post, tweet, message, and search. So these platforms are designed to promote usage and clicks, even to the point of addiction. Ads require eyeballs, and emotion aroused by pernicious content drives clicks and views. Erika Hall argues that the business model is "ad networks [are] parasitic on human connection." [125]

Laurie McNeill, who researches how people self-represent on blogs and SNSs, writes, "SNSs are set up for ease of (corporate) data mining. . . . As corporate-designed software, Facebook's algorithms reflect the interests and needs of the company." [126] Siva Vaidhyanthan, cultural historian and media scholar, labels this model "surveillance capitalism," wherein companies mine user engagement to craft detailed profiles that are monetized via precisely targeted advertising.[127] A business model based upon data harvesting deemphasizes user privacy. This is not the place for a thorough discussion of the rapidly growing debates about privacy and surveillance, but it is worth noting that these issues arise as much from the business model as from the technology of the Internet. And they most certainly play a critical role in how online engagement affects well-being, trust, and the vitality of social connections and communities. It is another important example of our central theme that how we use the Internet powerfully affects its social role.

Postscript: What Did We Learn about Virtual and Real Ties from the Epidemic?

After twenty years of research that suggested alloys of online and offline networks deeply matter, the coronavirus epidemic forced society into an unexpected experiment that has tested that hypothesis. As we write, we cannot know when America will emerge from the epidemic, much less what the quarantine experience will teach us about the power of alloys. We cannot, at this writing, say whether the epidemic will reveal the strengths of virtual ties or their weaknesses, nor answer the question most central to what we have explored here: Can virtual ties replace the in-person ties emphasized in *Bowling Alone*?

To arrive at any conclusions at this point about consequences—or still worse, to predict the future—would be foolhardy. Rather, we seek to extract lessons from the first six months of the epidemic about how online and offline social connections are related, with particular attention to implications for alloys.

The epidemic confounded two factors that are in principle distinct—a massive national crisis and a massive shift from face-to-face networks to virtual networks. Local and national crises often trigger an uptick in social capital, but that uptick is usually brief—six days after a blizzard, six weeks after a hurricane, six months after 9/11, and so on. But the shift from offline to online social networks could in principle have more long-lasting effects.

The epidemic underlined the need for social solidarity, because for the most part masking and social distancing served primarily to protect other people, not oneself. Wearing a cloth mask had only a minor effect on one's own safety, but a major effect on the safety of others. Thus the main reason for wearing a mask was altruism—stopping the spread of contagion. Mask-wearing was, according to early research, more common in communities that had had high levels of social capital prior to the epidemic.[128] Where people trusted that others would help them out in need, their optimism proved justified, and everyone benefited. When people expected the worst from one another, that too is what they got, and everyone was worse off for it. The epidemic provided powerful evidence of the power of social capital.

Social solidarity showed a significant uptick in the opening weeks of the epidemic. Initially, voluntary compliance with social distancing was remarkably high, with roughly half of Americans saying that they had not met up with anyone outside their household in the previous twenty-four hours.[129] But did that burst of national solidarity show that virtual ties are perhaps even better than face-to-face ties in sustaining social capital, or did it merely show that in the short run a massive crisis brings out the best in Americans? By the sixth month of the epidemic, as voluntary compliance waned, the second explanation began to seem more plausible.

The epidemic spurred vigorous use of the Internet. At one point, roughly half of all adults said that it was "essential" to them, and roughly one-third of all adults participated in a virtual gathering with friends or family. But the epidemic also revealed great digital divides as well: by age and education and factors correlated with education, such as race and class, as we noted earlier. Of adults under thirty, 48 percent took part in a virtual gathering, compared to about 21 percent of those over fifty; and 48 percent of college-educated Americans did so, compared to 19 percent of Americans who had not gone beyond high school.

Initially, at least, "online" began to feel more like a real place where you naturally connect with family and old friends. More people were forced to use the Internet to contact friends, which seemed to "normalize" its use, especially for the older generation. And this effect was multiplicative: as more people became familiar with the Internet, it became more useful to *other* people—the same "network effect" that a century ago had made phones increasingly useful to *everyone* the more people who had a phone.

Working at home got a boost for certain types of work that were already computer-intensive. Employees saved commuting time and could spend more time with family, pollution levels declined, and over the long run employers could save office space. Early estimates suggested that more than a third of all jobs in the economy could be done at home.[130] People learned to work in virtual teams.[131] But those advantages of the Internet were not shared with most Americans, who needed to show up at work in person, thus exacerbating socioeconomic and racial inequality. Of the bottom three income quintiles, just 35 percent to 42 percent worked from home, compared to 54 percent of the upper middle class and 71 percent of the top 20 percent of the income distribution.[132] As one group of researchers concluded, "the digital divide—or the fact that income and home Internet access are correlated—appears to explain much inequality we observe in people's ability to self-isolate."[133] Redress of America's deep inequalities will not come from the Internet—that lesson from the last twenty years was reconfirmed by the last six months.

Moreover, the lessons of the quarantine were more negative in other ways, reminding both employees and employers why they had resisted relying exclusively on telecommuting over the previous twenty years. Employers found that "there are serendipitous benefits to in-person collaboration that no number of Zoom meetings or Slack channels can replicate . . . [and] employees who telecommuted were more stressed out than those who left their work at the office."[134] Virtual meetings might be more *task*-efficient in a narrow sense, the shutdown suggested, but they were less socially (or even economically) efficient.

In the aftermath of the epidemic, the shift to working from home and the virtual meetings seem likely to persist, at least in certain occupations (telemedicine) and firms (Twitter). But for most employees, work in a purely virtual environment seems, at this writing, unlikely to persist. In short, the workplace is likely to continue to be dominated by various alloys of online and offline connections.

Mutual aid groups were initially reported to proliferate as the virus swept across the United States, strengthening neighborhood ties.[135] Americans used Nextdoor and other neighborhood apps to connect and coordinate, to organize neighborhood singalongs not unlike those in Italy, to help needy neighbors, and in general to relieve loneliness.[136] In principle, this phenomenon might foreshadow a strengthening of yet another alloy, as we noted when discussing Nextdoor earlier, but it is far too early to know if that will happen. CommonPlace[137] had been invented ten years earlier but did not catch on at that time, which suggests that this development was demand-driven, not technology-driven, reflecting a central theme of ours: that what the Internet becomes will depend more on our wants and needs than on any technological imperative.

The epidemic also highlighted the contrast between online and offline interaction in education. It forced parents and educators to replace face-to-face ties at school with virtual ones. Techno-optimistic education reformers like Sierra Filucci initially argued that "almost anything kids used to do offline before COVID-19 can now be done online with a few clicks or taps and a little creativity."[138] But COVID-19 quickly revealed the shortcomings of learning entirely online. Even parents in "good" school districts with high-quality facilities became unhappy with online classes, and homeschooling was much harder for poorer families, including those in working-class and rural areas.

The personal connection between teacher and student is crucial in learning, both cognitive and emotional, especially in the early years, as much prior research has shown. And that personal connection proved harder to sustain in distance learning. The "homework gap" and "summer loss gap" that had long been shown to be a disadvantage to poor kids were worsened by the epidemic.[139] In many homes, distance learning was a special challenge because of deficiencies in Internet access and in parental preparation/availability to take on the burdens of instruction. Consequently, most experts expected the switch to online learning to have left all students falling behind, while widening racial and class gaps in student achievement.[140]

The crisis revealed other weaknesses of virtual ties compared to face-to-face interaction. As it wore on, more and more people began to realize that humans are not wired for social distancing, and that face-to-face encounters are more effective for meaningful communication, sensitivity to emotions, and interpersonal trust.[141] AA meetings online, for example, struggled to create the same effect as in-person meetings.[142] At least in the initial months, the epidemic reminded Americans of the pain of loneliness and the importance of connection, and perhaps taught us that we're all in this together, but whether those lessons will endure remained uncertain. Before COVID-19, many assumed that the future of political organizing lay in social media, but the reliance on social media required by the quarantine convinced both sides of the aisle that Twitter or webcasts from home are not the equivalent of in-person campaigning. Similarly, it showed that electronic contact with dying parents is not the equivalent of bedside handholding. The unmistakable wave of "quarantine fatigue" that swept across parts of the U.S. in the fourth month of the shutdown, despite its costs in human lives, testified to the hunger for face-to-face connection felt by many Americans.

For many decades, evidence had accumulated that isolation and loneliness have serious costs in terms of health and happiness.[143] Emotional health deteriorated as the quarantine continued; the epidemic reinforced much research showing that social contact produces happiness by actually affecting the body's biochemistry.[144] Clinically-measured and self-reported depression surged, doubling during the epidemic, according to one Census Bureau study, though whether the surge was attributable to isolation or to fears about the disease or to economic anxiety remained unclear. The surge was much greater among younger adults and lower among older Americans, not what one would have expected if the depression simply reflected realistic risk of the disease.[145] Vivek H. Murthy and Alice T. Chen warned of a "social recession"—an epidemic of loneliness and isolation brought on by the virus.[146] And one observer opined that "Gen Z could come out of this with a permanent, lifelong, forged-in-disaster appreciation for physical connections over digital ones."[147]

The epidemic accentuated both the dark side and the usefulness of social media. Increased reliance on Internet connections led to more malignant hacking and cyberattacks, not just Zoom-bombing. "Twitter suffer[ed] from its usual cesspool dynamics, but now they're amplified by the crisis."[148] The Internet, as embodied in social networks and message boards like 4chan, increasingly transmitted fake news, quack cures, radical and cultish views, conspiracy theories, and authoritarian solutions.[149] On the other hand, social media exchanges among whistleblowers and private experts corrected bad information coming from official sources.[150]

In many ways, for good and bad, the epidemic essentially underscored and accelerated trends already visible beforehand. For example, on the good side, apps fostered neighborhood ties. On the bad side, preexisting geographic, class, and racial disparities became even more visible. We know from Daniel Aldrich's work that social capital is important in community resilience,[151] and the epidemic probably accentuated disparities in social capital.

The initial months of mainly virtual social interaction convinced many ordinary Americans why alloys matter and that face-to-face connections cannot simply be replaced by online networking. According to a Pew survey, 64 percent of Americans (and fully 69 percent of digital natives aged eighteen to twenty-nine) said that online or phone connections would be useful but *not* a substitute for in-person contact.[152] It is not surprising that pre-digital generations would feel the loss of offline "touch," but it is surprising that that seems to have been even more true of the Internet generation. It seems that the epidemic-induced shutdowns highlighted how important in-person interactions are as a buttress to online ones, which was probably not as visible before. In other words, unalloyed virtual ties may not have much social-capital "punch" without an admixture of face-to-face ties. As one digital native said, "online ties may be a multiplier of sorts, but zero times a multiplier is still zero."[153]

Although virtual ties appear better than nothing in the absence of all face-to-face ties, it is harder to convey nuance virtually, and much is lost in transmission. The epidemic experience has so far reinforced the view of those who argue that virtual ties can't replace the salubrious effects of real social ties on human well-being. At the same time, in some cases alloys of face-to-face and virtual ties proved their tensile strength; socially distanced neighborhood get-togethers, organized online, illustrated exactly this possibility. In short, the epidemic brought out the special virtues of online/offline alloys.

Even after the first few months, it also helped us see beyond crude debates about "the Internet—good or bad?" to a more nuanced understanding of which sorts of human functioning can be transferred online and which cannot. The epidemic suggested that "Can the Internet replace face-to-face social capital?" may be too broad a question. As Rabbi Brigitte Rosenberg, who praised virtual connections as a lifeline for her congregation, said, "virtual works, but sometimes it doesn't work for everything."[154] In our parlance, the rabbi is saying that we need strong alloys of online and offline connection to sustain our social relations. Some activities, like travel-free meetings and telemedicine, will likely transfer online fairly successfully, as we have discussed. Others, like K–12 education, proved not to work so well virtually. Neither did efforts to provide emotional support online.

Life in a pandemic is one of truncated sociability and worsening inequality. But the results of the experiment comparing online and offline connections won't be known for months, or even years, in the future. The outcome hinges on the answers to a number of key questions about the Internet and social capital. These questions emerged, to be sure, from the early months of the epidemic, but in a deeper sense they emerge from our conclusions about the last twenty years, and especially our emphasis on alloys and agency.

- To the extent that people's choices affect the role that the Internet plays in society, what (if anything) does the experience of the epidemic tell us about how people use the Internet and how that might change in the future?
- Will Americans be satisfied with the ability of available technology to maintain their social networks, or will they become disenchanted with these digital connections and leave these platforms, voting with their feet? Remembering that Internet entrepreneurs are not merely passive providers of Internet platforms, will tech companies find new ways of connecting online that make digital connections more attractive?
- Will digital divides deepen class, racial, and generational divides, or will the epidemic bring more and more people into the digital world as they use social networking?
- Will bridging social capital suffer as a result of the lack of natural third places online, or will social media begin to fill that role?
- Will Zoom fatigue and people's distaste for commuting lead to more thoughtful decisions about when we actually need to be physically present in a room together, when meetings are truly required, and when they can be accomplished remotely?
- Can we be more creative in designing not simply apps and platforms but more innovative alloys that combine online and offline networks, especially alloys that contain a larger portion of face-to-face activity and a relatively smaller portion of computer-mediated communication?
- Are there ways to create new and better alloys that encourage more efficient but also more serendipitous innovation?[155] For example, the epidemic proved that some sorts of work can be done online, but we know from much prior evidence that often the biggest new ideas come from chance face-to-face mingling (one reason why high-tech companies are concentrated in relatively few locations).[156] Similarly, the unprecedented nationwide Black Lives Matter protest marches offered new evidence on how social media can mobilize massive in-person protests, but at the same time the protests themselves revealed the power of face-to-face connection, since the "in real life" protests accomplished much more than an infinite number of "likes" or retweets could have done. It is unclear at this writing whether the BLM protests will create the sort of alloy (with strong underlying organization and mutual trust and solidarity) that could support durable change.[157]

Prediction is hard, as Yogi Berra said, especially about the future. We have traced the evolution of the Internet and especially social media over the first two decades or so of their existence, but we have not aspired to predict the future. However, it will surely be true in coming years, as it has been in the last twenty, that the Internet is what we make of it. Whether it will eventually become a powerful source of social capital or not is a question that ultimately rests in the hands of our readers, especially the younger generation. They can make the Internet what they want it to be—and the nation needs their energy and online know-how to craft alloys that will restore America's social capital.

Acknowledgments

For generous, skilled, timely, and good-humored help in the preparation of the afterword, we thank Robert Axelrod, Bernard Banet, Bob Bender, Aidan Connaughton, Pete Davis, Shaylyn Romney Garrett, Gabriel Karger, Lisa MacPhee, Alonso Perez-Putnam, Gabriel Perez-Putnam, Jonathan F. Putnam, Noah Putnam, Rosemary W. Putnam, Rafe Sagalyn, and Alexandra Samuel.

APPENDIX I

Measuring Social Change

MUCH OF THIS BOOK consists of systematic, quantitative evidence about social trends over the last half of the twentieth century. This appendix summarizes key methodological challenges involved in that exercise, as well as the most important sources of data on which I have drawn.

My primary strategy, as explained in chapter 1, has been to triangulate among as many independent sources of evidence as possible, following the model of researchers into global warming. Our exploration of social change is inevitably constrained by the fact that, just as in the case of global warming, no one thought ahead to collect the really perfect evidence that we now need—a half century's measurement of the reliability of friends or the helpfulness of strangers or the honesty of shopkeepers or the frequency of block parties. As a result, we need to look for convincing proof not in a single pair of polls, or even a single series of surveys, but instead for convergence across a number of different series, each carried out by different researchers. And where possible, we should look for change not merely in poll data, but also in institutions and behavior.

The core principle, thus, is this: *No single source of data is flawless, but the more numerous and diverse the sources, the less likely that they could all be influenced by the same flaw.* Two independent (though necessarily imperfect) strands of evidence are better than one, and more than two are better still, especially if they have *different* imperfections. What are the main sources of evidence used in this study—our equivalent of tree rings, ice cores, and weather records?

In some respects organizational records are the firmest indicators, for through them we can directly compare the civic involvement of Americans in the 1950s, the 1970s, and the 1990s. The assiduous record keeping of thousands of club secretaries and county clerks and church treasurers across the decades is much more reliable than frail recollections of "how things used to be." Much is held constant (or nearly so) in this comparison: the constituency of the group, the meaning of "membership," the assiduousness of information gathering. Of course, even these things can change. "Membership" in a union may not mean the same thing in 1998 as in 1938, and the occupation of "teamsters" has surely changed. Still, problems of comparability are less severe for organizational records than for most other sorts of data. Moreover, because organizations keep records over long periods, our comparisons can extend back decades or even centuries, giving us a longer perspective on recent events. Is a 10 percent slump in membership or contributions from one year to the next truly significant, or is it merely a commonplace down-tick? Only long-term records can really tell.

However, membership records have several grave defects as metrics of social change. First, organizations themselves have life cycles that may be independent of the vitality of the communities in which they exist. If the Elks club is fading, perhaps its place is being taken by myriad other organizations, all of them still too young and small and effervescent to worry about keeping careful membership records. If we confine ourselves to examining membership records of long-standing organizations, we will miss new and rapidly growing groups.

Another important caution follows from the fact that organizations have life cycles. Nothing whatever can be inferred about the civic vitality of a community from the *birth* rate of new organizations, unless at the same time we also examine the *death* rate of older ones. The discovery that, say, half of all environmental organizations now in existence were founded in the last decade proves absolutely nothing about organizational trends, unless we also know how many similar groups have disappeared over the same period.[1] This issue is especially problematic if (as is true, for example, of the Internal Revenue Service records of nonprofit organizations) a list of organizations is not pruned regularly to eliminate defunct organizations.

Third, not all community activity is embodied in record-keeping organizations—indeed, probably most is not. One scholar, for example, estimates that 80 percent of all community groups represent social "dark matter"—that is, without formal structure, without an address, without archives, without notice in newspapers, and thus invisible to conventional chroniclers.[2] If we confine our attention to membership rosters, we may miss massive change or massive stability. Worse yet, if community life is, for whatever reason, becoming richer, but less formally organized, tracking membership figures alone would lead us to precisely the wrong conclusion.

These deficiencies in organizational records can to some extent be offset by one of the most useful inventions of the twentieth century—the systematic social survey. A well-designed poll can provide a useful snapshot of opinions and behavior. Even better, a series of comparable surveys can yield a kind of social time-lapse photography. Just as one snapshot a day from a single camera pointed unvaryingly at the same garden patch can yield a marvelous movie of botanical birth and growth, so a single survey question, if repeated regularly, can produce a striking image of social change.

Moreover, if the question has been formulated deftly enough, it can encompass a more diverse and changing social landscape than the study of any single organization. Through surveys we can examine involvement not merely in the League of Women Voters, say, but in any club that a respondent thinks worth mentioning. We can assess attendance not merely at an official "town meeting," but at any local meeting. Best of all, surveys can capture informal activities—not merely voting, but chatting with your neighbor; not merely organizational membership, but poker games. Surveys, in short, can illuminate the "dark matter" of community life.

Yet for all their utility, surveys have at least four important limitations.

Comparability: Just as the camera in time-lapse photography must be motionless to capture motion, so survey questions must be (more or less) unchanging to capture change. For example, experienced pollsters know that the harder you probe, the more responses you get. Thus the number of organizational memberships that a poll uncovers is heavily dependent on the number of probes. So true is this that to the question "How many groups do you find the average American belongs to?" it is only a slight exaggeration to respond "As many as you'd like, if I ask hard enough."[3] Moreover, as survey researchers have become more sophisticated, they have discovered many other pitfalls for the unwary student of change: "order effects" (answers depend in part on the order in which questions are posed), "house effects" (different survey organizations obtain consistently different results to the same question), and so on. In other words, our social camera can be jiggled easily. It is especially risky to compare results from questions posed at different times by different survey organizations.

Only a few survey archives contain data carefully enough controlled to ensure that our social time-lapse photograph is reliable.

Continuity: The reliability of our time-lapse sequence is also very dependent on the number of snapshots at our disposal. *In assessing social change, two observations are better than one, but many is much better than two.* Literally nothing at all can be said sensibly about change from a single photo or a single survey. Though this point seems obvious, otherwise intelligent folks sometimes claim to detect directions of social change from a single observation, which is just as silly as to make a claim about global warming from a single glance at the thermometer.[4]

Data from two points in time offer some leverage for testing claims about change but are vulnerable to measurement inconsistency at either end. A single measurement error—a subtle change in question order, for example—might lead to a mistaken judgment about the overall trend. Or suppose that a survey of church attendance in 1964 was taken in the middle of August vacations and the same question in 1994 happened to be posed during Easter week. With only two points in time, we might well be misled into thinking that religious observance was booming in the 1990s. Just as it would be foolhardy for students of global warming to make much of a single pair of temperature readings two decades apart, so too in assessing social change, random fluctuations can invalidate judgments based on only a few data points.

Change measured at multiple points in time becomes exponentially more reliable; if a given variable increases steadily from time 1 to time 2, from time 2 to time 3, and so on to time 10, it becomes virtually impossible to conceive of a series of measurement slipups that might have produced the trend. In short, for reliable assessment of social change, we need not merely comparable measurements, but comparable measurements repeated as many times as possible. For that reason, in this book I have relied most heavily on surveys that posed the same question dozens—even hundreds—of times over the last quarter of the twentieth century.

Comprehensiveness: Just as in the case of membership rosters, our surveys must cover a wide range of activities. Even if a question is literally invariant, its accuracy as a measuring rod may change over time. We might consider a question about frequency of bowling as an indicator of informal social togetherness. However, if bowling were gradually replaced by softball or soccer as the leisure sport of choice among Americans, then an accurately reported decline in team bowling might simply have been offset by a rise in softball or soccer, both team sports.[5] So we must cast our net as widely as possible.

Timeliness: Since social change proceeds unevenly, *measurement periods must be matched to hypotheses about the scale and timing of change.* Our interest is not "social change" in the abstract. We want to know what, if anything, has happened to our communities over the last half century or so. Just as we could infer little about global warming by comparing yesterday to today, so too we can infer little about social change over the past several decades by examining evidence over the last few years—or over the last few centuries, for that matter. So we must always ask about any trend not just "What's changing?" but "What's changing over what period?" A fair test of our thesis requires comparable data over as much of the last three to five decades as possible.[6]

The good news is that several national survey archives provide comparable, continuous, and comprehensive evidence on the contours of social change. The bad news is that with rare exceptions, these collections did not begin before the mid-1970s.[7] There is reason to suspect that some important shifts in American community life began in the mid-1960s, but few of our cameras began operating until about a decade later. We cannot be sure what was happening before the shutter on our social time-lapse camera was first triggered, but the survey archives probably missed some of the most interesting action. This deficiency is one important reason for taking advantage of organizational records. It is also a reason for paying special attention to those few surveys that span the earlier period, such as the University of Michigan–NIMH study cited in chapters 3, 4, and 6.

One last issue of methodology: Should we measure absolute or relative change, and if relative, relative to what? Should we consider the absolute number of participants or contributions to some community purpose, or should we instead use some relative standard of comparison? Organizations and headline writers often boast of growing participation in absolute terms—"the XYZ Club has a record number of members this year!" "Record number of Angeleños go to the polls!" "Local church giving hits all-time high!" But absolute numbers can be badly misleading.

If the total vote rises by 5 percent, while voting-age population is rising by 10 percent, participation has actually fallen. Conversely, if membership in the Grange falls by 5 percent, while the number of farmers is falling by 50 percent, the involvement of the average farmer has actually risen. If membership in the local Parent-Teacher Association has fallen merely because there are fewer parents nowadays, we would not want to count that as evidence of civic decline. Conversely, if the number of lawyers in town doubled, while membership in the bar association grew by only 5 percent, it would be misleading to conclude that lawyers were becoming more active in professional affairs. In short, we generally should consider what economists call "market share": What proportion of *the eligible population* takes part in any given activity?[8]

One important (and, it turns out, highly controversial) instance of relative vs. absolute change is this: When examining changes in civic involvement, should we control for educational levels? The argument for doing so is simple and powerful. Education is one of the most important predictors—usually, in fact, *the* most important predictor—of many forms of social participation—from voting to chairing a local committee to hosting a dinner party. Moreover, educational levels of the American public rose very sharply during precisely the period of interest to us. So it seems logical to "control for" education, by asking, for example, about the civic involvement of the average college graduate. In effect, to control for education in this way is to assume that given the growth in educational levels, we should expect growth in civic involvement, and if we find declines *relative to educational levels*, that implies that some other factor must be depressing involvement. By analogy, if we found that vocabulary skills in America were steady or falling despite rising levels of education, we surely would look for some other factor (like TV, for example) that might have been simultaneously tending to depress literacy. At least until recently, to control for educational levels has been the conventional approach of social scientists in estimating changes in social and political participation.

Recently, however, some scholars have pointed out that many of the sociological effects of education may themselves be relative, not absolute.[9] If more people now have a college degree, perhaps the sociological significance of the credential has been devalued. Social status is, for example, associated with education, but we would not necessarily assume that just because more Americans are educated than ever before, America has a greater volume of social status than ever before. To the extent that education is merely about sorting people, not about adding to their skills and knowledge and civic values and social connections, it is misleading to "control for" educational change.

There is no agreement among scholars on this issue. The core issue is whether (holding constant my own education) I am less likely or more likely to participate civically if those around me become more educated. In some cases the effect of education may be relative, so that (intimidated by the eggheads around me) I may be less likely to speak up at a public meeting in a college town than I would in a more normal community. In these cases the effect of education is mainly *relative*, and we should not expect that rising educational levels would push up participation. In other cases it seems likely that my propensity to participate will actually rise with the level of education of my neighbors. I am more likely to join a reading group, for example, if I live in a community with lots of other educated readers. In these cases we should expect that rising levels of education should push up participation rates even faster.

Evidence uncovered in the course of this research strongly suggests that the effects of education on social participation are typically absolute, not relative.[10] My education increases my social participation, and generally speaking, your education does *not* lower my participation. So if we both graduate from college, we should both tend to become more civically engaged. Under these circumstances it would be appropriate to control for rising educational levels. However, doing so has the effect of amplifying declines in participation and minimizing increases, so given the nature of my argument, the more *conservative* course is *not* to control for education.

In the analyses reported in this book I generally *do* control for changes in population, but I do *not* usually control for changes in the educational composition of the population. This rule of thumb stacks the cards against my hypothesis. The upshot is that the evidence presented in this book may well *understate* the gross decline in civic engagement in America over the last half century.

Statistical controls are also relevant to another recurrent issue in this book, that of assessing causes and effects. Suppose that we are interested in the connection between TV watching and civic engagement, and suppose that we find that heavy TV watchers are rarely active in organizations. Before concluding that TV inhibits civic participation, however, we must consider other factors, such as social class, that might make this correlation spurious: perhaps working-class people watch more TV, whereas organizational leadership is monopolized by the middle class. One way to check this possibility is to control statistically for social class, in effect comparing the participation rates of people of the same class whose viewing habits differ.

Statistical techniques such as multiple regression allow us to control simultaneously for many possible confounding variables, particularly when (as, fortunately, in our case) very large survey archives are available. *Virtually every generalization in this book has been subjected to detailed statistical analysis of this sort, controlling simultaneously for age (or year of birth), gender, education, income, race, marital status, parental status, job status (working full-time, part-time, or not at all), and size of community of residence.* In addition, where relevant, I controlled for other background factors, including year of survey, region, financial worries, homeownership, residential mobility (both past and anticipated), commuting time, general leisure activity, self-reported time pressure, self-reported health, and other factors. To be sure, controls of this sort, though necessary, are not always sufficient to rule out spuriousness. For this reason I have ensured that the data that underlie our conclusions will be readily available to other researchers, so that they can explore alternative interpretations.[11] However, I have also undertaken due diligence myself in the analyses for this book to rule out obvious spuriousness. To keep complicated statistical apparatus from interfering with the presentation of my main conclusions, the graphs and charts here typically present the data without multivariate controls, but in each case I have also conducted extensive tests to be sure that the underlying relationship was not spurious.[12]

One final cosmetic issue about the figures in this book: In every case I present every available data point. Often, however, short-term fluctuations obscure the longer-term trends. For example, figure 2 presents annual data from the Department of Commerce on the number of political organizations. Even a cursory examination of this chart, however, reveals a clear biennial rhythm (more organizations in election years), along with a few other deviations from the longer trend (such as the modest dip in 1995). In this, as in all other graphs, I show both a dotted line linking the actual data points and a darker, smoother curve that conveys the longer-term trend. The darker lines (calculated simply as the best-fitting polynomial curves) are intended to ease reading of the figures, but purists who prefer the unvarnished data may simply ignore the darker lines.

What are the primary sources of our evidence? The two most widely used academic survey research archives for American social and political behavior are the National Election Studies (NES) and the General Social Survey (GSS). Virtually every two years since 1952, coinciding with national elections, the Survey Research Center of the University of Michigan has surveyed a sample of Americans about their political behavior (NES). Roughly every other year since 1974 the National Opinion Research Corporation at the University of Chicago has conducted a broadly similar set of surveys on social behavior (GSS). Both archives provide high-quality scientific evidence about changes in Americans' attitudes and behavior, and I have relied on both archives in this book. For our purposes the utility of the NES is limited, however, for it focuses on elections and gives little attention to everyday civic participation. The GSS covers a wider range of activities, although in the domains most central to our interests its continuous coverage is largely confined to formal group membership, church attendance, and social trust. Fortunately, in the course of this research my colleagues and I have discovered several other important survey archives to supplement the GSS and NES.[13]

Roughly ten times per year between September 1973 and October 1994 the Roper survey organization interviewed in person a national cross section of approximately 2,000 persons of voting age, yielding a survey archive of more than 410,000 respondents over more than two decades, the Roper Social and Political Trends data set.[14] The sampling method (a multistage, stratified probability sample with quotas for sex, age, and employed women) remained essentially constant over the entire period. Many questions of social and political significance were asked repeatedly over this period, and our analysis here draws frequently on this archive. Not all questions were asked in all surveys, and thus our analysis of evidence based on the Roper Social and Political Trends archive is sometimes based on much less than the entire sample of 410,000 respondents. (I have noted in such cases the specific surveys in which the relevant questions appeared.) However, one crucially important set of questions relevant to civic engagement (summarized in table 1) appeared on every single survey along with standard demographic information, and this massive sample enables us to examine even forms of participation, like running for public office, that are quite rare.

In the midst of this research my colleagues and I stumbled onto a second source of annual survey evidence on civic and social activities covering the last quarter of the twentieth century: DDB Needham Life Style surveys (DDB). Begun in 1975 and still continuing, these extraordinary surveys provide regular barometric readings on scores of social, economic, political, and personal themes, from international affairs and religious beliefs to financial worries and condom usage. With an annual sample of 3,500–4,000, this archive through 1999 contained more than 87,000 respondents over the last quarter of the twentieth century. To the extent that it can be shown to be methodologically reliable, the DDB Needham Life Style archive constitutes one of the richest known sources of data on social change in America in the last quarter of the twentieth century. Because of its novelty and importance, I present here some additional information about this archive.

Each year since 1975 the DDB Needham advertising agency has commissioned Market Facts, a commercial polling firm, to question a national panel of American households about their consumer preferences and behavior.[15] Most of the roughly twenty-page written questionnaire is taken up with inquiries about detergents, mutual funds, automobiles, and so on. However, every year a core set of questions has been posed about "life style" issues, including media usage, financial worries, social and political attitudes, self-esteem, and a wide range of social behavior, such as reading, travel, sports and other leisure activities, family life, and community involvement.

From the point of view of DDB Needham's commercial clients, these "life style" questions are valuable for planning marketing strategies, defining market niches, and drafting advertising copy. Are churchgoers more likely to send Christmas cards, for example? Are fast-food restaurants replacing the family dinner for two-career families? Are frequent moviegoers more liberal in their social attitudes? Are rock concert fans more likely than museum buffs to watch Monday Night Football?[16] From the point of view of social science, however, the DDB Needham Life Style data provide an unparalleled source of information on trends in social behavior over the last two decades.

However, the DDB Needham Life Style survey data are not without flaws. One important limitation is obvious and relatively easy to compensate for, but a second is more serious. The first is that until 1985 only married households were included in the sample. However, I have found few cases in which the observed *trends* between 1985 and 1999 differ significantly between married and single respondents, although in a number of cases there are modest differences in the *levels*. For example, married people attend church more often than single people do, while singles attend club meetings more often than married people, but the trends in both church- and clubgoing are essentially identical for the two groups. In all cases where this sampling peculiarity poses potential problems of analysis, I analyzed the data separately by marital status to confirm that the "missing 1975–84 singles" did not vitiate our substantive conclusions. Where the levels and/or trends in traits of interest vary by marital status, I have made an appropriate adjustment to track changes over the entire 1975–98 period.[17]

The second worrisome limitation is that the DDB Needham Life Style data come not from random samples of the population, but from a form of quota sampling called "mail panels." Participants in such surveys—which are frequently used by commercial polling firms—are initially self-selected. Given that the few people who choose to participate might differ significantly from the many who do not, this sampling procedure requires that we consider seriously the possibility of response bias in these data. I have assessed this potential problem in more detail elsewhere, but a brief overview is appropriate here.[18]

The sampling begins when Market Facts acquires from commercial list brokers the names, addresses, and sometimes demographic characteristics of very large numbers of Americans—from driver's license bureaus, telephone directories, and many other sources. Large samples from these lists are then invited by mail to express willingness in advance to respond periodically to mail and phone inquiries about commercial products and services, as well as other current issues.[19] According to Market Facts officials, the rate of favorable response to such invitations varies across different sectors of the population—from perhaps less than 1 percent among racial minorities and inner-city residents to perhaps 5–10 percent among middle-aged, middle-class "middle Americans." From this prerecruited "mail panel" (numbering perhaps five hundred thousand at any one time) are then drawn random, demographically balanced samples for the annual DDB Needham Life Style surveys (as well as hundreds of other commercial and other surveys throughout the year).[20] Each Life Style respondent is mailed a long written questionnaire that he or she is asked to complete and return within several weeks. At this stage the response rate (roughly 70–80 percent) is typically higher than for conventional random samples. As far as I have been able to ascertain, there has been no substantial change in these procedures over the last two decades, although less careful procedural records have been kept than would be characteristic of comparable academic archives, and in particular, systematic data on the rate of favorable responses to the initial mail invitations are lacking.

Compared with conventional random samples, the mail panel approach has several potential drawbacks.

1. Because the initial recruitment is by mail, literacy in English is an essential requirement, and thus the bottom of the educational ladder is underrepresented, as are non–English speakers.
2. Effective response rates are much lower among racial minorities.[21]
3. Adults under twenty-five are slightly underrepresented, probably because their mobility makes them harder to track.

Social traits that are especially common in those sections of the population are thus underrepresented in the DDB Needham Life Style sample. In round numbers, the sample contains 10 percent too few high school dropouts, 10 percent too few single respondents, 10 percent too many parents, and half as many racial minorities. Moreover, the sample may also underrepresent the highest and lowest categories of family income. These data reasonably represent the middle 80–90 percent of American society, but they do not well represent ethnic minorities, the very poor, the very rich, and the very transient.[22] They may also slightly overrepresent the portion of the public that is most engaged with the mass media. Thus a crucial question about the DDB Needham Life Style survey archive is the degree to which these known sample biases inhibit our ability to estimate social trends from these data.

How accurately do the DDB Needham Life Style data represent trends in American society? In the absence of a full census of social behavior—something that not even the U.S. Census Bureau believes in anymore—the two key questions here are as follows:

1. Do people who join a mail panel differ in substantively relevant ways from people who are willing to respond to conventional surveys?

2. Has the *degree* of difference between the Life Style panel and conventional surveys changed over time, thus rendering judgments about trends suspect?

If the answer to question 1 is "Yes," then in some respects the DDB Needham Life Style data may be inaccurate descriptively. Only if the answer to question 2 is also "Yes," however, will the *trends* in the Life Style data misrepresent trends as they would appear in a conventional random survey. A constant bias would be disconcerting, to be sure, but only a *changing* bias would affect our judgments about trends.

With respect to the quality of mail panel respondents, reassuring information is available from several studies that have directly compared results from mail panels and conventional samples. First, apart from the demographic disparity just described (fewer young, poor, and racial minorities in the mail panel), there are surprisingly few differences between the two approaches, even on variables that might be thought to be especially sensitive to the difference in technique. The two different samples do not differ in religious affiliation and religiosity; in public policy views (on tax policy, abortion, gun control); in their views about their own and the nation's economic circumstances; in their altruism (volunteering, philanthropy) or general "positivity"; in their basic consumer orientations, purchasing habits, ownership or use of common products; in their health or fitness; or in their leisure time. The only significant differences are 1) partisanship (mail panels are slightly less Democratic, probably because of the underrepresentation of racial minorities); and 2) media usage (mail panelists watch slightly more television and read slightly more newspapers).[23] That low response rates may not bias substantive results can also be inferred from a recent study that compared results from "easy to reach" and "hard to reach" samples. Aside from clear differences on racial issues, the upshot is that there are no significant differences on other issue stances, on media use, on engagement in daily activities, and on feelings about other people.[24]

Additional reassurance comes from a comparison between the two most widely reported national surveys of consumer confidence in the United States, one (from the University of Michigan) that relies on conventional random sampling and another (from the Conference Board) that relies on a mail panel. The long-run changes charted by the two methods have been very similar. (The semiannual correlation between the two indexes over more than three decades is $R^2 = .55$.) For fine-grained, month-to-month changes, one or the other of these two surveys might be preferred, but the broad-gauge impressions of annual trends that one would glean from the two are quite similar.

To explore more fully the reliability of DDB Needham Life Style data, I took advantage of the fact that this data set includes more than a dozen diverse questions that are comparable to questions posed on a regular basis over roughly the same time span in the General Social Survey. These measures include attitudes toward feminism, the legalization of marijuana and abortion, views of the Soviet Union, financial worries, military service, basic social values, smoking, video usage, hunting and gun ownership, and (especially relevant to our interests) social trust, church attendance, and leisure activities.[25] For each of these items, I posed three tests:

1. Do the *levels* of response on these variables differ between the two samples, taking into account obvious differences in question wording?
2. Do the *trends* that one would infer about the underlying trait differ between the two samples?
3. Do the underlying patterns of *demographic correlates* of these variables differ between the two samples?

As Steven Yonish and I report in detail elsewhere, in every case the answer is "No."[26] For purposes of describing and explaining this wide range of attitudes and behavior, the two surveys are virtually indistinguishable, despite marked differences in sampling (random vs. quota), questioning procedure (personal interviews vs. mail questionnaires), and in some cases question wording. Not only are the trends on all comparable items that I have found virtually identical in the two archives, but the deeper structure of relations between these items and demographic categories is also very similar.

According to the General Social Survey, for example, the probability that in 1990 a thirty-five-year-old single white mother with two years of college education and a part-time job who rented an apartment in a middle-size New England city favored marijuana legalization is 35 percent, whereas the comparable probability according to the DDB Needham Life Style data was 38 percent, a difference well within sampling error. Similarly, controlling simultaneously for year of survey, year of birth, marital status, employment status, parental status, education, income, race, region of the country, and type of residence, the GSS data suggest that women attend church exactly 5.3 more times per year than men, whereas the DDB Needham Life Style data imply that the difference between the sexes in churchgoing is 4.8 times per year—once again a difference well within sampling error. That the DDB Needham Life Style data pass this very stringent test of comparability with the GSS data—the most scientifically reputable data available on these topics—increases our confidence in the DDB Needham Life Style archive.

Finally, the two archives contain directly comparable questions about a range of leisure activities. Appendix table 1 shows the responses to a series of questions regarding "leisure or recreational activities . . . done in the past twelve months." The incidence of these

Appendix Table 1: Leisure Activities as Measured in Two National Survey Archives

Leisure Activities During Preceding Twelve Months (1993)		
General Social Survey wording *DDB Needham Life Style survey wording*	GSS	*Life Style*
Went out to see a movie in a theater	72%	70%
Went to the movies		
Recorded a TV program so you could watch it later	63%	70%
Videotaped a TV program on a VCR[a]		
Grew vegetables, flowers, or shrubs in garden	62%	68%
Worked in garden		
Participated in any sports activity, such as softball, basketball, swimming, golf, bowling, skiing, or tennis	59%	69%
Played softball and/or went swimming and/or played golf and/or went bowling and/or went skiing and/or played tennis[b]		
Attended an amateur or professional sports event	56%	56%
Attended a sporting event		
Went camping, hiking, or canoeing	44%	44%
Went camping and/or went hiking[c]		
Visited art museum or gallery	41%	47%
Visited an art gallery or museum		
Made art or craft objects, such as pottery, woodworking, quilts, or paintings	41%	48%
Worked on a crafts project (needlework, etc.)[d]		
Went hunting or fishing	37%	37%
Went hunting and/or went fishing		
Played a musical instrument like a piano, guitar, or violin	24%	23%
Played a musical instrument		
Went to classical music or opera performance	16%	17%
Went to classical concert		
Attended auto, stock car, or motorcycle race	16%	9%
Went to auto race[e]		

[a] *Life Style data are available for 1988–91 only. Figure here is for 1991.*
[b] *Since the Life Style questionnaire asked about each of these sports separately, in effect six separate probes were employed. This difference almost certainly inflated the Life Style results, relative to the single GSS question.*
[c] *Hiking was included in Life Style surveys in 1975–84 and 1996–97; figure for 1993 was interpolated. Canoeing was never included in Life Style surveys.*
[d] *Life Style data are available for 1994–97 only. Figure here is projected for 1993.*
[e] *Attendance at auto races was included in Life Style surveys only in 1997, and the figure is used here.*

Appendix Table 2: Algorithm for "Annualizing" Estimated Frequencies

GSS Response Alternatives	Imputed Score	DDB Needham Life Style Response Alternatives	Imputed Score
Never	0	None in the past year	0
Less than once a year	0.5	1–4 times	2
Once a year	1	5–8 times	6
Several times a year	6	9–11 times	10
Once a month	12	12–24 times	18
2–3 times a month	30	25–51 times	38
Nearly every week	40	52+ times	54
Every week	52		
More than once a week	60		

activities in the two surveys was astonishingly similar, well within the limits of sampling error. How many Americans went to the movies in 1993? GSS says 70 percent, DDB says 72 percent. How about hunting and fishing? GSS says 37 percent, DDB says 37 percent. How about classical concert–going? GSS says 16 percent, DDB says 17 percent. In other words, the profiles of leisure activities represented in the mail panel of the DDB Needham Life Style survey and in the random sample of the General Social Survey were essentially identical.[27]

In short, just as ice cores, though not infallible, are an invaluable source of information about climatic change, particularly when cross-checked against other measures, for the purposes of estimating basic trends in social participation over the last quarter of the twentieth century the DDB Needham Life Style archive is a valuable source of information, particularly if (as throughout the analyses reported in this book) the results from this archive are consistent with results from other modes of measurement.

Both the General Social Survey and the DDB Needham Life Style surveys typically ask respondents to estimate the frequency of various activities, such as church attendance, but the two surveys use slightly different categories for this purpose. In order to facilitate comparison between these two archives—and, more generally, to simplify presentation of estimated frequencies for various activities—I converted the raw data in each case into estimated annual frequencies, using the algorithm in appendix table 2. Reasonable observers might differ over exactly what "several times a year," for example, means in quantitative terms, but my basic results are not sensitive to exactly what integers are assigned to the various ranks.[28]

Another valuable data archive used frequently in this book derives from the Americans' Use of Time project, managed in recent decades by Professor John Robinson of the University of Maryland, based on careful time diaries kept by national samples of Americans in 1965, 1975, 1985, and 1995. Abundant details about these data are available in Robinson's book with Geoffrey Godbey, *Time for Life: The Surprising Ways Americans Use Their Time.*[29] One special feature of these data, however, deserves brief mention. One major advantage of this data archive is that it begins in 1965, just about the same time that (other data suggest) various forms of social capital began to decline. However, the 1965 data differed somewhat from the subsequent years, in that the 1965 sample excluded respondents who lived in areas with no city greater than fifty thousand in population, as well as households in which no member aged eighteen to sixty-five was part of the nonagricultural labor force. Since the 1965 sample excluded rural and retired families, the raw figures for that year slightly misrepresent what would have been found in a national sample that year. To estimate 1965 figures that are more nearly comparable to the later, nationwide data, I adjusted the raw data for 1965, using the observed differences in the 1975 and 1985 surveys between the full national sample and the subset of respondents who would have been included within the 1965 sampling frame. In addition, we weighted the raw data to ensure that each day of the week was equally represented in the final sample. These adjustments account for minor discrepancies between the results presented by Robinson and Godbey and the results reported here.

Sources for
Figures and Tables

FIGURE NUMBER	TITLE	SOURCE OF DATA
1	Trends in presidential voting (1820–1996), by region	Walter Dean Burnham, unpublished estimates of electoral turnout. For earlier estimates, see Walter Dean Burnham, "The Turnout Problem," in *Elections American Style*, James Reichley, ed. (Washington, D.C.: Brookings, 1987), 113–114.
2	Political organizations with regular paid staff, 1977–1996	U.S. Bureau of the Census, *County Business Patterns, 1977–1996* (Washington, D.C., various years). U.S. residential population in this and subsequent figures from *Statistical Abstract of the United States* (Washington, D.C.: U.S. Bureau of the Census, various years).
3	Citizen participation in campaign activities, 1952–1996	National Elections Studies survey archive, 1952–96.
4	Trends in civic engagement I	Roper Social and Political Trends survey archive, 1973–94.
5	Trends in civic engagement II	Roper Social and Political Trends survey archive, 1973–94.
6	Trends in civic engagement III	Roper Social and Political Trends survey archive, 1973–94.
7	The growth of national nonprofit associations, 1968–1997	National nonprofit organizations from *Encyclopedia of Associations* (Detroit, Mich.: Gale Research, various years), as reported in *Statistical Abstract of the United States* (various years).
8	Membership rate in 32 national chapter-based associations, 1900–1997	See appendix III for list of associations and relevant "constituency" for each. Membership data obtained from national headquarters of various associations and annual reports of those organizations, consulted at the Library of Congress, supplemented and confirmed by data from *World Almanac* (New York: Press Pub. Co. [New York World], various years), *Encyclopedia of Associations* (Detroit, Mich.: Gale Research, various years), histories of particular organizations (such as Gordon S. "Bish" Thompson, *Of Dreams and Deeds* [St. Louis: Optimist International, 1989], and Edward E. Grusd, *B'nai B'rith: The Story of a Covenant* [New York: Appleton-Century, 1966]), and the project on civic engagement directed by Professor Theda Skocpol at Harvard University. I am grateful to Professor Skocpol for exchanging membership data; she bears no responsibility for my interpretation of the data. Membership data for missing years were estimated by linear interpolation. Some organizations typically report membership figures including non-U.S. members, and those non-U.S. members typically constitute a growing fraction of total membership; wherever possible, we excluded such non-U.S. members from the data, in order to focus on trends within the United States. Data on population of underlying constituencies (such as wartime veterans, rural youth, and so on) from published and unpublished data from the U.S. Bureau of the Census, especially the *Statistical Abstract of the United States* (Washington, D.C.: U.S. Bureau of the Census, various years), and *Historical Statistics of the United States: Colonial Times to 1970* (Washington, D.C.: U.S. Bureau of the Census, 1975). Annual market share figures across the 1900–97 period were standardized, and those annual Z-scores were then averaged across all thirty-two organizations to generate figure 8.
9	The rise and fall of the PTA, 1910–1997	Membership numbers from PTA national headquarters. Number of families with children, 1950–97, from *Current Population Reports* (Washington, D.C.: U.S. Bureau of the Census, various years), Series P2, T1; for 1900–50, number of families with children estimated from public elementary and secondary school enrollment, as reported in number of family households and family *Historical Statistics of the United States*, series H420, cross-checked against number of family households and family size. Although these 1900–50 estimates are imprecise, they do not affect the basic pattern in figure 9. For example,

million families, for a PTA membership rate of eight. It is utterly implausible that the actual number of families was more than 25 million or less than 15 million, which gives bounds of seven and eleven for the PTA membership rate.

10 Active organizational involvement in the United States, 1973–1994

Roper Social and Political Trends survey archive, 1973–94.

11 Club meeting attendance dwindles, 1975–1999

DDB Needham Life Style survey archive, 1975–99.

12 Church membership, 1936–1999

Denominational data from Constant H. Jacquet, Jr., *Yearbook of American and Canadian Churches, 1984* (Nashville: Abingdon Press, 1984), 248, and later editions of this yearbook; *Statistical Abstract of the United States* (various years); and Benton Johnson, "The Denominations: The Changing Map of Religious America," *Public Perspective 4* (March/April 1993): 4. On methodological weaknesses of the denominational data, see notes in the *Yearbook of American and Canadian Churches, 1984* and later editions of this yearbook. Gallup Poll data from George H. Gallup, *The Gallup Poll: Public Opinion 1935–1971* (New York: Random House, 1972); George Gallup, Jr., *The Gallup Poll: Public Opinion* (Wilmington, Del.: Scholarly Resources Inc., various years); *Statistical Abstract of the United States, 1997*, table 86, based on surveys conducted by the Gallup Organization; Mayer, *Changing American Mind*, 379; and the Gallup Web site www.gallup.com/poll/indicators/indreligion.asp.

13 Trends in church attendance 1940–1999

Figure is based on average church attendance figures from the Gallup Poll ("last week," 1940–99), the Roper Social and Political Trends polls ("last week,"1974–98), the National Election Studies ("regularly," 1952–68; "almost weekly," 1970–98), the General Social Survey ("nearly every week," 1972–98), and the DDB Needham Life Style polls (at least "25 times last year," 1975–99). Results from the last three of these archives have been recalibrated to match the weekly attendance format of the first two archives; alternative calibration formulas would slightly affect the estimated level of attendance but would not alter the basic trends. The NES question format was changed in 1970 and again in 1990, but those changes do not appear to have substantially altered the results used to construct figure 13. As noted in text, questions have been raised about the reliability of the absolute level of church attendance reported in surveys.

14 Union membership in the United States, 1900–1998

Barry T. Hirsch and John T. Addison, *The Economic Analysis of Unions* (Boston: Allen & Unwin, 1986), 46–47 (table 3.1); Barry T. Hirsch and David A. Macpherson, *Union Membership and Earnings Data Book: Compilations from the Current Population Survey* (Washington, D.C.: Bureau of National Affairs, 1998), 10 (table 1).

15 Average membership rate in eight national professional associations, 1900–1997

See appendix III for list of professional associations and relevant "constituency" for each. Membership figures were obtained from the national headquarters of the respective associations, numbers of employed members of each profession from *Historical Statistics of the United States*, and unpublished data provided by the Bureau of Labor Statistics.

16 Social and leisure activities of American adults (1986–1990)

Roper Social and Political Trends archive, surveys of June 1986, April 1987, and June 1990.

17 Frequency of selected formal and informal social activities, 1975–1998

DDB Needham Life Style survey archive, 1975–98.

FIGURE NUMBER	TITLE	SOURCE OF DATA
18	Social visiting declines, 1975–1999	DDB Needham Life Style survey archive, 1975–99; Roper Social and Political Trends archive and *Roper Reports* (New York: Roper Starch Worldwide, various months); go out to friends' home: March of 1982, 1984, 1990, 1993, 1995; have friends in: November of 1975, 1977, 1985, 1988, 1993, 1996.
19	Family dinners become less common, 1977–1999	DDB Needham Life Style survey archive, 1977–99.
20	Bars, restaurants, and luncheonettes give way to fast food, 1970–1998	*1998 National Retail Census: Report to Retailers*, Jack Richman, ed. (New York: Audits & Surveys Worldwide, 1998).
21	The rise of card games in America, 1900–1951	Card sales from tax records: Jesse Frederick Steiner, *Americans at Play: Recent Trends in Recreation and Leisure Time Activities* (New York: McGraw-Hill, 1933), 138, updated with later data from the *Annual Report of the Commissioner of Internal Revenue* (Washington, D.C.: U.S. Department of the Treasury, various years) on excise tax on decks of playing cards; population aged fourteen and over: *Historical Statistics of the United States*, part I, 10, Series A 29–42.
22	Card playing and other leisure activities, 1975–1999	DDB Needham Life Style survey archive, 1975–99.
23	The decline of neighboring, 1974–1998	General Social Survey archive, 1974–98.
24	Informal socializing as measured in time diary studies, 1965–1995	Americans' Use of Time data archive, 1965–95. See appendix I for more details on this archive.
25	Stagnation in fitness (except walking)	DDB Needham Life Style survey archive, 1975–99.
26	The rise and decline of league bowling	American Bowling Congress *Annual Report, 1994* (Greendale, Wisc.: American Bowling Congress, 1994), updated with information from American Bowling Congress headquarters.
27	The growth of spectator sports, 1960–1998	*Historical Statistics of the United States: Statistical Abstract of the United States* (various years)
28	Volunteering fostered by clubgoing and churchgoing	DDB Needham Life Style survey archive, 1975–99.
29	*Schmoozing* and good works	DDB Needham Life Style survey archive, 1975–99.
30	Blood donation fostered by clubgoing and churchgoing	DDB Needham Life Style survey archive, 1981–84, 1986, 1992–94, and 1999. "Regular" blood donor means gave blood at least once in the last year or twice in the last three years or three times in the last five years.
31	The rise and fall of philanthropic generosity, 1929–1998	Contributions 1929–70: David Hammack and Dennis A. Young, eds., *Nonprofit Organizations in a Market Economy* (San Francisco: Jossey Bass, 1993), table 2.1; this series applies improved estimating procedures to the data provided in the *Internal Revenue Service Statistics of Income: Individual Income Tax Returns* and replaces earlier estimates such as series H399 in the 1975 edition of *Historical Statistics of the United States*. Like the earlier series, this one compensates for "overreporting" of contributions and contains estimates of contributions by those not reporting them to the Internal Revenue Service. The trends in both series are essentially identical, but the Hammack-Young series implies a slightly greater level of generosity throughout the period. Contributions 1967–98: *Giving USA 1998*, Ann

E. Kaplan, ed. (New York: American Association of Fund-Raising Counsel Trust for Philanthropy, 1998). Income: *Historical Statistics of the United States*, part I, 225, series F25, and Bureau of Economic Analysis, *National Income and Product Accounts* (U.S. Department of Commerce, Washington, D.C., 1998). The 1929–70 and 1967–98 series closely coincide for the four years in which they overlap (1967–70), suggesting that the two are generally comparable.

32   Trends in Protestant, Catholic, and United Way giving, 1920s–1990s

Protestant trends: John and Sylvia Ronsvalle, *The State of Church Giving through 1995* (Champaign, Ill.: emptytomb, 1997), 37. Catholic Trends: Andrew Greeley and William McManus, *Catholic Contributions: Sociology and Policy* (Chicago: Thomas More Press, 1987), updated in Andrew Greeley, *The Catholic Myth: The Behavior and Beliefs of American Catholics* (New York: Charles Scribner's Sons, 1990), 130, and further updated through 1989 by my own calculations from the General Social Survey archive, the source of Greeley's 1987–88 data. United Way: Data for numerator provided directly by United Way of America; for the period 1925–50, I have confirmed these data with the data given in F. Emerson Andrews, *Philanthropic Giving* (New York: Russell Sage Foundation, 1950), 142. Income data from Bureau of Economic Analysis, *National Income and Product Accounts*.

33   Reported charitable giving declined in the 1980s and 1990s

Unpublished data from Yankelovich Partners, Inc. (1981–99); Roper Political and Social Trends survey archives (November 1980, 1981, 1983, 1985, 1986, 1989, 1991, 1992, and 1994).

34   Volunteering up, community projects down, 1975–1999

DDB Needham Life Style survey archive, 1975–99.

35   Trends in volunteering by age category

DDB Needham Life Style survey archive, 1975–98.

36   Trends in participation in community projects by age category

DDB Needham Life Style survey archive, 1975–98.

37   Declining perceptions of honesty and morality, 1952–1998

1952, Ben Gaffin and Associates; 1965 and 1976, Gallup, 1998 *Washington Post* survey. The first three are taken from the POLL, online survey archive of the Roper Center for Public Opinion Research, University of Connecticut; the last from David S. Broder and Richard Morin, "Struggle over New Standards," *Washington Post* (December 27, 1998): A01.

38   Four decades of dwindling trust: adults and teenagers, 1960–1999

The primary sources for this figure are General Social Survey (1972–98); National Election Study (1964–98); DDB Needham Life Style survey archive (1975–99); Monitoring the Future survey archive (high school students, 1976–96). The first three sources are described in appendix I. The fourth is an annual survey conducted by the University of Michigan Survey Research Center and available through the Interuniversity Consortium for Political and Social Research. Additional data points were gleaned from the POLL online survey archive of the Roper Center for Public Opinion Research, University of Connecticut; Tom W. Smith, "Factors Relating to Misanthropy in Contemporary American Society," *Social Science Research* 26 (1997): 175; the World Values Surveys (1980, 1990, 1995), available from the Interuniversity Consortium for Political and Social Research; Robert E. Lane, "The Politics of Consensus in an Age of Affluence," *American Political Science Review* 59 (December 1965): 879; and Richard G. Niemi, John Mueller, and Tom W. Smith, *Trends in Public Opinion* (New York: Greenwood Press, 1989), 303. Missing data were excluded from all calculations. DDB Needham question is six-level agree/disagree item: "Most people are honest." The twenty-five-year trend for this question is essentially identical to that for the standard question "Most people can be trusted" vs. "You can't be too careful," although the absolute level of agreement to the DDB Needham question is c. 10 percent higher.

FIGURE NUMBER	TITLE	SOURCE OF DATA
39	Generational succession explains most of the decline in social trust	DDB Needham Life Style survey archive, 1975–1999.
40	The changing observance of stop signs	John Trinkaus, "Stop Sign Compliance: An Informal Look," *Psychological Reports* 50 (1982): 288; Trinkaus, "Stop Sign Compliance: Another Look," *Perceptual and Motor Skills* 57 (1983): 922; Trinkaus, "Stop Sign Compliance, A Further Look," *Perceptual and Motor Skills* 67 (1988): 670; Trinkaus, "Stop Sign Compliance: A Follow-up Look," *Perceptual and Motor Skills* 76 (1993): 1218; Trinkaus, "Stop Sign Compliance: A Final Look," *Perceptual and Motor Skills* 85 (1997): 217–218.
41	U.S. crime rates, 1960–1997	*Statistical Abstract of the U.S. 1997; Crime in the U.S. 1997* (Washington, D.C.: Federal Bureau of Investigation, 1998).
42	Employment in policing and the law soared after 1970	1900–70: *Historical Statistics of the United States,* part I, D589-D592, 144; 1970–96: *Statistical Abstract of the United States* and data provided directly by the Bureau of Labor Statistics (BLS). These data refer to actual employment, not professional qualification, so law school graduates who no longer practice law are excluded. Both the BLS and the Census Bureau have gone to great lengths to maintain the comparability of the operational definition of the various professions over time.
43	Explosive growth of national environmental organizations, 1960–1998	Post-1970: Bosso, "The Color of Money," and Bosso, "Facing the Future." Pre-1970: Mitchell, Mertig, and Dunlap, "Twenty Years of Environmental Mobilization." In a few cases I have interpolated data for missing years in order to avoid severe distortions in the series.
44	Initiatives on statewide ballots in the United States, 1900–1998	Data provided by M. Dane Waters of the Initiative and Referendum Institute.
45	The graying of protest demonstrations	Data for 1974 from Samuel H. Barnes, Max Kaase, et al. Political Action: An Eight Nation Study, 1973–76; for 1981 from M. Kent Jennings, Jan W. van Deth, et al. Political Action II, 1979–81; for 1980 and 1990 from World Values Study Group, World Values Survey, 1981–84 and 1990–93. All these survey archives are distributed through Interuniversity Consortium for Political and Social Research (University of Michigan: Ann Arbor, Michigan). Data for 1995 from World Values Survey provided directly by Ronald Inglehart.
46	Trends in telephones, calls, and letters	Household penetration: *Trends in Telephone Service* (Washington, D.C.: Federal Communications Commission, September 1999) staff estimates based on data from *Historical Statistics of the United States,* II: 783, except 1980 and 1990, which are from the decennial censuses. Prior to 1920 household penetration rates are estimates extrapolated from data on telephones per capita. Personal phone calls and letters: Roper Social and Political Trends survey archive, 1973–1994.
47	Working by choice and by necessity among American women, 1978–1999	DDB Needham Life Style survey archive, 1978, 1980–99.
48	More women work because they must, 1978–1999	DDB Needham Life Style survey archive, 1978, 1980–99.

49	Working full-time reduces community involvement	DDB Needham Life Style survey archive, 1978, 1980–99.
50	Community involvement is lower in major metropolitan areas	Roper Social and Political Trends survey archive, 1974–94.
51	Church attendance is lower in major metropolitan areas	DDB Needham Life Style survey archive, 1975–98.
52	The suburbanization of America, 1950–1996	For 1950–70: *Historical Statistics of the United States*, I: 40, series A276-287; for 1980–90, *1990 Census Population and Housing Unit Count* (Washington, D.C.: U.S. Bureau of the Census, 1995), table 48. For 1992 and 1995: data provided directly by Census Bureau. Note that to maintain comparability 1980 figures are based on standard metropolitan areas as defined in 1990.
53	Generational succession explains the demise of newspapers	General Social Survey archive, 1972–98.
54	Newshounds are a vanishing breed	DDB Needham Life Style survey archive, 1986–99.
55	A half century's growth in television watching, 1950–1998	*Nielsen Report on Television 1998* (New York: Nielsen, 1998); *Communications Industry Report, 1997* (New York: Veronis, Suhler & Associates, 1998); Cobbett S. Steinberg, *TV Facts* (New York: Facts on File, 1980). Data restricted to households with TV.
56	Screens proliferate in American homes	Data on VCRs and TV sets: *Statistical Abstract of the United States* (various years); computer and Internet usage, DDB Needham Life Style survey archive, 1988–99.
57	TV becomes an American habit, as selective viewing declines	Roper Social and Political Trends survey archive, 1975, 1979, 1985, and 1989.
58	Channel surfing is more common among younger generations	J. Walker Smith and Ann Clurman, *Rocking the Ages: The Yankelovich Report on Generational Marketing* (New York: HarperBusiness, 1997), 181, citing 1996 Yankelovich Monitor.
59	America watches TV all day every day	DDB Needham Life Style survey archive, 1993–98.
60	In the evening Americans, above all, watch TV	Roper Social and Political Trends survey archive, 1985 and 1989.
61	More TV means less civic engagement (among college-educated, working-age adults)	Roper Social and Political Trends survey archive, 1973, 1974, 1977, 1983, 1988, 1991, and 1993; analysis limited to respondents aged thirty to fifty-nine with at least some college education (N = 13149).
62	TV watching and volunteering don't go together	DDB Needham Life Style survey archive, 1975–98.
63	TV watchers don't keep in touch	DDB Needham Life Style survey archive, 1975–78.
64	TV watching and club meetings don't go together	DDB Needham Life Style survey archive, 1975–98.
65	TV watching and churchgoing don't go together	DDB Needham Life Style survey archive, 1975–98.

FIGURE NUMBER	TITLE	SOURCE OF DATA
66	TV watching and comity don't go together	DDB Needham Life Style survey archive, 1975–98 (1997–98 for "give finger to another driver").
67	Americans began cocooning in the 1970s	Roper Social and Political Trends survey archive, 1974–75, 1977, 1979.
68	TV watchers don't feel so great	DDB Needham Life Style survey archive, 1975–98.
69	Types of television programs and civic engagement, controlling for time spent watching TV	Roper Social and Political Trends survey archive, 1994, N = 1,482. Results based on probabilities calculated from logistic regression, generated using Monte Carlo simulation. Controls include education, household income, sex, age, race, marital status, employment status, size of community, year of study, watching prime-time TV, watching sports programs, and total time spent watching TV.
70	Membership in associations rises and falls with age	General Social Survey archive, 1972–94.
71a, 71b	Generational trends in civic engagement	Vote: National Election Study, 1952–96; newspaper readership: General Social Survey, 1972–98; social trust: General Social Survey, 1972–98; community project: DDB Needham Life Style, 1975–98; group membership: General Social Survey, 1974–94; interest in politics: DDB Needham Life Style, 1975–98; church attendance: General Social Survey, 1972–98; club attendance: DDB Needham Life Style, 1975–98.
72	Greed trumps community among college freshmen, 1966–1998	UCLA College Freshmen Survey Archive, 1966–98, as reported in Linda J. Sax et al., *The American Freshman* (Los Angeles: UCLA Higher Education Research Institute, 1998) and earlier volumes in this series.
73	Age-related differences in suicide rates, 1950–1995	*Sourcebook of Criminal Justice Statistics—1995*, Kathleen Maguire and Ann L. Pastore, eds. (Albany, N.Y.: Hindelang Criminal Justice Research Center, 1996), 365.
74	Growing generation gap in malaise	DDB Needham Life Style survey archive, 1975–99.
75	From generation to generation, patriotism wanes, materialism waxes	Wall Street Journal/NBC News Poll (July 1998).
76	Materialism grows in the final decades of the twentieth century	Roper Social and Political Trends archive, 1976, 1979, 1982, 1985, 1989, 1992, augmented for 1995 and 1997 from the relevant *Roper Reports* (New York: Roper Starch Worldwide, various years).
77	The meaning of community for successive generations	Yankelovich Partners, Inc. surveys, 1997–99.
78	Government spending, 1947–1998	Bureau of Economic Analysis, *National Income Accounts* (U.S. Department of Commerce, Washington, D.C., 1999).
79	Guesstimated explanation for civic disengagement, 1965–2000	Author's estimates from multiple analyses reported in section III.
80	Social capital in the American states	See sources for table 4 below.
81	Kids are better off in high-social-capital states	See sources for tables 4 and 5 below. Data on both variables available for 48 states.

#	Claim	Source
82	Schools work better in high-social-capital states	See sources for table 4 below. Our index of educational performance is based on the following: (1) State-level data from seven nationwide National Assessment of Educational Progress (NAEP) tests drawn from *Digest of Education Statistics: 1992, Digest of Education Statistics: 1995, NAEP 1996 Science Report Card for the Nation and the States,* and *NAEP 1996 Mathematics Report Card for the Nation and the States,* all published by the National Center for Education Statistics (Washington, D.C.: Department of Education, various years): reading proficiency for fourth-graders in 1994; science proficiency for eighth-graders in 1996; math proficiency for fourth-graders in 1992 and 1996; and math proficiency for eighth-graders in 1990, 1992, and 1996. (2) Participation-adjusted Scholastic Achievement Test (SAT) scores from Brian Powell and Lala Carr Steelman, "Bewitched, Bothered, and Bewildering: The Use and Misuse of State SAT and ACT Scores," *Harvard Educational Review* 66 (1996) 38. (3) Six convergent (though not identical) measures of high school dropout rates: the percentage of "status dropouts," ages sixteen to nineteen for 1990, as reported in *Digest of Education Statistics: 1992,* 13; the percentage of those aged sixteen to nineteen in the 1990 census who were not in regular school and had not completed twelfth grade or a GED, as reported in the *Statistical Abstract of the U.S., 1995*: 159; the percentage of those aged sixteen to nineteen in 1993–95 who were not enrolled in school and had not completed high school or a GED, as reported in *Kids Count 1997*; the "public high school graduation rate, 1989–1990," as reported in Victoria Van Son, *CQ's State Fact Finder* (Washington, D.C.: Congressional Quarterly, 1993), 106; and the high school completion rates for 1990–92 and for 1993–95 (*Digest of Education Statistics: 1997*). Data on both variables available for 48 states.
83	Kids watch less TV in high-social-capital states	See sources for table 4 below; NAEP measures of daily television watching by eighth-graders in 1990 and 1992 and fourth-graders in 1992, as reported in *Digest of Education Statistics: 1992* and *Digest of Education Statistics: 1995.* Data on both variables available for 44 states.
84	Violent crime is rarer in high-social-capital states	See sources for table 4 below; *Crime in the United States, 1997* (Washington, D.C.: Federal Bureau of Investigation, 1998). Data on both variables available for 48 states.
85	States high in social capital are less pugnacious	See sources for table 4 below; DDB Needham Life Style survey archive, 1976–98. Data on both variables available for 48 states.
86	Health is better in high-social-capital states	See sources for tables 4 and 6 below; Ichiro Kawachi, Bruce P. Kennedy, Kimberly Lochner, and Deborah Prothrow-Stith, "Social Capital, Income Inequality, and Mortality," *American Journal of Public Health* 87 (1997): 1491–1498. Data on both variables available for 48 states.
87	Americans don't feel as healthy as we used to	DDB Needham Life Style survey archive, 1975–99.
88	Social connectedness (at least in moderation) fosters happiness	DDB Needham Life Style survey archive, 1975–98.
89	Tax evasion is low where social capital is high	See sources for table 4 below; Internal Revenue Service criminal referrals and convictions per 100,000 population (1992–97) factor score, drawn from Transactional Records Access Clearinghouse, Syracuse University. Data on both variables available for 48 states.
90	Tolerance grows for racial integration, civil liberties, and gender equality	General Social Survey archive, 1974–96.
91	Social capital and tolerance go together	See sources for table 4 below; General Social Survey archive, 1974–96. Data on both variables available for 43 states.

FIGURE NUMBER	TITLE	SOURCE OF DATA
92	Social capital and economic equality go together	See sources for table 4 below; Kawachi, Kennedy, Lochner, and Prothrow-Stith, "Social Capital, Income Inequality, and Mortality." Data on both variables available for 48 states.
93	Social capital and civic equality go together	See sources for table 4 below; Roper Social and Political Trends survey archive, 1974–94. Data on both variables available for 42 states.
94	Associational density in 26 American communities, 1840–1940	Gerald Gamm and Robert D. Putnam, "The Growth of Voluntary Associations in America, 1840–1940," *Journal of Interdisciplinary History* 29 (1999): 511–557.
95	Founding and cumulative incidence of large membership associations	Theda Skocpol, "How Americans Became Civic," in *Civic Engagement in American Democracy*, Theda Skocpol and Morris P. Fiorina, eds. (Washington, D.C.: Brookings Institution Press, 1999): 54, figure 2–3.
96	Founding dates of contemporary U.S. associations	*Encarta 2000 New World Almanac* (Oxford: Helicon Publishing Ltd., 1998).

TABLE NUMBER	TITLE	SOURCE OF DATA
1	Trends in political and community participation	Roper Social and Political Trends archive, 1974–94.
2	Pace of introduction of selected consumer goods	Sue Bowden and Avner Offer, "Household Appliances and the Use of Time: The United States and Britain Since the 1920s," *Economic History Review* 47 (November 1994): 729, supplemented by data from the *Statistical Abstract of the United States* (various years)
3	All forms of civic disengagement are concentrated in younger cohorts	Newspaper readership: General Social Survey, 1972–98; all other forms of participation: Roper Social and Political Trends archive, 1974–94, supplemented by data on church attendance from *Roper Reports* (New York: Roper-Starch Worldwide, 1996–98).
4	Measuring social capital in the American states: Components of Social Capital Index	
	Served on committee for local organization last year	Roper Social and Political Trends archive, 1974–94.
	"Most people can be trusted" vs. "Can't be too careful"	General Social Survey, 1974–96.
	Agree "Most people are honest."	DDB Needham Life Style archive, 1975–98.
	Voting turnout in presidential elections	U.S. Census Bureau, 1988 and 1992.
	Served as officer of local organization last year	Roper Social and Political Trends archive, 1974–94.
	501(c)(3) charitable organizations per 1,000 pop.	*Non-profit Almanac, 1989* (San Francisco: Jossey-Bass, 1989).
	Attended club meetings: frequency last year	DDB Needham Life Style archive, 1975–98.
	Civic and social organizations per 100,000 pop.	County Business Patterns, Dept. of Commerce, 1977–92.
	Attended public meeting on town or school affairs	Roper Social and Political Trends archive, 1974–94.
	Organizational memberships per capita	General Social Survey, 1974–96.
	"I spend a lot of time visiting friends."	DDB Needham Life Style archive, 1975–98.
	Entertained at home: frequency last year	DDB Needham Life Style archive, 1975–98.
	Did volunteer work: frequency last year	DDB Needham Life Style archive, 1975–98.
	Worked on community project: frequency last year	DDB Needham Life Style archive, 1975–98.
5	Kids Count index of child welfare	Annie E. Casey Foundation (Baltimore, Md., 1999), Web site www.aecf.org/kidscount/index.htm.
6	Which state has the best health and health care	Morgan-Quitno Health Care State Rankings (1993–98), compiled by Morgan-Quitno Press (Lawrence, Kans.) and downloaded from www.morganquitno.com.
7	Indexes of tolerance for racial integration, gender equality, and civil liberties	General Social Survey, 1974–98.
8	Social capital and tolerance: Four types of society	Author's analysis.
9	Social capital innovations, 1870–1920	Founding dates from national headquarters of various associations, supplemented and confirmed by data from *World Almanac* (New York: Press Pub. Co. [New York World], various years), *Encyclopedia of Associations* (Detroit, Mich.: Gale Research, various years), and histories of particular organizations.

APPENDIX III

The Rise and Fall
of Civic and
Professional Associations

Organization	Founded	"Constituency" for calculating membership rate per 1,000	Growth in membership rate from 1940 to 1945 to peak year	Membership rate plateau begins	Year of peak membership rate	Membership rate plateau ends	Decline in membership rate from peak year to 1997	Membership rate (per 1,000) in peak year
Civic Associations								
4-H	1901	Rural youth	54%	1950	1950	1976	−26%	180
American Association of University Women	1881	Women with college degrees	15%	1930	1955	1955	−84%	53
American Bowling Congress	1895	Men aged 20 and over	434%	1964	1964	1979	−72%	83
American Legion	1919	All wartime veterans	10%	1940	1945	1945	−47%	274
B'nai B'rith	1843	Jewish men	90%	1947	1947	1965	−75% est.	78
Boy and Girl Scout adult leaders	1910–12	Youth aged 5–17	190%	1957	1957	1958	−18%	50
Boy Scouts and Girl Scouts	1910–12	Youth aged 5–17	134%	1957	1972	1973	−8%	156
Boy Scouts	1910	Boys aged 5–17	118%	1958	1972	1997	−5%	190
Girl Scouts	1912	Girls aged 5–17	174%	1956	1969	1971	−15%	125
Business and Professional Women (BPW)	1919	White-collar working women	51%	1949	1951	1951	−89%	17
Eagles	1898	Men aged 20 and over	82%	1947	1947	1950	−72%	29
Eastern Star, Order of the	1868	Women aged 20 and over	18%	1930	1930	1961	−73%	50
Elks	1868	Men aged 20 and over	107%	1962	1970	1977	−46%	25
General Federation of Women's Clubs	1890	Women aged 20 and over	56%	1949	1956	1956	−84%	16
Grange	1867	Rural population	42%	1951	1952	1955	−79%	16
Hadassah	1912	Jewish women	153%	1950	1983	1986	−15%	123
Jaycees	1915	Men aged 20–34	na	1973	1975	1978	−58%	5
Kiwanis	1915	Men aged 20 and over	94%	1956	1960	1966	−42%	5
Knights of Columbus	1882	Catholic males	46%	1949	1954	1959	−6%	14
League of Women Voters	1920	Women aged 20 and over	125%	1954	1965	1969	−61%	2
Lions	1917	Men aged 20 and over	129%	1957	1967	1976	−58%	9
Masons	1733	Men aged 20 and over	38%	1927	1927	1957	−71%	90
Moose (male members only)	1888	Men aged 20 and over	181%	1950	1980	1980	−35%	19
Moose (women members only)	1927	Women aged 20 and over	208%	1990	1990	1995	−3%	6
NAACP	1909	African Americans	69%	1944	1944	1969	−46%	31
Odd Fellows	1819	Men aged 20 and over	0%	1920	1920	1920	−94%	54
Optimists	1919	Men aged 20 and over	85%	1985	1990	1990	−24%	2
Parent-Teacher Association	1897	Families with children under 18	111%	1957	1960	1966	−60%	48
Red Cross (volunteers)	1881	Adults aged 20 and over	45%	1956	1956	1970	−61%	19

Rotary	1905	Men aged 20 and over	60%	1949	1967	1990	−25%	5
Shriners	1872	Men aged 20 and over	36%	1958	1960	1962	−59%	15
Veterans of Foreign Wars	1899	All wartime veterans	110%	1945	1945	1995	−9%	114
Women's Bowling Congress	1917	Women aged 20 and over	1121%	1965	1978	1978	−66%	54
Women's Christian Temperance Union	1874	Women aged 20 and over	4%	1920	1920	1920	−96%	11
Median	**1900**		**85%**	**1951**	**1959**	**1969**	**−58%**	**30**
Professional Associations								
American Bar Association	1878	Employed lawyers		1977	1977	1989		503
American Dental Association	1859	Active, licensed dentists		1960	1970	1970		960
American Institute of Architects	1857	Employed architects		c. 1950	1970	c. 1970		409
American Institute of Certified Public Accountants	1887	Employed accountants		1987	1992–93	1993		198
American Medical Association	1847	Licensed physicians		1949	1959	1959		745
American Nursing Association	1896	Registered nurses		na	Before 1977	na		At least 176
American Society of Mechanical Engineers	1880	Employed mechanical engineers		1951	1930	1993		400
American Institute of Electrical Engineers and Institute of Radio Engineers to 1961; Institute of Electrical and Electronics Engineers after 1961	1884	Employed electrical and electronic engineers		1952	1961	1961		620
Median	**1879**			**1952**	**1970**	**1970**		**456**

Notes: (1) In all cases where significant, non-U.S. members excluded from membership numbers

(2) Female members excluded from traditionally male fraternal organization membership numbers (although women Moose members broken out separately)

(3) World War II spike in Red Cross volunteers has been excluded from calculations about peak and rate of decline.

4-H

B'nai B'rith

American Assn of University Women

Boy and Girl Scout Adult Leaders

American Bowling Congress

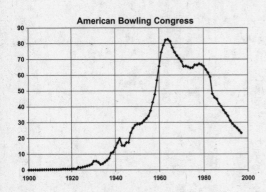

Boy and Girl Scouts

American Legion

Business and Professional Women

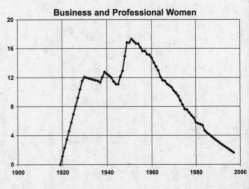

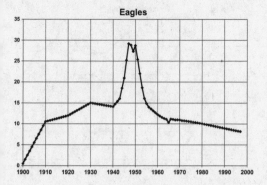

Eagles

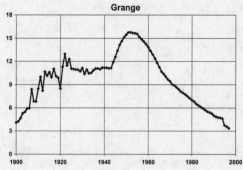

Grange

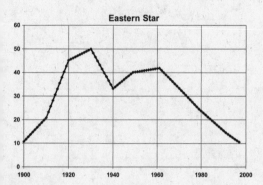

Eastern Star

Hadassah

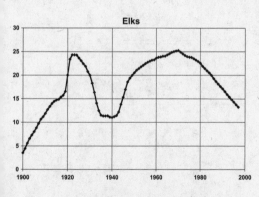

Elks

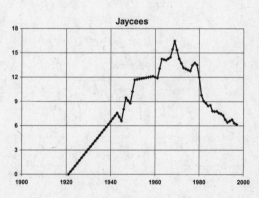

Jaycees

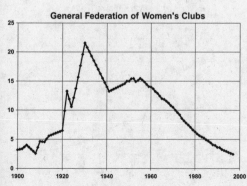

General Federation of Women's Clubs

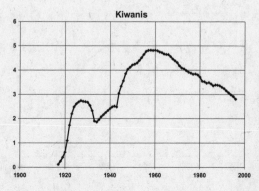

Kiwanis

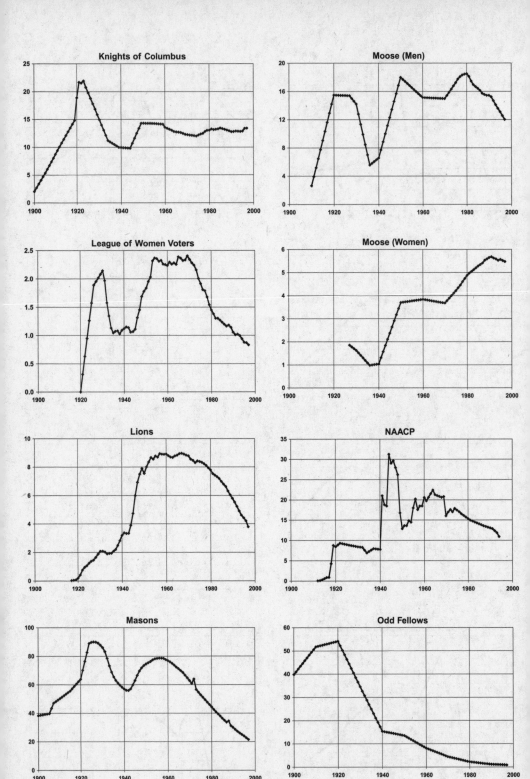

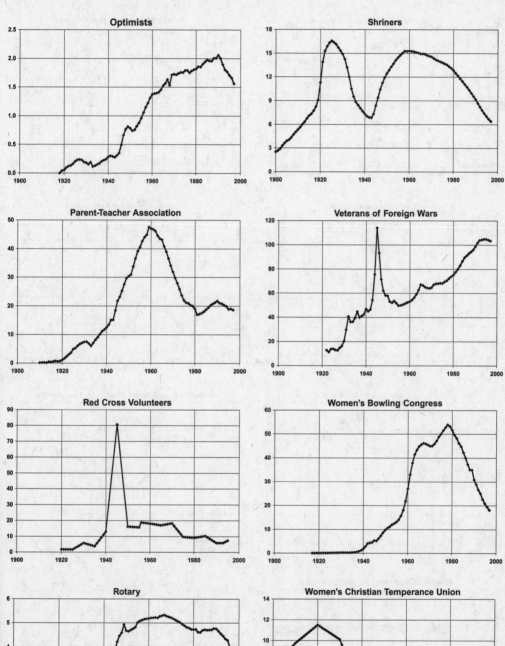

Optimists

Shriners

Parent-Teacher Association

Veterans of Foreign Wars

Red Cross Volunteers

Women's Bowling Congress

Rotary

Women's Christian Temperance Union

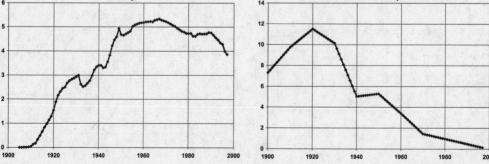

American Bar Association

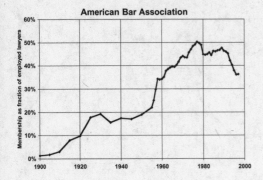

American Medical Association

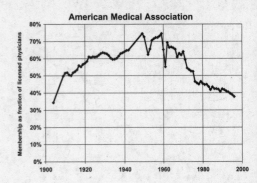

American Dental Association

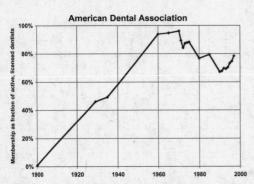

American Nursing Association

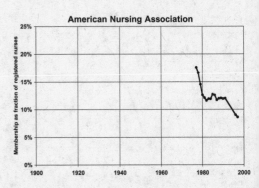

American Institute of Architects

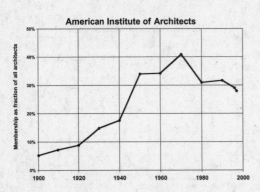

American Society of Mechanical Engineers

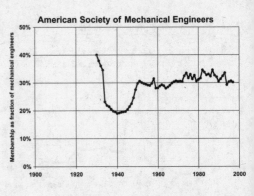

American Institute of Certified Public Accountants

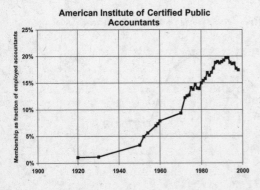

Electrical and Electronic Engineers

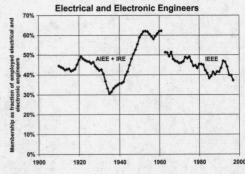

Notes

PREFACE

1. The drafting of this preface was interrupted by an unexpected bout of illness, and I am extremely grateful to Shaylyn Romney Garrett for stepping in to help craft my rough notes into this final version.

2. For a fuller account of how *Bowling Alone* came to be, see "The Story Behind This Book," pages 545–553 above.

3. For the best, quite critical, but fair-minded scholarly review of *Bowling Alone*, focused especially on the concept of "social capital," see Claude S. Fischer, "Bowling Alone: What's the Score?" *Social Networks* 27 (2005): 155–167. For independent assessments of the basic empirical claims of *Bowling Alone*, see, among other sources, Dora L. Costa and Matthew E. Kahn, "Understanding the American Decline in Social Capital, 1952–1998," *Kyklos* 56 (2003): 17–46; and U.S. Congress Joint Economic Committee, "What We Do Together: The State of Associational Life in America," Social Capital Project Report 01–17, May 15, 2017, https://www.jec.senate.gov/public/index.cfm/republicans/2017/5/what-we-do-together-the-state-of-associational-life-in-america.

4. See chapter 3 of the present book.

5. For extensive citations to relevant research, including updated curves for organizational membership, see Robert D. Putnam with Shaylyn Romney Garrett, *The Upswing: How America Came Together a Century Ago and How We Can Do It Again* (New York: Simon & Schuster, 2020), chapter 4.

6. See chapter 4 of the present book. For later data, see Robert D. Putnam and David Campbell, *American Grace: How Religion Divides and Unites Us* (New York: Simon & Schuster, 2010). For many more citations to relevant research, including updated curves for church membership and attendance, see Putnam with Garrett, *The Upswing*, chapter 4.

7. See chapter 5 of the present book; Barry T. Hirsch and David A. Macpherson, "Union Membership and Coverage Database from the Current Population Survey: Note," *Industrial and Labor Relations Review* 56, no. 2 (January 2003): 349–354 (updated annually at http://unionstats.com/). For a full discussion of the fate of unions in recent decades, see Putnam with Garrett, *The Upswing*, chapter 4.

8. See chapter 7 of the present book.

9. For discussion and citations related to recent trends in philanthropic giving, see Putnam with Garrett, *The Upswing*, chapter 4.

10. On social trust, see chapter 8 of the present book. For more on recent trends in social trust, see Putnam with Garrett, *The Upswing*, chapter 4.

11. For recent trends in volunteerism, see U.S. Congress Joint Economic Committee, "Further Thoughts on Volunteerism Trends and Data Issues," January 29, 2018, https://www.jec.senate.gov/public/index.cfm/republicans/analysis?ID=89B2FA75-F965-4B71-A4AB-95252C62C837.

12. See pages 127–133 of the present book.

13. For the basic evidence on political participation as of 2000, see chapter 2 of the present book.

14. On political alienation, see Putnam with Garrett, *The Upswing*, chapter 3.

15. For the basic argument about informal social interaction, see chapter 6 of the present book.

16. Miller McPherson, Lynn Smith-Lovin, and Matthew E. Brashears, "Social Isolation in America: Changes in

Core Discussion Networks over Two Decades," *American Sociological Review* 71, no. 3 (2006): 353–375, https://doi .org/10.1177/000312240607100301.

17. Claude S. Fischer, "The 2004 GSS Finding of Shrunken Social Networks: An Artifact?," *American Sociological Review* 74 (August 2009): 657–669; and Claude S. Fischer, *Still Connected: Family and Friends in America Since 1970* (New York: Russell Sage, 2011).

18. Matthew E. Brashears, "Small Networks and High Isolation?: A Reexamination of American Discussion Networks," *Social Networks* 33, no. 4 (2011): 331–341; and Matthew E. Brashears and Laura Aufderheide Brashears, "Do Contemporary People Have Fewer Friends Than They Used To?," in Robert Scott and Stephen Kosslyn, eds., *Emerging Trends in the Social and Behavioral Sciences* (Hoboken, N.J.: John Wiley and Sons, 2015).

19. Keith N. Hampton, Lauren F. Sessions, Eun Ja Her, and Lee Rainie, "Social Isolation and New Technology: How the Internet and Mobile Phones Impact Americans' Social Networks," Pew Internet and American Life Project, Pew Research Center, November 2009; see also Keith N. Hampton, Lauren F. Sessions, and Eun Ja Her, "Core Networks, Social Isolation, and New Media: How Internet and Mobile Phone Use Is Related to Network Size and Diversity," *Information, Communication & Society* 14, no. 1 (2011): 130–155, https://doi.org/10.1080/13691 18X.2010.513417.

20. Peter V. Marsden and Sameer B. Srivastava, "Trends in Informal Social Participation, 1974–2008," in Peter V. Marsden, *Social Trends in American Life: Findings from the General Social Survey Since 1972* (Princeton, N.J.: Princeton University Press, 2012), 240–264, https://doi.org/10.1515/9781400845569.

21. *Rochester Democrat and Chronicle*, Our Towns, March 7, 2001, 1.

22. Saguaro Seminar at the John F. Kennedy School of Government, Harvard University, 2000 Social Capital Community Benchmark Survey, https://ropercenter.cornell.edu/featured-collections/2000-social-capital-community -benchmark-survey.

23. See pages 290–294 of the present book.

24. Jed Sundwall, "Making People Powerful—Interview with Scott Heiferman from Meetup," NetSquared blog post, 2008, https://netsquared.org/blog/jedsundwall/making-people-powerful-interview-scott-heiferman-meetup.

25. "From Neighborliness to Social Capital," *Franconia Heritage News* 17 (April 2001).

26. *Wellness Bound* 2, no. 4 (2004).

27. See, for example, Edward S. Adams and Richard A. Saliterman, The Trusteeship of Legal Rulemaking, 30 HOFSTRA L. REV. 483 (2001), available at https://scholarship.law.umn.edu/faculty_articles/138; Jason Mazzone, "The Social Capital Argument for Federalism," *Southern California Interdisciplinary Law Journal* 11 (2001): 27–62, https://ssrn.com/abstract=933348; Jason Mazzone, "The Benefits of Social Capital," in Karen Christensen and David Levinson, eds., *Encyclopedia of Community: From the Village to the Virtual World* (Thousand Oaks, Calif.: Sage Publications, 2003); Mariana Zuleta Ferrari, "Trust in Legal Institutions: An Empirical Approach from a Social Capital Perspective," Oñati Socio-Legal Series 6, no. 5 (December 2016), Tilburg Law School Research Paper no. 02/2017, https://ssrn.com/abstract=2890155.

28. Bush offered this explanation in a seminar at Harvard, among other settings, on September 30, 2016. The article that he had read was Robert D. Putnam, "Bowling Alone: America's Declining Social Capital," *Journal of Democracy* 6 , no. 1 (January 1995): 65–78.

29. WMAL Radio, AIR Network, transcript of Rush Limbaugh, July 6, 2000, 12:30 p.m.

30. https://www.washingtonpost.com/news/wonk/wp/2015/03/06/the-terrible-loneliness-of-growing-up-poor-in -robert-putnams-america/.

31. Robert D. Putnam with Lewis Feldstein and Don Cohen, *Better Together: Restoring the American Community* (New York: Simon & Schuster, 2003).

32. Alan Ryan, "My Way," *New York Review of Books*, August 10, 2000.

CHAPTER 1: THINKING ABOUT SOCIAL CHANGE IN AMERICA

1. David Scott and Geoffrey Godbey, "Recreation Specialization in the Social World of Contract Bridge," *Journal of Leisure Research* 26 (1994): 275–295; Suzi Parker, "Elks, Lions May Go Way of the Dodo," *Christian Science Monitor*, August 24, 1998; John D. Cramer, "Relevance of Local NAACP Is Up for Debate," *Roanoke Times*, January 24, 1999; Dirk Johnson, "As Old Soldiers Die, V.F.W. Halls Fade Away," *New York Times*, September 6, 1999. I am grateful to Professor David Scott for information about the Glenn Valley Bridge Club; "Glenn Valley" is a pseudonym for a college town in central Pennsylvania.

2. Christine Wicker, "A Common Thread of Decency," *Dallas Morning News*, May 1, 1999; David Streitfeld, "The Last Chapter: After 50 Years, Vassar Ends Its Famed Book Sale," *Washington Post*, April 28, 1999, C1; Caroline Louise Cole, "So Many New Uniforms, but So Few Musicians," *Boston Sunday Globe Northwest Weekly*, September 5, 1999, 1.

3. Jeffrey A. Charles, *Service Clubs in American Society: Rotary, Kiwanis, and Lions* (Urbana: University of Illinois Press, 1993), 157.

4. Eric Larrabee and Rolf Meyersohn, *Mass Leisure* (Glencoe, Ill.: Free Press, 1958), 359, as quoted in Foster Rhea Dulles, *A History of Recreation: America Learns to Play*, 2nd ed. (New York: Appleton-Century-Crofts, 1965), 390.

5. *Life*, February 21, 1964, 91, 93. I am grateful to Rob Paarlberg for spotting this remarkable issue in a Maine flea market.

6. Robert E. Lane, *Political Life: Why People Get Involved in Politics* (Glencoe, Ill.: Free Press, 1959), 94; Daniel Bell and Virginia Held, "The Community Revolution," *The Public Interest* 16 (1969): 142.

7. In fact, turnout in 1976 was 53 percent and falling. See Richard A. Brody, "The Puzzle of Political Participation in America," in *The New American Political System*, ed. Anthony King (Washington, D.C.: American Enterprise Institute for Public Policy Research, 1978).

8. George H. Gallup, *The Gallup Poll: Public Opinion 1935–1971* (New York: Random House, 1972); Karlyn Bowman, "Do You Want to Be President?," *Public Perspective* 8 (February/March 1997): 40; Robert E. Lane, "The Politics of Consensus in an Age of Affluence," *American Political Science Review* 59 (December 1965): 879; and Richard G. Niemi, John Mueller, and Tom W. Smith, *Trends in Public Opinion* (New York: Greenwood Press, 1989), 303. The version of the "trust" question used in the 1940s, 1950s, and 1960s is not directly comparable to the one that has become standard in most recent years.

9. See Thomas R. Rochon, *Culture Moves: Ideas, Activism, and Changing Values* (Princeton, N.J.: Princeton University Press, 1998), xiii–xiv.

10. Doug McAdam, *Freedom Summer* (New York: Oxford University Press, 1988), 14–15.

11. James Q. Wilson, "Why Are We Having a Wave of Violence?" *The New York Times Magazine*, May 19, 1968, 120.

12. Lyda Judson Hanifan, "The Rural School Community Center," *Annals of the American Academy of Political and Social Science* 67 (1916): 130–138, quotation at 130. Ever the practical reformer, Hanifan was self-conscious about using the term *capital* to encourage hard-nosed businessmen and economists to recognize the productive importance of social assets. Having introduced the idea of social capital, he observes, "That there is a great lack of such social capital in some rural districts need not be retold in this chapter. The important question at this time is: How can these conditions be improved? The story which follows is an account of the way a West Virginia rural community in a single year actually developed social capital and then used this capital in the improvement of its recreational, intellectual, moral, and economic conditions." His essay, which included a list of practical exercises for community-based activists, was originally prepared in 1913 for West Virginia schoolteachers as "a handbook for community meetings at rural schoolhouses," and it was subsequently incorporated in L. J. Hanifan, *The Community Center* (Boston: Silver, Burdett, 1920). I am grateful to Brad Clarke for first spotting this usage of the term *social capital*.

13. John R. Seeley, Alexander R. Sim, and Elizabeth W. Loosley, *Crestwood Heights: A Study of the Culture of Suburban Life* (New York: Basic Books, 1956); Jane Jacobs, *The Death and Life of Great American Cities* (New York: Random House, 1961); Glenn Loury, "A Dynamic Theory of Racial Income Differences," in *Women, Minorities, and Employment Discrimination*, ed. P. A. Wallace and A. LeMund (Lexington, Mass.: Lexington Books, 1977), 153–188; Pierre Bourdieu, "Forms of Capital," in *Handbook of Theory and Research for the Sociology of Education*, ed. John G. Richardson (New York: Greenwood Press, 1983), 241–258; Ekkehart Schlicht, "Cognitive Dissonance in Economics," in *Normengeleitetes Verhalten in den Sozialwissenschaften* (Berlin: Duncker and Humblot, 1984), 61–81; James S. Coleman, "Social Capital in the Creation of Human Capital," *American Journal of Sociology* 94 (1988): S95–S120; and James S. Coleman, *Foundations of Social Theory* (Cambridge, Mass.: Harvard University Press, 1990). See also George C. Homans, *Social Behavior: Its Elementary Forms* (New York: Harcourt, Brace & World, 1961), 378–98. Except for a brief acknowledgment by Coleman of Loury's work, I can find no evidence that any of these theorists were aware of any of the preceding usages. For a comprehensive overview of the conceptual history of "social capital," see Michael Woolcock, "Social Capital and Economic Development: Toward a Theoretical Synthesis and Policy Framework," *Theory and Society* 27 (1998): 151–208.

14. Ronald S. Burt, *Structural Holes: The Social Structure of Competition* (Cambridge, Mass.: Harvard University Press, 1992); Ronald S. Burt, "The Contingent Value of Social Capital," *Administrative Science Quarterly* 42 (1997): 339–365; and Ronald S. Burt, "The Gender of Social Capital," *Rationality & Society* 10 (1998): 5–46; Claude S. Fischer, "Network Analysis and Urban Studies," in *Networks and Places: Social Relations in the Urban Setting*, ed. Claude S. Fischer (New York: Free Press, 1977), 19; James D. Montgomery, "Social Networks and Labor-Market Outcomes: Toward an Economic Analysis," *American Economic Review* 81 (1991): 1408–1418, esp. table 1.

15. In earlier work I emphasized this public dimension of social capital almost to the exclusion of the private returns to social capital. See Robert D. Putnam, "The Prosperous Community: Social Capital and Public Affairs," *The American Prospect* 13 (1993): 35–42, on which the present text draws. For a literature review that highlights the private returns almost to the exclusion of the collective dimension, see Alejandro Portes, "Social Capital: Its Origins and Applications in Modern Sociology," *Annual Review of Sociology* 22 (1998): 1–24.

16. Robert Frank in private conversation.

17. Xavier de Souza Briggs, "Social Capital and the Cities: Advice to Change Agents," *National Civic Review* 86 (summer 1997): 111–117.

18. *U.S. News & World Report* (August 4, 1997): 18. Fareed Zakaria, "Bigger Than the Family, Smaller Than the State," *New York Times Book Review*, August 13, 1995: 1, pointed out that McVeigh and his co-conspirators spent evenings together in a bowling alley and concluded that "we would all have been better off if Mr. McVeigh had gone bowling alone." Sometimes, as in certain cults or clans, even the *internal* effects of social capital can be negative, but these are less common than negative *external* effects.

19. In *Making Democracy Work: Civic Traditions in Modern Italy* (Princeton, N.J.: Princeton University Press, 1993), I ignored the possibility that social capital might have antisocial effects, but I recognized this possibility explicitly in "The Prosperous Community," published that same year.

20. So far as I can tell, credit for coining these labels belongs to Ross Gittell and Avis Vidal, *Community Organizing: Building Social Capital as a Development Strategy* (Thousand Oaks, Calif.: Sage, 1998), 8.

21. Mark S. Granovetter, "The Strength of Weak Ties," *American Journal of Sociology* 78 (1973): 1360–1380; Xavier de Souza Briggs, "Doing Democracy Up Close: Culture, Power, and Communication in Community Building," *Journal of Planning Education and Research* 18 (1998):1–13.

22. As quoted in Richard D. Brown, "The Emergence of Voluntary Associations in Massachusetts," *Journal of Voluntary Action Research* 2 (April 1973): 64–73, at 69. See also Ashutosh Varshney, *Ethnic Conflict and Civic Life: Hindus and Muslims in India* (New Haven, Conn.: Yale University Press, 2000).

23. Alexis de Tocqueville, *Democracy in America*, ed. J. P. Mayer, trans. George Lawrence (Garden City, N.Y.: Doubleday, 1969), 506. See also Wilson Carey McWilliams, *The Idea of Fraternity in America* (Berkeley: University of California Press, 1973), and Thomas Bender, *Community and Social Change in America* (Baltimore, Md.: Johns Hopkins University Press, 1978).

24. David Hackett Fischer, *Paul Revere's Ride* (New York: Oxford University Press, 1994).

25. Barry Wellman, "The Community Question Re-Evaluated," in *Power, Community, and the City*, Michael Peter Smith, ed. (New Brunswick, N.J.: Transaction 1988), 81–107, quotation at 82–83. Pamela Paxton, "Is Social Capital Declining in the United States? A Multiple Indicator Assessment," *American Journal of Sociology* 105 (1999): 88–127.

26. *The Public Perspective* 8 (December/January 1997): 64; Robert Wuthnow, "Changing Character of Social Capital in the United States," in *The Dynamics of Social Capital in Comparative Perspective*, Robert D. Putnam, ed. (2000, forthcoming); *The Public Perspective* 10 (April/May 1999): 15; *Wall Street Journal*, June 24, 1999, A12; Mark J. Penn, "The Community Consensus," *Blueprint: Ideas for a New Century* (spring 1999). Respondents with no opinion are excluded.

27. For example, figures 31–33 present data from six independent sources on trends in philanthropy, but I have also discovered four additional sources that confirm the basic pattern, and those sources are mentioned briefly in the notes. For additional discussion of methodology, see the appendixes.

28. Emma Jackson, "Buddy Had Kidney to Spare," *Ann Arbor News* (January 5, 1998). Thanks to Michael Dover for his elegant posting of this story in the Nonprofit and Voluntary Action listserv, www.arnova.org/arnova_l.htm, January 6, 1998.

CHAPTER 2: POLITICAL PARTICIPATION

1. In the mid-1970s Americans were about twice as likely to take an active role in political campaigns as were citizens in Britain, Germany, Austria, and the Netherlands; Samuel H. Barnes, Max Kaase, et al., *Political Action: Mass Participation in Five Western Democracies* (Beverly Hills, Calif.: Sage, 1979), 541–542. Nearly twenty years later Americans tied for third place among forty democracies (old and new) in the frequency with which we sign petitions, though Americans ranked twentieth out of forty in the frequency with which we discuss politics with our friends; Russell Dalton, *Citizen Politics: Public Opinion and Political Parties in Advanced Western Democracies*, 2nd ed. (Chatham, N.J.: Chatham House, 1996), 74. On turnout, see Dalton, *Citizen Politics*, 45.

2. Turnout figures here are from the *Statistical Abstract of the United States* (various years), based in turn on surveys by the Census Bureau. The numbers in figure 1, based on actual returns from the various states and state-by-state calculations of the eligible electorate, are probably slightly more accurate. However, every source describes essentially the same relative decline. On local turnout, see Sidney Verba, Kay Lehman Schlozman, and Henry E. Brady, *Voice and Equality: Civic Voluntarism in American Politics* (Cambridge, Mass.: Harvard University Press, 1995), 69. Strictly speaking, voting can be a highly individual act, and in that sense it need not embody social capital. On the other hand, much evidence (beginning with the earliest studies of voting) makes clear that voting is almost always a socially embedded act and that turnout and social engagement are highly correlated. That fact plus the ready availability of measures of turnout across both time and space make it a very useful proxy measure of social involvement.

3. Dalton, *Citizen Politics*; Raymond E. Wolfinger and Steven J. Rosenstone, *Who Votes?* (New Haven, Conn.: Yale University Press, 1980); Frances Fox Piven and Richard A. Cloward, *Why Americans Don't Vote* (New York: Pantheon Books, 1988). Ruy Teixeira, *The Disappearing American Voter* (Washington, D.C.: Brookings Institution, 1992), 29–30, summarizes the facts through 1992, *before* the introduction of motor voter registration. Data on motor voter spending from National Association of Secretaries of State. Stephen Knack, "Drivers Wanted: Motor Voter and the Election of 1996," *PS: Political Science and Politics* 32 (June 1999): 237–243, finds that without motor voter, turnout in 1996 would have fallen even further.

4. Figure 1 is confined to presidential elections, but the pattern for off-year elections is the same. I am grateful to Professor Walter Dean Burnham for his latest unpublished estimates of electoral turnout throughout American history. For earlier estimates, see Walter Dean Burnham, "The Turnout Problem," in *Elections American Style*, ed. A. James Reichley (Washington, D.C.: Brookings Institution Press, 1987), 113–114. In addition to the exclusion of blacks from voting rolls, one-party control in the South lowered white turnout, too. See V. O. Key, *Southern Politics in State and Nation* (New York: Knopf, 1949), and Piven and Cloward, *Why Americans Don't Vote*, ch. 3.

5. James DeNardo, "The Turnout Crash of 1972," in *Politicians and Party Politics*, ed. John G. Geer (Baltimore, Md.: Johns Hopkins University Press, 1998), 80–101.

6. According to Burnham, turnout in the 1998 election in the states outside the old Confederacy was the lowest since 1818. The decline in turnout in the North in the early years of the twentieth century was also attributable to political reforms, such as registration requirements, that increased obstacles to turnout, whereas the post-1960 decline has occurred in an environment conducive to high levels of voting. The three-decade decline after 1896 was exaggerated by the introduction of women's suffrage in 1920, which temporarily depressed the turnout for the next two elections. In 1971 the voting age was lowered to eighteen, but that played only a minor role in the overall decline in turnout over the last four decades.

7. See Philip E. Converse, *The Dynamics of Party Support: Cohort Analyzing Party Identification* (Beverly Hills, Calif.: Sage, 1976); Glenn Firebaugh, "Methods for Estimating Cohort Replacement Effects," in *Sociological Methodology 1989*, ed. C. C. Clogg (Oxford: Basil Blackwell, 1989), 243–62; and William G. Mayer, *The Changing American Mind: How and Why American Public Opinion Changed Between 1960 and 1988* (Ann Arbor: University of Michigan Press, 1993). A third process of change—life cycle change—often masks, or masquerades as, aggregate change. However, unless the age structure of the population changes, pure life cycle change produces no social change at all, since children simply reproduce the cycle traced by their parents. Over the last half of the twentieth century changes in the age structure of the U.S. population were directly *opposite* to the aggregate changes in political and social participation; that is, participation *increased* when the proportion of the population in their peak joining years was *declining* because of the baby boom (1945–65), and participation *decreased* when the proportion of the population in their peak joining years was *growing* as the boomers matured (1965–2000). In other words, taking life cycle factors into account more explicitly would actually magnify the participation trends I discuss.

8. Author's calculation from Roper Social and Political Trends archive.

9. Warren E. Miller and J. Merrill Shanks, *The New American Voter* (Cambridge, Mass.: Harvard University Press, 1996), 69, conclude the most exhaustive study of this question: "Generational differences in voting rates ... translated into a continual national decline in turnout because of the demographic machinery of generational replacement."

10. Stephen Knack, "Social Altruism and Voter Turnout: Evidence from the 1991 NES Pilot Study" (College Park: University of Maryland, 1992), M. Margaret Conway, *Political Participation in the United States*, 2nd ed. (Washington, D.C.: CQ Press, 1991), 135; James A. McCann, "Electoral Participation and Local Community Activism: Spillover Effects, 1992–1996" (paper presented at the annual meeting of the American Political Science Association, Boston, September 1998) and the research cited there.

11. Verba, Schlozman, Brady, *Voice and Equality*, 23–24 *et passim*. On the decline in turnout, see Brody, "The Puzzle of Political Participation"; Wolfinger and Rosenstone, *Who Votes?*; Teixeira, *The Disappearing American Voter*; Steven J. Rosenstone and John Mark Hansen, *Mobilization, Participation, and Democracy in America* (New York: Macmillan, 1993); and Miller and Shanks, *The New American Voter*.

12. Verba, Schlozman, Brady, *Voice and Equality*, 362 *et passim*, and Michael X. Delli Carpini and Scott Keeter, *What Americans Know About Politics and Why It Matters* (New Haven, Conn.: Yale University Press, 1996), 116–134, 196–199.

13. Throughout this book, since the frequency of activities varies widely, I generally emphasize the *rate* of decline rather than the *absolute amount* of decline. In other words, both a change from 50 percent to 40 percent of the population engaging in some activity, and from 5 percent to 4 percent, represent declines of one-fifth, or 20 percent. Because our samples are generally very large, even small absolute differences are statistically highly significant. In the Roper data the long-run linear trend in the fraction of the public expressing "a good deal of interest" in current events fell from roughly 50 percent in 1974 to roughly 38 percent in 1998. In the DDB Needham Life Style surveys agreement that "I am interested in politics" slumped from 52 percent in 1975–76 to 42 percent in 1998–99. A separate series of Roper questions (available in *Roper Reports* [New York: Roper Starch Worldwide, 1995–1998]—not in the Roper Social and Political Trends survey archive) found that the number of Americans who discussed politics "in the last week" fell more or less steadily from 51 percent in 1980 to 28 percent in 1996.

14. When political interest in the DDB Needham Life Style surveys and interest in current events in the Roper surveys are each regressed on year of birth and year of survey, the regression coefficient for year of birth is quite high, while the coefficient for year of survey is virtually insignificant. In other words, the trends are entirely attributable to intercohort, not intracohort, change. On this methodology, see Firebaugh, "Methods for Estimating Cohort Replacement Effects," 243–62. Stephen Earl Bennett, "Young Americans' Indifference to Media Coverage of Public Affairs," *PS: Political Science & Politics* 31 (September 1998):540, 539, reports that "individuals between 18 and 29 years of age are less likely than those over 30 to read, listen to, or watch political news stories, and less likely to pay close attention to media coverage of public affairs." See also Delli Carpini and Keeter, *What Americans Know About Politics*, 170.

15. Times Mirror Center for the People and the Press, "The Age of Indifference" (Washington, D.C.: Times Mirror Center, June 28, 1990). Delli Carpini and Keeter, *What Americans Know About Politics*, 172, confirm that "the knowledge gap ... is driven more by generational than life cycle processes."

16. According to the National Election Studies, in the two presidential elections of the 1950s, 37 percent of voters over 60 and 27 percent of voters under thirty said they were "very much interested" in the election. In the two presidential elections of the 1990s, the equivalent figures were 40 percent for those over sixty and 15 percent for those under thirty.

17. Joseph A. Schlesinger, "The New American Political Party," *American Political Science Review* 79 (December 1985):1152–1169; Larry Sabato, *The Party's Just Begun* (Glenview, Ill.: Scott, Foresman, 1988); John H. Aldrich, *Why Parties?* (Chicago: University of Chicago Press, 1995), esp. 15, 260. Author's analysis of National Election Studies, 1952–96.

18. Sabato, *The Party's Just Begun*, 76. Figure 2 is based on the number of political organizations nationwide liable for Social Security taxes, adjusted for the growth in national population.

19. On declining party identification, see Miller and Shanks, *The New American Voter*, ch. 7; Rosenstone and Hansen, *Mobilization, Participation, and Democracy*, ch. 5; and Russell J. Dalton, "Parties without Partisans: The Decline of Party Identifications Among Democratic Publics," (Irvine: University of California at Irvine, 1998). Independents are much less attentive to politics and public affairs and much less likely to participate. See Angus Campbell, Philip E. Converse, Warren E. Miller, and Donald E. Stokes, *The American Voter* (New York: John Wiley & Sons, Inc., 1960), and Miller and Shanks, *The New American Voter*.

20. Participation has declined in presidential election years more than in midterm years. Roughly half of the decline in presidential year activities and virtually all of the downward trend in midterm activities is due to generational replacement. Two other forms of campaign involvement are also measured in the National Election Studies: 1) displaying one's political preferences, by wearing a button, putting a campaign sticker on one's car, or putting up a sign at one's house; and 2) making a campaign contribution. Both show irregular changes, due in part perhaps to changes in question wording.

21. Author's analysis of National Election Studies. The question on party contacting is: "Did anyone from one of the political parties call you up or come around and talk to you about the campaign?"

22. Marshall Ganz, "Voters in the Crosshairs: How Technology and the Market Are Destroying Politics," *The American Prospect* 16 (winter 1994): 100–109; Aldrich, *Why Parties?*; and R. Kenneth Godwin, "The Direct Marketing of Politics," in *The Politics of Interests*, ed. Mark Petracca (Boulder, Colo.: Westview Press, 1992), 308–325. Data on campaign spending from Stephen J. Wayne, *The Road to the White House 1996: The Politics of Presidential Elections* (New York: St. Martin's Press, 1996), 30, 46; Herbert B. Asher, *Presidential Elections and American Politics: Voters, Candidates, and Campaigns Since 1952*, 5th ed. (Pacific Grove, Calif.: Brooks/Cole, 1992), 210–211; and Common Cause (August 1999). One exception to the decline of grassroots organization—the Christian Right—is discussed in chapter 9.

23. John Aldrich and Richard G. Niemi, "The Sixth American Party System: Electoral Change, 1952–1992," in

Broken Contract: Changing Relationships Between Americans and Their Government, ed. Stephen C. Craig (Boulder, Colo.: Westview Press, 1995), 87–109.

24. Verba, Schlozman, and Brady, *Voice and Equality,* 71–73; 77; 518. Members of a political club fell from 8 percent to 4 percent of the adult population, while contributors to a party or candidate rose from 13 percent to 23 percent.

25. The Roper Social and Political Trends polls continued after December 1994, but the raw data are no longer available to academic researchers. Moreover, the wording and format of the crucial questions changed significantly in January 1995, so that direct comparison with the earlier data is no longer possible. However, trends in the data gathered *after* the change in format show continued decline on virtually all items at least through 1998. For details on this archive, see appendix I.

26. Within sampling error, the results from the Roper surveys in figure 4 and the National Elections studies in figure 3 are quite consistent. Each data point in the Roper graph is based on roughly ten times as many interviews as each data point in the NES graph, and thus the trends in the Roper data are much smoother than those in the National Election Studies. Mediamark Research annual surveys show a comparable drop of 38 percent between the early 1980s and the late 1990s in the frequency of "actively work[ing] for a political party or candidate." I am grateful to Mediamark and Julian Baym for sharing these data.

27. Of the 64,210 randomly chosen Americans interviewed by Roper over the four years between 1973 and 1976, exactly 500 (or 0.78 percent) reported that they had been an office seeker or officeholder in the previous 12 months. By 1991–94 that figure had sunk to 0.66 percent. Because of the very large samples involved, there is less than one chance in twenty-five that the time trend is a statistical fluke.

28. Author's analysis of Roper Social and Political Trends data. Mediamark Research surveys show a drop of roughly 25 percent between the early 1980s and the late 1990s in the frequency of "taking an active part in some local civic issue" and a drop of 35 percent in the frequency of "addressing a public meeting."

29. For further discussion of ballot initiatives, see chapter 9. The Roper data on petition-signing contradict evidence, in Dalton, *Citizen Politics,* 76, that petition signing became more common between 1975 and 1990. The Roper surveys are much larger and more frequent than those cited by Dalton. Another possible explanation for the divergence is that the surveys cited by Dalton inquired whether the respondent had "ever" signed a petition, whereas the Roper question was focused on "the last twelve months." Since younger respondents are more likely to have signed a petition, slow growth in Dalton's "lifetime" figure might be consistent with decline in the "annual" rate measured by Roper. Nine national surveys conducted between 1974 and 1985 by the Food Marketing Institute (FMI) on behalf of the nation's supermarkets found a decline from 46 percent in 1974–77 to 30 percent in 1983–85 in the proportion of people who said they had sought to get neighbors to sign a petition; *Consumer Attitudes and the Supermarket* (Washington, D.C.: Food Marketing Institute, 1983, 1985, 1994, 1995, 1996). These three are the only sources of which I am aware that provide time-series data on petitioning. Roper data on letters to Congress appear inconsistent with data in Verba, Schlozman, and Brady, *Voice and Equality,* 73, but FMI surveys tend to confirm the Roper results, for the FMI data show a 40 percent decline between 1974–75 and 1984–85 in the proportion of respondents who had "written a letter to Congress demanding that the government do something." Some researchers report an increase in mail received in Congress, but that is consistent with decreased writing by individuals, if (as seems true anecdotally) a growing fraction of Congressional mail represents mass mailings by lobbying organizations; see Malcolm E. Jewell and Samuel C. Patterson, *The Legislative Process in the United States,* 3rd ed. (New York: Random House, 1977), 306–307; Stephen E. Frantzich, *Write Your Congressman: Constituent Communications and Representation* (New York: Praeger, 1986); David Thelen, *Becoming Citizens in the Age of Television* (Chicago: University of Chicago Press, 1996). The Roper data suggest a 14 percent decline in letters to the editor between 1973 and 1994, but the DDB Needham data suggest a roughly 10 percent increase in this activity between 1987 and 1998. Mediamark Research surveys show a drop of 15 percent between the early 1980s and the late 1990s in the frequency of writing a letter to the editor, a roughly 20 percent drop in writing an elected official "about a matter of public business," a 30 percent drop in the frequency of "personally visit[ing]" an elected official to express a point of view," and a 35–40 percent drop in writing or telephoning a radio or TV station. All in all, the balance of the evidence strongly suggests that over the last two to three decades Americans grew less likely to express their views on public matters.

30. The Roper data contradict claims by Everett Carll Ladd, "The Data Just Don't Show Erosion of America's 'Social Capital,'" *Public Perspective* 7 (June/July 1996): 17, citing evidence in Verba, Schlozman, and Brady, *Voice and Equality,* that the proportion of Americans involved in community collaboration increased between 1967 and 1987. Verba and his colleagues themselves have not claimed (and say privately they do not believe) that evidence from a single pair of surveys should outweigh evidence of continuous change measured in the more than two hundred separate Roper polls conducted monthly over twenty years.

31. Stephen Knack, "Civic Norms, Social Sanctions and Voter Turnout," *Rationality and Society* 4 (April 1992): 146–47, argued that the decline in voting represents weaker social connectedness. Knack was one of the first scholars to call attention to the general weakening of social attachments in recent years. See his "Why We Don't Vote—Or Say 'Thank You,'" *Wall Street Journal,* December 31, 1990, and Norval D. Glenn, "Social Trends in the United States," *Public Opinion Quarterly* 51 (winter 1987): S109–S126.

32. Lori Weber, *The Effects of Democratic Deliberation on Political Tolerance* (Ph.D. diss., University of Colorado, 1999), 24–42, reports that "social" forms of participation (such as attending meetings) are associated with increased political tolerance, whereas "individual" forms of participation (such as contacting officials) are not.

33. In 1947 the median American adult had completed nine years of formal schooling; in 1998 that figure was about thirteen. According to the Census Bureau, the fraction of adults who had completed high school rose from 31 percent in 1947 to 82 percent in 1998.

34. Author's analysis of Harris polls archived at the University of North Carolina Institute for Research in the Social Sciences.

CHAPTER 3: CIVIC PARTICIPATION

1. Tocqueville, *Democracy in America*, 513–517.

2. A Gallup poll in 1981 ranked America at the top of twelve industrialized democracies in the frequency of membership in voluntary associations; the 1991 World Values Survey found that among thirty-five nations, the United States tied with Norway for fourth, lagging behind Sweden, Iceland, and the Netherlands. See Verba, Schlozman, and Brady, *Voice and Equality*, 80, and Robert D. Putnam, "Bowling Alone: America's Declining Social Capital," *Journal of Democracy* 6 (January 1995): 65–78.

3. Murray Hausknecht, *The Joiners* (New York: Bedminster Press, 1962); Nicholas Babchuk and Alan Booth, "Voluntary Association Membership: A Longitudinal Analysis," *American Sociological Review* 34 (February 1969): 31–45.

4. Gale Research Company, *Encyclopedia of Associations*, as quoted in the Statistical Abstract of the United States (various years); Allan J. Cigler and Burdett A. Loomis, eds., *Interest Group Politics*, 3rd ed. (Washington, D.C.: CQ Press, 1991), 11; Kay Lehman Schlozman and John T. Tierney, *Organized Interests and American Democracy* (New York: Harper & Row, 1986); Jack L. Walker, *Mobilizing Interest Groups in America: Patrons, Professions, and Social Movements* (Ann Arbor: University of Michigan Press, 1991); Frank R. Baumgartner and Beth L. Leech, *Basic Interests: The Importance of Groups in Politics and in Political Science* (Princeton, N.J.: Princeton University Press, 1998), esp. 102–106.

5. David Horton Smith, "National Nonprofit, Voluntary Associations: Some Parameters," *Nonprofit and Voluntary Sector Quarterly* 21 (spring 1992): 81–94. I confirmed Smith's findings, comparing random samples of two hundred associations *with individual members* from various editions of the *Encyclopedia of Associations* (Detroit: Gale Research Co, 1956, 1968, 1978, 1988, and 1998). Average membership per association fell from 111,000 in 1956 to 13,000 in 1998. I am grateful to Adam Hickey for his able assistance on this and other assignments.

6. In 1971, 19 percent of all national nonprofit associations had their headquarters in Washington; by 1981 29 percent did, according to Robert H. Salisbury, "Interest Representation: The Dominance of Institutions," *American Political Science Review* 78 (March 1984): 64–76. See also Cigler and Loomis, *Interest Group Politics*, 3rd ed., and Smith, "National Nonprofit, Voluntary Associations."

7. Theda Skocpol, "Advocates without Members: The Recent Transformation of American Civic Life," in *Civic Engagement in American Democracy*, eds. Theda Skocpol and Morris P. Fiorina (Washington, D.C.: Brookings Institution Press, 1999), 461–509.

8. Jeffrey M. Berry, *Lobbying for the People: The Political Behavior of Public Interest Groups* (Princeton, N.J.: Princeton University Press, 1977), 42. After canvasing major national newspapers, the *Congressional Quarterly*, the *Encyclopedia of Associations*, and a wide array of registered lobbyists, Berry (p. 14) concluded that "this survey represents an extremely high percentage—surely above 80 percent—of the true number of public interest groups that existed at the time of the interviewing (September 1972–June 1973)."

9. These figures are calculated from the survey reported in Walker, *Mobilizing Interest Groups in America*. Among the citizens' groups, the correlation between date of founding and the presence of chapters with individual members was r = -.17, statistically significant at the .01 level. On the anomaly of public-interest groups without members, see Frank J. Sorauf, *The Wall of Separation* (Princeton, N.J.: Princeton University Press, 1976); Berry, *Lobbying for the People*; Michael T. Hayes, "The New Group Universe," in *Interest Group Politics*, 2nd ed., ed. Allan J. Cigler and Burdett A. Loomis (Washington, D.C.: Congressional Quarterly Press, 1986), 134; and Theda Skocpol, "Civic America, Then and Now," in Putnam, *Dynamics of Social Capital in Comparative Perspective*.

10. Charles R. Morris, *The AARP: America's Most Powerful Lobby* (New York: Times Books, 1996), 23–43. Cristine L. Day, *What Older Americans Think: Interest Groups and Aging Policy* (Princeton, N.J.: Princeton University Press, 1990), 66.

11. Sociologists use the term *primary associations* to refer to one's most intimate connections—the family and intimate friends—and *secondary associations* to refer to less intimate connections, such as churches, unions, and community organizations. For a prescient analysis, see Bernard Barber, "Participation and Mass Apathy in Associations," in *Studies in Leadership*, ed. A. W. Gouldner (New York: Harper, 1950).

12. Some of these organizations, of course, provide their members with commercial services, like group insurance or high-fashion T-shirts, but in this role they are indistinguishable from other mail-order firms.

13. Data on membership in veterans organizations from the General Social Survey, 1974–94; data on number of living veterans from the Veterans Administration. Data on membership in unions from the Department of Labor annual survey; data on numbers of labor unions from the *Encyclopedia of Associations*.

14. Christopher J. Bosso, "The Color of Money: Environmental Groups and the Pathologies of Fund Raising," in *Interest Group Politics*, 4th ed., ed. Allan J. Cigler and Burdett A. Loomis (Washington, D.C.: Congressional Quarterly, 1995), 101–130, esp. 117, and interviews with staff members. On direct-mail marketing by "citizens groups," see Jeffrey M. Berry, *The Interest Group Society*, 3rd ed. (New York: Longman, 1997), 77–80; and Paul E. Johnson, "Interest Group Recruiting: Finding Members and Keeping Them," in *Interest Group Politics*, 5th ed., ed. Allan J. Cigler and Burdett A. Loomis (Washington, D.C.: Congressional Quarterly Press, 1998), 35–62.

15. Figure 8 is intended only as a rough summary of the experiences of more than thirty separate organizations; interested readers are urged to consult the separate charts for each organization, given in appendix III. Given the inevitable uncertainty about membership data extending across an entire century and the unavoidable arbitrariness about which groups to include, the details of figure 8 should not be overinterpreted. I have sought to encompass all large national chapter-based civic organizations in the 1950s and 1960s plus any that came into existence thereafter (none did) plus a selection of smaller "niche" organizations, like Hadassah, NAACP, Optimists, and the 4-H. (Labor unions and professional associations are excluded from figure 8 but discussed in chapter 5.) Because the broad outlines of figure 8 are echoed in most of this diverse group of organizations, I am fairly confident that it represents broad historical trends in the membership of such organizations. In order to bias figure 8 *against* my hypothesis—declining membership in the last third of the twentieth century—I excluded several large nineteenth-century associations that moved toward extinction in the first half of the twentieth century, such as the Redmen fraternal group, though I included a

few that remained strong after World War II, such as the Odd Fellows. Including all such groups would diminish the apparent growth in associational vitality in the first half of the twentieth century and magnify the decline thereafter. These inclusions or exclusions would not, however, decisively alter the broad profile of figure 8. For each organization listed in appendix III, I calculated annual national membership as a fraction of the relevant population—PTA membership per one thousand families with children, American Legion membership per one thousand veterans, Hadassah membership per one thousand Jewish women, and so on. For missing years, I interpolated membership from adjacent years. To weight each organization equally, regardless of its size and market share, I computed "standard scores" for each organization, comparing its market share in a given year to its average market share over the century as a whole, and then averaged the standard scores of all organizations in a given year. Because of this standardization method, the vertical axis measures not absolute membership rates, but trends relative to the century-long average. I am grateful to Professor Theda Skocpol for many illuminating discussions about the history of associations in America, as well as for generously sharing data collected in her own research project on this theme. However, I alone am responsible for the evidence and conclusions presented here. See Theda Skocpol, with the assistance of Marshall Ganz, Ziad Munson, Bayliss Camp, Michele Swers, and Jennifer Oser, "How America Became Civic," in *Civic Engagement in American Democracy*, eds. Skocpol and Fiorina, 27–80.

16. Though quantitative data on nineteenth-century associationism are scarce, it appears that the only period of unambiguous decline in associational activity between 1865 and 1965 was from 1930 to 1935. For some evidence and relevant historiography, see Gerald Gamm and Robert D. Putnam, "The Growth of Voluntary Associations in America, 1840–1940," *Journal of Interdisciplinary History* 29 (spring 1999), 511–557. John Harp and Richard J. Gagan, "Changes in Rural Social Organizations: Comparative Data from Three Studies," *Rural Sociology* 34 (1969): 80–85, report that organizational density was unchanged between 1924 and 1936 and then increased by 50 percent by 1964—independent confirmation of figure 8.

17. American civic life also quickened after 1865 and after 1918, but both those postwar booms proved reasonably durable, even in the face of substantial economic dislocation, whereas the slump after 1960 began and persisted in periods of prosperity. In other words, the post-1960 slump should not be interpreted as merely some reversion to prewar "normalcy."

18. Babchuk and Booth, "Voluntary Association Membership," 34.

19. Susan Crawford and Peggy Levitt, "Social Change and Civic Engagement: The Case of the PTA," in *Civic Engagement in American Democracy*, ed. Skocpol and Fiorina, 249–296, quotation at 250–251.

20. PTO gains could account at most for only a fraction of PTA losses. *The Third PTA National Education Survey* (Los Angeles: Newsweek, 1993) found that two-thirds of all households that belonged to *any* school-based group belonged to the PTA, so even on the utterly improbable assumption that there were *no* nonaffiliated PTOs in 1960, the hypothetical increase in nonaffiliated groups could not equal the decline in PTA-affiliated membership. Moreover, at least one of the largest nonaffiliated local groups—the United Parents Associations of New York City—itself experienced massive membership drops after the early 1960s. See Sam Dillon, "A Surge in Advocacy Within Parent Groups," *New York Times*, October 13, 1993.

21. Tom W. Smith, "Trends in Voluntary Group Membership: Comments on Baumgartner and Walker," *American Journal of Political Science* 34 (August 1990): 646–661, quotation at 647 (emphasis added).

22. Frank R. Baumgartner and Jack L. Walker, "Survey Research and Membership in Voluntary Associations," *American Journal of Political Science* 32 (November 1988): 908–928; Smith, "Trends in Voluntary Group Membership."

23. Joseph Veroff, Elizabeth Douvan, and Richard A. Kulka, *The Inner American: A Self-Portrait from 1957 to 1975* (New York: Basic Books, 1981).

24. Veroff, Douvan, and Kulka, *Inner American*, 17.

25. Only the rubric of "social groups" (ranging from country clubs to sports teams), which accounted for roughly one membership in five, did not decline over these two decades; the rate of membership in this category rose from 13 percent to 16 percent.

26. Each of these survey archives is described in detail in appendix I.

27. In fifteen separate surveys between 1974 and 1994 the General Social Survey asked Americans "whether or not you are a member of" each of fifteen specific types of groups, from "fraternal groups" to "church-related groups," as well as a catch-all category of "other." Only limited subsamples of the GSS in 1993 and 1994 were asked the relevant question, so the results from those years are less reliable.

28. These data are drawn from the 1987 General Social Survey. A 1973 Louis Harris survey (study number 2343 at the University of North Carolina Institute for Research in the Social Sciences) found that 48 percent of all organizational members had served at one time as a club officer, virtually identical to the 1987 GSS figure.

29. Author's analysis of data from Roper Social and Political Trends archive.

30. William Safire, "On Language," *New York Times*, August 13, 1989.

31. See appendix I for methodological details.

32. John P. Robinson and Geoffrey Godbey, *Time for Life: The Surprising Ways Americans Use Their Time*, 2nd ed. (University Park: Pennsylvania State University Press, 1999). I am grateful both to Professor Robinson for sharing the Americans' Use of Time archive and to Dan Devroye for careful analysis of the data. Our results differ slightly from those reported by Robinson and Godbey, because we have weighted the data 1) to correct for sampling anomalies in the 1965 survey; and 2) to assure equal weight to diaries from each day of the week. The most important of these adjustments corrects for the fact that the 1965 samples excluded households in communities of less than thirty-five thousand or in which everyone was retired.

33. Author's analysis of Americans' Use of Time archive.

34. The weekly scale-up formula used here assumes that a person who reported activity on Wednesday would not also have reported activity on Thursday. Since that approximation is probably slightly inaccurate, the overall figures in the text probably slightly overestimate the total fraction of people who participate over the course of a week. However, this rough approximation is very unlikely to affect the size and direction of change over time. All the trends in time usage reported in this book are highly significant in statistical terms.

35. *Statistical Abstract of the United States 1997*, table 406, supplemented by unpublished data from the Bureau of Economic Analysis, U.S. Department of Commerce.

CHAPTER 4: RELIGIOUS PARTICIPATION

1. Seymour Martin Lipset, "Comment on Luckmann," in *Social Theory for a Changing Society*, ed. Pierre Bourdieu and James S. Coleman (Boulder, Colo.: Westview Press, 1991), 185–88, quotation at 187.

2. Phillip E. Hammond, *Religion and Personal Autonomy: The Third Disestablishment in America* (Columbia: University of South Carolina Press, 1992), xiv.

3. Roger Finke and Rodney Stark, *The Churching of America, 1776–1990: Winners and Losers in Our Religious Economy* (New Brunswick, N.J.: Rutgers University Press, 1992), esp. 16.

4. E. Brooks Holifield, "Towards a History of American Congregations," in *American Congregations, Volume 2: New Perspectives in the Study of Congregations*, ed. James P. Wind and James W. Lewis (Chicago: University of Chicago Press, 1994), 23–53, quotation at 24.

5. Wade Clark Roof and William McKinney, *American Mainline Religion: Its Changing Shape and Future* (New Brunswick, N.J.: Rutgers University Press, 1987), 6.

6. Sara Terry, "Resurrecting Hope," *The Boston Globe Magazine* (July 17, 1994), p. 22.

7. Hammond, *Religion and Personal Autonomy*, appendix A, 178–184; Holifield, "Towards a History of American Congregations," 44.

8. Verba, Schlozman, and Brady, *Voice and Equality*, esp. 282–83, 317–33, 377–84, and 518–21; Theodore F. Macaluso and John Wanat, "Voting Turnout & Religiosity," *Polity* 12 (fall 1979): 158–69; John M. Strate, Charles J. Parrish, Charles D. Elder, and Coit Ford, III, "Life Span Civic Development and Voting Participation," *American Political Science Review* 83 (June 1989): 443–64; Steven A. Peterson, "Church Participation and Political Participation: The Spillover Effect," *American Politics Quarterly* 20 (January 1992): 123–39; Fredrick C. Harris, "Something Within: Religion as a Mobilizer of African-American Political Activism," *Journal of Politics* 56 (February 1994): 42–68; Kenneth D. Wald, Lyman A. Kellstedt, and David C. Leege, "Church Involvement and Political Behavior," in *Rediscovering the Religious Factor in American Politics*, ed. David C. Leege and Lyman A. Kellstedt (Armonk, N.Y.: M. E. Sharpe, 1993), esp. 130; Rosenstone and Hansen, *Mobilization, Participation, and Democracy in America*, 158.

9. Author's analysis of General Social Survey and DDB Needham Life Style data, controlling for education, income, full-time employment, gender, marital and parental status, urban/rural residence, age, and race. This strong correlation between religiosity and associationism was reported in the 1950s by Hausknecht, *The Joiners*, 54, and Bernard Lazerwitz, "Membership in Voluntary Associations and Frequency of Church Attendance," *Journal for the Scientific Study of Religion* 2 (October 1962): 74–84.

10. Author's analysis of 1996 National Election Study.

11. In the DDB Needham Life Style surveys, attendance at church and agreement that "religion is important in my life" are more powerful predictors of club attendance, volunteering, visiting with friends, and entertaining at home than is education. On virtually all measures of civic engagement in the Roper Social and Political Trends surveys, the difference between those who attended church last week and those who did not is as large as the difference between high school and college graduates.

12. Author's analysis of a Scripps-Howard/Ohio University national survey of interpersonal communication, June 1997.

13. Virginia A. Hodgkinson and Murray S. Weitzman, *Giving and Volunteering in the United States: 1996 Edition* (Washington, D.C.: Independent Sector, 1996), 5, 14, 121–31; Virginia A. Hodgkinson, Murray S. Weitzman, and Arthur D. Kirsch, "From Commitment to Action: How Religious Involvement Affects Giving and Volunteering," and Mordechai Rimor and Gary A. Tobin, "Jewish Giving Patterns to Jewish and Non-Jewish Philanthropy," both in *Faith and Philanthropy in America*, ed. Robert Wuthnow, Virginia A. Hodgkinson, and associates (San Francisco: Jossey-Bass, 1990), 93–114; 134–164. For partially contradictory evidence, see John Wilson and Thomas Janoski, "The Contribution of Religion to Volunteer Work," *Sociology of Religion* 56 (summer 1995): 137–52.

14. Kenneth D. Wald, *Religion and Politics in the United States* (New York: St. Martin's Press, 1987), 29–30. See also Strate et al., "Life Span Civic Development," 452.

15. Ram A. Cnaan, Amy Kasternakis, and Robert J. Wineburg, "Religious People, Religious Congregations, and Volunteerism in Human Services: Is There a Link?" *Nonprofit and Voluntary Sector Quarterly* 22 (spring 1993): 33–51; Elton F. Jackson, Mark D. Bachmeier, James R. Wood, and Elizabeth A. Craft, "Volunteering and Charitable Giving: Do Religious and Associational Ties Promote Helping Behavior?" *Nonprofit and Voluntary Sector Quarterly* 24 (spring 1995): 59–78; John Wilson and Marc Musick, "Who Cares? Toward an Integrated Theory of Volunteer Work," *American Sociological Review* 62 (October 1997): 694–713. In the DDB Needham Life Style surveys, church attendance is a much more powerful predictor of volunteering than is agreement that "religion is important to my life."

16. Data in this paragraph are from the 1998 National Congregational Survey, as reported in Mark Chaves, "Religious Congregations and Welfare Reform: Who Will Take Advantage of 'Charitable Choice'?" *American Sociological Review* 64 (1999): 836–46, and Mark Chaves, "Congregations' Social Service Activities" (Washington, D.C.: The Urban Institute, Center on Nonprofits and Philanthropy, 1999). Somewhat higher but less representative rates of activity are reported in Virginia A. Hodgkinson, Murray S. Weitzman, and associates, *From Belief to Commitment: The Community Service Activities and Finances of Religious Congregations in the United States: 1993 Edition* (Washington, D.C.: Independent Sector, 1993), esp. 31, and Ram A. Cnaan, *Social and Community Involvement of Religious Congregations Housed in Historic Religious Properties: Findings from a Six-City Study* (Philadelphia: University of Pennsylvania School of Social Work, 1997). See also John J. DiIulio, Jr., "Support Black Churches: Faith, Outreach, and the Inner-City Poor," *The Brookings Review* 17 (spring 1999): 42–45. Glenn C. Loury and Linda Datcher Loury, "Not by Bread Alone," *The Brookings Review* 15 (winter 1997): 10–13; Samuel G. Freedman, *Upon this Rock: The Miracles of a Black Church* (New York: HarperCollins, 1993); and Mark R. Warren, "Community Building and Political

Power: A Community Organizing Approach to Democratic Renewal," *American Behavioral Scientist* 41 (September 1998): 78–92.

17. Aldon D. Morris, *The Origins of the Civil Rights Movement: Black Communities Organizing for Change* (New York: Free Press, 1984), quotation at 4. See also McAdam, *Freedom Summer*, and Doug McAdam, *Political Process and the Development of Black Insurgency 1930–1970* (Chicago: University of Chicago Press, 1982).

18. Fredrick C. Harris, *Something Within: Religion in African-American Political Activism* (New York: Oxford University Press, 1999), esp. 59, 63–64; C. Eric Lincoln and Lawrence H. Mamiya, *The Black Church in the African American Experience* (Durham, N.C.: Duke University Press, 1990); Mary Pattillo-McCoy, "Church Culture as a Strategy of Action in the Black Community," *American Sociological Review* 63 (December 1998): 767–784. The greater religiosity of African Americans is confirmed by the General Social Survey, National Election Study, Roper Social and Political Trends surveys, and DDB Needham Life Style archives, as well as Verba, Schlozman, and Brady, *Voice and Equality*.

19. C. Eric Lincoln, "The Black Church and Black Self-Determination" (paper presented at the annual meeting of the Association of Black Foundation Executives, Kansas City, Missouri, April 1989).

20. See Mayer, *The Changing American Mind*, 375–76. According to the Gallup poll (www.gallup.com/poll /indicators/indreligion.asp), the fraction of Americans who say that "religion is very important in my life," fell from 75 percent in 1952 to 52 percent in 1978, but then recovered somewhat to 60 percent in 1999. According to the DDB Needham Life Style archive, the fraction who "definitely" or "generally" agree that "religion is important in my life" has slipped from 57 percent in 1981 to 50 percent in 1999. By contrast, the Princeton Religious Index, which measures belief in God, religious preference, belief that God can answer today's problems, church membership, confidence in organized religion, feeling that clergy are honest, view of religion as very important in one's life, and church or synagogue attendance fell sharply and more or less continuously from 1961 to 1994: C. Kirk Hadaway and David A. Roozen, *Rerouting the Protestant Mainstream: Sources of Growth and Opportunities for Change* (Nashville, Tenn.: Abingdon Press, 1995), 43–44.

21. Professor Martin Marty of the University of Chicago, as quoted in "Spiritual America," *U.S. News & World Report*, April 4, 1994.

22. Robert Wuthnow, *The Crisis in the Churches: Spiritual Malaise, Fiscal Woe* (New York: Oxford University Press, 1997), vi. On the secularization debate, see Jeffrey K. Hadden, "Toward Desacralizing Secularization Theory," *Social Forces* 65 (March 1987): 587–611, Frank J. Lechner, "The Case against Secularization: A Rebuttal," *Social Forces* 69 (June 1991): 1103–19; and the special "Symposium: Surveys of U.S. Church Attendance," *American Sociological Review* 63 (February 1998): 111–45.

23. R. Stephen Warner, "Work in Progress toward a New Paradigm for the Sociological Study of Religion in the United States," *American Journal of Sociology* 98 (March 1993): 1044–93, esp. 1049.

24. Denominational data from *Yearbook of American and Canadian Churches, 1984*, ed. Constant H. Jacquet Jr. (Nashville, Tenn.: Abingdon Press, 1984), 248, and later editions of this yearbook; *Statistical Abstract of the United States, 1994*; Benton Johnson, "The Denominations: The Changing Map of Religious America," *Public Perspective* 4 (March/April 1993): 4. For a discussion of the methodological weaknesses of the denominational data, see notes in the *Yearbook of American and Canadian Churches, 1984* and later editions of this yearbook. Gallup poll data from *Statistical Abstract of the United States*, 1997 (table 86), based on surveys conducted by the Gallup Organization, Inc.; George Gallup, Jr., *The Gallup Poll: Public Opinion* (Wilmington, Del.: Scholarly Resources Inc., 1986 and other years), the Gallup Web site, www.gallup.com/poll/indicators/indreligion.asp, and Mayer, *The Changing American Mind*, 379. In later years this series combines multiple surveys into a single annual average. Norval D. Glenn, "The Trend in 'No Religion' Respondents to U.S. National Surveys, Late 1950s to Early 1980s," *Public Opinion Quarterly* 51 (fall 1987): 293–314; *Religion in America: 1992–1993*, ed. Robert Bezilla (Princeton, N.J.: Princeton Religion Research Center, 1993), 40.

25. The longest-term, most widely reported evidence comes from a standard Gallup poll question, asked regularly since 1939, "Did you yourself happen to attend church [or synagogue] in the last seven days?" A similar question appears in the 1974–93 Roper Social and Political Trends archive: "Which of the following things have you personally done in the last week? . . . Gone to church or religious service." Between 1952 and 1968 the National Election Studies asked respondents, "Would you say you go to church regularly, often, seldom or never?" and after 1968 they were asked, "Would you say you go to (church/synagogue) every week, almost every week, once or twice a month, a few times a year, or never?" Since 1967 the National Opinion Research Center (later the General Social Survey) has asked, "How often do you attend religious services?" and since 1975 the DDB Needham Life Style survey has asked, "How many times in the last twelve months did you attend church or other place of worship?" The weekly attendance estimate in the text represents the range of the Roper and Gallup results, and a similar figure is implied by the DDB Needham and GSS estimates of twenty to twenty-five church attendances per year.

26. These data are from the Gallup poll and the National Election Study series. The NIMH surveys cited in note 23 in chapter 3 found a 20 percent decline in church attendance between 1957 and 1976—a result consistent with the other survey evidence from that period.

27. The five archives, and the respective change that each records, are Gallup polls (down 4 percent from 1975–76 to 1998–99), National Election Studies (down 6 percent from 1970–72 to 1996–98), Roper Social and Political Trends (down 19 percent from 1974–75 to 1997–98), General Social Survey (down 13 percent from 1974–75 to 1997–98), and DDB Needham Life Style (down 15 percent from 1975–76 to 1998–99). A sixth archive graciously made available by Yankelovich Partners Inc. asks about at least "occasional" attendance; since this threshold is lower, the data are not sufficiently comparable to be included in figure 13, but this barometer, too, fell by nearly a quarter from 64 percent in 1978–80 to 49 percent in 1997–99.

28. Figure 13 is based on the average weekly church attendance figures from the Gallup poll (1940–99), the Roper Social and Political Trends polls (1974–96), the National Election Studies (1952–92), the DDB Needham Life Style polls (1975–99), and the General Social Survey (1972–98). Results from the last three of these archives have been recalibrated to match the "weekly church attendance" format of the first two archives. Alternative calibration

formulas would alter the absolute level of church attendance reported, but would not alter the basic trends. The NES question format was changed in 1970 and again in 1990, but those changes did not substantially alter the results used to construct figure 13.

29. See C. Kirk Hadaway, Penny Long Marler, and Mark Chaves, "What the Polls Don't Show: A Closer Look at U.S. Church Attendance," *American Sociological Review* 58 (December 1993): 741–52; Mark Chaves and James C. Cavendish, "More Evidence on U.S. Catholic Church Attendance," *Journal for the Scientific Study of Religion* 33 (December 1994): 376–81; and "Symposium: Surveys of U.S. Church Attendance." According to the 1996 General Social Survey, only 2 percent of people who did not attend church "last week" report that they attended some *other* type of religious event or meeting. Thus the standard question does not "miss" a significant number of people who attend, say, prayer meetings *instead of* church services.

30. Surveys summarized here include the 1952 National Election Study, which found 23 percent membership in religious groups, excluding church membership; a 1955 survey, reported by Hausknecht, *The Joiners* (25 percent); the 1987 General Social Survey (14 percent); a 1989 survey, reported by Verba, Schlozman, and Brady, *Voice and Equality* (8 percent); and the 1996 National Election Study (13 percent). The wording of the relevant questions varied slightly across these five surveys, but since more probes were used in the later surveys, the decline in religious group memberships between the 1950s and the 1980s–1990s was, if anything, probably underestimated.

31. According to the General Social Survey, membership in a "church-related group" gradually declined from 43 percent in 1974 to 34 percent by the 1990s. The 1987 GSS discovered that roughly half of these reported memberships are simply church membership. Since church membership itself was not falling that fast, the gross figures must reflect a decline at least that sharp among respondents who participated in other religious groups. Further evidence that this question taps intense involvement in a religious community is the fact that barely one-third (32–35 percent) of mainline Protestants report membership in church-related groups as compared to nearly two-thirds (63 percent) of evangelicals, fundamentalists, and Mormons. See Roof and McKinney, *American Mainline Religion*, 83–84, and Robert Wuthnow, "Mobilizing Civic Engagement: The Changing Impact of Religious Involvement," in *Civic Engagement in American Democracy*, ed. Skocpol and Fiorina, 331–63.

32. See also Stanley Presser and Linda Stinson, "Data Collection Mode and Social Desirability Bias in Self-Reported Religious Attendance," *American Sociological Review* 63 (February 1998): 137–45. A striking 50 percent decline in time devoted to church appears in time diary data gathered from children aged three to twelve in 1981 and 1997, according to Sandra L. Hofferth and Jack Sandberg, "Changes in American Children's Time, 1981–1997" (paper presented at the annual meeting of the American Sociological Association, Chicago, Ill., August 1999), 30.

33. Author's analysis of the GSS, Roper, NES, NIMH, and DDB Needham Life Style data, as well as the time diary data. (The Gallup data are not available for secondary analysis by outside scholars.) The statistical methodology underlying this conclusion is described in Firebaugh, "Methods for Estimating Cohort Replacement Effects." See also James A. Davis, "Changeable Weather in a Cooling Climate atop the Liberal Plateau: Conversion and Replacement in Forty-Two General Social Survey Items, 1972–1989," *Public Opinion Quarterly* 56 (fall 1992): 261–306, esp. 301.

34. On life cycle and generational patterns in American religious behavior, see Michael Hout and Andrew M. Greeley, "The Center Doesn't Hold: Church Attendance in the United States, 1940–1984," *American Sociological Review* 52 (June 1987): 325–345; Mark Chaves, "Secularization and Religious Revival: Evidence from U.S. Church Attendance Rates, 1972–1986," *Journal for the Scientific Study of Religion* 28 (December 1989): 464–477; Glenn Firebaugh and Brian Harley, "Trends in U.S. Church Attendance: Secularization and Revival, or Merely Lifecycle Effects," *Journal for the Scientific Study of Religion* 30 (December 1991): 487–500; Ross M. Stolzenberg, Mary Blair-Loy, and Linda J. Waite, "Religious Participation in Early Adulthood: Age and Family Life Cycle Effects on Church Membership," *American Sociological Review* 60 (February 1995): 84–103.

35. Author's analysis of Roper Social and Political Trends (1974–1998) and General Social Survey (1972–1998) archives.

36. Wade Clark Roof, *A Generation of Seekers: The Spiritual Journeys of the Baby Boom Generation* (San Francisco: Harper, 1993); David A. Roozen and William McKinney, "The 'Big Chill' Generation Warms to Worship: A Research Note," *Review of Religious Research* 31 (March 1990): 314–322; Tom W. Smith, "Counting Flocks and Lost Sheep: Trends in Religious Preference Since World War II," GSS Social Change Report, no. 26 (Chicago: National Opinion Research Center, January 1991), 9; and Hadaway and Roozen, *Rerouting the Protestant Mainstream*, 40–42.

37. Roof and McKinney, *American Mainline Religion*, 18–19; 7–8; 32–33.

38. On religious mobility, see Smith, "Counting Flocks and Lost Sheep," esp. 20; Hadaway and Marler, "All in the Family"; and Robert Wuthnow, *The Restructuring of American Religion: Society and Faith since World War II* (Princeton, N.J.: Princeton University Press, 1988); esp. 88–91. On cults, see Roger Finke and Rodney Stark, *The Churching of America, 1776–1990*, 239–245.

39. Wade Clark Roof, "America's Voluntary Establishment: Mainline Religion in Transition," in *Religion and America: Spiritual Life in a Secular Age*, ed. Mary Douglas and Steven Tipton (Boston: Beacon Press, 1983), 132, 137.

40. R. Stephen Warner, "Work in Progress toward a New Paradigm for the Sociological Study of Religion in the United States," 1076–78.

41. Roof and McKinney, *American Mainline Religion*, 170. See also John C. Green and James L. Guth, "From Lambs to Sheep: Denominational Change and Political Behavior," in *Rediscovering the Religious Factor in American Politics*, ed. David C. Leege and Lyman A. Kellstedt (Armonk, N.Y.: M. E. Sharpe, 1993), 105, 114; and Smith, "Counting Flocks and Lost Sheep," esp. 19–22.

42. Hammond, *Religion and Personal Autonomy*, 7–8 (quotation), 30, 43, 55; Stephen Carter, *The Culture of Disbelief* (New York: Basic Books, 1993).

43. Presser and Stinson, "Data Collection Mode," 144. Each of these two archives of time series data from youth surveys includes hundreds of thousands of respondents, so the trends are highly reliable.

44. The coefficient of variation for annualized measures of church attendance rose from 0.9 (1974–75) to 1.1 (1998–99) in both the General Social Survey and the DDB Needham Life Style archives and from 7.5 (1975) to 17.3 (1995) in the Americans' Use of Time archive. See also Glenn, "Trend in 'No Religion' Respondents," 309.

488 NOTES

45. Between 1980 and 1990 the five states that experienced the greatest *increase* in adherence to a Christian church were Mississippi, Alabama, Louisiana, South Carolina, and Georgia, while the five states that experienced the greatest *decrease* were Vermont, New Hampshire, Maine, Oregon, and Massachusetts. See *Statistical Abstract of the United States: 1996*, table 89. See also Hammond, *Religion and Personal Autonomy*, esp. 165. On the other hand, this regional polarization in religiosity does *not* appear in the General Social Survey, Roper Social and Political Trends, or DDB Needham Life Style data.

46. See Smith, "Counting Flocks and Lost Sheep"; Roof and McKinney, *American Mainline Religion*, 16; and Finke and Stark, *The Churching of America*, 248, on change between 1945–52 and 1985 in market share by denomination. The same pattern—increases in market share for Catholics and "none," declines for Protestants and Jews—appears in the Gallup poll (1947–99), the National Election Studies (1948–88), the annual UCLA Survey of College Freshmen (1966–97), the Roper Social and Political Trends surveys (1974–94), and the General Social Survey (1974–98). Roper surveys report a decline in the Protestant share of the population from 62 percent in 1973–74 to 50 percent in 1991–92; Harris Poll, a decline from 67 percent in 1966 to 55 percent in 1992; the GSS, a decline from 63 percent in 1972 to 53 percent in 1998; and the Gallup poll, a decline from 70 percent in 1962 to 55 percent in 1999. A virtually identical decline of 22 percent in the Protestant share of U.S. population from 1966 to 1991 is implied in Hadaway and Roozen, *Rerouting the Protestant Mainstream*, 30. The Protestant share of the U.S. population also declined between 1890 and 1906, because of massive immigration of Catholics and Jews from southern and Eastern Europe, but that decline was almost surely less than 10 percent. See Finke and Stark, *The Churching of America*, 113.

47. The terms *evangelical* and *fundamentalist* are used somewhat loosely to refer to churches that emphasize acceptance of Jesus as one's personal savior (the "born again" experience), a more or less literal reading of the Bible, and the obligation of Christians to spread the word of God, though there are sharp theological, social, and political differences within this broad category. On trends in evangelical and fundamentalist church membership, see Penny Long Marler and C. Kirk Hadaway, "New Church Development and Denominational Growth (1950–1988): Symptom or Cause?" in *Church and Denominational Growth*, ed. David A. Roozen and C. Kirk Hadaway (Nashville, Tenn.: Abingdon Press, 1993), 47–86; Smith, "Counting Flocks and Lost Sheep," esp. 10 and 16; Finke and Stark, *The Churching of America*, esp. 248; Roof and McKinney, *American Mainline Religion*; Wuthnow, *The Restructuring of American Religion*; Wuthnow, "Mobilizing Civic Engagement"; Tom W. Smith, "Are Conservative Churches Growing?" *Review of Religious Research* 33 (June 1992): 305–329; David Roozen, "Denominations Grow as Individuals Join Congregations," in Roozen and Hadaway, *Church and Denominational Growth*, 15–35; and Wade Clark Roof, "America's Voluntary Establishment: Mainline Religion in Transition," 137–38.

48. Author's analysis of GSS, Roper, NIMH, NES, and Americans' Use of Time survey data. See also Hout and Greeley, "The Center Doesn't Hold," and Presser and Stinson, "Data Collection Mode." Smith ("Counting Flocks and Lost Sheep," 14) notes that between 1958 and 1986 the proportion of the U.S. population attending Protestant services in an average week dropped 6.6 percentage points, while the Catholic proportion dropped 4.6 percentage points. According to the Roper Social and Political Trends data, the comparable declines between 1974–75 and 1991–92 were 6.1 percentage points for Protestants and 2.1 percentage points for Catholics. Hout and Greeley argue that the entire decline in church attendance over the last thirty years is due to a onetime jump in Catholic disaffection over Vatican social policies, but that thesis is inconsistent with two facts. First, the slump in participation rates among Catholics is a continuing one. Second, declining observance among Protestants appears not in lower rates of attendance *among* members, but in lower rates of membership itself.

49. Darren E. Sherkat and Christopher G. Ellison, "The Politics of Black Religious Change: Disaffiliation from Black Mainline Denominations," *Social Forces* 70 (December 1991): 431–54, and Sherry Sherrod DuPree and Herbert C. DuPree, "The Explosive Growth of the African American Pentecostal Church," in *Yearbook of American and Canadian Churches* (Nashville, Tenn.: Abingdon Press, 1993), 7–10. According to the Roper Social and Political Trends data, between 1974 and 1994 weekly church attendance declined by 2.7 percentage points per decade (or roughly 11 percent overall) among blacks, as compared with a decline of 3.2 percentage points (or roughly 15 percent overall) among nonblacks. Over the same period, according to the GSS data, membership in church groups declined by roughly 18 percent among blacks, as compared to 16 percent for nonblacks.

50. Finke and Stark, *The Churching of America*; Christian Smith, *American Evangelicalism: Embattled and Thriving* (Chicago: University of Chicago Press, 1998); and William G. McLoughlin, *Revivals, Awakenings, and Reform: An Essay on Religion and Social Change in America, 1607–1977* (Chicago: University of Chicago Press, 1978).

51. Wade Clark Roof, "America's Voluntary Establishment: Mainline Religion in Transition," 134.

52. Wuthnow, "Mobilizing Civic Engagement," 6. Catholics are more likely than Protestants to attend church, but Protestants as a group are more likely to engage in other socioreligious activities; see Verba, Schlozman, and Brady, *Voice and Equality*, 246–47; 320–25.

53. Here I draw heavily on Wuthnow, "Mobilizing Civic Engagement" and Wilson and Janoski, "The Contribution of Religion to Volunteer Work," 138, 149–50. For the contrary argument that evangelical Protestants are fully involved in civic affairs, see Smith, *American Evangelicalism*, but also the critical review of this book by Mark Chaves in *Christian Century* 116 (1999): 227–29.

54. George Marsden, "Preachers of Paradox: The New Religious Right in Historical Perspective," in Douglas and Tipton, *Religion and America*, 150–168, quotation at 161; philanthropy figures calculated from the General Social Survey, 1987–89.

55. Nancy Tatom Ammerman, *Bible Believers: Fundamentalists in the Modern World* (New Brunswick, N.J.: Rutgers University Press, 1987), George Will, "Chuck Colson's Miracle," *Washington Post*, May 30, 1999, p. B07; Joe Loconte, "Jailhouse Rock of Ages," *Policy Review* 84 (July/August 1997): 12–14; Chaves, "Religious Congregations and Welfare Reform."

56. Wuthnow, "Mobilizing Civic Engagement."

57. Wuthnow, "Mobilizing Civic Engagement," 14; see also Wilson and Janoski, "The Contribution of Religion to Volunteer Work," 138, and Fredrick C. Harris, "Religious Institutions and African American Political Mobilization," in *Classifying By Race*, ed. Paul E. Peterson (Princeton, N.J.: Princeton University Press, 1995). Wuthnow and

Hodgkinson, *Faith and Philanthropy in America*, ch. 8, report that liberal Protestant churches are more involved than conservative churches in thirty-five different public activities—indeed all such activities except right-to-life protests.

CHAPTER 5: CONNECTIONS IN THE WORKPLACE

1. War is associated with increases in union membership throughout American history and also in other countries. See Richard B. Freeman, "Spurts in Union Growth: Defining Moments and Social Processes," in *The Defining Moment: The Great Depression and the American Economy in the Twentieth Century*, ed. Michael D. Bordo, Claudia Goldin, and Eugene N. White (Chicago: University of Chicago Press, 1998), 265–295; and Gary N. Chaison and Joseph B. Rose, "The Macrodeterminants of Union Growth and Decline," in *The State of the Unions*, Industrial Relations Research Association Series, ed. George Strauss, Daniel G. Gallagher, and Jack Fiorita (Madison, Wis.: IRRA, 1991), 3–45, esp. 33.

2. A national survey in 1953 found that 23 percent of the respondents belonged to labor unions, the single most common type of membership in voluntary associations. See Charles R. Wright and Herbert H. Hyman, "Voluntary Association Memberships of American Adults: Evidence from National Sample Surveys," *American Sociological Review* 23 (June 1958): 284–294. To be sure, union membership is more likely to be merely nominal than membership in other voluntary associations, in part because union shop rules mean that some union memberships are not voluntary at all. On the other hand, as late as 1987, according to the General Social Survey, nearly half of all union members (46 percent) said that they were actively involved in union affairs.

3. Paul Weiler, "The Representation Gap in the North American Workplace," unpublished lecture, as quoted in Chaison and Rose, "The Macrodeterminants of Union Growth and Decline," 13.

4. For various interpretations of union decline, see William T. Dickens and Jonathan S. Leonard, "Accounting for the Decline in Union Membership, 1950–1980," *Industrial & Labor Relations Review* 38 (April 1985): 323–334; Leo Troy, "The Rise and Fall of American Trade Unions," in *Unions in Transition: Entering the Second Century*, ed. Seymour Martin Lipset (San Francisco: ICS Press, 1986), 75–109; Michael Goldfield, *The Decline of Organized Labor in the United States* (Chicago: University of Chicago Press, 1987); Chaison and Rose, "The Macrodeterminants of Union Growth and Decline"; and Freeman, "Spurts in Union Growth." Henry S. Farber, "Extent of Unionization in the United States," in *Challenges and Choices Facing American Labor*, ed. Thomas A. Kochan (Cambridge, Mass.: MIT Press, 1985), 15–43, statistic at 38, estimates that structural factors account for 40 percent of the total decline, whereas Richard B. Freeman and James L. Medoff, *What Do Unions Do?* (New York: Basic Books, 1984), put the figure at roughly 55–60 percent. Chaison and Rose, "The Macrodeterminants of Union Growth and Decline," estimate that the change in industrial composition accounts for no more than 25 percent of the total decline.

5. Troy, "The Rise and Fall of American Trade Unions," 87; and *Statistical Abstract of the United States: 1997*, table 691; *Union Data Book 1998* (Washington, D.C.: Bureau of National Affairs, 1998).

6. Henry S. Farber and Alan B. Krueger, "Union Membership in the United States: The Decline Continues," National Bureau of Economic Research working paper no. W4216 (Cambridge, Mass.: National Bureau of Economic Research, 1992), 17–18.

7. Peter J. Pestillo, "Can the Unions Meet the Needs of a 'New' Work Force?" *Monthly Labor Review* 102 (February 1979): 33. In the DDB Needham Life Style surveys, agreement that "unions have too much power in America" dropped from 79 percent in 1977 to 55 percent in 1998.

8. For the 1950s, see Murray Hausknecht, *The Joiners*; and the 1952 National Election Study. For the 1980s and 1990s, see the General Social Survey; Verba, Schlozman, and Brady, *Voice and Equality*; and the 1996 National Election Study.

9. Author's analysis of General Social Survey. On the other hand, the fraction of the population in professional or higher managerial jobs rose by about this same amount. Among those eligible to join professional associations there is a slight downward trend (not statistically significant) in membership rates over time.

10. Figure 15 is intended as a rough summary of the experiences of eight separate organizations. The standardization technique in figure 8 is used here. Since data are not available for all eight for the entire period, constructing yearly averages involves some arbitrariness. See appendix III for separate charts for each of the eight organizations. Membership figures were obtained from the national headquarters of the respective associations, numbers of professionals from *Historical Statistics of the United States: Colonial Times to 1970* (Washington, D.C.: U.S. Bureau of the Census, 1975) and unpublished data from the Bureau of Labor Statistics. In each case I divided total membership by the number of people actually employed in that profession nationwide, cross-checking between government and associational statisticians. Figures for employed mechanical engineers for 1930 and 1940 are estimates. Only CPAs may become members of the American Institute of Certified Public Accountants, but consistent historical data are available only for all accountants, not just CPAs. Figure 15 thus understates membership among CPAs, but the broad trend—rising market share from 1900 to 1980–90 and then slipping—is probably accurate.

11. This pattern applies to a number of other professional associations, such as the National Society of Professional Engineers, but we were unable to construct satisfactory data series to chart the decline in detail.

12. Facing membership decline, many organizations added new categories of "affiliates" for students, apprentices, workers in allied fields, and so on. This practice raised the numerator of the "market share" fraction without any compensating adjustment in the denominator (people employed in that profession), so figure 15 tends, if anything, to understate the post-1970s slump.

13. The fraction of all surgeons who belong to the American College of Surgeons was 62 percent in 1975 and 64 percent in 1996. The fraction of all anesthesiologists in the American Society of Anesthesiology fell from 72 percent in 1970 to 65 percent in 1996.

14. Thanks to Kristin Goss and David Pinto-Duschinsky for exceptional help in preparing this section.

15. Alan Wolfe, "Developing Civil Society: Can the Workplace Replace Bowling?" *The Responsive Community* 8:2 (spring 1998), 41–47, quotations at 44. See also Maria T. Poarch, "Ties That Bind: U.S. Suburban Residents on the Social and Civic Dimensions of Work," *Community, Work & Family* 1 (1998): 125–147.

16. *Statistical Abstract of the United States, 1998*, table 644.

17. Arlie Russell Hochschild, *The Time Bind: When Work Becomes Home and Home Becomes Work* (New York: Henry Holt, 1997).

18. Maria T. Poarch, "Civic Life and Work: A Qualitative Study of Changing Patterns of Sociability and Civic Engagement in Everyday Life," (Ph.D. diss., Boston University, 1997), 166.

19. Michael Novak, *Business as a Calling* (New York: Free Press, 1996), quotation at 146–50; Thomas H. Naylor, William H. Willimon, and Rolf Österberg, *The Search for Meaning in the Workplace* (Nashville, Tenn.: Abingdon Press, 1996); Carolyn R. Shaffer and Kristin Anundsen, *Creating Community Anywhere: Finding Support and Connection in a Fragmented World* (New York: Perigree, 1993).

20. Paul Osterman, "How Common Is Workplace Transformation and How Can We Explain Who Does It?" *Industrial and Labor Relations Review* 47 (January 1994): 173–188; Peter Cappelli, *The New Deal at Work: Managing the Market-Driven Workforce* (Boston: Harvard Business School Press, 1999): 146–147, and the works cited there; Claudia H. Deutsch, "Communication in the Workplace; Companies Using Coffee Bars to Get Ideas Brewing," *New York Times*, November 5, 1995; Arlie Russell Hochschild, "There's No Place Like Work," *New York Times Magazine*, April 20, 1997, p. 53.

21. Ellen Galinsky, James T. Bond, and Dana E. Friedman, *The Changing Workforce* (New York: Families and Work Institute, 1993), 24; James T. Bond, Ellen Galinsky, and Jennifer E. Swanberg, *The 1997 National Study of the Changing Workforce* (New York: Families and Work Institute, 1998), 106, 103, 161. On friendship at work, see sources cited in endnote 24. Author's analysis of a Scripps-Howard/Ohio University national survey of interpersonal communication, June 1997.

22. *Gallup Poll Social Audit on Black/White Relations in the United States*, Executive Summary (Princeton, N.J.: Gallup Organization, June 1997); Peter Marsden, "Core Discussion Networks of Americans," *American Sociological Review* 52 (1987): 122–131; Diana C. Mutz and Jeffrey J. Mondak, "Democracy at Work: Contributions of the Workplace Toward a Public Sphere," unpublished manuscript, April 1998.

23. In addition to evidence later in this chapter, see also the discussion of figure 77 in chapter 14.

24. Claude S. Fischer, *To Dwell Among Friends: Personal Networks in Town and City* (Chicago: University of Chicago Press, 1982); Barry Wellman, R. Y. Wong, David Tindall, and Nancy Naxer, "A Decade of Network Change: Turnover, Persistence and Stability in Personal Communities," *Social Networks* 19 (1997): 27–50; Bruce C. Straits, "Ego-Net Diversity: Same- and Cross-Sex Co-worker Ties," *Social Networks* 18 (1996): 29–45; Gwen Moore, "Structural Determinants of Men's and Women's Personal Networks," *American Sociological Review* 53 (1990): 726–735; Stephen R. Marks, "Intimacy in the Public Realm: The Case of Co-workers," *Social Forces* 72 (1994): 843–858; Peter Marsden, "Core Discussion Networks of Americans."

25. Thomas R. Horton and Peter C. Reid, *Beyond the Trust Gap: Forging a New Partnership Between Managers and Their Employers* (Homewood, Ill.: Business One Irwin, 1991), 3; Cappelli, Bassi, et al., *Change at Work*, 67–69; and more generally, Cappelli, *New Deal at Work*; and Charles Heckscher, *White Collar Blues: Management Loyalties in an Age of Corporate Restructuring* (New York: Basic Books, 1995).

26. Cappelli, *New Deal at Work*, 17; on outplacement, see Horton and Reid, *Beyond the Trust Gap*, 9.

27. In 1989, 63 percent of workers said that employees were less loyal to their companies than ten years earlier, while only 22 percent said employees were more loyal: Horton and Reid, *Beyond the Trust Gap*, 10, citing a survey by Yankelovich Clancy Shulman. While restructuring hurts employee commitment, it often boosts productivity. See Cappelli, *New Deal at Work*, 45–46, 122–136, and Cappelli, Bassi, et al., *Change at Work*, 53–65, 79–84.

28. Heckscher, *White Collar Blues*, quotations at 6, 12, 49, 73. In a few firms Heckscher found a new form of limited community: "I'll do my best for you while I'm here, but neither of us sees this as a long-term relationship." See also Horton and Reid, *Beyond the Trust Gap*, 9–10, 40–43; Cappelli, Bassi, et al., *Change at Work*, 79–84; and Richard Sennett, *The Corrosion of Character: The Personal Consequences of Work in the New Capitalism* (New York: W. W. Norton, 1998).

29. Cappelli, *New Deal at Work*, 14.

30. Points of Light Foundation, *Corporate Volunteer Programs: Benefits to Business*, Report 1029, Fact Sheet (Washington, D.C., n.d.); Hodgkinson and Weitzman, *Giving and Volunteering 1996*, 4–111; *Giving and Volunteering in the United States: Findings from a National Survey, 1999 Executive Summary* (Washington, D.C.: Independent Sector, 1999). The fraction of volunteers who report being asked specifically by their employer is even lower—about 7–8 percent.

31. Lawrence Mishel, Jared Bernstein, and John Schmitt, *The State of Working America: 1998–99*, Economic Policy Institute (Ithaca, N.Y.: Cornell University Press, 1998), esp. 227–235; Cappelli, *New Deal at Work*, 133–135.

32. Mishel, Bernstein, and Schmitt, *State of Working America*, 242–250; Cappelli, *New Deal at Work*, 136–144; Cappelli, Bassi, et al., *Change at Work*, 73–78; Sharon R. Cohany, "Workers in Alternative Employment Arrangements: A Second Look," and Steven Hipple, "Contingent Work: Results from the Second Survey," both in *Monthly Labor Review* (November 1998): 3–35.

33. Ronald S. Burt and Marc Knez, "Trust and Third-Party Gossip," in Roderick M. Kramer and Tom R. Tyler, eds., *Trust in Organizations: Frontiers of Theory and Research* (Thousand Oaks, Calif.: Sage Publications, 1996), 68–89, esp. 77; Katherine J. Klein and Thomas A. D'Aunno, "Psychological Sense of Community in the Workplace," *Journal of Community Psychology* 14 (October 1986): 365–377, esp. 368; Fischer, *To Dwell Among Friends*. According to 1986 GSS data, the fraction of one's close friends who are co-workers is only two-thirds as great for part-time workers as for full-time workers.

34. Jeanne S. Hurlbert, "Social Networks, Social Circles, and Job Satisfaction," *Work and Occupations*, 18 (1991): 415–430; Randy Hodson, "Group Relations at Work: Solidarity, Conflict, and Relations with Management," *Work and Occupations* 24 (1997): 426–452; Ronni Sandroff, "The Power of Office Friendships," *Working Mother* (November 1997): 35–36, and the works cited there.

35. *Gallup Poll Monthly*, no. 332 (May 1993): 21; and http:\\www.gallup.com (October 1999); respondents with "no opinion" are excluded. Cheryl Russell, *The Master Trend: How the Baby Boom Generation Is Remaking America*

(New York: Plenum Press, 1993), 64. Author's analysis of General Social Survey, 1972–98: job satisfaction fell from c. 65 percent to c. 61 percent among workers fully content with their financial situation, from c. 48 percent to c. 43 percent among those more or less content with their finances, and from c. 36 percent to c. 30 percent among those dissatisfied with their finances. Glenn Firebaugh and Brian Harley, "Trends in Job Satisfaction in the United States by Race, Gender, and Type of Occupation," *Research in the Sociology of Work* 5 (1995): 87–104, report no change in job satisfaction through the 1980s, and Bond, Galinsky, and Swanberg, *The 1997 National Study of the Changing Workforce*, ch. 7, found modest growth in job satisfaction between 1977 and 1997. On the other hand, Cappelli, *New Deal at Work*, 122–123, reports that after decades of relative stability, several proprietary survey archives found declining job satisfaction after the early 1980s. I have found no hard evidence on incivility and aggression at work over time, though most Americans believe that it has grown; see John Marks, "The American Uncivil Wars," *U.S. News & World Report*, April 22, 1996; Joel H. Neuman and Robert A. Baron, "Aggression in the Workplace," in *Antisocial Behavior in Organizations*, eds. Robert A. Giacalone and Jerald Greenberg (Thousand Oaks, Calif.: Sage Publications, 1996), 37–67; and Christine M. Pearson, Lynne H. Andersson, and Judith W. Webner, "When Workers Flout Convention: A Study of Workplace Incivility" (unpublished ms., Chapel Hill: University of North Carolina, 1999).

36.   Wolfe, "Developing Civil Society," 45.

37.   John R. Aiello, "Computer-Based Work Monitoring: Electronic Surveillance and Its Effects," *Journal of Applied Social Psychology* 23 (1993): 499–507; Cynthia L. Estlund, "Free Speech and Due Process in the Workplace," *Indiana Law Journal* 71 (1995): 101–151; David C. Yamada, "Voices from the Cubicle: Protecting and Encouraging Private Employee Speech in the Post-Industrial Workplace," *Berkeley Journal of Employment and Labor Law* 19 (1998): 1–51; "More U.S. Firms Checking E-Mail, Computer Files, and Phone Calls" (New York: American Management Association, April 1999). Thanks to Jason Mazzone for his contribution to this section.

CHAPTER 6: INFORMAL SOCIAL CONNECTIONS

1.   Every single bivariate correlation among the dozens of measures in the DDB Needham Life Style and Roper data sets of the *macher* activities listed in the text is strongly positive, controlling for education, age, gender, race, and marital status. All but two of the scores of correlations among the several dozen measures of the listed *schmoozer* activities are strongly positive, controlling for the same demographic factors. The distinction between involvement in formal community organizations and involvement in informal social activities appears clearly in factor analyses of both the Roper and DDB Needham surveys. The correlation between formal and informal involvement is positive, but modest.

2.   All generalizations in the next two paragraphs are confirmed by multiple regression analysis of the demographic correlates of church and club attendance, volunteering, visiting friends, entertaining at home, playing cards, visiting bars, and the like, in both the Roper Social and Political Trends and DDB Needham Life Style archives.

3.   Data on letter writing and phone calls from Roper Social and Political Trends and DDB Needham Life Style archives; data on gifts from *Gallup Poll Monthly* 293 (February 1990): 31, and International Communications Research Survey Research Group, on behalf of Sears Corporation, 1997; data on greeting cards and time with friends from the DDB Needham Life Style archive; data on computer usage from "Computer Use in the United States," U.S. Census Bureau (Washington, D.C.: Department of Commerce, 1999), 5, 9. According to time diaries women spend more time than men visiting with friends and informally conversing. Claude S. Fischer, *America Calling: A Social History of the Telephone* (Berkeley: University of California Press, 1992), quotation at 235. Fischer shows that women everywhere have always been much heavier users of home phones. Even in the liberated 1990s young women were "more likely than males to express concern and responsibility for the well-being of others," according to Ann M. Beutel and Margaret Mooney Marini, "Gender and Values," *American Sociological Review* 60 (1995): 436–448, and Constance A. Flanagan et al., "Ties That Bind: Correlates of Adolescents' Civic Commitments in Seven Countries," *Journal of Social Issues* 54 (1998): 4457–4475. Differences in "social cognition" between men and women may even have a genetic basis. See D. H. Skuse et al., "Evidence from Turner's Syndrome of an Imprinted X-Linked Locus Affecting Cognitive Function," *Nature* 387 (June 1997): 705–708.

4.   Author's analysis of DDB Needham Life Style archive.

5.   Karen V. Hansen, *A Very Social Time: Crafting Community in Antebellum New England* (Berkeley: University of California Press, 1994), 80.

6.   Herbert Gans, *The Urban Villagers* (Glencoe, Ill.: Free Press, 1962); Fischer, *To Dwell Among Friends*; and Wellman, "The Community Question Reevaluated."

7.   Robert R. Bell, *Worlds of Friendship* (Beverly Hills, Calif.: Sage, 1981); Marsden, "Core Discussion Networks of Americans."

8.   This question was posed to national samples of roughly two thousand each in 1982, 1984, 1990, 1993, and 1995. Answers add to more than 100 percent because more than a single evening out could have been cited.

9.   Roper national samples of approximately 2,000 each in June 1986, April 1987, and June 1990 were asked about a wide variety of social and leisure activities, as indicated in figure 16.

10.   The disparity between hosting and going out reflects the fact that guests outnumber hosts at most parties.

11.   Author's analysis of the Americans' Use of Time archive.

12.   Author's analysis of DDB Needham Life Style archives. Because the various Roper (past week; past month) and Life Style (past year) questions are formulated differently, one cannot directly compare responses, but the patterns are quite consistent. For example, the relative frequency of restaurant dining, home entertaining, club meetings, visits to bars, movies, and sporting events is virtually the same in all three types of surveys.

13.   Author's analysis of DDB Needham Life Style surveys.

14.   According to the DDB Needham Life Style data, as figure 17 shows, over the last quarter of the twentieth century the average annual frequency was twelve card games and five movies.

15.   The top half of figure 18 is based on DDB Needham Life Style data; the bottom half is based on Roper Social and Political Trends data. Because sampling and wording differ between these two archives, the two halves of figure 18

are not directly comparable, but the fact that two such different archives show similar declines in social visiting is all the more significant. DDB Needham Life Style surveys also show that dinner parties (given or attended) declined from 7.1 per year in the mid-1970s to 3.7 in the late 1990s. Yankelovich Partners Inc. report that agreement that "I have very little room in my life for new friends these days" rose from 23 percent in 1985–86 to 32 percent in 1998–99. (I am grateful to Yankelovich Partners for sharing these data.) Mediamark Research annual surveys show a drop of one-fifth between the early 1980s and the late 1990s in the frequency of "entertaining friends or relatives at home." Finally, eight times between 1938 and 1990 Gallup pollsters asked about one's "favorite way of spending an evening." Over the whole period "dancing" and "playing cards and games" dropped sharply, and after the 1970s "visiting with friends" and "dining out" also dropped. "Watching TV" and "home with family" rose over this period, suggesting a cocooning pattern consistent with the Roper and DDB Needham data. On the other hand, because of changes in wording, I am less confident about the Gallup trends. (See George Gallup, Jr., *The Gallup Poll: Public Opinion* [Wilmington, Del.: Scholarly Resources Inc., 1986], 104, 130.) According to the General Social Survey, the frequency of spending a social evening with "friends who live outside the neighborhood" more than once a month rose from 40 percent in 1974–76 to 44 percent in 1994–96. Of the six national survey archives that I have discovered with trend data on friendship over the last several decades, this is the only series that does *not* show a significant decline. (Unlike other measures of friendship, this GSS metric is also inexplicably more common among men than women.) See also Robert J. Sampson, "Local Friendship Ties and Community Attachment in Mass Society: A Multilevel Systemic Model," *American Sociological Review* 53 (October 1988): 766–779; Fischer, *To Dwell Among Friends*; Claude S. Fischer, Robert M. Jackson, et al., *Networks and Places: Social Relations in the Urban Setting* (New York: Free Press, 1977).

16. According to DDB Needham Life Style data, restaurant dinners rose from eighteen annually in 1975–76 to twenty-two in 1998–99 for married people and declined from 19 in 1985–86 to eighteen in 1998–99 for single people. The National Restaurant Association (NRA) reported (www.restaurant.org/RUSA/trends/craving.htm) that the number of "commercially prepared dinners per week" was 1.2 in 1981, 1985, and 1991, and 1.3 in 1996. Of "commercially prepared" food, moreover, a rapidly growing share is take-out, so restaurant dining has slipped. Both the NRA and Life Style data suggest that the only significant increase in eating out over the last several decades is at breakfast. Real annual per capita spending on food and drink outside the home rose almost imperceptibly over the last three decades from $476 in 1967 (in 1997 dollars) to $499 in 1997. See U.S. Bureau of the Census, "Annual Benchmark Report for Retail Trade: January 1988 Through December 1997," Current Business Reports, Series BR/97-RV (Washington, D.C.: 1998). According to Consumer Expenditure Surveys by the Bureau of Labor Statistics, spending on food away from home as a fraction of all food spending was stationary over the period 1984–1997, rising cyclically during prosperous periods to a peak of 43 percent and falling during recessions to a low of 38 percent, with no long-term trend at all. This same business cycle pattern in dining out appears in Roper Social and Political Trends data from the early 1970s to the early 1990s, with no secular trend. The NPD time diary study described in endnote 40 below shows a slight trend away from eating out over the decade of the 1990s. In short, *none* of the available evidence suggests that dining out has significantly increased over the last several decades.

17. According to a Roper Social and Political Trends question posed three times between 1986 and 1994 (as summarized in *Roper Reports 94–10* [New York: Roper Starch Worldwide, 1995]), 62 percent of Americans prefer "getting together with friends in your home," whereas 31 percent prefer "going out with friends to a restaurant, bar, or club." Over this period, those who preferred going out slipped from 34 percent to 28 percent, while the fraction who volunteered that they were not interested in spending time with friends at all rose from 2 percent to 6 percent. In fact, this growing stay-at-home sentiment applies to virtually all leisure activities measured in the Roper surveys, from movies to music to take-out food.

18. According to the DDB Needham Life Style surveys, picnics per year among American adults fell from 4.9 per year in 1975 to 2.0 per year in 1999. John P. Robinson, "Where's the Boom?" *American Demographics* (March 1987): 36, reported a 20 percent decline in picnicking between 1962 and 1982.

19. Author's analysis of DDB Needham Life Style survey archive. The fraction of married respondents in the DDB Needham Life Style surveys who agree that "we usually have a big weekend family breakfast" fell from 57 percent in 1975 to 45 percent in 1995. Although the frequency of family meals differs between couples with and without children, the trends over time are identical.

20. Single-person households doubled from 13 percent in 1960 to 26 percent in 1998, while the fraction of married couple households fell from 74 percent to 53 percent. See Lynne M. Casper and Ken Bryson, "Household and Family Characteristics: March 1998 (Update)," *Current Population Reports*, P20–515 (Washington, D.C.: U.S. Bureau of the Census, October 1998).

21. *Roper Reports 97–5* (New York: Roper Starch Worldwide, 1997), 186–191, based on surveys in 1976, 1986, 1990, 1995, and 1997. Confirming this trend, Sandra Hofferth and Jack Sandberg, "Changes in American Children's Time, 1981–1997," PSC Research Report No. 98-431 (Ann Arbor, Mich.: University of Michigan Population Studies Center, 1998), report that the time that children spend on weekday family meals declined 20 percent between 1981 and 1997, while family conversational time was cut in half.

22. Author's analysis from Roper Social and Political Trends surveys (augmented by data from *Roper Reports 1995-3* (New York: Roper Starch Worldwide, 1995), General Social Surveys, and DDB Needham Life Style surveys, using annualization formula in appendix I and linear regression to estimate slope.

Survey	Question Wording	Time Span	Singles Trend	Married Trend
Roper	Went out to bar, night club or disco in previous week?	1982–1995	−39%	−60%
GSS	How often do you go to a bar or tavern?	1974–1998	−31%	−41%
DDB	How many times last year did you go to a bar or tavern?	1988–1999	−21%	−13%

23. Data in figure 20 from Jack Richman, ed., "1998 National Retail Census," in *Report to Retailers* (New York: Audits & Surveys Worldwide, 1998). Until 1998 "coffee bars and shops" were not broken out by Audits & Surveys as a separate category within "other." I am grateful to Audits & Surveys for these data.

24. George Ritzer, *The McDonaldization of Society: An Investigation into the Changing Character of Contemporary Social Life*, rev. ed. (Thousand Oaks, Calif.: Pine Forge Press, 1996), 132–136.

25. Ray Oldenburg, *The Great Good Place: Cafes, Coffee Shops, Community Centers, Beauty Parlors, General Stores, Bars, Hangouts, and How They Get You Through the Day* (New York: Paragon House, 1989).

26. See Oswald Jacoby and Albert H. Morehead, *The Fireside Book of Cards* (New York: Simon & Schuster, 1957), 17, on 1940 survey. Until the 1950s every pack of playing cards sold in America was subject to a special tax. We have updated data in Jesse Frederick Steiner, *Americans at Play: Recent Trends in Recreation and Leisure Time Activities* (New York: McGraw-Hill, 1933), 138, with later Treasury reports.

27. For evidence on generalizations in this paragraph, see David Scott, "Narrative Analysis of a Declining Social World: The Case of Contract Bridge," *Play and Culture* 4 (February 1991): 11–23, at 11; Babchuk and Booth, "Voluntary Association Membership," 34; Bonnie H. Erickson and T. A. Nosanchuk, "How an Apolitical Association Politicizes," *Canadian Review of Sociology and Anthropology* 27 (May 1990): 206–219; and David Scott and Geoffrey C. Godbey, "An Analysis of Adult Play Groups: Social Versus Serious Participation in Contract Bridge," *Leisure Sciences* 14 (January/March 1992): 47–67.

28. Author's analysis of DDB Needham Life Style data. Mediamark Research annual surveys show a comparable drop of roughly 40 percent in the frequency of playing cards between the early 1980s and the late 1990s.

29. This calculation assumes, following the DDB Needham Life Style survey data, 8.4 games per adult per year (declining at the rate of .4 games per year), 192 million adults, 3.5 adults per game.

30. Author's analysis of DDB Needham Life Style data. Between 1981 and 1998 card playing dropped by 36 percent among people sixty and over, but by 48 percent among people under sixty. In the mid-1970s younger people played cards more often than their elders, but by the 1990s this pattern had been reversed. Age data supplied by the American Contract Bridge League, Memphis, Tennessee.

31. Children's board games are rapidly being replaced by play-alone computer games, fueling (according to Adam Pertman, "Board Games? No Dice," *Boston Globe*, December 16, 1998) "a fundamental societal shift away from an emphasis on community-based values and behavior."

32. Author's analysis of DDB Needham Life Style surveys, 1977–96.

33. Author's analysis of GSS surveys, using the annualization algorithm given in appendix I.

34. The University of Michigan-NIMH study cited in endnote 23 of chapter 3 found that the percentage of American adults who "got together" with friends and relatives at least once a week fell from 65 percent in 1957 to 58 percent in 1976, a statistically significant decline. The fraction of Detroit-area residents who "got together" with their neighbors at least once a week fell from 44 percent in 1955 to 32 percent in 1959 and to 24 percent in 1971. Author's analysis of data from the University of Michigan-NIMH study and from Detroit Area Study, made available through the Inter-university Consortium for Political and Social Research.

35. Author's analysis of National Election Study of 1996.

36. See Barrett A. Lee, R. S. Oropesa, Barbara J. Metch, and Avery M. Guest, "Testing the Decline-of-Community Thesis: Neighborhood Organizations in Seattle, 1929 and 1979," *American Journal of Sociology* 89 (1984):1161–1188, quotation at 1165; Alexander von Hoffman, *Local Attachments: The Making of an American Urban Neighborhood, 1850–1920* (Baltimore, Md.: Johns Hopkins University Press, 1994). See also Robert A. Rosenbloom, "The Neighborhood Movement: Where Has It Come From? Where Is It Going?" *Journal of Voluntary Action Research* 10 (April/June 1981): 4–26; Matthew A. Crenson, *Neighborhood Politics* (Cambridge, Mass.: Harvard University Press, 1983); John R. Logan and Gordana Rabrenovic, "Neighborhood Associations: Their Issues, Their Allies, and Their Opponents," *Urban Affairs Quarterly* 26 (1990): 68–94; and Robert Fisher, *Let the People Decide: Neighborhood Organizing in America*, 2nd ed. (New York: Twayne Publishers, 1994). Robert C. Ellickson, "New Institutions for Old Neighborhoods," *Duke Law Journal* 48 (1998): 75–110, esp. 81, presents evidence that homeowners associations ("residential community associations") have recently proliferated, in large part as a marketing device for new suburban developments.

37. *Criminal Victimization and Perceptions of Community Safety in 12 Cities, 1998* (Washington, D.C.: U.S. Department of Justice, 1999): 21. Another 61 percent of the respondents said they and their neighbors had agreed to watch out for one another's safety, illustrating the enduring importance of "natural" social capital, but unfortunately the study provides no evidence on its changing importance over time.

38. See James R. Gillham and George A. Barnett, "Decaying Interest in Burglary Prevention, Residence on a Block with an Active Block Club, and Communication Linkage: A Routine Activities Approach," *Journal of Crime & Justice* 17 (1994): 23–48 and the extensive literature cited there, especially at 24.

39. Author's analysis of Americans' Use of Time data. For further details, see appendix I. Our analysis here is limited to "primary" activities, excluding, for example, conversation while primarily engaged in child care or work. Because of an inconsistency in the coding of phone conversations in 1965, the figure for informal conversations in that year is imprecise. The participation rate for all informal socializing for 1965 almost certainly lies between 58 and 68 percent, and the mean time per day almost certainly lies between seventy-eight and eighty-nine minutes. The dotted lines in figure 24 reflect the midpoint of these bands of uncertainty. If "informal conversation" is excluded from the analysis to avoid this uncertainty, the thirty-year decline in time spent "visiting with friends" remains highly significant. Robinson and Godbey, *Time for Life*, 170 and 176, confirm a substantial decline in informal socializing between 1965 and 1985. In the DDB Needham Life Style archive the fraction of Americans, both married and single, who report that they "spend a lot of time visiting friends" has slipped by about 10 percent over the past decade or two.

40. *Time Lines: How Americans Spent Their Time During the 90s* (Rosemont, Ill.: NPD Group, July 1999). Every year between 1992 and 1999 the NPD Group asked three thousand adults to record their activities every thirty minutes during a twenty-four-hour period. My analysis weights men and women equally and weekday and weekend reports

appropriately to produce a "synthetic week." I am grateful to Harry Balzer and his colleagues at NPD for sharing their results with me; they are not responsible for my interpretations.

41. Author's analysis of DDB Needham Life Style, General Social Survey, Americans' Use of Time, and Roper Social and Political Trends data archives.

42. On single-person households, see endnote 20 above. According to the General Social Survey, the fraction of all adults who are married with children under 19 fell from 32 percent in 1975 to 24 percent in 1998.

43. Author's calculations from surveys of sports participation conducted on behalf of the National Sporting Goods Association (NSGA; 1986–97), the Sporting Goods Manufacturers Association (SGMA; 1987–97), and the DDB Needham Life Style surveys (1985–98), as well as a report on the National Health Interview Surveys (NHIS) of the National Center for Health Statistics (1985–95) as reported in John P. Robinson and Geoffrey Godbey, "Has Fitness Peaked?" *American Demographics*, September 1993, 36–42, updated by author's analysis of 1995 NHIS data from the NCHS. The NSGA results are based on persons aged seven and over who engaged in a given sport at least twice in the previous year. The SGMA results are based on persons aged six and over who engaged in the sport at least once in the previous year. The Life Style results are based on adults who engaged in the sport at least once in the previous year. The NHIS results are based on adults who had participated in the sport in the previous two weeks. Each of these four archives is based on surveys with tens of thousands of Americans, and each posed somewhat different questions to somewhat different populations. Nevertheless, with few exceptions, both levels and trends are consistent across the four series. (Thus this evidence is more credible than the evidence from the General Social Survey, based in some cases on only a few hundred interviews a year.) Among the dozens of different sports measured in these four archives, the only significant discrepancies involve hiking (up in the NSGA studies, down in the SGMA and Life Style studies) and bicycling (down in the NSGA, SGMA, and Life Style surveys, but up in the NHIS). The NSGA data are sometimes reported (as in the *Statistical Abstract of the United States*, for example) without adjusting for overall population growth. This practice gives a misleading impression of buoyancy in American athletic habits.

44. The NSGA surveys report a decline of 32 percent between 1986 and 1997; the SGMA surveys a decline of 36 percent between 1987 and 1997; the Life Style surveys a decline of 34 percent between 1983 and 1996; the NHIS a decline of roughly 25 percent between 1985 and 1995. All four concur that in the late 1990s no more than ten million American adults played softball at least four times a year. By contrast, the Amateur Softball Association, as recorded in the *Statistical Abstract of the United States*, claimed an unvarying figure of exactly forty-one million players every year over the last decade or two. I found no other source consistent with that figure; it may represent administrative lethargy rather than actual surveys.

45. According to the DDB Needham Life Style archive, exercise at home declined from an annual national average of eighteen times per year in 1984 to thirteen times per year in 1998. By contrast, the NSGA, SGMA, and NHIS data, based on as little as a single episode per year, suggest growth in home exercise over those years. This evidence suggests that many newly purchased treadmills and other exercise equipment may sit unused in America's basements after a single, hopeful tryout. In any event, exercise on a home treadmill is hardly an occasion for building social capital.

46. According to the NSGA surveys, the proportion of all Americans aged seven and over who played soccer at least twice a year grew from 4 percent in 1986 to 6 percent in 1997, and the comparable figures for basketball were 10 percent and 13 percent. Meanwhile, over the same period the proportion who played baseball fell from 7 percent to 6 percent, football (touch plus tackle) from roughly 9 percent to roughly 8 percent, softball from 10 percent to 7 percent, and volleyball from 11 percent to 7 percent. In short, the gain of 5 percentage points for soccer and basketball must be offset against the aggregate loss of 9 points for the other four sports. According to the SGMA surveys, participation in the "big six" team sports (as proportion of population aged six and over) declined from about 72 percent in 1987 to 62 percent in 1997. In short, both archives agree that participation in team sports declined by roughly 10–15 percent over the most recent decade. Aggregate participation in thirty-six different sports activities (weighted by frequency of participation) measured by the NSGA in 1987 and 1997—from treadmills to trap shooting and from powerboating to power walking—fell by about 5 percent. The equivalent figure for forty-nine different sports measured by the SGMA is a decline of 4 percent.

47. Data in this paragraph are from the DDB Needham Life Style archive. Swimming among twenty-somethings fell from about twelve times a year in the early 1980s to less than half that in 1998, while swimming among people sixty and over remained constant at about four times a year. Between 1989 and 1998, attendance at health clubs more than doubled among those over sixty (from an average of once a year to more than twice a year), while health club attendance declined among eighteen- to twenty-nine-year-olds from six times a year to five. This same pattern—greater declines in younger age groups—is confirmed in the National Center for Health Statistics surveys in 1985 and 1990; see Robinson and Godbey, "Has Fitness Peaked?," 38, 42. John P. Robinson, "Where's the Boom?," 34–37, summarizes recreational surveys in 1965 and 1982: People forty-five and over in 1982 were more active than people that age in 1965, whereas people under twenty-five in 1982 were less active than people that age in 1965.

48. According to the 1998 *State of the Industry Report* of the Sporting Goods Manufacturers Association, "One disturbing trend is the overall decline in physical fitness and sports/fitness-related activity among youngsters in America. . . . [Between 1986 and 1997] the number of 12–17-year-olds who participated in any sport, fitness or team activity, on a 'frequent' basis, increased by only 2.9% to 13 million youth [equivalent to a 4 percent *decline* on a per capita basis]." See also "Is Working Out Uncool?" *American Demographics*, March 1996 and *America's Youth in the 1990s*, ed. Robert Bezilla (Princeton, N.J.: Gallup International Institute, 1993), 228. On the other hand, Hofferth and Sandberg, "Changes in American Children's Time," report that time spent on sports outside of school by preadolescents aged three to twelve increased from 2½ hours in 1981 to 4 hours in 1997.

49. Youth membership in organized soccer leagues, standardized for numbers of youth aged five to nineteen, more than tripled between 1980 and 1995, according to the Soccer Industry Council. On the other hand, both SGMA and NSGA data suggest that nationwide per capita growth in soccer participation stagnated after 1990, especially among adolescents. See also *Youth Indicators 1996: Trends in the Well-Being of American Youth* (Washington, D.C.: National Center for Education Statistics, 1996), Indicator 41.

50. An upbeat report by the Sporting Goods Manufacturers Association, *Gaining Ground: A Progress Report on Women in Sports, 1998*, concedes (p. 3) that "except in the 6–11 age group, there has been little change in the overall percent of females who play sports frequently." In fact, the report shows that regular sports participation by women aged twenty-five to thirty-five declined from 8.3 percent in 1987 to 5.8 percent in 1997. Ironically, the beneficiaries of Title IX appear less likely to participate in sports as adults than their older sisters.

51. After rapid growth in the early 1980s, membership in health clubs (according to the International Health, Racquet & Sports Club Association) rose from 80 per 1,000 adults in 1987 to 102 per 1,000 adults in 1995. These figures are virtually identical to DDB Needham Life Style figures for people who report nine or more health club visits in the previous year. Based on as little as a single visit, SGMA surveys show a 51 percent growth between 1987 and 1997.

52. Data in this and the previous paragraph are from the DDB Needham Life Style archive. According to the 1998 survey, 29 percent of American adults played cards at least nine times in the previous year, compared to 9 percent who visited a health club that often. Even among college-educated twenty-something singles, health club visits edge out card games only four to three. Participation in jogging, health clubs, and exercise classes combined was virtually constant from 1989 to 1999. The growth in exercise walking is entirely concentrated among Americans over fifty. The senior boom in exercise walking appears in all four data sets on sports participation. On obesity, see K. M. Flegal, et al., "Overweight and Obesity in the United States: Prevalence and Trends, 1960–1994," *International Journal of Obesity and Related Metabolic Disorders* 22 (January 1998): 39–47, and Ali H. Mokdad, et al., "The Spread of the Obesity Epidemic in the United States, 1991–1998," *Journal of the American Medical Association* 282 (October 27, 1999): 1519–1522.

53. NSGA data suggest that bowling participation rates grew about 6 percent between 1986 and 1997, compared to a 1 percent increase in SGMA data, a 1 percent decline in NHIS data, and a 6 percent decline in DDB Needham Life Style data. In short, participation in bowling (unlike most sports) has just about kept pace with population growth.

54. Author's analysis of NSGA, SGMA, and DDB Needham Life Style surveys. Among all physical activities, walking, swimming, working out, and bicycling are more common, and fishing is tied, though falling behind. Basketball and pool are the next most popular sports, but have only about three-quarters as many participants as bowling.

55. Author's analysis of DDB Needham Life Style surveys. According to the 1996 survey, Americans in their twenties bowled 2.4 times per year and went in-line skating 1.7 times per year. On cosmic bowling, see Lisa Chadderdon, "AMF Is on a Roll," *Fast Company*, September 1998, 132.

56. Data from the American Bowling Congress.

57. Figure on annual bowlers from *Statistical Abstract of the United States: 1998*, table 437, 265. Other sources give the somewhat lower estimate of 54 million for annual bowling participants. The Committee for the Study of the American Electorate, "Turnout Dips to 56-Year Low" (Washington, D.C.: CSAE, November 5, 1998), at www.epn.org/csae/cgans4.html reported that 72.5 million Americans voted in 1998.

58. Attendance at horse and greyhound racing and jai-alai collapsed with the rise of legalized gambling in the 1980s and is excluded from figure 27. We are, it appears, increasingly gambling alone. Seasonally adjusted Roper survey data on whether the respondent had gone out to watch a sports event in the preceding week show a modest increase from roughly 8 percent in the early 1970s to roughly 10–12 percent in the late 1980s. According to a 1993 survey three to five times as many people watch sports on TV as attend games; see *Public Perspective* 5 (March/April 1994), 98. To some extent the growth in spectatorship at professional sports events (and quasi-professional events, like college football and basketball) is offset by a decline in spectatorship at amateur sports events like high school football and basketball, a trade-off that probably reflects a net decline in community connectedness.

59. In unpublished analyses of the DDB Needham Life Style survey archive for 1997–1998, Thad Williamson (Department of Government, Harvard University, 1999) found that, controlling for age, sex, education, and financial, marital, and parental status, and general leisure activity level, attendance at live sporting events is positively associated with civic engagement. However, this "pro-civic" effect of sports spectatorship appears confined to *amateur* sporting events—Little League, high school football, and college soccer.

60. Author's analysis of DDB Needham Life Style surveys.

61. Author's analysis of DDB Needham Life Style surveys. According to National Endowment for the Arts surveys of arts participation, lifetime exposure to music lessons declined from 47 percent in 1982 to 40 percent in 1992.

62. *Music USA 1997* (Carlsbad, Calif.: National Association of Music Merchants, 1997): 37–38.

CHAPTER 7: ALTRUISM, VOLUNTEERING, AND PHILANTHROPY

1. Robert B. Westbrook, *John Dewey and American Democracy* (Ithaca, N.Y.: Cornell University Press, 1991), 164. See also Theda Skocpol, "America's Voluntary Groups Thrive in a National Network," *The Brookings Review* 15 (fall 1997): 16–19. I am grateful to Gerald Gamm and Celia Borenstein for the story about Providence.

2. Everett Carll Ladd, *The Ladd Report* (New York: Free Press, 1999), 131–145.

3. Andrew Carnegie, "Wealth," *North American Review* 148 (June 1889), 653–664.

4. F. Emerson Andrews, *Philanthropic Giving* (New York: Russell Sage Foundation, 1950), 141. Professionalization of philanthropy accelerated at the end of the twentieth century; for example, membership in the National Society of Fund Raising Executives grew tenfold from 1,900 in 1979 to 18,800 in 1997.

5. *The Chronicle of Philanthropy*, October 30, 1997; Debra Blum, "United States Has 7 Charities per 10,000 People, Study Shows," *The Chronicle of Philanthropy*, August 7, 1997. Tax laws help explain the boom in newly organized charities.

6. Tocqueville, *Democracy in America*, 526. Sources for previous paragraph: Volunteering: Hodgkinson and Weitzman, *Giving and Volunteering* 1996, 3; they find that informal helping, though perhaps underreported, accounts for less than one-quarter of all volunteering. Philanthropy: Ann E. Kaplan, ed., *Giving USA 1998* (New York: AAFRC Trust for Philanthropy, 1998). Blood: E. L. Wallace, et al., "Collection and Transfusion of Blood and Blood Components in the United States, 1992," *Transfusion* 35 (October 1995): 802–812. According to the Harris Poll #88 (December 24, 1996), 76 percent of blood donors cite "wanting to help others" as the reason for their donation. 1989 survey:

Lichang Lee, Jane Allyn Piliavin, and Vaughn R. A. Call, "Giving Time, Money, and Blood: A Comparative Analysis" (Madison, Wisc.: University of Wisconsin, 1998). All three estimates are inflated by the public's desire to appear altruistic, but their relative standing is probably accurate.

7. *Giving and Volunteering: 1996*, 35–38, and Jane Allyn Piliavin and Hong-Wen Charng, "Altruism: A Review of Recent Theory and Research," *Annual Review of Sociology* 16 (1990): 27–65, esp. 56.

8. The following generalizations are commonly reported in the scientific literature and confirmed by the author's analysis of DDB Needham Life Style and Roper Social and Political Trends archives, as well as *Giving and Volunteering* survey data for 1996.

9. Paul G. Schervish and John J. Havens, "Do the Poor Pay More? Is the U-Shaped Curve Correct?" *Nonprofit and Voluntary Sector Quarterly* 24 (spring 1995): 79–90.

10. Author's analysis of DDB Needham Life Style and Roper Social and Political Trends surveys. (In the DDB Needham Life Style data, regular blood donation is slightly lower in rural areas than in big cities, but that is not the usual finding.) On size-of-place differences in altruism, see Charles Korte and Nancy Kerr, "Responses to Altruistic Opportunities in Urban and Nonurban Settings," *Journal of Social Psychology* 95 (April 1975): 183–184; James S. House and Sharon Wolf, "Effects of Urban Residence on Interpersonal Trust and Helping Behavior," *Journal of Personality and Social Psychology* 36 (1978): 1029–1043; Thomas C. Wilson, "Settlement Type and Interpersonal Estrangement: A Test of the Theories of Wirth and Gans," *Social Forces* 64 (September 1985): 139–150; Nancy Mehrkens Steblay, "Helping Behavior in Rural and Urban Environments: A MetaAnalysis," *Psychological Bulletin* 102 (November 1987): 346–356; Jane Allyn Piliavin, "Why Do They Give the Gift of Life? A Review of Research on Blood Donors Since 1977," *Transfusion* 30 (June 1990): 444–459; David Horton Smith, "Determinants of Voluntary Association Participation and Volunteering: A Literature Review," *Nonprofit and Voluntary Sector Quarterly* 23 (fall 1994): 243–263; and Julian Wolpert, *Patterns of Generosity in America: Who's Holding the Safety Net?* (New York: Twentieth Century Fund Press, 1993).

11. On age, philanthropy, and volunteering, in addition to the author's analysis of the DDB Needham Life Style and Roper Social and Political Trends surveys, see the *Giving and Volunteering* series; Charles T. Clotfelter, *Federal Tax Policy and Charitable Giving* (Chicago: University of Chicago Press, 1985); Anne Statham and Patricia Rhoton, "Mature and Young Women's Volunteer Work, 1974–1981" (Columbus, Ohio: Center for Human Resource Research, Ohio State University, February 1986); Richard B. Freeman, "Working for Nothing: The Supply of Volunteer Labor," National Bureau of Economic Research working paper no. 5435 (Cambridge, Mass.: National Bureau of Economic Research, January 1996); and Wilson and Musick, "Who Cares?" My interest in philanthropy is as an indicator of altruism and social capital among ordinary Americans, rather than as a sustainer of the nonprofit sector, so I have not concentrated on giving by the wealthy, although unpublished work by Boston College sociologist Paul Schervish suggests that such giving constitutes a growing fraction of American philanthropy. Teresa Odendahl, *Charity Begins at Home: Generosity and Self-Interest Among the Philanthropic Elite* (New York: Basic Books, 1990), and Francie Ostrower, *Why the Wealthy Give: The Culture of Elite Philanthropy* (Princeton, N.J.: Princeton University Press, 1995), show that social capital among the wealthy themselves is crucial to their giving.

12. On work and volunteering, see David Horton Smith, "Determinants of Voluntary Association Participation and Volunteering"; Richard B. Freeman, "Working for Nothing"; and Lewis M. Segal, *Four Essays on the Supply of Volunteer Labor and Econometrics* (Ph.D. diss., Northwestern University, 1993). Both DDB Needham Life Style and Roper Social and Political Trends survey archives confirm that volunteering is higher among part-time employees than among either full-time employees or those with no paid employment.

13. *Giving and Volunteering 1996*, 6. This source (at 4-131) reports that the strongest single predictor of how much people volunteer is the strength of their informal ties to others in community organizations.

14. Figure 28 and the associated discussion are based on the author's analysis of the DDB Needham Life Style archives and substantiated by the Gallup Poll-Independent Sector *Giving and Volunteering* data.

15. Author's analysis of DDB Needham Life Style survey data. These relationships persist under stringent controls for other demographic predictors.

16. John Wilson and Marc Musick, "Who Cares?"; and John Wilson and Marc Musick, "Attachment to Volunteering," *Sociological Forum* 14 (June 1999): 243–272. Family ties—a special form of social capital—are also highly predictive of volunteering. Volunteering runs in families, as does spontaneous helping. See *Giving and Volunteering 1996*, 4-90; Segal, *Four Essays*; Freeman, "Working for Nothing," 8–9.

17. *Giving and Volunteering: 1996*, 6, 4-92 to 4-95. Richard D. Reddy, "Individual Philanthropy and Giving Behavior," in *Participation in Social and Political Activities*, ed. David Horton Smith and Jacqueline Macaulay (San Francisco: Jossey-Bass, 1980), 370–399, summarizes seven studies between 1957 and 1975: the more participation, the more contributions. Roper Social and Political Trends survey data on charitable giving confirm this pattern. In a multiple regression analysis giving is best predicted by civic engagement (especially organizational leadership and attendance at meetings), followed by year of birth and education.

18. According to the DDB Needham Life Style surveys, 15 percent of regular church- and/or clubgoers are regular blood donors, compared with fewer than 10 percent of nonmembers. According to the Roper Social and Political Trends surveys, 20 percent of people who have served as an officer or committee member of a local organization or who have attended a local public meeting in the last year have also given blood, compared with 10 percent of other Americans. In multiple regression analyses of both DDB Needham and Roper surveys the strongest predictors of blood donation are age and gender (women and the elderly give blood less often, presumably for physiological reasons), full-time employment (presumably because of blood donation at work), church and club attendance, frequency of volunteering, small-town residence, and education, in that order. On philanthropy, altruism, and social capital, see Reddy, "Individual Philanthropy and Giving Behavior"; Piliavin and Charng, "Altruism"; Jane Allyn Piliavin and Peter L. Callero, *Giving Blood: The Development of an Altruistic Identity* (Baltimore, Md.: Johns Hopkins University Press, 1991); Amato, "Personality and Social Network Involvement as Predictors of Helping"; and Krzysztof Kaniasty and Fran H. Norris, "In Search of Altruistic Community: Patterns of Social Support Mobilization Following Hurricane Hugo," *American Journal of Community Psychology* 23 (August 1995): 447–477.

19. Gabriel Berger, *Factors Explaining Volunteering for Organizations in General, and Social Welfare Organizations in Particular* (Ph.D. diss., Brandeis University, 1991); and Amato, "Personality and Social Network Involvement as Predictors of Helping." Without random-assignment experiments—in which some people are required to attend church and civic organizations and others are prevented from doing so—we cannot exclude that some unmeasured "social propensity" wholly explains the linkages among giving, volunteering, and community involvement, but the detailed pattern of correlations makes this unlikely.

20. See *Giving and Volunteering: 1996* and Alvin W. Drake, Stan N. Finkelstein, and Harvey M. Sapolsky, *The American Blood Supply* (Cambridge, Mass.: MIT Press, 1982). "Being asked" is a powerful determinant of who volunteers, even after controlling for other social and personality traits. See Berger, *Factors Explaining Volunteering*; Freeman, "Working for Nothing"; and Richard B. Freeman, "Give to Charity?—Well, Since You Asked" (Cambridge, Mass.: Harvard University, 1993).

21. For evidence on the propositions in this paragraph, see Wilson and Musick, "Who Cares?"; Amato, "Personality and Social Network Involvement as Predictors of Helping"; Harvey Hornstein, *Cruelty and Kindness: A New Look at Aggression and Altruism* (Englewood Cliffs, N.J.: Prentice-Hall, 1976), esp. 133; and *Giving and Volunteering: 1996*, 4-88. This source (at 4-129-31) ranks youthful volunteering as the single strongest predictor of adult volunteering, controlling for dozens of other social and psychological factors. The link between social connectedness and giving and volunteering remains powerful under controls for all relevant demographic factors, including education, wealth, age, gender, and marital and work status; in fact, measures of social connectedness often reduce the demographic correlations to insignificance. These conclusions (based on the author's analyses of DDB Needham Life Style, Roper Social and Political Trends, and Independent Sector data archives, using a score of different measures of community involvement and altruistic behavior) are confirmed by Hausknecht, *The Joiners*, 100, 109; Paul R. Amato, "Personality and Social Network Involvement as Predictors of Helping Behavior in Everyday Life," *Social Psychology Quarterly* 53 (March 1990): 31–43; Smith, "Determinants of Voluntary Association Participation and Volunteering"; Jackson, et al., "Volunteering and Charitable Giving"; and Wilson and Musick, "Who Cares?"

22. Ladd, "The Data Just Don't Show Erosion of America's 'Social Capital,'" 17.

23. Data from *Statistical Abstract of the United States: 1997*.

24. "Tithe: to contribute or pay a tenth part of one's annual income." *The American Heritage Dictionary of the English Language, Third Edition* (New York: Houghton Mifflin Company, 1992).

25. All historical estimates of personal philanthropy are somewhat rough, so it is essential to find consistent long-term data series. Sources for figure 3 are given in appendix II. Our analysis concentrates on giving by living individuals, since this is most relevant to social capital. In the finances of the nonprofit sector, a partially offsetting trend has been the growth in charitable foundations and in bequests from wealthy patrons, but those developments reflect the bull market more than changes in altruism. Meanwhile, corporate philanthropy as a share of pretax income rose sharply in the early 1980s and has slumped since then. See *Giving USA: 1998* for details on all nonindividual philanthropy. An independent source for the first half of the period covered by figure 31, the *U.S. Treasury Department Report on Private Foundations* (Washington, D.C.: Government Printing Office, 1965), 67, estimated that between 1929 and 1962 gifts from living individuals as a fraction of adjusted gross income increased by 78 percent. Several independent sources confirm the downward trend in the second half of the period covered by figure 31: 1) the Filer Commission report, *Giving in America: Toward a Stronger Voluntary Sector* (Washington, D.C.: Commission on Private Philanthropy and Public Needs, 1975), 82–83, which reported a decline of 15 percent in personal philanthropy between 1960 and 1972; and 2) the Department of Labor's regular Consumer Expenditure Survey, which shows a steady decline in household contributions as a fraction of after-tax income from 3.4 percent in 1984–85 to 2.7 percent in 1996–97, a decline of more than one-fifth in little more than a decade. For technical reasons described in John and Sylvia Ronsvalle, *The State of Church Giving through 1995* (Champaign, Ill.: empty tomb, 1997), chapter 6, the *Giving USA* data used in figure 31 may *understate* the decline since 1967, but I accept them here, as the methodologically conservative practice. The oscillations in giving in the late 1980s reflect the changes in tax laws affecting deductions for charitable contributions. For example, contributions were made fully deductible for all taxpayers in 1986, a provision that was reversed that same year.

26. Sources for figure 32 are given in appendix II. According to *Roper Reports 95-4* (New York: Roper Starch Worldwide, 1995), 19 percent of Americans gave to United Way in the previous twelve months, compared with 53 percent for churches and synagogues, 23 percent for all medical charities combined, 16 percent for all youth groups, 7 percent for all environmental organizations, and so on. United Way donors are demographically more representative than other major donor groups, which are often concentrated in a single social niche. (For example, environmentalist donors are concentrated among the highly educated, youth group donors among parents of school-age children, and so on.) Thus United Way giving is an unusually good proxy for national trends in secular generosity. The data on Protestant giving in figure 32 cover ten mainline denominations plus the Southern Baptist Convention. After 1968 data are available for a fuller sample of twenty-nine Protestant denominations, including most of the major evangelical bodies. Those more complete data show an even *steeper* decline (down 17 percent between 1968 and 1996) than the trend line in figure 32. Each of the time series discussed in this section—total giving, Protestant giving, Catholic giving, and United Way giving—comes from an entirely independent source, so their concurrence on trends in giving over the last four decades is especially probative.

27. According to John and Sylvia Ronsvalle, *The State of Church Giving through 1995*, 24–27, between 1968 and 1995 religious giving as a fraction of disposable income fell from 6.1 percent to 4.1 percent among members of eight denominations affiliated with the National Association of Evangelicals and from 3.3 percent to 2.9 percent among members of eight denominations affiliated with the mainline National Council of Churches of Christ.

28. These figures are based on the full twenty-nine-denomination Protestant sample from John and Sylvia Ronsvalle, *The State of Church Giving through 1995*, updated through 1997 from John and Sylvia Ronsvalle, *The State of Church Giving through 1997* (Champaign, Ill.: empty tomb, 1999), 42.

29. This figure is calculated from figure 32; a virtually identical decline of 57 percent between 1963 and 1984 in Catholic giving as a fraction of income is given by John and Sylvia Ronsvalle, "A Comparison of the Growth in

Church Contributions with United States Per Capita Income," in *Yearbook of American and Canadian Churches: 1989*, ed. Constant H. Jacquet Jr. (Nashville, Tenn.: Abingdon Press, 1989), 275. Peter Dobkin Hall and Colin B. Burke, "Voluntary, Nonprofit, and Religious Entities and Activities," in *Historical Statistics of the United States: Millennial Edition* (New York: Cambridge University Press, 2000), present data on philanthropic giving to the Roman Catholic Church for 1929–59. Though not directly comparable to our data for 1960–89, the Hall data show that giving per Catholic (as a fraction of national per capita income) dropped 49 percent from 1929 to 1945 and recovered by 7 percent between 1945 and 1960. Thus, over the last seven decades of the twentieth century, Catholic and Protestant giving per capita (as a fraction of income) appear to have followed roughly parallel tracks—sharply down during the depression, modestly up after the war, steadily down after 1960.

30. Author's analysis from Roper Social and Political Trends surveys and Yankelovich Monitor results generously made available by Yankelovich Partners, Inc. In the Roper surveys respondents are asked which of a wide variety of activities "you personally have done in the last month," ranging from "been to a dentist" to "rented a pre-recorded video," as well as "made a contribution to a charity." To avoid seasonal variation this question is always posed in October. In the Yankelovich surveys respondents are asked which of a range of religious activities "you do at least occasionally," including attending a house of worship, reading a Holy Book, volunteering, praying, and so on. These data are broadly consistent with comparable results reported in *Giving and Volunteering in the United States, 1999* (Washington, D.C.: Independent Sector, 2000), although this series of surveys began only in 1987.

31. Religious estimate from John and Sylvia Ronsvalle, *The State of Church Giving through 1995*, 48–49; estimates for United Way and total giving are author's calculations from data supplied by United Way and *Giving USA*.

32. Wuthnow, *The Crisis in the Churches*.

33. Greeley and McManus, *Catholic Contributions*, 63.

34. Robert Wuthnow, "The Changing Character of Social Capital in the United States," in Putnam, *Dynamics of Social Capital in Comparative Perspective*; and Diane Colasanto, "Voluntarism: Americans Show Commitment to Helping Those in Need," *Gallup Report* (November 1989): 19. By contrast, several other sources of evidence do *not* confirm any growth in average volunteering. *Giving and Volunteering in the United States, 1999*, based on the biennial surveys by the Independent Sector, reports a modest, continuing slump in average hours of volunteering per week from 2.1 in 1987 to 1.9 hours in 1999, mainly because regular volunteering is being replaced by irregular or sporadic volunteering. Over the last three decades social psychologists have carried out many studies of "spontaneous helping"—returning lost property, assisting strangers, and so on. Nancy Mehrkens Steblay, in "Helping Behavior in Rural and Urban Environments," examined sixty-five such studies and found that helping had declined over time in urban settings, with no compensating rise outside cities.

35. "Regular" attendance means attending church at least weekly *and* attending at least one club meeting a month. Regular community involvement in this sense fell from 22 percent in 1975 to 9 percent in 1999, whereas those who *never* attend either church or club meetings rose from 11 percent to 20 percent. Volunteering among regular church- and clubgoers rose from fifteen to twenty-four times per year, whereas the rate among those who never attend either church or clubs rose from .8 to 2.8 times per year.

36. Wilson and Musick, "Attachment to Volunteering." *Giving and Volunteering in the United States, 1999*: 1, reports that fully 41 percent of all self-declared volunteers in 1999 "contributed time only sporadically and considered it a one-time activity."

37. Figure 35 and figure 36 are based on the author's analysis of the DDB Needham Life Style archive. Entries are calculated by regressing frequency of volunteering or community projects on year within each age category, multiplying by twenty-three years and dividing by the initial score. However, change in mean scores between 1975–76 and 1997–98—or even simply change in the fraction of volunteers—for each age category yields essentially the same result. Each figure combines data for single and married adults, but the same pattern appears in each category considered separately. Among people over sixty, singles volunteer more than married people, whereas in the middle-aged bracket, singles volunteer less. Presumably, seniors volunteer to help overcome social isolation, whereas middle-aged people do so as a by-product of family ties. Data from the Independent Sector *Giving and Volunteering* biennial surveys between 1987 and 1999, though more volatile and less robust than the DDB Needham data, also show increasing volunteerism among respondents over forty-five (especially among those over seventy-five), coupled with little or no growth among those under forty-five.

38. According to the National Fire Protection Association, volunteer fire personnel nationwide dropped from 884,600 in 1983 to 803,350 in 1997, while professionals rose from 226,600 to 275,700. Most communities under 50,000 are protected by volunteer fire departments. According to the *Comprehensive Report on Blood Collection and Transfusion in the United States 1997* (Bethesda, Md.: National Blood Data Resource Center, May 1999), 29, nationwide blood donations per capita (excluding self-directed donations) fell by roughly 20 percent between 1987 and 1997. The fraction of the public who said that giving blood was one way to get AIDS fell from 48 percent in August 1989 to 24 percent in June 1995, according to *Public Opinion Online* (Roper Center at University of Connecticut, Storrs), accession numbers 0126019 and 0197588. Data from 1979 to 1987, though not directly comparable to the later data, suggests a rising rate of blood donation, but the post-1987 decline is already greater than the earlier rise. Surveys over the last quarter century have consistently found that blood donation drops sharply after age fifty, so the decline began just as people born in 1937 (the last of what chapter 14 terms "the long civic generation") left the donor pool. On generational factors in the decline of blood donation, see also Eric Nagourney, "Blood Shortage: Answers Scarce, Too," *New York Times*, October 5, 1999, D8.

39. Kristin A. Goss, "Volunteering and the Long Civic Generation," *Nonprofit and Voluntary Sector Quarterly* 28 (1999): 378–415. See also Susan Chambré, "Volunteerism by Elders: Past Trends and Future Prospects," *Gerontologist* 33 (April 1993): 221–228.

40. Robinson and Godbey, *Time for Life*; John P. Robinson, Perla Werner, and Geoffrey Godbey, "Freeing Up the Golden Years," *American Demographics*, October 1997, 20–24.

41. Controlling for age, education, year, gender, income, church attendance, club attendance, and marital and parental status, volunteering is *positively* correlated with interest in politics and *negatively* correlated with agreement

that "honest men cannot get elected." Among frequent volunteers, 58 percent say they are interested in politics, compared to 41 percent of nonvolunteers. Only 42 percent of frequent volunteers agree that "honest men cannot get elected," as opposed to 49 percent of nonvolunteers. This correlation between volunteering and political engagement was steadily positive over the last quarter century.

CHAPTER 8: RECIPROCITY, HONESTY, AND TRUST

1. David Hume (*A Treatise of Human Nature*, book 3, part 2, section 5 [1740]), as quoted in Robert Sugden, *The Economics of Rights, Co-operation and Welfare* (Oxford: Basil Blackwell, 1986), 106.

2. Michael Taylor, *Community, Anarchy, and Liberty* (New York: Cambridge University Press, 1982), 28–29. See also Alvin W. Gouldner, "The Norm of Reciprocity: A Preliminary Statement," *American Sociological Review* 25 (April 1960): 161–178.

3. Tocqueville, *Democracy in America*, 525–528.

4. Francis Fukuyama, *Trust* (New York: Free Press, 1995); Rafael La Porta, Florencio Lopez-de-Silanes, Andrei Shleifer, and Robert W. Vishny, "Trust in Large Organizations," *American Economic Review Papers and Proceedings* 87 (May 1997): 333–338; Stephen Knack and Philip Keefer, "Does Social Capital Have an Economic Payoff? A Cross-country Investigation," *Quarterly Journal of Economics* 112 (1997): 1251–1288; and Kenneth J. Arrow, "Gifts and Exchanges," *Philosophy and Public Affairs* 1 (summer 1972): 343–362.

5. Ichiro Kawachi, Bruce P. Kennedy, and Kimberly Lochner, "Long Live Community: Social Capital as Public Health," *The American Prospect*, November/December 1997, 56–59.

6. For evidence that generalized social trust (trust in the absence of evidence to the contrary) is unrelated to gullibility (trust in the presence of evidence to the contrary), see Julian B. Rotter, "Interpersonal Trust, Trustworthiness, and Gullibility," *American Psychologist* 35 (January 1980): 1–7.

7. I am grateful to Russell Hardin for clarifying this important distinction for me. See his "Street Level Epistemology of Trust," *Politics & Society* 21 (December 1993): 505–529.

8. Diego Gambetta, "Can We Trust Trust?" in *Trust: Making and Breaking Cooperative Relations*, ed. Diego Gambetta (Oxford: Blackwell, 1988), 221.

9. Mark Granovetter, "Economic Action and Social Structure: The Problem of Embeddedness," *American Journal of Sociology* 91 (November 1985): 481–510; Coleman, *Foundations*, 300–321; Putnam, *Making Democracy Work*, ch. 6; Margaret Levi, "Social and Unsocial Capital: A Review Essay of Robert Putnam's *Making Democracy Work*," *Politics & Society* 24 (March 1996): 45–55; Edward Glaeser, David Laibson, Jose Scheinkman, and Christine Soutter, "What Is Social Capital? The Determinants of Trust and Trustworthiness," National Bureau of Economic Research working paper no. 7216 (Cambridge, Mass.: National Bureau of Economic Research, July 1999).

10. Bernard Williams, "Formal Structures and Social Reality," in Gambetta, *Trust*, 3–13; Ronald S. Burt and Marc Knez, "Trust and Third-Party Gossip," in *Trust in Organizations*, ed. Roderick M. Kramer and Tom R. Tyler (Thousand Oaks, Calif.: Sage Publications, 1996), 68–89. This distinction between thin and thick trust is close (but not identical) to the distinction that Toshio Yamagishi and Midori Yamagishi, "Trust and Commitment in the United States and Japan," *Motivation and Emotion* 18 (June 1994): 129–66, draw between "trust" and "commitment."

11. Rotter ("Interpersonal Trust, Trustworthiness, and Gullibility," 2) defines "the generalized other" as "a person or group with whom one has not had a great deal of personal experience." Across forty-three states for which data are available, organizational density (based on the Roper Social and Political Trends surveys) and social trust (based on the General Social Survey and the DDB Needham Life Style surveys) are correlated $R^2 = .52$.

12. "Thick trust" and "thin trust" represent the ends of a continuum, for "thick trust" refers to trust with a short radius, encompassing only others who are close to the truster, sociologically speaking, and "thin trust" refers to trust with a long radius, encompassing people at a greater social distance from the truster.

13. Wendy M. Rahn and John E. Transue, "Social Trust and Value Change: The Decline of Social Capital in American Youth, 1976–1995," *Political Psychology* 19 (September 1998): 545–565, quotation at 545.

14. For evidence of the generalizations in this paragraph, see John Brehm and Wendy Rahn, "Individual-Level Evidence for the Causes and Consequences of Social Capital," *American Journal of Political Science* 41 (July 1997): 999–1023; Eric Uslaner, "Faith, Hope, and Charity: Trust and Collective Action" (College Park: University of Maryland, 1995); John T. Scholz, "Trust, Taxes, and Compliance," in *Trust and Governance*, Russell Sage Foundation Series on Trust, vol. 1, ed. Valerie A. Braithwaite and Margaret Levi (New York: Russell Sage Foundation, 1998), 135–166; Young-dahl Song and Tinsley E. Yarbrough, "Tax Ethics and Taxpayer Attitudes: A Survey," *Public Administration Review* 38 (September/October 1978): 442–452; Steven M. Sheffrin and Robert K. Triest, "Can Brute Deterrence Backfire? Perceptions and Attitudes in Taxpayer Compliance," in *Why People Pay Taxes: Tax Compliance and Enforcement*, ed. Joel Slemrod (Ann Arbor: University of Michigan Press, 1992), 193–218; John T. Scholz and Mark Lubell, "Trust and Taxpaying: Testing the Heuristic Approach to Collective Action," *American Journal of Political Science* 42 (April 1998): 398–417; Stephen Knack, "Civic Norms, Social Sanctions, and Voter Turnout," 145; Rotter, "Interpersonal Trust, Trustworthiness, and Gullibility"; and unpublished analysis of a 1991 Roper survey by Robert B. Smith (Cambridge, Mass., June 1998); I am grateful to Dr. Smith for sharing this analysis. For details about the survey, see *Public Attitude Monitor 1991* (Wheaton, Ill.: Insurance Research Council, 1991). According to the DDB Needham Life Style data, controlling for various demographic factors, social trust is associated with frequent attendance at club meetings and church services, as well as with more frequent blood donation.

15. A lively debate is under way about the direction of the causal arrows among these factors. The debate is important and yet complicated both theoretically and empirically. However, it is only tangential to my concern here. For an important first step in the experimental exploration of these issues, see Glaeser, Laibson, Scheinkman, and Soutter, "What Is Social Capital?"

16. Across individuals, across countries, and across time, social and political trust are, in fact, correlated, but social scientists are very far from agreement about why. Some believe that a native disposition to credulity explains both. Some believe that both are influenced by the same thing—prosperity, government performance, or whatever. Some

believe that one leads to the other through a complicated chain of causation; for example, perhaps low social trust leads to political conflict which lowers government performance which reduces trust in government. For a range of views, see Levi and Braithwaite, *Trust and Governance*; Susan Pharr and Robert D. Putnam, eds., *What's Troubling the Trilateral Democracies?* (Princeton, N.J.: Princeton University Press, 2000); Robert Wuthnow, "The Changing Character of Social Capital in the United States"; Brehm and Rahn, "Individual-Level Evidence"; Tom W. Smith, "Factors Relating to Misanthropy in Contemporary American Society," *Social Science Research* 26 (June 1997): 170–196; and Ken Newton, "Social and Political Trust," in *Critical Citizens: Global Support for Democratic Government*, ed. Pippa Norris (Oxford: Oxford University Press, 1999).

17. For empirical evidence that this question taps trust in strangers, see Eric Uslaner, *Moral Foundations of Trust* (forthcoming).

18. Kenneth Newton, "Social Capital and Democracy," *American Behavioral Scientist* 40 (March/April 1997): 575–586.

19. Author's analysis of GSS and DDB Needham Life Style survey archives, using comprehensive controls for other demographic characteristics. Independent analysis of the GSS confirms these patterns; see Smith, "Factors Relating to Misanthropy."

20. For evidence supporting the generalizations of this paragraph, see *Uniform Crime Rates for the United States 1997* (Washington, D.C.: Federal Bureau of Investigation, 1998), available at www.fbi.gov/ucr/Cius_97/97crime/97crime.pdf; Brehm and Rahn, "Individual-Level Evidence"; Alfred DeMaris and Renxin Yang, "Race, Alienation, and Interpersonal Mistrust," *Sociological Spectrum* 14 (October/December 1994): 327–349; Tom W. Smith, "Factors Relating to Misanthropy"; Korte and Kerr, "Response to Altruistic Opportunities in Urban and Nonurban Settings," 183–84; Stanley Milgram, "The Experience of Living in Cities," *Science* 167 (March 1970): 1461–1468; unpublished analysis by Robert B. Smith, as cited in note 14; and Paul Blumberg, *The Predatory Society: Deception in the American Marketplace* (New York: Oxford University Press, 1989), 163.

21. Intriguing international evidence on the accuracy of reports about generalized reciprocity come from a study sponsored by *Reader's Digest*. Four hundred wallets with $50 in cash and the names and addresses of their putative owners were left on city streets in fourteen different European countries. The rate at which the wallets were returned intact closely corresponded ($r = .67$) to the national score on the standard social trust question. In other words, where citizens report that "most people can be trusted," they're generally right, and where citizens report that "you can't be too careful in dealing with people," they're right, too. This fascinating result is reported in Knack and Keefer, "Does Social Capital Have an Economic Payoff?," 1257.

22. Social psychologists have found evidence that social trust is *both* a more or less stable feature of an individual's psyche *and* a cognitive response to changing circumstance and context. See, for example, Sharon G. Goto, "To Trust or Not to Trust: Situational and Dispositional Determinants," *Social Behavior and Personality* 24 (1996): 119–132. Eric Uslaner in his forthcoming *The Moral Foundations of Trust* argues that generalized or thin trust derives from personal optimism, which in turn derives from childhood experience.

23. Robert Wuthnow, "The Role of Trust in Civic Renewal," *The National Commission on Civic Renewal*, working paper no. 1 (College Park: University of Maryland, 1997). Glaeser, Laibson, Scheinkman, and Soutter, "What Is Social Capital?" argue that the standard question predicts behavioral trustworthiness, not trust.

24. In *The Cynical Americans: Living and Working in an Age of Discontent and Disillusion* (San Francisco: Jossey-Bass, 1989), Donald L. Kanter and Philip H. Mirvis report that 72 percent of the workers surveyed agreed that "there is a growing loss of basic trust and faith in other people."

25. Lane, "Politics of Consensus," 879; and Niemi, Mueller, and Smith, *Trends in Public Opinion*, 303, report that agreement that "most people can be trusted" climbed from 66 percent in 1942–48 to 77 percent in 1963–64 and thereafter fell to 71 percent in 1966 and to 56 percent by 1983. These data cannot be compared with responses to the standard trust question used elsewhere in this book, for the surveys cited in this note posed only the single phrase "most people can be trusted," whereas the standard question offers a choice between "most people can be trusted" and "you can't be too careful." Adding the distrustful alternative lowers measured trust by about twenty percentage points.

26. The surveys summarized in figure 38 are these:

Survey Archive	Period	Trust in Earliest Year	Trust in Latest Year	Relative Change Per Decade
NORC–General Social Survey	1972–1998	48%	39%	−7%
National Election Study	1964–1998	55%	40%	−8%
DDB Needham Life Style	1975–1999	42%	25%	−16%
Monitoring the Future (high school students)	1976–1996	46%	24%	−23%

Sources for figure 38 are described in appendix I. In all cases *except* the DDB Needham Life Style surveys, the same question was used in all these surveys: "Generally speaking, would you say that most people can be trusted, or that you can't be too careful in dealing with people?" DDB Needham surveys offered six levels of agreement or disagreement with the view that "Most people are honest." Because this version lacks an explicit distrustful alternative, it gains roughly 20 percent more agreement, but in other respects, this question behaves like the double-barreled version. To make this question more nearly comparable to the others, I have used the percentage of respondents who "definitely" or "generally" agree, but this cutting point does not affect the conclusions in any way.

27. On youthful social distrust, see Rahn and Transue, "Social Trust and Value Change." Professor Rahn deserves credit for first spotting the generational basis for long-term trends in social capital in America.

28. The evidence in this paragraph is drawn from the author's analysis of the DDB Needham Life Style and General Social Survey archives. Following the method explicated by Firebaugh, "Methods for Estimating Cohort Replacement Effects," most if not all of the aggregate decline in social trust is attributable to cohort replacement. This is entirely consistent with the sharp declines in social trust across successive high school classes, as found in the Monitoring the Future surveys between 1976 and 1996. For independent confirmation of cohort-related declines in social trust, see Smith, "Factors Relating to Misanthropy." This conclusion is unaffected by the exact cutting points between successive generations.

29. Robert M. Groves and Mick P. Couper, *Nonresponse in Household Interview Surveys* (New York: John Wiley & Sons, Inc., 1998), 155–187. See also John Goyder, *The Silent Minority: Nonrespondents on Sample Surveys* (Cambridge, U.K.: Polity Press, 1987), esp. 64; John Brehm, *The Phantom Respondents: Opinion Surveys and Political Representation* (Ann Arbor: University of Michigan Press, 1993), and Joop J. Hox and Edith D. de Leeuw, "A Comparison of Nonresponse in Mail, Telephone, and Face-to-Face Surveys," *Quality & Quantity* 28 (November 1994): 329–344. For a contrary view, see Tom W. Smith, "Trends in Survey Non-Response," *International Journal of Public Opinion Research* 7 (1995): 157–171.

30. According to Louis Harris & Associates polls, available in the University of North Carolina Institute for Research in Social Science Data Archive, 15 percent of respondents reported unlisted phone numbers in 1974–76, as compared with 25 percent in 1997. Independently, Survey Sampling Inc. found that the fraction of unlisted households rose from 22 percent in 1984 to 30 percent in 1997: "Sacramento Is Most Unlisted," *The Frame: A Quarterly Newsletter for Survey Researchers* (March 1997), at www.worldopinion.com/newsstand.taf?f=a&id=1248. On call screening, see William G. Mayer, "The Rise of the New Media," *Public Opinion Quarterly* 58 (spring 1994): 124–146, table at 146, based on Roper polls; Robert W. Oldendick and Michael W. Link, "The Answering Machine Generation: Who are They and What Problem Do They Pose for Survey Research?" *Public Opinion Quarterly* 58 (summer 1994): 264–273, at 268; and Michael W. Link and Robert W. Oldendick, "Call Screening: Is It Really a Problem for Survey Research?" *Public Opinion Quarterly* 63 (1999): 577–589.

31. On mail census returns, see Mick P. Couper, Eleanor Singer, Richard A. Kulka, "Participation in the 1990 Decennial Census: Politics, Privacy, Pressures," *American Politics Quarterly* 26 (January 1998): 59–80, as well as Census Bureau data provided by Kristin Goss and Stephen Knack, to whom I am grateful. In dress rehearsals for the 2000 census, the Census Bureau found that civic participation was a very strong predictor of census participation, much stronger than exposure to advertising designed to encourage census participation. See Nancy Bates and Sara Buckley, "Reported Exposure to Paid Advertising and Likelihood of Returning a Census Form," (paper presented to fifty-fourth annual conference of the American Association for Public Opinion Research, St. Petersburg, Fla., May 1999).

32. On road rage, see Matthew L. Wald, "Temper Cited as Cause of 28,000 Road Deaths a Year," *New York Times*, July 18, 1997. For a skeptical view, see Michael Fumento, " 'Road Rage' Versus Reality," *Atlantic Monthly*, August 1998. Fumento, however, reports that crashes at stoplights increased by 14 percent in the period 1992–1996, with the number of fatal crashes at stoplights increasing by 19 percent. Tolerance of speeding in towns rose steadily from 20 percent in 1990 to 46 percent in 1997, while tolerance of speeding on the open highway remained stable at about 50 percent, according to the *Public Attitude Monitor* 5 (Wheaton, Ill.: Insurance Research Council, 1997), 8. On Gallup poll results, see George Gallup Jr. and Frank Newport, "Americans Take Their Automobiles Seriously," *Gallup Poll Monthly*, no. 308 (May 1991): 46–61, esp. 58–59 and *Gallup Poll Monthly* (August 1997): 60. For additional confirmation, see *The Public Perspective* 8 (December/January 1997): 64.

33. See appendix II for the sources for figure 40. Thanks to Stephen Knack for this citation.

34. Figure 41 draws on data from the FBI's Uniform Crime Reports both for the aggregate of all crime (violent and nonviolent) and for murder. Measures of the murder rate are more reliable but are closely tied to family discord and to the ups and downs of drug wars and are thus less than ideal as a generic indicator of national law-abidingness. National Crime Survey victimization rates are not available before the 1970s.

35. See, for example, Fox Butterfield, "Decline of Violent Crimes Is Linked to Crack Market," *New York Times*, December 28, 1998.

36. I want to thank Sam Bowles for initially suggesting this approach.

37. This is true whether measured in terms of total U.S. population or in terms of total employment. See also Richard L. Abel, *American Lawyers* (New York: Oxford University Press, 1989).

38. Richard H. Sander and E. Douglass Williams, "Why Are There So Many Lawyers? Perspectives on a Turbulent Market," *Law and Social Inquiry Journal* 14 (1989), 433.

39. Statistics in this and the previous paragraphs are drawn from *Historical Statistics of the United States:* Series D589–D592; *Statistical Abstract of the United States* (various years), series no. 637; and data provided directly by the Bureau of Labor Statistics.

40. Robert Clark, "Why So Many Lawyers," *Fordham Law Review* 61 (1993): 275.

41. See Marc Galanter, "The Day After the Litigation Explosion," *Maryland Law Review* 46 (fall 1986): 3–39; Marc Galanter, "Beyond the Litigation Panic," *New Directions in Liability Law*, ed. Walter Olson (New York: The Academy of Political Science, 1988), 18–30; Marc Galanter, "Real World Torts: An Antidote to Anecdote," *Maryland Law Review* 46 (1996): 1093–1160; Marc Galanter and Thomas Palay, *Tournament of Lawyers* (Chicago: University of Chicago Press, 1991).

42. Marc Galanter, "The Faces of Mistrust: The Image of Lawyers in Public Opinion, Jokes, and Political Discourse," *University of Cincinnati Law Review* 66 (spring 1998): 805–845, quotation at 806–807.

43. R. J. Gilson and R. H. Mnookin, "Disputing Through Agents: Cooperation and Conflict Between Lawyers in Litigation," *Columbia Law Review* 94 (1994): 509–66, as cited in Tom R. Tyler, "Trust and Democratic Governance," in *Trust and Governance*, Valerie Braithwaite and Margaret Levi, eds. (New York: Russell Sage Foundation, 1999), 269–294, at 288.

CHAPTER 9: AGAINST THE TIDE? SMALL GROUPS, SOCIAL MOVEMENTS, AND THE NET

1. Robert Wuthnow, *Sharing the Journey: Support Groups and America's New Quest for Community* (New York: Free Press, 1994), especially 45–46, 59–76, 170, 320.

2. Theodora Penny Martin, *The Sound of Our Own Voices: Women's Study Clubs 1860–1910* (Boston: Beacon Press, 1987), quotations at 172; and Theda Skocpol, *Protecting Soldiers and Mothers: The Political Origins of Social Policy in the United States* (Cambridge, Mass.: Harvard University Press, Belknap Press, 1992).

3. Ellen Slezak, *The Book Group Book* (Chicago: Chicago Review Press, 1993), 14.

4. James A. Davis, *Great Books and Small Groups* (Glencoe, Ill.: Free Press, 1961), as well as author's analysis of 1996 National Election Study, correlating membership in literary, study, and discussion groups with other forms of community involvement, controlling for other demographic factors.

5. Robert Oliphant, "My Say," *Publishers Weekly*, January 4, 1985, 72; Mary Mackay, "Booking a Group Adventure," *Belles Lettres: A Review of Books by Women* 8 (summer 1993): 26. The Study Circle Resource Center and the Kettering Foundation sponsor study and reading groups around the country.

6. Surveys carried out in 1967 (Sidney Verba and Norman H. Nie, *Participation in America: Political Democracy and Social Equality* [New York: Harper & Row, 1972]) and 1996 (National Election Study) found essentially identical rates of participation (4 percent) in literary, artistic, study, or discussion groups. The author's analysis of the General Social Survey found no significant net change in membership in such groups between 1974 and 1994 and a significant decline if we control for educational and marital changes. According to the staff of the Great Books program, a national program for reading groups established in 1947, they have half as many participants now as in the 1960s.

7. Alfred H. Katz, *Self-Help in America: A Social Movement Perspective* (New York: Twayne Publishers, 1993); Irving Peter Gellman, *The Sober Alcoholic: An Organizational Analysis of Alcoholics Anonymous* (New Haven, Conn.: College and University Press, 1964); Nan Robertson, *Getting Better: Inside Alcoholics Anonymous* (New York: William Morrow, 1988), 88, 155–56.

8. Author's analysis of National Election Study of 1996; Morton A. Lieberman and Lonnie R. Snowden, "Problems in Assessing Prevalence and Membership Characteristics of Self-Help Group Participants," *Journal of Applied Behavioral Science* 29 (June 1993): 166–180.

9. Wuthnow, *Sharing the Journey*, 158.

10. Lieberman and Snowden, "Problems in Assessing Prevalence and Membership Characteristics of Self-Help Group Participants," 176–178. For contrasting views about self-help groups, see Frank Riessman and David Carroll, *Redefining Self-Help: Policy and Practice* (San Francisco: Jossey-Bass, 1995); Katz, *Self-Help in America* (1993); and Wendy Kaminer, *I'm Dysfunctional, You're Dysfunctional: The Recovery Movement and Other Self-Help Fashions* (Reading, Mass.: Addison-Wesley, 1992).

11. Alfred H. Katz and Eugene I. Bender, eds., *The Strength In Us: Self-Help Groups in the Modern World* (New York: Franklin Watts, 1976), 6.

12. Riessman and Carroll, *Redefining Self-Help*; Katz, *Self-Help in America*.

13. Author's analysis of 1996 National Election Study. Lieberman and Snowden, "Problems in Assessing Prevalence and Membership Characteristics of Self-Help Group Participants," 170.

14. Wuthnow, *Sharing the Journey*, 3–6. Wuthnow reports (322) that larger "small" groups (with more than twenty members) do encourage participants to become focused on wider issues, but smaller "small" groups (with ten or fewer members) do not. See also Wuthnow's *Loose Connections: Joining Together in America's Fragmented Communities* (Cambridge, Mass.: Harvard University Press, 1998).

15. Jack L. Walker, *Mobilizing Interest Groups in America*, esp. 35–40; W. Douglas Costain and Anne N. Costain, "The Political Strategies of Social Movements: A Comparison of the Women's and Environmental Movements," *Congress and the Presidency* 19 (spring 1992): 1–27.

16. Rochon, *Culture Moves*.

17. McAdam, *Freedom Summer*, 63–64, and 217 ff.; Doug McAdam and Ronnelle Paulsen, "Specifying the Relationship between Social Ties and Activism," *American Journal of Sociology* 99 (November 1993): 640–667; Morris, *Origins of the Civil Rights Movement*; Edward J. Walsh and Rex H. Warland, "Social Movement Involvement in the Wake of a Nuclear Accident: Activists and Free Riders in the TMI [Three Mile Island] Area," *American Sociological Review* 48 (December 1983): 764–780; Sara Diamond, *Roads to Dominion: Right-Wing Movements and Political Power in the United States* (New York: Guilford Press, 1995); John D. McCarthy, "Pro-Life and Pro-Choice Mobilization: Infrastructure Deficits and New Technologies," in *Social Movements in an Organizational Society: Collected Essays*, ed. Mayer N. Zald and John D. McCarthy (New Brunswick, N.J.: Transaction Books, 1987), 49–66, esp. 55–56; Rochon, *Culture Moves*, ch. 4.

18. Mario Diani, "Social Movements and Social Capital: A Network Perspective on Movement Outcomes," *Mobilization: An International Journal* 2 (September 1997): 129–147; Carmen Sirianni and Lewis Friedland, "Social Capital and Civic Innovation: Learning and Capacity Building from the 1960s to the 1990s" (paper presented at the annual meeting of the American Sociological Association, Washington, D.C., 1995); and www.cpn.org/sections/new_citizenship/theory/socialcapital_civicinnov.html.

19. McAdam, *Freedom Summer*, 132, 190; Kenneth T. Andrews, "The Impacts of Social Movements on the Political Process: The Civil Rights Movement and Black Electoral Politics in Mississippi," *American Sociological Review* 62 (1997): 800–819.

20. Debra C. Minkoff, "Producing Social Capital," *American Behavioral Scientist* 40 (March/April 1997): 606–619.

21. Margit Mayer, "Social Movement Research and Social Movement Practice: The U.S. Pattern," in *Research on Social Movements: The State of the Art in Western Europe and the USA*, ed. Dieter Rucht (Boulder, Colo.: Westview Press, 1991): 47–120, quotation at 64.

22. John D. McCarthy, "Pro-Life and Pro-Choice Mobilization," 58.

23. McCarthy, "Pro-Life and Pro-Choice Mobilization"; Suzanne Staggenborg, *The Pro-Choice Movement: Organization and Activism in the Abortion Conflict* (New York: Oxford University Press, 1991), 5–6, 146.

24. Interviews with NARAL state officials.

25. Minkoff, "Producing Social Capital," 613.

26. Sidney Tarrow has argued both sides of this debate. For his theory of "cycles of protest," which end in exhausted quiescence, see Sidney Tarrow, *Power in Movement: Social Movements and Contentious Politics*, 2nd ed. (New York: Cambridge University Press, 1998), esp. 141–160. On the other hand, for his speculations about a new, permanently active "movement society," see David S. Meyer and Sidney Tarrow, "A Movement Society: Contentious Politics for a New Century," in *The Social Movement Society: Contentious Politics for a New Century*, ed. David S. Meyer and Sidney Tarrow (Lanham, Md.: Rowman and Littlefield, 1998), 1–28, esp. 4. Ronald Inglehart, *Modernization and Postmodernization: Cultural, Economic, and Political Change in 43 Societies* (Princeton, N.J.: Princeton University Press, 1997), esp. 313, argues that "elite-challenging" behavior has become more common. For arguments that social movements end up as conventional interest groups or "professional movement organizations," see Frances Fox Piven and Richard A. Cloward, *Poor People's Movements: Why They Succeed, How They Fail* (New York: Vintage Books, 1977), and John D. McCarthy and Mayer Zald, *The Trend of Social Movements in America: Professionalization and Resource Mobilization* (Morristown, N.J.: General Learning Press, 1973).

27. Morris, *Origins of the Civil Rights Movement*, 182–185, 191; McAdam, *Freedom Summer*; Anne N. Costain, *Inviting Women's Rebellion: A Political Process Interpretation of the Women's Movement* (Baltimore, Md.: Johns Hopkins University Press, 1992), esp. 79–121; Debra Minkoff, "The Sequencing of Social Movements," *American Sociological Review* 62 (October 1997): 779–799, esp. 789; and Anne Costain, Richard Braunstein, and Heidi Berggren, "Framing the Women's Movement," in *Women, Media, and Politics*, ed. Pippa Norris (New York: Oxford University Press, 1997), 205–220.

28. Riley E. Dunlap and Angela G. Mertig, eds., *American Environmentalism: The U.S. Environmental Movement, 1970–1990* (New York: Taylor and Francis, 1992); Costain and Costain, "The Political Strategies of Social Movements"; and Donald Snow, *Inside the Environmental Movement: Meeting the Leadership Challenge* (Washington, D.C.: Island Press, 1992), 9.

29. All post-1970 membership data for environmental groups in this chapter are drawn from Christopher J. Bosso, "The Color of Money: Environmental Groups and the Pathologies of Fund Raising," in Cigler and Loomis, *Interest Group Politics*, 4th ed., 101–130; and Christopher J. Bosso, "Facing the Future: Environmentalists and the New Political Landscape," in *Interest Group Politics*, 6th ed., Allan J. Cigler and Burdett A. Loomis, eds. (Washington, D.C.: Congressional Quarterly Press, 1999). Thanks to Professor Bosso for help in understanding the environmental movement. For the period prior to 1970 I have drawn on Robert Cameron Mitchell, Angela G. Mertig, and Riley E. Dunlap, "Twenty Years of Environmental Mobilization: Trends Among National Environmental Organizations," in Dunlap and Mertig, *American Environmentalism*, 11–26. In a few cases, I have interpolated data for missing years.

30. Robert C. Mitchell et al., "Twenty Years. . . ," 17; Bosso, "Color of Money," 117.

31. Unsourced quotations and data in the following three paragraphs are from Paul E. Johnson, "Interest Group Recruiting: Finding Members and Keeping Them," in Cigler and Loomis, *Interest Group Politics*, 5th ed., 35–62; and Bosso, "Color of Money," esp. 113–115. See also Grant Jordan and William Maloney, *The Protest Business? Mobilizing Campaign Groups* (Manchester, England: Manchester University Press, 1997).

32. Mitchell, Mertig, and Dunlap, "Twenty Years of Environmental Mobilization," 13.

33. Bosso, "Color of Money," 113–114.

34. Gregg Easterbrook, "Junk-Mail Politics," *New Republic*, April 25, 1988, 21, as cited in Jeffrey M. Berry, *The Interest Group Society*, 3rd ed. (New York: Longman, 1997), 77.

35. Andrew S. McFarland, *Common Cause: Lobbying in the Public Interest* (Chatham, N.J.: Chatham House Publishers, 1984), 46.

36. Email from assistant director of "membership and marketing" of a major environmental organization.

37. R. Kenneth Godwin, *One Billion Dollars of Influence* (Chatham, N.J.: Chatham House, 1988), 55–65, and the works cited there; John D. McCarthy, "Pro-Life and Pro-Choice Mobilization," 49–66, esp. 62–63.

38. Of the thirty-two associations represented in figure 8, only those two nineteenth-century giants whose membership had peaked in the 1920s (the Women's Christian Temperance Union and the International Order of Odd Fellows) lost as many as 85 percent of their remaining members from their post–World War II peak through the end of the twentieth century.

39. Christopher J. Bosso, review of *The Protest Business? Mobilizing Campaign Groups*, by Grant Jordan and William Maloney, *American Political Science Review* 93 (June 1999): 467.

40. Linda L. Fowler and Ronald G. Shaiko, "The Grass Roots Connection: Environmental Activists and Senate Roll Calls," *American Journal of Political Science* 31 (August 1987): 484–510, quotation at 490.

41. Financial contributions to tertiary groups are fully accounted for in the data already presented in chapter 7 on trends in philanthropy, as summarized in figure 31.

42. Kelly Patterson, "The Political Firepower of the National Rifle Association," in Cigler and Loomis, *Interest Group Politics*, 5th ed., 130.

43. John D. McCarthy, "Pro-Life and Pro-Choice Mobilization," 62.

44. Tarrow, *Power in Movement*, 133.

45. Jordan and Maloney, *The Protest Business*, 191. This survey was conducted among British members of these two organizations, though there is no reason to doubt that the results apply as well to American members. Godwin, *One Billion Dollars of Influence*, 48, argues that "for many groups, the objective is a quiescent contributor, not an active member."

46. Jordan and Maloney, *The Protest Business*, 169.

47. McCarthy and Zald, *The Trend of Social Movements*, 3. Ronald G. Shaiko, "More Bang for the Buck," in Cigler and Loomis, *Interest Group Politics*, 3rd ed., 124.

48. Bosso, "Facing the Future." See also Mitchell, Mertig, and Dunlap, "Twenty Years of Environmental Mobilization," 21–23.

49. In his classic study, *Political Parties* (Glencoe, Ill.: Free Press, 1962 [1911]), Robert Michels argued that even the most democratically inspired organizations inevitably fell under the influence of a small elite.

50. "Yogurt-eaters for Wilderness," *Sierra* (January/February 1989), 22, as cited in Philip A. Mundo, *Interest Groups: Cases and Characteristics* (Chicago: Nelson-Hall, 1992), 178. We asked representatives in two or three states for each national environmental organization with state or local chapters to estimate what fraction of their members did more than contribute financially. Estimates ranged from 1.5 percent to 15 percent, figures that are unlikely to be underestimates. In 1998 there were 27,082 Rotarians in Texas, according to Rotary International Membership Services (Evanston, Ill.). Rotary members must attend 60 percent of all weekly meetings, but most aim for 100 percent.

51. Riley E. Dunlap and Angela G. Mertig, "The Evolution of the U.S. Environmental Movement from 1970 to 1990: An Overview," in Dunlap and Mertig, *American Environmentalism*, 6 (emphasis added).

52. Gallup data cited in Riley E. Dunlap, "Trends in Public Opinion Toward Environmental Issues: 1965–1990," in Dunlap and Mertig, *American Environmentalism*, 113, and Gallup/CNN/USA Today poll, April 13–14, 1999.

53. Survey data in this paragraph from the General Social Survey, 1993–94. The GSS estimates seem to be greatly exaggerated. During the 1990s membership in all major environmental organizations combined averaged six to seven million a year. That figure includes much double counting, since the average member donates to several others on the list and remains a contributor for three years. However, assuming that *all* members contributed to only *one* organization and left after *two* years, a maximum of sixteen million Americans, or 8 percent of all adults, could have contributed over five years, as compared with the GSS-based rate of 49 percent. Plausible estimates for subnational environmental giving could not close that gap.

54. Unpublished results from Yankelovich Partners, Inc. archives. *Roper Reports* 97-3 (New York: Roper Starch Worldwide, 1997), 117–121, reports that between 1989 and 1997 everyday recycling by Americans rose sharply (e.g., "separating garbage from recyclable material . . . on a regular basis" jumped from 14 percent to 39 percent), probably because of the proliferation of local recycling programs, but that "writing letters to politicians expressing opinions on environmental issues . . . on a regular basis [or] from time to time" slumped from 20 percent to 17 percent. In writing this book, I contacted a dozen experts, both academics and activists, on grassroots environmentalism. Without exception they believed that grassroots environmental activity was on the rise. With one exception, however, none could cite hard evidence for this impression. The exception was a series of directories of state and local environmental groups prepared by the National Wildlife Federation (NWF) annually since 1968. The raw number of such organizations listed in successive years has grown. However, over these thirty years NWF got better at finding such groups, and once we take that improvement into account, the directories tell a story of *decline*. For example, of groups shown in the 1999 directory with founding dates before 1968, only one-third had been listed in the 1968 directory. Even modest adjustment for this early undercounting converts apparent growth into actual decline. Thanks to Arkadi Gerney for help with this research. Other alleged evidence of growth in grassroots environmental organizations, such as that presented in Nicholas Freudenberg and Carol Steinsapir, "Not in Our Backyards: The Grassroots Environmental Movement," in *American Environmentalism: The U.S. Environmental Movement, 1970–1990*, edited by Riley E. Dunlap and Angela G. Mertig (New York: Taylor & Francis, 1992), 29, is seriously flawed by the fact that most lists of grassroots groups are never purged of defunct organizations. Another bit of evidence against the supposed growth of environmental activism over the last several decades comes from the annual UCLA survey of hundreds of thousands of college freshmen. The proportion who rated "becoming involved in programs to clean up the environment" an important goal in life fell from 45 percent in 1972 to 19 percent in 1998; see Linda J. Sax et al., *The American Freshman* (Los Angeles: UCLA Higher Education Research Institute, 1998) and earlier volumes in this series. In the 1990s an antienvironmental movement arose, especially in the West, under the labels of "Wise Use" and "property rights," but I have not found any hard evidence on grassroots involvement in it.

55. On the religious Right, see Robert C. Liebman and Robert Wuthnow, eds., *The New Christian Right: Mobilization and Legitimation* (Hawthorne, N.Y.: Aldine Publishing Company, 1983); Diamond, *Roads to Dominion*; Justin Watson, *The Christian Coalition: Dreams of Restoration, Demands for Recognition* (New York: St. Martin's Press, 1997); and Smith, *American Evangelicalism*. In 1998 the Christian Coalition claimed 1.7 million members with over 1,425 chapters. Subsequent reports suggested that those claims were vastly inflated and that the Christian Coalition was primarily a direct-mail operation. See Laurie Goodstein, "Coalition's Woes May Hinder Goals of Christian Right," *New York Times*, August 2, 1999.

56. Wuthnow, *The Restructuring of American Religion*, 173–214.

57. Robert Wuthnow, "The Political Rebirth of American Evangelicals," in Liebman and Wuthnow, *The New Christian Right*, 167–185.

58. Smith, *American Evangelicalism*, 39.

59. James L. Guth, John C. Green, Lyman A. Kellstedt, and Corwin E. Smidt, "Onward Christian Soldiers: Religious Activist Groups in American Politics," in Cigler and Loomis, *Interest Group Politics*, 4th ed., 55–76.

60. Guth, Green, Kellstedt, and Smidt, "Onward Christian Soldiers," 63, 73.

61. The generalizations in this paragraph are drawn from James L. Guth, Lyman A. Kellstedt, Corwin E. Smidt, and John C. Green, "Thunder on the Right: Religious Interest Group Mobilization in the 1996 Election," in Cigler and Loomis, *Interest Group Politics*, 5th ed., 169–192.

62. Data generously supplied by M. Dane Waters of the Initiative and Referendum Institute. See M. Dane Waters, "A Century Later—The Experiment with Citizen-Initiated Legislation Continues," *The Public Perspective* (special issue: *America at the Polls: 1998*) 10 (December/January 1999): 123–144, esp. 128.

63. David D. Schmidt, *Citizen Lawmakers: The Ballot Initiative Revolution* (Philadelphia: Temple University Press, 1989).

64. David B. Magleby, "Direct Legislation in the American States," in *Referendums around the World*, eds. David Butler and Austin Ranney (Washington, D.C.: AEI Press, 1994): 230–233.

65. Caroline J. Tolbert, Daniel H. Lowenstein, and Todd Donovan, "Election Law and Rules for Using Initiatives," in *Citizens as Legislators: Direct Democracy in the United States*, eds. Shaun Bowler, Todd Donovan, and Caroline J. Tolbert (Columbus: Ohio State University Press, 1998): 35 (emphasis added). See also other chapters in the Bowler, Donovan, and Tolbert volume; David B. Magleby, *Direct Legislation: Voting on Ballot Propositions in the United States* (Baltimore, Md.: Johns Hopkins University Press, 1984); Thomas E. Cronin, *Direct Democracy: The Politics of Initiative, Referendum, and Recall* (Cambridge, Mass.: Harvard University Press, 1989); and M. Dane Walters, "A Century Later—The Experiment with Citizen-Initiated Legislation Continues."

66. For evidence on the propositions in this paragraph, see Betty H. Zisk, *Money, Media, and the Grass Roots: State Ballot Issues and the Electoral Process* (Newbury Park, Calif.: Sage, 1987), quotation at 246; Cronin, *Direct Democracy*, esp. 110–116; Tolbert, Lowenstein, and Donovan, "Election Law"; Magleby, "Direct Legislation in the American States." Thanks to Benjamin Deufel for his able help on this topic.

67. Zisk, *Money, Media, and the Grass Roots*, 250.

68. Kevin Djo Everett, "Professionalization and Protest: Changes in the Social Movement Sector, 1961–1983," *Social Forces* 70 (June 1992): 957–975.

69. Debra E. Blum, "Men's Group Lays Off Entire Staff," *The Chronicle of Philanthropy*, March 12, 1998. Promise-Keepers subsequently resumed operations, but remained about half as large organizationally a year after Stand in the Gap as before. See "Promise Keepers at a Prayerful Crossroads; One Year After Mall Rally, Men's Religious Group Grapples with Message, Money," *Washington Post*, October 7, 1998.

70. Evidence for the generalizations in this paragraph comes from Verba, Schlozman, and Brady, *Voice and Equality*, 50, 60, 88–89; Dalton, *Citizen Politics*, 67–85; Matthew Crozat, "Are the Times A-Changin'? Assessing the Acceptance of Protest in Western Democracies," in Meyer and Tarrow, *The Social Movement Society*, 59–81; and author's analysis of General Social Survey data (1973; 1996), Political Action Studies (1974; 1981), Roper Social and Political Trends surveys (1978; 1980; 1985; 1994), and the World Values Surveys (1980; 1990; 1995). Confirming the "graying" of protest demonstrations shown in figure 45, Roper surveys found that the fraction of all self-proclaimed protesters who were forty-five and over doubled from 17 percent in 1978 to 32 percent in 1994. Dalton notes that data from the five Political Action and the World Values Surveys conducted between 1974 and 1995 show that the fraction of adults who had *ever* joined a boycott rose from 16 percent in 1974 to 19 percent in 1995; had *ever* joined a lawful demonstration rose from 12 percent to 16 percent; had *ever* participated in a wildcat strike rose from 2 percent to 4 percent; and had *ever* participated in a sit-in remained constant at 2 percent. These same surveys show, however, that the average age of all adults who had ever demonstrated rose steadily from thirty-five in 1974 to forty-six in 1995; the modal protester throughout this period was the aging veteran of the sixties.

71. Meyer and Tarrow, "A Movement Society," 8.

72. For all phone calls: Federal Communications Commission, *Statistics of Communications Common Carriers* (formerly *Statistics of the Communication Industry in the U.S.*) (Washington, D.C.: Government Printing Office, 1945–1999). For all personal calls in 1982: Fischer, *America Calling*, 226; for trends in long-distance personal calls and letters: author's analysis of Roper Social and Political Trends survey archive plus Roper Reports for August 1995. For 1998 usage: Pew Research Center for the People & the Press, *Biennial News Consumption Survey*, www.people-press.org/med98que.htm.

73. For predictions about the telephone's social impact, see Ithiel de Sola Pool, *Forecasting the Telephone: A Retrospective Technology Assessment of the Telephone* (Norwood, N.J.: Ablex Publishing, 1983); Sidney Aronson, "Bell's Electrical Toy: What's the Use? The Sociology of Early Telephone Usage," and Asa Briggs, "The Pleasure Telephone: A Chapter in the Prehistory of the Media," both in *The Social Impact of the Telephone*, ed. Ithiel de Sola Pool (Cambridge, Mass.: MIT Press, 1977); Fischer, *America Calling*, quotation at 82. Thanks to David Campbell for his review of the social effects of telephony.

74. Pool, "Introduction," in *Social Impact of the Telephone*, ed. Pool, 4.

75. Alan H. Wurtzel and Colin Turner, "The Latent Functions of the Telephone: What Missing the Extension Means," in *Social Impact of the Telephone*, ed. Pool, 246–61.

76. Sidney H. Aronson, "The Sociology of the Telephone," *International Journal of Comparative Sociology* 12 (September 1971): 162; Fischer, *America Calling*, 195; Malcolm M. Willey and Stuart A. Rice, *Communication Agencies and Social Life* (New York: McGraw-Hill, 1933); Martin Mayer, "The Telephone and the Uses of Time," in *Social Impact of the Telephone*, ed. Pool, 225–45, quotations at 226 and 230.

77. Fischer, *America Calling*, 3, 242, 253, 265–66.

78. Daniel J. Boorstin, *The Americans: The Democratic Experience* (New York: Vintage Books, 1974), 391.

79. Technological diffusion: table 2 below and the associated discussion; time usage: John Robinson, Shawn Levin, and Brian Hak, "Computer Time," *American Demographics*, August 1998; Internet usage: figure 56 below and "64.2 Million American Adults Regularly Use the Internet," Mediamark press release (May 12, 1999), at www.mediamark.com/mri/docs/pres_s99.htm.

80. Youth and Internet: *Project Vote Smart/Pew Charitable Trusts 1999 Survey* (Philipsburg, Mont.: Project Vote Smart, 1999), (www.votesmart.org/youthsurvey.phtml?checking=/, accessed October 5, 1999); AARP Web site: "Silver Stringers Get New Life on Line," *Boston Globe*, December 25, 1998.

81. Religious services: "God Goes Online," *Wall Street Journal*, March 26, 1999, W1; prayer: Joshua Cooper Ramo, "Finding God on the Web," *Time*, December 16, 1996, 60–65; "Praying on the Internet," *Christian Century*, April 16, 1997; weddings: "The Knot: Weddings for the Real World Launches Wedding Day," *Business Wire*, June 24, 1997; funerals and grief counseling: "Post-mortems Meet Modems: Online Funerals Is Mourners' Way to Go," Associated Press, in the *Sacramento Bee*, August 25, 1996, A7; Sarah Wyatt, "Comfort and Counsel in Times of Grief," *New York Times*, August 18, 1997; virtual demonstrations and lobbying: "We Shall All Log-On: Digital Demonstrators Unite on the Web," *Wall Street Journal*, December 3, 1998, B1; Rebecca Fairley Raney, "Flash Campaigns: Online Activism at Warp Speed," *New York Times*, June 3, 1999; Internet and community: William A. Galston, "(How)

Does the Internet Affect Community? Some Speculations in Search of Evidence," in *democracy.com? Governance in a Networked World*, eds. Elaine Ciulla Kamarck and Joseph S. Nye, Jr. (Hollis, N.H.: Hollis Publishing, 1999), 45–61.

82. Philip Aspden and James E. Katz, "A Nation of Strangers?" *Communications of the ACM* 40 (December 1997): 81–86; "The Internet News Audience Goes Ordinary," Pew Research Center for the People & the Press (www .people-press.org/tech98mor.htm, accessed on August 15, 1999), esp. 15; author's analysis of DDB Needham Life Style survey archive. See also Bruce Bimber, "Information and Civic Engagement in America: Political Effects of Information Technology" (unpublished ms., University of California at Santa Barbara, 1999) for a similar finding.

83. Barry Wellman, Janet Salaff, Dimitrina Dimitrova, Laura Garton, Milena Gulia, and Caroline Haythornthwaite, "Computer Networks as Social Networks: Collaborative Work, Telework, and Virtual Community," *Annual Review of Sociology* 22 (1996): 213–238, quotation at 213, and Barry Wellman and Milena Gulia, "Virtual Communities as Communities: Net Surfers Don't Ride Alone," in *Communities in Cyberspace*, Marc A. Smith and Peter Kollock, eds. (New York: Routledge, 1999), 167–194, quotation at 188.

84. Starr Roxanne Hiltz and Murray Turoff, *The Network Nation: Human Communication Via Computer* (Reading, Mass.: Addison-Wesley, 1978), as quoted in Nitin Nohria and Robert G. Eccles, "Face-to-Face: Making Network Organizations Work," in *Networks and Organizations: Structure, Form, and Action*, Nitin Nohria and Robert G. Eccles, eds. (Boston: Harvard Business School Press, 1992), 289; Michael Strangelove, "The Internet, Electric Gaia and the Rise of the Uncensored Self," *Computer-Mediated Communication Magazine* 1 (September 1994), 11.

85. Howard Rheingold, *The Virtual Community: Homesteading on the Electronic Frontier* (Reading, Mass.: Addison-Wesley, 1993), 1; John Perry Barlow, Sven Birkets, Kevin Kelly, and Mark Slouka, "What Are We Doing On-Line," *Harper's* (August 1995): 35–46, quotation at 40.

86. John Seely Brown and Paul Duguid, *The Social Life of Information* (Boston: Harvard Business School Press, 2000), quotation at 31; Laura Garton and Barry Wellman, "Social Impacts of Electronic Mail in Organizations: A Review of the Research Literature," *Communication Yearbook* 18 (Thousand Oaks, Calif.: Sage, 1995), 434–453, esp. 445–447.

87. Michael L. Dertouzos, *What Will Be: How the New World of Information Will Change Our Lives* (San Francisco: HarperEdge, 1997), 157–160.

88. Rheingold, *Virtual Community*, 422; Starr Roxanne Hiltz and Murray Turoff, *The Network Nation*, rev. ed. (Cambridge, Mass.: MIT Press, 1993); Peter Steiner, "On the Internet, No One Knows You're a Dog," *New Yorker*, July 5, 1993, 61.

89. Lee Sproull and Sara B. Kiesler, *Connections: New Ways of Working in the Networked Organization* (Cambridge, Mass.: MIT Press, 1991).

90. Peter Kollock and Marc A. Smith, "Communities in Cyberspace," in *Communities in Cyberspace*, Smith and Kollock, eds. (New York: Routledge, 1999), 3–25, quotation at 13.

91. Mark S. Bonchek, *From Broadcast to Netcast: The Internet and the Flow of Political Information*, Ph.D. diss. (Harvard University, 1997), esp. 99–109.

92. Brown and Duguid, *Social Life of Information*, 226.

93. Author's analysis of DDB Needham Life Style surveys on Internet usage; *Falling Through the Net II: New Data on the Digital Divide* (Washington, D.C.: National Telecommunications and Information Administration, 1999), at www.ntia.doc.gov/ntiahome/net2/falling.html accessed on July 1, 1999; Manuel Castells, *The Rise of the Network Society* (Cambridge, Mass.: Blackwell, 1996), 363–64; Pippa Norris, "Who Surfs? New Technology, Old Voters, & Virtual Democracy," in Kamarck and Nye, *democracy.com*, 71–94; Pippa Norris, "Who Surfs Café Europa? Virtual Democracy in the U.S. and Western Europe," paper presented at the Annual Meeting of the American Political Science Association (Atlanta, September 1999).

94. Dertouzos, *What Will Be*, 299.

95. Albert Mehrabian, *Silent Messages: Implicit Communications of Emotions and Attitudes*, 2nd ed. (Belmont, Calif.: Wadsworth, 1981), iii, as cited in Brittney G. Chenault, "Developing Personal and Emotional Relationships Via Computer-Mediated Communication," *Computer-Mediated Communication Magazine* 5 (May 1998): 1, at www .december.com/cmc/mag/1998/may/chenault.html, as consulted October 16, 1999. On evolution and honesty, see Robert H. Frank, *Passions Within Reason: The Strategic Roles of the Emotions* (New York: Norton, 1988).

96. Research comparing face-to-face and computer-mediated communication is extensive. See Nohria and Eccles, "Face-to-Face," esp. 292–299, from which the quotation is taken; Sara Kiesler, Jane Siegel, and Timothy W. McGuire, "Social Psychological Aspects of Computer-Mediated Communication," *American Psychologist* 39 (1984): 1123–1134; L. K. Trevino, R. H. Lengel, and R. L. Daft, "Media Symbolism, Media Richness, and Media Choice in Organizations: A Symbolic Interactionist Perspective," *Communication Research* 14 (1987): 553–574; Lee Sproull and Sara Kiesler, "Computers, Networks, and Work," *Scientific American* 265 [3] (1991): 116–127; Poppy Lauretta McLeod, "An Assessment of the Experimental Literature on Electronic Support of Group Work: Results of a Meta-Analysis," *Human-Computer Interaction* 7 (1992): 257–280; Joseph B. Walther, "Interpersonal Effects in Computer-Mediated Interaction: A Relational Perspective," *Communication Research* 19 (1992): 52–90; Joseph B. Walther, "Anticipated Ongoing Interaction Versus Channel Effects on Relational Communication in Computer-Mediated Interaction," *Human-Computer Interaction* 20 (1994): 473–501; M. Lea and R. Spears, "Love at First Byte? Building Personal Relationships over Computer Networks," in *Understudied Relationships: Off the Beaten Track*, eds. J. T. Wood and S. Duck (Newbury Park, Calif.: 1995), 197–233; Garton and Barry Wellman, "Social Impacts"; Susan G. Straus, "Technology, Group Process, and Group Outcomes: Testing the Connections in Computer-Mediated and Face-to-Face Groups," *Human-Computer Interaction* 12 (1997): 227–265, esp. 233–236; Elena Rocco, "Trust Breaks Down in Electronic Contexts but Can Be Repaired by Some Initial Face-to-Face Contact," *Computer-Human Interaction* [CHI] *Proceedings* (Los Angeles, Calif.: April 1998), 492–502. Scientists do not yet agree on which differences between face-to-face and computer-mediated communication account for the different outcomes—the richer "social presence" in face-to-face settings, slower communication in text-based settings, the greater presumption of ongoing

relations in face-to-face settings, or something else. Brown and Duguid, *Social Life of Information*, 41–52, provide a useful overview of the differences between negotiating in real life and in cyberspace.

97. Brown and Duguid, *Social Life of Information*, 61. On flaming, see Martin Lea, Tim O'Shea, Pat Fung, and Russell Spears, " 'Flaming' in Computer-Mediated Communication: Observations, Explanations, Implications," in *Contexts of Computer-Mediated Communication*, Martin Lea, ed. (New York: Harvester Wheatsheaf, 1992), 89–112; Garton and Wellman, "Social Impacts," 441–442; and Straus, "Technology," 234–235. Rocco ("Trust Breaks Down") found that brief face-to-face interaction prior to computer-mediated communication improved cooperation.

98. Nohria and Eccles, "Face-to-Face," 300–301; Andrew Cohill and Andrea Kavanaugh, *Community Networks: Lessons from Blacksburg, Virginia* (Norwood, Mass.: Artech House, 2000).

99. Galston, "(How) Does the Internet Affect Community?"

100. Brid O'Connaill, Steve Whittaker, and Sylvia Wilbur, "Conversations over Video Conferences: An Evaluation of the Spoken Aspects of Video-Mediated Communication," *Human-Computer Interaction* 8 (1993): 389–428; Abigail J. Sellen, "Remote Conversations: The Effects of Mediating Talk with Technology," *Human-Computer Interaction* 10 (1995): 401–444.

101. Marshall van Alstyne and Erik Brynjolfsson, "Electronic Communities: Global Village or Cyberbalkanization?" (1996), web.mit.edu/marshall/www/Abstracts.html, accessed on October 1, 1999. See Bruce Bimber, "The Internet and Political Transformation: Populism, Community, and Accelerated Pluralism," *Polity* 31 (1998): 133–60, for a related argument that the Internet will encourage "the fragmentation of the present system of interest-based group politics."

102. Stephen Doheny-Farina, *The Wired Neighborhood* (New Haven, Conn.: Yale University Press, 1996), 16.

103. I am grateful to Paul Resnick for continuing instruction and thoughtful reflection on the Internet and social capital.

104. *Time*, September 27, 1999; Robert Kraut, Michael Patterson, Vicki Lundmark, and Sara Kiesler, "Internet Paradox: A Social Technology That Reduces Social Involvement and Psychological Well-Being?" *American Psychologist* 53 (September 1998): 1017–1031.

105. Emmanuel Koku, Nancy Nazer, and Barry Wellman, "Netting Scholars: Online and Offline," *American Behavioral Scientist* 43 (2000, forthcoming). Keith N. Hampton and Barry Wellman, "Netville On-line and Off-line: Observing and Surveying a Wired Suburb," *American Behavioral Scientist* 43 (November/December 1999): 475–492, report that residents of a wired suburb of Toronto used computer-mediated communication primarily to reinforce ties with neighbors rather than to extend their social networks beyond the bounds of physical space. Wellman also reports in "The Global Village Isn't So Global," *Connections* 22 (1999): 14–16, that a pilot study of email usage among University of California graduate students found that nearly two-thirds of their messages were from the Bay Area and fully half from within Berkeley itself. I am grateful to Barry Wellman for many helpful insights into the theme of this section as well as his BMW expertise. For additional evidence that telecommunications and face-to-face communication are complementary, not competitive, see Jess Gaspar and Edward L. Glaeser, "Information Technology and the Future of Cities," *Journal of Urban Economics* 43 (1998): 136–156.

106. Dertouzos, *What Will Be*, 300; Brown and Duguid, *Social Life of Information*, 226, quoting Dan Huttenlocher.

CHAPTER 10: INTRODUCTION

1. Morris Janowitz, *The Community Press in an Urban Setting: The Social Elements of Urbanism*, 2nd ed. (Chicago: University of Chicago Press, 1967), xvii; Fischer, Jackson, et al., *Networks and Places*, 201–203.

2. Wuthnow, *Sharing the Journey*, 6.

3. For an analogous point, see Robert J. Sampson, "Local Friendship Ties," 766–779.

4. Author's analysis of General Social Survey, DDB Needham Life Style, and Roper Social and Political Trends archives. Henry E. Brady, Kay L. Schlozman, Sidney Verba, and Laurel Elms, "Who Bowls? Class, Race, and Political Inequality, 1973–1994" (paper delivered at the annual meeting of the American Political Science Association, Boston, September 1998), confirm the absence of class differences in civic disengagement.

5. Generalizations in this paragraph are based on author's analysis of DDB Needham Life Style, Roper Social and Political Trends, and General Social Survey archives, controlling for other demographic factors, including sex, race, marital, parental, and employment status, age, income and financial worries, and homeownership.

6. On the role of education in explaining differences in political participation, see Verba, Schlozman, and Brady, *Voice and Equality*; and Norman H. Nie, Jane Junn, and Kenneth Stehlik-Barry, *Education and Democratic Citizenship in America* (Chicago: University of Chicago Press, 1996), as well as appendix I.

7. *Statistical Abstract of the United States 1998* (Washington, D.C.: U.S. Census Bureau, 1998), supplemented by author's analysis of General Social Survey.

8. As noted earlier, synergistic effects might blur or eliminate the individual-level correlation between two factors that were causally related in the aggregate.

CHAPTER 11: PRESSURES OF TIME AND MONEY

1. Verba, Schlozman, and Brady, *Voice and Equality*, 129; *Giving and Volunteering: 1996*, 4–112; Robinson and Godbey, *Time for Life*, 231; author's multivariate analysis of DDB Needham Life Style and GSS surveys. In the DDB Needham surveys, for example, the fraction of Americans who "stayed late at work" at least once a month in the previous year climbed steadily from 29 percent in 1985 to 38 percent in 1999.

2. Ellen R. McGrattan and Richard Rogerson, "Changes in Hours Worked Since 1950," *Federal Reserve Bank of Minneapolis Quarterly Review* 22 (winter 1998): 2–19. For a recent balanced and comprehensive overview of trends in work hours, see *Report on the American Workforce 1999* (Washington, D.C.: Department of Labor, 1999), ch. 3.

As discussed below, this aggregate stability conceals large reallocations of hours worked across subgroups of the population.

3. Robinson and Godbey, *Time for Life*, 339. Free time is all time *not* spent on work, household, family and personal care, shopping, eating, and sleeping. On the debate about trends in work hours, see Robinson and Godbey, *Time for Life*; Juliet B. Schor, *The Overworked American* (New York: Basic Books, 1991); McGrattan and Rogerson, "Changes in Hours"; Mary T. Coleman and John Pencavel, "Changes in Work Hours of Male Employees, 1940–1988," *Industrial and Labor Relations Review* 46 (January 1993): 262–283; Mary T. Coleman and John Pencavel, "Trends in Market Work Behavior of Women Since 1940," *Industrial and Labor Relations Review* 46 (July 1993): 653–676; Laura Leete and Juliet B. Schor, "Assessing the Time Squeeze Hypothesis: Hours Worked in the United States, 1969–1989," *Industrial Relations* 33 (January 1994): 25–43; Barry Bluestone and Stephen Rose, "Overworked *and* Underemployed," *The American Prospect* 31 (March/April 1997): 58–69; Mishel, Bernstein, and Schmitt, *The State of Working America*, esp. 17–18, 123.

4. Author's analysis of Harris polls, obtained from the Louis Harris poll archive at the University of North Carolina. Robinson and Godbey, *Time for Life*, 126–129. Time diary data are generally more reliable than survey recall questions, and they show less work time and more leisure time.

5. Schor, *The Overworked American*; Robinson and Godbey, *Time for Life*, 217–218; *Report on the American Workforce 1999*, 95, 100.

6. Juliet Schor, "Civic Engagement and Working Hours: Do Americans Really Have More Free Time Than Ever Before?" in *Working Time, Overwork and Underemployment: Trends, Theory and Policy Perspectives*, eds. Lonnie Golden and Deborah M. Figart (London: Routledge, 2000 forthcoming).

7. Author's analysis of General Social Survey and DDB Needham Life Style data, controlling for sex, race, year of birth, year of survey, education, income, financial worries, region, size of city, marital, parental and employment status, self-reported health, expected mobility, homeownership, and mean commuting time in county of residence. Our DDB Needham index of time pressure is based on four closely intercorrelated items, the first three of them agree-disagree statements: 1) "I work very hard most of the time"; 2) "I have a lot of spare time" (scoring reversed); 3) "I feel I am under a great deal of pressure most of the time"; and 4) "How often during the past 12 months did you stay late at work?"

8. Richard B. Freeman, "Working for Nothing: The Supply of Volunteer Labor," National Bureau of Economic Research working paper no. 5435 (Cambridge, Mass.: National Bureau of Economic Research, 1996), 28–34; Verba, Schlozman, Brady, *Voice and Equality*, 352–358, esp. footnote 40; and Kay Lehman Schlozman, Henry E. Brady, Sidney Verba, Jennifer Erkulwater, and Laurel Elms, "Why Can't They Be Like We Were? Life Cycle, Generation, and Political Participation" (paper presented at the annual meeting of the American Political Science Association, Atlanta, September 1999); author's analysis of DDB Needham Life Style survey data.

9. John Robinson, "The Time Squeeze," *American Demographics*, February 1990. Time pressure and TV dependence are also strongly negatively correlated in the DDB Needham data.

10. Author's analysis of DDB Needham Life Style data.

11. Author's analysis of DDB Needham Life Style data. Financial anxiety is measured by four agree-disagree statements: "No matter how fast our income goes up we never seem to get ahead" (agree); "Our family is too heavily in debt today" (agree); "We have more to spend on extras than most of our neighbors do" (disagree); and "Our family income is high enough to satisfy nearly all our important desires" (disagree). All four show an increase in financial worry between 1975 and 1999 (especially in the first half of that period); all four are strongly correlated with civic and social disengagement, with standard demographic controls. Of course, the negative correlation between social engagement and financial worry does not prove causation. Perhaps investments in social capital act as buffers against economic reversals, or perhaps socially engaged individuals are more easily satisfied economically than other, more materialistic individuals. (Thanks to Lara Putnam for these points.) In any event, controlling for financial worry only faintly diminishes the basic declines in civic and social engagement discussed in section II.

12. Juliet B. Schor, *The Overspent American: Upscaling, Downshifting, and the New Consumer* (New York: Harper, 1999); Robert H. Frank, *Luxury Fever: Why Money Fails to Satisfy in an Era of Excess* (New York: Free Press, 1999). For more evidence of growing materialism, see figure 76.

13. Marie Jahoda, Paul Lazarsfeld, and Hans Zeisel, *Marienthal* (Chicago: Aldine-Atherton, 1933 [1971]); Eli Ginzberg, *The Unemployed* (New York: Harper and Brothers, 1943); Richard C. Wilcock and Walter H. Franke, *Unwanted Workers* (New York: Free Press of Glencoe, 1963).

14. Generalizations in this paragraph and the next are based on author's analysis of DDB Needham Life Style, Roper Social and Political Trends, and General Social Survey archives. In the GSS electoral turnout and group membership are positively correlated with financial satisfaction, controlling for income, education, age, sex, race, marital and parental status, and year of survey.

15. Caroline Hodges Persell, "The Interdependence of Social Justice and Civil Society" (New York: New York University, 1996); W. Lance Bennett, "The UnCivic Culture: Communication, Identity, and the Rise of Lifestyle Politics," *PS: Political Science & Politics* 31 (December 1998): 741–761.

16. Author's analysis of DDB Needham Life Style surveys.

17. Robert Wuthnow, "Changing Character of Social Capital in the United States." Burnham, "Turnout Problem," offers evidence that between the mid-1960s and the mid-1980s, turnout declined twice as rapidly among blue-collar workers as among their white-collar colleagues. Although I find little evidence that civic disengagement has been concentrated in the lower classes, my analysis of polls from 1966 to 1998 from the Harris poll archive at the University of North Carolina suggests that alienation has grown more rapidly at the bottom of the social hierarchy. In this sense, I find some support for the "marginality" interpretation as regards political attitudes and behavior.

18. Theda Skocpol, "Unraveling from Above," *The American Prospect*, March/April 1996, 20–25.

19. Author's analysis of the DDB Needham Life Style, General Social Survey, and Roper Social and Political Trends archives, using a wide range of indicators of both social participation and socioeconomic privilege. See also Verba et al., "Who Bowls?"

20. This generalization is based on extensive multivariate analysis of the General Social Survey, the DDB Need-

ham Life Style archives, and the Roper Social and Political Trends archives, predicting measures of civic engagement from many demographic factors, including income and financial worries, plus year of survey. The time trend is cut by no more than 5–10 percent, even under the most stringent of economic controls, both objective and subjective.

21. Bureau of Labor Statistics; Coleman and Pencavel, "Trends in Market Work Behavior of Women." McGrattan and Rogerson, "Changes in Hours," estimate that weekly paid working hours per woman increased by about seven hours between 1960 and 1990. Leete and Schor, "Assessing the Time Squeeze," estimate women's paid labor increased five hours per week from 1969 to 1989; *Report on the American Workforce*, 84, estimates an increase of six hours per week from 1976 to 1998. These studies use different methods and cover different periods but converge on an estimated increase of roughly one more hour per day in paid labor by the average woman over these three decades. Based on time diary data, Robinson and Godbey, *Time for Life*, 346, estimate that between 1965 and 1995 the increase in paid labor hours for all women amounted to eight hours per week, whereas the decline in housework and child care amounted to thirteen hours per week, leaving a net gain of about five hours per week in discretionary free time.

22. Ithiel de Sola Pool and Manfred Kochen, "Contacts and Influence," *Social Networks* 1 (1978–79): 5–51; Patricia Klobus Edwards, John N. Edwards, and Ann DeWitt Watts, "Women, Work, and Social Participation," *Journal of Voluntary Action Research* 13 (January/March 1984): 7–22; author's analysis of Roper Social and Political Trends and GSS archives. Robinson and Godbey, *Time for Life* report that nonemployed women spend more time on activity in voluntary associations than their fully employed counterparts. That is confirmed by evidence from the DDB Needham archive, as reported in figure 49.

23. Author's analysis of Roper Social and Political Trends archives. Holding standard demographic factors constant, full-time employment among women is linked with modest increases in local organizational leadership, signing petitions, writing Congress, and other public forms of community engagement.

24. Author's analysis of DDB Needham Life Study surveys, predicting civic engagement from work status among single moms, controlling for all standard demographic variables.

25. Author's analysis of DDB Needham Life Style surveys and the Americans' Use of Time archive. Verba, Schlozman, and Brady, *Voice and Equality*, 259, find that men are more active in politics and women more active in religious institutions; they find no gender difference in secular, nonpolitical participation.

26. Author's analysis of DDB Needham Life Style surveys. The generalizations in this paragraph refer to the net effect of full-time work, controlling for education, race, financial worries, residential mobility, marital and parental status, year of birth, and year of survey. This same pattern appears in the Americans' Use of Time archive, as reported by Laura Tiehen, "Has Working Caused Married Women to Volunteer Less? Evidence from Time Diary Data 1965 to 1993," paper delivered at the 28th Annual Conference of the Association for Research on Nonprofit Organizations and Voluntary Action (ARNOVA), Washington, D.C., November 4–6, 1999. In the Roper Social and Political Trends data, too, husbands of full-time employees attend church less frequently, holding other demographic factors constant.

27. Author's analysis of General Social Survey (membership in school service organizations), DDB Needham Life Style surveys (for club attendance), and Americans' Use of Time archive (for time allocation).

28. The full question is: "In today's society, many women work at home as full-time homemakers, and many women work and are paid for jobs outside the home. Other women combine both worlds by working part-time. Which of the alternatives below best describes what you do, along with the main reason behind your choice? (1) Full time homemaker, because I get personal satisfaction from being a homemaker and do not care to work outside my home; (2) Full-time homemaker, because I feel I should be at home to take better care of my children, even though I would like to work; (3) Employed part-time, because I get personal satisfaction from working at least some time outside my home; (4) Employed part-time, because the money I earn at my part-time job helps out with the family finances; (5) Employed full-time because I get personal satisfaction from my job; (6) Employed full-time, because the income I earn contributes to the family finances." As noted in appendix I, the DDB Needham Life Style surveys did not include single respondents prior to 1985. To extend our analysis of trends back to 1978, I imputed the distribution of work status and preferences for single women between 1978 and 1984, on the basis of observed trends for single women in 1985–99. No conclusion in the text would be altered, however, if we limited our analysis to 1985–99, although the degree of change in women's work status would be truncated.

29. This finding is confirmed by the Roper finding that "the proportion of [all] women who say they would rather stay home than go to work stood at 53 percent in 1992, up from 43 percent in 1985, a reversal of the downward trend in this statistic since the early 1970s." Russell, *Master Trend*, 65. Caution is necessary in assessing the details of figure 48, given the special character of the DDB Needham Life Style sample described in appendix I. I have no reason to doubt the pattern in figure 48, but I have found no other archives that contain the overtime information on women's work preferences necessary to confirm it.

30. Columns in figure 49 represent unstandardized OLS regression coefficients for dummy variables representing the various female work status, controlling for education, year of birth, year of survey, marital and parental status, financial worries, and expected future mobility. Absent financial worries, low income has no net effect on civic engagement.

31. The same pattern appears in the General Social Survey; in Nicholas Zill, "Family Change and Student Achievement: What We Have Learned, What It Means for Schools," in *Family-School Links: How Do They Affect Educational Outcomes?*, eds. Alan Booth and Judith Dunn (Mahwah, N.J.: Lawrence Erlbaum, 1996), 23; and in Marc Musick and John Wilson, "Women's Labor Force Participation and Volunteer Work," paper presented at the annual meeting of the Association for Research on Nonprofit Organizations and Voluntary Action (Washington, D.C.: 1999).

32. These estimates control for education, age, financial security, and marital and parental status.

33. Women who *choose* to work (whether full-time or part-time) are even less likely to attend church than those who work out of necessity. Self-selection may be relevant in this case, in the sense that women who are highly observant religiously may be more likely to choose a traditional family role.

34. I explored possible interactions among work, parental, and marital status in affecting women's social interaction. Except among single moms, as discussed above, full-time work inhibits social connectedness, whatever the woman's marital and parental status.

510 NOTES

35. Multivariate analysis of the DDB Needham data suggests that women who are not employed full-time invest their additional free time in civic activities, whereas men who are working part-time do not.

36. Author's analysis of data from the General Social Survey. My previous work drew exclusively on the GSS measure of formal membership and was therefore led to the guess—firmly contradicted by the more abundant evidence now available—that full-time employment might not impede women's social participation. See my "Tuning In, Tuning Out: The Strange Disappearance of Social Capital in America," *PS: Political Science and Politics* 28 (December 1995): 664–683; and "The Strange Disappearance of Civic America," *The American Prospect*, winter 1996, 34–48.

37. My back-of-the-envelope estimate of the effects of women's entry into the labor force is this: The largest difference in club attendance is between homemakers by choice and full-time workers by necessity—2 meetings annually. Between 1978 and 1999, according to our data, roughly one person in ten (net) moved from the most "club-friendly" to the least "club-friendly" category. Thus if *no* women had moved into the workplace over this period, that might have "saved" .2 club meetings per adult annually, whereas the actual decline over these same years (as shown in chapter 3) was roughly 5 meetings per year. Comparable calculations for other forms of civic engagement converge on a rough estimate that 10 percent of the total drop might be linked to this factor. This calculation ignores the effect of a wife's work on her husband's civic activity, but that effect is small in the aggregate. These individual correlations between work status and engagement disregard synergistic effects of women entering the labor force—if, for example, the fact that some women took a job also cut club-going among those who stayed home.

38. Author's analysis of DDB Needham Life Style and Roper Social and Political Trends archives. Affluence in the DDB Needham Life Style analysis was defined as the lowest quartile of financial anxiety. Over these two decades the number of affluent housewives fell by two-thirds to only 8 percent of working-age women. Affluence in the Roper Social and Political Trends analysis (absent a direct measure of financial anxiety) was defined as the highest quartile of income.

39. The effects of women working and financial worries discussed in this chapter cannot simply be added together, since the two factors themselves overlap, as we have seen. My best guess is that *together* they account for roughly one-tenth of the total decline in social connectedness.

CHAPTER 12: MOBILITY AND SPRAWL

1. Sally Ann Shumaker and Daniel Stokols, "Residential Mobility as a Social Issue and Research Topic," *Journal of Social Issues* 38 (1982): 1–19, and author's analysis of DDB Needham Life Style surveys.

2. J. Miller McPherson and William G. Lockwood, "The Longitudinal Study of Voluntary Association Memberships: A Multivariate Analysis," *Journal of Voluntary Action Research* 9 (January/December 1980): 74–84; Wolfinger and Rosenstone, *Who Votes?*, esp. 50–54; Robert J. Sampson, "Linking the Micro- and Macrolevel Dimensions of Community Social Organization," *Social Forces* 70 (September 1991): 43–64; Sampson, "Local Friendship Ties"; Steven J. Rosenstone and John Mark Hansen, *Mobilization, Participation, and Democracy in America*, esp. 157–58; Verba, Schlozman, and Brady, *Voice and Equality*, 452–455; Johanne Boisjoly, Greg J. Duncan, and Sandra Hofferth, "Access to Social Capital," *Journal of Family Issues* 16 (September 1995): 609–631; Hausknecht, *Joiners*, 47–48; author's analysis of the DDB Needham Life Style surveys, controlling for standard demographic factors, including age, sex, race, education, income, and marital, parental, and employment status.

3. Sampson, "Local Friendship Ties"; Robert D. Crutchfield, Michael R. Geerken, and Walter R. Gove, "Crime Rate and Social Integration: The Impact of Metropolitan Mobility," *Criminology* 20 (November 1982): 467–478; Robert Audette, Robert Algozzine, and Michelle Warden, "Mobility and School Achievement," *Psychological Reports* 72 (April 1993): 701–702; John Eckenrode, Elizabeth Rowe, Molly Laird, and Jacqueline Brathwaite, "Mobility as a Mediator of the Effects of Child Maltreatment on Academic Performance," *Child Development* 66 (August 1995): 1130–1142; and John Hagan, Ross MacMillan, and Blair Wheaton, "New Kid in Town: Social Capital and the Life Course Effects of Family Migration on Children," *American Sociological Review* 61 (June 1996): 368–385. For counterevidence, see Peter H. Rossi, *Why Families Move* (Beverly Hills, Calif.: Sage, 1980); and Fischer, Jackson, et al., *Networks and Places*, 177–184.

4. Larry E. Long, *Migration and Residential Mobility in the United States* (New York: Russell Sage Foundation, 1988); Shumaker and Stokols, "Residential Mobility"; *Historical Statistics of the United States* I: 646; *Statistical Abstract of the United States* 1998; U.S. Census Bureau, "Housing Vacancies and Homeownership," at www.census.gov/hhes/www/housing/hvs/historic/histt14.html; Fischer, Jackson, et al., *Networks and Places*, 191–192; author's analysis of National Election Study and DDB Needham Life Style surveys. One recent study suggests that mobility in the second half of the twentieth century may have been higher than in the period between 1860 and 1920, but this study, too, finds lower mobility in 1960–90 than in 1940–60; see Patricia Kelly Hall and Steven Ruggles, "Moving Through Time: Internal Migration Patterns of Americans, 1850–1990," paper presented at the Social Science History Association meetings (Fort Worth, Tex.: November 1999). Although the average American has been in the same locality for more than two decades, we change residences about every 5 years—renters every 2.1 years, homeowners every 8.2 years; Randolph E. Schmid, "Americans Move about Every 5 Years," Associated Press, October 29, 1998, citing Census Bureau study. One possible exception to declining mobility is that younger single people may be slightly more mobile now than their counterparts were several decades ago, but this trend is much too limited to account for the aggregate decline in social connectedness. Author's analysis of DDB Needham Life Style surveys; Matthew Klein, "Where America Lives," *American Demographics*, January 1998, citing National Association of Home Builders.

5. Author's analysis of DDB Needham Life Style, Roper Social and Political Trends, and General Social Survey archives, controlling for education, age, race, income, marital status, and residential stability. Residents of big cities and their suburbs are less likely to engage in every one of the dozen civic activities measured in the Roper Social and Political Trends surveys, especially running for office, serving as an officer or committee member of a local organization, attending a public meeting, and making a speech. See also John Eric Oliver, *Civil Society in Suburbia: The Effects of Metropolitan Social Contexts on Participation in Voluntary Organizations* (Ph.D. diss., University of California at Berkeley, 1997), esp. 64, and Hausknecht, *Joiners*, 18–21.

6. This pattern appears for virtually all of the dozens of indicators of civic involvement in both the DDB Needham Life Style and the Roper Social and Political Trends data, controlling for all standard demographic variables. The exact categorization of city size differs between the two archives, as indicated in figure 50 and figure 51, but in both archives at each step up in size from rural areas to major metropolitan areas civic engagement decreases.

7. The DDB Needham Life Style survey includes questions about where the respondent would prefer to live—big city or small town, city or suburb. When actual location and preferred location are both included in multiple regression analysis of social participation measures, actual location is always significant and preferred location rarely so.

8. John D. Kasarda, Stephen J. Appold, Stuart H. Sweeney, and Elaine Sieff, "Central-City and Suburban Migration Patterns: Is a Turnaround on the Horizon?" *Housing Policy Debate* 8 (1997): 307–358.

9. Mark Twain (1867) quoted in Bayrd Still, *Urban America: A History with Documents* (Boston: Little, Brown, 1974), 198; Henry George, *Progress and Poverty* (1884) excerpted in *City and Country in America*, ed. David R. Weimer (New York: Appleton-Century-Crofts, 1962), 60.

10. The Roper Social and Political Trends surveys hint at a civic "boom and bust" cycle in small towns and rural areas in the late 1980s, a pattern that blurs the secular trend downward in those settings, but this pattern does not appear in the DDB Needham Life Style, General Social Survey, or National Election Study surveys, so it is most likely a statistical fluke.

11. Ad for Park Forest Homes, Inc., November 8, 1952, quoted in William H. Whyte, Jr., *The Organization Man* (New York: Simon & Schuster, 1956), 284.

12. Whyte, *Organization Man*, quotation at 287; Herbert J. Gans, *The Levittowners: Ways of Life and Politics in a New Suburban Community* (New York: Pantheon Books, 1967); Claude S. Fischer and Robert Max Jackson, "Suburbanism and Localism," in Fischer et al., *Networks and Places*, 117–138; Seeley, Sim, and Loosley, *Crestwood Heights*. By contrast, Bennett M. Berger, *Working Class Suburb: A study of Autoworkers in Suburbia* (Berkeley: University of California Press, 1960), and Basil G. Zimmer and Amos H. Hawley, "The Significance of Membership in Associations," *American Journal of Sociology* 65 (September 1959): 196–201, found little or no unusual community involvement in early postwar suburbs.

13. Peter O. Muller, *Contemporary Suburban America* (Englewood Cliffs, N.J.: Prentice-Hall, 1981); Gregory R. Weiher, *The Fractured Metropolis: Political Fragmentation and Metropolitan Segregation* (Albany: State University of New York Press, 1991); Douglas Massey and Mitchell Eggers, "The Spatial Concentration of Affluence and Poverty During the 1970s," *Urban Affairs Quarterly* 29 (December 1993): 299–315; Evan McKenzie, *Privatopia: Homeowner Associations and the Rise of Residential Private Government* (New Haven, Conn.: Yale University Press, 1994); and Edward J. Blakely and Mary Gail Snyder, *Fortress America: Gated Communities in the United States* (Washington, D.C.: Brookings Institution, 1997). McKenzie reports that homeowners associations nationwide mushroomed from 10,000 in 1970 to 150,000 in 1992, representing 32 million Americans.

14. www.concordhomes.com/co/co_greenfield.html. Ironically, Greenfield is only a few miles from Whyte's Park Forest.

15. Blakely and Snyder, *Fortress America*; J. Eric Oliver, "The Effects of Metropolitan Economic Segregation on Local Civic Participation," *American Journal of Political Science* 43 (January 1999): 186–212, quotation at 205. Serious research on gated communities is in its infancy.

16. M. P. Baumgartner, *The Moral Order of a Suburb* (New York: Oxford University Press, 1988); Duany and Plater-Zyberk, quoted in William Schneider, "The Suburban Century Begins," *The Atlantic Monthly*, July 1992, 33–44, at 37.

17. Lewis Mumford, *The Culture of Cities* (New York: Harcourt, Brace, 1938), 412; Robert E. Lang and Karen A. Danielsen, "Gated Communities in America: Walling Out the World?" *Housing Policy Debate* 8 (1997): 873

18. Kenneth T. Jackson, *Crabgrass Frontier: The Suburbanization of the United States* (New York: Oxford University Press, 1985), quotation at 272, 279–80.

19. Robert Fishman, *Bourgeois Utopias: The Rise and Fall of Suburbia* (New York: Basic Books, 1987); Joel Garreau, *Edge City: Life on the New Frontier* (New York: Anchor Books, 1991); James Howard Kunstler, *The Geography of Nowhere: The Rise and Decline of America's Man-Made Landscape* (New York: Simon & Schuster, 1993); *The New Urbanism: Toward an Architecture of Community*, ed. Peter Katz (New York: McGraw-Hill, 1994); Thomas W. Hanchett, "U.S. Tax Policy and the Shopping Center Boom of the 1950s and 1960s," *American Historical Review* 101 (October 1996): 1082–1110; Kenneth T. Jackson, "All the World's a Mall: Reflections on the Social and Economic Consequences of the American Shopping Center," *American Historical Review* (October 1996): 1111–1121; Margaret Crawford, "The World in a Shopping Mall," in *Variations on a Theme Park: The New American City and the End of Public Space*, Michael Sorkin, ed. (New York: Noonday Press, 1992); Jackson, *Crabgrass Frontier*, 265.

20. *Statistical Abstract of the United States: 1998*, 636; *The Public Perspective* 10 (February/March 1999): 26; Brad Edmondson, "In the Driver's Seat," *American Demographics*, March 1998, at www.americandemographics.com; and National Association of Home Builders from Census data, at www.nahb.com/facts/forecast/sf.html (consulted January 27, 2000).

21. Data in this and the previous two paragraphs from Patricia S. Hu and Jennifer R. Young, "Summary of Travel Trends: 1995 Nationwide Personal Transportation Survey," prepared for U.S. Department of Transportation (Oak Ridge, Tenn.: Center for Transportation Analysis, Oak Ridge National Laboratory, January 1999), www.cta.ornl.gov/npts/1995/Doc/trends_report18.pdf, 1995 data adjusted for comparability with earlier surveys; *Statistical Abstract of the United States: 1998*, 636; *Our Nation's Travel: 1995 National Personal Transportation Survey Early Results Report* (Washington, D.C.: U.S. Department of Transportation, 1998), "Work at Home in 1997," a report from the Bureau of Labor Statistics, http://stats.bls.gov/news.release/homey.nws.htm; William G. Deming, "Work at Home: Data from the CPS," *Monthly Labor Review* (February 1994): 14–20; Patricia L. Mokhtarian and Dennis K. Henderson, "Analyzing the Travel Behavior of Home-Based Workers in the 1991 CALTRANS Statewide Travel Survey," *Journal of Transportation and Statistics* (October 1998): 25–41; David Schrank and Tim Lomax, *The 1999 Annual Urban Mobility Study* (College Station: Texas Transportation Institute, Texas A&M University, 1999), at http://mobility.tamu.edu/. *Our Nation's Travel* estimates solo commuting at 80 percent in 1995; Gallup (www.gallup.com) estimates it at 90 per-

cent in December 1998. Other data on commuting time converge on an estimate of twenty minutes each way, rising over time. These include the decennial census (1980–90), the Roper Social and Political Trends surveys (1973–98), and the Americans' Use of Time studies (1965–85). *Roper Reports* 98–3 (New York: Roper Starch Worldwide, 1998), 150, which provides the longest, most up-to-date time series, suggests that even accounting for home-based work, employees who commute more than twenty minutes rose from 29 percent in 1973 to 38 percent in 1999. *Report on the American Workforce 1999*, 117, shows that the share of the workforce who did *any* work at home, including self-employment or taking work home at night, slipped from 18.3 percent in 1991 to 17.7 percent in 1997.

22. Edmondson, "In the Driver's Seat."

23. Author's analyses of DDB Needham Life Style, Roper Social and Political Trends, and Americans' Use of Time survey archives, controlling for all standard demographic variables. In the Roper and Use of Time surveys commuting time is based on the respondent's own estimate, whereas in the DDB Needham analysis the measure is the mean commuting time in the respondent's county of residence. All approaches converge on the estimate that ten minutes more commuting means 10 percent less participation across many measures of civic engagement.

24. In metropolitan areas with more than two million inhabitants the fraction who generally or definitely would prefer to live in a big city rather than in a small town fell from 38 percent in 1975 to 31 percent in 1999. For the debate about suburbia and the auto, see Jane Holtz Kay, *Asphalt Nation: How the Automobile Took Over America and How We Can Take It Back* (New York: Crown, 1997); Richard Moe and Carter Wilkie, *Changing Places: Rebuilding Community in the Age of Sprawl* (New York: Henry Holt, 1997); and James Q. Wilson, "Cars and Their Enemies," *Commentary* 104 (July 1997): 17–23.

25. Verba and Nie, *Participation in America*, 236, 247.

26. The fraction of the population living in metropolitan areas has grown by roughly ten percentage points since the mid-1970s, and the civic penalty associated with such areas is, in round numbers, 20 percent, as suggested by figure 50, figure 51, and our analysis of the effects of commuting time. If Americans still lived spatially where we did in the mid-1970s, the aggregate level of community involvement might be roughly 2 percent higher, as compared with the drops of 20–40 percent registered in section II. This calculation is rough-and-ready and disregards synergistic effects.

CHAPTER 13: TECHNOLOGY AND MASS MEDIA

1. T. S. Eliot, *New York Post*, September 22, 1963.

2. Sue Bowden and Avner Offer, "Household Appliances and the Use of Time: The United States and Britain Since the 1920s," *Economic History Review* 47 (November 1994): 729, supplemented by data from the *Statistical Abstract of the United States*.

3. Tocqueville, *Democracy in America*, 517–518.

4. Author's analysis of General Social Survey, DDB Needham Life Style, and Roper archives, controlling for year of birth, sex, education, income, marital, parental and work status, size of city, race, and homeownership. Regular newspaper readers are roughly 10–20 percent more likely to participate in all the ways cited in the text. See also Pippa Norris, "Does Television Erode Social Capital? A Reply to Putnam," *PS: Political Science & Politics* 29 (September 1996): 474–80, esp. 479; *So Many Choices, So Little Time* (Vienna, Va.: Newspaper Association of America, 1998), 15, 18; and Delli Carpini and Keeter, *What Americans Know About Politics*.

5. *Statistical Abstract of the United States* (various years) and *Historical Statistics of the United States*.

6. Author's analysis of the General Social Survey archive; *So Many Choices, So Little Time*; *Statistical Abstract of the United States*; and Stu Tolley, "The Abyss That Is Destroying Daily Newspaper Reading" (Vienna, Va.: Newspaper Association of America, 1998), at www.naa.org/marketscope/research/cohort.htm.

7. According to the 1998 DDB Needham Life Style survey, half of all Americans who read the news in a newspaper also watch the evening network news on TV, as compared with only one-quarter of those who do not read a newspaper. This correlation persists under stringent controls for all standard demographic factors.

8. Author's analysis of DDB Needham Life Style 1998 survey archive; Jack M. McLeod, Katie Daily, Zhongshi Guo, William P. Eveland, Jr., Jan Bayer, Seungchan Yang, and Hsu Wang, "Community Integration, Local Media Use and Democratic Processes," *Communication Research* 23 (1996): 179–209; Norris, "Does Television Erode Social Capital?"; Staci Rhine, Stephen Earl Bennett, and Richard S. Flickinger, "Americans' Exposure and Attention to Electronic and Print Media and Their Impact on Democratic Citizenship" (paper presented at the annual meeting of the Midwest Political Science Association, Chicago, 1998).

9. Pew Research Center for the People & the Press, *Internet News Takes Off*, biennial news consumption survey at www.people-press.org/med98rpt.htm; *Times Mirror* Center, "Age of Indifference"; William G. Mayer, "The Polls-Poll Trends: Trends in Media Usage," *Public Opinion Quarterly* 57 (June 1993): 593–611; Stephen Earl Bennett and Eric W. Rademacher, " 'The Age of Indifference' Revisited: Patterns of Political Interest, Media Exposure, and Knowledge among Generation X," in *After the Boom: The Politics of Generation X*, eds. Stephen C. Craig and Stephen Earl Bennett (Lanham, Md.: Rowman & Littlefield, 1997); and Cliff Zukin, *Generation X and the News: Road Closed?* (Radio and Television News Directors Foundation, 1997), at www.rtndf.org/rtndf/genx/index.html. Richard Davis and Diana Owen, *New Media and American Politics* (New York: Oxford University Press, 1998), 136, report that in 1975 nearly half of all households watched network news *every evening*, compared with one-quarter in 1997.

10. Pew Center, *Internet News Takes Off*; Norris, "Who Surfs?" 80–82; author's analysis of the 1998 DDB Needham Life Style survey archive, which is the source of the generalization about CNN in the text.

11. Author's analysis of DDB Needham Life Style 1996–98 survey archive: respondents who say that they rely primarily on the Internet for news are *less* likely than other Americans to volunteer, to spend time with friends, to trust others, and so on.

12. *Statistical Abstract of the United States* (various years); Veronis, Suhler & Associates, *Communications Industry Report: Five-Year Historical Report* (1991–95) (New York: Veronis, Suhler & Associates, 1996); Cobbett S. Steinberg, *TV Facts* (New York: Facts on File, 1980); Russell, *Master Trend*, 59; "People, Opinion, and Polls: American Popular Culture," *Public Perspective*, August/September 1995: 47; Robert T. Bower, *The Changing Television Audi-*

ence in America (New York: Columbia University Press, 1985), esp. 33, 46; George Comstock et al., *Television and Human Behavior* (New York: Columbia University Press, 1978); George Comstock, *Evolution of American Television* (Newbury Park, Calif.: Sage Publications, 1989); and Doris A. Graber, *Mass Media and American Politics* (Washington, D.C.: CQ Press, 1993).

13. Data in this paragraph exclude time when television is merely on in the background. Comstock, *Evolution of American Television*, 17, reports that "on any fall day in the late 1980s, the set in the average television owning household was on for about eight hours." According to Eurodata TV (*One Television Year in the World: Audience Report*, April 1999), the United States ranks third out of forty-seven nations in viewing hours per day, behind only Japan and Mexico. Thanks to Pippa Norris for advice about the media and participation. Robinson and Godbey, *Time for Life*, 136–153, 340–341.

14. *Statistical Abstract of the United States* (various years); *Kids & Media @ The New Millennium* (Menlo Park, Calif.: Henry J. Kaiser Family Foundation, 1999), 13. Data on Internet access in figure 56 are from the DDB Needham Life Style archive; these data are quite consistent with other surveys of Internet usage, such as the Nielsen and IntelliQuest surveys summarized in *Nua Internet Surveys* (Dublin, Ireland: Nua Ltd., 1999), at www.nua.ie/surveys /how_many_online/n_america.htlml (consulted December 11, 1999) and the January 1999 report by the Pew Research Center for the People & the Press, www.people-press.org/tech98sum.htm.

15. *Where Does the Time Go? The United Media Enterprises Report on Leisure in America* (New York: Newspaper Enterprise Association, 1983), 10; author's analysis of DDB Needham Life Style archive. Preference for a quiet evening at home rose from 68 percent in 1975 to 77 percent in 1999. Those who agreed were also more likely to agree that "TV is my primary form of entertainment."

16. Kunstler, *Geography of Nowhere*, 167.

17. Paul William Kingston and Steven L. Nock, "Time Together Among Dual Earner Couples," *American Sociological Review* 52 (June 1987): 391–400; Zukin, *Generation X and the News*; Diane Crispell, "TV Soloists," *American Demographics*, May 1997, 32; Robert Kubey and Mihaly Csikszentmihalyi, *Television and the Quality of Life: How Viewing Shapes Everyday Experience* (Hillsdale, N.J.: Lawrence Erlbaum, 1990), 74; *Kids & Media*, 62–63. As early as 1996, of the 76 percent of kids (ages nine to seventeen) who had their own bedroom, 59 percent had their own television, 55 percent had a cable/satellite hookup, 36 percent a video game system, and 39 percent a VCR; source: www.yankelovich.com/press3.htm.

18. Author's analysis of Roper Social and Political Trends surveys in 1979, 1985, 1989, and 1993; David E. Campbell, Steven Yonish, and Robert D. Putnam, "Tuning In, Tuning Out Revisited: A Closer Look at the Causal Links between Television and Social Capital," paper presented at the Annual Meeting of the American Political Science Association (Atlanta, Ga., September 1999). Thanks to my coauthors for their many insights into this topic. They are, however, not responsible for my conclusions here.

19. Thanks to Steve Yonish for spotting this line as part of his research duties watching late-night movies.

20. Author's analysis of Roper Social and Political Trends archive. More than half of the trend in figure 57 reflects generational differences. Generation more strongly predicts habitual viewing than does any other demographic characteristic. See also Campbell, Yonish, and Putnam, "Tuning In, Tuning Out Revisited."

21. Barbara Schneider and David Stevenson, *The Ambitious Generation: America's Teenagers, Motivated but Directionless* (New Haven, Conn.: Yale University Press, 1999), 189–211.

22. Figure 59 is limited to weekday watching, but the figures for weekend watching are similar. These surveys do not reveal how much time *during* each period was occupied by TV viewing; thus they somewhat exaggerate the fraction of the public viewing TV at any given moment. For confirmation of these patterns of TV viewing, see Kubey and Csikszentmihalyi, *Television and the Quality of Life*, 75 (for the United States); and Michael Argyle, *Social Psychology of Everyday Life* (New York: Routledge, 1991), 111 (for the United Kingdom).

23. Author's analysis of DDB Needham Life Style survey data, 1993–98. The TV-during-dinner rate is 39 percent for married couples with children at home and 55 percent for other adults. An additional 7 percent of all adults say that the TV was on in the background during dinner. According to *America's Youth in the 1990s*, Bezilla, ed., 39, and Catherine McGrath, "Busy Teenagers," *American Demographics*, July 1998, 37–38, in 1990, 39 percent of teenagers reported that TV was on during dinner, a figure that had risen to 50 percent by 1997.

24. Author's analysis of Roper Social and Political Trends archive, based on surveys in 1985 and 1989. The figure for watching TV includes both news (58 percent) and other programs (68 percent).

25. All estimates in this and the following two paragraphs are based on multivariate logistic regression analyses of Roper surveys from 1973, 1974, 1977, 1983, 1988, 1991, and 1993, controlling for education, income, marital, parental, and work status, sex, age, race, region, and city size. Only social class (as measured by education and income) rivals television viewing as a predictor of all twelve forms of civic participation in the Roper archive. Figure 61 is limited to working-age, college-educated respondents and to four common measures of participation to illustrate that the negative correlation is strong even within the most civically engaged segment of the population, but the pattern is found across all subsets of the population and all measures of participation. Of working-age, college-educated Americans, 17 percent reported watching less than an hour of TV per day, 54 percent one to three hours, and 29 percent more than three hours. For the population as a whole, the equivalent figures were 12 percent, 43 percent, and 45 percent.

26. This estimate is intended only to indicate the potential order of magnitude of the effect of television on civic engagement: civic engagement declined roughly 40 percent over the last third of the century, and additional TV viewing over those years might account for a 10 percent decline.

27. This pattern appears in both the Roper Social and Political Trends data and the DDB Needham Life Style data; see Campbell, Yonish, and Putnam, "Tuning In, Tuning Out Revisited."

28. Evidence in this paragraph comes from Roper Social and Political Trends surveys in 1973–75, 1988, and 1993; see Campbell, Yonish, and Putnam, "Tuning In, Tuning Out Revisited."

29. All generalizations in this and the following six paragraphs are based on the author's analysis of the DDB Needham Life Style survey archive. The fraction of respondents who agree that "television is my primary form of entertainment" has tended to rise from about 47 percent in the 1970s to about 53 percent in the 1990s. (Inexplicably, the

fraction surged sharply to 60–65 percent in 1987–88 and then declined somewhat, but the secular trend is upward.) Of those who rely on TV for entertainment, 47 percent also concede that "I'm what you'd call a couch potato," as compared with 17 percent of other Americans. Based on the time slots per day in which they report watching TV, those who say that TV is their primary form of entertainment watch about 40 percent more TV than other Americans. This question effectively singles out the one American in every two who is most dependent upon television entertainment.

30. Figures 62 to 66 present bivariate relationships, but all generalizations in this paragraph and the previous one are based on multiple regression analysis, controlling for sex, race, year of birth, year of survey, education, income, financial worries, region, size of city, marital, parental, and employment status, self-reported physical health, expected mobility, homeownership, self-reported time pressure, and mean commuting time in county of residence. In virtually every case, the respondent's self-described dependence on television for entertainment (measured on a six-point scale) is one of the two or three strongest predictors; it is the single most consistent predictor across all measures of public and private sociability.

31. Author's analysis of the DDB Needham Life Style archive. Religiosity is measured by agreement that "religion is important in my life."

32. The DDB Needham Life Style surveys between 1975 and 1998 include three hundred female college grads aged thirty to forty-four in the financially most secure third of the population and living in New England or the mid-Atlantic states. The statistics in the text compare civic involvement among the 28 percent of these women who agree that "TV is my primary form of entertainment" and the 72 percent who disagree. These comparisons thus control for sex, region, education, financial worries, and age, the five factors most closely correlated with reliance on televised entertainment. For the measure of life contentment, see chapter 20.

33. Robinson and Godbey, *Time for Life*, 139–144; Harwood K. McClerking and Kristina C. Miler, "The Deleterious Effect of Television Viewership on Membership in Voluntary Organizations" (paper prepared for the annual meeting of the Southern Political Science Association, Norfolk, Va., November 1997); Harwood K. McClerking, Kristina C. Miler, and Irfan Nooruddin, "Must See TV? A Non-Random Assignment Model of Television and Membership" (paper prepared for the annual meeting of the American Political Science Association, Boston, September 1998); and Pippa Norris, "Blaming the Messenger? Television and Civic Malaise," in Pharr and Putnam, *What's Troubling the Trilateral Democracies?*

34. Tay Keong Tan, "Silence, Sacrifice, and Shoo-Fly Pies: An Inquiry Into the Social Capital and Organizational Strategies of the Amish Community in Lancaster County, Pennsylvania" (Ph.D. diss., Harvard University, 1998).

35. *The Impact of Television: A Natural Experiment in Three Communities*, ed. Tannis MacBeth Williams (Orlando, Fla.: Academic Press, 1986). Thanks to David Campbell for reviewing the literature on the effects of television on community life.

36. Williams, *Impact of Television*, 2.

37. Ibid., 166.

38. Ibid., 178.

39. William A. Belson, "Effects of Television on the Interests and Initiative of Adult Viewers in Greater London," *British Journal of Psychology* 50 (1959): 145–158; Wilbur Schramm, Jack Lyle, and Edwin B. Parker, *Television in the Lives of our Children* (Stanford, Calif.: Stanford University Press, 1961), on the United States; J. R. Brown, J. K. Cramond, and R. J. Wilde, "Displacement Effects of Television and the Child's Functional Orientation to Media" in *The Uses of Mass Communications: Current Perspectives on Gratifications*, eds. Jay G. Blumler and Elihu Katz (Beverly Hills, Calif.: Sage, 1974), on Scotland; John P. Murray and Susan Kippax, "Children's Social Behavior in Three Towns with Differing Television Experience," *Journal of Communication* 28 (1978): 19–29, on Australia; and Diana C. Mutz, Donald F. Roberts, and D. P. van Vuuren, "Reconsidering the Displacement Hypothesis: Television's Influence on Children's Time Use," *Communication Research* 20 (1993): 51–75, on South Africa. Karl Erik Rosengren and Sven Windahl, *Media Matter: TV Use in Childhood and Adolescence* (Norwood, N.J.: Ablex, 1989), report counterevidence from a study of Swedish children.

40. Richard G. Niemi and Jane Junn, *Civic Education: What Makes Students Learn* (New Haven, Conn.: Yale University Press, 1999); Alan S. Zuckerman, "First Steps into Politics: The Political Bases of the Decisions of Young People to Engage in Political Discussion" (Providence, R.I.: Brown University, 1998); Jay Braatz and Robert D. Putnam, "Community-Based Social Capital and Educational Performance: Exploring New Evidence" (Cambridge, Mass.: Harvard University, 1999); John Condry, "Thief of Time, Unfaithful Servant: Television and the American Child," *Daedalus* 122 (winter 1993): 259–278; William T. Bielby, "The Cost of Watching Television: A Longitudinal Assessment of the Effect of Heavy Viewing on Earnings," working paper (Boston: Harvard University School of Public Health, n.d.); George Comstock and Haejung Paik, *Television and the American Child* (New York: Academic Press, 1991), 72, 86.

41. Author's analysis of DDB Needham Life Style and Roper Social and Political Trends archives, controlling for education, income, urbanism, age, marital and parental status, job status, sex, race, and region. The same pattern appears in both archives. Rolf Meyersohn, "Television and the Rest of Leisure," *Public Opinion Quarterly* 32 (spring 1968): 102–112.

42. Comstock et al., *Television and Human Behavior*; John P. Robinson, "Television and Leisure Time: A New Scenario," *Journal of Communication* 31 (winter 1981): 120–130; Comstock, *Evolution of American Television*; Bower, *Changing Television Audience*; Robinson and Godbey, *Time for Life*; Kubey and Csikszentmihalyi, *Television and the Quality of Life*; Brehm and Rahn, "Individual-Level Evidence," 1015, and Brehm and Rahn, personal communication; Schramm, Lyle, and Parker, *Television in the Lives of our Children*; Comstock and Paik, *Television and the American Child*; Mutz, Roberts, and van Vuuren, "Reconsidering the Displacement Hypothesis." Author's analysis of the DDB Needham Life Style surveys from 1993 to 1998; 39 percent of respondents who watched TV during two time slots or fewer a day "generally" or "definitely" agreed that "I am a homebody," as compared with 50 percent of those who watched during six or more time slots. See also my "Tuning In, Tuning Out."

43. Increased cocooning during the 1970s is confirmed by DDB Needham Life Style surveys of 1975–76. Activities that respondents reported doing more often were staying home, spending time with family and friends, dining with the family, and watching TV—in short, relaxing at home alone or with family and friends. Activities said to be declining were entertaining at home, going out to dinner, and going to the movies—in short, going out or formally entertaining.

44. Author's analysis of Roper Social and Political Trends surveys in 1974, 1975, 1977, and 1979. Controlling for sex, age, education, and city size, as well as parental, marital and work status, respondents who said they were watching *more* television than in the past were 25–35 percent less likely to participate in community activities than were those who said they were watching *less* than in the past. See also Campbell, Yonish, and Putnam, "Tuning In, Tuning Out Revisited."

45. Kubey and Csikszentmihalyi, *Television and the Quality of Life*. These authors review research on the psychological effects of television viewing. See also Neil Postman, *Amusing Ourselves to Death: Public Discourse in the Age of Show Business* (New York: Viking, 1985).

46. Kubey and Csikszentmihalyi, *Television and the Quality of Life*, 164–165.

47. Michael Argyle, *Social Psychology of Everyday Life*, 110; Bowden and Offer, "Household Appliances," 735–736.

48. Kubey and Csikszentmihalyi, *Television and the Quality of Life*, 138–139.

49. Bowden and Offer, "Household Appliances," 739–741.

50. Data in this and the following paragraph from author's analysis of DDB Needham Life Style archive. Three closely correlated agree-disagree items were combined into a factor score of malaise: 1) "I get more headaches than most people," 2) "I have trouble getting to sleep," and 3) "I frequently get indigestion." Each symptom is independently correlated with dependence on TV, but insomnia is the *least* closely linked, so the basic correlation is *not* a function of insomniacs who watch late-night TV for distraction. "High" in figure 68 refers to the top third of the population in frequency of headaches, indigestion, and insomnia. I cannot exclude the possibility that heavy doses of TV ads for headache, indigestion, and insomnia remedies increase hypochondria.

51. Bowden and Offer, 737–738; Robinson, "TV and Leisure," 129; F. Thomas Juster, "Preferences for Work and Leisure," in *Time, Goods, and Well-Being*, F. Thomas Juster and Frank P. Stafford, eds. (Ann Arbor: Institute for Social Research, University of Michigan, 1985), 333–351; Robinson and Godbey, *Time for Life*, 242–250. In the DDB Needham Life Style data, reliance on TV for entertainment is a powerful predictor of unhappiness (as measured in chapter 20), roughly equivalent to financial worries and being single (typically found to be the strongest predictor of unhappiness).

52. Robinson and Godbey, *Time for Life*, 149.

53. Sources for this paragraph and the next: Joshua Meyrowitz, *No Sense of Place: The Impact of Electronic Media on Social Behavior* (New York: Oxford University Press, 1985), 318; Roderick P. Hart, *Seducing America: How Television Charms the Modern Voter* (New York: Oxford University Press, 1994); Shanto Iyengar, *Is Anyone Responsible? How Television Frames Political Issues* (Chicago: University of Chicago Press, 1991); Allan McBride, "Television, Individualism, and Social Capital," *PS: Political Science & Politics* 31 (September 1998): 542–552; Lawrence K. Grossman, *The Electronic Republic: Reshaping Democracy in the Information Age* (New York: Penguin, 1995).

54. A controversial line of research under the rubric of the "mean world effect" argues that heavy TV watching is associated with symptoms of misanthropy, such as overestimating crime rates. See George Gerbner, Larry Gross, Michael Morgan, and Nancy Signorielli, "The 'Mainstreaming' of America: Violence Profile No. 11," *Journal of Communication* 30 (summer 1980): 10–29; Anthony N. Dobb and Glenn F. Macdonald, "Television Viewing and Fear of Victimization: Is the Relationship Causal?" *Journal of Personality and Social Psychology* 37 (1979): 170–179; Paul M. Hirsch, "The 'Scary World' of the Nonviewer and Other Anomalies: A Re-analysis of Gerbner et al.'s Findings on Cultivation Analysis, Part I," *Communication Research* 7 (October 1980): 403–456; Michael Hughes, "The Fruits of Cultivation Analysis: A Re-examination of the Effects of Television Watching on Fear of Victimization, Alienation, and the Approval of Violence," *Public Opinion Quarterly* 44 (1980): 287–303; Comstock, *The Evolution of American Television*, 265–269; L. J. Shrum, Robert S. Wyer, Jr., and Thomas C. O'Guinn, "The Effects of Television Consumption on Social Perceptions: The Use of Priming Procedures to Investigate Psychological Processes," *Journal of Consumer Research* 24 (March 1998): 447–458. Brehm and Rahn, "Individual-Level Evidence," Dhavan V. Shah, "Civic Engagement, Interpersonal Trust, and Television Use: An Individual-Level Assessment of Social Capital," *Political Psychology* 19 (September 1998): 469–496, and my own analysis of the DDB Needham data suggest that the link between distrust and TV viewing is probably spurious.

55. Author's analysis of DDB Needham Life Style surveys. Thanks to Rusty Silverstein, Dan Devroye, David Campbell, and Steve Yonish for help with this research. Credit for inspiring this line of work belongs to Shah, "Civic Engagement."

56. Figure 69 is drawn from Campbell, Yonish, and Putnam, "Tuning In, Tuning Out Revisited."

57. J. Philipe Rushton, "Television and Prosocial Behavior," in *Television and Behavior: Ten Years of Scientific Progress and Implications for the Eighties*, eds. David Pearl, Lorraine Bouthilet, and Joyce Lazar (Rockville, Md.: National Institute of Mental Health, U.S. Department of Health and Human Services, 1982), 248–258, and Susan Hearold, "A Synthesis of 1,043 Effects of Television on Social Behavior," in *Public Communication and Behavior*, vol. 1, ed. George Comstock (New York: Academic Press, 1986), 65–133.

58. Joseph Turow, *Breaking Up America: Advertisers and the New Media World* (Chicago: University of Chicago Press, 1997).

59. Nielsen Media Research, *1998 Report on Television* (New York: 1998), 19, 23.

60. Rahn and Transue, "Social Trust and Value Change"; George Gerbner, Larry Gross, Michael Morgan, and Nancy Signorielli, "Growing Up with Television: The Cultivation Perspective," in *Media Effects: Advances in Theory and Research*, ed. Jennings Bryant and Dolf Zillman (Hillsdale, N.J.: Lawrence Erlbaum Associates, 1994), 17–41, quotation at 31; Alexander W. Astin, *What Matters in College* (San Francisco: Jossey-Bass, 1993), 310.

61. Robert E. Lane, "The Road Not Taken: Friendship, Consumerism, and Happiness," *Critical Review* 8

(fall 1994): 521–554; Nicholas Zill and John Robinson, "The Generation X Difference," *American Demographics* 17 (April 1995): 24–31.

62. Sven Birkerts, *The Gutenberg Elegies* (Boston: Faber and Faber, 1994), 214–215.

CHAPTER 14: FROM GENERATION TO GENERATION

1. Among DDB Needham Life Style respondents who denied that TV was their primary entertainment, lived in towns under 50,000, had a household income in the top third nationally, and were married with only the husband working full-time, club meetings annually fell from sixteen in the 1970s to nine in the 1990s. Among Roper respondents who watched less than one hour of television a day, lived in towns under 250,000, had an above-average income, and were either wives not employed full-time or married males, those who took part in *none* of the twelve forms of civic participation rose from 17 percent in the 1970s to 28 percent in the 1980s and to 37 percent in the 1990s. Frank Bryan found that in a sample of about seventy-five Vermont towns with an average population of about 1,000, town meeting attendance fell from about 27 percent of registered voters in 1970–73 to about 15 percent in 1998. Frank M. Bryan, personal communication and *Real Democracy* (unpublished ms., 1999), as cited in Joseph F. Zimmerman, *The New England Town Meeting: Democracy in Action* (Westport, Conn.: Praeger, 1999), 93–97.

2. Author's analysis of DDB Needham Life Style, Roper Social and Political Trends, General Social Survey, and National Election Studies archives, using standard demographic controls.

3. Both life cycle and generational effects may be at work simultaneously. For technical treatments of this methodological issue, see note 7, chapter 2.

4. Author's analysis of GSS, Roper, and DDB Needham Life Style survey archives; Babchuk and Booth, "Voluntary Association Membership"; and S. Cutler, "Age Differences in Voluntary Association Membership," *Social Forces* 55 (1976): 43–58.

5. Wendy Rahn deserves credit for emphasizing the generational basis of declines in social capital.

6. To maximize reliability, table 3 aggregates several years of surveys at each end of the two-decade period. Except for union membership and church attendance, for which abundant confirmation is available in other surveys, every entry in table 3 is based on 5,000–7,500 interviews, so even small absolute differences are highly reliable.

7. In the Americans' Use of Time archive, too, the declines in activity in both religious and secular organizations are almost entirely intergenerational.

8. David Butler and Donald Stokes, *Political Change in Britain: The Evolution of Electoral Choice* (London: Macmillan, 1974).

9. Figure 71 draws on interviews over a quarter-century span (roughly 1970–75 to roughly 1995–2000) to estimate the civic engagement by year of birth. To control for life cycle effects early and late in life, figure 71 excludes respondents under twenty-five and over eighty. Too few respondents born in the late nineteenth century appear in these surveys to reliably discern differences among successive birth cohorts. However, those scant data (not broken out in figure 71) suggest that the turn of the last century might have been an era of rising civic engagement. Similarly, too few respondents born after 1970 have yet appeared in national surveys to be confident about their generational profile, although slender results suggest that the forty-year generational plunge in civic engagement might be bottoming out. Section II showed that declines in the civic engagement are substantial, even without controls for education, but to clarify generational differences, figure 71 holds constant the educational composition of the various birth cohorts. To offset the relatively small year-by-year samples and to control for educational differences, figure 71 charts five-year moving averages for respondents with less than high school, high school, and more than high school education. Figure 71 abstracts from life cycle and period effects, but the analyses that underlie this figure have explored other possible interpretations, and I do not believe that the generational interpretation is seriously misleading in any material respect. The operational measures are Vote: National Election Studies (1952–96) presidential year voting; newspaper: General Social Survey (1972–98) read newspaper every day; social trust: GSS (1972–98) agree "most people can be trusted"; community project: DDB (1975–98) worked on at least one community project in previous year; group membership: GSS (1974–94) member of at least one group; interest in politics: DDB (1975–98) agree "I am interested in politics"; church: GSS (1972–98) attend church at least "nearly every week"; club: DDB (1975–98) attended nine or more club meetings in previous year.

10. See Zukin, *Generation X and the News*.

11. The 1910–40 generation also seems more civic than its elders, at least to judge by the few people born in the late nineteenth century who appeared in these samples.

12. In an unpublished comment on an earlier version of my argument here.

13. Miller and Shanks, *New American Voter*, 57.

14. Ithiel de Sola Pool, "Public Opinion," in *Handbook of Communication*, ed. Ithiel de Sola Pool et al. (Chicago: Rand McNally, 1973), 818–821.

15. Author's analysis of the National Election Studies, Roper Social and Political Trends, DDB Needham Life Style, and GSS archives. The gap in presidential turnout between those aged twenty-one to twenty-nine and those aged fifty and over rose from 16 percent in the 1960s and 1970s to 25 percent in the 1980s and 1990s. See also Times Mirror Center, "Age of Indifference," 25.

16. Author's analysis of the Roper Social and Political Trends archive. During these years the fraction of the adult population aged forty-five and older increased slightly from 44 percent to 48 percent.

17. Michael X. Delli Carpini, *Stability and Change in American Politics: The Coming of Age of the Generation of the 1960s* (New York: New York University Press, 1986); Paul C. Light, *Baby Boomers* (New York: W. W. Norton, 1988); and Cheryl Russell, *The Master Trend*.

18. Light, *Baby Boomers*, 123–125.

19. Delli Carpini, *Stability and Change*, 150.

20. Russell, *The Master Trend*; Delli Carpini, *Stability and Change*; M. Kent Jennings and Richard G. Niemi,

Generations and Politics: A Panel Study of Young Adults and Their Parents (Princeton, N.J.: Princeton University Press, 1981); and author's analysis of Roper Social and Political Trends and DDB Needham Life Style archives.

21. Delli Carpini, Stability and Change in American Politics, 326.

22. Light, Baby Boomers, 32, 136, and 49, citing Richard Easterlin, Birth and Fortune: The Impact of Numbers on Personal Welfare (New York: Basic Books, 1980).

23. Jennings and Niemi, Generations and Politics, 215–226; Light, Baby Boomers, 28; Daniel Yankelovich, "How Changes in the Economy Are Reshaping American Values," in Values and Public Policy, Henry J. Aaron, Thomas E. Mann, and Timothy Taylor, eds. (Washington, D.C.: Brookings, 1994), 16–53.

24. Russell, The Master Trend.

25. Rahn and Transue, "Social Trust and Value Change." See also the High School and Beyond surveys conducted by the U.S. Department of Education, National Center for Education Statistics, in 1974, 1984, and 1994, as well as R. A. Easterlin and E. M. Cummings, "Private Materialism, Personal Self-Fulfillment, Family Life and Public Interest: The Nature, Effects, and Causes of Recent Changes in the Values of American Youth," Public Opinion Quarterly 55 (winter 1991): 499–533.

26. Author's analysis of Monitoring the Future survey archive, provided through the Interuniversity Consortium for Political and Social Research at the University of Michigan. The decline is from 14–15 percent in the mid-1970s to 10–11 percent in the mid-1990s. Because these samples are very large, these estimates are highly reliable.

27. Author's analysis of the Monitoring the Future archive. "Undecided" responses are excluded from this analysis, although their inclusion would not affect the basic trend.

28. Bennett and Rademacher, "The 'Age of Indifference' Revisited"; Zukin, Generation X and the News; Diana Owen and Molly W. Sonner, " 'Think Globally, Act Locally': Why Political Science Underestimates the NEXT Generation" (paper prepared for the annual meeting of the Midwest Political Science Association, Chicago, April 1995); Diana Owen, "Mixed Signals: Generation X's Attitudes toward the Political System," in Craig and Bennett, After the Boom, 85–106; Times Mirror Center, "The Age of Indifference," 26–28; and author's analysis of the Roper Social and Political Trends archive. Since figure 72 holds life cycle constant, the lower participation rates of X'ers cannot be attributed simply to their youth.

29. Myrna Weissman, Martha Livingston Bruce, Philip J. Leaf, Louise P. Florio, and Charles Holzer III, "Affective Disorders," in Psychiatric Disorders in America: The Epidemiological Catchment Area Study, Lee N. Robins and Darrel A. Regier, eds. (New York: Free Press, 1991), 53–80, quotation at 80. This source includes an appendix reviewing and dismissing possible methodological flaws in this evidence.

30. Martin E. P. Seligman, "Boomer Blues," Psychology Today, October 1988, 50–55, quotation at 50. See also Gerald L. Klerman, "The Current Age of Youthful Melancholia: Evidence for Increase in Depression among Adolescents and Young Adults," British Journal of Psychiatry 152 (1988): 4–14; Gerald L. Klerman and Myrna Weissman, "Increasing Rates of Depression," Journal of American Medical Association 261 (1989): 2229–2235; Martin E. P. Seligman, Learned Optimism (New York: Pocket Books, 1990); Cross-National Collaborative Group, "The Changing Rate of Depression: Cross-National Comparisons," Journal of American Medical Association 268 (December 2, 1992): 3098–3105; Peter M. Lewisohn, Paul Rohde, John R. Seeley, and Scott A. Fischer, "Age-Cohort Changes in the Lifetime Occurrence of Depression and Other Mental Disorders," Journal of Abnormal Psychology 102 (1993): 110–120; and Eric Fombonne, "Depressive Disorders: Time Trends and Possible Explanatory Mechanisms," in Psychosocial Disorders in Young People: Time Trends and Their Causes, ed. Michael Rutter and David J. Smith, eds. (New York: John Wiley & Sons, Inc., 1995), 544–615.

31. Sourcebook of Criminal Justice Statistics—1995, ed. Kathleen Maguire and Ann L. Pastore (Albany, N.Y.: Hindelang Criminal Justice Research Center, 1996), 365. See also U.S. Public Health Service, The Surgeon General's Call to Action to Prevent Suicide (Washington, D.C.: 1999), and the research cited there. On the low suicide rates among those I term "the long civic generation," see Max A. Woodbury, Kenneth G. Manton, and Dan Blazer, "Trends in U.S. Suicide Mortality Rates 1968 to 1982: Race and Sex Differences in Age, Period and Cohort Components," International Journal of Epidemiology 17 (1988): 356–362, esp. 360. For broadly comparable patterns in other nations, see C. Pritchard, "New Patterns of Suicide by Age and Gender in the United Kingdom and the Western World 1974–1992: An Indicator of Social Change?" Social Psychiatry and Psychiatric Epidemiology 31 (1996): 227–234.

32. Michael Rutter and David J. Smith, "Towards Causal Explanations of Time Trends in Psychosocial Disorders of Young People," in Psychosocial Disorders in Young People, Rutter and Smith, eds., 807.

33. On our index of malaise, see note 50, chapter 13. Some symptoms of malaise show life cycle effects—sleeplessness slightly increases with age, while headaches decrease with age—but life cycle differences are screened out of figure 74. "High" malaise means in the top third of all respondents over these twenty-five years, but any reasonable cut point would produce the same results. Financial worries have grown in the younger cohort over the last quarter century, and financial worries in turn produce headaches, indigestion, and sleepless nights. When our index of financial worries is added to a multiple regression prediction for malaise (including sex, education, age, reliance on TV for entertainment, and an interactive term for age and year), the unstandardized regression coefficient on the interactive term—a statistical measure of the growing generation gap—is cut by roughly 60 percent but remains highly significant.

34. Ed Diener, "Subjective Well-Being," Psychological Bulletin 95 (1984): 542–575, esp. 554. W. A. Stock, M. A. Okun, M. J. Haring, and R. W. Witter, "Age and Subjective Well-being: A Meta-analysis," in R. J. Light (ed.), Evaluation Studies: Annual Review, vol. 8 (Beverly Hills, Calif.: Sage, 1983), 279–302; D. D. Witt, G. D. Lowe, C. W. Peek, and E. W. Curry, "The Changing Relationship between Age and Happiness: Emerging Trend or Methodological Artifact?" Social Forces 58 (1979): 1302–1307; and author's analysis of DDB Needham Life Style archive. For our index of life contentment, see chapter 20.

35. Schneider and Stevenson, Ambitious Generation, 189–211, quotation at 192; Seligman, "Boomer Blues," 52, 55.

36. L. I. Pearlin, M. A. Lieberman, E. G. Menaghan, and J. T. Mullan, "The Stress Process," Journal of Health and Social Behavior 22 (1981): 337–356; P. Cohen, E. L. Struening, G. L. Muhlin, L. E. Genevie, S. R. Kaplan,

518 NOTES

and H. B. Peck, "Community Stressors, Mediating Conditions and Wellbeing in Urban Neighborhoods," *Journal of Community Psychology* 10 (1982): 377–391; A. Billings and R. Moos, "Social Support and Functioning among Community and Clinical Groups: A Panel Model," *Journal of Behavioral Medicine* 5 (1982): 295–311; Nan Lin and W. M. Ensel, "Depression-Mobility and Its Social Etiology: The Role of Life Events and Social Support," *Journal of Health and Social Behavior* 25 (1984): 176–188; G. A. Kaplan, R. E. Roberts, T. C. Camacho, and J. C. Coyne, "Psychosocial Predictors of Depression," *American Journal of Epidemiology* 125 (1987): 206–220.

37. This generalization summarizes the author's extensive multivariate analysis of dozens of measures of civic engagement and social capital in the Roper Social and Political Trends survey archive, the DDB Needham Life Style survey archive, the General Social Survey, the National Election Studies, the Americans' Use of Time archive, the Monitoring the Future archive, and others. (Generational analysis of the Roper Social and Political Trends surveys is seriously complicated by the fact that "age"—and thus year of birth—is crudely measured in these surveys, so regression analysis of these data provide less clear-cut support for the generational interpretation. On the other hand, see table 3 for evidence of the role in generation in the Roper data.) The central question in these analyses was this: *By what fraction is the trend over time* (the unstandardized regression coefficient for year of survey, for example) *reduced when generation is controlled* (by entering year of birth in the regression, for example)? As discussed earlier, for some indicators of civic engagement—voting, church attendance, newspaper readership, interest in public affairs, and social trust—virtually *all* net change over the last third of the twentieth century is attributable to generational change. This pattern can be seen, for example, in figures 39 and 53 and in the fact that if both year of birth and year of survey are included in the same regression, year of survey becomes virtually insignificant as a predictor of these measures. For other indicators of social capital, like club meetings and family dining, somewhat less than half of the trend is eliminated when generation is controlled. For some measures of *schmoozing*, such as playing cards and entertaining at home, controls for generation have little or no effect on the trends.

38. William Graham Sumner, *Folkways: A Study of the Sociological Importance of Usages, Manners, Customs, Mores, and Morals* (Boston: Ginn, 1911), 12–13; Lewis A. Coser, *The Functions of Social Conflict* (Glencoe, Ill.: Free Press, 1956); Arthur A. Stein, "Conflict and Cohesion," *Journal of Conflict Resolution* 20 (1976): 142–172; Theda Skocpol, Ziad Munson, Marshall Ganz, and Andrew Karch, "War and the Development of American Civil Society," paper prepared for annual meeting of the American Sociological Association (Chicago, August 1999); Susan J. Ellis, and Katherine H. Noyes, *By the People: A History of Americans as Volunteers*, rev. ed. (San Francisco: Jossey-Bass, 1990), quotation at 13.

39. Charles, *Service Clubs*, 15–16, 31.

40. Thanks to Wendy Rahn and Theda Skocpol for illuminating discussions of the effects of war, especially World War II, on social capital and civic engagement. See Theda Skocpol, with the assistance of Marshall Ganz, Ziad Munson, Bayliss Camp, Michele Swers, and Jennifer Oser, "How Americans Became Civic," in *Civic Engagement in American Democracy*, eds. Skocpol and Fiorina, 27–80, and Tom Brokaw, *The Greatest Generation* (New York: Random House, 1998).

41. John Morton Blum, *V Was for Victory: Politics and American Culture during World War II* (New York: Harcourt, Brace, Jovanovich, 1976), 339; author's analysis of the General Social Survey (1974–94) and the DDB Needham Life Style archive (1983–88). Veterans are *not* more engaged civically than other men of their generation. The enduring effects of World War II on the civic habits of those who lived through it were not limited to the battlefield. Or perhaps the brutalizing effects of combat counterbalanced its communitarian effects.

42. Richard R. Lingeman, *Don't You Know There's a War On? The American Home Front, 1941–1945* (New York: G. P. Putnam's Sons, 1970), 71; Bill Gold, quoted in Roy Hoopes, *Americans Remember the Home Front: An Oral Narrative* (New York: Hawthorne, 1977), xii.

43. Richard Polenberg, *War and Society: The United States, 1941–1945* (New York: J. B. Lippincott, 1972), 17.

44. Polenberg, *War and Society*, 29–30.

45. The Crosby jingle appears in a taped collection of wartime memorabilia, *The Home Front, 1938–1945* (Petaluma, Calif.: The Mind's Eye, 1985).

46. Lingeman, *Don't You Know*, 237, estimates 335,000 tons; Polenberg, *War and Society*, 16, suggests 450,000 tons. The president's appeal is quoted at Polenberg, *War and Society*, 16.

47. Lingeman, *Don't You Know*, 52, 59, 62, 250; Red Cross national membership records.

48. Lingeman, *Don't You Know*, 251.

49. Julie Siebel, "Silent Partners/Active Leaders: The Association of Junior Leagues, The Office of Civilian Defense, and Community Welfare in World War II" (Ph.D. diss., University of Southern California, 1999).

50. Polenberg, *War and Society*, 132, citing W. Lloyd Warner, "The American Town," in *American Society in Wartime*, William Fielding Ogburn, ed. (Chicago: University of Chicago Press, 1943), 45–46.

51. Jeffrey G. Williamson and Peter H. Lindert, *American Inequality: A Macroeconomic History* (New York: Academic Press, 1980), esp. 53–54 and 82–92, data at 54 and 315. See also Polenberg, *War and Society*, 94. World War I had similarly sharply reduced economic inequality, but the equalizing effect of that war vanished within a year or two, whereas the more egalitarian distribution of wealth and income after World War II persisted and even improved until the early 1970s.

52. Polenberg, *War and Society*, 137. In retrospect one might be surprised that as much as 80 percent of Americans believed that using the black market was *never* justified.

53. Polenberg, *War and Society*, 140–145, quotation at 143. Brian M. Downing, *The Paths of Glory: War and Social Change in Twentieth-Century America* (forthcoming, 2000), argues that the war's disruptive effects of community outweighed its positive effects.

54. Personal communication, Robert Rosenheck, M.D. (New Haven, Conn., Veterans' Administration).

55. Blum, *V Was for Victory*, 340.

56. Thanks to Professor Rahn for the data for figure 75, drawn from a July 1998 *Wall Street Journal*/NBC News Poll.

57. Author's analysis of Roper Social and Political Trends archive through 1991, augmented for 1994 and 1996

from the relevant *Roper Reports* (New York: Roper Starch Worldwide, various years). "Material luxuries" in figure 76 refers to respondents who chose *at least two* of the following six items as part of the definition of "the good life": a job that pays more than average, a swimming pool, a vacation home, really nice clothes, a second color TV set, a second car. Controlling for income, education, marital status, sex, and city size, both year of survey and year of birth are highly significant predictors of materialism, but year of birth (representing generational differences) is by far the strongest predictor.

58. The alternatives offered were these: my family; my old friends; my new friends; the people in my neighborhood; my church/synagogue; the people I work with; my local community; reading local newspapers; the organizations or groups I belong to; parents of my children's friends; reading special interest magazines; the people I meet online on the computer. More than one alternative could be chosen. To simplify figure 77, I have consolidated "old" and "new" friends and eliminated "parents of my children's friends" and "special interest magazines." Overall, 9 percent mentioned magazines and 28 percent of parents with children at home mentioned other parents; neither alternative differed significantly by generation. "Co-workers" is calculated on the basis only of respondents who work at least part-time outside the home. The cohort breakdown was determined by Yankelovich Partners and excludes respondents born after 1978; to simplify figure 77, I have omitted the baby boomers (born 1946–64); almost without exception they fall midway between the other two cohorts. There are no significant differences among the surveys in 1997, 1998, and 1999; figure 77 presents the average for these three years. Thanks to Yankelovich Partners for making these data available.

59. William James, "The Moral Equivalent of War" (New York: American Association for International Conciliation, 1910).

CHAPTER 15: WHAT KILLED CIVIC ENGAGEMENT? SUMMING UP

1. Theodore Caplow, Howard M. Bahr, John Modell, and Bruce Chadwick, *Recent Social Trends in the United States: 1960–1990* (Montreal: McGill-Queen's University Press, 1991), 47, 106, 11; U.S. Bureau of the Census, Current Population Reports, Series P20-509, "Household and Family Characteristics: March 1997," and earlier reports. Author's analysis of General Social Survey.

2. All generalizations in the preceding paragraphs are based on the author's analysis of the Roper Social and Political Trends, DDB Needham Life Style, Americans' Use of Time archive, General Social Survey, and National Election Studies archives, controlling for all standard demographic characteristics. This conclusion differs from my speculation in "Tuning In, Tuning Out" and is based on a much broader range of evidence on the links between family structure and social connectedness.

3. Verba, Schlozman, and Brady, *Voice and Equality*, 241–247.

4. Author's analysis of General Social Survey, Roper Social and Political Trends, and DDB Needham Life Style archives. White support for segregation is measured by this question in the GSS: "If you and your friends belonged to a social club that would not let blacks join, would you try to change the rules so that blacks could join?" Similar results obtain if white racism is measured by support for residential segregation or antimiscegenation laws.

5. Fukuyama, *Trust*, 313–314. On the debate about whether government programs "crowd out" philanthropy and volunteering and erode social capital, see Paul L. Menchik and Burton A. Weisbrod, "Volunteer Labor Supply," *Journal of Public Economics* 32 (1987): 159–183; Susan Chambre, "Kindling Points of Light: Volunteering as Public Policy," *Nonprofit and Voluntary Studies Quarterly* 18 (1989): 249–268; Richard Steinberg, "The Theory of Crowding Out: Donations, Local Government Spending, and the 'New Federalism,'" in *Philanthropic Giving*, Richard Magat, ed. (New York: Oxford University Press, 1989), 143–156; Marvin Olasky, *The Tragedy of American Compassion* (Washington, D.C.: Regnery Gateway, 1992); Peter Dobkin Hall, *Inventing the Nonprofit Sector* (Baltimore, Md.: Johns Hopkins University Press, 1992), 1–83; Robert Moffitt, "Incentive Effects of the U.S. Welfare System: A Review," *Journal of Economic Literature* 30 (1992): 1–61; Deborah Stone, "The Durability of Social Capital," *Journal of Health Politics, Policy, and Law* 20 (1995): 689–694; and J. David Greenstone and Paul E. Peterson, *Race and Authority in Urban Politics: Community Participation and the War on Poverty* (New York: Russell Sage Foundation, 1973).

6. Statewide differences in levels of social capital, as discussed in section IV, are substantial, closely intercorrelated, and reasonably stable, at least from the 1970s to the 1990s.

7. Putnam, "Tuning In, Tuning Out," 671.

8. Daniel Bell, *The Cultural Contradictions of Capitalism*, 20th anniv. ed. (New York: Basic Books, 1996); Robert E. Lane, *The Market Experience* (New York: Cambridge University Press, 1991).

9. Charles H. Heying, "Civic Elites and Corporate Delocalization: An Alternative Explanation for Declining Civic Engagement," *American Behavioral Scientist* 40 (1997): 657–668.

10. Another possible explanation for civic disengagement is the rising crime rate during the 1970s and 1980s. However, if we control for other influences on connectedness (education, race, income, generation, gender, marital, parental, and job status, financial worries, city size, homeownership, residential mobility, commuting time, and TV dependence), *neither* the objective crime rate in the surrounding county *nor* the subjective fear of crime is correlated with such measures of civic engagement as club meeting attendance, home entertaining, visiting friends, interest in politics, or engaging in community projects. I find no evidence that the civic disengagement described in section II is a result of increased crime.

11. These rough estimates of the relative importance of various causal factors are derived from multiple regression analyses across all the major data sets in this study and all the major indicators of social and political participation. In effect, I asked, "How much would civic participation or social capital have declined if the relevant causal factor—the fraction of women in the workforce, economic anxiety, suburbanization, TV viewing, and so forth—had *not* changed over the last third of the twentieth century?" Necessarily, this approach abstracts from minor differences across various measures and assumes away any synergistic effects. However, as a general summary it does no violence to the underlying evidence.

CHAPTER 16: INTRODUCTION

1. Kenneth J. Arrow, "Gifts and Exchanges," *Philosophy and Public Affairs* 1 (summer 1972): 357.

2. The measure of group membership is from the General Social Survey as described in chapter 3 and is available for forty states. The measures of public meetings and local organizational leadership are from the Roper archive as described in chapter 2 and are available for forty-three states. The measures of club meetings, volunteering, and community projects are from the DDB Needham archive as described in chapters 3 and 7 and are available for forty-eight states.

3. The specific questions from the DDB Needham archive: "I spend a lot of time visiting friends" (agree-disagree) and "How often in the last year did you entertain at home?" They are available for forty-eight states.

4. The specific questions are from the DDB Needham archive ("Most people are honest"), available for forty-eight states, and the General Social Survey ("Most people can be trusted" vs. "You can't be too careful"), available for forty-one states. Though entirely distinct methodologically these two statewide measures of social trust are quite convergent (r = .79 for all available states; r = .85 for the thirty-eight states for which at least one hundred respondents are available in each survey).

5. Our measure of turnout is simply the average percentage of the voting-age population who voted in the presidential elections of 1988 and 1992, as reported in the *U.S. Statistical Abstract, 1994*: 289. These data are available for all fifty states.

6. Our measure of the incidence of nonprofit (501[c]3) organizations is simply the number of such organizations in each state in 1989 (as reported in the *Non-Profit Almanac* for 1992–93), divided by the state's population in 1990. (I thank Professor Tom W. Rice for pointing me to these data.) This measure is stable over time; the 1989 measure that we use is very strongly correlated (r = .89) with the same measure in 1992. Our measure of the incidence of civic associations is the mean number of "civic and social associations" (SIC 8640) reported annually from 1977 to 1992 by the Commerce Department, divided by the state's population in each year. Both sets of data are available for all fifty states.

7. Of the ninety-one possible bivariate correlations among these fourteen indicators, eighty-eight are statistically significant in the proper direction at the .05 level or better, and none are in the wrong direction. The mean intercorrelation across the ninety-one is r = .56. This concordance is impressive, given that the underlying data come from three independent survey archives and three different government agencies. The summary index is simply the average of the standardized scores on the fourteen component measures. To maximize the number of cases, we computed this average even for those few cases in which data were missing on as many as five of the underlying fourteen indicators; this procedure enabled us to include all states except Alaska and Hawaii in our analysis. Effectively, this index is identical to the factor score from a principal components analysis of the fourteen component variables.

8. The few exceptions from the surprisingly smooth gradients in figure 80 are intuitively explicable—Nevada is unusually low, whereas Mormon Utah is relatively high.

9. One other plausible measure of social capital—church attendance—is empirically quite unrelated with the other indicators used here. The fraction of all respondents in the 1974–94 General Social Survey who report attending religious services at least "nearly every week" is essentially uncorrelated with our Social Capital Index (r = -.06). Some states with high levels of religious observance (Alabama, for example) are very low on our measure of community-based social capital, but other relatively religious states (Minnesota, for example) are very high in social capital. Conversely, South Dakota is high on social capital but low on church attendance, while Hawaii is relatively low on both.

10. Tocqueville, *Democracy in America*, 81.

11. Our measure of social capital at the state level in the 1980s and 1990s is correlated R^2 = .52 with the measure of "state political culture" invented by Daniel J. Elazar, *American Federalism: A View from the States* (New York: Crowell, 1966), based on descriptions of state politics in the 1950s and subsequently quantified by Ira Sharkansky, "The Utility of Elazar's Political Culture," *Polity* 2 (1969): 66–83. In a fascinating and important study, Tom W. Rice and Jan L. Feldman, "Civic Culture and Democracy from Europe to America," *Journal of Politics* 59 (1997): 1143–1172, report that "the civic attitudes of contemporary Americans bear a strong resemblance to the civic attitudes of the contemporary citizens of the European nations with whom they share common ancestors," even though the last direct contact with the "mother country" may have been several generations ago.

CHAPTER 17: EDUCATION AND CHILDREN'S WELFARE

1. Urie Bronfenbrenner, Phyllis Moen, and James Garbarino, "Child, Family, and Community," in Ross D. Parke, ed. *Review of Child Development Research*, vol. 7. (Chicago: University of Chicago Press, 1984).

2. Kids Count Index from Annie E. Casey Foundation (Baltimore, Md., 1999), Web site: www.aecf.org/kids count/index.htm.

3. The Pearson's r correlation coefficient is +0.80. A score of 1 would represent perfect linear association; social scientists generally consider scores above .40 to constitute strong correlation.

4. This conclusion is based on ten ordinary least squares multivariate regression analyses. The units of observation were the fifty states, excluding D.C. The following ten dependent variables were used: births per one thousand females aged fifteen to seventeen in 1995; percent of children in poverty in 1995; percent of babies born at subnormal weight in 1995; percent of teens (sixteen to nineteen) not attending school and not working in 1995; infant mortality rate in 1995; child death rate (aged one to fourteen) in 1995; percent of teens (sixteen to nineteen) who are high school dropouts; death rate of teens (fifteen to nineteen) by accident, homicide, and suicide in 1995; arrest rate of juveniles (ten to seventeen) for violent crimes in 1995; as well as the comprehensive Kids Count index for 1997. In each regression model, the following control variables were included simultaneously: the state poverty rate (1987–92); the fraction of the 1990 population that was white; the fraction of all families with children that are headed by single parents; and the fraction of adults who have graduated from high school. In the full models, the poverty rate was a significant (p <.05 or better) predictor of seven negative outcomes; meanwhile, a low score on the Social Capital Index

was a significant predictor of five negative outcomes. Racial composition and the fraction of families headed by single parents were significant in four and three of the models, respectively, but the magnitude of the effect was small, and these predictors were also associated in the *wrong direction* in two and three of the models, respectively. Adult high school graduation rates linked in the *wrong direction* for seven of the ten variables. The fraction of adults who are college grads was also explored, but it also performed poorly as a predictor. In predicting the overall measure of child welfare, only poverty and social capital had a major independent effect, both at the .001 level of statistical significance.

5. Jill E. Korbin and Claudia J. Coulton, "Understanding the Neighborhood Context for Children and Families: Combining Epidemiological and Ethnographic Approaches," in Jeanne Brooks-Gunn, Greg J. Duncan, and J. Lawrence Aber, eds., *Neighborhood Poverty, Volume II* (New York: Russell Sage Foundation, 1997), 65–79. See also Susan P. Lumber and Maury A. Nation, "Violence within the Neighborhood and Community," in *Violence against Children in the Family and the Community*, eds. Penelope K. Trickett and Cynthia J. Schellenbach (Washington, D.C.: American Psychological Association, 1998), 191–194; Robert J. Sampson, Jeffrey D. Morenoff, and Felton Earls, "Beyond Social Capital: Spatial Dynamics of Collective Efficacy for Children," *American Sociological Review* 64 (1999): 633–660.

6. James Garbarino and Deborah Sherman, "High-Risk Neighborhoods and High-Risk Families: The Human Ecology of Child Maltreatment," *Child Development* 51 (1980): 188–198.

7. D. K. Runyan, W. M. Hunter, et al., "Children Who Prosper in Unfavorable Environments: The Relationship to Social Capital," *Pediatrics* 101 (January 1998): 12–18; Howard C. Stevenson, "Raising Safe Villages: Cultural-Ecological Factors that Influence the Emotional Adjustment of Adolescents," *Journal of Black Psychology* 24 (1998): 44–59; A. J. De Young, "The Disappearance of 'Social Capital' in Rural America: Are All Rural Children 'At Risk'?" *Rural Special Education Quarterly* 10 (1989): 38–45.

8. Ronald A. Wolk, ed., *Quality Counts: A Report Card on the Condition of Public Education in the 50 States* (Washington, D.C.: Editorial Projects in Education, 1997), 3.

9. Excluding the District of Columbia from analysis, we find that the Social Capital Index is correlated with each of seven National Assessment of Educational Progress tests administered in the 1990s: fourth-grade math, 1992: $r = .81$; fourth-grade math, 1996: $r = .67$; eighth-grade math, 1990: $r = .90$; eighth-grade math 1992: $r = .91$; eighth-grade math, 1996: $r = .88$; fourth-grade reading, 1994: $r = .68$; eighth-grade science, 1996: $r = .85$. In addition, the Social Capital Index is correlated with state average scores on the Scholastic Assessment Test (1993), adjusted for test-participation rates across states ($r = .67$). The Social Capital Index is also negatively correlated with the state high school dropout rate aggregated over the period 1990–95 ($r = -.79$).

10. Author's analysis of state-level data on educational performance and data from the DDB Needham Life Style and Roper Social and Political Trends archives, aggregated to the state level, along with state-level data on racial composition, poverty, and educational levels of the adult population. All analyses of state educational performance in this chapter control for single-parent rate, 1984–90; pupil-teacher ratio, 1988–90; state poverty rate, 1987–90; percent of population nonwhite, 1990; mean personal per capita income, 1980–90; income inequality (Gini coefficient), 1990; fraction of adult population with at least high school degree, 1990; total educational spending per pupil, 1989–90 to 1991–92 (in real dollars) and mean teacher salaries, 1989, both adjusted for differences in state cost of living; fraction of elementary and secondary students in public schools; Catholic percentage of state population; and a composite survey-based measure of religious observance.

11. Strictly speaking, the statistical analysis suggests that to bring North Carolina's educational performance to the level of Connecticut merely by adjusting the student-teacher ratio would require a cut in average class size of twenty to twenty-five pupils per class, but the average class size in North Carolina at the time these data were collected was actually seventeen students. This fact represents statistically the practical impossibility of relying solely on smaller class size to fix educational problems.

12. Author's analysis of state-level data on educational performance and data from the DDB Needham Life Style and Roper Social and Political Trends archives, aggregated to the state level.

13. In a multivariate regression with an index of student misbehavior as the dependent variable, community social capital had a standardized beta of -.612, compared with .333 for single-parent rate, .261 for fraction of the adult population with at least four years of high school, and .226 for the pupil-teacher ratio. All were significant at $p < .05$ or better (social capital was significant at $p = .0002$). Other demographic, economic, and educational variables that were included in the initial model were nonsignificant. The dependent variable was an index composed of high school teachers' perceptions of the seriousness of four problems: student weapon possession, absenteeism, and apathy, as well as student-on-student violence.

14. P. W. Cookson, *School Choice: The Struggle for the Soul of American Education* (New Haven, Conn.: Yale University Press, 1994); Sharon G. Rollow and Anthony S. Bryk, "The Chicago Experiment: The Potential and Reality of Reform," *Equity and Choice* 9, no. 3 (spring 1993): 22–32.

15. James S. Coleman and Thomas Hoffer, *Public and Private High Schools: The Impact of Communities* (New York: Basic Books, 1987), 94, 133–135, 231, 229. For contrary evidence, see Stephen L. Morgan and Aage B. Sørensen, "A Test of Coleman's Social Capital Explanation of School Effects," *American Sociological Review* 64 (1999): 661–681.

16. Anne T. Henderson and Nancy Berla, *A New Generation of Evidence: The Family Is Critical to Student Achievement* (Washington, D.C.: National Committee for Citizens in Education, 1994), 1.

17. Roger G. Barker and Paul V. Gump, *Big School, Small School: High School Size and Student Behavior* (Stanford, Calif.: Stanford University Press, 1964); Kenneth R. Turner, "Why Some Public High Schools Are More Successful in Preventing Dropout: The Critical Role of School Size," unpublished dissertation, Harvard University Graduate School of Education, 1991.

18. Anthony S. Bryk, Valerie E. Lee, and Peter B. Holland, *Catholic Schools and the Common Good* (Cambridge, Mass.: Harvard University Press, 1993). For example, a public school in the fiftieth percentile for teacher enjoyment of work would move to the eighty-fourth percentile if Catholic school "communal organization" were adopted. Likewise, a fiftieth percentile public school that became more communal would move to the eighty-ninth per-

centile for staff morale; the thirtieth percentile for rates of class cutting; the twenty-eighth percentile for classroom disorder; and the sixty-sixth percentile for student interest in academics. See page 288.

19. Bryk, Lee, and Holland, *Catholic Schools* (1993), 314.

20. James P. Comer and Norris M. Haynes, *Summary of School Development Program Effects* (New Haven, Conn.: Yale Child Study Center, 1992).

21. James P. Comer, *School Power: Implications of an Intervention Project* (New York: Free Press, 1980), 126–28. See also Wendy Glasgow Winters, *African-American Mothers and Urban Schools: The Power of Participation* (New York: Lexington Press, 1993).

22. Anthony S. Bryk and Barbara Schneider, "Social Trust: A Moral Resource for School Improvement," in G. G. Whelage and J. A. White, eds., *Rebuilding the Village: Social Capital and Education in America* (London: Falmer Press, forthcoming). See also Donald Moore, "What Makes These Schools Stand Out?" (Chicago: Designs for Change, April 1998), 1–19 and 83–103.

23. That smaller schools foster greater student engagement in curricular and extracurricular activities is a common finding among educational researchers, as is the generalization that extracurricular participation in school is a strong predictor of civic engagement in later life. See sources cited in note 17 above and in note 4 of chapter 24.

24. Coleman, "Social Capital in the Creation of Human Capital."

25. Frank F. Furstenberg Jr. and Mary Elizabeth Hughes, "The Influence of Neighborhoods on Children's Development: A Theoretical Perspective and a Research Agenda," in Jeanne Brooks-Gunn, Greg J. Duncan, and J. Lawrence Aber, eds., *Neighborhood Poverty: Volume II* (New York: Russell Sage Foundation, 1997), 43.

26. Nancy Darling and Lawrence Steinberg, "Community Influences on Adolescent Achievement and Deviance," in Brooks-Gunn, Duncan, and Aber, eds. *Neighborhood Poverty: Volume II*, 120–131; Jay Teachman, Kathleen Paasch, and Karen Carver, "Social Capital and the Generation of Human Capital," *Social Forces* 75 (1999): 1343–1359.

27. Frank F. Furstenberg Jr. and Mary Elizabeth Hughes, "Social Capital and Successful Development among At-Risk Youth," *Journal of Marriage and the Family* 57 (August 1995): 580–592.

28. Ernest T. Pascarella and Patrick T. Terenzini, *How College Affects Students: Findings and Insights from Twenty Years of Research* (San Francisco: Jossey-Bass, 1991); Uri Treisman, "Studying Students Studying Calculus: A Look at the Lives of Minority Mathematics Students in College," *College Mathematics Journal* 23 (1992): 362–372; Alexander W. Astin, "What Matters in College," *Liberal Education* (fall 1993): 4–14; Alexander W. Astin, "Involvement in Learning Revisited: Lessons We have Learned," *Journal of College Student Development* 37 (1996): 123–134.

CHAPTER 18: SAFE AND PRODUCTIVE NEIGHBORHOODS

1. Robert J. Sampson and Jeffrey D. Morenoff, "Ecological Perspectives on the Neighborhood Context of Urban Poverty: Past and Present," in Jeanne Brooks-Gunn, Greg J. Duncan, and J. Lawrence Aber, eds., *Neighborhood Poverty: Volume II* (New York: Russell Sage Foundation, 1997), 1–22; Robert J. Sampson, "The Community" in *Crime*, James Q. Wilson and Joan Petersilia, eds. (San Francisco: Institute for Contemporary Studies Press, 1995), 193–216.

2. Jacobs, *Death and Life of Great American Cities*, 56.

3. The Pearson's *r* correlation coefficient between the average murder rate in a state (1980–95) and the Social Capital Index is -0.8 where -1.0 would constitute a perfect negative linear association.

4. In a multiple regression, with the fifty states as units of analysis, the best-fitting model includes four statistically significant variables: the Social Capital Index, the mean poverty rate (1987–90), the fraction of the population that is white (1990), and the fraction of the population classified as urban (1990). Other variables that were entered but not found to be statistically significant were mean single parent rate (1984–90); personal per capita income (1990, in $1992); fraction of the population with at least four years of college education (1990); fraction of the population with at least four years of high school (1990); fraction of the population that is Catholic; Gini index of income inequality (1990); and responses to the DDB Needham Life Style survey question about "worry that my family may become a victim of crime." If the causal arrow ran from high crime to low social capital, as fear of crime inhibited social intercourse, then controlling for fear of crime should eliminate the crime–social capital correlation, but it does not; the partial correlation of crime and social capital remains a highly significant *r* = -.53. Mitchell B. Chamlin and John K. Cochran, "Social Altruism and Crime," *Criminology* 35 (1997): 203–227, report that (controlling for other relevant factors, such as poverty, inequality, race, residential mobility, and family structure) crime is lower in cities where the ratio of United Way contributions to city income is higher, another indication of social capital.

5. Sheldon Hackney, "Southern Violence," *American Historical Review* 73 (1969): 906–925, quotation at 925; Richard E. Nisbett and Dov Cohen, *Culture of Honor: The Psychology of Violence in the South* (Boulder, Colo.: Westview Press, 1996); Raymond D. Gastil, "Homicide and a Regional Culture of Violence," *American Sociological Review* 36 (1971): 412–427; Steven F. Messner, "Regional and Racial Effects on the Urban Homicide Rate: The Subculture of Violence Revisited," *American Journal of Sociology*, 88 (1983): 997–1007; and (for a critical view) Colin Loftin and Robert H. Hill, "Regional Subculture and Homicide: An Examination of the Gastil-Hackney Thesis," *American Sociological Review* 39 (1974): 714–724.

6. This conclusion is based on extensive multivariate predictions of the murder rate 1980–95 in the fifty states, based on poverty rates, income level, income inequality, educational levels, degree of urbanism, and racial composition, along with our standard measure of social capital and the north-south distinction. In virtually all specifications, when social capital is introduced, the north-south distinction becomes insignificant. The most robust predictors across various models are the percentage of nonwhites in the population, the poverty rate, urbanism, and social capital, all of equivalent significance. Among the thirty-nine states outside the old Confederacy, the bivariate correlation between social capital and the murder rate is a very strong *r* = -.74.

7. Author's analysis of DDB Needham Life Style surveys. Here too the effects of social capital masquerade as regional differences. Southerners appear more pugnacious than northerners, but once we control for differences in

social capital, those regional differences disappear, whereas if we control for region (by looking only at northern states, for example), the negative correlation between social capital and physical truculence persists.

8. On neighborhood effects, see Christopher Jencks and Susan E. Mayer, "The Social Consequences of Growing Up in a Poor Neighborhood," in L. E. Lynn Jr. and M. G. H. McGeary, eds., *Inner-City Poverty in the United States* (Washington, D.C.: National Academy Press, 1990), 111–186; and Martha A. Gephart, "Neighborhoods and Communities as Contexts for Development," in Jeanne Brooks-Gunn, Greg J. Duncan, and J. Lawrence Aber, eds., *Neighborhood Poverty: Volume 1* (New York: Russell Sage Foundation, 1997), 1–43.

9. W. N. Evans, W. E. Oates, and R. M. Schwab, "Measuring Peer Group Effects: A Study of Teenage Behavior," *Journal of Political Economy* 100 (1992): 966–991. Greg J. Duncan, James P. Connell, and Pamela K. Klebanov, "Conceptual and Methodological Issues in Estimating Causal Effects of Neighborhoods and Family Conditions on Individual Development," in Brooks-Gunn, Duncan, and Aber, eds., *Neighborhood Poverty: Volume I*, 219–250; and Jencks and Mayer, "Social Consequences."

10. Anne C. Case and Lawrence F. Katz, "The Company You Keep: The Effects of Family and Neighborhood on Disadvantaged Youths," National Bureau of Economic Research working paper no. 3705 (Cambridge, Mass.: National Bureau of Economic Research, 1991); M. E. Ensminger, R. P. Lamkin, and N. Jacobson, "School Leaving: A Longitudinal Perspective Including Neighborhood Effects," *Child Development* 67 (1996): 2400–2416.

11. Susan E. Mayer and Christopher Jencks, "Growing Up in Poor Neighborhoods: How Much Does It Matter?" *Science*, March 17, 1989, 1441–1445; and Ingrid Gould Ellen and Margery Austin Turner, "Does Neighborhood Matter? Assessing Recent Evidence," *Housing Policy Debate* 8 (1997): 833–866.

12. Furstenberg and Hughes, "The Influence of Neighborhoods on Children's Development"; Margery Austin Turner, Ingrid Gould Ellen, Sheila O'Leary, and Katherine Carnevale, "Location, Location, Location: How Does Neighborhood Environment Affect the Well-Being of Families and Children?" unpublished ms., May 1997.

13. Turner, Ellen, O'Leary, and Carnevale, "Location, Location, Location."

14. Robert J. Sampson, "Family Management and Child Development: Insights from Social Disorganization Theory," in Joan McCord, ed., *Facts, Framework, and Forecasts: Advances in Criminological Theory*, vol. 3 (New Brunswick, N.J.: Transaction Publishers, 1992), 63–93.

15. See chapter 6.

16. William Julius Wilson, *The Truly Disadvantaged* (Chicago: University of Chicago Press, 1987), 144.

17. Elijah Anderson, *Streetwise: Race, Class, and Change in an Urban Community* (Chicago: University of Chicago Press, 1990), 4, 69, 72.

18. Robert J. Sampson, Stephen W. Raudenbush, and Felton Earls, "Crime: A Multilevel Study of Collective Efficacy," *Science* 277 (August 15, 1997): 918–924.

19. R. J. Sampson and W. B. Groves, "Community Structure and Crime: Testing Social Disorganization Theory," *American Journal of Sociology* 94, no. 4 (1989): 774–802. See also Edward L. Glaeser, Bruce Sacerdote, and Jose A. Scheinkman, *Crime and Social Interactions*, National Bureau of Economic Research working paper no. 5026 (Cambridge, Mass.: National Bureau of Economic Research, 1995).

20. Ora Simcha-Fagan and Joseph E. Schwartz, "Neighborhood and Delinquency: An Assessment of Contextual Effects," *Criminology* 24, no. 4 (1986): 667–703.

21. Darling and Steinberg, "Community Influences on Adolescent Achievement and Deviance," 120–131.

22. Elijah Anderson, *Code of the Street: Decency, Violence, and the Moral Life of the Inner City* (New York: Norton, 1999).

23. Darling and Steinberg, "Community Influences."

24. Herbert C. Covey, Scott Menard, and Robert J. Franzese, *Juvenile Gangs*, 2nd ed. (Springfield, Ill.: Charles C. Thomas Publisher, 1997), 23–30, 161–185.

25. I am grateful to Karen Ferree for her review of the literature on gangs and social capital.

26. Joan W. Moore, *Homeboys* (Philadelphia: Temple University Press, 1978).

27. Ruth Horowitz, *Honor and the American Dream* (New Brunswick, N.J.: Rutgers University Press, 1983), 187.

28. Shakur's appalling experiences are described in Kody Scott [Sanyika Shakur], *Monster: The Autobiography of an L.A. Gang Member* (New York: Penguin, 1994).

29. Moore, *Homeboys*.

30. John Hagedorn and Perry Macon, *People and Folks: Gangs, Crime and the Underclass in a Rustbelt City* (Chicago: Lakeview Press, 1988).

31. Martín Sánchez Jankowski, *Islands in the Street: Gangs and American Urban Society* (Berkeley: University of California Press, 1991).

32. Ko-Lin Chin, "Chinese Gangs and Extortion," in Ronald Huff, ed., *Gangs in America* (Newbury Park, Calif: Sage Books, 1990).

33. Jankowski, *Islands*; Moore, *Homeboys*.

34. Kristin A. Goss, " 'We All Have to Come Together: Moms' Role in Disarming Kids in the Nation's Capital," master's thesis, Duke University, 1996.

35. Paul A. Jargowsky, "Beyond the Street Corner: The Hidden Diversity of High-Poverty Neighborhoods," *Urban Geography* 17 (1996): 579–603.

36. Carol B. Stack, *All Our Kin: Strategies for Survival in a Black Community* (New York: Harper & Row, 1974), 28.

37. Elliot Liebow, *Tally's Corner: A Study of Negro Street Corner Men* (Boston: Little, Brown, 1967), argues instead that among the unmarried and unemployed men who hang out on urban streets, social relations are superficial and transient. Lee Rainwater's *Behind Ghetto Walls*, a study of St. Louis's infamous Pruitt-Igoe housing project (Chicago: Aldine De Gruyter, 1970), describes a world of alienation and distrust, both within the family and among neighbors.

38. At least one author has challenged the assumption that extended kin networks are necessarily good for low-income people. When members of the kin group use or sell drugs, these networks become transmission belts passing

drug use down through the generations. See Eloise Dunlap, "The Impact of Drugs on Family Life and Kin Networks in the Inner-City African-American Single Parent Household," in Adele V. Harrell and George E. Peterson, eds., *Drugs, Crime, and Social Isolation: Barriers to Urban Opportunity* (Washington, D.C.: Urban Institute Press, 1992).

39. Mary Benin and Verna M. Keith, "The Social Support of Employed African American and Anglo Mothers," *Journal of Family Issues* 16 (1995): 275–297; R. Kelly Raley, "Black-White Differences in Kin Contact and Exchange Among Never Married Adults," *Journal of Family Issues* 16 (1995): 77–103; Dennis P. Hogan, David J. Eggebeen, and Clifford C. Clogg, "The Structure of Intergenerational Exchanges in American Families," *American Journal of Sociology* 98 (1993): 1428–1458; Dennis P. Hogan, Ling-Xin Hao, and William L. Parish, "Race, Kin Networks, and Assistance to Mother-Headed Families," *Social Forces* 68 (1990): 797–812.

40. Wesley G. Skogan, "Community Organizations and Crime," in Michael Tonry and Norval Morris, eds., *Crime and Justice: A Review of Research*, volume 10 (Chicago: University of Chicago Press, 1988).

41. Wesley Skogan and Susan Hartnett, *Community Policing: Chicago Style* (New York: Oxford University Press, 1997), quotation at 160; Christopher Winship and Jenny Berrien, "Boston Cops and Black Churches," *Public Interest* 136 (1999): 52–68.

CHAPTER 19: ECONOMIC PROSPERITY

1. Fukuyama, *Trust*; La Porta et al., "Trust in Large Organizations"; Knack and Keefer, "Does Social Capital Have an Economic Payoff?"

2. Economist Glenn C. Loury, one of several independent "inventors" of the concept of social capital, did so to capture the fact that even if the human and financial capital advantages of white Americans were neutralized, their richer connections to mainstream American institutions—their "social capital"—would give them an advantage unavailable even to middle-class members of minority communities. See Glenn C. Loury, "The Economics of Discrimination: Getting to the Core of the Problem," *Harvard Journal of African American Public Policy* 1 (1992): 91–110.

3. Mary Corcoran, Linda Datcher, and Greg Duncan, "Most Workers Find Jobs through Word of Mouth," *Monthly Labor Review* (August 1980): 33–35; Montgomery, "Social Networks and Labor-Market Outcomes"; Burt, "Contingent Value of Social Capital"; Maura A. Belliveau, Charles A. O'Reilly III, and James B. Wade, "Social Capital at the Top: Effects of Social Similarity and Status on CEO Compensation," *Academy of Management Journal* 39 (1996): 1568–1593; Joel M. Podolny and James N. Baron, "Resources and Relationships in the Workplace: Social Networks and Mobility in the Workplace," *American Sociological Review* 62 (1997): 673–693.

4. Mark S. Granovetter, *Getting a Job* (Cambridge, Mass.: Harvard University Press, 1974); Granovetter, "The Strength of Weak Ties."

5. Jay MacLeod, *Ain't No Making It: Aspirations and Attainment in a Low-Income Neighborhood*, 2nd ed. (Boulder, Colo.: Westview Press, 1985).

6. Joleen Kirschenmann and Kathryn M. Neckerman, " 'We'd Love to Hire Them, But . . . ': The Meaning of Race for Employers," in Christopher Jencks and Paul E. Peterson, eds., *The Urban Underclass* (Washington, D.C.: Brookings Institution, 1991), 203–232; David T. Ellwood, "The Spatial Mismatch Hypothesis: Are There Teenage Jobs Missing in the Ghetto?" in Richard B. Freeman and Henry J. Holzer, eds., *The Black Youth Employment Crisis* (Chicago: University of Chicago Press, 1986), 147–185.

7. John D. Kasarda, "Urban Change and Minority Opportunities," in Paul E. Peterson, ed., *The New Urban Reality* (Washington, D.C.: Brookings Institution, 1985); John D. Kasarda, "Urban Industrial Transition and the Underclass," *Annals of the American Academy of Political and Social Science* 501 (January 1989): 26–47.

8. John D. Kasarda, "Urban Industrial Transition and the Underclass"; Henry J. Holzer, "The Spatial Mismatch Hypothesis: What Has the Evidence Shown?" *Urban Studies* 28, no. 1 (1991): 105–122.

9. Katherine M. O'Regan, "The Effect of Social Networks and Concentrated Poverty on Black and Hispanic Youth Employment," *Annals of Regional Science* 27, no. 4 (December 1993): 327–342.

10. Roger Waldinger, *Still the Promised City?* (Cambridge, Mass.: Harvard University Press, 1996); Ivan Light, *Ethnic Enterprise in America: Business and Welfare Among Chinese, Japanese, and Blacks* (Berkeley: University of California Press, 1972).

11. James H. Johnson, Jr., Elisa Jayne Bienenstock, and Walter C. Farrell, Jr., "Bridging Social Networks and Female Labor Force Participation in a Multi-Ethnic Metropolis," in *Prismatic Metropolis: Analyzing Inequality in Los Angeles*, Lawrence D. Bobo, Melvin L. Oliver, James H. Johnson, Jr., and Abel Valenzuela, eds. (New York: Russell Sage Foundation, 2000).

12. Corcoran, Datcher, and Duncan, "Most Workers Find Jobs through Word of Mouth"; and Gary P. Green, Leann M. Tigges, and Irene Browne, "Social Resources, Job Search, and Poverty in Atlanta," *Research in Community Sociology* 5 (1995): 161–182.

13. Richard B. Freeman, "Who Escapes? The Relation of Churchgoing and Other Background Factors to the Socioeconomic Performance of Black Male Youths from Inner-City Tracts," in Richard B. Freeman and Henry J. Holzer, eds., *The Black Youth Employment Crisis* (Chicago: University of Chicago Press, 1986), 353–376.

14. Burt, *Structural Holes*; Burt, "The Contingent Value of Social Capital"; Nan Lin, "Social Networks and Status Attainment," *Annual Review of Sociology* 25 (1999): 467–487, and the works cited there; Brian Uzzi, "Embeddedness in the Making of Financial Capital: How Social Relations and Networks Benefit Firms Seeking Financing," *American Sociological Review* 64 (1999) 481–505; Paul Dimaggio and Hugh Louch, "Socially Embedded Consumer Transactions: For What Kinds of Purchases Do People Most Often Use Networks?" *American Sociological Review* 63 (1998): 619–637.

15. Philip Kasinitz and Jan Rosenberg, "Missing the Connection: Social Isolation and Employment on the Brooklyn Waterfront," *Social Problems* 43, no. 2 (May 1996): 180–196.

16. Loïc J. D. Wacquant and William Julius Wilson, "The Cost of Racial and Class Exclusion in the Inner City," *Annals of the American Academy of Political and Social Science* 501 (1990): 8–25.

17. Kasinitz and Rosenberg, "Missing the Connection."

18. Manuel Pastor, Jr., and Ara Robinson Adams, "Keeping Down with the Joneses: Neighbors, Networks, and Wages," *Review of Regional Studies* 26, no. 2 (1996): 115–145.

19. Green, Tigges, and Browne, "Social Resources."

20. Ibid.

21. Catherine Zimmer and Howard Aldrich, "Resource Mobilization Through Ethnic Networks: Kinship and Friendship Ties of Shopkeepers in England," *Sociological Perspectives* 30 (1987): 422–445.

22. Alejandro Portes and Julia Sensenbrenner, "Embeddedness and Immigration: Notes on the Social Determinants of Economic Action," *American Journal of Sociology* 98, no. 6 (May 1993): 1320–1350; Woolcock; "Social Capital and Economic Development."

23. Kenneth Temkin and William Rohe, "Social Capital and Neighborhood Stability: An Empirical Investigation," *Housing Policy Debate* 9, no. 1 (1998): 61–88.

24. This history of Tupelo's development is borrowed from the excellent account by Vaughn L. Grisham, Jr., *Tupelo: The Evolution of a Community* (Dayton, Ohio: Kettering Foundation, 1999).

25. AnnaLee Saxenian, *Regional Advantage: Culture and Competition in Silicon Valley and Route 128* (Cambridge, Mass.: Harvard University Press, 1994), 36.

26. Dara Elizabeth Menashi, *Making Public/Private Collaboration Productive: Lessons for Creating Social Capital*, unpublished doctoral dissertation, John F. Kennedy School of Government, Harvard University, 1997.

27. Saxenian, *Regional Advantage*, 161.

28. Michael J. Piore and Charles F. Sable, *The Second Industrial Divide: Possibilities for Prosperity* (New York: Basic Books, 1984).

29. Francis Fukuyama, *Trust*; William G. Ouchi, "Markets, Bureaucracies and Clans," *Administrative Science Quarterly* 25, no. 1 (March 1980): 129–141; Lynne G. Zucker, "Production of Trust: Institutional Sources of Economic Structure, 1840–1920," *Research in Organizational Behavior* 8 (1986): 53–111.

30. Walter W. Powell, Kenneth W. Koput, and Laurel Smith-Doerr, "Interorganizational Collaboration and the Locus of Innovation: Networks of Learning in Biotechnology," *Administrative Science Quarterly* 41 (1996): 116–145; Jane A. Fountain, "Social Capital: A Key Enabler of Innovation," in *Investing in Innovation: Toward a Consensus Strategy for Federal Technology Policy*, L. M. Branscomb and J. Keller, eds. (Cambridge, Mass.: MIT Press, 1998): 85–111.

31. For recent work on social capital and economic development, see *Social Capital: A Multifaceted Perspective*, Partha Dasgupta and Ismail Serageldin, eds. (Washington, D.C.: The World Bank, 2000); *Social Capital and Poor Communities*, Susan Saegert, J. Phillip Thompson, and Mark R. Warren, eds. (forthcoming); and Michael Woolcock, *Using Social Capital: Getting the Social Relations Right in the Theory and Practice of Economic Development* (Princeton, N.J.: Princeton University Press, 2000).

CHAPTER 20: HEALTH AND HAPPINESS

1. For comprehensive overviews of the massive literature on health and social connectedness, see James S. House, Karl R. Landis, and Debra Umberson, "Social Relationships and Health," *Science* 241 (1988): 540–545; Lisa F. Berkman, "The Role of Social Relations in Health Promotion," *Psychosomatic Medicine* 57 (1995): 245–254; and Teresa E. Seeman, "Social Ties and Health: The Benefits of Social Integration," *Annual of Epidemiology* 6 (1996): 442–451. Other useful recent overviews include Benjamin C. Amick III, Sol Levine, Alvin R. Tarlov, and Diana Chapman Walsh, eds., *Society and Health* (New York: Oxford University Press, 1995), esp. Donald L. Patrick and Thomas M. Wickizer, "Community and Health," 46–92; Richard G. Wilkinson, *Unhealthy Societies: From Inequality to Well-Being* (New York: Routledge, 1996); Linda K. George, "Social Factors and Illness," in *Handbook of Aging and the Social Sciences* 4th ed., Robert H. Binstock and Linda K. George, eds. (New York: Academic Press, 1996), 229–252; Frank W. Young and Nina Glasgow, "Voluntary Social Participation and Health," *Research on Aging* 20 (1998): 339–362; Sherman A. James, Amy J. Schulz, and Juliana van Olphen, "Social Capital, Poverty, and Community Health: An Exploration of Linkages," in *Using Social Capital*, Saegert, Thompson, and Warren, eds.

2. B. H. Kaplan, J. C. Cassel, and S. Gore, "Social Support and Health," *Medical Care* (supp.) 15, no. 5 (1977): 47–58. L. F. Berkman, "The Relationship of Social Networks and Social Support to Morbidity and Mortality," in S. Cohen and S. L. Syme, eds., *Social Support and Health* (Orlando, Fla.: Academic Press, 1985), 241–262; J. S. House, D. Umberson, and K. R. Landis, "Structures and Processes of Social Support," *Annual Review of Sociology* 14 (1988): 293–318. Ichiro Kawachi, Bruce P. Kennedy, and Roberta Glass, "Social Capital and Self-Rated Health: A Contextual Analysis," *American Journal of Public Health* 89 (1999): 1187–1193.

3. Lisa Berkman, "The Changing and Heterogeneous Nature of Aging and Longevity: A Social and Biomedical Perspective," *Annual Review of Gerontology and Geriatrics* 8 (1988): 37–68; Lisa Berkman and Thomas Glass, "Social Integration, Social Networks, Social Support, and Health," in *Social Epidemiology*, Lisa F. Berkman and Ichiro Kawachi, eds. (New York, Oxford University Press, 2000), 137–174; T. E. Seeman, L. F. Berkman, and D. Blazer, et al., "Social Ties and Support and Neuroendocrine Function: The MacArthur Studies of Successful Aging," *Annals of Behavioral Medicine* 16 (1994): 95–106; Sheldon Cohen, "Health Psychology: Psychological Factors and Physical Disease from the Perspective of Human Psychoneuroimmunology," *Annual Review of Psychology* 47(1996): 113–142.

4. Berkman and Glass, "Social Integration, Social Networks, Social Support, and Health."

5. Kawachi et al., "Social Capital and Self-Rated Health."

6. The Pearson's r coefficient between the fraction reporting they were in fair or poor health and the (demographically weighted) state mistrust ranking (low, medium, high) was 0.71; the r coefficient between fraction of population in fair/poor health and the (demographically weighted) state "helpfulness" ranking (low, medium, high) was -0.66.

7. The Pearson's r coefficient between the Social Capital Index and the Morgan-Quitno health index (1991–98) across the fifty states equals 0.78, which is strong by conventional social science standards; the comparable correlation between the Social Capital Index and the age-adjusted all-cause mortality rate is -.81. Thanks to Ichiro Kawachi for providing this measure of death rates.

8. Thanks to Kimberly Lochner for bringing the history of Roseto to my attention and for introducing me to the literature on the health effects of social connectedness. The key studies of Roseto are J. G. Bruhn and S. Wolf, *The Roseto Story: An Anatomy of Health* (Norman, Okla.: University of Oklahoma Press, 1979); S. Wolf and J. G. Bruhn, *The Power of Clan: The Influence of Human Relationships on Heart Disease* (New Brunswick, N.J.: Transaction Publishers, 1993); B. Egolf, J. Lasker, S. Wolf, and L. Potvin, "The Roseto Effect: A Fifty-Year Comparison of Mortality Rates," *American Journal of Epidemiology* 125, no. 6 (1992): 1089–1092.

9. L. F. Berkman and S. L. Syme, "Social Networks, Host Resistance and Mortality: A Nine Year Follow-up of Alameda County Residents," *American Journal of Epidemiology* 109 (1979): 186–204.

10. J. House, C. Robbins, and H. Metzner, "The Association of Social Relationships and Activities with Mortality: Prospective Evidence from the Tecumseh Community Health Study," *American Journal of Epidemiology* 116, no. 1 (1982): 123–140. This finding held for men only.

11. House, Robbins, and Metzner (1982); this finding held for women only. T. E. Seeman, G. A. Kaplan, L. Knudsen, R. Cohen, and J. Guralnik, "Social Network Ties and Mortality among the Elderly in the Alameda County Study," *American Journal of Epidemiology* 126, no. 4 (1987): 714–723; this study found that social isolation predicted mortality only in people over sixty.

12. D. Blazer, "Social Support and Mortality in an Elderly Community Population," *American Journal of Epidemiology* 115, no. 5 (1982): 684–694; K. Orth-Gomer and J. V. Johnson, "Social Network Interaction and Mortality," *Journal of Chronic Diseases* 40, no. 10 (1987): 949–957.

13. L. Welin, G. Tibblin, K. Svardsudd, B. Tibblin, S. Ander-Peciva, B. Larsson, and L. Wilhelmsen, "Prospective Study of Social Influences on Mortality," *The Lancet*, April 20, 1985, 915–918; Frederick J. Manning and Terrence D. Fullerton, "Health and Well-Being in Highly Cohesive Units of the U.S. Army," *Journal of Applied Social Psychology* 18 (1988): 503–519.

14. Sheldon Cohen et al., "Social Ties and Susceptibility to the Common Cold," *Journal of the American Medical Association* 277 (June 25, 1997): 1940–1944.

15. A. Colantonio, S. V. Kasl, A. M. Ostfeld, and L. Berkman, "Psychosocial Predictors of Stroke Outcomes in an Elderly Population," *Journal of Gerontology* 48, no. 5 (1993): S261–S268.

16. Young and Glasgow, "Voluntary Social Participation and Health."

17. Angus Deaton and C. H. Paxson, "Aging and Inequality in Income and Health," *American Economic Review* 88 (1998): 252, report "there has been no improvement, and possibly some deterioration, in health status across cohorts born after 1945, and there were larger improvements across those born before 1945."

18. R. C. Kessler et al., "Lifetime and 12-Month Prevalence of DSM-III-R Psychiatric Disorders in the United States, *Archives of General Psychiatry* 51 (1994): 8–19; C. J. Murray and A. D. Lopez, "Evidence-Based Health Policy—Lessons from the Global Burden of Disease Study," *Science* 274 (1996): 740–743; L. I. Pearlin et al., "The Stress Process"; G. A. Kaplan et al., "Psychosocial Predictors of Depression"; A. G. Billings and R. H. Moos, "Life Stressors and Social Resources Affect Posttreatment Outcomes Among Depressed Patients," *Journal of Abnormal Psychiatry* 94 (1985): 140–153; C. D. Sherbourne, R. D. Hays, and K. B. Wells, "Personal and Psychosocial Risk Factors for Physical and Mental Health Outcomes and Course of Depression among Depressed Patients," *Journal of Consulting and Clinical Psychology* 63 (1995): 345–355; and T. E. Seeman and L. F. Berkman, "Structural Characteristics of Social Networks and Their Relationship with Social Support in the Elderly: Who Provides Support," *Social Science and Medicine* 26 (1988): 737–749. I am indebted to Julie Donahue for her fine work on this topic.

19. L. I. Pearlin, M. A. Lieberman, E. G. Menaghan, J. T. Mullan, "The Stress Process," *Journal of Health and Social Behavior* 22, no. 4 (1981): 337–356; A. Billings and R. Moos, "Social Support and Functioning Among Community and Clinical Groups: A Panel Model," *Journal of Behavioral Medicine* 5, no. 3 (1982): 295–311; G. A. Kaplan, R. E. Roberts, T. C. Camacho, and J. C. Coyne, "Psychosocial Predictors of Depression," *American Journal of Epidemiology* 125, no. 2, (1987), 206–220; P. Cohen, E. L. Struening, G. L. Muhlin, L. E. Genevie, S. R. Kaplan, and H. B. Peck, "Community Stressors, Mediating Conditions and Well-being in Urban Neighborhoods," *Journal of Community Psychology* 10 (1982): 377–391; David G. Myers, "Close Relationships and Quality of Life," in D. Kahneman, E. Diener, and N. Schwartz, eds., *Well-being: The Foundations of Hedonic Psychology* (New York: Russell Sage Foundation, 1999).

20. Michael Argyle, *The Psychology of Happiness* (London: Metheun, 1987); Ed Diener, "Subjective Well-being," *Psychological Bulletin* 95 (1984): 542–575; Ed Diener, "Assessing Subjective Well-being," *Social Indicators Research*, 31 (1994): 103–157; David G. Myers and Ed Diener, "Who Is Happy?" *Psychological Science* 6 (1995): 10–19; Ruut Veenhoven, "Developments in Satisfaction-Research," *Social Indicators Research*, 37 (1996): 1–46; and works cited there.

21. In these data and in most studies the effect of marriage on life happiness is essentially identical among men and women, contrary to some reports that marriage has a more positive effect on happiness among men.

22. Income in successive Life Style surveys is measured in terms of income brackets, defined in dollars of annual income. To enhance comparability over time, we have translated each of these brackets in each annual survey into its mean percentile ranking in that year's income distribution. The effect of income measured in percentiles on contentment is not linear, but that is offset by the fact that the translation of income in dollars to income percentiles is also not linear. Thus the "happiness equivalent" of any particular change in income is accurate in its order of magnitude, but not in detail.

23. The results here are based on multiple regression analyses on the DDB Needham Life Style sample, including age, gender, education, income, marital status, as well as our various measures of civic engagement. The results are essentially identical for men and women, except that the effects of education and of social connections on happiness are slightly greater among women. Income, education, and social connections all have a greater effect among single people than among married people. For example, the effects of club meetings on the happiness of single people is twice as great as on the happiness of married people. In other words, absent marriage, itself a powerful booster of life contentment, other factors become more important. Conversely, even among the poor, uneducated, and socially isolated, marriage provides a fundamental buffer for contentment.

24. Author's analysis of DDB Needham Life Style and Harris poll data.
25. Martin E. P. Seligman, "Boomer Blues," *Psychology Today*, October 1988, 50–55.

CHAPTER 21: DEMOCRACY
1. Though this bon mot is widely attributed to Wilde, I have been unable to confirm that attribution.
2. Joseph Schumpeter, *Capitalism, Socialism, and Democracy* (London: Harper and Brothers, 1942).
3. Jefferson to Kercheval, July 12, 1816, in Merrill Peterson, ed., *Writings* (New York: Library of America, 1984), 1227, quoted in James P. Young, *Reconsidering American Liberalism* (Boulder, Colo.: Westview Press, 1996), 86.
4. Tocqueville, *Democracy in America*, 511.
5. Text from John Stuart Mill, *Considerations on Representative Government* (1861), at english-www.hss.cmu.edu/philosophy/mill-representative-govt.txt.
6. John Dewey, *The Public and Its Problems*, as cited in Robert B. Westbrook, *John Dewey and American Democracy* (Ithaca, N.Y.: Cornell University Press, 1991), 314.
7. James Madison, *Federalist*, 10.
8. Michael Schudson, *The Good Citizen: A History of American Civic Life* (New York: Free Press, 1998), 55.
9. See, for example, Peter L. Berger and Richard John Neuhaus, *To Empower People: From State to Civil Society* (Washington, D.C.: AEI Press, 1977; 1996).
10. Tocqueville, *Democracy in America*, 190.
11. Amy Gutmann, "Freedom of Association: An Introductory Essay," in Amy Gutmann, ed., *Freedom of Association* (Princeton, N.J.: Princeton University Press, 1998), 3.
12. Karl-Dieter Opp and Christiane Gern, "Dissident Groups, Personal Networks, and Spontaneous Cooperation: The East German Revolution of 1989," *American Sociological Review* 58 (1993): 659–680.
13. Tocqueville, *Democracy in America*, 515.
14. William Kornhauser, *The Politics of Mass Society* (Glencoe, Ill.: Free Press, 1959), 73.
15. Verba, Schlozman, Brady, *Voice and Equality*, 304–333.
16. William A. Muraskin, *Middle-Class Blacks in a White Society: Prince Hall Freemasonry in America* (Berkeley: University of California Press, 1975), 27.
17. Verba, Schlozman, Brady, *Voice and Equality*, 378.
18. Frederick C. Harris, "Religious Institutions and African American Political Mobilization," in Paul Peterson, ed., *Classifying by Race* (Princeton, N.J.: Princeton University Press, 1995), 299. The evidence suggests that churches organized congregationally, such as Protestant denominations, tend to provide more opportunities for parishioners to build civic skills than do hierarchically organized churches, including Catholic and evangelical denominations. Protestants are three times as likely as Catholics to report opportunities to exercise civic skills. Verba, Schlozman, Brady, *Voice and Equality*, 321–322, 329.
19. Verba, Schlozman, Brady, *Voice and Equality*, 385.
20. Jon Elster, ed., *Deliberative Democracy* (Cambridge, UK: Cambridge University Press, 1998); Amy Gutmann and Dennis Thompson, *Democracy and Disagreement* (Cambridge, Mass.: Harvard University Press, 1996); J. Bohman, *Public Deliberation* (Cambridge, Mass.: MIT Press, 1996); C. Nino, *The Constitution of Deliberative Democracy* (New Haven, Conn.: Yale University Press, 1996).
21. Gutmann "Freedom of Association," 25.
22. See, for example, Will Kymlicka, "Ethnic Associations and Democratic Citizenship," in Gutmann, *Freedom of Association*, 177–213.
23. See Michael Walzer, "The Civil Society Argument," in Ronald Beiner, ed., *Theorizing Citizenship* (Albany: State University of New York Press, 1995).
24. Michael Hanks, "Youth, Voluntary Associations, and Political Socialization," *Social Forces* 60 (1981): 211–223.
25. David Sally, "Conversation and Cooperation in Social Dilemmas: A Meta-Analysis of Experiments from 1958 to 1992," *Rationality and Society* 7, no. 1 (1995): 58–92.
26. Gutmann and Thompson, *Democracy and Disagreement*, 52–53.
27. See, for example, Nancy Rosenblum, *Membership and Morals* (Princeton, N.J.: Princeton University Press, 1998); Daniel Schulman, "Voluntary Organization Involvement and Political Participation," *Journal of Voluntary Action Research* 7 (1978): 86–105.
28. Theodore J. Lowi, *The End of Liberalism: Ideology, Policy, and the Crisis of Public Authority* (New York: Norton, 1969); Jonathan Rauch, *Demosclerosis: The Silent Killer of American Government* (New York: Times Books, 1994).
29. Michael Walzer, "The Civil Society Argument," in Ronald Beiner, ed., *Theorizing Citizenship* (Albany: State University of New York Press, 1995).
30. See, for example, Hausknecht, *The Joiners*; Verba, Schlozman, Brady, *Voice and Equality*; and David Horton Smith, "Determinants of Voluntary Association Participation and Volunteering: A Literature Review," *Nonprofit and Voluntary Sector Quarterly* 23, no. 3 (fall 1994): 243–263.
31. E. E. Schattschneider, *The Semisovereign People: A Realist's View of Democracy in America* (New York: Holt, Rinehart & Winston, 1960).
32. Seymour Martin Lipset, *Political Man: The Social Bases of Politics* (Garden City, N.Y.: Doubleday, 1960); Samuel Stouffer, *Communism, Conformity and Civil Liberties* (New York: Doubleday, 1955); Sheri Berman, "Civil Society and the Collapse of the Weimar Republic," *World Politics* 49 (April 1997): 401–429.
33. Samuel P. Huntington, "The Democratic Distemper," *The Public Interest* 41 (fall 1975): 9–38.
34. Rosenblum, *Membership and Morals*, 155.
35. Morris P. Fiorina, "Extreme Voices: The Dark Side of Civic Engagement," in Skocpol and Fiorina, eds., *Civic Engagement in American Democracy*. Fiorina's anecdote is insightful, and his concluding call for more civic

engagement is correct. Unfortunately, some passages of his essay confuse a) a high degree of citizen participation in a community with b) a system of representation or a decision-making process that privileges citizen participation, however few the participants may be. The former is a behavioral characteristic, the latter an institutional one. (The two may be linked causally or historically, but they are not the same thing.) Confusingly, Fiorina uses the term *civic engagement* to refer to both, but his essay demonstrates the "dark side" of b), not the dark side of a). Contrary to the essay's title, his evidence shows the dark side of civic *disengagement*.

36. Generalizations in this and the following paragraph are drawn from the author's analysis of Roper Social and Political Trends archives. Ideological self-description is based on this question: "Now, thinking politically and socially, how would you describe your general outlook—as being very conservative, moderately conservative, middle-of-the-road, moderately liberal, or very liberal?"

37. I have calculated the linear trend between 1974 and 1994 for each of the twelve basic forms of participation for each of the five categories of ideological self-identification and expressed the net change over the twenty-one years as a fraction of the participation rate in 1974. This approach is less sensitive to annual outliers than other possible measures and allows easier comparisons across the different forms of participation, but any reasonable metric yields the same conclusion: The more extreme the self-declared ideological position, the smaller the relative decline in participation rates over these two decades.

38. Gabriel Weimann, "On the Importance of Marginality: One More Step in the Two-Step Flow of Communication," *American Sociological Review* 47 (December 1982): 764–773; Gabriel Weimann, "The Strength of Weak Conversational Ties in the Flow of Information and Influence," *Social Networks* 5 (1983): 245–267; Matthew A. Crenson, "Social Networks and Political Processes in Urban Neighborhoods," *American Journal of Political Science* 22, no. 3 (August 1978): 578–594. Michael MacKuen and Courtney Brown, "Political Context and Attitude Change," *American Political Science Review* 81 (June 1987): 471–490; Robert Huckfeldt and John Sprague, *Citizens, Politics, and Social Communication: Information and Influence in an Election Campaign* (New York: Cambridge University Press, 1995).

39. Cathy J. Cohen and Michael C. Dawson, "Neighborhood Poverty and African American Politics," *American Political Science Review* 87 (1993): 286–302.

40. Michael Schudson, "What If Civic Life Didn't Die?" *The American Prospect* 25 (1996): 17–20, quotation at 18.

41. Tarrow, *Power in Movement*, 133.

42. Theda Skocpol, "Advocates without Members: The Recent Transformation of American Civic Life," in Skocpol and Fiorina, eds., *Civic Engagement in American Democracy*, 505–506.

43. Peter Skerry, "The Strange Politics of Affirmative Action," *Wilson Quarterly* (Winter 1997): 39–46.

44. James T. Hamilton, "Testing for Environmental Racism: Prejudice, Profits, Political Power?," *Journal of Policy Analysis and Management* 14, no. 1 (1995): 107–132.

45. Robert D. Putnam with Robert Leonardi and Raffaella Nanetti, *Making Democracy Work: Civic Traditions in Modern Italy* (Princeton, N.J.: Princeton University Press, 1993).

46. Daniel Elazar, *American Federalism: A View from the States* (New York: Crowell, 1966).

47. Ira Sharkansky, "The Utility of Elazar's Political Culture," *Polity* 2 (1969): 66–83.

48. The Pearson's r correlation coefficient is 0.77, where 1.0 signifies a perfect linear relationship.

49. Charles A. Johnson, "Political Culture in American States: Elazar's Formulation Examined," *American Journal of Political Science* 20 (1976): 491–509; Ira Sharkansky, *Regionalism in American Politics* (Indianapolis, Ind.: Bobbs-Merrill, 1970); Richard A. Joslyn, "Manifestations of Elazar's Political Subcultures: State Public Opinion and the Content of Political Campaign Advertising," John Kincaid, "Political Culture and the Quality of Urban Life," and Susan Welch and John G. Peters, "State Political Culture and the Attitudes of State Senators Toward Social, Economic Welfare, and Corruption Issues," all in *Political Culture, Public Policy and the American States*, John Kincaid, ed. (Philadelphia: Institute for the Study of Human Issues, 1982), 59–80; 121–149; 151–159; Tom W. Rice and Alexander F. Sumberg, "Civic Culture and Government Performance in the American States," *Publius* 27 (1997): 99–114; Maureen Rand Oakley, "Explaining the Adoption of Morality Policy Innovations: The Case of Fetal Homicide Policy," paper presented at the Annual Meeting of the American Political Science Association (Atlanta, Ga., September 1999).

50. Patronage politics are often based on bonding social capital. While they may lead to inefficient government and reinforce ethnic cleavages, they are often highly effective at political mobilization.

51. Margaret Weir, "Power, Money, and Politics in Community Development," in Ronald F. Ferguson and William T. Dickens, eds., *Urban Problems and Community Development* (Washington, D.C.: Brookings Institution Press, 1999).

52. Jeffrey M. Berry, Kent E. Portney, and Ken Thomson, *The Rebirth of Urban Democracy* (Washington, D.C.: Brookings Institution Press, 1993).

53. In a regression analysis predicting compliance rates across states, only the Social Capital Index proved to be a statistically significant variable. Other variables—per capita income, income inequality, racial composition, urbanism, education—were not significant. On the role of social capital and trust in undergirding compliance, see Tyler, "Trust and Democratic Governance."

54. Young-dahl Song and Tinsley E. Yarbrough, "Tax Ethics and Taxpayer Attitudes: A Survey," *Public Administration Review* 38 (1978): 442–452; Steven M. Sheffrin and Robert K. Triest, "Can Brute Deterrence Backfire: Perceptions and Attitudes in Taxpayer Compliance," in *Why People Pay Taxes: Tax Compliance and Enforcement*, Joel Slemrod, ed. (Ann Arbor: University of Michigan Press, 1992), 193–222; Scholz and Lubell, "Trust and Taxpaying"; and Scholz, "Trust, Taxes, and Compliance."

55. Martha E. Kropf and Stephen Knack, "Viewers Like You: Community Norms and Contributions to Public Broadcasting," unpub. ms. (Kansas City: University of Missouri, Kansas City Department of Political Science, 1999).

56. Jennifer M. Coston, Terry Cooper, and Richard A. Sundeen, "Response of Community Organizations to the Civil Unrest in Los Angeles," *Nonprofit and Voluntary Sector Quarterly* 22 (1993): 357, and Krzysztof Kaniasty and Fran H. Norris, "In Search of Altruistic Community: Patterns of Social Support Mobilization Following Hurricane Hugo," *American Journal of Community Psychology*, 23 (1995): 447–477. The literature on small-group solidarity and

military effectiveness is enormous, and much of it is directly relevant to social-capital theory. See Edward A. Shils and Morris Janowitz, "Cohesion and Disintegration in the Wehrmacht in World War II," *Public Opinion Quarterly* 12 (1948): 280–315; Samuel A. Stouffer et al., *The American Soldier* (Princeton, N.J.: Princeton University Press, 1949); and Anthony Kellett, *Combat Motivation: The Behavior of Soldiers in Battle* (Boston: Kluwer-Nijhoff, 1982).

CHAPTER 22: THE DARK SIDE OF SOCIAL CAPITAL

1. Henry David Thoreau, "Life without Principle," *Atlantic Monthly* XII (1863): 484–495, as quoted in McWilliams, *Idea of Fraternity in America*, 296.

2. Sinclair Lewis, *Babbitt* (New York: Harcourt, Brace & World, 1950 [1922]): 203. The *American Heritage Dictionary of the English Language*, 3rd ed. (New York: Houghton Mifflin, 1992), defines "babbitt" as "a member of the middle class whose attachment to its business and social ideals is such as to make that person a model of narrow-mindedness and self-satisfaction."

3. *The Collected Works of Walter Bagehot*, ed. Norman St John-Stevas (London: The Economist, 1965–1986), vol. iii, 243.

4. Gallup Poll Social Audit (various years); John L. Sullivan, James E. Piereson, and George E. Marcus, *Political Tolerance and American Democracy* (Chicago: University of Chicago Press, 1982), esp. 26–53; Glenn, "Social Trends in the United States"; John Mueller, "Trends in Political Tolerance," *Public Opinion Quarterly* 52 (1988): 1–25; Davis, "Changeable Weather in a Cooling Climate atop the Liberal Plateau"; Benjamin I. Page and Robert Y. Shapiro, *The Rational Public: Fifty Years of Trends in Americans' Policy Preferences* (Chicago: University of Chicago Press, 1992); Thomas C. Wilson, "Trends in Tolerance Toward Rightist and Leftist Groups, 1976–1988," *Public Opinion Quarterly* 58 (1994): 539–556; George E. Marcus, John L. Sullivan, Elizabeth Theiss-Morse, and Sandra L. Wood, *With Malice Toward Some: How People Make Civil Liberties Judgments* (New York: Cambridge University Press, 1995); Howard Schumann, Charlotte Steeh, Lawrence Bobo, and Maria Krysan, *Racial Attitudes in America: Trends and Interpretations*, rev. ed. (Cambridge, Mass.: Harvard University Press, 1997). Scholars have hotly debated whether tolerance in general has grown, or only tolerance toward some specific (leftist) groups; the current consensus seems to be that tolerance has shifted but has also grown in general.

5. Schudson, *The Good Citizen*; Alan Wolfe, *One Nation After All* (New York: Viking Press, 1998).

6. Sources for data in the previous two paragraphs: Schumann et al., *Racial Attitudes in America*, 104–105; 117; archives of Pew Research Center for the People & the Press (www.people-press.org/); Gallup Poll Social Audit (various years); and author's analysis of General Social Survey and DDB Needham Life Style archives. Researchers disagree about whether the favorable trends in white responses to questions about race might simply reflect political correctness rather than real changes in behavior, but most believe that the changes are too big and too consistent to be written off.

7. I draw this image from Amy Gutmann's articulate critique of communitarian political philosophy: "Communitarian Critics of Liberalism," *Philosophy & Public Affairs* 14 (1985): 308–322, at 319.

8. Schudson, *The Good Citizen*, 307 (emphasis added).

9. Sources for evidence in previous two paragraphs: author's analysis of General Social Survey archive and the 1996 Adult Civic Involvement survey of the National Household Education Survey of the U.S. Department of Education; Berry, Portney, and Thomson, *Rebirth of Urban Democracy*, 220–221; Samuel C. Stouffer, *Communism, Conformity and Civil Liberties* (New York: Doubleday, 1956); Clyde Z. Nunn, Harry J. Crockett, and J. Allen Williams, Jr., *Tolerance for Nonconformity* (San Francisco: Jossey-Bass, 1978); Herbert McClosky and Alida Brill, *Dimensions of Tolerance: What Americans Believe about Civil Liberties* (New York: Russell Sage Foundation, 1983); James L. Gibson and Richard D. Bingham, *Civil Liberties and Nazis: The Skokie Free Speech Controversy* (New York: Praeger, 1985); Page and Shapiro, *Rational Public*; John L. Sullivan, Patrick Walsh, Michal Shamir, David G. Barnum, and James L. Gibson, "Why Are Politicians More Tolerant? Selective Recruitment and Socialization Among Political Elites in New Zealand, Israel, Britain, and the United States," *British Journal of Political Science* 23 (1993): 51–76. Not all studies have found a *positive* correlation between tolerance and civic engagement, but none have found a *negative* correlation. Lori Weber, *The Effects of Democratic Deliberation on Political Tolerance* (Ph.D. diss., University of Colorado, 1999), 24–42, drawing on the surveys from Verba, Schlozman, and Brady, *Voice and Equality*, found that "social" forms of political participation (such as attending meetings) are associated with increased political tolerance, whereas "individual" forms of political participation (such as contacting officials) are not. On the other hand, dozens of studies have linked religious participation to political intolerance, controlling for potential confounding variables; see, for example, Stouffer, *Communism, Conformity and Civil Liberties*; Nunn, Crockett, and Williams, *Tolerance for Nonconformity*; and Kathleen Beatty and Oliver Walter, "Religious Preference and Practice: Reevaluating Their Impact on Political Tolerance," *Public Opinion Quarterly* 48 (1984): 318–329.

10. I have aggregated at the state level all three measures of tolerance outlined in table 7. Reasonably reliable estimates of average tolerance are available for forty-five states. In the interests of economy, figure 91 combines all three measures of tolerance—for gender and racial diversity and for civil liberties—into a single index, because across the states all those measures are quite closely correlated. However, precisely the same pattern applies to each measure taken separately. Figure 91 presents the bivariate relationship between social capital and tolerance, but the link is highly robust in multivariate analysis and is equally strong for any or all of the individual measures of tolerance taken separately. Controlling for education, income, race, urbanism, income inequality, and even region (north/south), the Social Capital Index is significantly correlated with tolerance for gender equality (r = .48), with support for civil liberties (r = .44), with racial tolerance among whites (r = .45), and the composite index of tolerance shown in figure 91 (r = .50). Social capital is a far stronger predictor of state-level tolerance than any or all of these standard socioeconomic factors.

11. Other researchers have also noted that the growth in tolerance is driven mostly by differences between the prewar and postwar generations, rather than by differences among more recent generations. See Davis, "Changeable Weather in a Cooling Climate atop the Liberal Plateau"; Thomas C. Wilson, "Trends in Tolerance toward Rightist

and Leftist Groups, 1976–1988: Effects of Attitude Change and Cohort Succession," *Public Opinion Quarterly* 58 (1994): 539–556; Schumann et al., *Racial Attitudes in America*; Kevin A. Hill, "Generations and Tolerance: Is Youth Really a Liberalizing Factor?" in Craig and Bennett, *After the Boom*; and Kenneth H. Stehlik-Barry, "The Growth of Political Tolerance 1976–96," paper prepared for presentation at the Annual Meeting of the American Political Science Association (Boston, September 3–6, 1998).

12. Gallup Social Audit survey, 1997, available at www.gallup.com/Special_Reports/black-white.htm.

13. Amy Gutmann, "An Introductory Essay," 19, 25.

14. Robert D. Plotnick, Eugene Smolensky, Eirik Evenhouse, and Siobhan Reilly, "The Twentieth Century Record of Inequality and Poverty in the United States" (Madison, Wisc.: University of Wisconsin Institute for Research on Poverty Discussion Paper no. 1166-98, 1998); Williamson and Lindert, *American Inequality*.

15. On the growth of economic inequality in the last three decades of the twentieth century, see Edward N. Wolff, *Top Heavy: A Study of the Increasing Inequality of Wealth in America* (New York: Twentieth Century Fund Press, 1995); Mishel, Bernstein, and Schmitt, *State of Working America*, 37–90.

16. The measure of economic equality used in figure 92 is based on the distribution of income; specifically, it is 1- the Gini index of income inequality. Many different measures of economic equality are available, but any reasonable alternative sustains the same basic conclusion: Social capital and economic equality are positively correlated. The index of civic equality used in figure 93 is based on class differences in rates of political participation, as measured in the Roper Social and Political Trends surveys. For each of the twelve forms of political participation measured in those surveys—signing petitions, attending public meetings, and so on—we constructed the ratio of the logged incidence in the top quintile of the income distribution to the bottom quintile of the income distribution. These various measures of civic inequality were themselves highly intercorrelated, and from them (excluding the one based on running for office, which was abnormally distributed) we constructed a factor score. The scoring was reversed so that a positive number signifies relatively high civic equality or, in other words, relatively little difference in the frequency of civic participation between the wealthiest and the poorest fifth of the population. I am very grateful to Bruce P. Kennedy for constructing this measure, although I alone am responsible for its use here.

17. Private communication.

18. I am grateful to Lara Putnam for clarifying these dilemmas.

CHAPTER 23: LESSONS OF HISTORY: THE GILDED AGE AND THE PROGRESSIVE ERA

1. What follows, while consistent with conventional historical accounts, makes no pretense to be a comprehensive survey of the history of America between 1865 and 1920. For overviews of the Gilded Age and Progressive Era, see Nell Irvin Painter, *Standing at Armageddon: The United States, 1877–1919* (New York: Norton, 1987); Richard L. McCormick, "Public Life in Industrial America, 1877–1917," in *The New American History*, ed. Eric Foner (Philadelphia: Temple University Press, 1990), 93–117; John Whiteclay Chambers II, *The Tyranny of Change: America in the Progressive Era, 1890–1920* (New York: St. Martin's Press, 1992); Sean Dennis Cashman, *America in the Gilded Age: From the Death of Lincoln to the Rise of Theodore Roosevelt*, 3rd ed. (New York: New York University Press, 1993); *The Gilded Age: Essays on the Origins of Modern America*, ed. Charles W. Calhoun (Wilmington, Del.: Scholarly Resources, 1996); Mark Wahlgren Summers, *The Gilded Age: or, The Hazard of New Functions* (Upper Saddle River, N.J.: Prentice-Hall, 1997); Steven J. Diner, *A Very Different Age: Americans of the Progressive Era* (New York: Hill & Wang, 1998); Sidney M. Milkis and Jerome M. Mileur, eds., *Progressivism and the New Democracy* (Amherst, Mass.: University of Massachusetts Press, 1999). Classic interpretations include Benjamin Parke De Witt, *The Progressive Movement: A Non-partisan, Comprehensive Discussion of Current Tendencies in American Politics* (Seattle: University of Washington Press, 1968 [1915]); Richard Hofstadter, *The Age of Reform: From Bryan to F.D.R.* (New York: Alfred A. Knopf, 1985 [1955]); Samuel P. Hays, *The Response to Industrialism, 1885–1914* (Chicago: University of Chicago Press, 1957); Robert H. Wiebe, *The Search for Order: 1877–1920* (New York: Hill and Wang, 1967); Thomas Bender, *Toward an Urban Vision: Ideas and Institutions in Nineteenth Century America* (Baltimore, Md.: Johns Hopkins University Press, 1982); and Paul Boyer, *Urban Masses and Moral Order in America: 1820–1920* (Cambridge, Mass.: Harvard University Press, 1978). As a nonhistorian, I repeat the plea of the English sociologist T. H. Marshall: "It is the business of historians to sift [a] miscellaneous collection of dubious authorities and give to others the results of their careful professional assessment. And surely they will not rebuke the sociologist for putting his faith in what historians write." T. H. Marshall, *Class, Citizenship, and Social Development* (New York: Doubleday & Co., 1964), 35.

2. *Historical Statistics of the United States*, vol. 2, 958–959; Cashman, *America in the Gilded Age*, 100; Calhoun, *Gilded Age*, xii; and Howard Husock, "Elks Clubs, Settlement Houses, Labor Unions and the Anti-Saloon League: Nineteenth and Early Twentieth-Century America Copes with Change," John F. Kennedy School of Government case no. C105–97–1381.0 (Cambridge, Mass.: Harvard University, 1997), 1–2. In this chapter I draw often on this summary; I am grateful to Howard Husock for his skilled presentation of our evidence, as well as his extensive knowledge of the Progressive Era.

3. Quoted in Cashman, *America in the Gilded Age*, 19.

4. Cashman, *America in the Gilded Age*, 8–9, 23. On "island communities," see Wiebe, *Search for Order*.

5. Diner, *Very Different Age*, 49; Summers, *Gilded Age*, 283; Ralph Nelson, *Merger Movements in American Industry: 1895–1956* (Princeton, N.J.: Princeton University Press, 1959); Devra L. Golbe and Lawrence J. White, "Mergers and Acquisitions in the U.S. Economy: An Aggregate and Historical Overview," in *Mergers and Acquisitions*, ed. Alan J. Auerbach (Chicago: University of Chicago Press, 1988), 25–47, esp. figures 9.7 and 9.8 at 273 and 275; *Mergers and Acquisitions*, ed. Gregory Marchildon (Cambridge, Mass.: Cambridge University Press, 1991); Patrick Gaughan, *Mergers, Acquisitions, and Corporate Restructurings* (New York: John Wiley & Sons, Inc., 1996). For recent data, see Mergerstat at www.mergerstat.com/free_reports/free_reports_m_and_a_activity.html.

6. Glenn Porter, "Industrialization and the Rise of Big Business," in Calhoun, *Gilded Age*, 9, 14–15.

7. Thomas C. Cochran and William Miller, *The Age of Enterprise: A Social History of Industrial America* (New

York: Harper, 1961), 230, as cited in Husock, "Elks Clubs, Settlement Houses . . . ," 2; *Historical Statistics of the United States*, vol. 1, 224–225.

8. Wahlgren Summers, *Gilded Age*, 138, 122; Cashman, *America in the Gilded Age*, 354; Painter, *Standing at Armageddon*, xix–xx; Eric Arnesen, "American Workers and the Labor Movement in the Late Nineteenth Century," in Calhoun, *Gilded Age*, 42–43; Williamson and Lindert, *American Inequality*; and Claudia Goldin and Lawrence F. Katz, "The Returns to Skill across the Twentieth Century United States," unpublished ms. (Cambridge, Mass.: Harvard University Department of Economics, 1999). Economic historians seem to agree that inequality rose from the 1830s or 1840s to roughly 1910 (with the fastest increase coming early in that period), that it leveled off and perhaps declined from roughly 1910 to roughly 1940, that it certainly declined from roughly 1940 to roughly 1970, and that it certainly rose from roughly 1970 on. Reductions in inequality were concentrated around World Wars I and II.

9. Arnesen, "American Workers," 42; McCormick, "Public Life," 103. Real GNP per capita grew every year between 1896 and 1912 except for modest recessions in 1902, 1904, and 1907–1908, according to *Historical Statistics*, vol. 1, 224.

10. *Historical Statistics*, vol. 1, 8, 11–12; Robert G. Barrows, "Urbanizing America," in Calhoun, *Gilded Age*, 91–110. "Urban" was defined by the Census Bureau in this period as any place with a population of 2,500 or more. Roughly half of the new city dwellers were from the rural U.S. and half were foreign immigrants.

11. *Historical Statistics*, vol. 1, 105–06; Calhoun, *Gilded Age*, xiii; Cashman, *America in the Gilded Age*, 146. Despite these waves of immigrants, the foreign-born fraction of the population rose only from 13.2 percent in 1860 to 14.5 percent in 1910. In 1997 that figure was 9.7 percent: Dianne Schmidley and Herman A. Alvarado, "The Foreign-Born Population in the United States: March 1997 (Update)," *Current Population Reports*, no. P20–507 (Washington, D.C.: U.S. Census Bureau, March 1998).

12. Diner, *Very Different Age*, 5.

13. Cashman, *America in the Gilded Age*, 92; see also Diner, *A Very Different Age*, 101.

14. Husock, "Elks Clubs, Settlement Houses . . . ," 4, citing Cochran and Miller, *Age of Enterprise*; Painter, *Standing at Armageddon*, xx.

15. Painter, *Standing at Armageddon*, 172; McCormick, "Public Life in Industrial America," 103; Cashman, *America in the Gilded Age*, 20; Wahlgren Summers, *Gilded Age*, 4.

16. Quoted in Cashman, *America in the Gilded Age*, 354.

17. Quoted in James T. Patterson, *America in the Twentieth Century: A History*, 2nd ed. (New York: Harcourt Brace Jovanovich, 1983), 33.

18. Stacy A. Cordery, "Women in Industrializing America," in Calhoun, *Gilded Age*, 111–135.

19. Henry Adams, *The Education of Henry Adams: An Autobiography* (Boston: Houghton Mifflin, 1961 [1918]), 53.

20. Husock, "Elks Clubs, Settlement Houses . . . ," 4; Painter, *Standing at Armageddon*, xxii; Cashman, *America in the Gilded Age*, 148. Reliable crime statistics for the nineteenth century are scant, but homicide—generally considered a bellwether of violent crime—sharply increased during the first decades of the twentieth century. See Ted Robert Gurr, "Historical Trends in Violent Crime: A Critical Review of the Evidence," in *Crime and Justice: An Annual Review of Research*, vol. 3, ed. Michael Tonry and Norval Morris (Chicago: University of Chicago Press, 1981), 295–353, esp. figure 2 at 325; and Bureau of Justice Statistics, "Homicide Trends in the U.S.," at www.ojp.usdoj.gov/bjs.

21. Jacob Riis, *How the Other Half Lives* (New York: Penguin Books, 1997 [1890]), 6.

22. As cited in Painter, *Standing at Armageddon*, xxii–xxiii.

23. Josiah Strong, *The Twentieth Century City* (New York: Baker and Taylor, 1898), 181, as quoted in Richard Hofstadter, *The Age of Reform: From Bryan to F.D.R.* (New York: Knopf, 1955), 175.

24. Don S. Kirschner, *The Paradox of Professionalism: Reform and Public Service in Urban America, 1900–1940* (New York: Greenwood Press, 1986), 179; Jon C. Teaford, *The Unheralded Triumph: City Government in America, 1870–1900* (Baltimore, Md.: Johns Hopkins University Press, 1984); Terrence J. McDonald, *The Parameters of Urban Fiscal Policy: Socio-Economic Change and Political Culture in San Francisco, 1860–1906* (Berkeley: University of California Press, 1986); Barrows, "Urbanizing America," in Calhoun, *Gilded Age*, 107; Lincoln Steffens, *The Shame of the Cities* (New York: Hill and Wang, 1957 [1904]), 2.

25. Diner, *A Very Different Age*, 5. Charles W. Calhoun, "The Political Culture: Public Life and the Conduct of Politics," in *Gilded Age*, ed. Calhoun, 185–213, criticizes conventional stereotypes of politicians in the Gilded Age.

26. Cashman, *America in the Gilded Age*, 36–72, 100–134; Arnesen, "American Workers and the Labor Movement," 39–61.

27. Painter, *Standing at Armageddon*, xxix; Cashman, *America in the Gilded Age*, 97–98; Wahlgren Summers, *Gilded Age*, 174–178; Joseph R. Gusfield, *Symbolic Crusade: Status Politics and the American Temperance Movement* (Urbana: University of Illinois Press, 1963); Bordin, *Woman and Temperance*; Paul Aaron and David Musto, "Temperance and Prohibition in America: A Historical Overview," in *Alcohol and Public Policy: Beyond the Shadow of Prohibition*, eds. Mark H. Moore and Dean R. Gerstein (Washington, D.C.: National Academy Press, 1981), 127–181.

28. McCormick, "Public Life in Industrial America," 110; Cashman, *America in the Gilded Age*, 238–240, 242; Wahlgren Summers, *Gilded Age*, 156–161, 259; Leslie H. Fishel, Jr., "The African-American Experience," in Calhoun, *Gilded Age*, 137–161.

29. Wahlgren Summers, *Gilded Age*, 157; McWilliams, *Idea of Fraternity in America*, 503; Eileen L. McDonagh, "Race, Class, and Gender in the Progressive Era," in *Progressivism*, eds. Milkis and Mileur, 145–191.

30. *Emporia* (Kan.) *Gazette*, February 1, 1912, quoted in Jean B. Quandt, *From the Small Town to the Great Community: The Social Thought of Progressive Intellectuals* (New Brunswick, N.J.: Rutgers University Press, 1970), 17.

31. Diner, *Very Different Age*, 45.

32. Quandt, *Small Town to Great Community*, 23–35. Thanks to Brad Clarke for his review of Progressive political thought.

33. William Allen White, *The Old Order Changeth: A View of American Democracy* (New York: Macmillan, 1910), 250–252.

34. As quoted in Michael J. Sandel, *Democracy's Discontent: America in Search of a Public Philosophy* (Cambridge, Mass.: Harvard University Press, 1996), 208.

35. Quandt, *Small Town to Great Community*, 44–45, quoting Mary Parker Follett, *The New State* (New York: Longmans, Green, 1918), 251.

36. Quandt, *Small Town to Great Community*, 39, 41.

37. Robert Park, *Society: Collective Behavior, News and Opinion, Sociology and Modern Society*, ed. Everett Cherrington Hughes et al. (Glencoe, Ill.: Free Press, 1955 [1918]), 147, as quoted in Quandt, *Small Town to Great Community*, 146; John Dewey, *The Public and Its Problems* (Denver, Colo.: Alan Swallow, 1927), 138–139.

38. Clarke Chambers, *Seedtime of Reform: American Social Service and Social Action, 1918–1933* (Minneapolis: University of Minnesota Press, 1963); Kathleen D. McCarthy, *Noblesse Oblige: Charity and Cultural Philanthropy in Chicago, 1849–1929* (Chicago: University of Chicago Press, 1982); Paul Starr, *The Social Transformation of American Medicine* (New York: Basic Books, 1982); Judith Ann Trolander, *Professionalism and Social Change: From the Settlement House Movement to Neighborhood Centers, 1886 to the Present* (New York: Columbia University Press, 1987); William H. Wilson, *The City Beautiful Movement* (Baltimore, Md.: Johns Hopkins University Press, 1989); Robyn Muncy, *Creating a Female Dominion in American Reform, 1890–1935* (New York: Oxford University Press, 1991); Robert Fisher, *Let the People Decide: Neighborhood Organizing in America*, 2nd ed. (New York: Twayne Publishers, 1994); Steven G. Brint, *In an Age of Experts: The Changing Role of Professionals in Politics and Public Life* (Princeton, N.J.: Princeton University Press, 1994).

39. Painter, *Standing at Armageddon*, xliii; Wahlgren Summers, *Gilded Age*, 119; Patterson, *America in the Twentieth Century*, 40.

40. Diner, *Very Different Age*, 203–205; Patterson, *America in the Twentieth Century*, 40.

41. Walter Lippman, *Drift and Mastery* (Englewood Cliffs, N.J.: Prentice-Hall, 1961 [1914]), 92, quoted in Sandel, *Democracy's Discontent*, 205–206, emphasis added.

42. Booth Tarkington, *The Turmoil* (New York: Grosset & Dunlap, 1915), 2, as quoted in Barrows, "Urbanizing America," in Calhoun, *Gilded Age*, 91.

43. Barrows, "Urbanizing America," in Calhoun, *Gilded Age*, 91. Cooley quoted in *Roderick D. McKenzie on Human Ecology*, ed. Amos H. Hawley (Chicago: University of Chicago Press, 1968), 72.

44. Quandt, *Small Town to Great Community*, 5, 7.

45. Benjamin Disraeli, *Sybil, or, The Two Nations* (London: H. Colburn, 1845), bk. 2, ch. 5; Quandt, *Small Town to Great Community*, 19.

46. Quandt, *Small Town to Great Community*, 10.

47. Boyer, *Urban Masses*, esp. 161; Charles, *Service Clubs*, 25; Bender, *Urban Vision*; Hays, *Response to Industrialism*; Quandt, *Small Town to Great Community*, esp. 28; McWilliams, *Idea of Fraternity*, esp. 484.

48. Woodrow Wilson, *The New Freedom* (New York: Doubleday, Page & Company, 1913), as cited in Diner, *Very Different Age*, frontispiece and 200.

49. McWilliams, *Idea of Fraternity*, 487.

50. McCormick, "Public Life in Industrial America," in Foner, *New American History*, 103–104.

51. Skocpol, "How Americans Became Civic."

52. Theda Skocpol, "Civic America, Then and Now," in Putnam, *Dynamics of Social Capital in Comparative Perspective*; Wahlgren Summers, *Gilded Age*, 49.

53. For extensive bibliography, see Gamm and Putnam, "Growth of Voluntary Associations."

54. For methodological details, see Gamm and Putnam, "Growth of Voluntary Associations," from which figure 94 and some of the associated text are drawn.

55. See Glenn R. Carroll, "Organizational Ecology," *Annual Review of Sociology* 10 (1984): 71–93, esp. figure 2c at 88.

56. Skocpol, "How Americans Became Civic." The ratio for those that were *ever* that large is 29 of 58. More than half of all such large membership organizations that are still in existence (however attenuated) were founded in the 1870–1920 period—24 of 43.

57. *Encarta 2000 New World Almanac 2000*. Not all major associations are included in this list, but it appears to be broadly representative of American associations. A similar analysis of all associations listed in the 1999 *World Almanac* yielded virtually identical results. Claudia Goldin and Lawrence F. Katz, "The Shaping of Higher Education: The Formative Years in the United States, 1890 to 1940," *Journal of Economic Perspectives* 13 (1999): 37–61, and National Bureau of Economic Research working paper no. W6537 (April 1998), show that 1890–1910 was also the peak period in American history for founding universities and learned societies.

58. For the four previous paragraphs, see W. S. Harwood, "Secret Societies in America," *North American Review* 164 (1897): 617, 620, and David T. Beito, *From Mutual Aid to the Welfare State: Fraternal Societies and Social Services, 1890–1967* (Chapel Hill: University of North Carolina Press, 2000), quotations at 14, 10, 3, 27. Beito makes clear that one central function of fraternal organizations was to provide life, health, and accident insurance, and as those functions were assumed by private enterprise and government, beginning in the 1920s and 1930s, the fraternal orders lost an important part of their rationale.

59. McCormick, "Public Life in Industrial America," in Foner, *New American History*, 108; Skocpol, *Protecting Soldiers and Mothers*, ch. 6; Painter, *Standing at Armageddon*, esp. 105.

60. Diner, *Very Different Age*, 72, 76–101, quotation at 92. See also Beito, *From Mutual Aid to the Welfare State*, ch. 2, on mutual aid in immigrant communities.

61. Rowland Berthoff, *An Unsettled People: Social Order and Disorder in American History* (New York: Harper & Row, 1971), 273; Diner, *Very Different Age*, 91.

62. W. E. B. Du Bois, *The Philadelphia Negro: A Social Study* (New York: Schocken Books, 1967 [1899]),

224–233, as cited in Loretta J. Williams, *Black Freemasonry and Middle-Class Realities* (Columbia: University of Missouri Press, 1980), 85; Jesse Thomas Moore, Jr., *A Search for Equality: The National Urban League, 1910–1961* (University Park: Pennsylvania State University Press, 1981); Ralph Watkins, "A Reappraisal of the Role of Volunteer Associations in the African American Community," *Afro-Americans in New York Life and History* 14 (1990): 51–60; Evelyn Brooks Higginbotham, *Righteous Discontent: The Women's Movement in the Black Baptist Church, 1880–1920* (Cambridge: Harvard University Press, 1993); Firor Scott, "Most Invisible of All"; Diner, *Very Different Age*, 141–147; Wahlgren Summers, *Gilded Age*, 288. This pattern of growth is substantiated by unpublished evidence from the project described in Gamm and Putnam, "Growth of Voluntary Associations."

63. E. Brooks Holifield, "Toward a History of American Congregations," in James P. Wind and James W. Lewis, eds., *American Congregations*, vol. 2 (Chicago: University of Chicago Press, 1994), 23–53, quotation at 39–41.

64. Higginbotham, *Righteous Discontent*, 7; Arthur S. Link and Richard L. McCormick, *Progressivism* (Wheeling, Ill.: Harlan Davidson, 1983), 23; Cashman, *America in the Gilded Age*, 370; McWilliams, *Idea of Fraternity*, 479–481. On Chautauqua, see Theodore Morrison, *Chatauqua: A Center for Education, Religion, and the Arts in America* (Chicago: University of Chicago Press, 1974), quotation at 181.

65. Painter, *Standing at Armageddon*, 44, 95, *et passim*; Husock, "Elks Clubs, Settlement Houses . . . ," 7; Leo Troy, *Trade Union Membership, 1897–1962* (New York: National Bureau of Economic Research; distributed by Columbia University Press, 1965), 2. Membership faltered from 1905 to 1909, but then resumed its growth.

66. Cochran and Miller, *Age of Enterprise*, 235.

67. Boyer, *Urban Masses*; LeRoy Ashby, *Saving the Waifs: Reformers and Dependent Children, 1890–1917* (Philadelphia: Temple University Press, 1984); Dominick Cavallo, *Muscles and Morals: Organized Playgrounds and Urban Reform, 1880–1920* (Philadelphia: University of Pennsylvania Press, 1981); Lela B. Costin, "Unraveling the Mary Ellen Legend: Origins of the 'Cruelty' Movement," *Social Service Review* 65 (1991): 203–223; Michael B. Katz, "Child-Saving," *History of Education Quarterly* 26 (1986): 413–424; Macleod, *Building Character in the American Boy*; Franklin M. Reck, *The 4-H Story* (Chicago: National Committee on Boys and Girls Club Work, 1951); Michael Rosenthal, *The Character Factory: Baden-Powell and the Origins of the Boy Scout Movement* (New York: Pantheon Books, 1984); Claudia Goldin, "America's Graduation from High School: The Evolution and Spread of Secondary Schooling in the Twentieth Century," *Journal of Economic History* 58 (1998): 345–374.

68. Wahlgren Summers, *Gilded Age*, 177.

69. Husock, "Elks Clubs, Settlement Houses . . . ," 9; Painter, *Standing at Armageddon*, 107; McCormick, "Public Life in Industrial America," in Foner, *New American History*, 109; Diner, *Very Different Age*, 21–23; and Allen F. Davis, *Spearheads for Reform: The Social Settlements and the Progressive Movement, 1890–1914* (New Brunswick, N.J.: Rutgers University Press, 1984). For alternative perspectives on the settlement house movement, see Ruth Hutchinson Crocker, *Social Work and Social Order: The Settlement House Movement in Two Industrial Cities, 1889–1930* (Urbana: University of Illinois Press, 1992), and Elizabeth Lasch-Quinn, *Black Neighbors: Race and the Limits of Reform in the Settlement House Movement* (Chapel Hill: University of North Carolina Press, 1993) and the works cited there.

70. Peter Levine, *The New Progressive Era: Toward a Fair and Deliberative Democracy* (Boulder, Colo.: Rowman & Littlefield, 2000), xi. Peter G. Filene, "An Obituary for 'The Progressive Movement,'" *American Quarterly* 22 (1970): 20–34.

71. Myron T. Scudder, "Rural Recreation: A Socializing Factor," *Country Life* 40 (March 1912): 175–190, quotation at 185–86. See also Cavallo, *Muscles and Morals*, 8.

72. Michael Sandel, *Democracy's Discontent*, 210; McWilliams, *Idea of Fraternity*, 475.

73. Husock, "Elks Clubs, Settlement Houses . . . ," 8; Marvin Lazerson, "Urban Reform and the Schools: Kindergartens in Massachusetts, 1870–1915," *History of Education Quarterly* (summer 1971), 115–142; and Michael Steven Shapiro, *Child's Garden: The Kindergarten Movement from Froebel to Dewey* (University Park: Pennsylvania State University Press, 1983). Thanks to Melissa Buis for work on this and other important aspects of social capital in American history.

74. McCormick, "Public Life in Industrial America," in Foner, *New American History*, 107. American social science was born in this period as a handmaiden of reformism; see Anthony Oberschall, "The Institutionalization of American Sociology," in *The Establishment of Empirical Sociology: Studies in Continuity, Discontinuity, and Institutionalization*, ed. Anthony Oberschall (New York: Harper & Row, 1972), esp. 198, and Dorothy Ross, *The Origins of American Social Science* (Cambridge, U.K.: Cambridge University Press, 1991). For a thoughtful, thorough account of the Progressives' commitment to civic engagement and deliberative democracy, see Levine, *New Progressive Era*.

75. Diner, *Very Different Era*, 21, 202.

76. Ida M. Tarbell, *All in the Day's Work: An Autobiography* (New York: Macmillan, 1939), 82, as cited in Painter, *Standing at Armageddon*, 72; Painter, *Standing at Armageddon*, 211, 245; Diner, *Very Different Age*, 210.

77. Skocpol, "How Americans Became Civic," 61.

78. Kevin Mattson, *Creating a Democratic Public: The Struggle for Urban Participatory Democracy During the Progressive Era* (University Park: Pennsylvania State University Press, 1998), quotations at 56, 59. For a similar tale, see David C. Hammack, "Community Foundations: The Delicate Question of Purpose," reprinted in *Making the Nonprofit Sector in the United States: A Reader*, David C. Hammack, ed. (Bloomington: Indiana University Press, 1998), 330–353.

79. Gamm and Putnam, "Growth of Voluntary Associations"; Claudia Goldin and Lawrence Katz, "Human Capital and Social Capital: The Rise of Secondary Schooling in America, 1910–1940," *Journal of Interdisciplinary History* 29 (1999): 683–723; Link and McCormick, *Progressivism*, 9.

80. Jon C. Teaford, *The Unheralded Triumph*; Kenneth Fox, *Better City Government: Innovation in American Urban Politics, 1850–1937* (Philadelphia: Temple University Press, 1977); Martin J. Schiesl, *The Politics of Efficiency: Municipal Administration and Reform in America, 1880–1920* (Berkeley: University of California Press, 1977); Link and McCormick, *Progressivism*, 28–32.

81. See the trilogy of historian Morton Keller: *Affairs of State: Public Life in Late Nineteenth-Century America*

(Cambridge, Mass.: Harvard University Press, 1977); *Regulating a New Economy: Public Policy and Economic Change in America, 1900–1933* (Cambridge, Mass.: Harvard University Press, 1990); and *Regulating a New Society: Public Policy and Social Change in America, 1900–1933* (Cambridge, Mass.: Harvard University Press, 1994); Skocpol, *Protecting Soldiers and Mothers.*

82. Skocpol, *Protecting Soldiers and Mothers,* 321–372; Elisabeth S. Clemens, "Securing Political Returns to Social Capital: Women's Associations in the United States, 1880s–1920s," *Journal of Interdisciplinary History* 29 (1999): 613–638.

83. Link and McCormick, *Progressivism,* esp. ch. 3, "Social Justice and Social Control"; McCormick, "Public Life in Industrial America," in Foner, *New American History,* 110–114; McWilliams, *Idea of Fraternity,* 498–502; Philip J. Ethington, "The Metropolis and Multicultural Ethics: Direct Democracy versus Deliberative Democracy in the Progressive Era," in *Progressivism,* eds. Milkis and Mileur, 192–225, quotation at 192. On turnout, see chapter 2, figure 1, in the present book.

84. Linda Gordon, *Heroes of their Own Lives: The Politics and History of Family Violence, Boston 1880–1960* (New York: Penguin, 1988); Painter, *Standing at Armageddon,* xii.

85. C. H. Henderson, "The Place and Function of Voluntary Associations," *American Journal of Sociology* 1 (1895): 327–334; Louis Wirth, "Urbanism as a Way of Life," *American Journal of Sociology* 44 (1938): 1–24; Arthur M. Schlesinger, "Biography of a Nation of Joiners," *American Historical Review* 50 (October 1944): 1–25; and Oscar and Mary Handlin, *The Dimensions of Liberty* (Cambridge, Mass.: Belknap Press of Harvard University Press, 1961).

86. Quoted in Kirschner, *Paradox of Professionalism,* 15.

87. Husock, "Elks Clubs, Settlement Houses . . . ," 6. The second Ku Klux Klan also had anti-immigrant, anti-Catholic, anticrime, and fundamentalist components and was strongest in the Midwest, not the South.

CHAPTER 24: TOWARD AN AGENDA FOR SOCIAL CAPITALISTS

1. The Saguaro Seminar is composed of thirty-three accomplished thinkers and doers who meet regularly to develop actionable ideas to increase Americans' connectedness to one another and to community institutions. Participants come from diverse backgrounds, professions, and parts of the country; they have included Xavier de Souza Briggs, Bliss Browne, Kirbyjon Caldwell, John DiIulio, E. J. Dionne, Carolyn Doggett, Lewis Feldstein, Chris Gates, Stephen Goldsmith, Amy Gutmann, Henry Izumizaki, Louise Kennedy, Vanessa Kirsch, Carol Lamm, Liz Lerman, Glenn Loury, John Mascotte, Martha Minow, Mark Moore, Barack Obama, Peter Pierce, Ralph Reed, Paul Resnick, Kris Rondeau, Tom Sander, Juan Sepúlveda, Robert Sexton, Harry Spence, George Stephanopoulos, Dorothy Stoneman, Lisa Sullivan, Jim Wallis, Vin Weber, and William Julius Wilson. None bears any responsibility for my recommendations here. More information about the Saguaro Seminar can be found by contacting the Seminar staff at the John F. Kennedy School of Government, Harvard University, or at ksgwww.harvard.edu/saguaro. For a complementary compendium of recommendations for revitalizing American democracy, see Levine, *New Progressive Era.*

2. Delli Carpini and Keeter, *What Americans Know About Politics and Why It Matters;* A. D. Lutkus et al., *The NAEP 1998 Civics Report Card for the Nation* (Washington, D.C.: U.S. Department of Education, National Center for Education Statistics, 1999).

3. Fred M. Newmann and Robert A. Rutter, "The Effects of High School Community Service Programs on Students' Social Development" (Washington, D.C.: National Institute of Education, December 1983); Virginia Hodgkinson and Murray S. Weitzman, *Volunteering and Giving Among Teenagers 12 to 17 Years of Age* (Washington, D.C.: Independent Sector, 1997); Richard Battistoni, "Service Learning and Democratic Citizenship," *Theory into Practice* 35 (1997): 150–156; Thomas Janoski, Mark Musick, and John Wilson, "Being Volunteered? The Impact of Social Participation and Pro-Social Attitudes on Volunteering," *Sociological Forum* 13 (September 1998): 495–519; Alan Melchior and Larry Orr, *Evaluation of National and Community Service Programs, Overview: National Evaluation of Serve-America (Subtitle B1)* (Washington, D.C.: Corporation for National Service, October 20, 1995); Alexander W. Astin and Linda J. Sax, "How Undergraduates Are Affected by Service Participation," *Journal of College Student Development* 39, no. 3 (May/June 1998): 251–263; Dwight E. Giles Jr. and Janet Eyler, "The Impact of a College Community Service Laboratory on Students' Personal, Social, and Cognitive Outcomes," *Journal of Adolescence* 17 (1994): 327–339; Richard G. Niemi, Mary Hepburn, and Chris Chapman, "Community Service by High School Students: A Cure for Civic Ills?" *Political Behavior* (forthcoming, 2000) and the works cited there. "Service learning" refers to community service that is coupled to classwork, and most observers believe that it is more effective in inculcating civic habits. In 1999 about 57 percent of U.S. students in grades 6–12 participated in some form of community service, up from 49 percent in 1996; on the other hand, only slightly more than half of them (30 percent of all students) engaged in service learning. See "Youth Service-Learning and Community Service among 6th- through 12th-Grade Students in the United States, 1996 and 1999" (Washington, D.C.: National Center for Education Statistics, 1999).

4. James Youniss, Jeffrey A. McLellan, and Miranda Yates, "What We Know about Engendering Civic Identity," *American Behavioral Scientist* (March/April 1997): 620–631; Elizabeth Smith, "Extracurricular Activities and Political Participation: Exploring the Connection," paper presented at 1998 Midwestern Political Science Association, unpublished ms., 1998; Michael Hanks, "Youth, Voluntary Associations, and Political Socialization," *Social Forces* 60 (1981): 211–223; Verba, Schlozman, and Brady, *Voice and Equality,* 423–442, 449, 452; Paul Allen Beck and M. Kent Jennings, "Pathways to Participation," *American Political Science Review* 76 (1982): 94–108; David Ziblatt, "High School Extracurricular Activities and Political Socialization," *Annals of the American Academy of Political and Social Science* 361 (1965): 20–31; John Wilson and Thomas Janoski, "Contribution of Religion to Volunteer Work," *Sociology of Religion* 56 (1995): 137–152; Nicholas Zill, Christin Winquist Nord, and Laura Spencer Loomis, "Adolescent Time Use, Risky Behavior, and Outcomes: An Analysis of National Data" (at http://aspe.os.dhhs.gov/hsp/cyp/xstimuse.htm).

5. Sandra E. Black and Lisa M. Lynch, "How to Compete: The Impact of Workplace Practices and Information Technology on Productivity" (Cambridge, Mass.: National Bureau of Economic Research working paper Series

#6120, August 1997); *Report on the American Workforce 1999*, 103. More generally on issues of work, family, and community, see the publications of the Families and Work Institute at www.familiesandwork.org/.

6. One group experimenting in this area is Working Today (www.workingtoday.org).

7. For a reasoned discussion of alternatives for reducing sprawl, see Richard Moe and Carter Wilkie, *Changing Places: Rebuilding Community in the Age of Sprawl* (New York: Henry Holt, 1997).

8. For an overview, see William Fulton, *New Urbanism: Hope or Hype for American Communities?* (Cambridge, Mass.: Lincoln Institute of Land Policy, 1996). The Congress for the New Urbanism (www.cnu.org) forged a charter to which builders, architects, planners, government officials, and others subscribe.

9. For nuanced first-person impressions of Celebration, see Douglas Frantz and Catherine Collins, *Celebration, U.S.A.: Living in Disney's Brave New Town* (New York: Henry Holt, 1999), and Andrew Ross, *The Celebration Chronicles: Life, Liberty and the Pursuit of Property Value in Disney's New Town* (New York: Ballantine Books, 1999).

10. John L. McKnight and John P. Kretzmann, *Building Communities from the Inside Out: A Path Toward Finding and Mobilizing a Community's Assets* (Chicago, Ill.: ACTA Publications, 1993); Harry C. Boyte and Nancy N. Kari, *Building America: The Democratic Promise of Public Work* (Philadelphia: Temple University Press, 1996). The Texas Industrial Areas Foundation, led by Ernesto Cortes, has pioneered many effective community organizing techniques; for a useful overview, see Mark Russell Warren, *Social Capital and Community Empowerment: Religion and Political Organization in the Texas Industrial Areas Foundation* (Ph.D. diss., Harvard University Department of Sociology, 1995). On CDCs and social capital, see *Urban Problems and Community Development*, Ferguson and Dickens, eds., and Xavier de Souza Briggs and Elizabeth Mueller, *From Neighborhood to Community: Evidence on the Social Effects of Community Development* (New York: Community Development Research Center, New School for Social Research, 1997).

11. William G. McLoughlin, *Revivals, Awakenings, and Reform*; Marshall William Fishwick, *Great Awakenings: Popular Religion and Popular Culture* (New York: Haworth Press, 1995); Anne Boylan, *Sunday School: The Formation of an American Institution, 1790–1880* (New Haven, Conn.: Yale University Press, 1988); Boyer, *Urban Masses and Moral Order*, 34–53.

12. Diane Winston, *Red-Hot and Righteous: The Urban Religion of the Salvation Army* (Cambridge, Mass.: Harvard University Press, 1999).

13. In 1995 a number of evangelicals, spearheaded by Jim Wallis of Sojourners, formed an evangelical coalition spanning the political spectrum from ultra-liberal to ultra-conservative. See Jim Wallis, *Faith Works* (New York: Random House, 2000). See also Howard Husock, "Bringing Back the Settlement House," *The Public Interest* 109 (Fall 1992): 53–72.

14. Lewis A. Friedland, Jay Rosen, and Lisa Austin, *Civic Journalism: A New Approach to Citizenship* (1994) at www.cpn.org/sections/topics/journalism; Jay Rosen and Paul Taylor, *The New News v. the Old News: Press and Politics in the 1990s* (New York: Twentieth Century Fund Press, 1992); James Fallows, *Breaking the News* (New York: Vintage Books, 1997); Frank Denton and Esther Thorson, "Civic Journalism: Does It Work?" (a Special Report for the Pew Center for Civic Journalism, 1997), available at www.pewcenter.org/doingcj/research/r_doesit.html. For a thoughtful critique, see Charlotte Grimes, "Whither the Civic Journalism Bandwagon?" Discussion Paper D-36, Joan Shorenstein Center on Press and Politics (John F. Kennedy School of Government, Harvard University: 1999).

15. Keith Hampton and Barry Wellman, "Examining Community in the Digital Neighborhood: Early Results from Canada's Wired Suburb," in *Lecture Notes in Computer Science*, Toru Ishida and Katherine Isbister, eds. (Berlin: Springer-Verlag, 2000); Andrea Kavanaugh, "The Impact of the Internet on Community: A Social Network Analysis" (Blacksburg, Va.: Blacksburg Electronic Village, Virginia Polytechnic Institute and State University, 1999); Andrew S. Patrick, "Personal and Social Impacts of Going On-Line: Lessons from the National Capital FreeNet" (Ottawa, Canada: Communications Research Center, 1997), at http://debra.dgbt.doc.ca/services-research/survey/impacts. Caution is appropriate in assessing these early returns, especially given the possibility of self-selection. More generally, see Douglas Schuler, *New Community Networks: Wired for Change* (New York: Addison-Wesley, 1996).

16. For information on some of the projects cited here, see: Liz Lerman Dance Exchange at www.danceexchange.org/lizhome.html; Roadside Theater at www.appalshop.org/rst/99rstabt.htm; Baltimore Museum of Art at www.artbma.org; Galley 37 at www.gallery37.org. See also *Opening the Door to the Entire Community: How Museums Are Using Permanent Collections to Engage Audiences* (New York: Lila Wallace Reader's Digest Fund, November 1998), available at www.wallacefunds.org/lilaframesetpub.htm.

17. On Indianapolis's Front Porch Alliance, see www.indygov.com/mayor/fpa/. On neighborhood government, see Berry, Portney, and Thomson, *The Rebirth of Urban Democracy*.

AFTERWORD: HAS THE INTERNET REVERSED THE DECLINE OF SOCIAL CAPITAL?

1. Dan Balz and Emily Guskin, "Poll Finds Universal Lifestyle Changes, Rising Stress and Growing Fears About Catching Coronavirus," *Washington Post*, March 27, 2020, https://www.washingtonpost.com/politics/poll-finds-universal-lifestyle-changes-rising-stress-and-growing-fears-about-catching-coronavirus/2020/03/26/11360bb2-6f5e-11ea-b148-e4ce3fbd85b5_story.html.

2. For further treatment of the theory of social capital, see pages 19–24 of the present book, as well as Robert D. Putnam and Kristin A. Goss, "Introduction," in Robert D. Putnam, ed., *Democracies in Flux: The Evolution of Social Capital in Contemporary Society* (New York: Oxford University Press, 2002).

3. Marshall van Alstyne and Erik Brynjolfsson, "Electronic Communities: Global Village or Cyberbalkans?" (1996), http://web.mit.edu/marshall/www/Abstracts.html, accessed on October 1, 1999.

4. Of our speculations about potential obstacles to Internet-based social capital, only one proved shortsighted, but the error was a doozy! We speculated that bandwidth limitations would inhibit the transmission of high-fidelity images and thus impede nonverbal communication. Technology quickly overcame the bandwidth problem, although during the Zoom boom of 2020 some users did find it hard to read the tiny faces on crowded screens.

5. See page 180 of the present book.

6. Peter Schwartz and Peter Leyden, "The Long Boom: A History of the Future, 1980–2020," *Wired*, July 1, 1997, https://www.wired.com/1997/07/longboom/.

7. John Perry Barlow, "A Declaration of the Independence of Cyberspace," Electronic Frontier Foundation, February 8, 1996, https://www.eff.org/cyberspace-independence.

8. Joseph Bernstein, "Alienated, Alone and Angry: What the Digital Revolution Really Did to Us," *BuzzFeed News*, December 17, 2019, https://www.buzzfeednews.com/article/josephbernstein/in-the-2010s-decade-we-became-alienated-by-technology.

9. Paul Hitlin, "Internet, Social Media Use and Device Ownership in U.S. Have Plateaued After Years of Growth," Pew Research Center, September 28, 2018, https://www.pewresearch.org/fact-tank/2018/09/28/internet-social-media-use-and-device-ownership-in-u-s-have-plateaued-after-years-of-growth/.

10. Kim Parker and Ruth Igielnik, "On the Cusp of Adulthood and Facing an Uncertain Future: What We Know about Gen Z So Far," Pew Research Center, May 14, 2020, https://www.pewsocialtrends.org/essay/on-the-cusp-of-adulthood-and-facing-an-uncertain-future-what-we-know-about-gen-z-so-far/?utm_source=pew+research+center&utm_campaign=1be8fdcbcc-weekly_2020_05_16&utm_medium=email&utm_term=0_3e953b9b70-1be8fdcbcc-399483209.

11. "Social Media Fact Sheet," Pew Research Center, June 12, 2019, https://www.pewresearch.org/internet/fact-sheet/social-media/. See also Diana Orcés, "Who Uses Social Media Most Frequently?," Public Religion Research Institute, May 22, 2020, https://www.prri.org/spotlight/who-uses-social-media-most-frequently/.

12. Monica Anderson and Jingjing Jiang, "Teens, Social Media & Technology 2018," Pew Research Center, May 31, 2018, https://www.pewresearch.org/internet/2018/05/31/teens-social-media-technology-2018/.

13. Because turnover in popular sites is so rapid, the details in figure B are likely to be outdated before long, especially for teenagers, but they capture an important pre-COVID-19 reality.

14. Sources for the chart: Andrew Perrin and Monica Anderson, "Share of U.S. Adults Using Social Media, Including Facebook, Is Mostly Unchanged Since 2018," Pew Research Center, April 10, 2019, https://www.pewresearch.org/fact-tank/2019/04/10/share-of-u-s-adults-using-social-media-including-facebook-is-mostly-unchanged-since-2018/; Anderson and Jiang, "Teens, Social Media & Technology 2018." TikTok is excluded from the chart only because it was not included in the Pew survey.

15. Kevin Roose, *Rabbit Hole*, podcast, *New York Times*, April 22, 2020–June 4, 2020, https://www.nytimes.com/column/rabbit-hole.

16. Cristos Goodrow, "You Know What's Cool? A Billion Hours," YouTube Official Blog, February 27, 2017, https://youtube.googleblog.com/2017/02/you-know-whats-cool-billion-hours.html.

17. For evidence that the trends in conventional or "face-to-face" social capital discussed in *Bowling Alone* have continued in the same direction in the ensuing years, see Robert D. Putnam and Shaylyn Romney Garrett, *The Upswing* (New York: Simon & Schuster, 2020), chapter 4.

18. Claude S. Fischer, "Technology and Community: Historical Complexities," *Sociological Inquiry* 67 (February 1997): 113–118.

19. Sara Wilson, "The Era of Antisocial Social Media," *Harvard Business Review*, February 5, 2020, https://hbr.org/2020/02/the-era-of-antisocial-social-media.

20. Michael Castleman, "Dueling Statistics: How Much of the Internet Is Porn?," *Psychology Today*, November 3, 2016, https://www.psychologytoday.com/us/blog/all-about-sex/201611/dueling-statistics-how-much-the-internet-is-porn.

21. Many, perhaps even most, platforms have multiple uses, so any classification scheme has overlapping gray areas (for example, YouTube, Reddit, and Tumblr), while some platforms (podcasts) are very much like pre-digital media (for example, talk radio). In this necessarily limited overview of social media, we must forgo such details of classification.

22. Kevin Roose, "The Coronavirus Crisis Is Showing Us How to Live Online," *New York Times*, March 17, 2020, updated April 2, 2020, https://www.nytimes.com/2020/03/17/technology/coronavirus-how-to-live-online.html.

23. Kaveri Subrahmanyam et al., "Online and Offline Social Networks: Use of Social Networking Sites by Emerging Adults," *Journal of Applied Developmental Psychology* 29, no. 6 (2008): 420–433, https://doi.org/10.1016/j.appdev.2008.07.003; Nicole B. Ellison, Charles Steinfield, and Cliff Lampe, "Connection Strategies: Social Capital Implications of Facebook-Enabled Communication Practices," *New Media & Society* 13, no. 6 (September 2011): 873–892, doi:10.1177/1461444810385389; Lee Rainie and Barry Wellman, *Networked: The New Social Operating System* (Cambridge, Mass.: MIT Press, 2012).

24. For one illustration, see Adrien Chen, "Unmasking Reddit's Violentacrez, the Biggest Troll on the Web," *Gawker*, October 12, 2012, https://gawker.com/5950981/unmasking-reddits-violentacrez-the-biggest-troll-on-the-web.

25. Putnam personally experienced this transition. During the semester that Zuckerberg invented Facebook at Harvard, one of his roommates happened to be a student in Putnam's small undergraduate seminar, so that class became a beta tester. Obviously, all the "friends" in that Facebook group were friends who would see each other face-to-face at least weekly. "Friend" was not merely a cybermetaphor. When Facebook went global, however, suddenly anyone on Facebook anywhere in the world could "friend" anyone else, regardless of whether they knew each other. Since Putnam became somewhat visible, he now gets daily friend requests from unknown people (or bots?) around the world. As a matter of principle, he has refused to accept requests from people he's not met face-to-face, so all his "friends" are also friends.

26. Charles Croom, Bay Gross, Larry D. Rosen, and Brad Rosen, "What's Her Face(book)? How Many of Their Facebook 'Friends' Can College Students Actually Identify?," *Computers in Human Behavior* 56 (March 2016): 135–141, https://doi.org/10.1016/j.chb.2015.11.015.

27. Alistair G. Sutcliffe, Jens F. Binder, and Robin I. M. Dunbar, "Activity in Social Media and Intimacy in Social Relationships," *Computers in Human Behavior* 85 (August 2018): 227–235, https://doi.org/10.1016/j.chb.2018.03.050.

28. Mark Zuckerberg, "One of our big focus areas for 2018 is making sure the time we all spend on Facebook is time well spent," Facebook, January 11, 2018, https://www.facebook.com/zuck/posts/10104413015393571;

Mark Zuckerberg, "Bringing the World Closer Together," Facebook, June 22, 2017, https://www.facebook.com/notes/mark-zuckerberg/bringing-the-world-closer-together/10154944663901634/.

29. Zuckerberg, "Bringing the World Closer Together."

30. For a discussion of the challenges facing Facebook groups, see Ashley Carman, "Facebook Groups Are Falling Apart Over Black Lives Matter Posts," *The Verge*, June 5, 2020, https://www.theverge.com/2020/6/5/21279319/facebook-group-moderation-black-lives-matter-movement.

31. Pete Davis, "CommonPlace," https://petedavis.org/tag/commonplace/; https://nextdoor.com/neighborhood/fairwayoaksabilene–abilene–tx/.

32. Keith Hampton, Lauren Sessions Goulet, Eun Ja Her, and Lee Rainie, "Overview" to "Social Isolation and New Technology," Pew Research Center, November 4, 2009, 5–11.

33. Hunt Allcott et al., "The Welfare Effects of Social Media," National Bureau of Economic Research working paper no. 25514 (Cambridge, Mass.: National Bureau of Economic Research, January 2019, rev. November 2019), https://doi.org/10.3386/w25514. As we shall discuss later, the Allcott team randomly encouraged some subjects to use Facebook frequently and paid others to abstain from using it, a research design that comes close to a pure test of causation, not mere correlation.

34. See, for example, Jeffrey Boase and Barry Wellman, "Personal Relationships: On and Off the Internet," in Anita L. Vangelisti and Daniel Perlman, eds., *The Cambridge Handbook of Personal Relationships* (Cambridge: Cambridge University Press, 2006), 709–723.

35. Andrea Miconi, "Review of Lee Rainie and Barry Wellman, Networked: The New Social Operating System," *International Journal of Communication* 7 (2013), Book Review: 954–959.

36. Shelley Boulianne, "Social Media Use and Participation: A Meta-Analysis of Current Research," *Information, Communication & Society* 18, no. 5 (2015): 524–538, https://doi.org/10.1080/1369118X.2015.1008542.

37. Andrea Geraci et al., "Broadband Internet and Social Capital," IZA Discussion Papers 11855, Institute of Labor Economics (IZA), September 2018. Geraci and colleagues also found, though, that Internet access apparently had no effect one way or the other on informal social interaction, such as talking with neighbors or meeting with friends.

38. Scott Wallsten, "What Are We Not Doing When We Are Online?," in Avi Goldfarb, Shane M. Greenstein, and Catherine E. Tucker, eds., *Economic Analysis of the Digital Economy* (Chicago: University of Chicago Press, 2015), 55–82.

39. Allcott et al., "The Welfare Effects of Social Media." See also Roger Patulny and Claire Seaman, "'I'll Just Text You': Is Face-to-Face Social Contact Declining in a Mediated World?," *Journal of Sociology* 53, no. 2 (June 2017): 285–302, https://doi.org/10.1177/1440783316674358.

40. Sherry Turkle, *Alone Together: Why We Expect More from Technology and Less from Each Other*, rev. ed. (New York: Basic Books, 2017). Several experiments have found that smartphone use during face-to-face social interaction appears to interfere with the pleasure usually associated with in-person interaction. See Jean M. Twenge, "The Sad State of Happiness in the United States and the Role of Digital Media," in John F. Helliwell, Richard Layard, and Jeffrey D. Sachs, eds., *World Happiness Report 2019* (New York: Sustainable Development Solutions Network, 2019), chapter 5, https://worldhappiness.report/ed/2019/the-sad-state-of-happiness-in-the-united-states-and-the-role-of-digital-media/. For an opposing, skeptical view, see Claude S. Fischer, "Smartphones Aren't Anti-Social," *Boston Review*, September 30, 2015, http://bostonreview.net/blog/claude-fischer-sherry-turkle-smart-phone-social-communication.

41. Emily A. Vogels, "10 Facts About Americans and Online Dating," Pew Research Center, February 6, 2020, https://www.pewresearch.org/fact-tank/2020/02/06/10-facts-about-americans-and-online-dating/.

42. Michael J. Rosenfeld, Reuben J. Thomas, and Sonia Hausen, "Disintermediating Your Friends: How Online Dating in the United States Displaces Other Ways of Meeting," *Proceedings of the National Academy of Sciences* 116, no. 36 (September 2019): 17753–17758, doi: 10.1073/pnas.1908630116.

43. Eli J. Finkel, Paul W. Eastwick, Benjamin R. Karney, Harry T. Reis, and Susan Sprecher, "Online Dating: A Critical Analysis from the Perspective of Psychological Science," *Psychological Science in the Public Interest* 13, no. 1 (January 2012): 3–66, https://doi.org/10.1177/1529100612436522.

44. Rebecca Heino, Nicole Ellison, and Jennifer Gibbs, "Relationshopping: Investigating the Market Metaphor in Online Dating," *Journal of Social and Personal Relationships* 27 (2010): 427–447, 10.1177/0265407510361614.

45. Vogels, "10 Facts About Americans and Online Dating."

46. Monica Anderson et al., "Public Attitudes Toward Political Engagement on Social Media," Pew Research Center, July 11, 2018, https://www.pewresearch.org/internet/2018/07/11/public-attitudes-toward-political-engagement-on-social-media/.

47. W. Lance Bennett and Alexandra Segerberg, "The Logic of Connective Action: Digital Media and the Personalization of Contentious Politics," *Information, Communication & Society* 15, no. 5 (June 2012): 739–768, https://doi.org/10.1080/1369118X.2012.670661.

48. Shelley Boulianne, "Social Media Use and Participation: A Meta-Analysis of Current Research," *Information, Communication & Society* 18, no. 5 (March 2015): 524–538, https://doi.org/10.1080/1369118X.2015.1008542.

49. See pages 152–153 and 338 in the present book.

50. David Karpf, "Analytic Activism and Its Limitations," *Social Media + Society* 4, no. 1 (January 2018): 6. On the complementary role of Internet and face-to-face organizing, see Lara Putnam and Theda Skocpol, "Middle America Reboots Democracy," *Democracy: A Journal of Ideas*, February 20, 2018, https://democracyjournal.org/arguments/middle-america-reboots-democracy/; Hahrie Han, "When Does Activism Become Powerful?," *New York Times*, December 16, 2019, https://www.nytimes.com/2019/12/16/opinion/activism-power-victories.html; and Dana Fisher, *American Resistance: From the Women's March to the Blue Wave* (New York: Columbia University Press, 2019).

51. Hahrie Han, *How Organizations Develop Activists: Civic Associations and Leadership in the 21st Century* (New York: Oxford University Press, 2014); Nicole Carty, "The Key to Saving the World in the Era of Social Media May Be Real Human Connection," *Medium*, March 25, 2019, https://medium.com/@nicolecarty/the-key-to-saving-the-world-in-the-era-of-social-media-may-be-real-human-connection-41ba6e74b21. See also Zeynep Tufekci, *Twitter and Tear Gas: The Power and Fragility of Networked Protest* (New Haven, Conn.: Yale University Press, 2017).

52. See pages 44–46 in the present book.

53. Kevin Lewis, Kurt Gray, and Jens Meierhenrich, "The Structure of Online Activism," *Sociological Science* 1 (February 2014): 1–9, doi: 10.15195/v1.a1.

54. Ben McGuire, "Political Organizing in the Digital Age: Why Campaigns Need to Integrate Traditional and Digital Organizing," *Kennedy School Review*, August 22, 2018, https://ksr.hkspublications.org/2018/08/22/political-organizing-in-the-digital-age-why-campaigns-need-to-integrate-traditional-and-digital-organizing/.

55. Kay Lehman Schlozman, Sidney Verba, and Henry E. Brady, "Weapon of the Strong?: Participatory Inequality and the Internet," *Perspectives on Politics* 8, no. 2 (2010): 487–509, especially 491–492, doi:10.1017 /S1537592710001210; "Social Media Fact Sheet," Pew Research Center, June 12, 2019, https://www.pewresearch.org /internet/fact-sheet/social-media/; Eszter Hargittai, "Potential Biases in Big Data: Omitted Voices on Social Media," *Social Science Computer Review* 38, no. 1 (2020): 10–24, https://doi.org/10.1177/0894439318788322.

56. Dana Floberg, "The Racial Digital Divide Persists," *Free Press*, December 13, 2018, https://www.freepress .net/our-response/expert-analysis/insights-opinions/racial-digital-divide-persists.

57. Kathryn Zichuhr and Aaron Smith, "Digital Differences," Pew Research Center, April 13, 2012, http:// pewinternet.org/~/media//Files/Reports/2012/PIP_Digital_differences_041312.pdf; Andrew Perrin, "Digital Gap Between Rural and Nonrural America Persists," Pew Research Center, May 31, 2019, https://www.pewresearch.org/fact -tank/2019/05/31/digital-gap-between-rural-and-nonrural-america-persists/.

58. Eszter Hargittai and Amanda Hinnant, "Digital Inequality: Differences in Young Adults' Use of the Internet," *Communication Research* 35 (October 2008): 602–621; Fred Rothbaum, Nancy Martland, and Joanne Beswick Jannsen, "Parents' Reliance on the Web to Find Information about Children and Families: Socio-Economic Differences in Use, Skills and Satisfaction," *Journal of Applied Developmental Psychology* 29 (March–April 2008): 118–128; Eszter Hargittai and Yuli Patrick Hsieh, "Digital Inequality," in William H. Dutton, ed., *The Oxford Handbook of Internet Studies* (New York: Oxford University Press, 2013), 129–150.

59. danah boyd, *It's Complicated: The Social Lives of Networked Teens* (New Haven, Conn.: Yale University Press, 2014), 171–174.

60. Cass Sunstein, quoted in Dan Kopf, "Social Media's Effect on Democracy Is 'Alexander Hamilton's Nightmare,'" *Quartz*, March 17, 2017, https://qz.com/933150/cass-sunstein-says-social-medias-effect-on-democracy-is-al exander-hamiltons-nightmare/. This question of the impact of contact across ideological lines on polarization is controversial, since some studies seem to find that more contact with one's opponents can increase extreme polarization. See Christopher A. Bail et al., "Exposure to Opposing Views on Social Media Can Increase Political Polarization," *Proceedings of the National Academy of Sciences* 115, no. 37 (September 2018): 9216–9221, doi: 10.1073 /pnas.1804840115.

61. Putnam and Garrett, *The Upswing*, chapter 3, provides detailed citations to the literature supporting the generalizations in this paragraph.

62. Ethan Kaplan, Jörg Spenkuch, and Rebecca Sullivan, "Measuring Geographic Polarization: Theory and Long-Run Evidence," January 2019, http://econweb.umd.edu/~kaplan/big_sort_APSA.pdf.

63. Nolan McCarty, Keith T. Poole, and Howard Rosenthal, *Polarized America: The Dance of Ideology and Unequal Riches*, 2nd ed. (Cambridge, Mass.: MIT Press, 2016); Shanto Iyengar, Gaurav Sood, and Yphtach Lelkes, "Affect, Not Ideology," *Public Opinion Quarterly* 76, no. 3 (September 2012): 405–431, https://doi.org/10.1093/poq/nfs038.

64. Yphtach Lelkes, "Mass Polarization: Manifestations and Measurements," *Public Opinion Quarterly* 80, no. S1 (2016): 392–410.

65. Joshua A. Tucker et al., "Social Media, Political Polarization and Political Disinformation: A Review of the Scientific Literature," March 2018, https://ssrn.com/abstract=3144139.

66. Yphtach Lelkes, Gaurav Sood, and Shanto Iyengar, "The Hostile Audience: The Effect of Access to Broadband Internet on Partisan Affect," *American Journal of Political Science* 61, no. 1 (January 2017): 5–20, https://doi .org/10.1111/ajps.12237.

67. Miller McPherson, Lynn Smith-Lovin, and James M. Cook, "Birds of a Feather: Homophily in Social Networks," *Annual Review of Sociology* 27 (2001): 415–444.

68. danah boyd, *It's Complicated*, 167–171.

69. Ibid., 158–159.

70. Eytan Bakshy, Solomon Messing, and Lada A. Adamic, "Exposure to Ideologically Diverse News and Opinion on Facebook," *Science* 348, no. 6239 (June 2015): 1130–1132, https://doi.org/10.1126/science.aaa1160.

71. Bail et al., "Exposure to Opposing Views on Social Media Can Increase Political Polarization."

72. R. Kelly Garrett, "Echo Chambers Online?: Politically Motivated Selective Exposure Among Internet News Users," *Journal of Computer-Mediated Communication* 14, no. 2 (January 2009): 265–285, https://doi.org/10.1111 /j.1083-6101.2009.01440.x; Solomon Messing and Sean J. Westwood, "Selective Exposure in the Age of Social Media: Endorsements Trump Partisan Source Affiliation When Selecting News Online," *Communication Research* 41, no. 8 (December 2014): 1042–63, https://doi.org/10.1177/0093650212466406; Bakshy, Messing, and Adamic, "Exposure to Ideologically Diverse News and Opinion on Facebook"; Matthew Barnidge, "Exposure to Political Disagreement in Social Media Versus Face-to-Face and Anonymous Online Settings," *Political Communication* 34, no. 2 (April 2017): 302–321, https://doi.org/10.1080/10584609.2016.1235639; Yonghwan Kim, "The Contribution of Social Network Sites to Exposure to Political Difference: The Relationships Among SNSs, Online Political Messaging, and Exposure to Cross-Cutting Perspectives," *Computers in Human Behavior* 27, no. 2 (March 2011): 971–977, https:// doi.org/10.1016/j.chb.2010.12.001; Yonghwan Kim, Shih-Hsien Hsu, and Homero Gil de Zúñiga, "Influence of Social Media Use on Discussion Network Heterogeneity and Civic Engagement: The Moderating Role of Personality Traits: Social Media & Personality Traits," *Journal of Communication* 63, no. 3 (June 2013): 498–516, https://doi .org/10.1111/jcom.12034; Patrick Ferrucci, Toby Hopp, and Chris J. Vargo, "Civic Engagement, Social Capital, and Ideological Extremity: Exploring Online Political Engagement and Political Expression on Facebook," *New Media & Society* 22, no. 6 (June 2020): 1095–1115, https://doi.org/10.1177/1461444819873110; Pablo Barberá and Gonzalo Rivero, "Understanding the Political Representativeness of Twitter Users," *Social Science Computer Review* 33,

no. 6 (December 2015): 712–729, https://doi.org/10.1177/0894439314558836. For a contrary view, see Levi Boxell, Matthew Gentzkow, and Jesse M. Shapiro, "Greater Internet Use Is Not Associated with Faster Growth in Political Polarization Among US Demographic Groups," *Proceedings of the National Academy of Sciences* 114, no. 40 (October 2017): 10612–10617, https://doi.org/10.1073/pnas.1706588114; or Matthew Gentzkow and Jesse M. Shapiro, "Ideological Segregation Online and Offline," *Quarterly Journal of Economics* 126, no. 4 (November 2011): 1799–1839, https://doi.org/10.1093/qje/qjr044.

73. Quoted in Peter Wehner, "Jonathan Haidt Is Trying to Heal America's Divisions," *The Atlantic*, May 24, 2020, https://www.theatlantic.com/ideas/archive/2020/05/jonathan-haidt-pandemic-and-americas-polarization/612025/.

74. Molly J. Crockett, "Moral Outrage in the Digital Age," *Nature Human Behaviour* 1, no. 11 (November 2017): 769–771, https://doi.org/10.1038/s41562-017-0213-3; Bakshy, Messing, and Adamic, "Exposure to Ideologically Diverse News and Opinion on Facebook"; Matthew Barnidge, "The Role of News in Promoting Political Disagreement on Social Media," *Computers in Human Behavior* 52 (November 2015): 211–218, https://doi.org/10.1016/j.chb.2015.06.011. See also Karsten Müller and Carlo Schwarz, "Fanning the Flames of Hate: Social Media and Hate Crime," 2018, https://warwick.ac.uk/fac/soc/economics/research/c...373–2018_schwarz.pdf; Karsten Müller and Carlo Schwarz, "Making America Hate Again?: Twitter and Hate Crime Under Trump," October 31, 2019, doi: 10.2139/ssrn.3149103.

75. Elizabeth Suhay, Emily Bello-Pardo, and Brianna Maurer, "The Polarizing Effects of Online Partisan Criticism: Evidence from Two Experiments," *International Journal of Press/Politics* 23, no. 1 (January 2018): 95–115, https://doi.org/10.1177/1940161217740697; Allcott et al., "The Welfare Effects of Social Media."

76. Jeff Horwitz and Deepa Seetharaman, "Facebook Executives Shut Down Efforts to Make the Site Less Divisive," *Wall Street Journal*, May 26, 2020, https://www.wsj.com/articles/facebook-knows-it-encourages-division-top-executives-nixed-solutions-11590507499.

77. Leticia Bode, "Pruning the News Feed: Unfriending and Unfollowing Political Content on Social Media," *Research & Politics* 3, no. 3 (2016): 1–8.

78. Gregory Asmolov, "The Disconnective Power of Disinformation Campaigns," *Journal of International Affairs* 71, no. 1.5 (2018): 69–76.

79. Eli Pariser, *The Filter Bubble: What the Internet Is Hiding from You* (New York: Penguin Press, 2011).

80. Lev Muchnik, Sinan Aral, and Sean J. Taylor, "Social Influence Bias: A Randomized Experiment," *Science* 341, no. 6146 (August 2013): 647–651, https://doi.org/10.1126/science.1240466. After a period of five months, a single positive initial vote artificially increased the mean rating of a story by 25 percent.

81. Jaime E. Settle, *Frenemies: How Social Media Polarizes America* (Cambridge: Cambridge University Press, 2018).

82. Disinformation is intentional, while misinformation is not necessarily.

83. Horwitz and Seetharaman, "Facebook Executives Shut Down Efforts."

84. Cass R. Sunstein, *#Republic: Divided Democracy in the Age of Social Media* (Princeton, N.J.: Princeton University Press, 2017).

85. See chapter 20 of the present book; see also John Helliwell and Robert D. Putnam, "The Social Context of Well-Being," *Philosophical Transactions of the Royal Society* (London), Series B, 359 (August 31, 2004): 1435–1446; John F. Helliwell, Haifang Huang, and Shun Wang, "Social Capital and Well-Being in Times of Crisis," *Journal of Happiness Studies* 15, no. 1 (2014): 145–162; John F. Helliwell, Haifang Huang, and Shun Wang, "The Social Foundations of World Happiness," in John F. Helliwell, Richard Layard, and Jeffrey D. Sachs, eds., *World Happiness Report 2017* (New York: Sustainable Development Solutions Network, 2017), chapter 2; and John F. Helliwell, Haifang Huang, Shun Wang, and Max Norton, "Social Environments for World Happiness," in John F. Helliwell, Richard Layard, Jeffrey D. Sachs, and Jan Emmanuel De Neve, eds., *World Happiness Report 2020* (New York: Sustainable Development Solutions Network, 2020), chapter 2.

86. John F. Helliwell and Haifang Huang, "Comparing the Happiness Effects of Real and On-Line Friends," *PLoS ONE* 8, no. 9 (2013): e72754, doi: 10.1371/journal.pone.0072754. For contrary evidence based on a much smaller sample, see Rachel Grieve, Kate Witteveen, Georgina Tolan, and Jessica Marrington, "Face-to-Face or Facebook: Can Social Connectedness Be Derived Online?," *Computers in Human Behavior* 29 (2013): 604–609, 10.1016/j.chb.2012.11.017.

87. Christina Sagioglou and Tobias Greitemeyer, "Facebook's Emotional Consequences: Why Facebook Causes a Decrease in Mood and Why People Still Use It," *Computers in Human Behavior* 35 (2014): 359–363, https://doi.org/10.1016/j.chb.2014.03.003.

88. Holly B. Shakya and Nicholas A. Christakis, "Association of Facebook Use with Compromised Well-Being: A Longitudinal Study," *American Journal of Epidemiology* 185, no. 3 (February 2017): 203–211, https://doi.org/10.1093/aje/kww189.

89. Fabio Sabatini and Francesco Sarracino, "Online Social Networks and Trust," *Social Indicators Research* 142, no. 1 (February 2019): 229–260, https://doi.org/10.1007/s11205-018-1887-2. To explore the direction of causation, they exploit the fact that different areas within Italy got high-speed Internet access at different times.

90. Neza Stiglic and Russell M. Viner, "Effects of Screentime on the Health and Well-Being of Children and Adolescents: A Systematic Review of Reviews, *BMJ Open* 9, no. 1 (January 2019): e023191, doi:10.1136/bmjopen-2018-023191; K. C. Madhav, Shardulendra Prasad Sherchand, and Samendra Sherchan, "Association Between Screen Time and Depression Among US Adults," *Preventive Medicine Reports* 8 (August 2017): 67–71, doi:10.1016/j.pmedr.2017.08.005.

91. Compare Jean M. Twenge, "Have Smartphones Destroyed a Generation?," *The Atlantic*, September 2017, with Alexandra Samuel, "Yes, Smartphones Are Destroying a Generation, but Not of Kids," JSTOR Daily, August 8, 2017, https://daily.jstor.org/yes-smartphones-are-destroying-a-generation-but-not-of-kids/, and Amy Orben and Andrew K. Przybylski, "The Association Between Adolescent Well-Being and Digital Technology Use," *Nature Human Behavior* 3 (2019): 173–182, https://doi.org/10.1038/s41562-018-0506-1.

92. Jean M. Twenge, "The Sad State of Happiness in the United States and the Role of Digital Media," in Helli-

well, Layard, and Sachs, eds., *World Happiness Report 2019*, chapter 5; Melissa G. Hunt, Rachel Marx, Courtney Lipson, and Jordyn Young, "No More Fomo: Limiting Social Media Decreases Loneliness and Depression," *Journal of Social and Clinical Psychology* 37, no. 10 (2018): 751–768, https://doi.org/10.1521/jscp.2018.37.10.751; Hunt Allcott, Luca Braghieri, Sarah Eichmeyer, and Matthew Gentzkow, "The Welfare Effects of Social Media," *American Economic Review* 110, no. 3 (2020): 629–676; and Roberto Mosquera, Mofioluwasademi Odunowo, Trent McNamara, Xiongfei Guo, and Ragan Petrie, "The Economic Effects of Facebook," *Experimental Economics* 23 (2020): 575–602, https://doi.org/10.1007/s10683-019-09625-y.

93. Moira Burke and Robert E. Kraut, "The Relationship Between Facebook Use and Well-Being Depends on Communication Type and Tie Strength: Facebook and Well-Being," *Journal of Computer-Mediated Communication* 21, no. 4 (July 2016): 265–281, https://doi.org/10.1111/jcc4.12162.

94. On loneliness, see Keith N. Hampton, Lauren F. Sessions, and Eun Ja Her, "Core Networks, Social Isolation and New Media: How Internet and Mobile Phone Use Is Related to Network Size and Diversity," *Information, Communication & Society* 14, no. 1 (2011): 130–155; Eric Klinenberg, *Going Solo: The Extraordinary Rise and Surprising Appeal of Living Alone* (New York: Penguin, 2012); John T. Cacioppo and William Patrick, *Loneliness: Human Nature and the Need for Social Connection* (New York: W. W. Norton, 2009); Jacqueline Olds and Richard S. Schwartz, *The Lonely American: Drifting Apart in the Twenty-first Century* (Boston: Beacon Press, 2009); "All the Lonely Americans?," Report of U.S. Congress Joint Economic Committee, August 22, 2018, https://www.jec.senate.gov/public/index.cfm/republicans/2018/8/all-the-lonely-americans; Vivek H. Murthy, *Together: The Healing Power of Human Connection in a Sometimes Lonely World* (New York: Harper Wave, 2020).

95. Rebecca Nowland, Elizabeth A. Necka, and John T. Caciopppo, "Loneliness and Social Internet Use: Pathways to Reconnection in a Digital World?," *Perspectives on Psychological Science* 13, no. 1 (2018): 70–87, https://doi.org/10.1177/1745691617713052.

96. Carty, "The Key to Saving the World in the Era of Social Media May Be Real Human Connection."

97. Francis Fukuyama, *Trust: The Social Virtues and the Creation of Prosperity* (New York: Free Press, 1995); and see pages 134–147 above.

98. See Putnam and Garrett, *The Upswing*, 158–162.

99. Angelo Antoci et al., "Civility and Trust in Social Media," *Journal of Economic Behavior & Organization* 160 (April 2019): 83–99, https://doi.org/10.1016/j.jebo.2019.02.026; Sabatini and Sarracino, "Online Social Networks and Trust"; Paolo Massa, Martino Salvetti, and Danilo Tomasoni, "Bowling Alone and Trust Decline in Social Network Sites," in *2009 Eighth IEEE International Conference on Dependable, Autonomic and Secure Computing* (Chengdu: IEEE, 2009), 658–663, https://doi.org/10.1109/DASC.2009.130.

100. Mei Alonzo and Milam Aiken, "Flaming in Electronic Communication," *Decision Support Systems* 36, no. 3 (January 2004): 205–213, https://doi.org/10.1016/S0167-9236(02)00190-2; Claire Hardaker, "Trolling in Asynchronous Computer-Mediated Communication: From User Discussions to Academic Definitions," *Journal of Politeness Research* 6, no. 2 (July 2010), https://doi.org/10.1515/jplr.2010.011.

101. Cliff Lampe et al., "Crowdsourcing Civility: A Natural Experiment Examining the Effects of Distributed Moderation in Online Forums," *Government Information Quarterly* 31, no. 2 (April 2014): 317–326, https://doi.org/10.1016/j.giq.2013.11.005; Russell Spears and Martin Lea, "Social Influence and the Influence of the 'Social' in Computer-Mediated Communication," in Martin Lea, ed., *Contexts of Computer-Mediated Communication* (London: Harvester Wheatsheaf, 1992), 30–65; Abraham H. Foxman and Christopher Wolf, *Viral Hate: Containing Its Spread on the Internet* (New York: Palgrave Macmillan, 2013).

102. Pasek, more, and Romer, "Realizing the Social Internet? Online Social Networking Meets Offline Civic Engagement."

103. Joseph B. Walther et al., "Self-Generated versus Other-Generated Statements and Impressions in Computer-Mediated Communication: A Test of Warranting Theory Using Facebook," *Communication Research* 36, no. 2 (April 2009): 229–253, https://doi.org/10.1177/0093650208330251.

104. Daniel Halpern and Jennifer Gibbs, "Social Media as a Catalyst for Online Deliberation?: Exploring the Affordances of Facebook and YouTube for Political Expression," *Computers in Human Behavior* 29, no. 3 (2013): 1159–1168.

105. Andrew Chadwick, *Internet Politics: States, Citizens, and New Communication Technologies* (New York: Oxford University Press, 2006), 27.

106. Daegon Cho and K. Hazel Kwon, "The Impacts of Identity Verification and Disclosure of Social Cues on Flaming in Online User Comments," *Computers in Human Behavior* 51 (October 2015): 363–372, https://doi.org/10.1016/j.chb.2015.04.046.

107. Diana C. Mutz and Byron Reeves, "The New Videomalaise: Effects of Televised Incivility on Political Trust," *American Political Science Review* 99, no. 1 (February 2005): 1–15, https://doi.org/10.1017/S0003055405051452; Porismita Borah, "Does It Matter Where You Read the News Story?: Interaction of Incivility and News Frames in the Political Blogosphere," *Communication Research* 41, no. 6 (August 2014): 809–827, https://doi.org/10.1177/0093650212449353.

108. Zizi Papacharissi, "Democracy Online: Civility, Politeness, and the Democratic Potential of Online Political Discussion Groups," *New Media & Society* 6, no. 2 (April 2004): 259–283, https://doi.org/10.1177/1461444804041444; Shiv R. Upadhyay, "Identity and Impoliteness in Computer-Mediated Reader Responses," *Journal of Politeness Research* 6, no. 1 (January 2010), https://doi.org/10.1515/jplr.2010.006.

109. Rishab Nithyanand, Brian Schaffner, and Phillipa Gill, "Online Political Discourse in the Trump Era," *arXiv:1711.05303*, November 14, 2017, http://arxiv.org/abs/1711.05303.

110. Zack Beauchamp, "Our Incel Problem," *Vox*, April 23, 2019, https://www.vox.com/the-highlight/2019/4/16/18287446/incel-definition-reddit.

111. Eun-Ju Lee, "Deindividuation Effects on Group Polarization in Computer-Mediated Communication: The Role of Group Identification, Public-Self-Awareness, and Perceived Argument Quality," *Journal of Communication* 57, no. 2 (June 2007): 385–403, https://doi.org/10.1111/j.1460-2466.2007.00348.x.

112. "Third places" is a term coined by sociologist Ray Oldenburg and refers to places where people spend time between home ("first" place) and work ("second" place): *The Great Good Place: Cafes, Coffee Shops, Bookstores, Bars, Hair Salons, and Other Hangouts at the Heart of a Community* (New York: Marlowe & Company, 1999). For one interesting study of a possible online third place, see Constance A. Steinkuehler and Dmitri Williams, "Where Everybody Knows Your (Screen) Name: Online Games as 'Third Places,'" *Journal of Computer-Mediated Communication* 11, no. 4 (July 2006): 885–909, https://doi.org/10.1111/j.1083-6101.2006.00300.x.

113. Robert Wulff, "The Impact of E-Commerce on Retail Real Estate," Center for Real Estate Entrepreneurship at George Mason University School of Business, June 6, 2018, http://business.gmu.edu/blog/realestate/2018/06/06/impact-e-commerce-retail-real-estate/.

114. Alistair Gray, "US Shopping Mall Vacancies Hit 8-Year High," *Financial Times*, October 3, 2019, https://www.ft.com/content/a4919eec-e58b-11e9-9743-db5a370481bc.

115. Dan Kopf, "Americans Spend Two Hours Less a Month on Shopping Than They Did 15 Years Ago," *Quartz*, July 31, 2019, https://qz.com/1677747/americans-are-spending-way-less-time-shopping/.

116. Ryan Raffaelli, "Reframing Collective Identity in Response to Multiple Technological Discontinuities: The Novel Resurgence of Independent Bookstores," November 2017, https://hbswk.hbs.edu/Documents/pdf/2017-11-15%20Indie%20Bookstore%20Resurgence_Ryan%20Raffaelli_Extended%20Abstract_HBSWK.PDF.

117. Andria Cheng, "Bookstores Find Growth as 'Anchors of Authenticity,'" *New York Times*, June 23, 2019, https://www.nytimes.com/2019/06/23/business/independent-bookstores.html.

118. See chapter 5 above.

119. Alan Wolfe, "Developing Civil Society: Can the Workplace Replace Bowling?," *The Responsive Community* 8, no. 2 (Spring 1998): 41–47; Cynthia Estlund, *Working Together: How Workplace Bonds Strengthen a Diverse Democracy* (New York: Oxford University Press, 2003).

120. Helaine Olen, "Telecommuting Is Not the Future," *Washington Post*, May 20, 2020, https://www.washingtonpost.com/opinions/2020/05/20/telecommuting-is-not-future/.

121. Kenneth Olmstead, Cliff Lampe, and Nicole B. Ellison, "Social Media and the Workplace," Pew Research Center, June 2016, https://www.pewresearch.org/internet/2016/06/22/social-media-and-the-workplace/. Roughly half of all workers say their employers have policies about social media use, which seems to be another obstacle to workplace-based social capital.

122. Claude S. Fischer, "Technology and Community: Historical Complexities," *Sociological Inquiry* 67, no. 1 (Winter 1997): 115.

123. Kevin Roose, "Welcome to the Rabbit Hole," *New York Times*, April 16, 2020, https://www.nytimes.com/2020/04/16/technology/rabbit-hole-podcast-kevin-roose.html.

124. We are grateful to Alexandra Samuel for calling this important point to our attention.

125. Annalee Newitz, "A Better Internet Is Waiting for Us," *New York Times*, November 30, 2019, https://www.nytimes.com/interactive/2019/11/30/opinion/social-media-future.html.

126. Laurie McNeill, "There Is No 'I' In Network: Social Networking Sites and Posthuman Auto/Biography," *Biography* 35, no. 1 (Winter 2012): 75–76.

127. Siva Vaidhyanathan, *Antisocial Media: How Facebook Disconnects Us and Undermines Democracy* (New York: Oxford University Press, 2018).

128. John M. Barrios et al., "Civic Capital and Social Distancing During the Covid-19 Pandemic," NBER working paper no. 27320 (Cambridge, Mass. National Bureau of Economic Research, June 2020) http://www.nber.org/papers/w27320; Ruben Durante et al., "Asocial Capital: Civic Culture and Social Distancing During COVID-19," Einaudi Institute for Economics and Finance working paper no. 20/12, May 2020, http://www.eief.it/eief/images/WP_20.12.pdf; Pol Campos-Mercade et al., "Prosociality Predicts Health Behaviors During the COVID-19 Pandemic," University of Zurich, Department of Economics, working paper no. 346, May 17, 2020, https://ssrn.com/abstract=3604094; and Abel Brodeur et al., "Stay-At-Home Orders, Social Distancing and Trust," IZA Discussion Papers from Institute of Labor Economics, No. 13234, May 2020, https://econpapers.repec.org/paper/izaizadps/dp13234.htm.

129. "COVID-19 in America: Concerns About the Crisis, Application of Social Distancing and Current Financial Impact," https://ssrs.com/covid-19-in-america/; David Lazer et al., "The State of the Nation: A 50-State COVID-19 Survey, April 2020, https://www.kateto.net/COVID19%20CONSORTIUM%20REPORT%20April%2030%202020.pdf.

130. Jonathan I. Dingel, Brent Neiman, "How Many Jobs Can Be Done at Home?," National Bureau of Economic Research working paper no. 26948 (Cambridge, Mass.: National Bureau of Economic Research, April 2020, rev. June 2020), https://www.nber.org/papers/w26948.

131. Balz and Guskin, "Poll Finds Universal Lifestyle Changes, Rising Stress and Growing Fears About Catching Coronavirus." For more data on work at home (for example, 20 percent reported "working from home due to the coronavirus"), see https://ssrs.com/covid-19-in-america/.

132. E. J. Dionne, Jr., "There Are Two Paths Out of This Crisis. Which Will We Choose?," *Washington Post*, April 12, 2020, https://www.washingtonpost.com/opinions/after-the-virus-will-we-choose-solidarity-or-division/2020/04/12/0acc7594-7b67-11ea-9bee-c5bf9d2e3288_story.html. For more data, see Richard V. Reeves and Jonathan Rothwell, "Class and COVID: How the Less Affluent Face Double Risks," Brookings Institution, March 27, 2020, https://www.brookings.edu/blog/up-front/2020/03/27/class-and-covid-how-the-less-affluent-face-double-risks/.

133. Lesley Chiou and Catherine Tucker, "Social Distancing, Internet Access and Inequality," National Bureau of Economic Research working paper no. 26982 (Cambridge, Mass.: National Bureau of Economic Research, April 2020), http://www.nber.org/papers/w26982.

134. Olen, "Telecommuting Is Not the Future."

135. Charlie Warzel, "Feeling Powerless About Coronavirus? Join a Mutual-Aid Network," *New York Times*, March 23, 2020, https://www.nytimes.com/2020/03/23/opinion/coronavirus-aid-group.html.

136. See John Herrman, "Neighbors Are Reaching Out on Nextdoor," *New York Times*, March 25, 2020, https://www.nytimes.com/2020/03/25/style/nextdoor-neighbors-coronavirus.html; Heather Kelly, "Suddenly, Nextdoor Is

Filled with Kind Neighbors. But Also New Kinds of Shaming," *Washington Post*, March 26, 2020, https://www.wash ingtonpost.com/technology/2020/03/26/nextdoor-coronavirus-nicer/; Dearbhla Gavin, "This Billion-Dollar Startup Helps Neighbors and Local Businesses Stay Connected and Help Each Other During the COVID-19 Lockdown," *Business Insider*, May 19, 2020, https://www.businessinsider.sg/nextdoor-this-startup-helps-neighbors-connect-during -the-covid-19-lockdown-2020–5.

137. Pete Davis, "CommonPlace," blog post, petedavis.org, December 2014, https://petedavis.org/tag/common place/.

138. Jessica Guynn, "COVID-19 Social Distancing: Together Apart, Screen Times Connects Isolated Kids with Family, Friends," *USA Today*, March 27, 2020, https://www.usatoday.com/story/tech/2020/03/27/coronavirus-covid -19-social-distancing-screen-time-parents-children-zoom-facetime-fortnite-minecraft/5084998002/.

139. See Brooke Auxier and Monica Anderson, "As Schools Close Due to the Coronavirus, Some U.S. Students Face a Digital 'Homework Gap,' " Pew Research Center, March 16, 2020, https://www.pewresearch.org/fact -tank/2020/03/16/as-schools-close-due-to-the-coronavirus-some-u-s-students-face-a-digital-homework-gap/; "Locked Out of the Virtual Classroom," *New York Times*, March 27, 2020, https://www.nytimes.com/2020/03/27/opinion /coronavirus-internet-schools-learning.html; Dana Goldstein, "The Class Divide: Remote Learning at 2 Schools, Private and Public, *New York Times*, May 9, 2020, https://www.nytimes.com/2020/05/09/us/coronavirus-public-private -school.html?action=click&module=Top%20Stories&pgtype=Homepage.

140. Dana Goldstein, "Research Shows Students Falling Months Behind During Virus Disruptions," *New York Times*, June 6, 2020, https://www.nytimes.com/2020/06/05/us/coronavirus-education-lost-learning.html.

141. Kate Murphy, "Why Zoom Is Terrible," *New York Times*, April 29, 2020, https://www.nytimes .com/2020/04/29/sunday-review/zoom-video-conference.html. Note that concern about video quality was mentioned in the original edition of *Bowling Alone*: see page 177 above.

142. Virginia Heffernan, "Staying Sober During a Lockdown," *New York Times*, April 2, 2020, updated April 3, 2020, https://www.nytimes.com/2020/04/02/nyregion/coronavirus-alcoholics-anonymous-on-line.html?algo =top_conversion &fellback=false&imp_id=43761600&imp_id=96638103&action=click&module=trending&pgtype =Article&region=Footer.

143. Some of this research was summarized in the original edition of *Bowling Alone*: see chapter 20 above. More recently, see Julianne Holt-Lunstad, "The Potential Public Health Relevance of Social Isolation and Loneliness: Prevalence, Epidemiology, and Risk Factors," *Public Policy & Aging Report* 27, no. 4 (January 2018): 127–130, https://doi .org/10.1093/ppar/prx030; Murthy, *Together*; Daniel S. Hamermesh, "Lock-Downs, Loneliness and Life Satisfaction," National Bureau of Economic Research working paper no. 27018 (Cambridge, Mass.: National Bureau of Economic Research, April 2020), http://www.nber.org/papers/w27018.

144. Arthur C. Brooks, "How Social Distancing Could Ultimately Teach Us How to Be Less Lonely," *Washington Post*, March 20, 2020, https://www.washingtonpost.com/opinions/how-social-distancing-could-ultimately-teach -us-how-to-be-less-lonely/2020/03/20/ca459804-694e-11ea-9923-57073adce27c_story.html; Jennifer L. Merolla et al., "Oxytocin and the Biological Basis for Interpersonal and Political Trust," *Political Behavior* 35, no. 4 (2013): 753–776.

145. Alyssa Fowers and William Wan, "A Third of Americans Now Show Signs of Clinical Anxiety or Depression, Census Bureau Finds Among Coronavirus Pandemic," *Washington Post*, May 26, 2020, https://www.washington post.com/health/2020/05/26/americans-with-depression-anxiety-pandemic/?arc404=true.

146. Vivek H. Murthy and Alice T. Chen, "The Coronavirus Could Cause a Social Recession," *The Atlantic*, March 22, 2020, https://www.theatlantic.com/ideas/archive/2020/03/america-faces-social-recession/608548/.

147. Jon Steinberg, the creative director for Epic, a production and publishing company, quoted in Nellie Bowles, "Coronavirus Ended the Screen-Time Debate. Screens Won," *New York Times*, April 21, 2020, https://www .nytimes.com/2020/03/31/technology/coronavirus-screen-time.html.

148. Lindsay Crouse, "There Is No More IRL Now," *New York Times*, March 16, 2020, https://www.nytimes .com/2020/03/16/opinion/coronavirus-social-media.html.

149. Jason Slotkin, "U.K. Cellphone Towers Ablaze as Conspiracy Theories Link 5G Networks to COVID-19," NPR, April 4, 2020, https://www.npr.org/sections/coronavirus-live-updates/2020/04/04/827343675/u-k-cellphone -towers-ablaze-as-conspiracy-theories-link-5g-networks-to-covid-19.

150. Yong Xiong, Hande Atay Alam, and Nectar Gan, "Wuhan Hospital Announces Death of Whistleblower Doctor Li Wenliang," CNN, February 7, 2020, https://www.cnn.com/2020/02/06/asia/li-wenliang-coronavirus-whistle blower-doctor-dies-intl/index.html; Sheri Fink and Mike Baker, " 'It's Just Everywhere Already': How Delays in Testing Set Back the U.S. Coronavirus Response," *New York Times*, March 10, 2020, https://www.nytimes.com/2020/03/10/us /coronavirus-testing-delays.html; Scott Gottlieb, MD (@ScottGottliebMD), "THREAD: A review of Catch-22 when it comes to #Coronavirus . . . ," Twitter, February 2, 2020, 1:49 p.m., https://twitter.com/ScottGottliebMD/status /1224042220665307137.

151. Daniel P. Aldrich and Michelle A. Meyer, "Social Capital and Community Resilience," *American Behavioral Scientist* 59, no. 2 (2015): 254–260.

152. Monica Anderson and Emily A. Vogels, "Americans Turn to Technology During COVID-19 Outbreak, Say an Outage Would Be a Problem," Pew Research Center, March 31, 2020, https://www.pewresearch.org /fact-tank/2020/03/31/americans-turn-to-technology-during-covid-19-outbreak-say-an-outage-would-be-a-problem/#more -360949.

153. Email from Gabriel Perez-Putnam to author.

154. Rabbi Brigitte Rosenberg quoted in Judy Woodruff, Courtney Norris, and Alison Thoet, "How Religious Leaders Are Keeping the Faith During COVID-19," *PBS NewsHour*, April 28, 2020, https://www.pbs.org/newshour /show/how-religious-leaders-are-keeping-the-faith-during-covid-19.

155. "Glimpses of a Silver Lining in the Great Lockdown," *Financial Times*, April 24, 2020, https://www.ft.com /content/5d62f752-857a-11ea-b555-37a289098206.

156. Edward L. Glaeser and Joshua D. Gottlieb, "The Wealth of Cities: Agglomeration Economies and Spatial Equilibrium in the United States," *Journal of Economic Literature* 47, no. 4 (2009): 983–1028; Edward Glaeser,

Triumph of the City: How Our Greatest Invention Makes Us Richer, Smarter, Greener, Healthier, and Happier (New York: Penguin Press, 2011). See also chapter 1 of the present book and (on pandemics and cities), Edward L. Glaeser, "Cities and Pandemics Have a Long History," *City Journal*, Spring 2020, https://www.city-journal.org/cities-and-pandemics-have-long-history.

157. John Eligon and Kimiko de Freytas-Tamura, "Today's Activism: Spontaneous, Leaderless, but Not Without Aim," *New York Times*, June 3, 2020, https://www.nytimes.com/2020/06/03/us/leaders-activists-george-floyd-protests.html; Joshua Keating, "The George Floyd Protests Show Leaderless Movements Are the Future of Politics," *Slate*, June 9, 2020, https://slate.com/news-and-politics/2020/06/george-floyd-global-leaderless-movements.html.

APPENDIX I: MEASURING SOCIAL CHANGE

1. For examples of this error, see Lester M. Salamon, "The Rise of the Nonprofit Sector," *Foreign Affairs* 73 (1994): 109–122, esp. 111, and Nicholas Freudenberg and Carol Steinsapir, "Not in Our Backyards: The Grassroots Environmental Movement," in *American Environmentalism: The U.S. Environmental Movement, 1970–1990*, edited by Riley E. Dunlap and Angela G. Mertig (New York: Taylor & Francis, 1992), 29.

2. David Horton Smith, "The Rest of the Nonprofit Sector: Grassroots Associations as the Dark Matter Ignored in Prevailing 'Flat Earth' Maps of the Sector," *Nonprofit and Voluntary Sector Quarterly* 26 (June 1997): 115–131.

3. Verba, Schlozman, Brady, *Voice and Equality*, 62, report that in response to a single question about membership in organizations—"for example, unions or professional associations, fraternal groups, recreational organizations, political issue organizations, community or school groups, and so on"—49 percent of all respondents claimed at least one membership. In response to subsequent probing about nineteen specific types of organizations, fully 79 percent mentioned one or more affiliations.

4. Experts who know better sometimes violate this elementary precept; see, for example, Andrew Kohut, "Trust and Citizen Engagement in Metropolitan Philadelphia: A Case Study" (Washington, D.C.: Pew Research Center on the People & the Press, 1997), and American Association of Retired Persons, *Maintaining America's Social Fabric: The AARP Survey of Civic Involvement* (Washington, D.C.: AARP, 1996).

5. These oft cited counterexamples (such as Nicholas Lemann, "Kicking in Groups: Alleged Decline of America's Communal Capital," *Atlantic Monthly* [April 1996]: 22–27; Robert J. Samuelson, "'Bowling Alone' Is Bunk," *Washington Post* [April 10, 1996]: A19) are, in fact, fallacious. As reported in chapter 6, four different national survey archives confirm that softball playing *fell* by a third between the mid-1980s and the late 1990s. Soccer, though unquestionably of growing importance, involves only a tiny proportion of all adults, even as spectators. According to the Sporting Goods Association of America, less than 20 percent of all American schoolchildren played soccer more than once in 1993. Since less than 30 percent of Americans are parents of schoolchildren, less than 6 percent of all adults in 1993 were parents of youth soccer players; by contrast, that same year 18 percent of all adults bowled more than once. Bowlers, in short, are three times as common in America as soccer parents. Even if—quite implausibly—every single soccer mom and dad in America began to show up regularly at their children's games, their numbers would not offset the decline in league bowling. In fact, the DDB Needham Life Style surveys suggest that parental attendance at sporting events was actually *lower* in the 1990s than in the 1970s. Regular soccer moms and dads do build social capital, but they are too rare, relatively speaking, to constitute a significant countertrend.

6. For a critique that indiscriminately mixes data about "change" over a year or two and "change" over half a century, see Everett C. Ladd, "The Data Just Don't Show Erosion of America's 'Social Capital,'" *The Public Perspective* 7 (June/July 1996): 5–22.

7. Of the four primary survey series on which we can draw, the General Social Survey began in 1972, the Roper Social and Political Trends surveys began in 1974, and the DDB Needham Life Style surveys began in 1975. The National Election Studies began in 1952, but their long-term coverage is limited primarily to national electoral and campaign behavior.

8. Another instance of this issue of absolute vs. relative change involves money. As explained in chapter 7, generosity should be measured by the fraction of personal income (or national income) that is given to charity, not the absolute number of dollars.

9. Norman H. Nie, Jane Junn, and Kenneth Stehlik-Barry, *Education and Democratic Citizenship in America* (Chicago: University of Chicago Press, 1996).

10. John Helliwell and Robert D. Putnam, "Education and Social Capital," unpublished ms.

11. Information about access to all the major data archives used in this research is available at www.bowlingalone.com.

12. Figures 53, 65, and 73 *do* incorporate multivariate controls.

13. NES data are available from the Interuniversity Consortium for Political and Social Research at the University of Michigan. GSS data are available from the Roper Center for Public Opinion Research at the University of Connecticut (Storrs).

14. The raw data from these surveys were deposited with the Roper Center for Public Opinion Research at the University of Connecticut (Storrs). However, because of archiving difficulties, the data themselves became available for analysis only recently, thanks to the efforts of a joint team from Harvard University and the University of California at Berkeley. I am grateful to Steve Yonish and to Henry Brady and his colleagues for their Herculean efforts in this Augean task. For an earlier analysis of political participation based on the aggregate Roper data, see Rosenstone and Hansen, *Mobilization, Participation, and Democracy*. Roper polling continued after December 1994, but the raw data after that date are unavailable to academic researchers, and in any event the format of the crucial questions changed significantly at that time, so that direct comparison with the prior data is no longer possible. Results for the first survey in 1995 show a sharp onetime upward ratcheting for every single one of the dozen civic activities, but from that new higher benchmark, each activity then resumed its downward trend. In other words, although the analysis of the Roper data in this book is limited to 1973–94, there is reason to believe that the declines in civic engagement continued after

that period. Aggregate results from Roper surveys between 1995 and 1998 used in this book are drawn from the bimonthly *Roper Reports* (New York: Roper Starch Worldwide, 1995–98), which can be consulted at the Roper Center at the University of Connecticut.

15. I am grateful to Dhavan Shah, a former graduate student at the University of Minnesota, and his instructor, Professor William Wells, for alerting me to the existence of the DDB Needham Life Style surveys. Marty Horn, Doug Hughes, Chris Callahan, and their colleagues at DDB Needham generously made these data available for analysis and responded to subsequent inquiries. Sid Groeneman and his colleagues at Market Facts helped me to understand the methodology used and its potential advantages and disadvantages. For background, see *Life Style and Psychographics*, ed. William D. Wells (Chicago: American Marketing Association, 1974), and William D. Wells, "Psychographics: A Critical Review," *Journal of Marketing Research* 12 (1975): 196–213.

16. The answer to all these questions is "Yes."

17. This adjustment involves estimating the "level" difference between married and single respondents over the 1985–99 period, using that difference to estimate the annual scores for single respondents during the 1975–84 period and then estimating the annual population score during the 1975–84 period by creating a "synthetic" sample with the appropriate fraction of married and single respondents. In the few cases where the "level" difference between married and single respondents changed over 1985–99, I projected that difference backward for the 1975–84 period. This procedure assumes away any nonlinear interaction in the effects of year and marital status, but I found no evidence of such interaction in any of the variables of interest in this study.

18. Robert D. Putnam and Steven Yonish, "How Important Is Response Rate? An Evaluation of a 'Mail Panel' Survey Archive," unpublished ms. (Cambridge, Mass.: Harvard University, 1999).

19. Respondents are occasionally offered a nominal gift—a packet of Post-it notes and a tiny tote bag, for example—for completing a particularly burdensome questionnaire.

20. Sid Groeneman ("Multi-purpose Household Panels and General Samples: How Similar and How Different?" paper presented at the annual meeting of the American Association for Public Opinion Research, Danvers, Mass., 1994; emphasis in the original) reports that the sample is "drawn to approximate actual distributions of household income, population density, panel member's age, and household size *within the 9 Census divisions.*" Weights are then applied to the actual respondents to match the demographic composition of the final sample to the target population. Questionnaires are mailed to roughly 5,000 respondents; usable responses are received from an average of 3500–4000 respondents.

21. This is also true for conventional sampling, but the disparity is greater for mail panels.

22. Though the questions are not exactly comparable, there is evidence that DDB data contains 10 percent too many homeowners, as compared with GSS data. There is also some evidence that the undersampling of the less educated has been somewhat reduced in more recent years.

23. Groeneman, "Multi-purpose Household Panels," compared panel and nonpanel samples using data obtained from Market Facts mail panel and random digit dialing surveys. The discrepancy in party identification, though statistically significant, is very slight. In 1996 the NES found 39 percent Democrats, 28 percent Republicans, and 33 percent Independents; in that same year the Life Style sample reported 37 percent Democrats, 31 percent Republicans, and 32 percent Independents.

24. Andrew Kohut, "Conservative Opinions Not Underestimated, but Racial Hostility Missed" (Washington, D.C.: Pew Research Center on the People & the Press, 1998). See also Penny Visser, Jon Krosnick, Jesse Marquette, and Michael Curtin, "Mail Surveying for Election Forecasting: An Evaluation of the *Columbus Dispatch* Poll," *Public Opinion Quarterly* 60 (1996): 181–227.

25. I have found no paired questions in the two surveys that would call into question the essential comparability of the two data sets. That is, I have not singled out comparisons that support my conclusion.

26: Putnam and Yonish, "How Important Is Response Rate?"

27. I also compared DDB Needham Life Style results in 1982 and 1984 with simultaneous, roughly comparable evidence from the Roper surveys regarding dining out, moviegoing, and attending a sporting event. The Roper questions asked, "Did you happen to engage in this activity this last *week?*" whereas the Life Style questions asked, "How often last *year* did you engage in this activity?" When the Roper "last week" responses are converted to "times per year" (by multiplying by 52), the results are virtually identical to the Life Style responses (dinner out: nineteen times per year for each; movies: five times per year for each; sports event: four times per year in the Roper surveys, five times per year in the Life Style surveys).

28. Across entire GSS sample, our interval scores correlate $R^2 = .99$ with those generated by an entirely independent algorithm that I discovered after defining mine (Michael Hout and Andrew Greeley, "Exchange on Overreporting of U.S. Church Attendance," *American Sociological Review* 63 [1998]: 116).

29. 2nd edition (University Park: Pennsylvania State University, 1999). I am grateful to Professor Robinson for making selected data from the 1995 wave of this study available for my analysis.

The Story
Behind This Book

THE EXISTENCE of this book refutes its central premise. My argument claims, among other things, a decline of generalized reciprocity—the practice of helping others with no expectation of gain. Yet without unsolicited, unexpected, and unrequited generosity beyond imagining, I could not have written this book. I want to describe here just how indebted I am to others.

In retrospect, work on this book began in earnest in 1992, as I was completing *Making Democracy Work*, a twenty-year study of local government in Italy. I was fresh from a stint as dean of the Kennedy School of Government, where I had focused on the problems of American democracy. It gradually dawned on me that one of the conclusions of the Italian research—that democracy depended on social capital—might have implications for contemporary America.

Over the next two years, with support and encouragement from the late Joel Orlen and the American Academy of Arts and Sciences, I convened a series of academic workshops on social capital and its implications for economic development, urban poverty, and American democracy. Eventually Peter B. Evans, Susan Pharr, and Theda Skocpol joined me in guiding this project, and I learned a great deal from their conceptual perspectives, which differed in important respects from my own. Our work was generously supported by the Carnegie Corporation, the Ford Foundation, and the Rockefeller Foundation. I am grateful to Alberta Arthurs, Clifford Chanin, Barbara Finberg, Peter Goldmark, David Hamburg, Michael Lipsky, Geraldine Mannion, and their colleagues for their willingness to invest in ideas whose theoretical rigor and practical payoff were uncertain. I am also grateful to them—and to three chance acquaintances from the world of journalism, David Boldt, Jonathan S. Cohn, and Paul Solman—for gently but firmly pressing me to carry the discussion beyond academic circles.

I began idly to explore what statistical evidence I could find that might reveal trends in civic engagement in America, not at all sure whether hard data would substantiate my hunch. Harold A. Pollack, my "research team" at that point, rounded up the initial evidence with skill, energy, and "show me" skepticism. By early 1994 we had accumulated enough data on things like membership in the PTA and fraternal organizations to move beyond the stage of pure anecdote. Over breakfast that spring a generous friend, Peter Ackerman, mentioned that trends in league bowling seemed to fit my evolving generalization. A few weeks later, hearing that story, my colleague Jack Donahue mused that Americans seemed to be "bowling alone," and we agreed that that might be a nice title for a paper I was then mulling. I was already getting by with more than a little help from my friends.

As had been my habit in previous research projects, I planned to compose a preliminary version of my argument, listen to critical commentary from my colleagues, and then reformulate a more refined version. At the invitation of Axel Hadenius, Dietrich and Marilyn Rueschemeyer, and Björn Wittrock, I agreed to present some initial reflections at a pair of academic conferences in August 1994 in Uppsala, Sweden. By May I wrote a friend that I hoped "to spend 1995 finishing a slim volume on this topic for more than an academic audience." (Readers of this tome will know that I missed that target in more ways than one.) In January 1995 an abridged version of the Uppsala paper was published in a respected but little-known periodical, the *Journal of Democracy*. Without warning, a deluge struck.

Until January 1995 I was (as one critic later observed with perfect accuracy) "an obscure academic." Although I had published scores of books and articles in the previous three decades (many of them, I immodestly believed, of greater scholarly elegance than "Bowling Alone"), none had attracted the slightest public attention. Now I was invited to Camp David, lionized by talk-show hosts, and (the secular equivalent of canonization in contemporary America) pictured with my wife, Rosemary, on the pages of *People*. The explanation was not late-blooming genius, but the simple fact that I had unwittingly articulated an unease that had already begun to form in the minds of many ordinary Americans. (This period quickly taught me the power of the media spotlight to elicit personal reactions: spontaneous generosity from friends, relatives, colleagues, and total strangers soon made me the proud owner of one of the country's finest collections of bowling tchotchkes—from bowling pins and towels to bowling ties and salt-and-pepper sets.) The hubbub was intoxicating, but as I wrote to two friends in February 1995, "Pretty heady stuff, but it has kept me away from my computer, where I'm supposed to be working out a fuller version. . . . We may be running a risk of our marketing operation getting too far out in front of our product development."

I was acutely aware that the thesis with which I was now associated rested on limited evidence. To deepen the argument, I needed more time and more help. Generous supporters, including the Aspen Institute's Nonprofit Sector Research Fund, Colin Campbell (and the Rockefeller Brothers Fund), Craig Dykstra and Susan Wisely (and the Lilly Endowment), Charles Heck (and the Trilateral Commission), Paul Light and Rebecca Rimel (and the Pew Charitable Trusts), and Frank Weil (and the Norman Foundation), stepped in to offer encouragement and crucial resources. I am especially grateful that although the benefactors who supported this stage of the project were eager for conclusions about "what is to be done," they showed great respect for the importance of getting the facts straight before moving too quickly to possible solutions.

To get the facts straight, I needed to acquaint myself with many new literatures. Much of my argument—and indeed much of this book—involved simply integrating masses of relevant research that had already been honed by experts in a dozen separate fields over several decades. To accomplish that task in less than a lifetime required help. I doubt that any research project has ever been blessed with a more resourceful, thoughtful, and energetic group of collaborators than this one. Steadily refreshed with new recruits over the years, the team developed a tradition of regular meetings at which individual reports were presented, and the ensuing debates were among the most intellectually rewarding of my life. Although virtually all the participants shared a conviction that we were exploring a topic of considerable importance, some of the most searching criticisms of my theories came from this group. By 1999 the roster of researchers had lengthened to nearly half a hundred, including Cindy Adams, Neil Allison, Maryann Barakso, Ben Berger, Jay Braatz, Melissa Buis, David E. Campbell, Brad Clarke, Zoe Clarkwest, Ben Deufel, Dan Devroye, Karen Ferree, Kate Fitzpatrick, Archon Fung, Arkadi Gerney, Kristin Goss, Louise Hayes, Isadora Helfgott, Adam Hickey, Scott Jacobs, Bertram Johnson, Jeffrey Kling, Lisa Laskin, Kristen Lasky, Jonathan Leeman, Kimberly Lochner, Karen Mapp, Stephen Marshall, Jason Mazzone, Victor Mendiola, Rob Mickey, Elizabeth Morton, Chad Noyes, Amy Perlmutter, David Pinto-Duschinsky, John Rector, A.J. Robinson, Emily Ryo, Alexandra Samuel, Andrew Schneller, Rustin Silverstein, Zach Stern, Hannah Stires, Maurits van der Veen, Geoffrey Vaughan, Christian Warren, Mark Warren, Aaron Wicks, and Steve Yonish. Of this group, several deserve special mention for the duration and intensity of their involvement and the extraordinary creativity of their contributions at virtually all stages of the project: Melissa Buis, David Campbell, Ben Deufel, Arkadi Gerney, Kristin Goss, Adam Hickey, Jason Mazzone, and Steve Yonish. Working from my rough notes and outline, Kristin Goss deftly drafted the initial version of much of what became Section IV of this book.

The first wave of publicity that had greeted my argument as 1995 opened was excessively complimentary, not least because other scholars, such as Steve Knack, Wendy Rahn, Michael Walzer, and Robert Bellah and his coauthors of *Habits of the Heart*, had already expressed similar concerns about civic disengagement. On the other hand, the very notoriety of "Bowling Alone" invited others to offer contrary interpretations of a still slender body of evidence that was, admittedly, ambiguous. The inevitable backwash as 1995 closed was not pleasant—"Bowling Alone Is Bunk," ran one memorable headline—but the criticism was instructive and ultimately more productive than the praise.

In the debate that followed I learned much from my critics, including writers like Carles Boix, Bob Edwards, Michael W. Foley, Charles Heying, Patricia Landolt, Nicholas Lemann, Daniel N. Posner, and Alejandro Portes. More gratifying, in the ensuing years some of the most incisive public critics also provided wise and time-consuming private counsel. For this unusual collegiality, well beyond the norm in our contentious profession, I am especially grateful to Marshall Ganz, Kenneth Newton, Pippa Norris, Michael Schudson, Theda Skocpol, Richard M. Valelly, and Robert Wuthnow. As the evidence became clearer, some critics and I converged toward a shared diagnosis, but differences remained. The conventional addendum to acknowledgments that those kind enough to have offered advice bear no responsibility for the result is uniquely pertinent here.

My own confidence in the argument of "Bowling Alone" was unexpectedly shaken early in 1996 when John Helliwell, an economist friend with whom I was collaborating on related research, and I discovered that the published version of the General Social Survey (on which I had relied for some crucial evidence) was flawed. Correcting the computational errors had the effect of diminishing the apparent decline in formal group membership. My only consolation was that we had uncovered the error before my critics. Throughout this period I valued not merely John's friendship and scholarly acumen, but also his steady commitment to following the evidence where it led.

Meanwhile, continuing to be lucky in my collaborations, I began work with Gerald Gamm, a political historian, on the evolution of civic associations in America since Tocqueville's time. Over the next several years Gerald patiently tutored me in the cautious subtleties of the historian's craft, while sharing my enthusiasm for our unexpected discoveries.

The most commonly cited weakness of "Bowling Alone" had been clear to me from the start—by drawing primarily on evidence about declining membership in specific formal groups, I had ignored the possibility of offsetting increases in other groups or in informal types of connectedness. For some alleged counterexamples, like soccer matches and softball games, hard work unearthed hard evidence, and they turned out mostly to be illusory, but that momentary clarification left undiminished the possibility that other overlooked forms of social capital were expanding. I simply could think of no source of systematic evidence on civic engagement in general, and still less on such ephemera as picnics and card games. My colleagues Kristin Goss and Steve Yonish spent hundreds of hours in endlessly resourceful (but usually fruitless) searches for systematic evidence of what we called "unobtrusive indicators" of social connectedness.

One initial breakthrough came when we learned of the possibility that a hitherto unanalyzed survey treasure trove—what I describe in appendix I as the Roper Social and Political Trends archive—might be retrievable. Henry Brady, head of the Survey Research Center at the University of California, while firmly agnostic about my claims of civic disengagement, generously agreed to share the task of acquiring the data and readying them for analysis. The archive proved much dustier than we had expected, but a year's hard work by Steve Yonish at Harvard and Dorie Apollonio, Andrea Campbell, and Laurel Elms at Berkeley eventually yielded an archive of unparalleled value. Even skeptics in our group were impressed by this massive new evidence of civic disengagement.

Ironically, an even more startling discovery first appeared in mid-1997 in a footnote to a graduate student critique of "Bowling Alone" sent to me by Wendy Rahn. I profited from dozens of such missives, but none turned out to be more instructive than this paper by Dhavan Shah, then a student of William Wells at the University of Minnesota, which alerted me to the existence of the DDB Needham Life Style survey archive. Steve Yonish gained access to these data, and with the help of Jim Crimmins, Chris Callahan, Marty Horn, and Doug Hughes of DDB

Needham and Sid Groeneman of Market Facts, as described in appendix I, a truly unique resource was added to our repertoire. Someone had been keeping track of picnics and card games, after all, and to our collective astonishment the new data seemed to show that "Bowling Alone" might actually have understated the depth and breadth of the social transformation under way in America. To validate and analyze the new evidence would add two years to the project but deepen our confidence that we were on to something.

Throughout these years I felt torn between the twin imperatives of accuracy and action. To Tom Rochon, a longtime friend and unconvinced critic, I had written in April 1994:

> Though it proves nothing, I have to report a striking distinction between the reactions of academic audiences and of public audiences. Academics *always* want to know whether it's really true that we are disengaging— what about the new social movements? the Internet? 12-step groups? new age encounter groups? etc., etc. They almost *never* have any comments on what could be done about it, if it *were* true. Public audiences almost *never* ask whether it is true, because it rings so true to their own experience. They are *always* deeply concerned about how to fix the problem. Their questions are tougher.

Already I had begun casual conversations about the practical implications of my theories with Lewis Feldstein, president of the New Hampshire Charitable Foundation, whom I had met through mutual friends. By the following spring those conversations ripened into a formal proposal for what came to be the Saguaro Seminar on Civic Engagement in America. Over the next five years my collaboration with Lew blossomed into one of the most enjoyable and productive of my professional life. Drawing on a lifetime of practical idealism, he inspired me to see our evolving research in a broader framework. Lew also had practical skills in planning and managing an incipient social movement that I utterly lacked. Lew bears no responsibility for where my argument has ended up, but no one is more responsible for its focus not merely on what has happened, but also on what we should do about it.

By 1997, in collaboration with Tom Sander and, somewhat later, Chris Gates, president of the National Civic League, Lew and I had recruited a blue-ribbon group of civic leaders and scholars from across the country to join the Saguaro Seminar. (We settled upon that name because the southwestern saguaro cactus, which grows mostly unseen for decades before throwing up those marvelous trunks that in turn host myriad plant and animal communities, seemed a suitable metaphor for social capital.) The Saguaro Seminar was generously supported by the Carnegie Corporation of New York, the Lilly Endowment, the John D. and Catherine T. MacArthur Foundation, the Charles Stewart Mott Foundation, the Surdna Foundation, the Rockefeller Brothers Fund, the Rockefeller Foundation, and the Lila Wallace Reader's Digest Fund. The Saguaro participants were unstinting with their time, their experience, and their creativity as we struggled together to define an actionable national agenda for civic revitalization. My colleagues in the Saguaro Seminar are identified in chapter 24, which also draws heavily on the inspiration of our meetings. A fuller report on our conclusions will appear shortly after this book.

Throughout this research I reveled in unexpected support and wisdom from a wide range of acquaintances, old and new. Rafe Sagalyn, my exceptional literary agent, proved to be a sturdy thick-and-thin friend and guide, sharing and yet channeling my enthusiasms toward a publishable manuscript. Nick Mitropoulos, who embodies the classic Hellenic virtues of good friendship and good citizenship along with the classic Beantown virtues of loyalty and connections, materialized at my elbow at every difficult moment over the last decade to offer encouragement and solve problems. Angela Glover Blackwell, then vice president of the Rockefeller Foundation and deeply skeptical about aspects of my argument, nevertheless provided crucial support, while working patiently to help me understand her insights. The late Michael Bruno, vice president and chief economist at the World Bank, Partha Dasgupta, chair of the Faculty of Economics and Politics at Cambridge University, and Ismail Serageldin, vice president for Sustainable Development at the World Bank, all generously provided encouragement for a novice trespassing disciplinary boundaries. William A. Galston, a distinguished political philosopher and senior adviser in the White House, shared and encouraged my enthusiasm for liberal communitarianism, while cautioning me to be sure I had the facts straight. Michael Woolcock, whom I originally "met" as the anonymous author of a brilliant (but critical) journal article I had been asked to review, became a good friend and co-conspirator in the nascent social capital movement. When I sought to understand how social capital was being re-created at the grass roots, Ernie Cortes introduced me to Texas, Milda Hedblom and Rip Rapson to Minnesota, and Ethan Seltzer and Lynn Youngbar to Oregon. Marcia Sharp offered crisp, valuable advice at several key junctures. Ed Skloot of the Surdna Foundation and Simon & Schuster's Alice Mayhew—each supportive yet eager for more rapid progress than I was capable of—provided constant stimulation; I regret that in different ways I caused each of them frustration. Last, but far from least, the most ruthlessly candid, intellectually demanding, and constructively creative editor of every page of this book—as of all my work for the last decade and more—was my daughter, Lara Putnam.

Hundreds of scholars, researchers, and ordinary citizens wrote with encouragement and critical thoughts—too many to acknowledge individually, but all made an impact. Only a pair of improbable illustrations will have to serve: General Bernard Trainor penned a long account of the history of U.S. Marine Corps efforts to ensure small-unit solidarity, with an eye toward potential lessons for civilian life; while Professor David Scott of Texas A&M wrote me out of the blue about his research on the sociology of bridge, an exchange that led eventually to the opening lines of this book. I deeply regret that I cannot acknowledge individually each of the contributions that arrived "over the transom," for more than any bit of statistical evidence they convinced me that America's springs of civic renewal still run strong.

In the course of this research many colleagues and organizations generously shared data from projects of their own, including Julian Baym of Mediamark, Christopher J. Bosso, Steven Brint, Frank M. Bryan, Margot Cella of the

Food Marketing Institute, Anne Costain, Russell Dalton, Ronald Inglehart, Ann Kaplan of the AAFRC Trust for Philanthropy, Ichiro Kawachi, Bruce Kennedy, William G. Mayer, Peter Nardulli, Lisa Parmalee of the Roper Center at the University of Connecticut, John P. Robinson, Theda Skocpol, Robert Smith, M. Dane Waters, and Don Winter and J. Walker Smith of Yankelovich Partners. Staff members at scores of civic organizations were unstinting with their time and expertise, retrieving elusive records and filling in historical details. I particularly laud the skill, conscientiousness, and courtesy of nearly a score of experts in the Bureau of the Census, the Bureau of Labor Statistics, the Library of Congress, and other government departments, who responded promptly and efficiently to inquiries from me and my research team and whose expertise and energy repeatedly put the lie to stereotypes about government officials.

I am grateful to many colleagues who in the course of this project have given me especially detailed and insightful help and advice, some (but, at my peril, not all) of which I have accepted. They include Joel Aberbach, Lorien Abroms, Robert Axelrod, Benjamin Barber, Daniel Bell, Lisa F. Berkman, Peter Berkowitz, Derek Bok, Harry Boyte, Xavier de Souza Briggs, Steven Brint, Richard Cavanagh, Mark Chaves, the late James S. Coleman, Susan B. Crawford, Russell Dalton, Jack Donahue, Michael A. Dover, Lewis Feldstein, Claudia Goldin, Sid Groeneman, Vaughn L. Grisham, Jr., Glenn Firebaugh, Robert Frank, Marc Galanter, Gerald Gamm, Peter Dobkin Hall, David Halpern, Russell Hardin, Frederick C. Harris, Scott Hemphill, Virginia Hodgkinson, Bonnie Honig, Howard Husock, Helen Ingram, Kathleen Hall Jamieson, Christopher Jencks, Lawrence F. Katz, Morton Keller, Gary King, Robert Keohane, Robert Klitgaard, Steven Knack, Margaret Levi, Seymour Martin Lipset, Glenn Loury, Robert Luskin, Doug McAdam, Eileen McDonagh, Steven Macedo, Jane Mansbridge, Peter Marsden, John D. McCarthy, David G. Myers, Carl Milofsky, Martha Minow, Mark Moore, Katherine Newman, Richard Niemi, Susan Olzak, Elinor Ostrom, Virginia Park, David Pinto-Duschinsky, Jane Piliavin, Fred Pryor, Wendy Rahn, Paul Resnick, Tom Rochon, Nancy Rosenblum, Robert I. Rotberg, Peter Rowe, Kay Schlozman, Juliet Schor, Dhavan Shah, Dietlind Stolle, Janet Topolsky, Eric Uslaner, Sidney Verba, Robert Vos, Mark Warren, Margaret Weir, Barry Wellman, Edwenna Werner, Grant Williams, Shirley Williams, Thad Williamson, John Wilson, Alan Wolfe, Michael Woolcock, Robert Wuthnow, Alan Zaslavsky, and Alan Zuckerman.

In addition to these professional colleagues, students too numerous to single out spotted deficiencies in my argument and evidence, increased my peripheral vision by alerting me to unexpectedly relevant ideas in adjacent disciplines, and (above all) strengthened my confidence that (despite what might be too easily inferred from some evidence in this book) the ingenuity and idealism of the younger generations represent a potent resource for civic renewal.

This research turned out to be substantially more demanding than I had envisioned, and one grievous consequence was that I repeatedly fell short of my responsibilities on several related projects. Nevertheless, my collaborators on these projects showed great forbearance, while continuing to supply extraordinary intellectual stimulation and personal friendship. I especially want to express my deep appreciation to Jean-Claude Casanova, Charles Heck, and the late Seizaburo Sato, collaborators in the Trilateral Commission project on Democracy in the Contemporary World; to Eva Cox, Peter Hall, Takashi Inoguchi, Claus Offe, Victor M. Pérez-Díaz, Bo Rothstein, Dirk Rumberg, Theda Skocpol, Volker Then, Jean-Pierre Worms, and Robert Wuthnow, my collaborators and supporters on the Bertelsmann Science Foundation project on the dynamics of social capital in Europe, North America, and East Asia; and to my close friend and colleague Susan J. Pharr, who assumed leadership of the Ford-sponsored project on Democracy in the Trilateral World. Meanwhile my faculty colleagues in Harvard's Department of Government and Kennedy School of Government challenged and enriched my research, often in ways of which they were unaware, while bearing with gracious collegiality the burdens that I let slide while immersed in this seemingly endless project.

The project was successively hosted by the Weatherford Center for International Affairs, headed by Jorge I. Dominguez, and the Taubman Center for State and Local Government, headed by Alan Altshuler. I have enjoyed the personal friendship of Jorge and of Alan for more than two decades, and each has been unstinting in his support of this research. I am also grateful to Deans Jeremy R. Knowles and Joseph S. Nye for both intellectual and organizational encouragement.

In the course of this research I benefited almost beyond belief from the hard work and expertise of colleagues who have kept the operation moving forward, including Cindy Adams, Lisa Adams, Annette Mann Bourne, Jeffrey Boutwell, Alicia Carrasquillo, Zoe Clarkwest, Anne Emerson, Kate Fitzpatrick, Sarah Hagan, Roger Labrie, Steve Minicucci, Marisa Murtagh, Erin Quinn, Julissa Reynoso, Karen Rogers, Barbara Salisbury, Corinne Schelling, and Katie Tenney.

Despite all the help I have just enjoyed recounting, this book and the associated efforts to contribute to a renaissance of American democracy would not have come to fruition without the extraordinary role played by my two professional partners, Louise Kennedy and Tom Sander. They turned a chaos of good intentions into a marvelous adventure.

When Tom joined the project, I told him that someone needed to wake up each morning worrying about how to mobilize America's civic energies, and it was not going to be me. Intensely intelligent, driven by an outsize civic conscience, Tom has labored for four frenzied years on every aspect of this project. Everything about the Saguaro Seminar—from its inscrutable title to its roster of distinguished participants, from its exhaustively planned meetings to its final report—is Tom's handiwork. This book, too, bears indelible marks of his energy and creativity. When I mused one afternoon about trends in lawyering, for example, he worked day and night to track down numbers, catalog interpretations, and adjudicate discrepancies. Without authorization, he carved out a role as the project's whistle-blower, looking behind every generalization to see if I had short-circuited the truth. He is a wonderful colleague.

For five extraordinary years Louise has managed my professional life, a bedrock of stable good sense, exquisite tact, and fabled loyalty. Masquerading mostly under the innocent-sounding title of "executive assistant," she has masterminded a score of conferences and workshops, overseen half a hundred research assistants, kept the books for a multimillion-dollar budget, designed and executed media strategy, soothed ruffled feathers, buffered my enthusiasms and despairs, planned and replanned hundreds of trips, strategized about social change, reminded me of my manners, and (on the side) directed the Saguaro Seminar's work on culture and the arts and designed our Web site. Her judgment on matters large and small is impeccable. Most important, she, like Tom, never faltered in the conviction that we were on a worthy mission.

Not every author is as fortunate as I in having a loving and supportive family. Christin Campbell, Mario Perez, and Jonathan and Lara Putnam good-naturedly ribbed me about how long it was taking (as did everyone else I know!) at the same time that they offered innumerable insights and words of encouragement. My mother, Ruth Putnam, and my late parents-in-law, Louis and Zelda Werner, gracefully accepted my absences, while providing extraordinary exemplars of "the long civic generation." In uncounted ways my wife, Rosemary, enabled my addiction to this project. She drew on her professional experience as librarian to catalog the tens of thousands of documents, manuscripts, reports, and clippings that the project accumulated. At the same time Rosemary endured—almost always with good cheer—the fact that I spent most of the past five years in our house on Frost Pond, New Hampshire, working on this project, while she commuted each weekend. When the going was difficult, she buoyed my spirits, and when my ego soared, she reminded me to call my mom. Everyone needs a best friend; I am blessed to be married to mine.

Frost Pond, N.H.
December 1999

Index

Page numbers in *italics* refer to figures and tables.

Cortes, Ernesto, 408
cotton economy, 323
country clubs, 22
crack cocaine, 144
crime, 20, 137
  ecological theories of, 307–8
  neighborhood effects and, 310–18
  poverty and, 307, 312–13, 314
  rates of, 107, 144, *144*, 146, 205, 207,
    296, 308–10, *309*, 318, 368
  reform and, 370, 373–74
  regional differences in, 309–10
  victims of, 138, 308
Croatian immigrants, 390
Croly, Herbert, 377, 382
Crosby, Bing, 269
Crucible, The (Miller), 354
Crystal Cathedral, 66
Csikszentmihalyi, Mihaly, 238–40
cultural activities, 404, 411–12
  see also specific cultural activities

dairy industry, 323
Dallas, Tex., 15
Dance Exchange, 411–12
dancing, 217, 411–12
Danielsen, Karen, 210
Darley, John M., 93*n*
dating, interracial, 352
Davis, James C., 357
Dawson, Michael C., 343
day care centers, 270, 345
Dayton, Ohio, 283
D-Day, 259
DDB Needham Life Style survey, 59, 60,
    98, 109, 196, 214, 223, 226, 240,
    243, 263, 265, 310, 333, 420–24, *423*
death:
  premature, 326, 329
  see also suicide
*Death and Life of Great American Cities,
    The* (Jacobs), 308
Debs, Eugene, 392
declensionist narratives, 24–26
defense spending, 281
  see also military
delinquency, *see* crime
Delli Carpini, Michael, 257–58
democracy, 173, 336–49, 381
  civic skills developed in, 337, 338–44
  extremism in, 338, 340–42

face-to-face interactions in, 336–44
participatory, 18, 336–49, 367
psychic engagement and, 342–43;
  see also politics and public affairs,
  interest in
self-interest in, 135
see also citizenship, citizens; government; politics and public affairs
Democratic Party, 37, 185, 269
demonstrations and rallies, 35, 41, *41*,
    44, 152, 156, 158, 160, 164–65,
    165, 170, 186, 259, 346, 392
Demosclerosis (Rauch), 340
dentists, 83
Denver, Colo., 371
depression, 179, 234, 239, 261–65, 299,
    326, 331–35
Depression, Great, *see* Great Depression
Dertouzos, Michael L., 172, 175, 179
de Souza Briggs, Xavier, 21, 23
Detroit, Mich., 318, 343
Detroit Free Press, 240
Dewey, John, 116, 337, 377, 378, 397,
    404
Diana, Princess of Wales, 244
dictatorships, 173
diet, 327, 329
  see also eating
Dietrich, Marlene, 269
digital divide, 174–75, 411
Dilbeck, Pat, 16
DiMaggio, Joe, 271
Dimaggio, Paul, 321
Diner, Steven, 371, 374
dining out, 96, 97, 100, 101–2, *102*
dinner parties, 94, 97, 100, 108, 110,
    183, 185, 186, 203, 231, 234, 237,
    265–66, 278, 279, 291, 329, 333,
    334, 335, 352, 362
direct mail, 39, 154, 156–59, 160, 164
disease, 370, 373
  see also health
Disraeli, Benjamin, 380
divorce, 27, 96, 146–47, 151, 187, 258,
    259, 267, 277–79
  see also marriage
dog walking, 228
Doheny-Farina, Stephen, 178
Dole, Bob, 32
Dorchester Temple Baptist Church, 66
Dorr, Rheta Childe, 396

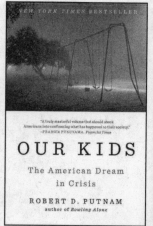
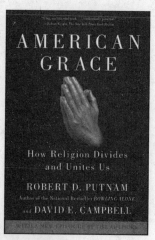
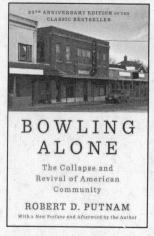
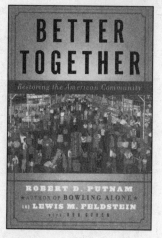